# Tolley's Property Taxes 2002–03

Fifteenth Edition



by

**Robert W Maas** FCA FTII FIIT TEP

of Blackstone Franks

Tolley
LexisNexis™

**Members of the LexisNexis Group worldwide**

| | |
|---|---|
| United Kingdom | LexisNexis Butterworths Tolley, a Division of Reed Elsevier (UK) Ltd, Halsbury House, 35 Chancery Lane, London, WC2A 1EL, and 4 Hill Street, Edinburgh EH2 3JZ |
| Argentina | LexisNexis Argentina, Buenos Aires |
| Australia | LexisNexis Butterworths, Chatswood, New South Wales |
| Austria | LexisNexis Verlag ARD Orac GmbH & Co KG, Vienna |
| Canada | LexisNexis Butterworths, Markham, Ontario |
| Chile | LexisNexis Chile Ltda, Santiago de Chile |
| Czech Republic | Nakladatelství Orac sro, Prague |
| France | Editions du Juris-Classeur SA, Paris |
| Hong Kong | LexisNexis Butterworths, Hong Kong |
| Hungary | HVG-Orac, Budapest |
| India | LexisNexis Butterworths, New Delhi |
| Ireland | Butterworths (Ireland) Ltd, Dublin |
| Italy | Giuffrè Editore, Milan |
| Malaysia | Malayan Law Journal Sdn Bhd, Kuala Lumpur |
| New Zealand | LexisNexis Butterworths, Wellington |
| Poland | Wydawnictwo Prawnicze LexisNexis, Warsaw |
| Singapore | LexisNexis Butterworths, Singapore |
| South Africa | LexisNexis Butterworths, Durban |
| Switzerland | Stämpfli Verlag AG, Berne |
| USA | LexisNexis, Dayton, Ohio |




A CIP Catalogue record for this book is available from the British Library.

First edition published 1986

ISBN 0 7545 51671 7

Typeset by Letterpart Ltd, Reigate, Surrey
Printed and bound in Great Britain by Butler & Tanner Ltd, Frome, Somerset

## Preface

The structuring of property transactions is one of the most difficult areas of tax planning. Each transaction needs to be considered individually. At the same time one transaction can affect the tax status of another carried out by the same person. As few property transactions of any size are wholly financed by the taxpayer, the structure of a transaction is frequently dictated, or at least heavily influenced, by the requirements of third parties. Furthermore, the ease with which interests in land can be created or subdivided frequently means that the tax implications of a proposal on several different owners need to be considered.

VAT in relation to property can be extremely complex and getting it wrong can be expensive and I am finding in practice that I am spending an increasing amount of time on VAT problems. Frequently, structuring a transaction slightly differently can give a vastly different VAT result. In the meantime there is no sign of a decrease in the number of VAT tribunal decisions that have to be considered.

I have tried in this book not only to explain the law – and the problems where the law is not clear cut – but to put this into the context of the types of transaction that are likely to take place in practice. I hope that this will help property owners and developers and others who deal in property to understand the transaction, as well as pointing their professional advisors towards the relevant legislative provisions themselves.

I would like to thank readers of earlier editions who have drawn to my attention areas of the text that needed clarification. I welcome such help and hope that readers will continue to write to Tolley's with suggestions for improvement. More than 30 years of experience of property taxation has taught me that there are always new things to be learnt in this field.

I would also like to take the opportunity of thanking others involved in the production of this book, in particular Maggie O'Callaghan for typing the original manuscript, Jill Holland for typing the additional material for this edition and Lance Blackstone and my other partners at Blackstone Franks for their helpful comments on various aspects of the text.

The law referred to in this book in general reflects the position at 1 September 2002.

London EC1, October 2002 **R W MAAS**

# Contents

# Table of Statutes

# Table of Statutory Instruments

| | | |
|---|---|---|
| **1992/613** | **Council Tax (Administration and Enforcement) Regulations 1992** | 20.30, 20.58, 20.79 |
| | Regs 3, 4 | 20.39 |
| | Regs 5, 6 | 20.40 |
| | Reg 7 | 20.43 |
| | Regs 8-10 | 20.44 |
| | Reg 11 | 20.45 |
| | (1)-(4) | 20.63 |
| | (1) | 20.56 |
| | (2) | 20.56, 20.79 |
| | (2)-(5) | 20.81 |
| | (6), (7) | 20.52 |
| | (10) | 20.63 |
| | Reg 12 | 20.46 |
| | Regs 14-16 | 20.47 |
| | Regs 18, 19 | 20.48 |
| | Reg 20 | 20.49 |
| | Reg 21 | 20.50, 20.51 |
| | Regs 22, 23 | 20.53 |
| | Reg 24(1)-(3), (6) | 20.54 |
| | Reg 25(4)-(6), (9) | 20.56 |
| | Reg 26 | 20.56 |
| | Reg 27 | 20.57 |
| | Reg 28 | 20.57 |
| | Reg 29(1) | 20.79 |
| | Reg 30 | 20.74 |
| | Regs 33-35 | 20.59 |
| | Reg 36 | 20.60 |
| | Reg 37 | 20.61 |
| | Reg 38 | 20.62 |
| | Reg 39(1)-(7) | 20.64 |
| | Reg 40 | 20.64 |
| | Reg 41(1), (2) | 20.65 |
| | Reg 41(3) | 20.61 |
| | Regs 42-44 | 20.65 |
| | Reg 45 | 20.66 |
| | Reg 46 | 20.67 |
| | Regs 47, 48 | 20.68 |
| | Reg 49 | 20.70 |
| | Reg 50 | 20.69 |
| | Reg 52(1)-(3) | 20.71 |
| | Reg 54 | 20.72 |
| | Reg 56 | 20.80 |
| | Reg 58 | 20.83 |
| | Sch 5 | 20.66 |
| **1992/1725** | **Housing (Northern Ireland) order** | 17.50 |
| **1992/2941** | **Council Tax (Exempt Dwellings) (Amendment) Order 1992** | 20.7 |
| **1992/2942** | **Council Tax (Additional Provisions for Discount Regards) (Amendment) Regulations 1992** | 20.22 |
| **1992/3008** | **Council Tax (Administration and Enforcement) (Amendment) Regulations 1992** | 20.30 |
| **1992/3121** | **VAT (Place of Supply of Services) Order** | |
| | Reg 5 | 17.250 |
| **1992/3222** | **VAT (Input Tax) Order 1992** | |
| | Art 6 | 17.14 |

# Table of Cases

All cases referred to in this book are listed below under the names of both parties unless the Commissioners of Inland Revenue were one party, when only the other party is listed.

# Abbreviations and References

| | | |
|---|---|---|
| ACT | = | Advance Corporation Tax |
| C & E | = | Customs & Excise |
| CAA 1990 | = | Capital Allowances Act 1990 |
| CCAB | = | Consultative Committee of Accountancy Bodies |
| CGT | = | Capital Gains Tax |
| CGTA 1979 | = | Capital Gains Tax Act 1979 |
| CIR | = | Commissioners of Inland Revenue |
| Col | = | Column |
| Customs | = | Customs & Excise |
| EIS | = | Enterprise Investment Scheme |
| FA | = | Finance Act |
| IBA | = | Industrial Buildings Allowance |
| ICTA 1988 | = | Income and Corporation Taxes Act 1988 |
| IHT | = | Inheritance Tax |
| IHTA 1984 | = | Inheritance Tax Act 1984 |
| LGFA | = | Local Government Finance Act |
| NAV | = | Net Annual Value |
| para | = | paragraph |
| reg | = | regulation |
| s | = | section |
| SA | = | Stamp Act 1891 |
| Sch | = | Schedule |
| SI | = | Statutory Instrument |
| TCGA 1992 | = | Taxation of Chargeable Gains Act 1992 |
| TMA 1970 | = | Taxes Management Act 1970 |
| UK | = | United Kingdom |
| VAT | = | Value Added Tax |
| VATA 1983 | = | Value Added Tax Act 1983 |

| | | |
|---|---|---|
| AC | = | Law Reports, Appeal Cases (Incorporated Council of Law Reporting for England and Wales, 3 Stone Buildings, Lincoln's Inn, London WC2A 3XN) |
| All E R | = | All England Law Reports (Butterworth & Co (Publishers) Ltd, 88 Kingsway, WC2B 6AB) |
| BTC | = | British Tax Cases (CCH Editions Ltd, Telford Road, Bicester, Oxon OX6 0XD) |
| Ch | = | Law Reports, Chancery Division |
| Ex D | = | Exchequer Division |
| IR | = | Irish Reports (Law Reporting Council, Law Library, Four Courts, Dublin) |
| ITC | = | Irish Tax Cases (Government Publications, 1 & 3 GPO Arcade, Dublin 1) |
| KB | = | Law Reports, King's Bench Division |
| QBD | = | Law Reports, Queen's Bench Division |
| SC | = | Court of Session Cases |

STC = Simon's Tax Cases (Butterworth & Co (Publishers) Ltd, as above)

TC = Official Reports of Tax Cases (HMSO, PO Box 276, London SW8 5DT)

WLR = Weekly Law Reports (Incorporated Council of Law Reporting for England and Wales, as above)

*Chapter 1*

# Introduction

**1.1** Property transactions are different from most business operations for a number of reasons. As the unit cost is very high it is important to consider the structure of each individual transaction rather than the business as a whole. Because it is possible to make a very large profit on a single transaction the Inland Revenue are likely to try very hard to contend that such profit is income rather than a capital gain – which in many cases is taxed less heavily – if there is any doubt as to the status of a transaction. For the same reason taxpayers frequently seek ways to transform a trading profit into a capital gain – or to try to arrange things so that it arises outside the UK – with the result that a large number of anti-avoidance provisions have been introduced over the years in an attempt to thwart such moves.

**1.2** By means of leases and joint ownership it is easier than with most other types of asset to dispose of interests in a property whilst retaining a share in the ownership, or a reversionary or subsidiary interest in the property. Every site or building is unique, so that virtually every property transaction is different in one or more respects from every other. The needs and desires of landowners and developers differ considerably and the structure of a transaction may often need to be varied to accommodate the special wishes of, say, the vendor of part of a site who wants a lease in the redevelopment, of the landowner who wants to retain a share in the rental income from a development or who wants to exercise a degree of control over the appearance of the development, of the financier who wants temporarily to own the site to maximise his security, of the developer who may have a number of alternative ways of financing the development, or of the two owners of a property company whose ability to leave their funds in the company and whose needs for income may be vastly different.

**1.3** The wide variety of uses to which property can be put, the volume of tax legislation aimed at property, and the propensity of landowners and developers to maintain a large degree of flexibility in relation to their holdings, in particular as regards the length of time for which they intend to retain a particular property, makes tax planning both important and at the same time often very difficult. The problems are aggravated by the fact that the exact manner in which a transaction is structured can significantly affect the tax payable. Perhaps worse, it is relatively easy to walk unwittingly into tax traps by looking only at the end result of a series of transactions and missing the tax consequences of some of the steps leading up to that result.

**1.4** A further problem is that the inter-relationship between different taxes is far more important when planning property transactions than with most types of business. In particular, VAT needs to be considered with care as some property disposals attract VAT whereas most do not, and expenditure is likely to consist of a mixture of exempt items, such as land purchases, and standard-rated ones, such as fees and building work. Furthermore, in those cases where receipts are normally exempt the taxpayer is sometimes entitled to opt to bring them into the scope of VAT if he so wishes. Whilst at first sight it is difficult to envisage anyone volunteering to be taxed if he does not have to be, it is likely to be sensible to make such an election in many cases. The position is further complicated by the fact that a structure that is attractive from a VAT point of view – or indeed a stamp duty viewpoint – can often give rise to serious adverse income tax or corporation tax consequences. It is accordingly important, when considering tax on property transactions, to be able to take an overall view of all the problems involved.

**1.5** The purpose of this book is to attempt to review the tax provisions that need to be considered in relation to property transactions and to relate them to one another. Chapters 6 to 9 look at specific types of property transactions, the acquisition and disposal of property as a trading transaction, the holding of property as an investment, the carrying out of property development, and the refurbishment of existing buildings. It is intended that each of these chapters should be able to stand on its own so that those not expert in tax can dip into them as required without having to peruse the entire book to ascertain the sorts of things that they need to think about. This inevitably involves a degree of duplication, as points dealt with elsewhere in the book which are of major importance to such types of transaction have also been examined in these four chapters in the specific context of the transaction involved. It is hoped that this element of duplication does not unduly distract the reader who wishes to read the book from cover to cover.

**1.6** Clearly, in considering tax on property companies or property transactions, account needs to be taken of the general tax law. It is always difficult to determine how much of the tax system as a whole one needs to explain when dealing with a specialist area. It is hoped that this book will be useful to the property owner or developer without a detailed knowledge of tax as well as the tax practitioner, and in achieving this aim a degree of compromise is inevitable. No attempt has been made to explain corporation tax or capital gains tax in any detail but sufficient of the basic principles have had to be included to enable the non-expert to see his property transactions in the context of his overall position. Clearly, however, these explanations of general principles should be looked on as guidelines and not as a detailed exposition of the general tax system, and the reader will need to look elsewhere for the caveats and exceptions that there is not space to mention here.

**1.7** Chapters 11, 17, 18 and 19, which deal with tax on chargeable gains, value added tax, inheritance tax (formerly capital transfer tax) and stamp duty respectively, are restricted to a consideration of the provisions of those taxes that either relate wholly to property or which tend to affect property far more than other assets. As such they are by no means exhaustive. No attempt has been made in these three chapters to cover reliefs or anti-avoidance provisions that can apply to property as much as to other assets, but are not specific to property as such.

**1.8** Readers of *Tolley's Anti-Avoidance Provisions* by the same author may find a sense of familiarity when reading parts of chapters 3 and 12 and much of chapter 14. The author has to confess that having given detailed consideration to such complex anti-avoidance provisions in his earlier book he has nothing useful to add and has therefore 'borrowed' the appropriate sections as he felt that for the sake of completeness these provisions needed to be covered here. By contrast it is not sought to consider here in depth the anti-avoidance provisions mentioned in chapter 15. These are not specifically property related and the chapter is intended to flash warning lights, leaving the would-be tax avoider to refer elsewhere for a detailed consideration of the relevant provisions.

**1.9** Finally, for those not expert in tax, it may be helpful to put property tax in context in relation to the tax system as a whole. A basic distinction is drawn in tax law between property bought for resale and that bought as a long-term investment. The tax treatment of these two categories is very different. Accordingly, before considering what the tax effect of a property transaction is likely to be, it is important to ascertain whether it is a dealing transaction or an investment transaction. This applies not only where property is acquired by individuals but also where it is acquired by companies.

**1.10** Irrespective of whether the building is bought for investment or resale the rental income produced from the building is taxed under the special rules of Schedule A. These are considered in chapter 2. To avoid rental income being converted into capital by the use of premiums for short leases, the legislation contains provisions designed to tax part of such a premium as if it were income. These are considered in chapter 3.

**1.11** There are two special areas of general tax law that are of particular relevance to property. The first is that most property transactions are financed partly by borrowings and the owner will want to ensure that he can obtain tax relief on such borrowings. The rules for the allowability of loan interest are considered in chapter 4.

**1.12** The second area is that much of the expenditure on buildings can qualify for capital allowances where the building is held as an investment. These allowances can be significant and can be set against the tax on the rental income produced by the building. The appropriate rules are considered in chapter 10.

*Chapter 2*

# Rents

## Introduction

**2.1** Rents from land and property in the UK are normally taxed under Schedule A. The Schedule A rules have altered radically in recent years, for income tax purposes from 6 April 1995 and for corporation tax from 1 April 1998. Between those dates there were two distinct systems, one for income tax and the other for corporation tax. Income tax is payable by individuals and trusts. It is also payable by overseas companies that invest in UK property but do not carry on a UK trade. Corporation tax is payable by UK companies and by non-UK trading companies.

**2.2** The position between 6 April 1995 and 31 March 1998 was very confused by the method that the government chose to incorporate the new system in the tax legislation. There were two *sections 15* and *21* of *ICTA 1988*, the sections as originally enacted (and amended up to 1994) which applied for corporation tax, and the sections as amended by *FA 1995, s 39* which applied for income tax.

This chapter is split into four sections.

1. The current rules which apply for income tax purposes from 1995/96 and for corporation tax purposes from 1 April 1998 (2.3–2.56).

2. The old corporation tax Schedule A rules which applied up to 31 March 1988 – and also applied for income tax purposes up to 1994/95 (2.57–2.92).

3. Property income of non-UK residents (2.93–2.99).

4. Particular matters that apply to both the old and the current Schedule A systems, namely the treatment of service charges, dilapidations, rent-a-room relief for letting space in one's own residence, rents taxable under Case I of Schedule D, furnished holiday lettings, tipping rights, income from overseas properties and anti-avoidance.

## The Current Rules

**2.3** Tax is now charged under Schedule A on annual profits arising from a business carried on for the exploitation, as a source of rents or other receipts, of any estate, interest or rights in or over land in the UK. Any transaction entered into for such exploitation of the above rights must of course be regarded as entered into in the course of such a business. All such businesses or transactions entered into by a particular person or partnership are treated as a single business (*ICTA 1988, s 15(1)* as substituted by *FA 1998, Sch 5 para 1*). This business is called a 'Schedule A business'.

**2.4** The receipts taxable under Schedule A are explicitly stated to include:

(*a*) receipts in respect of a licence to occupy or otherwise use land or in respect of the exercise of any other right over land; and

(*b*) rentcharges, ground annuals, feu duties and other annual payments reserved in respect of, or charged on or issuing out of, the land.

**2.5** The right to use a caravan or a houseboat is regarded as a right taxable under Schedule A if the use to which the caravan or houseboat may be put in pursuance of the right is confined to use at a single location in the UK. For this purpose any structure designed or adapted for human habitation which is capable of being moved is regarded as a caravan (applying *s 29(1), Caravan Sites and Development Act 1960*) and a houseboat is defined as a boat or similar structure designed or adapted for use as a place of human habitation (*ICTA 1988, s 15 para 3*).

**2.6** In the case of furnished lettings, the amount payable for the use of the furniture as well as that for the use of the land is treated as Schedule A income, and expenses in connection with the provision of the furniture are treated as expenses of the Schedule A business. A furnished letting for this purpose is any letting where a sum (or other consideration other than money) is payable in respect of the use of the premises (or caravan or houseboat) and the person entitled to the use of the premises is also entitled to the use of furniture in connection with that use. However, a trade which consists in, or involves, making furniture available for use in premises is not a furnished letting. It is not clear what this seeks to exclude. It appears to exclude a separate trade of leasing furniture, but, if so, it is odd that it was thought necessary as it is hard to imagine anyone thinking that such an activity could fall within the above wording (*ICTA 1988, s 15 para 4*).

**2.7** The following activities are specifically excluded from the scope of Schedule A:

(*a*) profits arising from the occupation of land. These will normally constitute a trade taxable under Case 1 of Schedule D (see 2.123). This will exclude trades such as property dealing, operating hotels and furnished lettings where there is a large degree of services;

(*b*) farming and market gardening – which are taxed under Case 1 of Schedule D by virtue of *ICTA 1988, s 53(1)* (see 22.9);

(*c*) mines, quarries and other concerns taxed under Case 1 of Schedule D by virtue of *ICTA 1988, s 55* (see 22.16);

(*d*) the income from (and expenses of) tied premises – which is taxed as a trading receipt under *ICTA 1988, s 98* (see 22.32);

(*e*) rent receivable in connection with mines, quarries and other concerns which is taxed under Schedule D by virtue of *ICTA 1988, s 119–121* (see 22.18–22.22);

(*f*) rent, etc. in respect of electric line wayleaves to the extent that this is taxable under Schedule D by virtue of *ICTA 1988, s 120(1)* (see 22.28).

(ICTA 1988, s 15(1)).

Although not specifically excluded in the legislation, Schedule A also does not tax

(*g*) annual interest, e.g. under a mortgage, which is taxable under Case III of Schedule D;

(*h*) profits from the occupation of woodlands managed on a commercial basis and with a view to the realisation of profits – which are exempt from tax (see chapter 16). Receipts from woodlands not meeting these requirements is probably not income at all for tax purposes.

**2.8** If a non-UK company has both Schedule A transactions chargeable to corporation tax and Schedule A transactions chargeable to income tax it is treated as carrying on two separate Schedule A businesses, an income tax one and a corporation tax one (*ICTA 1988, s 15(1A)*). It is difficult to envisage such circumstances occurring. The obvious one is where the company is carrying on a trade in the UK through a branch and lets part of the trading premises (which would create a corporation tax Schedule A business) and also owns UK investment properties unconnected with the trade (which would give rise to an income tax Schedule A business). However, it would be odd to structure a company in this way. The trading operations would normally be carried on by a separate company to the investment transactions.

**2.9** Despite the all-embracing nature of this charging section, rents can, in some cases, be assessable under Case I or Case VI of Schedule D. Such cases are considered later in this chapter (see 2.123).

**2.10** Income tax under Schedule A is charged on (and payable by) the person receiving or entitled to the income (*ICTA 1988, s 21(1)* as substituted by *FA 1998, Sch 5 para 4*). The word 'receiving' is odd, although this word was also used in the old legislation. An agent may well 'receive' the income. However, unlike with interest, where they will tax the agent as the person in receipt of the income, the Revenue have never sought to tax an agent under Schedule A (apart from the special provisions that used to apply for taxing non-residents).

## Computation of Profits

**2.11** The profits of a Schedule A business are computed in the same way as those of a trade for periods of accounts beginning after 6 April 1999 (*ICTA 1988, s 21A(1)*). This means that they must be computed on an accounting basis which gives a true and fair view subject to any adjustment required or authorised by law and from 24 July 2002 means that they must be prepared in accordance with generally accepted accounting practice (*FA 1998, s 42* as amended by *FA 2002, s 103(5)*). 'Generally accepted accounting practice' means generally accepted accounting practice with respect to accounts of UK companies that are intended to give a true and fair view, and has the same meaning in relation to individuals, entities other than companies and non-UK companies as it has in relation to UK companies (*ICTA 1988, s 836A* inserted by *FA 2002, s 103(2)*). In practical terms the same basis also applies before 6 April 1999.

**2.12** What is taxed is the profits or gains arising in the year, i.e. the fiscal year (*ICTA 1988, s 21(2)*). The Revenue have stated that accounts should be prepared to 5 April (or 31 March if the taxpayer is prepared to treat this as co-terminous with 5 April), and, unlike in earlier years, insist that the computation of profits or gains is time-apportioned over the fiscal year if accounts are prepared to a date other than 5 April (or 31 March). The exception to this is partnerships. From 1997/98 Schedule A income of a partnership is included in the partnership tax return and therefore computed on the basis of the partnership's accounting year. Where a partnership's Schedule A or furnished letting income was calculated on an account basis for 1994/95 the Revenue allowed the 1995/96 and 1996/97 income to stay on an accounts basis (Tax Bulletin Number 18, August 1995). Where it was on a fiscal year basis or a preceding year accounts basis a transitional adjustment had to be made. Guidance on how to calculate this is given in Tax Bulletin Number 21, February 1996. It is a question of fact whether the Schedule A income of a trading partnership is ancillary income of that partnership or income of a separate parallel partnership, to which the concession would not apply. It is also a question of fact whether the mere joint ownership of property constitutes a partnership. To do so it would of itself need to constitute the carrying on of a business jointly with a view to profit, which is not normally the case with a joint investment (Tax Bulletin Number 20, December 1995).

**2.13** As indicated earlier, all of a person's UK properties together form his Schedule A business (*ICTA 1988, s 21(4)*). A partnership is treated as a separate person for this purpose. Accordingly, the pre-self assessment restrictions on the set-off of a deficit on one property against income from another no longer apply. In particular there are no special rules for property let at less than a full rent, even if let at a nominal figure to a connected person – although in such a case it may be difficult to show that expenditure on the property was incurred wholly and exclusively for the purposes of the Schedule A business and there could be Schedule E consequences for the tenant (see 22.49). Furthermore the disposal of a property no longer forfeits relief for unrelieved losses in respect of that property; the loss can be carried forward against future Schedule A income from other properties. On the other hand a partner will not be able to set his share of a partnership Schedule A loss against income from his personal properties, and vice versa. The Revenue have said that where property is owned jointly (and, as will normally be the case, the letting activity does not amount to a partnership) and one of the joint owners takes responsibility for the overall supervision of the letting, if the name and address of that 'managing owner' is shown on the other co-owner's tax returns, questions relating to the letting will normally be made only to the managing owner (Tax Bulletin 25, October 1996). It is understood that they will also be content for a co-owner's share of the net letting income to be shown as a single figure in his return (other than of course for the managing owner).

**2.14** The Revenue regard expenditure incurred on legal and professional fees on the first letting or subletting of a property as capital unless the lease is for a year or less. Such expenses of renewing a lease will be revenue if the lease is for less than 50 years, but any part relating to a premium on the renewal is capital. Where there is a change of tenant the new lease can normally be regarded as a renewal if it follows closely on the previous one and is on broadly similar terms. This does not apply if there is some other substantial use, such as owner occupation, between lettings or if a short lease is replaced by a long one (IR 150 and Tax Bulletin 26, December 1996).

**2.15** The special rules in *ICTA 1988, ss 103* to *106, 108* and *109*, and *110* (post-cessation receipts) and *109A* (post-cessation expenditure) which apply on a discontinuance of a trade are specifically applied to the profits of a Schedule A business (*ICTA 1988, s 21B*). It is unlikely that they will often apply. The transitional rules (see 2.52 below) generally made it sensible to adopt a full earnings basis of accounting for a Schedule A business that existed in 1994/95 whereas the post-cessation receipt provisions are aimed at concessional accounting bases. Furthermore the post-cessation expenditure rules do not cover payments of rent under the privity of contract rules in respect of leases previously owned and assigned to a purchaser, the most likely type of post-cessation expense for a Schedule A business. They relate only to negligence, and product liability and similar claims and the related costs and to bad debts and related costs. One effect of calculating the profits of a Schedule A business under Schedule D, Case I rules is to apply all the Case I legal decisions, including that in *Odeon Associated Theatres Ltd v Jones* (see 9.4) which was effectively excluded by the old Schedule A rules. Relief for 'pre-trading' expenditure in the seven years prior to the commencement of a Schedule A business can be claimed in the year that the business commences in the same way as with a trade (*ICTA 1988, s 401(1)*). The specific relief for redundancy payments in *ICTA 1988, s 579* and *580* and for training courses for employees and counselling services for employees in *ICTA 1988, ss 588* to *589B* are specifically applied to employees of a Schedule A business (*ICTA 1988, s 21A(2)*). So are the specific rules on apportionment (*ICTA 1988, s 72*), business entertainment expenses (*ICTA 1988, s 577*), expenditure involving crime (*ICTA 1988, s 577A*), consideration for restrictive undertakings (*FA 1988, s 73(2)*), deduction of emolument paid more than nine months after the end of the accounting year (*FA 1989, s 43*), expenses in connection with unapproved retirement benefit schemes (*FA 1989, s 76*) and expenditure in connection with the provision of security assets or services (*FA 1989, s 112–113*; *ICTA 1988, s 21A(2)*).

**2.16** The basic Schedule D, Case I computational rules in *ICTA 1988, ss 74–99* and *FA 1992, s 42* and *46(1)(2)* are also specifically applied (*ICTA 1988, s 21A(2)*). So are the special income tax rules on changes in the persons engaged in carrying on a trade (*ICTA 1988, s 113*), the corporation tax provision where a company begins or ceases to carry on a trade (*ICTA 1988, s 337(1)*) and the special provisions on a change of accountancy basis (*FA 1988, s 44* and *Sch 6* (*ICTA 1988, s 21B*)). These are not dealt with in this book.

**2.17** There are also a few provisions that are excluded from applying for Schedule A purposes, namely *ICTA 1988, s 82* (disallowance of certain interest paid to non-UK residents), *ICTA 1988, s 87* (deduction of taxable proportion of a premium) and *ICTA 1988, ss 96, 98* (farming and market gardening and tied premises) (*ICTA 1988, s 21A(4)*). The last two are not relevant as the trades concerned are specifically excluded from Schedule A (see 2.7). *Section 87* is not needed as there are separate Schedule A rules giving relief for a premium paid. These are considered at 3.32–3.40. The exclusion of *section 82* preserves the deductibility of certain overseas interest payments for Schedule A purposes that has applied since 1994.

**2.18** There is also a special rule in relation to mutual business. The transactions or relationships involved in mutual business are treated as if they were transactions or relationships between persons between whom no relationship of mutuality existed. Any surplus or deficit on such a business is regarded as a (taxable) Schedule A profit or loss. The person in receipt of that profit, i.e. who is taxable on it, is the person who would be treated as the person entitled to the profit if the business were not a mutual one. This special rule is overridden by *ICTA 1988, s 488* in respect of co-operative housing associations (*ICTA 1988, s 21C*, inserted by *FA 1998, Sch 5 para 5*).

**2.19** Unfortunately the draftsman has opted not to define mutual business. It presumably means any type of mutual business. The effect of *section 21C* is therefore to exclude Schedule A income from the tax exemption for profits from mutual trading enunciated by the House of Lords in 1887 in *Styles v New York Life Assurance Co (2 TC 460)*.

**2.20** The Revenue made no special concession for expenditure on repairing or reinstating a building arising from bomb damage in relation to buildings in Docklands and Manchester in 1996. If this expenditure (net of insurance recoveries) does not qualify as repairs under the normal rules it will not be deductible, i.e. to the extent that it relates to improvements or alterations, and if the work is so extensive that it amounts to the replacement of one building by another (albeit identical) one it is capital expenditure. They accept that the use of different materials or building methods reflecting technological advances since the building was erected is still likely to be repairs. Where improvements were carried out prior to 1 April 2001, ESC B4 allowed a deduction in computing Schedule A income for the estimated cost of repairs obviated by the improvement or alteration, but this concession has been withdrawn. Some people are concerned that the effect of the withdrawal is to now make such expenditure capital. In some cases it may well do so, but it is probable that the decision in *Conn v Robins Bros Ltd (43 TC 266)* (see 9.9) will give the same effect in most cases. Indeed it seems likely that ESC B4 was intended to apply the effect of that decision to Schedule A and that it has been withdrawn as it is no longer needed now that Schedule A profits are calculated using Schedule D, Case I principles. If the original steel frame of a building remains standing and it is reused the Revenue accept that the rebuilding is not the replacement of the building (Tax Bulletin 26, December 1996).

**2.21** It should be stressed that a Schedule A business is not a trade; Schedule A simply adopts the Schedule D, Case I rules on the computation of profits. Therefore the profits of a Schedule A business are not earned income and so do not become pensionable. An income tax Schedule A loss cannot be carried backwards or set against other income. It can only be carried forward against future Schedule A income. This could cause problems with bad debts. In the past where a debt for unpaid rent proved bad, relief was, in theory at least, given by adjusting the income for the year in which it was receivable. Under the new rules the bad debt is an expense of the year it becomes bad. If that is after the property is sold there may be no future income to set it against with the result that the relief is effectively lost. Curiously, if the taxpayer only owned one letting property he could be in a better position than if he owned several. This is because the disposal of that property will normally give rise to a cessation of the Schedule A business and *ICTA 1988, s 109A(4)* (introduced by *FA 1995, s 90*) gives relief for post-cessation bad debts against general income of the year in which it proves bad, whereas if the Schedule A business continues the bad debt will be an expense which can be relieved only against future income from that business.

**Loan Interest Payable**

**2.22** For income tax purposes loan interest is treated like any other expense. The special rules contained in chapter 4 that applied up to 5 April 1995 no longer apply (*FA 1995, s 42*). Furthermore *ICTA 1988, s 82*, which restricts the deduction for interest paid to non-residents in computing trading profits, is specifically excluded from applying to a Schedule A business so such interest can be deducted (*FA 1995, Sch 6 para 13*). Where a swap, cap or other interest rate hedging contract is taken out the hedging costs will constitute deductions of the Schedule A business and any hedging gain will be taxable income of that business. The calculation should normally be on an accruals basis (Tax Bulletin 25, October 1996).

**2.23** Where a loan is both for a Schedule A business and a non-business qualifying purpose, relief obviously cannot be claimed both as a trading expense and as a charge on income (*FA 1995, Sch 6 para 17*).

**2.24** For corporation tax purposes loan interest is not deducted in calculating the Schedule A income. Instead it is dealt with under the loan relationship rules. A net debit on loan relationships can be set against a Schedule A profit, which normally creates the same overall result as if the interest had been deductible.

*Receipts and Payments on Sale of Land*

**2.25** Where receipts or outgoings of the vendor are apportioned between the parties on a sale of land, the part attributable to the period falling after completion is treated as being received or paid, as the case may be, by the purchaser immediately after the completion (*ICTA 1988, s 40(1)(2)*). Similarly receipts or payments of the purchaser relating to the period prior to the completion must be treated as having been received or paid by the vendor prior to completion. Only the balance of the receipt or payment is, of course, then treated as received by or paid to the actual recipient or payer (*ICTA 1988, s 40(3)*).

*Land Managed as One Estate*

**2.26** Where land in one ownership was managed as one estate at 5 April 1963 and the owner for the time being makes or has made an appropriate election (which must be made within twelve months of the end of the first year of assessment or accounting period of his ownership or such later time as the Revenue may allow, and can only be made if the immediately preceding owner also did so), special rules apply (*ICTA 1988, s 26*). The owner is treated as if he were entitled to rent for any unlet part of the estate (other than any part occupied by him wholly and exclusively for purposes connected with the management of the estate or for the purpose of a trade, profession or vocation) on a daily basis at a rate equal to the annual value of that part under *ICTA 1988, s 837*. If any part of the estate is let under a lease not at a full rent the rent for that part must similarly be increased to the annual value (*ICTA 1988, s 26(1)*). Prior to 1998/99 it also had to be assumed that the notional rent arose from a lease at full rent (not being a tenant's repairing lease).

**2.27** In return for agreeing to be taxed on this notional income the taxpayer can deduct the whole of the (allowable) expenses of running the estate from the aggregate rents from the estate. Any new property added to the estate after 5 April 1963 cannot be regarded as part of the estate and the expenses applicable to such property must therefore be segregated. This does not apply to property which at 5 April 1963 was owned by a trust in which the current owner had a contingent interest and managed as one estate with his personal property (*ICTA 1988, s 26(4)(5)*).

**2.28** Between 6 April 1998 and 5 April 2001 (1 April 2001 for corporation tax) excess expenses in respect of the notionally let part of the estate could only be deducted from actual rents on the remainder of the estate, not from rents generally. Any excess could be carried forward against future rents from the estate (*ICTA 1988, s 26(2A)* inserted by *FA 1998, Sch 5 para 7(4)*), (*FA 1998, s 39*). If the estate included a building or land that had been designated as a historic building (and the requisite undertakings remained in force) under *FA 1975, s 34(1)*, *FA 1976, s 77* or *IHTA 1984, s 31* and another part of the estate was transferred to a trust approved by the Treasury under *IHTA 1984, Sch 4 para 1* (maintenance funds for historic buildings), the trust property was treated as remaining part of the estate – and the trust expenditure as estate expenditure (*ICTA 1988, s 27*). This extension to *section 26* of course also ceased on 5 April 2001 (*FA 1998, s 39*).

*Sporting Rights*

**2.29** Up to 1997/98 if the owner (or other person entitled to possession) of any land usually let sporting rights over it but in a particular year did not do so, expenditure in that year that would have qualified for a deduction if the rights had been let could be treated as deductible from rents under a lease at full rent (*ICTA 1988, s 29(1)*). This enabled relief for that expenditure to be obtained as an expense of the Schedule A business (or under the old rules by setting it against rents from leases at full rent under *ICTA 1988, s 25(7)* (see 2.80 below)). Sporting rights for this purpose were the rights of fowling, shooting, or fishing, or of taking or killing game, deer or rabbits (*ICTA 1988, s 29(5)*). If the sporting rights were exercised by the owner or by any other person at the owner's invitation (or, if they were owned by a close company, by a director or participator of that company), the expenditure available for relief had to be reduced by the price which that person might reasonably have been expected to pay if he had given full consideration for such exercise. No such restriction was needed if the exercise of the rights constituted a benefit in kind taxable under Schedule E by virtue of *ICTA 1988, s 154* (*ICTA 1988, s 29(2)(3)*). If the owner of the rights was a company, the relief had to be calculated for the year of assessment and apportioned (presumably on a time basis) between the accounting periods falling wholly or partly within that year (*ICTA 1988, s 29(4)*). It was presumably felt fairest to calculate relief on an annual basis, as such rights were normally exercisable during only part of the year. This provision was repealed for 1998/99 onwards (*FA 1998, Sch 5 para 10*). When sporting rights were let for part of a year and used by the owner, etc., for part, the rules of course excluded from relief expenditure applicable to the period of the owner's use.

*Alternative Accommodation*

**2.30** Where a person lets his own private residence, the cost of providing alternative accommodation for himself cannot, of course, be deducted (*Wylie v Eccott (6 TC 128)*; *Smith v Irvine (27 TC 381)*).

## Capital Allowances

*Machinery and Plant*

**2.31** Capital allowances can be claimed for machinery and plant used by a person entitled to rent or other receipts taxable under Schedule A for the maintenance, repair or management of premises in respect of which the rent, etc. arises. This is achieved by treating the person's Schedule A business (or in the case of a company liable to corporation tax all the activities which would have constituted its Schedule A business had the income tax rules applied (other than any taxable under Case VI of Schedule D)) as a qualifying activity (*CAA 2001, s 15(1)(b)*). In the case of furnished holiday accommodation, the part of the Schedule A business (or deemed Schedule A business) that consists of the commercial letting of such accommodation is treated for capital allowances as a separate trade, i.e. a second pool of plant and machinery in relation to such accommodation must be kept separate from the main Schedule A business pool (*CAA 2001, ss 15(1)(a), 249(1)*). Allowances can also be claimed for plant and machinery incorporated in the building itself. These are considered at 10.5 onwards below.

**2.32** Capital allowances on plant or machinery are not claimable on assets used for furnished lettings of residential property. Instead the Revenue will allow relief for replacement of furniture, etc. on a renewal basis – which of course means that no tax relief is given until the initial furniture wears out. Alternatively, an annual depreciation allowance can be claimed. This will normally be 10% of the rent, net of council tax and water rates and any other services paid for by the landlord which are normally liabilities of the tenant. Where a different method of allowing for depreciation applied prior to 6 April 1975 in a particular case this has normally been allowed to continue (Inland Revenue Press Release 13 October 1977). If detailed accounts are not submitted it would be wise to at least indicate on the tax return if some basis other than the normal 10% of net rents figure has been used. The Schedule A apportionment rules on the purchase or sale of land (see *ICTA 1988, s 40(5)*) apply. The 10% deduction covers such things as cookers, washing machines, dishwashers, suites, beds, curtains, linen, crockery and cutlery. It does not however preclude the landlord from claiming as repairs the replacement of fixtures such as baths, washbasins and toilets which would not normally be removed if the property were vacated or sold (ESC B47).

**2.33** Capital allowances on machinery and plant are normally given in taxing the Schedule A business in the same way as in a trade. The special rules apply subject to the override in *ICTA 1988, s 32(1B)* (*FA 1995, Sch 6 para 33*).

**2.34** Capital allowances are normally treated as an expense in calculating the profits of the Schedule A business in the same way as with a trade. This is achieved by deeming the Schedule A business for capital allowance purposes to be a trade set up after 5 April 1995.

**2.35** *Section 9(1)–(3)* of the *CAA 1990* (inserted by *FA 1995, Sch 6 para 29* and amended by *FA 1998, Sch 5 para 47*) extends the relief for industrial buildings allowances. Such allowances are given as a trading expense of an actual or deemed Schedule A business as if it were a trade which commenced after 5 April 1995 (1 April 1998 for corporation tax). For corporation tax, the initial allowance is given by reference to the date the expenditure is incurred, if it is let at that time, or when the building is used for any purpose, if later, and writing-down allowances are given on the balance at the end of the chargeable period for which the allowance is made together with any balancing allowances or charges arising on disposals. The rules effectively relieve 'pre-trading' expenditure by creating a loss in the deemed business which can be carried forward until the real Schedule A business commences. The same procedure applies where an industrial building is temporarily disused (*CAA 1990, s 15ZA* inserted by *FA 1998, Sch 5 paras 48, 49* replacing *CAA 1990, s 15(2A)* inserted by *FA 1995, Sch 6 para 30*). Similar rules apply to agricultural buildings allowances under *CAA 1990, s 132* (*FA 1995, Sch 6 para 35*) and to capital allowances for assured tenancies (given on expenditure incurred before 15 March 1988 only).

**2.36** Prior to 1997/98 (or for accounting periods ending before 1 April 1997 for a company) capital allowances and balancing charges were given by adding (or deducting in the case of a balancing charge) the allowances to (from) the deductible expenditure in respect of the premises (*ICTA 1988, s 32(3)*). They accordingly augmented a loss in relation to those premises. They could not be given against any other type of income (*ICTA 1988, s 32(3)*). Allowances could not, of course, also be claimed for the same machinery or plant against trading profits (*ICTA 1988, s 32(7)*). The taxpayer had to elect to claim allowances. Such an election applied for the year of assessment or accounting period in which it was made and for subsequent accounting periods (*ICTA 1988, s 32(5)*). The election could apply either to all machinery and plant used for the maintenance of the particular premises or to any class of such machinery or plant. In the latter case the election had to be made before any assessment (for any year) incorporating a deduction for repairs or management of the premises has been finally determined (*ICTA 1988, s 32(6)*). *Section 32* was repealed by *FA 1997, Sch 15 para 1.*

### *Sea Walls*

**2.37** If the owner or tenant of any premises incurs expenditure on making a sea wall or other embankment necessary to protect the premises against encroachment of the sea or of any tidal river he can treat one twenty-first of that expenditure as an allowable deduction from the rent for those premises for that and the next twenty years of assessment (*ICTA 1988, s 30(1)*). Obviously a deduction cannot be claimed under this provision if capital allowances have been claimed for the expenditure under some other provision. If the whole of the taxpayer's interest in the premises is subsequently transferred (by operation of law or otherwise) to any other person, e.g. on a sale, the transferee takes over the entitlement to the deduction for future years. In the year of transfer it must be apportioned between the two in such manner as may be just. If part of the taxpayer's interest is transferred the transferee becomes entitled to such part of the deduction as is properly referable to that part of the premises (*ICTA 1988, s 30(2)*). If the expenditure was incurred by the tenant his interest will be deemed to have been transferred on the expiry of his lease:

(*a*) to any incoming lessee, if he makes a payment to the outgoing lessee in respect of the sea wall; or

(*b*) to his immediate landlord in any other case.

(*ICTA 1988, s 30(3)*).

**2.38** It is not clear what happens if the tenant is granted a new lease of the same premises on the expiry of his original lease. Although illogical, it appears that the right to the allowance will automatically devolve on the landlord as the tenant probably cannot make a payment to himself to bring himself within (*a*).

**2.39** In the case of a company the allowances must be calculated for a year of assessment and apportioned between the accounting periods falling wholly or partly into that year (*ICTA 1988, s 30(4)*).

**2.40** A person who acquires a property with the benefit of a sea wall, etc. needs to enquire from the vendor whether any expenditure has been incurred in the previous 21 years which gave rise to a deduction under this provision as the benefit of these can pass to the purchaser.

## Schedule A Losses – Income Tax

**2.41** A Schedule A loss is carried forward against any future income from the Schedule A business (*ICTA 1988, s 379A(1)*). It cannot be set against income from other sources with the exception that a rental loss by a builder from a property held as trading stock can by concession be allowed as a trading expense instead of being carried forward under Schedule A (Inspector's Manual, IM 1959). Where a taxpayer has only one letting property it may be difficult to determine when his Schedule A business ceases so that the losses cease to be relievable. It is probable that the sale of that property does not itself create a cessation provided that there is an intention to acquire further letting properties. On the other hand *ICTA 1988, s 15(1)* states that 'all the businesses and transactions carried on . . . by any particular person . . . so far as they are businesses or transactions the profits or gains of which are chargeable to tax under [Schedule A], are to be treated . . . as . . . a single business'. This appears to deem a person to have one single Schedule A business lasting throughout his entire life, irrespective of whether or not he owns property at any particular time. Such an interpretation would however render the specific incorporation of the rules on post-cessation income and expenses applicable only in rare circumstances which may induce the courts to refrain from a literal interpretation of *section 21(4)*. The Revenue's views on *ICTA 1988, s 53(2)*, a similar provision, may also apply here (see 22.9). They consider that a significant gap in the activities brings the deemed trade to an end.

**2.42** Where the Schedule A business includes an agricultural estate (see 2.44) allowable expenses of which have been deducted in arriving at the loss, part of the Schedule A loss can be set against any income of the taxpayer for the same or the next tax year (*ICTA 1988, s 379A(2)(b)*). The relevant part is the lower of the Schedule A loss, the allowable agricultural expenses plus capital allowances (less balancing charges), or the taxpayer's 'relievable income' for the year (*ICTA 1988, s 379A(3)(4)*). This relief must be claimed within 12 months of 31 January after the end of the year of loss, i.e. within approximately 22 months of the end of the tax year (*ICTA 1988, s 379A(3)*).

**2.43** The allowable agricultural expenses are the disbursements or expenses attributable to the agricultural estate which are deductible in respect of maintenance, repairs, insurance or management of the estate, but excluding any loan interest (*ICTA 1988, s 379A(8)*). This will not necessarily include all the expenses in relation to the estate which are deductible in arriving at the Schedule A loss. For example rent of the land does not fall into either of the four heads specified but is an expense of the Schedule A business. Any allowable expenses attributable solely to part of the estate not used for the purposes of husbandry must also be excluded, as must be the non-husbandry part of expenses incurred partly for the agricultural part of the estate and partly for the non-agricultural part (*ICTA 1988, s 379A(9)*).

**2.44** An agricultural estate means land, including buildings, managed as one estate and including any land, houses or other buildings in the UK occupied wholly or mainly for the purposes of husbandry (*ICTA 1988, s 379A(10)*).

**2.45** The relief can also be claimed if there are no allowable agricultural expenses but net capital allowances (i.e. less balancing charges) (*ICTA 1988, s 379A(2)(a)*). Prior to 1997/98 the reference to capital allowances excluded allowances for plant and machinery in let buildings to the extent that the lessee did not use it or used it for purposes other than those of a trade (*ICTA 1988, s 379A(2)*). Curiously this appears to have precluded relief if the tenant sublet the building even if the subtenant was carrying on a trade.

**2.46** A person's relievable income is his total income for the year after deducting Schedule A losses brought forward (to the extent of the Schedule A income) and after deducting relief under *section 379A(3)* for the balance of the previous year's loss (*ICTA 1988, s 379A(6)*).

**2.47** Unrelieved Schedule A deficits or losses brought forward from the old Schedule A system are treated as (new system) Schedule A losses. So are Case VI losses incurred before 1995/96 from transactions which would have arisen in the course of the Schedule A business had they taken place in 1995/96, e.g. from furnished lettings (*FA 1995, Sch 6 para 19(2)*). Unrelieved interest on letting properties carried forward to 1995/96 under *ICTA 1988, s 355(4)* is also treated as a brought forward Schedule A loss (*FA 1995, Sch 6 para 19(3)*).

**Schedule A Losses – Corporation Tax**

**2.48** A Schedule A loss of a company arising after 1 April 1998 can be set against total profits of the accounting period (*ICTA 1988, s 392A(1)* inserted by *FA 1998, Sch 5 para 28*). It can also be surrendered to another group company under the group relief rules (*ICTA 1988, s 403* as amended by *FA 1998, Sch 5 para 29*). Alternatively the loss can be carried forward and treated as a Schedule A loss in the next accounting period (*ICTA 1988, s 392A(2)*) but it cannot be surrendered as group relief in that later period (*ICTA 1988, s 403 ZD(3)* inserted by *FA 1998, Sch 5 para 28*). By concession a rental loss suffered by a builder from a property held as trading stock can be allowed as a trading expense instead of being carried forward under Schedule A (Inspector's Manual, IM 1959).

**2.49** If an investment company ceases to carry on its Schedule A business while remaining an investment company any unrelieved Schedule A loss is not lost; it is carried forward as if it were a management expense (*ICTA 1988, s 392A(3)*).

**2.50** Except where the Schedule A business is carried on in the exercise of a statutory function paragraphs 2.48 and 2.49 above do not apply to the extent (if any) that the Schedule A business is not carried on on a commercial basis. For this purpose a business (or part of a business) is carried on on a commercial basis if it is carried on either with a view to making a profit or so as to afford a reasonable expectation of profit. If there is a change in the manner in which the business (or part) is carried on, it is treated as being carried on throughout the accounting period of change in the way in which it is being carried on at the end of that accounting period (*ICTA 1988, s 392A(5)–(7)*). It is not clear what happens in such a case. It appears that the loss cannot be carried forward at all. This contrasts with a trading loss incurred in such circumstances which can be carried forward against future profits from the trade under *ICTA 1988, s 385*.

**2.51** If there is a change in the ownership of a company carrying on a Schedule A business to which any of *ICTA 1988, 768B(1)*, *768C* or *768(1)* applies (broadly speaking, there is a major change in the nature or conduct of the business, or it is revived after the scale of the business has become negligible), a Schedule A loss arising before the change of ownership cannot be carried forward to an accounting period beginning after the change in ownership. For this purpose the accounting period in which the change takes place is split into two, the second starting immediately after the change in ownership (*ICTA 1988, s 768D* inserted by *FA 1998, Sch 5 para 31*).

## The Transitional Income Tax Rules

**2.52** The *Finance Act 1995* does not contain any transitional rules for the change to the new system. This was dealt with informally on the basis of a published guidance note which the Revenue issued to their staff and published generally on 10 February 1995. The concept is that there should be a fair and reasonable result in the transition. There are two main problems. The changeover meant that rent received in advance in March 1995 was taxable in 1994/95 under the old basis and most of it was taxable again in 1995/96 under the new. This was normally dealt with by excluding the doubly taxed amount from the 1994/95 figure. The other problem is that some people previously dealt with Schedule A on an accounts basis. This is not permissible under the current system (other than for partnerships). Such people would have income and expenses either not taxed or taxed twice. In such a case the 1994/95 assessment was on an average figure. For interest payments the idea was to ensure that a person obtained twelve months tax relief each year. In general the adjustment to achieve fairness was made to the 1994/95 figures (although any additional relief for interest was given in 1995/96). This was because payments on account for 1996/97 tax were based on the 1995/96 assessment so it would have caused problems if that were an artificially depressed figure. Tax Bulletin Number 20 (December 1995) contains some worked examples.

## Letting Ceasing in 1995/96

**2.53** The above rules did not apply if a taxpayer was taxable under Schedule A, or Case VI of Schedule D on furnished lettings, for 1994/95 on rent from a source which ceased in 1995/96, e.g. the property was sold or became occupied by the owner as his private residence, and the taxpayer did not commence another Schedule A business in the course of 1995/96. Instead the taxpayer was taxable for 1995/96 under the 1994/95 rules (*FA 1995, s 39(5)*). The idea was of course that there was little point in going over to the new system where the letting would not continue. The source must cease to be a Schedule A source not only for the taxpayer but for any other person. The reason for this is not readily apparent. It is presumably intended as an anti-avoidance provision but as it is not limited to connected persons the taxpayer will not necessarily know that the property is no longer to be let if he sells it. It is not clear whether commencing a Schedule A business during the course of 1995/96 refers to the subsequent acquisition of a new property or if it also includes the retention of other pre-1995/96 properties which become a Schedule A business by virtue of the statute. It is probably the latter. Where the old rules continue, the relief for interest paid under *ICTA 1988, s 355(1)(b)* also continues for 1995/96 (*FA 1995, s 42(4)*). Where the Schedule A source continued beyond 1995/96 but ceased in 1996/97 the taxpayer could use the old rules for both 1995/96 and 1996/97 if he wished (para 9.103 of SAT 1 and Tax Bulletin 25, October 1996) – but as he was not able to obtain any relief for interest (because of the repeal of *ICTA 1988, s 255(1)(b)*) this was not normally a sensible thing to do if there was a mortgage on the property.

## Transitional Corporation Tax Rules

**2.54** *FA 1998, Sch 5 paras 65–76* contains transitional corporation tax rules to cover the change in the basis in the computation of Schedule A income from 1 April 1998. To the extent that a receipt or expense had been taken into account under the old rules (or would have been if the person concerned had been chargeable to tax – *paragraph 71*) it had to be excluded from the computation under the new ones (*paragraph 66*). Conversely any receipt not taxed or expense not allowed under the old rules had to be brought into account as if it were received or incurred on 1 April 1998 (*paragraph 67*). Pre-commencement expenditure incurred before 1 April 1998 which is deemed to have been incurred when the Schedule A business commenced cannot be carried back to the time it was actually incurred (*paragraph 68*). Where an estate, interest or rights in or over land is transferred from one person to another these rules apply as if the two were a single person (*paragraph 69*). This appears to apply even if the transferor and transferee are at arm's length, although it is not clear in practice how the one is to know what the other has done.

**2.55** Where relief for uncollectable rent was given prior to 1 April 1998 and the amount is recovered after that date the recovery must be treated as a Schedule A receipt arising after 1 April 1998. If a pre-1 April 1998 rental amount is recognised as irrecoverable after that date, relief is given as a bad debt of the Schedule A business, not by re-opening the earlier year's assessment (*paragraph 70*).

**2.56** An unrelieved Case VI loss at 1 April 1998 is treated as a Schedule A loss to the extent to which it relates to activities which after 1 April 1998 would form part of a Schedule A business – and as an overseas Schedule A business loss if it would have formed part of such a business (*paragraph 72*). For group relief purposes, where the accounting period spans 1 April 1998 the parts of the loss arising before and after that date are computed separately (*paragraph 75*). If a source of Schedule A (or property related Schedule D, Case VI) income ceased in the accounting period spanning 1 April 1998 the old rules applied for the entire period unless the source was acquired either during that accounting period or in the preceding 12 months (*paragraph 73*). If it was acquired in such a period it appears that the pre and post 1 April 1998 rental income needed to be computed separately. The logic of this is not readily apparent.

## The Old Corporation Tax Schedule A Rules to 31 March 1998 (and Income Tax Rules to 1994/95)

**2.57** The old system taxed

(*a*) rents under leases of land in the UK,

(*b*) rent charges, ground annuals, feu duties, and other annual payments received in respect of UK land or issuing out of it, and

(*c*) any other receipts arising to a person from, or by virtue of, his ownership of an estate or interest in (or a right over)

  (i) UK land, or

  (ii) any incorporeal hereditament or incorporeal heritable subject in the UK.

(*ICTA 1988, s 15(1)*).

### Computation of Income under Schedule A

**2.58** Tax was charged on the rent or receipts to which a person became entitled in an accounting period or, for income tax purposes up to 1994/95, the year of assessment (*ICTA 1988, s 15(1)*). In other words if a person was entitled to rent he was taxable on it whether he received it or not. This is a major departure from the general rule (which applies to income other than trading profits) that 'receivability without receipt is nothing'. In practice the Revenue were prepared to accept the adoption of an accounts basis for income tax purposes in many cases. They often required a full set of accounts including a balance sheet, although in practice did not always insist on this. The accounting year adopted was treated as co-terminous with the year of assessment in which it ended (Revenue Pamphlet IR 27 paras 102–104 – this booklet was withdrawn for other reasons but this practice remained unchanged). If a person's total gross rents were under £15,000 (under £10,000 prior to 6 April 1992), there was no need to itemise expenses; it was sufficient to show gross rents, total expenses and net rents.

#### *Relief for Unpaid Rents*

**2.59** This basic rule was modified to allow relief for certain bad debts. The taxpayer was treated as never having become entitled to the rent if he 'proved' (*a*) that he has not received an amount of rent, etc. to which he was entitled, and

(*b*) the non-receipt either

(i) was attributable to the default of the tenant (or other person by whom it was payable) and the taxpayer had taken any reasonable steps available to him to enforce payment, or

(ii) was due to the taxpayer having waived payment without consideration in order to avoid hardship – normally to the tenant, although the wording is wide enough to cover hardship to a third party, e.g. the relief applied if a head landlord waived rent due from his tenant because he knew this would enable the tenant to waive rent due from his sub-tenant who suffered hardship.

(*ICTA 1988, s 41(1)*).

**2.60** The use of the word 'proved' should particularly be noted. This placed the onus firmly on the taxpayer to demonstrate that he qualified for relief.

**2.61** Some Inspectors of Taxes expected a landlord to have taken legal action against a tenant to fall within (*b*)(i) in 2.59 above, but most accepted that where landlord and tenant were at arm's length the steps to be taken to seek to extract money from a recalcitrant tenant were a matter of commercial judgement and granted relief where the landlord opted not to expend further funds in an effort to recover the lost rent.

**2.62** If the tenant subsequently paid any part of the irrecoverable rent after relief had been allowed under *section 41* the landlord (or his executors if he was dead) had to notify the Inland Revenue within six months of the receipt. The Revenue then adjusted the assessment – for the year in which the rent fell due. They were empowered to make such an adjustment at any time up to six years after the end of the year of assessment in which the receipt took place (*ICTA 1988, s 41(2)*). *Section 41* was repealed with effect from 1 April 1998 (*FA 1998, Sch 5 para 21*). Any recovery is now treated as a receipt of the landlord's Schedule A business (see 2.3).

*Lettings to Connected Persons*

**2.63** The general rule that rents were assessable by reference to the dates they were receivable did not apply where the rent was payable in arrears, it was a trading expense or a management expense of the tenant or licensee (or he was otherwise entitled to deduct it in computing profits or gains for tax purposes), and landlord and tenant were connected with one another. In such circumstances the recipient was taxable on the rent on an accruals basis (*ICTA 1988, s 33A*; *F(No 2)A 1992, s 57*). This was an anti-avoidance provision introduced to 'prevent manipulation' of the Schedule A rules, although it will be apparent that its effect was far wider and that it applied to many innocent transactions.

**2.64** This special rule did not apply to rents accrued before 10 March 1992. This led to some strange results in 1991/92 and 1992/93.

*Example 1*

Joe owns a property which he lets to his family trading company, Joe's Enterprises Ltd, at a rent of £15,000 p.a. The rent is receivable annually in arrears on 30 April, the company's accounting date.

Joe's assessable income is as follows:

| | | | |
|---|---|---|---|
| 1991/92 | rent receivable on 30 April 1991 | £15,000 | |
| | Add rent accrued<br>10 March 1992 – 5 April 1992<br>27/365 × £15,000 | 1,109 | £16,109 |
| 1992/93 | rent receivable on 30 April 1992 | 15,000 | |
| | Less rent from 10 March 1992<br>taxed in 1991/92 | 1,109 | |
| | | 13,891 | |
| | Add rent accrued<br>1 May 1992 – 5 April 1993<br>338/365 × £15,000 | 13,890 | 27,781 |
| 1993/94 | rent accrued<br>6 April 1993 – 5 April 1994 | | 15,000 |

**2.65** The special rules applied not only if the parties were connected persons at the time the rent accrued, but also if they were connected persons at some earlier period during the currency of the lease, unless they ceased to be connected before 10 March 1992 (*ICTA 1988, s 33A(1)(c)*). The *ICTA 1988, s 839* definition of connected persons (see Appendix 1) applied (*ICTA 1988, s 33A(4)*).

*Example 1A*

Joe's Enterprises Ltd in *Example 1* is sold to Mighty Conglomerates plc in June 1994. On 1 September 1995 the trade of Joe's Enterprises Ltd is transferred to a fellow subsidiary, Combined Enterprises Ltd, which also takes an assignment of the lease. Joe has no shares in Mighty Conglomerates plc.

Joe's assessable income is as follows:

| | | | |
|---|---|---|---|
| 1994/95 | rent accrued 6 April 1994 – 5 April 1995 (as, although Joe's Enterprises Ltd ceased to be connected with Joe in June 1994, it was connected at an earlier time during the lease) | | £15,000 |
| 1995/96 | rent accrued 6 April 1995 – 31 August 1995 148/365 × £15,000 | | 6,082 |
| 1996/97 | rent due 30 April 1996 | 15,000 | |
| | Less rent accrued 6 April 1995 – 31 August 1995 | 6,082 | 8,918 |
| | (as Joe and Combined Enterprises Ltd have never been connected persons the normal Schedule A rules apply from 1 September 1995) | | |
| 1997/98 | rent due 30 April 1997 | | 15,000 |

**2.66** If the above provisions would otherwise apply but for the fact that the connected person who was entitled to a tax deduction for rent (or some other sum, such as a payment under a licence) in respect of the land was not the tenant but a third party, such as a subtenant, the landlord again had to calculate his rents on an accruals basis even though his tenant may have been an unconnected person (*ICTA 1988, s 33B(1)(2)*). This applied irrespective of whether the third party's payment was rent or other sum. The only qualification was that it was payable in arrears (*ICTA 1988, s 33B(4)*). These provisions ceased to apply from 1 April 1998 (*FA 1998, Sch 5 para 14*).

### *Agricultural Land*

**2.67** Where an estate consisted of or included agricultural land, any surplus of allowable expenditure (including capital allowances) over rents and other receipts taxable under the old style Schedule A (whether from the estate or other properties, and after deduction of all amounts deductible under Schedule A) could be set against other income of the taxpayer (*ICTA 1988, s 33(1)*). It had to be set primarily against agricultural income, i.e. income chargeable under Schedule D in respect of farming or market gardening in the UK. The amount eligible for relief against other income could not exceed the surplus expenditure that would have arisen if the estate had not included any part used wholly for purposes other than husbandry, and the expenditure had excluded a proportionate part of the expenditure relating to land used only partly for husbandry, i.e. only the part of the loss applicable to agricultural usage of the land qualified for offset against general income (*ICTA 1988, s 33(2)*). For the purpose of *section 33* an estate means any land (including houses or other buildings) managed as one estate; and agricultural land means land, houses or other buildings in the UK occupied wholly or mainly for the purpose of husbandry (*ICTA 1988, s 33(3)*). It should particularly be noted that whether or not the land was managed as one estate is a question of fact – the existence or otherwise of an election under *ICTA 1988, s 26* (see 2.26) is not relevant for this purpose. This provision ceased to apply from 1 April 1998 (*FA 1998, Sch 5 para 13*).

**Expenses under Schedule A**

**2.68** In computing assessable income under the old style Schedule A deductions could only be made for payments made by the taxpayer in respect of

(*a*) maintenance, repairs, insurance or management,

(*b*) any services provided by him otherwise than by way of maintenance or repairs which he was obliged to provide but for which he received no separate consideration (it is not clear if 'obliged' means legally obliged or if it can include something the landlord felt morally constrained to incur to protect his good name),

(*c*) rates or other charges on the occupier which the person chargeable was obliged to defray, and

(*d*) any rent, rentcharge, ground annual, feu duty or other periodical payment reserved in respect of, or charged on, or issuing out of, the land.

(*ICTA 1988, s 25(2)*).

**2.69** If an expense could not be brought within one of the above heads it could not be deducted. The Schedule D, Case I and II 'wholly and exclusively' test did not apply. Interest was not deductible even if it could be brought within one of these heads (*ICTA 1988, s 25(2)*). It could, however, be deducted from net Schedule A income. The appropriate rules are considered in chapter 4. Council tax is a property tax and as such should fall within 2.68(*c*) or (*d*) if paid by the landlord. Its predecessor, the community charge, was not, but where a landlord paid the collective community charge (which was assessable on the landlord where a building was in multi-occupation) this was deductible for Schedule A purposes to the extent that he was unable to collect it from his tenants (Inland Revenue Press Release 10 November 1989).

**2.70** Somewhat surprisingly, where improvements (or additions or alterations) to a property obviated the need to carry out maintenance or repairs, the Revenue used to allow the estimated cost of the repairs to be deducted (Inland Revenue Extra-Statutory Concession B4). This concession did not apply if the alterations, etc. were so extensive as to amount to a reconstruction of the property, or if there was a change of use of the property which would have made it unnecessary to carry out the repairs or maintenance in any event. It has been withdrawn from 1 April 2001.

**2.71** The expense also had to be incurred in respect of a period falling within the currency of the lease of the premises to which it related. In the case of a payment for maintenance or repairs it additionally had to be incurred by reason of dilapidations attributable to such a period – and after the time when the taxpayer became the landlord if he acquired the property with the lease already in place (*ICTA 1988, s 25(3)(4)*). The Schedule D case of *Odeon Associated Theatres Ltd v Jones (48 TC 257)* which allows a Case I deduction in certain circumstances for repairs attributable to dilapidations arising before the acquisition of the premises (see 9.4 below) accordingly had no application for Schedule A purposes. Expenditure on such dilapidations up to 5 April 1995 was allowed as a deduction by concession where the immediately preceding landlord was the husband or wife (or a trustee for the husband or wife) of the taxpayer or of a person for whom the taxpayer acts as trustee (Inland Revenue Extra-Statutory Concession A21). The heading to the concession read 'property passing from husband to wife (or vice versa) on death' but the wording is not so limited, so it probably also applies after an *inter vivos* transfer. The concession was withdrawn as it was felt unnecessary under the new Schedule A rules as these should automatically give relief – it is not clear how, as such expenditure would probably be capital in the hands of the new owner under the *Law Shipping* principle.

**2.72** In the case of a lease at full rent the currency of the lease was deemed to include any 'previous qualifying period'. This is any period

(*a*) during which the taxpayer was the landlord in respect of a previous lease (at full rent) of the premises, or

(*b*) which was a void period starting with either the termination of a previous lease at full rent or the acquisition by the taxpayer of the interest in the premises giving him the right to possession.

(*ICTA 1988, s 25(5)*).

**2.73** A period could not be a previous qualifying period if a non-qualifying period, e.g. one where the property was not let at a full rent, intervened between it and the grant of the lease (*ICTA 1988, s 25(5)*). A void period was one during which the taxpayer was not in occupation of the premises or of any part of them but was entitled to possession (*ICTA 1988, s 25(2)*). A period of owner occupation was not a void period.

*Example 1B*

Billy acquired a property on 10 May 1989. He renovated it and on completion of the works let it on 28 October 1989 for five years at a full rent. When the tenant moved out he looked for a new tenant without success. He then let it to a relative on 15 February 1995 on a temporary basis at a nominal rent. He managed to find a tenant willing to pay a full rent on 18 July 1995.

The period 10.5.1989 – 27.10.1989 is a previous qualifying period in respect of the lease commencing on 28.10.1989. Any expenses referable to dilapidations in that period can therefore be set against the rents under that lease.

The letting on 15.2.1995 prevents any previous period being a previous qualifying period in relation to the lease commencing on 18.7.1995. Prior losses cannot therefore be carried forward and used against the rent under that lease.

If the lease to the relative had been at a full rent all of the following would have been previous qualifying periods in relation to the lease commencing on 18.7.1995. Unrelieved expenditure in such periods could therefore be set against the rents under that lease.

| | | |
|---|---|---|
| 10.5.1989 | – 27.10.1989 | – a void period commencing with acquisition |
| 28.10.1989 | – 27.10.1994 | – a previous lease at full rent |
| 28.10.1994 | – 14.2.1995 | – a void period commencing with a previous lease at full rent |
| 15.2.1995 | – 17.7.1995 | – a previous lease at full rent |

**2.74** A lease was at full rent (for the purposes of all of *sections 25–31*) if the rent reserved under it (including an appropriate portion of any premium) was sufficient, taking one year with another, to defray the cost to the lessor of fulfilling his obligations under the lease and of meeting any expenses of maintenance, repairs, insurance and management of the premises subject to the lease, which fell to be borne by him (*ICTA 1988, s 24(7)*). The rent did not have to be a market rent. Nor did it have to be such as would show a profit to the landlord. He merely needed to expect to break even over a period. Indeed, as the definition does not take account of the possibility that the landlord may himself have to pay rent for the property, a lease could apparently be at full rent even though the landlord would make a consistent loss, provided that such loss does not exceed his rent payable. Conversely the fact that a rent was a market rent does not necessarily mean that it was at a full rent. If a rent payable by a controlled tenant was insufficient to cover the landlord's expenditure – which could happen where significant repairs were needed – it would not be a full rent and relief for past losses in respect of the premises would, at least in theory, be lost.

**2.75** If the necessary conditions were fulfilled during a period in respect of part of the premises only, that period was treated as a previous qualifying period in respect of that part, any necessary apportionments of both rent and expenditure being made (*ICTA 1988, s 25(6)*).

**2.76** If, by reason of a change of circumstances, a lease changed its status, e.g. a lease not at full rent became one at full rent, or a non-tenant's repairing lease at full rent became a tenant's repairing one, a new lease was deemed to come into existence at the time of the change (*ICTA 1988, s 25(8)*). If the taxpayer retained possession of part of the premises for the use of all the tenants a payment made in respect of those common parts was treated as if it had been made in respect of the tenanted parts (*ICTA 1988, s 25(9)*). If the leases of the tenanted parts did not all fall into the same category it was presumably necessary to apportion the expenditure on common parts between the different leases. The *Act* gave no guidance as to how this was to be done. Presumably a just and equitable basis would need to be used.

*Supplementary Provisions*

**2.77** Expenditure needed, as far as possible, to be deducted against income for the period in which it was paid. If it exceeded such income it had to be deducted in the earliest possible period in which relief could be given (*ICTA 1988, s 31(3)*). Where the income of a period was insufficient to allow the expenditure to be deducted the taxpayer could choose the order of set-off (*ICTA 1988, s 31(4)*). This restriction does not apply after 5 April 1998 (1 April 1998 for companies) (*FA 1998, Sch 5 para 12*).

**2.78** No deduction could be claimed for expenditure which was (or will be) balanced by the receipt of insurance monies, or recovered from or borne by some other person (unless the taxpayer would be chargeable under Schedule A by reference to the amount of the recovery). Nor could a deduction be taken for any amount payable under deduction of income tax (unless the taxpayer was a company) (*ICTA 1988, s 31(5)*). This is reasonable insofar as the deduction of tax gives basic rate relief for the payments. It does not give higher rate relief but, as such a payment would normally constitute an annual payment, this could be obtained against general income. An amount cannot of course be deducted twice (*ICTA 1988, s 31(6)*). This restriction does not apply after 5 April 1998 (1 April 1998 for companies) (*FA 1998, Sch 5 para 12*).

**2.79** For the purpose of the Schedule A legislation a lease includes an agreement for a lease, and any tenancy. It does not include a mortgage. References to a lessor or lessee include the successors in title to such a person. References to premises include any land (*ICTA 1988, s 24(1)*).

### Schedule A Losses

**2.80** In the first instance allowable expenses had to be deducted from the rent for the premises comprised in the lease (which was the rent of the relevant part of the building only, if it is in multi-occupation). A resultant loss in respect of premises (i.e. buildings but not land) let under a lease at a full rent (whether or not under a tenant's repairing lease) could be set against rents from other premises in the same or a subsequent year provided that those other premises were let at a full rent other than under a 'tenant's repairing lease' (*ICTA 1988, s 25(7)*). A tenant's repairing lease was one where the lessee was under an obligation to maintain the whole, or substantially the whole, of the premises comprised in the lease (*ICTA 1988, s 24(6)(c)*). This right of set-off applied not only to current losses. A brought forward loss on one property was eligible for relief against future rent from another provided that at the time such rents became due the property was still let and the loss was eligible for deduction against the then current income of the premises to which it related. Expenditure incurred during a void period in relation to the first property could also be set against rents from the second, provided that the void period followed a lease at a full rent and the expenditure would have been eligible for offset had that lease continued (*ICTA 1988, s 25(7)(b)*). Expenditure in a void period starting from the date of acquisition of the first property was probably not eligible for offset against rents from the second property. *Section 25(7)(b)* refers to 'a void period beginning with the termination of a lease at a full rent'. It may be that if the previous owner had let the property at a full rent the omission of any reference to the person chargeable would enable the period starting from the current owner's acquisition to fall within this wording.

**2.81** It may be helpful to summarise the rules on losses.

| | *Type of lease* | *Can set loss against income from* |
|---|---|---|
| (*a*) | at full rent, not a tenant's repairing lease | another lease at full rent, not a tenant's repairing lease |
| (*b*) | a tenant's repairing lease at full rent | a lease at full rent which is not a tenant's repairing lease |
| (*c*) | a lease not at full rent | the same property arising during the currency of the same lease only |

**2.82** *Section 25(8)* and *(9)* (see 2.76 above) again apply.

### Income Tax Basis of Assessment

**2.83** The assessment under Schedule A was on an 'actual' basis, i.e. the charge for a year of assessment was on the rents receivable for that year (*ICTA 1988, s 15(1)*). Where *section 33A* or *section 33B* applied (see 2.63 to 2.66 above), it was the rent accrued during that year. The due date for payment of tax was 1 January in the year of assessment (*ICTA 1988, s 5(1)*). In many cases the chargeable amount could not be known at that date. Accordingly, to avoid undue delay in collecting the tax, the assessment was initially based on the income of the preceding year and adjusted after the end of the year of assessment when the exact amount was known (*ICTA 1988, s 22(2)*). Except as mentioned below, provided that an assessment is based on the income of the preceding year there are no valid grounds of appeal against it. As *section 22(2)(b)* provided for automatic adjustments to be made after the end of the year of assessment there was strictly speaking no need to appeal against such an assessment.

**2.84** If the taxpayer sent a written statement to the Revenue before 1 January in the year of assessment (i.e. before the tax became payable) which:

(*a*) showed that since the beginning of the previous year of assessment he had ceased to possess one or more sources of income chargeable under Schedule A, e.g. he had sold a property,

(*b*) gave the aggregate of the rent and receipts relevant for the purpose of Schedule A to which he expected to become entitled in the current year, and

(*c*) showed both that those rents were less than the aggregate rents for the previous year and that if he had not sold the property the aggregate would not have been lower,

then, provided of course that the Inspector of Taxes was satisfied as to the accuracy of the statement, the assessment for the current year became the proportion of the assessment for the previous year that the rent receivable in the current year bore to that for the previous year (*ICTA 1988, s 22(3)*).

*Example 2*

Adam owned two properties, Whiteacre and Blackacre, throughout 1993/94. He sold Blackacre on 20 October 1994. He delivered a statement under *section 22(3)* to the Revenue on 20 December 1994. This showed rent receivable and expenses as follows:

| | *Rent* | *Expenses* | *Net Rent* |
|---|---|---|---|
| 1993/94 | £ | £ | £ |
| Whiteacre | 8,000 | 3,000 | 5,000 |
| Blackacre | 20,000 | 15,000 | 5,000 |
| | | | £10,000 |

| | Rent £ | Expenses £ | Net Rent £ |
|---|---|---|---|
| 1994/95 (to 20.12.1994) | | | |
| Whiteacre | 10,000 | 12,000 | (2,000) |
| Blackacre | 9,500 | 3,000 | 6,500 |
| | | | £4,500 |
| 1994/95 (anticipated to 5.4.1995) | | | |
| Whiteacre | 14,000 | 13,000 | 1,000 |
| Blackacre | 9,500 | 3,000 | 6,500 |
| | | | £7,500 |

The 1993/94 assessment will have been on £10,000. The provisional assessment for 1994/95 was on

$$\frac{23{,}500 \text{ (anticipated gross 1994/95 rents)}}{28{,}000 \text{ (gross 1993/94 rents)}} \times £10{,}000 = £8{,}392$$

In theory the Revenue could collect tax on this sum on 1 January 1995. After 5 April 1995 part of this tax would be refunded if the estimated net rental figure of £7,500 proves to be correct. In practice they are likely to collect tax initially on the £7,500 only, to avoid unnecessary work all round.

**2.85** There are a number of points that should be noted.

(*a*) Expenses for the then current year were irrelevant in this connection as the computation for *section 22(3)* purposes is based on the rents receivable.

(*b*) A statement under *section 22(3)* could be served only if gross rents fell because of a disposal of one of the properties. If the rents on Whiteacre for 1994/95 in the above example had been estimated at £19,000 no adjustment could have been made, as although Blackacre had been sold there would have been no reduction in the aggregate rents.

(*c*) If the tenant of Blackacre had moved out but the property had been retained no adjustment would have been competent, i.e. the provisional assessment would have been £10,000 for 1994/95 even though the rents had fallen as Blackacre had become vacant. It is not certain that this would be so if the owner had moved into Blackacre, as it is arguable that by becoming a private residence it would have ceased to be a source of income chargeable under Schedule A.

(*d*) There was no provision to enable the provisional assessment to be reduced below that for the previous year on the grounds that exceptionally heavy expenditure has had to be incurred on the properties in the current year.

**2.86** The special provisions set out above in relation to sporting rights (see 2.29), receipts and payments on sale of land (see 2.25), land managed as one estate (see 2.26) and sea walls (see 2.37–2.40) also applied under the old system. So does the comment at 2.30 on alternative accommodation. The rules on capital allowances (see 2.31–2.36) also applied under the old rules with the exception that capital allowances were not deducted in arriving at the Schedule A income. They were calculated separately and offset against the Schedule A income.

## Collection from Lessees and Agents

**2.87** The old style Schedule A charge was on the person receiving or entitled to the profits or gains in respect of which the tax was charged (*ICTA 1988, s 21(1)*). This did not apply where the person entitled to the income was within the charge to corporation tax (*ICTA 1988, s 21(2)*). Instead the normal corporation tax charging provisions applied in such circumstances.

**2.88** For years up to 1994/95 (1995/96 where the provisions of *FA 1995, s 39(5)* (see 2.53) apply), if tax was charged on a person who was not the occupier of the land (which was almost always the case) and that taxpayer (called the person in default) did not pay the tax, provision was made for it to be recovered from the occupier or some other person in certain circumstances (*ICTA 1988, s 23(1)*).

(*a*) The Collector of Taxes could require the occupier or any other lessee whose interest derived directly or indirectly from that of the person in default to pay the Collector on such date or dates as he specified such sum or sums as he required. The amount required to be paid in any period could not exceed the rent (or other sums) payable by that person in respect of the land at the end of that period to either the person in default or to a person deriving his interest from him (*ICTA 1988, s 23(2)(3)*). The payer was entitled to deduct the tax payment from any subsequent payment of rent due from him. If he deducted it from rent due not to the person in default but to an intermediate lessee, that lessee could in turn deduct the like amount from rent that he owed his landlord. If an intermediate lessee's rent payable was such that he could not recoup the deduction from payments he made in the following twelve months, he could reclaim the excess from the Revenue (*ICTA 1988, s 23(5)(6)*). The intention was obviously that the occupier or an intermediate lessee could be required to pay his rent to the Collector instead of to the landlord until the tax debt had been discharged. If the occupier or lessee who was required by the Collector to make the payments did not do so they could be recovered from him as if they were tax charged on him (*ICTA 1988, s 23(4)*).

(*b*) If rents or other receipts from land were received by an agent and Schedule A tax charged on his principal was unpaid, the Collector could require the agent to pay to the Collector any sums from time to time received by the agent on behalf of the principal, until the tax liability had been settled. The requirement extended to all receipts on account of rents or other receipts from land, including any amounts in the agent's hands when the notice was given by the Collector. The agent was liable to a penalty of up to £50 in relation to sums in hand at the date of the notice, plus a further £50 in relation to each subsequent receipt of rent, if he did not comply with such a notice (*ICTA 1988, s 23(7)(8)*).

*Section 23* of *ICTA 1988* was repealed for income tax purposes for 1995/96 onwards and for corporation tax for accounting periods ending on or after 31 March 1995. There was an exception where a source of income assessable in 1994/95 under Schedule A ceased during 1995/96 and the taxpayer did not set up and commence another Schedule A business in that year (*FA 1995, s 39(5)*).

**Receipts other than Rent**

**2.89** The only expenditure that could be deducted from Schedule A receipts which was not rent payable under a lease was

(*a*) so much of any payment made by the taxpayer as was made in respect of maintenance, repairs, insurance or management of premises to which the receipt relates, and which constituted an expense of the transaction under which the taxpayer became entitled to that receipt,

(*b*) so much of any rent, rentcharge, ground annual, feu duty or other periodical payment made by the taxpayer as was reserved in respect of (or was charged upon or issued out of) premises to which the receipt relates and constituted an expense of the transaction giving rise to the receipt,

(*c*) so much of any other payment, not being an expense of a capital nature, made by the taxpayer as constituted an expense of the transaction giving rise to the receipt, and

(*d*) if the taxpayer entered into a similar transaction in the same or an earlier year of assessment or accounting period, any amount falling within (*a*) to (*c*) in relation to that other transaction which could have been deducted from the receipt under the other transaction but for its being too small.

(*ICTA 1988, s 28*).

**Rents taxable under Case VI of Schedule D**

**2.90** Rents from furnished lettings were not normally taxable under Schedule A. They were taxable under Case VI of Schedule D, unless it could be shown that the lettings constituted a trading activity. Where Case VI applied the taxpayer could elect, within two years after the end of the relevant year of assessment or accounting period, for the rent to be apportioned between consideration for the occupation of the property and consideration for the use of the furniture, and for the former to be taxed under Schedule A (*ICTA 1988, s 15(1) para 4, (2)*). This course involved agreeing an apportionment of the rent with the Inland Revenue. As both Schedule A and Case VI were assessable on an actual basis there was normally no benefit in making such an election unless the taxpayer had Schedule A losses in respect of other properties. In such circumstances the election allowed part of the rent from the furnished property to be set against the losses. Strictly speaking, prior to 6 April 1992, this election could only be made in relation to rent receivable under a lease. *F(No 2)A 1992, s 58* formally extended the provision to other receipts, such as under a licence, although the change merely gave statutory force to a long-standing Revenue practice.

**2.91** There were no special rules laid down in the legislation as to the computation of Case VI profits. In practice they were normally calculated broadly on Schedule D, Case I principles. However, the income to be brought into account was undoubtedly only the amounts actually received in the year as the normal rule for taxing investment income (as opposed to trading profit) is that, in the absence of specific legislation (such as under Schedule A), it must have been received to attract a tax charge. Capital allowances on plant or machinery were not claimable on assets used for furnished lettings of residential property (*CAA 1990, s 61(2)*). Instead the Revenue allowed relief for replacement of furniture, etc. on a renewals basis – which of course meant that no tax relief was given until the initial furniture wore out. Alternatively an annual depreciation allowance could be claimed. This was normally 10% of the rent, net of council tax and water rates and any other services paid for by the landlord which are normally liabilities of the tenant. Where a different method of allowing for depreciation applied prior to 6 April 1975 in a particular case, this was normally allowed to continue (Inland Revenue Press Release 13 October 1977).

**2.92** Capital allowances could be claimed against income from furnished lettings of non-residential properties, although it is unusual for commercial premises to be let furnished other than where individual offices are let as serviced offices – where the charge to tax was normally under Case I of Schedule D rather than Case VI (*CAA 1990, s 61*).

## Non-residents

**2.93** A special scheme for rents payable to non-residents (called below the Non-Resident Landlords Scheme) was introduced from 1996/97 to fit in with self-assessment for individuals. *FA 1995, s 40* contains the enabling legislation for the new scheme and this is filled out by the *Taxation of Income from Land (Non-Residents) Regulations 1995* (*SI 1995 No 2902*). There are two options, to suffer tax by deduction at source or to opt into self-assessment. *Section 43* of *ICTA 1988* which imposed a tax charge on any UK agent (see 2.97) ceased to apply to payments after 5 April 1996 (*FA 1995, s 40(3)*). For the purpose of the Non-Resident Landlords Scheme an individual is non-resident if his usual place of abode is outside the UK. A trust or company is non-resident if it is managed and controlled outside the UK. A non-UK resident company is chargeable to income tax not corporation tax (except in relation to UK trading income and income ancillary to such trading income). It must therefore compute its taxable income in accordance with the income tax rules.

*Deduction of Tax at Source*

**2.94** In the absence of any action by the landlord, the tenant or, if he pays his rent to a UK agent, that agent (or if there are several UK agents the last in the chain), must deduct tax at source and account for it quarterly to the Inland Revenue, irrespective of whether the rent has been paid over to the landlord in that quarter. Payment into the landlord's UK account is not payment to an agent so the depositor has the obligation to deduct. A tenant is relieved of the obligation to account for tax where there is no agent if the gross rent is at the rate of £5,200 p.a. or less (*Reg 3(5)*). He may need to take care as the Revenue have said that there will be an obligation to account for tax if the rent is £100 per week and there are 53 rent days in the tax year (Taxline, March 1996, p 4). The deduction is based on the gross rents less specified expenses. Specified expenses means any amount paid in the quarter either by the tenant (or agent) or by another person at his direction that he can reasonably be satisfied are deductible under the Schedule A rules (*Reg 9*).

**2.95** If the payer does not deduct tax when he should the Inland Revenue nevertheless requires him to account to them for the sum that ought to have been deducted. It may not always be possible to recover the amount subsequently from the landlord. Great care needs to be taken where the tenant knows or suspects that the landlord's usual place of abode is outside the UK. However, the Inland Revenue have confirmed that the tenant would not be held liable for deducting tax at source if the landlord moves his usual place of abode outside the UK and the tenant is unaware that the move has taken place. In those circumstances the Revenue could still assess the non-resident landlord.

As the property is in the UK the Revenue can readily enforce payment by obtaining judgment against the landlord and, if this is not complied with, instituting bankruptcy proceedings.

**2.96** From the landlord's point of view the deduction of income tax creates a number of problems. Deduction at source is based on rents received by the agent (or paid by the tenant) whereas the landlord's Schedule A liability is calculable on an accruals basis. Mortgage interest is rarely paid by the agent or at his direction. In the case of residential property it is normally paid direct by the landlord and with commercial property the agent is normally instructed to pay the rents into the landlord's bank account with the lender, against which the lender debits the interest by arrangement with the landlord. In either case it is unlikely to be a specified expense. Capital allowances on plant in a building, and in the case of furnished lettings the 10% wear and tear allowance, are also not specified expenses. It is notoriously difficult with repairs and some other types of expense to determine the extent to which it qualifies as a Schedule A deduction or is disallowable as capital. An agent or tenant is likely to be very cautious and give the benefit of any doubt to the Revenue. He will be liable for a penalty if he takes into account something that the Revenue think he ought not to have been reasonably satisfied was deductible. Accordingly deduction at source is likely to result in payment of excessive tax – and the need for the landlord to file a self-assessment return to reclaim the over-deduction. If the landlord is an individual a possible advantage of deduction at source is that it is limited to basic rate tax and in practice the Revenue are likely to accept the deduction as satisfying the landlord's tax liability.

**2.97** Prior to 1995/96 a tenant had an obligation to deduct income tax at the basic rate from the gross rent and account for it to the Inland Revenue (*ICTA 1988, s 43(1)*). There was no obligation to make a deduction if the payment was made to a UK agent of the non-resident landlord. A payment into a UK bank account in the name of the non-resident was regarded as a payment to the non-resident and tax needed to be deducted. Where payment was made to a UK agent the non-resident was normally assessed in the name of the non-resident and the agent was personally liable for the non-resident's tax on the rents.

### *Self-assessment*

**2.98** The alternative of opting in to self-assessment requires the consent of the Inland Revenue. This will not be given unless the non-resident has a satisfactory tax history, i.e. for a non-resident who wants to self-assess for 2003/04 onwards he has filed his tax return/accounts and paid the tax for all years up to 2001/02. A non-resident who first invests in UK property after 5 April 1995 is automatically assumed to have a satisfactory tax history. An application to self-assess needs to be made to the Revenue as early as possible – for new purchases preferably well before completion. This is because the tenant or agent must deduct tax until he has been notified by the Inland Revenue not to do so. The application form must be completed by the landlord; it cannot be signed by the agent on his behalf. Permission to self-assess will be withdrawn if the non-resident incurs a tax surcharge or if he is tardy in supplying information to the Revenue. Once withdrawn the non-resident will have to wait two years before being again allowed to self-assess.

**2.99** Agents for a non-resident have to register with the Inland Revenue's Centre for Non-Residents in Bootle, irrespective of whether they deduct tax at source or all their clients self-assess. Agents have to make a quarterly return of tax due (on a global basis) and a detailed annual return. They are also subject to audit by the Inland Revenue.

## Service Charges

**2.100** There is no special tax regime applying to service charges, or to sinking or reserve funds set up under service charge arrangements. The tax position will depend on identifying and applying the legal effect of the provisions of each individual lease, although in practice the Revenue seem content to treat the amount as rent irrespective of its legal status (see 2.104).

**2.101** There are four main possibilities, although almost every lease is different, and the correct approach is not to try to ascertain into which of these categories the particular lease most nearly falls, but rather to identify the legal effect of that particular lease. The main possibilities are:

(*a*) the service charge is paid as additional rent;

(*b*) the service charge (including any reserve fund element) is paid under a covenant in the lease to reimburse to the landlord expenditure incurred by him;

(*c*) the service charge is payable to the landlord but the reserve fund element is payable to a trustee (who may be – and normally is – the landlord himself); and

(*d*) a separate management company takes on responsibility for maintaining the building and receives the service charge direct from the tenant.

The position is further complicated by *section 42* of the *Landlord and Tenant Act 1987* which requires service charge monies to be held on trust for the tenants in the case of most, but not all, residential properties. *Section 42* overrides a provision in the lease in relation to such monies. Worse, it is not clear from the statute precisely what the terms of that statutory trust are (see 2.111). Accordingly the tax treatment of interest arising from the investment of such funds is likely to be different from that suggested by the terms of the lease.

**2.102** Major tax problems are unlikely to occur in relation to service charges which merely recoup actual expenditure. The problems arise where a sinking or reserve fund is being built up. The VAT position can also be complex. This is considered at 17.211 onwards.

**Additional Rent**

**2.103** Where the service charge is receivable as additional rent the receipt is clearly taxable under Schedule A in the same way as the basic rent and the landlord can deduct the actual expenditure to the extent that he can bring it within the Schedule A rules (see 2.12 and 2.68 above). The effect will be to tax the landlord on money he receives in respect of contributions to a reserve fund or in respect of capital expenditure (as the definition of repairs under most service charge clauses will often include items that constitute improvements for tax purposes). Care may sometimes need to be taken to match receipts and payments where the service charge year is different from the landlord's accounting period – although it would be rare for any excess of service charge expenditure over service charge income falling in an accounting period to be so large as to exceed the total rents. If, although a landlord receives the service charge as additional rent, he is obliged by the lease to set aside the reserve fund element, this will in effect require him to appropriate his own (taxed) money for this purpose. If the reserve fund is required to be invested in such a case, the investment income will be income of the landlord and the tax payable on it will therefore be dependent on his tax position.

**Under Covenant**

**2.104** Where the service charge is receivable under a covenant in the lease it is probably strictly assessable under either Case I (as constituting a trade) or possibly Case VI of Schedule D. In practice the receipt is likely to be assessed under Schedule A although it does not strictly arise to the landlord 'by virtue of his ownership of an estate or interest in land'; it arises by virtue of the obligation to provide services that he has entered into. As a Case VI loss cannot be carried back and cannot be set against non-Case VI income – such as rents – any attempt to assess under Case VI needs to be resisted.

**Payable to a Trustee**

**2.105** If the reserve fund element of the service charge is payable by the tenant to a trustee the trust is a separate taxable entity, albeit that the sole trustee is normally the landlord, so the tax treatment of neither the contributions nor the income generated from their investment will be affected by the landlord's own tax position. As the trust will receive the sinking fund contributions as capital they would not themselves attract a tax charge. Income generated by the investment of the funds will belong to the trust and will be taxable. The tax rate will depend on the form of the trust – which is not always readily apparent, i.e. is it a discretionary trust or an interest in possession trust? If it is a discretionary trust the 34% rate applicable to trusts will be payable. If it is an interest in possession trust the tax rate within the trust will be 20% but each of the tenants will need to declare his share of the interest on his tax return and pay higher rate tax, or corporation tax, on it (subject to being given credit for the 20% paid). Because of the practical difficulties of collecting the tax in such circumstances the Revenue have been known to claim that the trust is an 'unincorporated association' and as such liable to corporation tax. As a trust is an entity recognised in law it is difficult to see how they could substantiate such a claim. Nevertheless, as the small companies rate of corporation tax of 20% would almost always apply, such treatment ought normally to be acceptable to tenants. It is interesting to note that in their 1991 consultative document on trusts the Revenue state (at para 14.31):

'Any income and gains from the investment of the service charges are taxed under the normal trust rules. Often . . . liability is at the sum of the basic and additional rates because the trustees have the power to accumulate any income which is not needed to meet current expenditure or have some discretion as to how the fund income should be used.'

**2.106** It also needs to be borne in mind that trusts have Inheritance Tax ('IHT') consequences and there is no exception in the IHT legislation for trusts set up under leases. There is probably no problem when money is paid into the trust as the tenant is fulfilling a contractual obligation and has no gratuitous intent to benefit anyone other than himself. If the trust is an interest in possession trust there will be a potential liability to IHT when the tenant disposes of his lease. This will bring about a cessation of his interest in possession, which will generate IHT on the difference between the disposal proceeds of the interest and the underlying value of the assets in the settlement attributable to that interest. The problem can be solved by the tenant attributing the appropriate proportion of the selling price to his interest in the reserve fund and reducing the amount attributable to his lease – although this may be unattractive to the purchaser from a CGT viewpoint. As the IHT is a liability of the trustees, and is thus in effect borne by the remaining tenants, consideration needs to be given to requiring the tenant, as a condition of giving him a licence to assign his lease, to reimburse any IHT payable.

**2.107** If the trust is a discretionary trust IHT charges can arise both on the application of the reserve fund monies and under the ten-yearly periodic charge if the life of the fund exceeds ten years. It is not at all clear how any IHT liability would be calculated. The rate depends on the rate payable by a deemed settlor at the time of creation of the settlement. Each tenant is probably the settlor of the amount he puts into the reserve fund – although it is unclear whether he 'settles' all his periodic payments at the time he signs the lease or if each payment is an additional settlement. Nor is it clear what assumptions are made as to the deemed settlor when the tenant is a company. The Revenue do not in practice seem to take these IHT points but it is probably unsafe to assume that they will never do so.

## Separate Management Company

**2.108** Probably the most satisfactory approach from a tax point of view, where it is wished to maintain a reserve fund, is to have a separate management company to handle the management of the building. This is very common with residential property but rare with commercial lettings. The management company is almost certainly carrying on a trade of providing the services but the 'profit' (i.e. the reserve fund) should be free of tax under the mutual trading principle provided that the requisite conditions are met. Mutual trading occurs where 'a member . . . makes a rateable contribution to a common fund, in which he and his co-partners are jointly interested . . . He pays according to an estimate of the amount which will be required for the common benefit' (*Styles v New York Life Assurance Co (2 TC 460)*). This is a good description of a service charge! The existence of a company does not destroy the mutuality but the receipt of service charges from a tenant who does not have an interest in the common fund probably does. This is why it is normal for each of the tenants to hold a share in the company. In theory the ownership of the company is not important. What is important is to be able to demonstrate that on a liquidation any surplus assets will be returned to the contributors to the common fund. The receipt of investment income, such as bank interest from the investment of the sinking fund, will not destroy the mutuality. Such income will however be chargeable to corporation tax. Where trading income is receivable from non-members it may be possible to separate those activities from the mutual activities. For example, if a company receives service charges for flats wholly from members and such charges from garages partly from members and partly from non-members, it may be possible to contend that the company is carrying on two distinct trading activities – servicing flats, which is a mutual trade, and servicing garages, the whole of the profit (if any) from which is chargeable to corporation tax. It is understood that the Revenue are sometimes prepared to treat servicing the flats of shareholders as a mutual trade and servicing the flats of other tenants as a taxable activity.

**2.109** The mutual trading concept does not apply for Schedule A, at least from 1998/99 onwards and probably also before that date. Accordingly where, as is normal with residential flat management companies, the management company is also the landlord, e.g. it is entitled to the ground rents on long leases, the mutual trading concept cannot apply. In practice in the past where such a company claimed to be exempt under mutual trading the Revenue normally accepted it. The Revenue now say that they accepted no tax was payable not under mutual trading principles but by concession. Where service charges received by occupier-controlled flat management companies were matched over a period of up to five years by admissible expenses no Schedule A charge was normally imposed (Tax Bulletin 37, September 1998).

**Deemed trusts under the Landlord and Tenant Act 1987**

**2.110** *Section 42* of the *Landlord and Tenant Act 1987* provides that service charge monies received in relation to residential property are to be held on trust to carry out the work with any surplus being held on trust for the tenants. The Revenue take the view that the correct accounting treatment in the light of this requirement is to treat the service charge monies as received as capital in the landlord's capacity as a trustee. Such monies will therefore not be income of the landlord for Schedule A purposes. It seems questionable whether this is a correct interpretation but as it is wholly favourable to taxpayers it seems unlikely that anyone will challenge it.

**2.111** The Revenue consider that income generated from the investment of service charge monies that are to be held on statutory trusts under *section 42* of the *Landlord and Tenant Act 1987* is taxable on the trustees at the 34% rate applicable to trusts. This is apparently because they consider that *section 42* contains 'an implied power to accumulate'. It is by no means certain that they are correct. The exact nature of the trust created by *section 42* is unclear. It is also unclear who is the settlor. *Subsection 3(a)* appears to create a purpose trust but such trusts are not recognised in English law (*re Endacott [1959] 3 All ER 562*). Accordingly, in trust law, the trust may well be a resultant trust for the benefit of the settlor. Where under the terms of a lease the landlord is entitled to receive the service charge without there being any requirement for him to put the monies into trust, the settlor of the *section 42* trust must be the landlord. Under the lease it is his money but the law requires him to take it and set up the trust. *Section 42(7)* provides that in certain circumstances the money is to revert to the person legally entitled to receive the service charge (which would normally be either the landlord or a separate management company or trust) and for that recipient to then pass the money to the landlord. Accordingly, if the landlord is the settlor, the trust must be a trust in which the settlor has retained an interest so that the income of that trust will be taxable on the settlor under *ICTA 1988, s 660A*. That seems fairly tough on the landlord as the statute requires the trust to be created in this particular format. Nevertheless that seems to be the tax effect. If the landlord is not the settlor of the *section 42* trust, then presumably the tenant is the settlor. If that is the case, the trust is again one in which the settlor has retained an interest because of section *42(3)(b)*. An alternative analysis is that the monies in the trust belong at all times to the tenants in equity, so that the income is taxable on the tenants at their tax rates. The landlord is taxable as a person in receipt of the income, but only at the basic rate. In practice the interest is unlikely to be large enough to justify the costs of an appeal so the Revenue view that the interest is taxable at 34% is likely to become a standard treatment.

**2.112** The *Landlord and Tenant Act 1987* applies only to England and Wales. For *section 42* to apply a payment must be made under the terms of the lease. The Act defines a service charge as 'an amount payable by a tenant of a dwelling, as part of or in addition to rent, which is payable directly or indirectly for services, repairs, maintenance or insurance or the landlord's costs of management, and the whole or part of which varies or may vary according to the relevant costs'. There is an exception for an 'exempt' landlord as defined in *section 58(1)* of the Act (mainly registered social landlords, local authorities and charitable housing trusts) (Tax Bulletin 48, August 2000).

### The Position of the Tenant

**2.113** The position of the tenant is considered at 12.8 below. The structuring of service charges and reserve funds will depend largely on commercial considerations, taking into account whether a reserve fund is needed, the protection the tenants want for any such fund, the need of the tenants to obtain a deduction, and the importance to the landlord of not paying tax on money that he is required to set aside for a specific purpose.

## Dilapidations

**2.114** Where the landlord receives a payment from the tenant for dilapidations on the expiry of the lease the tax treatment is unclear. Logically the receipt is compensation for the fact that the tenant has not delivered back the premises in the same state and as a result has reduced the value of the landlord's interest in the property. It is therefore consideration for a part disposal of the property in accordance with *TCGA 1992, s 22*. However that is not the Revenue view. They say that the tax treatment depends on what the landlord does with the premises. If he disposes of the premises or occupies them himself, they agree it is a capital receipt chargeable to capital gains tax. If he re-lets the premises and does not carry out the repairs, they consider it is a revenue receipt as it has the effect of filling a hole in the landlord's profits, i.e. it is compensation for the lower rent the property can now command (Property Income Manual PIM 2020). It is hard to follow the logic of this. The hole is not a temporary one. There is a permanent diminution in the value of the premises and that diminution is as much a capital 'loss' if the premises are re-let as if they are sold or owner occupied. If the money is used towards the cost of repairs, the revenue view is that it should be netted off against the expenditure as that expenditure has not been expended by the landlord to the extent that it has been made good by the former tenant (PIM 2020). Again this seems questionable.

## Rent-a-Room Relief

**2.115** For 1992/93 onwards a special relief applies to the furnished lettings of part of an only or main residence of an individual (*F(No 2)A 1992, s 59, Sch 10*). This relief, which the government call 'rent-a-room', exempts the gross rent from income tax if it is less than £4,250 (£3,250 up to 1996/97). If it exceeds that sum, the taxpayer is, in effect, allowed to claim a deduction in calculating the rent of such sum as will bring the aggregate deductions for expenses and interest up to £4,250. The rent must be assessable under Case I or Schedule A (or prior to 1995/96 Case VI of Schedule D) (*F(No 2)A 1992, Sch 10 para 2*). Electing under the pre-1995/96 rules to tax the part relating to use of the premises under Schedule A (see 2.90) would have taken it out of the scope of the relief. It would also have taken the part relating to the use of the furniture out of the scope of the relief as it applies only if 'all relevant sums', i.e. all sums accruing in respect of the use of furnished accommodation in the residence, or in respect of relevant goods or services supplied in connection with that use, are taxable under Case I or Case VI (*F(No 2)A 1992, Sch 10 para 2(2)*). Relevant goods and services means meals, cleaning, laundry and goods and services of a similar nature (*F(No 2)A 1992, Sch 10 para 8*). The relief of course covers not only rent for the premises but any other receipt in respect of such items.

**2.116** Although the relief is intended to apply only to residential accommodation some people think that it is drawn sufficiently broadly that it will also apply to a letting of a room in one's house for non-residential purposes. Accordingly it is sometimes suggested that the director of a family company might let a room in his house to his company for use as an office and escape tax on the rent. Anyone tempted to do this should be wary of simply not declaring the rent on the director's tax return. As the Revenue have made clear that they do not accept this view (Tax Bulletin, Issue 12, August 1994) it would be wise to draw the treatment adopted to the attention of the Revenue while at the same time claiming that it is not taxable. Apart from the intention of the legislation, there are two specific provisions that cast doubt on the above interpretation. *Sch 10 para 7* defines a residence as 'a building, or part of a building occupied or intended to be occupied as a separate residence'. This may exclude a room intended to be occupied as an office from being part of the residence at all. That certainly is how the Revenue interpret the wording. *Sch 10 para 5*, which deals with the position where there are joint owners of the property, refers to rent 'in respect of the use of residential accommodation in the residence'. It seems unlikely that the courts will hold that the Schedule allows a room to be let as commercial accommodation if there is a single owner but not if there are joint owners.

**2.117** The relief does not apply if in the year of assessment the individual is taxable in respect of any sums derived from a qualifying residence which are not 'relevant sums' accruing to him in respect of that residence (*F(No 2)A 1992, Sch 10 para 2(3)*). It is not readily apparent what this exclusion is intended to cover. It seems to apply if another part of the residence is let unfurnished so that an amount is taxable under Schedule A. It would also apply if the services provided include any which are not similar to meals, cleaning and laundry. For example, if the rent includes use of a garden, such a facility would not appear to be either in respect of use of the furnished accommodation or the use of relevant goods or services. It is difficult to discern any logic in denying relief in either of these circumstances.

**2.118** The property concerned must be a qualifying residence; that is, a property which is the individual's only or main residence at any time in the basis period for the year of assessment concerned (*F(No 2)A 1992, Sch 10 para 4*). A residence is defined as a building, or part of a building occupied or intended to be occupied as a separate residence, or a caravan or house boat. A building designed for permanent use as a single residence is to be treated as such notwithstanding that it is temporarily divided into two or more parts which are occupied as separate residences (*F(No 2)A 1992, Sch 10 para 7*). No guidance is given as to what is meant by temporarily divided. Suppose a person who owns a two-storey house puts a door at the foot of the stairs, lets the top part furnished to a family, and takes in a lodger in the bottom owner-occupied part. The property is undoubtedly occupied as two separate residences, one by the owner and the lodger and the other by the tenant family. If the door temporarily divides the property, the relief extends to the total rent received. If it does not, i.e. it either permanently divides it or divides it for longer than a short duration (whichever meaning the word temporary is intended to bear), the relief will apply only to the rent from the lodger. What if the upper part is let unfurnished? If the door divides the house temporarily, no relief at all is due. If it does not, relief is due on the rent from the lodger.

**2.119** As mentioned in 2.115 above, the relief applies only if the gross rents do not exceed £4,250 p.a. (£3,250 up to 1996/97) (*F(No 2)A 1992, Sch 10 para 6(b)*). The Treasury are empowered to alter this figure either upwards or downwards (*F(No 2)A 1992, Sch 10 para 6(a)*). If, at any time in the basis period during which the property is the individual's only or main residence, sums accrue to some other person in respect of the use of residential accommodation in the residence (or in respect of goods or services supplied in connection with that use), the limit is reduced to half, i.e. £2,125. For example, if the rent is received jointly by husband and wife, each will be able to receive £2,125 tax free. This will also apply where only one spouse receives rent, by virtue of *ICTA 1988, s 282A* (which requires income from jointly held property to be attributed to spouses in equal shares), unless an election is made under *section 282B*. Curiously, if the rent is received jointly by husband, wife and two children (who are either over 18 or bought a share of the house out of funds provided other than by their parents), each is entitled to £2,125, so increasing the total exempt amount in respect of the house to £8,500. The reason for this generosity on the part of the government where children are still living at home, is not readily apparent. However, it should be noted that if one of the joint recipients did not reside in the property (and thus could not qualify for 'rent-a-room'), the resident recipient would still only be entitled to £2,125 tax free.

**2.120** Where the exemption applies and a loss is incurred, the loss will not be an allowable loss (*F(No 2)A 1992, Sch 10 para 9(2)(b)*). Nor can capital allowances be claimed or a balancing charge be made (*F(No 2)A 1992, Sch 10 para 9(3)*). However, if a potential balancing charge plus the rent itself exceeds the £4,250 (or £2,125) figure, the exemption does not apply if the rents are taxable under Case I, although it did seem still to apply if they were taxable under Case VI as the legislation refers to 'machinery or plant provided for the purposes of any trade' (*F(No 2)A 1992, Sch 10 para 9(4)(5)*). To preserve the benefit of a loss, an election can be made for the exemption from tax not to apply (*F(No 2)A 1992, Sch 10 para 10*). Such an election has effect only for the year for which it is made; it does not affect the exemption for later years. It can also be withdrawn if this is beneficial – and it is discovered quickly, as both the election and a withdrawal need to be made within one year of the end of the year of assessment concerned (*F(No 2)A 1992, Sch 10 para 10(4)*). The Board of Inland Revenue have power to extend this time limit. Losses brought forward under *ICTA 1988, s 385* (or under *ICTA 1988, s 392* in relation to property related Case VI income) from years when 'rent-a-room' did not apply, can be carried forward for use in later years when an election for the exemption not to apply is in force.

**2.121** Where the gross rents exceed the £4,250 or £2,125 limit, an election can be made to adopt a limited relief. Where, as will usually be the case, the receipts for rent and services are treated as derived from a single source, the taxable income of the basis period is deemed to be A minus B where A is the gross rents and B is the individual's limit for the year, i.e. £4,250 or £2,125 as the case may be (*F(No 2)A 1992, Sch 10 para 11(2)(3)*). If the receipts are treated as derived from two or more sources, e.g. furnished letting and a trade of providing meals, the profits or gains of the basis period of each source are deemed to be C minus D. C is the gross income from the individual source and D is a fraction of the individual's limit for the year, namely the fraction that the gross income from that source bears to the aggregate gross income from all of the sources (*F(No 2)A 1992, Sch 10 para 11(4)(5)*). Where this election is made, no deduction can be claimed for expenses 'or any other matter' – which presumably means loan interest. Nor can capital allowances be claimed (*F(No 2)A 1992, Sch 10 para 11(6)(7)*). There is no bar on the Revenue raising a balancing charge though. Clearly, the election should only be made if the expenses and interest are under the individual's limit for the year as the overall effect of the election is to substitute £4,250 (£2,125) for the aggregate of the actual expenses, capital allowances and other deductions.

**2.122** The election must be made within one year after the end of the year of assessment for which it is to apply (*F(No 2)A 1992, Sch 10 para 12(2)(b)*). Once made it will also have effect for all future years until it is withdrawn (*F(No 2)A 1992, Sch 10 para 12(2)(a)*). Notice of withdrawal (which can apply to the first year if desired) must similarly be made within twelve months after the end of the year of assessment for which it is to have effect. A withdrawal will not prevent a fresh election being made for a subsequent year (*F(No 2)A 1992, Sch 10 para 12(4)*). If at any time while an election is in force, the rent drops below the £4,250 (or £2,125) limit, notice of withdrawal of the election is automatically deemed to have been given. It is deemed to be given at the very end of the notice period, not so that the Revenue can raise an assessment and then subsequently vacate it but to allow the Revenue the maximum period to raise any resultant assessment (although it is hard to envisage why they should need to do so (*F(No 2)A 1992, Sch 10 para 12(6)*)).

## Rents taxable under Case I of Schedule D

**2.123** Rents can be assessable under Case I of Schedule D as trading income in two circumstances. The first is where part of a trader's business premises is sublet. This is a concessional treatment to avoid the need to apportion outgoings. Statutorily rents are required to be taxed under Schedule A. For it to apply

(*a*) the accommodation must be temporarily surplus to business requirements, i.e. it must have been used or intended for use in the business and it must not be evident that it has become permanently surplus to business requirements,

(*b*) the property must be used partly for the business and partly let – as the object of the concession is to avoid the need to apportion outgoings on the property between trading and Schedule A expenses, and

(*c*) the rental income must be comparatively small (it is not clear in comparison with what).

(Tax Bulletin, Issue 10). In the past the concession was also given where premises formerly occupied in the trade were let temporarily pending their disposal but this treatment no longer appears acceptable.

**2.124** The second is where services provided by the landlord are of sufficient substance that the landlord is carrying on a trade of providing serviced accommodation. There are no hard and fast rules as to what is necessary to constitute a trade. It is a matter of degree. Most Inspectors of Taxes will regard cleaning and lighting of the common parts as insufficient and will look for the provision of services to individual rooms. The provision of meals to tenants will generally attract Case I treatment. The provision of cleaning to individual rooms and making up beds will frequently do so. Where a range of services is not provided to individual rooms most Inspectors will resist Case I treatment, although some may be sympathetic if the landlord is engaged virtually full-time in managing his properties and provides at least some services to tenants such as small repairs, window cleaning, etc.

**2.125** There are two leading cases, *Gittos v Barclay (55 TC 633)* and *Griffiths v Jackson (56 TC 583)*, in both of which the activities were held not to constitute a trade. However, the services seem to have been of a relatively minor nature and the decisions are not surprising. Mrs Gittos owned a number of holiday villas which she let out furnished. The services provided seem to have been limited to preparing the villas for tenants and cleaning up after them. No services seem to have been provided for individual tenants whilst they were in occupation of their villa. Mr Jackson, who had a full-time job elsewhere, rented properties to students. He supplied linen, which was laundered once a month, for lets of 13 weeks or less but not for longer lettings. He provided occasional food and other services – primarily the stocking of fridges before a tenant took up occupation. Again, however, few or no services appear to have been provided to a tenant once his occupation of the property had commenced.

**2.126** Following the decisions in *Gittos v Barclay* and *Griffiths v Jackson*, the Inland Revenue are in general seeking to recategorise from Case I to Case VI many lettings which they had previously accepted as constituting a trade. It has also become virtually impossible to establish that a new furnished letting activity constitutes a trade. It should be borne in mind that those cases did not actually decide that furnished lettings for which services are provided cannot constitute a trade, but rather that, on the particular facts of those cases, those lettings did not do so. This was confirmed in Parliament by the then Chief Secretary to the Treasury, Peter Rees QC, an eminent tax barrister (see 2.134 below). Those cases nevertheless make it far more difficult than before to establish that the lettings constitute a trade where the landlord is not intimately involved in providing services to the tenants of the accommodation. It may be helpful to mention that in *Griffiths v Jackson* Vinelott J said that the real question is whether the activities constitute the letting of furnished rooms or the activities of a lodging housekeeper and the distinction between the two 'is no doubt a narrow one, more particularly in these days of self-service hotels and motels, but the principle is clear'. He went on to quote with approval Lord Russell of

Kilowin in a rating case, *Westminster Council v Southern Railway Co ([1936] AC 511)*, who identified the main attributes of the keeper of a lodging house as the retention of a contractual right of access to the lodgers' rooms and control of the ingress and egress to and from the house.

**2.127** When considering whether to push for Case I treatment it is important to be conscious of the VAT position. Whilst rents from letting residential accommodation are normally exempt from VAT, the provision of sleeping accommodation in a 'similar establishment' to a hotel, inn or boarding house, and the letting of 'holiday accommodation' in a house or flat, are both liable to VAT at the 17½% standard rate (*VATA 1994, Sch 9 Group 1*). It is accordingly a difficult tightrope to walk to convince the Inland Revenue that the activities amount to a trade whilst keeping the income safe from Customs. Neither of the two above terms is exhaustively defined. Holiday accommodation is specifically stated to include all accommodation held out as such – a ploy that has often been used in the past to endeavour to take the property outside the protection of the *Rent Acts* (*Note 13* to *Group 1*). Premises in which furnished sleeping accommodation is provided and which are held out as being suitable for use by visitors or travellers is specifically stated to be a similar establishment to a hotel, etc. irrespective of whether or not meals are provided (*Notes 9* and *13* to *Group 1*).

## Furnished Holiday Lettings

**2.128** The widespread recategorisation by the Revenue of many serviced furnished lettings from Case I to Case VI caused general disquiet. This was particularly so among seaside landladies (most of whom would in any event probably have succeeded in establishing an entitlement to Case I treatment), who had long enjoyed the benefits of Case I treatment and were often engaged full-time in their letting activities during the holiday season, and were relying on obtaining capital gains tax roll-over relief and retirement relief. The law was accordingly amended by *FA 1984, s 50* (now re-enacted in *ICTA 1988, s 503*) to treat qualifying furnished holiday lettings as a trade for most tax purposes.

**2.129** A commercial letting of furnished holiday accommodation in the UK in respect of which the profits or gains are chargeable to tax under Case VI of Schedule D is to be treated as a trade for the purpose of the following provisions.

(*a*) *ICTA 1988, ss 380–390, 393, 394*: reliefs for trading losses, but as if *ICTA 1988, s 384(6)–(8)* and part of *(10)* were omitted after 1996/97 (1 April 1998 for corporation tax).

(*b*) *ICTA 1988, ss 623(2)(c), 644(2)(c)*: relevant earnings for retirement annuity relief and personal pensions purposes.

(*c*) *ICTA 1988, s 833(4)(c)*: income charged under Schedule E which is immediately derived by an individual from the carrying on of a trade, profession or vocation is earned income.

(*d*) *TCGA 1992, ss 152–157*: roll-over relief for replacement of business assets.

(*e*) *TCGA 1992, ss 163, 164, Sch 6*: retirement relief.

(*f*) *TCGA 1992, s 165, Sch 7*: relief for gifts of business assets.

(*g*) *TCGA 1992, s 253*: relief in respect of loans to traders.

(*TCGA 1992, s 241*; *ICTA 1988, s 503* as amended by *FA 1998, Sch 5 para 42*).

**2.130** A Schedule A business which consists of the commercial letting of furnished holiday accommodation in the UK is treated as if it were a trade chargeable to tax under Case I of Schedule D. Where part only of that Schedule A business consists of such lettings that part is treated as a Case I trade for the purpose of the above provisions.

**2.131** All such lettings made by a particular person, partnership or body of persons (e.g. a company) are to be treated as one trade (*ICTA 1988, s 503(1)(b)*).

**2.132** Prior to 1 April 1998 (1995/96 for income tax purposes) the activity was also treated as a trade for the following purposes.

(*a*) *ICTA 1988, s 5(2)*: this enabled the tax on trading income to be paid by two equal instalments, the first on 1 January in the year of assessment and the second on the following 1 July;

(*b*) *CAA 1990, Pt II, Chapter 1*: capital allowances on plant and machinery; and

(*c*) *ICTA 1988, s 401*: relief for trading expenses.

Head (*a*) is no longer needed following a change to the income tax system and the other two now follow automatically from calculating the profits of a Schedule A business as if it were a trade.

**2.133** It is difficult to think of any provision not on the list at 2.129 under which a person with furnished lettings would be at a disadvantage in having a deemed trade rather than a trade. It is equally difficult to see why the Chancellor at the time steadfastly resisted categorising furnished holiday letting as a trade but merely gave them the same major tax benefits as a trade attracts. It should be noted that this deeming only applies to furnished holiday lettings 'in respect of which the profits or gains are chargeable to tax under Case VI'. This clearly envisages that not all such lettings will fall into that category; some will be assessable under Case I and the treatment of such 'real' trades is unaffected by this legislation.

**2.134** Although some Inspectors of Taxes have suggested that furnished holiday lettings cannot constitute a trade, as stated at 2.126 the then Chief Secretary to the Treasury, Peter Rees QC, an eminent tax barrister, made clear during the 1984 Finance Bill debates that at least in his view this is incorrect. '*Clause 49* . . . was designed to relieve the position which was thought to have been disturbed by two cases recently heard in the High Court. One is called *Gittos v Barclay* and the other *Griffiths v Jackson* . . . I do not believe that those cases established that the fruits of holiday lettings were never to be taxed under Case I of Schedule D. High Court judges have held that in certain circumstances such income should be taxed under Case VI of Schedule D, but there is an area of uncertainty by reference to the general tax law . . . *Clause 49* is not intended to overturn the general principles that may have to be applied where a holiday letting does not measure up to the tests as they eventually emerge . . . A proprietor of holiday lettings who does not satisfy the tests as laid down will still be at liberty to take his chance by reference to the general law . . . and I repeat that the two cases to which I have referred do not seem to me to have established that the fruits of holiday lettings are always to be taxed under Case VI of Schedule D or that they are never to be taxed under Case I' (Hansard, Standing Committee A, 5 June 1984, Cols 737/8). It is also worthy of note that the Revenue's 'rent-a-room' press release of 18 June 1992 refers to 'Case I of Schedule D (the basis on which tax is charged when a taxpayer is regarded as carrying on a trade, which may be the case where substantial services are provided in connection with the furnished letting)'.

**2.135** And later, 'The income tax from some caravan parks will be assessable under Case I of Schedule D – that is, when they are run consistently on a commercial basis, when a range of services is provided, and so on' (*Ibid* Col 739).

**2.136** What is a commercial letting of furnished holiday accommodation? A letting is a commercial letting if it is on a commercial basis with a view to the realisation of profits (*ICTA 1988, s 504(2)(a)*). In *Brown v Richardson (1997 STC (SCD) 233 SpC 129)* the Special Commissioners held that 'profits' means commercial, not tax-adjusted, profits so account had to be taken of interest payable (which at that time was not a deduction in calculating the profits but a charge on income deductible from total income). They decided that even though the properties had been let on a commercial basis the interest on the loans used to purchase them was so great that the appellant had not proved the letting was with the view to making a profit. This case needs to be approached with caution. The taxpayer was claiming loss relief on a property which in the mortgage application he had described as a holiday home. The tribunal did not believe that the predominant reason for buying the property was to let it as furnished holiday accommodation and felt that the letting was primarily to obtain a contribution towards the running expenses of the property. That was the primary reason for their decision. Nevertheless the Revenue believe the case supports their view that

(*a*) profits, means commercial profits;

(*b*) a taxpayer's expressed intentions are not necessarily conclusive;

(*c*) where there is evidence to suggest a property was acquired primarily as a holiday or second home, the letting activity is likely to be with a view to generating income to offset costs rather than to realising profits; and

(*d*) the size of a mortgage can be so large that the projected profitability is jeopardised or the commercial credibility of the scheme as a whole becomes questionable.

They say that in such cases they would 'expect a written business plan to be prepared at the outset'. (Tax Bulletin, 31 October 1997). In the context of how small businesses normally operate, such an expectation is wholly unrealistic. This suggests that a lot of cases on the realisation of profit tests are likely to have to go before the Commissioners. A person lets accommodation if he permits another person to occupy it whether or not in pursuance of a lease (*ICTA 1988, s 504(9)*). Accommodation is furnished if the tenant is entitled to the use of furniture (*ICTA 1988, s 504(2)(b)*). Holiday accommodation is not specifically defined and would have its normal everyday meaning. However, it is specifically provided that accommodation is *not* to be treated as holiday accommodation unless:

(*a*) it is available for commercial letting to the public generally as holiday accommodation for periods which amount, in aggregate, to at least 140 days;

(*b*) the periods for which it is in fact let to the public generally as holiday accommodation under commercial lettings amount in aggregate to at least 70 days; and

(*c*) for a period comprising at least seven months (which need not be continuous but must include any month in which one of the 70 days in (*b*) above falls) it is not normally in the same occupation for a continuous period exceeding 31 days.

(*ICTA 1988, s 504(3)*).

**2.137** In the case of an individual (or other person who is not a company) the above tests must normally be met during the year of assessment (*ICTA 1988, s 504(4)(c)*). If the accommodation is first let by the taxpayer as furnished accommodation in the current year of assessment the tests are applied by reference to the twelve months starting from the date on which the property was first let (not first available for letting) (*ICTA 1988, s 504(4)(a)*). If it ceases to be let during the current year of assessment the tests are applied by reference to the twelve months ended on the date on which it was last let (*ICTA 1988, s 504(4)(b)*). In the case of a letting by a company the tests are normally applied by reference to the period of twelve months ending with the last day of the accounting period. If the accommodation was first let, or ceased to be let, by the company as furnished accommodation in the accounting period, the tests are applied for the first, or last, twelve months of letting in the same way as with an individual (*ICTA 1988, s 504(5)*).

**2.138** If, in a year of assessment or accounting period, a person lets furnished accommodation which is treated as holiday accommodation for *section 503* purposes ('the qualifying accommodation'), he can elect for the 70-day test under *section 504(3)(b)* to be applied to it and to any other accommodation specified in his claim which was let by him as furnished holiday accommodation during that year. Where such a claim is made, that other accommodation will be treated as holiday accommodation for the year if the number of days for which the qualifying accommodation and the other accommodation was let amounts on average to at least 70 days (*ICTA 1988, s 504(6)(7)*). Qualifying accommodation cannot be specified in more than one claim in respect of any one year of assessment or accounting period (*ICTA 1988, s 504(8)*). A claim under *section 504(6)* must be made within two years of the end of the year of assessment or accounting period to which it relates.

*Example 3*

Jack has two cottages, Westlea and Southlea, available for furnished holiday letting throughout the period 1 April to 30 October 2002. He actually lets Westlea for 100 days during this period and Southlea for 60 days.

Westlea qualifies as holiday accommodation but Southlea does not. If Jack elects for averaging, the days are aggregated, 100 + 60 = 160, and averaged over the two properties, 80 per property. Accordingly both properties will qualify as furnished holiday accommodation for 2002/03.

**2.139** It is not clear if averaging can apply to several properties. For example, if there was a third property, Eastlea, which was let for 65 days, could Jack claim that the average of the three was 75 days so that all qualify? The wording of *section 504(7)* suggests that he could. That of *section 504(8)* casts doubt on this. It is possibly merely intended to prevent double-counting, however, rather than to stop the surplus days on one property being averaged over more than one other.

**2.140** It should be noted that these provisions only apply to holiday lettings. They do not apply to student lettings or any other short-term furnished lettings. As nowadays people take holidays all over the country and not just at the seaside, it is likely to be difficult in many cases to determine whether or not a letting is a holiday let.

**2.141** Once a property qualifies as holiday accommodation for a year, the whole of the income from letting it, not merely income from letting it for use as holiday accommodation, qualifies as part of the income of the deemed trade. It is not necessary to apportion the income between income from holiday use and income from letting for other uses outside the holiday season.

**2.142** It should be noted that the test in 2.136(*c*) above is not concerned with what happens during the remaining five months of the year. The property could be let to a single individual for the entire five months. It is also possible, at least in theory, for the property to be let to the same person for two continuous 30-day periods in the seven months provided that they are separated by a gap. However the Revenue can be expected to scrutinise such a letting closely to ensure that such occupation by a single person is not 'normal' for the property.

**2.143** Relief cannot be claimed under *ICTA 1988, s 381* in respect of a loss in a year of assessment if any of the accommodation in respect of which the trade is carried on in that year was first let by him as furnished accommodation (even though not as holiday accommodation) more than three years before the beginning of the year of assessment (*ICTA 1988, s 503(3)(a)*), i.e. the trade is deemed for *section 381* purposes to start when furnished lettings began, not when letting as holiday accommodation began. Naturally, relief cannot be given for a loss both as a deemed trading loss and under some other provision, e.g. against Case VI income (*ICTA 1988, s 503(4)*). The profits or gains from furnished lettings of holiday accommodation chargeable under Case VI must be computed in accordance with Case I principles (*ICTA 1988, s 503(5)*).

**2.144** For capital gains tax purposes (i.e. (*d*) to (*g*) at 2.129 above), where in any year of assessment a person makes a commercial letting of furnished holiday accommodation, it is treated as having been used in that year only for the purposes of the trade of making such lettings (even if it is let for other purposes for part of the year) and that trade is deemed to have been carried on throughout the year (*TCGA 1992, s 241*). This does not apply to any period in the year of assessment during which the accommodation is neither let commercially nor available to be so let, unless it is prevented from being so let or available by any works of construction or repair. For example, if it was used as a private residence for part of the year an apportionment would be necessary.

**2.145** If a gain arises on the disposal of a property which was an individual's principal private residence and the base cost of that property was reduced by roll-over relief (because at the time of acquisition it was acquired as furnished holiday accommodation), the private residence exemption will not extend to the rolled-over gain. The latter is thus treated as the top part of the gain on the private residence and will be wholly taxed if it is less than the total gain on the disposal (*TCGA 1992, s 241*).

**2.146** If part only of a property is let as holiday accommodation, such apportionments must be made as appear to the Inspector, or, on appeal, the Commissioners, to be just and reasonable (*TCGA 1992, s 241*; *ICTA 1988, s 503(4)*).

## Tipping etc. rights

**2.147** A sum received for the grant of tipping rights on land has been held to be capital (*McClure v Petre (1988 STC 749)*). Once a site has been filled in it cannot again be exploited for tipping. Accordingly the owner has made a disposal of a valuable right attaching to the land, which is a capital disposal. Similarly a payment to acquire tipping rights is capital expenditure as a lasting benefit is obtained – albeit lasting only for a few years (*Rolfe v Wimpey Waste Management Ltd (1989 STC 454)*).

**2.148** Although a person carrying on a trade of waste disposal cannot obtain tax relief for the cost of the site itself he can claim relief for expenditure incurred after 6 April 1989 on either site preparation expenditure or expenditure on restoration after tipping has ended. Site preparation expenditure is written off over the useful life of the site. The amount deductible each year is

$$\begin{array}{c}\text{cumulative expenditure}\\\text{less part previously}\\\text{allowed}\end{array} \times \frac{\text{volume of waste deposited in the period of account}}{\begin{array}{c}\text{volume of waste}\\\text{deposited in the}\\\text{period}\end{array} + \begin{array}{c}\text{future capacity}\\\text{of the site}\end{array}}$$

(*ICTA 1988, s 91B(1)–(8)*).

Preparation includes expenditure on earthworks. A tipping licence under the *Control of Pollution Act 1974* or a waste management licence under the *Environmental Protection Act 1990* must have been held before tipping commenced to qualify for relief (*ICTA 1988, s 91B(1)(11)*). Where expenditure was first incurred on the site before 6 April 1989 a portion of that expenditure can also qualify for relief, namely the part that the unused capacity of the site at 6 April 1989 bears to its total capacity including the part utilised before that date (*ICTA 1988, s 91B(9)(10)*). Restoration payments are deductible when they are paid, provided that the trade is still being carried on at that time. The payment must be incurred to comply with the conditions of the tipping or waste management licence or a *Town and Country Planning Act 1990, s 106* or similar agreement. Waste disposal activities cover all or any of the collection, treatment, conversion and final depositing of waste materials (*ICTA 1988, s 91A*). The Revenue have given guidance on what is site preparation expenditure and what revenue expenditure on the creation of internal cells in Tax Bulletin 34, April 1998 and Tax Bulletin 51, Feb 2001.

## Income from Overseas Property

**2.149** Up to 1994/95 there were no special rules for taxing income from non-UK properties. The rules of Case V of Schedule D applied in the same way as for other overseas assets. Special rules were introduced for income tax purposes (but not for corporation tax – *ICTA 1988, s 65A(4)*) for 1995/96 onwards. These rules were repealed and replaced with new ones from 5 April 1998 for income tax purposes or 1 April 1998 for corporation tax, but although the wording has altered the new rules mirror the old. These rules also apply for corporation tax purposes (other than the restriction on travelling expenses) from 1 April 1998 (*ICTA 1988, s 70A* inserted by *FA 1998, Sch 5 para 25*). The profits from overseas properties are now calculated in the same way as for UK ones, i.e. the taxpayer is treated as operating a Schedule A business the income from which is calculated in the same manner as trading income (*ICTA 1988, s 65A(1)–(3)* introduced by *FA 1998, Sch 5 para 24*). If the land law in the country where the property is situated differs from that in the UK, they must be interpreted to produce the nearest possible result to the UK position (*ICTA 1998, s 65A(8)*).

**2.150** The Schedule A business in relation to overseas properties (called below the overseas Schedule A business) is separate from the Schedule A business for UK properties (*ICTA 1988, s 65A(4)*). Furthermore, although the overseas property activity is treated as if it were a Schedule A business in order to apply the Schedule A rules to it, the income remains taxable under Case V of Schedule D, not Schedule A (*ICTA 1988, s 65A(5)*). As the UK Schedule A business and the overseas Schedule A business are separate businesses, losses of one cannot be set against income from the other (*ICTA 1988, s 65A(6)*). The special rules for furnished holiday lettings (see 2.128) are not extended to overseas properties (*ICTA 1988, s 65A(7)*). Accordingly such lettings will normally form part of the taxpayer's overseas Schedule A business. Capital allowances apply to an overseas Schedule A business in the same way as to a UK one (*CAA 2001, s 15(1)(d)*). For income tax purposes only, *sections 80* and *81* of *ICTA 1988*, which contain special rules to grant relief for expenses connected with foreign trades and travel between separate UK and foreign trades, are not to apply to an overseas Schedule A business (*ICTA 1988, s 65A(6)*). In most, if not all cases this will deny relief for travelling expenses to visit the overseas property. This restriction does not apply for corporation tax.

**2.151** The full Schedule A loss rules are applied to overseas properties from 1998/99 but, of course, such losses can be set only against the profits of the overseas Schedule A business (*ICTA 1988, s 379B* inserted by *FA 1998, Sch 5 para 27*).

**2.152** For a continuing source which started before 6 April 1994, income under Case V was assessed on a preceding year basis up to 1995/96. The concept of the overseas Schedule A business did not change this, but required the income for the year to 5 April 1995 to be computed using the new rules but without relief for capital allowances (*FA 1995, s 41(5)(7)*).

**2.153** Where a taxpayer had more than one overseas letting property each property formed a separate overseas Schedule A business for 1995/96 and 1996/97 (*FA 1995, s 42(6)*). This prevented a loss on one overseas property being set against profits from another. The Case V rules actually contain no relief for losses (other than trading losses) but the Revenue by concession allowed a rental loss to be set against future income from the same property (ESC B25).

**2.154** In the same way as with a UK Schedule A business, the new system does not apply where the property ceased to be a letting property in 1995/96 and *FA 1995, s 39(5)* (see 2.53) would have excluded the new rules had the land been in the UK (*FA 1995, s 41(9)*).

**2.155** For corporation tax purposes, a loss on the company's overseas Schedule A business can be carried forward against future income from that business. This does not apply to the extent that the business is not being carried on on a commercial basis. The rules at 2.50 above apply to a loss arising in such circumstances. These appear to disallow relief for the loss entirely (*ICTA 1988, s 392B*, inserted by *FA 1998, Sch 5 para 28*). A loss in an overseas Schedule A business cannot be set against general income or surrendered under the group relief rules.

## Anti-Avoidance

### Rent Factoring

**2.156** An anti-avoidance provision to inhibit 'rent factoring' applies to transactions entered into by companies after 21 March 2000. The Revenue warned in 1999 that they were aware of an arrangement involving the grant of a lease of land intra-group and the sale of the entitlement to the rental stream (but not the lease) to a financial trader for a fixed period. They questioned whether the scheme worked but hoped that their warning would deter people from trying it. The introduction the following year of *FA 2000, s 110* suggests that their warning went unheeded. Furthermore, the legislation was timely as the efficacy of the arrangement that had come to their attention was subsequently upheld in *CIR v John Lewis Properties Ltd (2001 STC 1118)*.

**2.157** The provision applies to 'finance agreements' that transfer a right to receive rent in respect of land in the UK from one person to another otherwise than by means of a lease of that land (*ICTA 1988, s 43B* inserted by *FA 2000, s 110*). A person who receives a 'finance' amount under that agreement is treated as receiving it as rent in the chargeable period in which the agreement is entered into (not, if different, in that in which the amount is received). If he does not carry on a Schedule A business he is treated as receiving it in the course of such a business (*ICTA 1988, s 43B*).

**2.158** A 'transaction' is a finance agreement for this purpose if 'in accordance with generally accepted accounting practice for a company incorporated in any part of the UK' the accounts of a company which receives money under the transaction would record a financial obligation in relation to that receipt (whether as a lease creditor or otherwise) (*ICTA 1988, s 43A(1)(2)*). If a company is a member of a group, what needs to be looked at for the purpose of *s 43A(1)* is the accounting practice that applies to the group accounts (*ICTA 1988, s 43(3)*). It is not wholly clear what this means. *Subsection (1)* does not look at the accounting practice actually used by the company; it looks at that which would be used by a hypothetical company. The draftsman presumably intends that if there is more than one generally accepted accounting practice, the practice adopted in the group accounts must be taken to be the only acceptable one, but it seems questionable whether the wording achieves that.

**2.159** A company is treated as receiving money, so as to make a transaction a finance agreement, if it falls to be brought into account as a receipt for corporation tax purposes or, if the company is non-UK resident, would have done so if it had been UK resident (*ICTA 1988, s 43A(4)*).

**2.160** A 'finance amount' is any receipt within *ICTA 1988, s 43A(1)*. (*ICTA 1988, s 43B(3)*).

**2.161** There are a number of exceptions. The provision does not apply if:

(*a*) the term over which the financial obligation is to be reduced exceeds 15 years;

(*b*) except where the person who receives the money and the person from whom the right to receive rent is transferred are connected (within *ICTA 1988, s 839*), the arrangements for the reduction of the financial obligation substantially depend on a person's entitlement to capital allowances;

(*c*) the transaction falls within *ICTA 1988, s 36* (sale of land with a right to reconveyance) (see 3.17) so the receipt is already taxed as income;

(*d*) the transaction falls within *ICTA 1988, s 780* (certain sale and leasebacks) (see 12.25) which already taxes part of the receipt as income; or

(*e*) the capital sum in question is already taxed as income in computing the profits of a trade.

(*ICTA 1988, s 43C*).

**2.162** If under a finance agreement a lease is granted at a premium which generates a need to recognise a financial obligation within *ICTA 1988, s 43A(1)* (see 2.158) the person who receives the premium is taxed on it as if it were rent receivable in the chargeable period in which the agreement is made and in the course of a Schedule A business (*ICTA 1988, s 43D*). This does not apply if:

(*a*) the term over which the financial obligation is to be reduced exceeds 15 years,

(*b*) the length of the lease does not exceed 15 years (in which case *ICTA 1988, s 780* or *ICTA 1988, s 36* will tax the bulk of the premium as income),

(*c*) the length of the lease is not significantly different from the term over which the financial obligation is to be reduced (*ICTA 1988, s 43E(1)*), or

(*d*) exemption (*b*) or (*e*) in 2.161 applies to the receipt.

*ICTA 1988, s 38* (see 3.24) must be applied to ascertain the length of the lease for the purpose of (*b*) and (*c*) (*ICTA 1988, s 43E(2)*).

(*ICTA 1988, s 43E*).

**2.163** In applying these provisions 'rent' includes any sum taxable under Schedule A, a 'lease' includes an underlease, sublease, tenancy, licence or any agreement for any of these things (but not a mortgage), a 'premium' includes any like sum and any amount treated as a premium under *ICTA 1988, s 34(4)* or *(5)* (see 3.6 and 3.8) and 'sum' includes any consideration (*ICTA 1988, s 43G(2)*). References to a transfer of a right to receive rent include any arrangements under which rent ceases to form part of a company's taxable income (*ICTA 1988, s 43G(3)*). Special rules apply to insurance companies (*s 43F*).

**2.164** In calculating the term over which a financial obligation is to be reduced, no account is to be taken of any earlier period during which the arrangements for reduction differ from those which apply in a previous period in which the financial obligations were substantially reduced (unless the reduction results from a rent review on commercial terms) (*ICTA 1988, s 43E(4)*).

**2.165** It should be noted that these provisions apply only to companies, not to individuals or trusts. However, they will apply to a non-UK resident company, which is within the scope of income tax rather than corporation tax.

*Chapter 3*

# Premiums

**3.1** The consideration for the grant of a lease of land is not always simply an annual rent. The landlord may require payment of a capital sum for the grant of the lease. The rent would then normally be less than a market rent to take account of this capital sum (called a premium). In the absence of special provisions a landlord would effectively be able to convert income into capital by requiring a premium equal to the total of the annual market rents for the property, with the rent payable under the lease then being a nominal figure. This particularly applies to a short lease, where the tenant's cash flow position need not be seriously affected by, in effect, paying the whole of his rent in advance on signing the lease, particularly if the landlord is prepared to accept the premium by annual instalments. The legislation accordingly contains a number of special rules to prevent the avoidance of income tax by taking premiums and other capital payments in lieu of rent. This is done by treating part of the premium as additional rent.

## Treatment of Premiums on Leases of up to 50 Years as Rent

**3.2** If the payment of a premium is required under a lease the duration of which does not exceed 50 years (or otherwise under the terms subject to which such a lease is granted), part of the premium is taxed on the landlord as if it were rent. The taxable part is the amount of the premium reduced by one-fiftieth for each complete period of twelve months other than the first comprised in the term of the lease (*ICTA 1988, s 34(1)*). This deeming automatically treats the taxable amount as income of the landlord's Schedule A business (or prior to 1 April 1998 as a Schedule A receipt for corporation tax purposes and prior to 1995/96 for income tax purposes) (*ICTA 1988, s 34(1)* as amended by *FA 1995, Sch 6 para 9* and *FA 1998, s 40*).

*Example 4*

Jane grants a lease on 1 July 2002 for the period of 10 years 7 months to 31 January 2013 at a rent of £100 p.a. and a premium of £50,000.

Jane is taxable under Schedule A for 2002/03 (in addition to the rent) on:

| | | £ |
|---|---|---|
| Premium | | 50,000 |
| Complete years | 10 | |
| Reduction | $\frac{10-1}{50} \times 50{,}000$ | 9,000 |
| Additional rent | | £41,000 |

**3.3** The taxable amount can conveniently be expressed as 2% of the premium for each year by which the complete years in the term less 1 falls short of 50, i.e. in the above example the taxable amount could more directly be arrived at as

$$2\% \times (50 - (10 - 1)) = 82\% \text{ of } £50{,}000 = £41{,}000$$

For the algebraically-minded the *Act* expresses it as

$$P - \frac{(P \times Y)}{50}$$

where P is the premium and Y is the number of complete periods of twelve months (other than the first) comprised in the duration of the lease.

**Deemed Premiums**

**3.4** If the terms subject to which a lease is granted impose an obligation on the tenant to carry out any work on the premises the lease is deemed to have required the payment of a premium (in addition to any actual premium payable) of a sum equal to the amount by which the value of the landlord's interest in the property immediately after the commencement of the lease exceeds what its then value would have been if the obligation to carry out the works had not been imposed on the tenant (*ICTA 1988, s 34(2)*). The landlord's interest immediately after the commencement of the lease is a reversionary interest. Accordingly this effectively requires one to consider to what extent the value of the reversion will be increased by the expenditure when the lease falls in, and to discount this increase back to the commencement of the lease. In most cases where the tenant is required to fit out a shop or office this figure will be nil or very low, as at the expiry of the lease a new tenant would be likely to strip out the shopfront and most of the internal fittings and replace them in a different style, and an office would often need to be refurbished before it is re-let. A deemed premium may well arise, however, if the lease requires the tenant to erect a building or an extension or if it requires him to refurbish the premises and to make good dilapidations to the refurbished standard on the expiry of the lease. The VAT implications of such a provision are considered in 17.301.

**3.5** In practice the Revenue rarely assess deemed premiums under *ICTA 1988, s 34(2)* where the work is fitting out. Where they do it is normally as a result of pressure from the tenant, who is seeking a deduction (see 12.45 below). A charge under *section 34(2)* cannot arise if the work that has to be done by the tenant would have qualified for a deduction under *ICTA 1988, ss 25–30* if the expenditure had been incurred by the landlord, e.g. if it is work which constitutes an expense of the taxpayer's Schedule A business (or repairs prior to 1995/96) (*ICTA 1988, s 34(3)*).

**3.6** If under the terms subject to which a lease is granted a sum becomes payable by the tenant in lieu of all or part of the rent for any period, or as consideration for the surrender of the lease, such sum is again deemed to be an additional premium (*ICTA 1988, s 34(4)*). In such a case the income tax charge will be for the year of assessment in which the sum becomes payable by the tenant. In the case of a payment in lieu of rent, the taxable amount of the notional premium is calculated as if the duration of the lease were limited to that period.

*Example 5*

Karen granted a lease on 8 March 1998 for a term of 21 years at a rent of £10,000 p.a. with five-year reviews. It contains a right for the tenant to pay on any review date a capital sum equal to 400% of the reviewed rent instead of paying rent for the next review period. On the first review on 8 March 2003 the rent increased to £15,000 p.a. and the tenant opted to pay Karen £60,000 in lieu of the rent for the next 5 years.

Karen is deemed to have granted a 5-year lease from 8 March 2003 for a premium of £60,000. She is therefore taxed as if she had received additional rent for 2002/03 of

$$2\% \times (50 - (5 - 1)) = 92\% \text{ of } £60{,}000 = \underline{\underline{£55{,}200}}$$

**3.7** It should be borne in mind that *ICTA 1988, s 34(4)* applies only where the payment in lieu of rent or to terminate the lease is made under the terms subject to which the lease is granted (although *ICTA 1988, s 34(5)* – see 3.8 below – will catch a payment on a variation). If the tenant negotiates a surrender of a lease during its term under which he agrees to make a payment to the landlord, the payment is not within the *subsection*.

**3.8** If a sum (other than rent) becomes payable by the tenant as consideration for the variation or waiver of any of the terms of a lease, the lease is deemed to have required the payment of an additional premium to the landlord. For the purpose of computing the tax on that notional premium the lease is deemed to commence at the time the variation or waiver takes effect, to cease at the time that it ceases to have effect, and to have become payable at the time the contract providing for the variation or waiver is entered into (*ICTA 1988, s 34(5)*).

**3.9** A payment to induce a landlord to accept a surrender of a lease is almost certainly not within *subsection (5)* as this seems to envisage the lease continuing. A payment to the landlord as part of a settlement of an action by the landlord for forfeiture following a breach has been held to be a payment for the waiver or variation of a term of the lease and thus a premium under *section 34(5)* (*Banning v Wright (48 TC 421)*). Unlike with payments within *subsections (1)* to *(4)*, a payment within *section 34(5)* will not normally be envisaged in the original lease but will arise from a subsequent agreement.

**3.10** If a lease requires a payment to be made not to the landlord but to some other person the amount to be taxed as income is calculated in the normal way. It is not, however, taxed on the landlord under Schedule A. It is assessed on the recipient as if he had himself been the landlord. This makes it a receipt of the recipient's Schedule A business. If he does not have any Schedule A income of his own the effect of his deeming is also to deem him to carry on a Schedule A business. Prior to 1995/96 (1 April 1998 for corporation tax purposes) the charge was under Case VI of Schedule D. If the payment is for a variation or waiver (i.e. one within *section 34(5)*) it is taxed on the third party only if he is a connected person of the landlord (within *ICTA 1988, s 839* – see Appendix 1). If he is not, it is taxed on the landlord (*ICTA 1988, s 34(6)(7)* as amended by *FA 1995, Sch 6 para 9(5)* and *FA 1998, Sch 5 para 15*).

**3.11** If a premium is receivable by instalments the landlord can opt to pay the tax by instalments if he can satisfy the Revenue that he would otherwise suffer hardship. The number and amount of the instalments is at the discretion of the Revenue but they cannot be spread over more than eight years (*ICTA 1988, s 34(8)*). The Revenue normally expect the monies received to be used to pay the tax and will generally agree to instalments coinciding with the receipt of the consideration. If an instalment is paid late the Revenue charge interest only from the date the instalment fell due (Property Income Manual para 1220).

**3.12** The normal Schedule A basis of assessment (see 2.83 above) does not apply to the taxable part of a premium. Instead it is simply taxed on an actual basis for the year in which the lease is granted (*ICTA 1988, s 34(9)*).

## Schedule D Charge on Assignment of Lease Granted at an Undervalue

**3.13** *Section 34* applies only to premiums payable for the grant of a lease; it does not apply to a capital sum, often colloquially called a premium, payable on the assignment of a lease. Such a payment does not in general attract an income tax charge. There is, however, one exception. It would be relatively easy to avoid a charge under *section 34* by the landlord granting a lease to a connected person without asking a premium, with the connected person then collecting a capital sum from the prospective tenant for an assignment of the lease. *Section 35* is designed to prevent this.

**3.14** If the terms subject to which a lease of a duration of 50 years or less is granted are such that, having regard to values prevailing at the time, the landlord could have demanded a premium or a larger premium than he in fact received for the grant of the lease if it had been negotiated at arm's length (the difference being called below the 'amount foregone'), an income tax charge will arise if the lease is subsequently assigned for a capital sum. The amount of this charge is the sum that would have been taxable under *section 34(1)* (see 3.2 above) if the lower of the amount received on the assignment (less any premium paid for the grant of the lease) or the amount foregone had been received as a premium for the grant of the lease. Such sum is taxed on the assignor as a receipt of his Schedule A business (or of a notional Schedule A business if he does not have a Schedule A business of his own) (*ICTA 1988, s 35(2)*). The assignor does not have to be connected with the lessor. If he has obtained a lease at an undervalue the *Act* assumes that the lease was not granted at arm's length and that it is accordingly reasonable to impose a charge on the assignor. If the grant of the original lease was at arm's length then prima facie the amount foregone will be nil as the lease will have been granted on arm's length terms. Prior to 1995/96 the charge was under Case VI for income tax as well as corporation tax purposes. This provision does not apply if the premium concerned is already taxable under *ICTA 1988, s 43D(2)* (rent factoring) (see 2.156). That provision takes precedence.

**3.15** If the amount received on an assignment is less than the amount foregone a further charge will arise on a subsequent assignment until the full amount of the amount foregone has been brought into account.

*Example 6*

On 1 January 2000 April granted a 20-year lease to her sister May at rent of £1,000 p.a. and a premium of £2,000. If the transaction had been at arm's length April could have demanded a premium of £15,000. On 8 January May assigned the lease to her niece

June for a payment of £10,000. June occupied the premises for the purposes of her business. On 31 December 2002 she ceased trading and assigned the lease at arm's length for a payment of £20,000.

April is taxed under *section 34(1)* on the premium received of £2,000

| | | | |
|---|---|---|---|
| 2% of (50 – 19) × £2,000 | | | = £1,240 |
| The amount foregone is | | | |
| Arm's length premium | | 15,000 | |
| Premium received | | 2,000 | |
| Amount foregone | | £13,000 | |
| | | | £1,240 |
| May is taxed under *section 35* on the lesser of | | | |
| Payment received | 10,000 | | |
| *Less* premium paid | 2,000 | 8,000 | |
| Amount foregone | | 13,000 | |
| 2% × 31 × £8,000 | | | = £4,960 |
| June is taxed under *section 35* on the lesser of | | | |
| Payment received | 20,000 | | |
| *Less* premium paid | 10,000 | 10,000 | |
| Amount foregone | 13,000 | | |
| *Less* taxed on May | 8,000 | 5,000 | |
| 2% × 31 × £5,000 | | | = £3,100 |
| April is taxed in 1999/00, May in 2000/01 and June in 2002/03. It will be seen that all the charges are based on the taxable proportion at the date the premium is granted. | | | |
| | | | £9,300 |

It will also be seen that the charges aggregate to

2% × 31 × £15,000 = £9,300

**3.16** If the original landlord or any assignor or assignee wishes to know where he stands he can submit to his Inspector of Taxes a statement showing whether or not a charge to tax arises or could arise under *section 35* and, if so, the amount on which a charge may arise. If the Inspector is satisfied as to the accuracy of the statement he must certify its accuracy (*ICTA 1988, s 35(3)*). If he is not satisfied – and as he is not a valuer it is difficult to see how he can be satisfied – he does not appear to have to do anything. The Revenue's Property Income Manual tells Inspectors to refuse to give a certificate unless all the parties concerned are in agreement with the determination (para 1222). It is difficult to see any point in requesting such a certificate.

## Schedule D Charge on Sale of Land with Right to Reconveyance

**3.17** When a person grants a lease of property he gives up the right to possession for the period of the lease and recovers that right at its expiry. By 1963, when the provisions on premiums were introduced, the draftsmen were beginning to appreciate the ingenuity of taxpayers, and realised that a person could obtain the same effect as granting a lease at a premium by selling his land and buying it back for a lower figure at a later date. *Section 36* is designed to prevent the avoidance of income tax on a premium for a short lease by the use of this device.

**3.18** It operates where the terms subject to which an estate or interest in land is sold provide that it will be reconveyed at a future date to the vendor (or to a person connected with him within the terms of *ICTA 1988, s 839* – see Appendix 1) or that it may be required to be so reconveyed. It imposes a charge to income tax on the vendor on the amount, if any, by which the sale price exceeds the price at which it is to be reconveyed, reduced (if the earliest date that it can be required to be reconveyed falls two years or more after the sale) by one-fiftieth for each complete year (other than the first) in the period between the date of sale and the earliest date of reconveyance (*ICTA 1988, s 36(1)*).

*Example 7*

Joseph sold a property for £180,000 on 1 June 2002 on terms that the purchaser would resell it to him for £120,000 on 1 June 2007.

Joseph will be charged to income tax on:

| | £ |
|---|---|
| Sale price | 180,000 |
| Reconveyance price | 120,000 |
| | 60,000 |
| Less $\frac{1}{50}$th × (5 – 1) years | 4,800 |
| Taxable as income | £55,200 |

**3.19** The taxable amount is treated as a receipt of the vendor's Schedule A business (or a notional Schedule A business if he does not have other Schedule A income) (*ICTA 1988, s 36(1)*). Prior to 1995/96 (1 April 1998 for corporation tax purposes) it was taxable under Case VI of Schedule D. The amount is treated as received when the estate or interest is sold and is thus treated as income of the period in which that sale takes place. For this purpose the time of sale is the time when either an unconditional contract for sale is entered into, a conditional contract for sale becomes unconditional or an option or pre-emption right is exercised requiring the vendor to enter into an unconditional contract or sale (*ICTA 1988, s 36(4A), (4B)* inserted by *FA 1998, Sch 5 para 17*). This provision fixing the time did not apply prior to 1998/99 (1 April 1998 for corporation tax purposes).

**3.20** If the date of reconveyance is not fixed and the repurchase price varies with that date the price must be taken to be the lowest possible under the terms of the sale. If when the reconveyance takes place, the resale price is higher the owner can claim (within six years after the date of the reconveyance) repayment of the excess of the tax paid over the amount payable based on the actual date of reconveyance (*ICTA 1988, s 36(2)*). Presumably this claim needs to be made outside the tax return.

*Example 8*

Harry sold a property for £300,000 on 12 September 2002. The sale agreement provided that the tenant could resell the property to Harry at any time after 5 years and must resell it to him one month after the expiry of the 15th year if he has not done so earlier. The reconveyance price was expressed to be:

on a sale at end of year 5 £230,000
on a sale at end of year 15 £75,000
on a sale on intermediate date £230,000 less £15,500 for each complete year after the fifth.

The property was reconveyed at the beginning of year 9 for £183,500.

It must be assumed that the property will be reconveyed at the end of year 5 (the earliest date at which it can be reconveyed) for £75,000 (the lowest price at which it can be reconveyed).

Harry will therefore be charged to income tax for 2002/03 on:

| | £ |
|---|---|
| Sale price | 300,000 |
| Deemed reconveyance price | 75,000 |
| | 225,000 |
| *Less* $^1/_{50}$th × (5 – 1) years | 18,000 |
| Taxable as income | £207,000 |

Following the reconveyance Harry can have the charge reduced to:

| | £ |
|---|---|
| Sale price | 300,000 |
| Reconveyance price | 183,500 |
| | 116,500 |
| *Less* $^1/_{50}$th × (8 – 1) years | 16,310 |
| Taxable as income | £100,190 |

Clearly it is most unattractive to enter into that sort of an arrangement!

**3.21** The *Act* does not indicate how the tax is to be computed if the reconveyance price is not fixed. This would not happen in an avoidance situation as the owner would want to fix the amount of the difference between sale and repurchase price if that difference were a disguised premium. Suppose, however, that the owner of an historic building sells it with a right of first refusal to repurchase at market value in its current use in the event of the purchaser wishing to resell. He may be public-spirited and require this right to prevent the building being sold to a developer. The transaction will be within *section 36*. However, the repurchase price is not known. Hopefully the Revenue would say that the earliest date the property could be reconveyed is the day after the sale, at which time the reconveyance price would be equal to the sale price so that no charge could arise. The risk is that they would say that the lowest price at which the property could be reconveyed, e.g. following a nuclear holocaust, is £1. Accordingly, income tax should provisionally be paid on the full sale proceeds. This would be disastrous, particularly as if tax is paid initially and the reconveyance does not take place within 51 years of the sale – in which case the tax payable would be nil – no claim for repayment can be made until such time, if any, as the reconveyance actually takes place. The Revenue stated in 1978 that they were not aware of any bona fide commercial transactions ever having taken place that could fall within *section 36*. It is to be hoped that this happy state of affairs will continue to prevail!

**3.22** Without further anti-avoidance rules it would be possible to circumvent the above provisions by a sale coupled with a right to the grant of a long lease to the vendor at a future date for a premium of less than the sale price, or for no premium but at a nil or nominal rent. Accordingly it is provided that if the sale agreement provides for the grant of a lease (directly or indirectly out of the interest sold) to the vendor or to a connected person (within *ICTA 1988, s 839* – see Appendix 1) the grant of the lease must be regarded as equivalent to a reconveyance of the interest sold at a price equal to the amount of the premium (if any) paid for the lease plus the value (at the date of the initial sale) of the right to receive a conveyance of the reversion immediately after the lease begins to run (*ICTA 1988, s 36(3)*). The difference between the price that the purchaser pays and the value of his interest after granting the lease is of course the cost of obtaining the use of the property for the period between his purchase and the grant of the lease, which is the sum that would have been demanded as premium if he had taken a lease instead of entering into the sale and leaseback transaction. There is an exemption from *section 36(3)* where the lease is granted to the vendor (and begins to run) within one month of the sale. This is to ensure that normal commercial sale and leaseback transactions are not caught by *section 36*. This extension to *section 36(1)* does not apply where the sale proceeds constitutes a finance amount for the purpose of *ICTA 1988, s 43B* (rent factoring) (see 2.156). That provision applies instead.

## Rules for Ascertaining Duration of Leases

**3.23** Without rules for ascertaining the duration of leases it would be possible to disguise a lease of under 50 years as a long lease by, for example, granting a 60-year lease with a break clause after 30 years, perhaps coupled with such an enormous increase in rent that the tenant is bound to exercise the break option. To prevent such manipulation the following rules must be applied to determine the duration of a lease for the purpose of *sections 34–36*.

(*a*) Where any of the terms of the lease make it unlikely that the lease will continue beyond a particular date and the premium paid was not substantially greater than it would have been had the term expired on that date the lease cannot be regarded as having a term longer than one expiring on that date (*ICTA 1988, s 38(1)(a)*). For example, suppose a 55-year lease is granted containing a provision that the lease can be forfeited at any time after the 25th year if the tenant does not thereafter repaint the property once a week. It is improbable that the tenant will repaint weekly. Accordingly, it is likely that the lease will be forfeited a week after the expiry of the 25th year. The lease must therefore be regarded as being for 25 years plus a week.

(*b*) Where the terms of the lease include provision for the extension of the lease beyond a given date by notice given by the tenant, account may be taken of any circumstances making it likely that the lease will be extended (*ICTA 1988, s 38(1)(b)*). For example, suppose a 10-year lease contains an option for the tenant to extend the lease for a further 15 years and on taking possession the tenant installs equipment having a life of 25 years which it is uneconomic to install for 10 years only. It is likely that he will exercise the option to extend so the lease can be regarded as a 25-year lease. If the option to extend was exercisable by the landlord and not by the tenant the lease would be regarded as a 10-year lease even if it was obvious that there was an understanding that the lease would be extended.

(*c*) If the tenant (or a connected person within *ICTA 1988, s 839* – see Appendix 1) is, or may become, entitled to a further lease of the same premises (or of premises including the whole or part of the same premises) the term of the lease can (but not must) be treated as not expiring before the term of the further lease (*ICTA 1988, s 38(1)(c)*). For example, suppose a tenant enters into a lease for 10 years for a premium and simultaneously enters into a further lease of the same premises for 89 years commencing on the expiry of the first lease. The first lease can be treated as a 99-year lease. It may be thought that this is an improbable transaction. However, if a landlord is taxed on part of a premium the tenant is entitled to a deduction (if he is carrying on a trade or subletting the premises) spread over the term of the lease and equal to the amount taxed on the landlord (see 12.45–12.49 below). Accordingly where a landlord does not mind being taxed on a premium, such as if he has losses or is a property dealing company, it would be attractive to the tenant to pay a premium for a very short lease. *Section 38(1)(c)* was therefore introduced to stop the term of a lease being very short but being supplemented by a second lease, so that commercially the tenant had the security of a very long lease but the tax benefits of a very short one. Where it is appropriate to do so, all or part of any premium paid for either of the two leases can be attributed to the other (*ICTA 1988, s 24(3)*).

**3.24** The rules in 3.23 above must be applied by reference to the facts which were known or ascertainable at the time of the grant of the lease. In the case of a payment for a waiver or variation of a term of a lease which is treated as a premium under *section 34(5)* (see 3.8 above) the facts known at the time the variation agreement is entered into need to be considered (*ICTA 1988, s 38(2)*). In applying the above rules it must be assumed that all parties concerned act as if they were at arm's length (even if they are in fact connected) (*ICTA 1988, s 38(3)*). If any benefits other than vacant possession and beneficial occupation of the premises, or the right to receive rent at a reasonable commercial rate in respect of the premises, are conferred by the lease (or in connection with its grant), or payments are made that would not be expected to be made by parties acting at arm's length if no other benefits had been conferred, it must be assumed that the benefits would not have been conferred (or the payments made) had the lease been for a term ending before its stated expiry, i.e. *section 38(1)(a)* (see 3.23(*a*) above) cannot be applied so as to deem the lease to be for a shorter period than its expressed term. This does not apply if it can be shown that the benefits were not in fact conferred (or the payment made) for the purpose of securing a tax advantage by the use – or abuse – of the provisions relating to income tax on premiums for leases, etc. (*ICTA 1988, s 38(4)*).

**3.25** *Section 38* does not apply to leases granted before 13 June 1969 or a variation or waiver entered into before that date. Where any of the terms of such a lease include provision for the determination of the lease by either landlord or tenant it cannot be treated as being for a term extending beyond the earliest date on which it could be terminated by notice, and where any of the terms or any other circumstances make it unlikely that the lease will continue beyond a date, it cannot be treated as extending beyond that date. This is subject to the provisos that if the duration of a lease falls to be ascertained after it has come to an end it is not to be treated as for longer than the period for which it in fact subsisted, and if the duration falls to be ascertained during the subsistence of the lease the above rules must be applied in accordance with circumstances prevailing at the time, e.g. they cannot treat it as already having come to an end (*ICTA 1988, Sch 30 para 2(1), 4*). If the terms of a lease granted before 25 August 1971, or varied or waived before that date, provide for determination by notice given by the landlord, it cannot be treated as being for a term longer than one ending on the earliest date on which it could be so determined; the rules in 3.23(*a*) above are modified by ignoring whether or not the premium is substantially greater than would be appropriate for a lease expiring on an earlier date, and those in 3.23(*c*) above do not apply. The normal meaning of 'premium' is also modified in relation to such a lease (*ICTA 1988, Sch 30 para 3*).

## Power to Obtain Information

**3.26** If an Inspector of Taxes believes that any person has information relevant to the ascertainment of the duration of a lease for these purposes, he can require him to give the Inspector such information on the matters that he specifies in his letter of request as are in that person's possession. A solicitor cannot however be required (on a client matter) to do more than state that he was acting on behalf of a client and give the client's name and address (*ICTA 1988, s 38(5)*).

## Ancillary Points

**3.27** Where it appears to the Inspector that the determination of a taxable amount under *sections 34–36* may affect the tax liability of some other person, such as the tenant who will want to claim a deduction for the notional rent, he can notify that other person of the determination that he intends to make. If he does so the tenant, etc. has 30 days to object to the proposed determination. If he does not object he cannot later challenge the determination. If he objects and the calculation of the taxable amount cannot be resolved amicably between the landlord, the tenant, the Inspector, and anyone else interested, the matter goes before the General (or Special) Commissioners. At this hearing all of the affected parties have a right to take part in the proceedings and all (and their successors in title) will be bound by the determination made by the Commissioners. The Inspector is empowered to require any person to give such information as he may think necessary to decide whether a notification should be served on any person (*ICTA 1988, s 42*).

**3.28** Prior to 6 April 1996, where a premium or other payment within *sections 34–36* was paid to a non-resident, the tenant was under an obligation to deduct income tax at the basic rate from the taxable part of the premium (*ICTA 1988, s 43(2)*). It was apparently up to him to work out the taxable part. If he got it wrong the Revenue could still look to him for the tax that he should have deducted. The detailed rules are considered in 2.97 above.

**3.29** The position now is unclear. As the premium is deemed to be additional rent it is income of the landlord's Schedule A Business. *Regulation 1(2)(a)* of the *Taxation of Income from Land (Non-Residents) Regulations 1995* (*SI 1995 No 2902*) requires tax to be deducted from 'any payment . . . which constitutes income of a Schedule A business carried on by a non-resident'. The Regulations do not contain any specific rules regarding premiums. It was held in the Schedule E case of *CIR v Herd (66 TC 29)* that the reference to 'any payment' in the PAYE Regulations did not impose an obligation to deduct tax where part only of the payment was income. It may well be that the courts would interpret this regulation in the same way. On the other hand the Revenue have given no indication that the new rules were intended to remove the obligation to deduct tax from the Schedule A element of a premium on a lease. Interestingly, their booklet IR 150 (Taxation of Rents) states that tax has to be deducted 'from the income of your rental business' (para 542) but leaflet IR 140 (Non-resident landlords) tells the tenant only that he must deduct tax from rents.

**3.30** For the purpose of the above provisions any sum (other than rent) paid on or in connection with the granting of a tenancy will be presumed to be a premium unless sufficient other consideration for the payment can be shown to have been given (*ICTA 1988, s 24(2)*). *Section 24* contains definitions of a lease, premises and reversion. These are self-evident – with the possible exception of a premium, the normal meaning of which is extended to include any like sum payable either to the landlord, to his landlord, or to a connected person of either (within *ICTA 1988, s 839* – see Appendix 1).

**3.31** The provisions to allow relief in respect of rent not received in certain circumstances (see 2.59 above) apply equally to amounts receivable as premium or deemed premium under *section 34* or amounts taxable under Case VI of Schedule D under *sections 34(6), 35* and *36* (*ICTA 1988, s 41(3)*).

## Deduction of Premium Paid

**3.32** Where part of a premium or other payment to the landlord has become chargeable to income tax or treated as income of a Schedule A business under *section 34* or *35*, or would have become so chargeable but for any exemption from tax, e.g. where the landlord is a charity, or but for the operation of *section 37(1)* itself, the payer may be entitled to claim tax relief under either *ICTA 1988, s 37* or *ICTA 1988, s 87*. *Section 87* is considered in 12.45–12.49 below. *Section 37(1)* applies where the tenant himself receives a premium or deemed premium in respect of the premises; for example, on the grant of a sublease. It limits the charge on the tenant (or the amount treated as income of the Schedule A business) under *section 34* or *35* in relation to the premium he receives to the excess of the chargeable amount of that premium over 'the appropriate fraction of the amount chargeable on the superior interest' (*ICTA 1988, s 37(2)*).

**3.33** The amount chargeable on the superior interest is, of course, the amount on which the landlord is taxed. The appropriate fraction is the proportion of that amount that the length of the lease granted by the tenant bears to the length of the lease in relation to which he paid his premium, i.e.

$$\text{amount taxed on landlord} \times \frac{\text{length of lease for which tenant received premium}}{\text{length of lease for which tenant paid premium}}$$

**3.34** In both cases the length of the lease is the period treated as the duration of the lease under *section 34* (which can be less than the term of the lease either because it is deemed under *section 38* to have a specific duration, or because the sum paid relates to a variation, waiver, etc. for less than the whole term of the lease), or the duration remaining at the date of the assignment where the charge is under *section 35*.

*Example 9*

Leslie paid a premium of £80,000 on 6 April 2002 for a grant of a lease for a period of 40 years. She immediately granted a sublease for five years at a premium of £6,000.

Leslie is taxable under Sch A (in addition to her net rent received) on:

| | | £ |
|---|---|---|
| Taxable portion of premium received<br>2% × (50 – (5 – 1)) = 92% of £6,000 | | 5,520 |
| *Less* appropriate fraction of taxable portion of premium paid<br>2% × (50 – (40 – 1)) = 22% of £80,000 = | £17,600 | |
| 17,600 × 5/40 = | | 2,200 |
| | | £3,320 |

**3.35** If the sublease extends to part only of the premises only that part of the appropriate fraction of the amount chargeable on the superior interest which on a just apportionment relates to the part sublet can, of course, be deducted (*ICTA 1988, s 37(3)*).

**3.36** If a person who pays a premium grants a sublease under which no premium is payable (or the premium on which is insufficient to enable full relief for the amount taxable on the landlord to be given) he is treated as paying additional rent for the premises, which is deemed to become due from day to day during the period in respect of which the amount chargeable on the landlord arose, equal in total to that amount (*ICTA 1988, s 37(4)(5)*). In other words, the amount taxable on the landlord is spread on a day-to-day basis over the term of the lease (or rather its deemed term under *section 34* or *35*) and treated as rent payable by the tenant. If the tenant assigns his lease, the assignee takes over the right to the deduction for the unexpired period.

*Example 10*

Mary paid a premium of £60,000 on 18 May 2002 for a 10-year lease at a rent of £500 p.a. She granted a sublease for 5 years from 1 July 2002 at a rent of £7,500 p.a. payable monthly in advance. She sold the lease to Mark for £55,000 on 31 December 2003.

| *Mary* | £ | £ |
|---|---|---|
| Rent received 2002/03 10 months @ £625 | | 6,250 |
| *Less* rent paid | 500 | |
| notional additional rent | | |
| 2% × (50 – (10 – 1)) = 82% of £60,000 = £49,200 | | |
| proportion attributable to period 18.5.00 – 5.4.2001 | | |
| $\frac{323}{10 \times 365}$ days × 49,200 | 4,354 | |
| | | 4,854 |
| | | £1,396 |
| Rent received 2003/04 8 months @ £625 | | 5,000 |
| *Less* rent paid | 500 | |
| *Less* recovered from Mark on the assignment | 187 | |
| | 313 | |
| notional additional rent | | |
| $\frac{270}{10 \times 365}$ × 49,200 | 3,639 | |
| | | 3,952 |
| | | £1,048 |

| *Mark* | £ | £ |
|---|---|---|
| Rent received 2004/05 4 months @ £625 | | 2,500 |
| Less rent paid (under apportionment on acquisition) | 187 | |
| notional additional rent | | |
| $\frac{95}{10 \times 365}$ × 49,200 | 1,281 | |
| | | 1,468 |
| | | £1,032 |

**3.37** Where, as in *Example 9* above, full relief for the fraction of the amount chargeable on the landlord can be given against the premium on the sublease, no further relief can be given against the rent under that sublease. However, where relief is given under *section 37(2)* against the taxable part of the premium on a sublease, but the taxable part of that premium is less than the taxable portion of the premium paid to the landlord that is attributable to the term of the sublease, relief for the balance can be given against the rent – but only to the extent of the proportion which that balance bears to the taxable portion of the premium paid that is attributable to the sublease (*ICTA 1988, s 37(5)*).

*Example 11*

Suppose that Leslie in *Example 9* had granted her five-year sublease for a premium of £2,000 and a rent of £1,000 p.a. payable monthly in advance, and the ground rent payable under her lease was £100 p.a. payable annually in advance.

| | £ | £ |
|---|---|---|
| Her taxable rent for 2002/03 would be | | |
| Taxable portion of premium received | | |
| 2% × (50 – (5 – 1)) = 92% of £2,000 | 1,840 | |
| *Less* appropriate fraction of taxable portion of premium paid (as before) | 2,200 | NIL |
| Excess | 360 | |
| Rent received | | 1,000 |
| *Less* rent paid | 100 | |
| Notional additional rent | | |
| $\frac{360}{2,200} \times \frac{17,600}{40 \text{ years}}$ | 72 | 172 |
| | | £828 |

Over the first five years Leslie will therefore obtain relief of £1,840 + (5 × £72) = £2,200, or ⅛th of £17,600, which is what one would expect as the sublease covers ⅛th of the length of Leslie's lease.

**3.38** If the sublease extends to part only of the premises the relief due is calculated separately for that part and for the remainder (*ICTA 1988, s 37(6) proviso*).

**3.39** Where a person has granted a sublease for a term shorter than that of the headlease and subsequently grants a further sublease, relief under either *section 37(2)* or *(4)* as appropriate is of course available against the premium or rent from that subsequent lease.

*Example 12*

Leslie in *Example 11* granted a second sublease for five years at a premium of £6,000 on the expiry of the sublease on 5 April 2007.

The position will be:

Relief in the first 5 years as in *Example 11*

| | |
|---|---|
| £1,840 + (5 × £72) | £2,200 |
| Relief in year 6 against premium received as per *Example 9* | £2,200 |
| Relief available to be given against premium/rent on subsequent leases for year 11 onwards | £13,200 |

**3.40** No relief can be given under either *section 37* or *section 87* (see 12.45) in respect of an amount taxed on the landlord under *section 36*. Relief used to be given for such a sum but it was found to be open to abuse – an artificial tax avoidance scheme exploited what was intended as an anti-avoidance provision to generate tax relief for the cost of land and buildings. Rather than seek to block this abuse the government opted to withdraw the relief completely.

## Capital Gains Tax Relief

**3.41** The grant of a lease at a premium is a part disposal for capital gains tax purposes. The value of the property undisposed of, namely the reversion on the lease, accordingly needs to be ascertained and the normal A/(A+B) formula used to arrive at the allowable cost (*TCGA 1992, s 42, Sch 8 para 2*). Where part of the premium has been taxed under Schedule A under *section 34*, that taxed amount obviously needs to be excluded from the capital gains tax computation. This is achieved by *TCGA 1992, Sch 8 paras 5, 6*.

**3.42** The basic rule is that the amount taxed under Schedule A is excluded from capital gains tax, i.e. it is deducted from the premium, the net amount only being liable to capital gains tax (*TCGA 1992, Sch 8 para 5(1)*). For the purpose of applying the normal A/(A+B) formula that applies to part disposals in order to arrive at the part of the cost to be set against the premium, the gross premium still needs to be used in the denominator of the fraction (*TCGA 1992, Sch 8 para 5(1)*).

*Example 13*

Jane in *Example 4* (see 3.2 above) granted a lease at a premium of £50,000. Suppose the value of her freehold reversion following the grant of the lease was £140,000 and that the freehold property had originally cost her £160,000.

| | £ |
|---|---|
| Her chargeable gain will be | |
| Premium | 50,000 |
| *Less* part taxed under Sch A (see *Example 4*) | 41,000 |
| | 9,000 |
| *Less* allowable cost | |
| $\dfrac{\text{part of premium subject to CGT}}{\text{entire premium + reversion}} \times \text{cost}$ | |
| $\dfrac{9{,}000}{50{,}000 + 140{,}000} \times £160{,}000$ | 7,579 |
| Chargeable gain (ignoring indexation relief) | £1,421 |

**3.43** This treatment applies where the lease is granted out of a freehold or a long lease, i.e. one which is not a wasting asset – normally one of over 50 years. If a sublease is granted out of a lease which has 50 years or less to run at the time of granting the sublease (the length of the lease being determined in accordance with the rules set out in 11.18–11.37 below), a different approach is adopted. The amount which is taxed under Schedule A is deducted not from the consideration (the premium) but from the capital gain accruing on the receipt of the premium (*TCGA 1992, Sch 8 para 5(2)*). As will be seen from 11.30 below the capital gain in such circumstances is not calculated using the A/(A+B) formula and the special method of calculation makes the normal CGT treatment of the amount taxed under Schedule A inappropriate.

**3.44** The deduction from the gain is limited to the amount of the capital gain; it cannot create or increase a capital loss (*TCGA 1992, Sch 8 para 5(2)*).

**3.45** If income tax has been charged under *section 36* (sale of land with right to reconveyance) (see 3.17 above) the amount charged to income tax is similarly excluded from the sale proceeds received unless the sale is a part disposal when the sale proceeds are left unadjusted in the denominator of the part disposal fraction (*TCGA 1992, Sch 8 para 5(3)*) – or unless what is disposed of is the remainder of a lease, or a sublease out of a lease of 50 years or less, in which case the Schedule A amount is deducted from the gain (but it cannot create or increase a capital loss) (*TCGA 1992, Sch 8 para 5(3) proviso*).

**3.46** These rules displace *TCGA 1992, s 37* (exclusion of consideration chargeable to income tax) (*TCGA 1992, Sch 8 para 5(5)*). They apply where the Schedule A charge is on a deemed premium as well as where an actual premium is received (*TCGA 1992, Sch 8 para 5(4)*).

These are both instances where a cash sum is received. The reason that *paragraph 5(4)* does not include a deemed premium under *section 34(2)* (where the tenant is required to carry out works) is that the landlord would not have a capital gains tax disposal in such circumstances. Where a deemed premium arises under *section 34(2)* the amount on which the landlord is charged to tax is deemed to be enhancement expenditure attributable to his interest in the property, so capital gains tax relief will be obtainable on a subsequent disposal (*TCGA 1992, Sch 8 para 7*).

**3.47** If the payer of a premium for a lease has granted a sublease and is entitled to treat part of the premium that he pays as additional rent under *section 37(4)(5)* (see 3.36 above) any capital gains tax loss on the grant of the sublease is restricted by deducting from the loss the sum which he is entitled to claim as additional rent over the term of the sublease. This deduction can only eliminate the loss; it cannot convert it into a gain (*TCGA 1992, Sch 8 para 6(1)*).

*Example 14*

Leslie in *Example 11* see (3.37 above) paid a premium of £80,000 on 6 April 2001 for a 40-year lease and received a premium of £2,000 on the same day for the grant of a 5-year sublease.

Her capital gains tax computation on the premium received will be:

| | £ | £ |
|---|---|---|
| Premium received | | 2,000 |
| *Less* allowable portion of premium paid | | |
| take percentage for a 40-year lease 95.457 | | |
| take percentage for a 35-year lease 91.981 | | |
| $\frac{95.457 - 91.981}{95.457} \times £80{,}000$ | | 2,913 |
| Loss | | (913) |
| Restriction is made as follows: | | |
| taxable portion of premium paid applicable to period of sublease | 2,200 | |
| taxable portion of premium received (92%) | 1,840 | |
| excess relievable against rents | | 360 |
| Allowable loss | | £(553) |

**3.48** Where a Schedule A charge arises under *section 35* (see 3.14 above) in relation to the assignment of a lease granted at an undervalue, *TCGA 1992, s 37* (which excludes from capital gains tax amounts taxed as income) is not to apply (*TCGA 1992, Sch 8 para 6(2)*). The effect seems to be to subject the entire receipt to capital gains tax as well as charging part to income tax. It may be that the draftsman felt that where *section 35* applies the grant of the lease would normally have been a transaction otherwise than at arm's length, so that the lessee's capital gains tax base cost would be the market value of the lease at the time it was granted, i.e. the open market premium that could have been charged. Accordingly the amount of the undervalue taxed under *section 35* will already have been excluded from his capital gains tax computation. However, this would imply a capital gains tax charge on the lessor in relation to the undervalue, so there would still be double taxation overall.

## 'Premiums' for Assignments of Leases

**3.49** A payment for an assignment of an existing lease is generally described as a premium. However, except in the unusual circumstances covered by *section 35* (see 3.14 above), such a payment will not attract an income tax charge on the landlord, and will generate no income tax relief for the tenant. The receipt by the assignor is chargeable to capital gains tax in the normal way. He will have made a complete disposal of his interest in the lease. See further 11.18–11.37 below. If the assignor pays the incoming tenant a capital sum to induce him to take the assignment, that sum was normally not taxable prior to 9 March 1999. It is now normally taxable although spread over the period up to the first rent review. The new provisions do not address the problem of the assignor getting tax relief for the payment. He cannot normally obtain a Case I deduction for the payment (unless he held the lease as trading stock) (see 12.45 below). He cannot treat it as allowable expenditure for the purpose of claiming a capital loss on the lease either, as it does not fit into the restrictive rules of *TCGA 1992, s 38(1)(2)*. This problem is considered further at 3.56.

## Surrender of Leases

**3.50** The surrender of a lease will not normally attract an income tax charge under these rules even if the tenant makes a payment to the landlord for the surrender, unless that payment is under one of the terms subject to which the lease was granted (see 3.6–3.9 above). The landlord will of course be chargeable to capital gains tax on the receipt either under *TCGA 1992, Sch 8 para 3(2)* (see 11.24 below) or, more often, under *TCGA 1992, s 22(1)* as a capital sum derived from the landlord's interest in the property. The VAT aspects of reverse surrenders are dealt with at 17.100 onwards.

## 'Reverse Premiums'

**3.51** The expression 'reverse premium' is frequently used to describe a payment by a landlord to a tenant to induce him either to enter into a lease or to increase the rent payable under an existing lease. The tax treatment of a reverse premium is likely to depend on the facts of each individual case and in particular on the category into which the transaction falls. If the payment is to an existing tenant to induce him to pay an increased rent the reverse premium is in effect paid in consideration of his disposing of his existing right to occupy the premises at a favourable rent. As such he will have a part disposal of his lease and will realise a capital gain on the reverse premium less an apportioned part of his base cost of the lease (*TCGA 1992, s 22(1)(c)*).

**3.52** If the payment is to induce the tenant to enter into a new lease he starts with nothing. He is receiving the reverse premium as an inducement to persuade him to take on liabilities that he would not otherwise have undertaken. Prior to 9 March 1999 such a receipt was in practice normally a tax-free receipt. However, such reverse premiums are now normally taxable as income under *FA 1999, Sch 6*. This applies to reverse premiums received after 8 March 1999 unless the recipient was entitled to receive it immediately before that date. For the purpose of ascertaining whether such entitlement existed no account is to be taken of any arrangements made after that date (*FA 1999, s 54*).

**3.53** *FA 1999, Sch 6* applies where:

(*a*) a person receives a payment or other benefit by way of inducement in connection with a transaction entered into by him or a person connected with him;

(*b*) that transaction is one under which the person receiving the payment or other benefit (or the connected person) becomes entitled to an estate or interest in (or a right in or over) land; and

(*c*) the payment or other benefit is paid or provided by either:

- (i) the person by whom that estate, interest or right is granted (or was granted at an earlier time) (the grantor),
- (ii) a person connected with the grantor, or
- (iii) a nominee of the grantor (or a connected person of his) or a person acting on the directions of the grantor or of a connected person (*FA 1999, Sch 6 para 1(1)*).

**3.54** It should be particularly noted that:

(*a*) The payment must be by way of inducement. It is not clear what this means. For example, if a person is prepared to enter into a lease at £90,000 per annum and the prospective landlord suggests that instead he pays the prospective tenant £100,000 and the rent is increased to £115,000, it is not at all clear that the £100,000 is an inducement. It may be simply a commercial bargain under which one person is prepared to assume a liability to make a series of payments in consideration of an initial lump sum. When one purchases an annuity one would not normally describe the purchase price as an inducement to the insurance company to grant the annuity. The word 'inducement' implies an element of persuasion.

(*b*) It is not clear what is meant by 'other benefit'. The Revenue have said that this has to be a benefit in money's worth and would not cover the granting of a rent-free period. However, they resisted requests for this to be spelt out in the legislation. It obviously needs to be a benefit that can be valued (and that value taxed) but even a rent-free period has a value to the tenant even though that value cannot be realised by a sale of the benefit.

(*c*) Persons are connected if they are connected within the meaning of *ICTA 1988, s 839* (see Appendix 1) at any time when the relevant arrangements, i.e. any arrangements entered into in connection with the relevant transaction (either before, at the same time as, or after it), are entered into (*FA 1999, Sch 6 para 8*). A payment to a third party who is not a connected person will not be caught. For example an individual could agree to take a lease if a payment is made to his fiancée, his nephew, his uncle or his common-law spouse. Whilst the opportunity for such payments may not arise often it is worth looking out for them.

(*d*) The recipient (or connected person) must become entitled to an estate or interest in land in consequence of the transaction. *Schedule 6* will not therefore apply if a person already has that interest, e.g. where the reverse premium is paid to vary the terms of an existing lease.

(*e*) The premium must be paid or provided by the landlord or a connected person of his. Situations can arise where an existing tenant is prepared to pay a landlord to accept a surrender of his lease. If the tenant enters into an agreement with the landlord and an unconnected third party that in consideration of the third party taking a new lease from the landlord the existing tenant will make a payment to the third party, that payment will not fall within *Schedule 6*. Similarly a payment by a tenant to a third party to induce him to take an assignment of an existing lease will not fall within the *Schedule*. A payment by the landlord to induce the third party to take over an existing lease would do so though, unless the landlord himself initially took an assignment of his interest in the lease so that he is not the grantor of it.

**3.55** There are a number of statutory exceptions.

(*a*) A receipt is not caught to the extent that it reduces the recipient's expenditure qualifying for capital allowances under *CAA 2001, s 532* (see 8.5) (*FA 1999, Sch 6 para 5*). Where a tenant will carry out fitting out works it may be worth considering seeking a contribution to such costs instead of a reverse premium. Although this will restrict the tenant's capital allowances the resultant extra tax burden will be spread over a number of years and the landlord may be willing to increase the payment to reflect part of the benefit of his tax allowances if he can claim allowances under *CAA 2001, s 538* in relation to that contribution.

(*b*) A receipt by an individual which relates to premises occupied or to be occupied by him as his only or main residence is not caught (*FA 1999, Sch 6 para 6*).

(*c*) A payment as consideration for the acquisition of an estate or interest in land under a sale and lease back within *ICTA 1988, ss 779(1)* (see 12.15), *779(2)* (see 12.21) or *780(1)* (see 12.27) is obviously not caught (*FA 1999, Sch 6 para 7*) as those provisions contain their own tax regime.

**3.56** Where a reverse premium within *Schedule 6* is received for the purpose of a trade, profession or vocation carried on (or to be carried on) by the recipient it is taxed as a trading receipt of that trade (*FA 1999, Sch 6 para 2(2)*). In any other case it is treated as income of a Schedule A business. If the recipient already has a Schedule A business it is a receipt of that business (*FA 1999, Sch 6 para 2(3)*). If a person has significant Schedule A losses on other properties the diversion of a reverse premium to that person could be a means of utilising such losses. The effect in both cases is that the reverse premium is not normally taxed wholly in the year of receipt. It is normally spread on a straight-line basis over the lease term or, if shorter, the period to the review date on which the rent is first expected to be adjusted to a full market rent in accordance with UITF 12. If the landlord will accept reviews to say 95% of market rent this may allow the premium to be spread over the full lease term. Special rules apply for life insurance companies (*FA 1999, Sch 6 para 4*).

**3.57** The reverse premium is taxed wholly in the year of receipt if one or more of the parties to the arrangements under which it is paid are connected persons (within *ICTA 1988, s 839* — see Appendix 1) and the terms of those arrangements are not such as would reasonably have been expected if those persons had been dealing at arm's length, i.e. they differ to a significant extent from the terms which, at the time the arrangements were entered into, would be regarded as normal and reasonable in the market conditions then prevailing between persons dealing with each other at arm's length in the open market (*FA 1999, Sch 6 para 3(1)(4)*). The year of receipt for this purpose is the accounting year of the recipient in which the reverse premium is received. If the recipient receives it for the purposes of a trade, profession or vocation which has not yet commenced it is the accounting year in which the trade commences (*FA 1999, Sch 6 para 3(2)(3)(5)*).

**3.58** The Revenue have given their own views on the interpretation of the legislation (Tax Bulletin 44, December 1999). They consider that:

(*a*) The following will be taxable inducements:

(i) contributions towards specific tenant's costs such as fitting out, start up or relocation;

(ii) sums paid to third parties to meet obligations of the tenant, such as rent to a landlord under an existing lease or a capital sum to terminate an existing lease; and

(iii) the effective payment of cash by other means, for example the landlord's writing off a sum which the tenant owes.

It is questionable whether a payment to a third party ((ii) above) constitutes a benefit to the tenant – or if it does whether the payment is the quantum of the benefit – particularly as the legislation contains no machinery for valuing non-cash benefits. The Revenue do not deal with the more common case where the landlord takes an assignment of the prospective tenant's existing lease. Under that scenario, and indeed the payment of rent to the tenant's existing landlord, the 'benefit' to the tenant is virtually impossible to value in many cases as it is spread over an indefinite period and even then the cost cannot be quantified as this will depend on the ability to find a new tenant for the premises. Often a landlord takes an assignment of the prospective tenant's existing lease solely because he wants the tenant as an anchor tenant in his development and expects to be able to re-let the tenant's premises fairly easily. There is probably no benefit to the tenant in that event.

(*b*) The following are not caught because they do not involve any actual outlay:

(i) the grant of a rent-free period;

(ii) replacement by agreement of an existing lease at an onerous rent by a new lease at a lower rent; and

(iii) replacement by agreement of an existing lease by a new lease with less onerous conditions.

(*c*) The tenant does not receive a benefit if the landlord pays for tenant's fittings but reflects the expenditure in the rent.

(*d*) The payment by the tenant of fitting out costs or part of the building costs because he wants the work carried out to a specified standard is not caught even if the landlord reimburses all or part of the costs to him. (It is hard to imagine anyone thinking it might be.)

(*e*) A payment or other benefit to induce a person to buy a freehold building is not caught because a freehold cannot be 'granted', it can only be conveyed.

**3.59** When *Schedule 6* was introduced the government said that it was to clarify that law following the Privy Council decision in a New Zealand case, *CIR v Wattie (1998 STC 1160)* where an inducement payment to take a lease at a rent substantially above a market rate was held to be a capital receipt, albeit that it was admitted to be commercially, financially and mathematically linked to the rent. In practice, despite what the government said, the author cannot recollect having seen a pre 9 March 1999 reverse premium taxed as income. It is not by its nature income. It is not received in consideration of the tenant undertaking to provide services to the landlord. Admittedly a reverse premium has been held to be consideration for the provision of a service for VAT purposes (see 3.65) but the VAT legislation deems anything done for a consideration and which is not a supply of goods to be a supply of services. This statutory fiction does not apply for income tax. The cases of *Gallagher v Jones (1993 STC 537)* and *Johnston v Britannia Airways Ltd (1994 STC 763)* emphasised that the starting point for the computation of profits for tax purposes is generally accepted accounting principles. The Accounting Standards Board's statement UITF 12 requires a reverse premium to be written off against profits over the term of the lease. Some people fear that this treatment will convert a pre 9 March 1999 reverse premium into profits. This fear is probably unfounded. There is nothing in those cases to suggest that the accounting treatment can change the basic legal distinction between income and capital, and a reverse premium is by its nature a capital receipt. The reverse premium does not seem to come within the scope of Schedule A as a receipt 'arising to a person from or by virtue of his ownership of an estate or interest in or right over such land' (*ICTA 1988, s 15(1) para 1(c)*) and neither can the lease premium rules be applied as the payment is not a 'premium required under a lease, or otherwise under the terms subject to which a lease is granted' (*ICTA 1988, s 34(1)*). This view is supported by *ICTA 1988, s 780* (see 12.25 below). This was introduced to impose an income tax charge on part of an amount received where a tenant under a short lease either took a reverse premium or sold his lease and took back a sublease at a higher rent. The *section* would hardly have been introduced if such a receipt was already within the charge to income tax.

**3.60** A reverse premium that is not caught by *Schedule 6* and which is an inducement to take a new lease (as opposed to varying an existing one) does not seem to be within the scope of capital gains tax. This is charged on 'chargeable gains . . . accruing to a person on the disposal of assets' (*TCGA 1992, s 1(1)*). The author cannot see any asset that the tenant can have disposed of. The charge is extended by *TCGA 1992, s 22* to the case 'where any capital sum is derived from assets', but again it is not thought that this extension catches a reverse premium. The recipient of the premium does not derive it 'from' an asset. He derives it from agreeing to enter into a lease which has a negative market value. The Revenue seem to accept that the receipt is not taxable in such circumstances.

**3.61** If the inducement is to take a new lease of premises already occupied by the tenant on the expiration of his existing lease, the Revenue might contend that the receipt is in consideration of the tenant giving up his *Landlord and Tenant Act* rights deriving from the lease. However, it is difficult to envisage such a contention succeeding in the light of the decision in *Bayley v Rogers (53 TC 420)*, where it was held that a new lease granted following proceedings under the *Landlord and Tenant Act 1954* did not derive from the prior lease but was a separate asset.

**3.62** The other provision that might need to be considered is *ICTA 1988, s 776* (see chapter 14). However, for this to apply, either:

(*a*) land, or property deriving its value from land, must be acquired with the sole or main object of realising a gain from disposing of the land; or

(*b*) land must be held as trading stock; or

(*c*) land must be developed with the sole or main object of realising a gain from disposing of the land when developed.

**3.63** Assuming that the incoming tenant is intending to occupy the premises (so that condition (*a*) above will not apply) the receipt of a reverse premium will not normally fall into either of the two remaining categories.

**3.64** As far as the payer is concerned, if he is a property dealer he should have no difficulty in obtaining a deduction for the reverse premium as a trading expense. If he holds the property as an investment, he will need to demonstrate that the payment constituted enhancement expenditure (see 11.4(*b*) below). In many, if not most, cases it would clearly do so as the intention of making the payment is to enhance the investment value of the property. Similar considerations to those relating to payments to tenants to vacate premises would apply. These are discussed at 8.8 below. It may be more difficult to show that the expenditure is reflected in the state or nature of the asset at the time of its disposal though. It should particularly be noted that the legislation does not grant relief to the payer for a reverse premium taxed under *Schedule 6*. Nor does it convert the payment to income as far as the payer is concerned. He can obtain a deduction only where the basic tax rules will permit this.

**3.65** The VAT position on reverse premiums is considered at 17.100 onwards. Unfortunately the law is not clear cut. Broadly speaking, a reverse premium does not attract VAT. However, it is necessary to consider carefully whether the receipt is merely intended as an inducement to take up the lease or whether the payer receives some benefit other than entering into the lease, for which all or part of the sum might constitute consideration.

# Relief for Interest Payable

**4.1** Property owners frequently borrow funds to finance the acquisition of their properties or for carrying out works on them. In such circumstances it may be important to ensure that tax relief for the interest can be obtained. This is by no means automatic. The interest must often meet a number of conditions to attract a deduction for tax purposes.

**4.2** The rules on deduction of interest have changed significantly in recent years. For income tax purposes interest can be deducted either as a trading expense or a Schedule A expense. If it cannot qualify as either it may still be deductible as an annual payment. The most common example of interest as an annual payment used to be interest on a loan in connection with an individual's principal private residence. Interest paid after 5 April 2000 on loans to acquire properties is unlikely to be a charge on income (except on certain home income plans (see 4.10)). Interest as such is no longer deductible for corporation tax purposes (*s 337A* inserted by *FA 1996, Sch 14 para 15*); instead it is deductible as a debit on loan relationships. Different rules applied for company accounting periods ending before 1 April 1996.

## Income Tax

### Interest as a Trading or Schedule A Expense

**4.3** There are no special rules where the interest constitutes a trading expense or a Schedule A expense. As with any other expense, to qualify as a deduction the interest must be wholly and exclusively incurred for the purpose of the trade or Schedule A business (or overseas Schedule A business where relevant). Provided it does so and does not fall foul of any of the other exclusions in *ICTA 1988, s 74* it is deductible on an accruals basis in the same way as any other expense.

**4.4** Prior to 1995/96 interest was not deductible in computing Schedule A income. It was deductible as an annual payment and therefore had to meet the rules described below for annual payments. These rules also applied for 1995/96 in those cases where a taxpayer had Schedule A income in 1994/95 but this ceased entirely in 1995/96 (see

2.53). In particular the loan had to be for a qualifying purpose (see 4.13). It also had to meet the qualifying condition that the property was let at a commercial rent for more than 26 weeks in any period of 52 weeks, including the date on which the interest was payable and falling wholly or partly within the year of assessment in which it was paid, and when not so let had either to be available for letting at a commercial rent or prevented from being so available by works of construction or repair (*ICTA 1988, s 355(1)(b)*). The restriction to interest on the first £30,000 of borrowings and the limitation on the rate of relief (see 4.24) did not apply to interest on a letting property whether the income was taxable under Schedule A or, in the case of furnished lettings, Case VI of Schedule D.

**4.5** It is possible for interest to be capital. In a Privy Council case, *Wharf Properties Ltd v Commissioner of Inland Revenue (of Hong Kong) (1997) STC 351)* interest was held to be capital. The relevant head of the legislation prohibited the deduction of 'any expenditure of a capital nature'. Fortunately the equivalent UK legislation, *ICTA 1988, s 74(1)(f)*, 'any sum employed or intended to be employed as capital', contains a proviso that 'this paragraph shall not be treated as disallowing the deduction of any interest', so this decision is not directly relevant to the UK. It is useful for what it says about accounting principles though.

**4.6** If interest could qualify for relief both under the above tests and under the tests in para 4.4 the relief was given under *ICTA 1988, s 355(1)(b)* so that the restriction did not apply (*s 353(1C)*). This could have occurred where a taxpayer let his main residence whilst temporarily absent (see 4.36) or living in job-related accommodation (see 4.45). An election could be made for the relief to be given under the private residence rules instead (*s 353(1C)(1D)*). Such an election was not normally attractive unless the taxpayer had unrelieved losses on let properties.

**4.7** Relief for the interest could be given only against income from the letting of the same or any other land (or caravan or houseboat). If the interest exceeded the total rental income for the year of assessment in which it was paid the excess could be carried forward against future rents from the same or any other property. When the property to which such unrelieved interest related was sold, any unrelieved balance ceased to be eligible for carry forward against rents from other properties (*ICTA 1988, s 355(4)*). It is not wholly clear to what extent such brought-forward interest could be relieved in the year of sale. It is probable that it could be set against income from other properties for the entire year of assessment if the property was owned as a letting property at any time during the year. Where an election was made to split furnished letting income between rent for the land and rent for the furniture (see 2.90) it is likely that interest on other properties could be set only against the land element. Unrelieved interest at 5 April 1996 was converted into a Schedule A loss, so preserving the relief, provided that the taxpayer was carrying on a Schedule A business in 1995/96 (see 2.47).

**4.8** Where refurbishment work or improvements were carried out it needs to be remembered that no relief was due for interest paid more than six months prior to the property being let. Similarly interest relief could be lost if there was a gap between lettings of more than six months, although in most cases the interest payment date would fall within six months of the previous letting if it did not come within six months of the new one.

**4.9** A rentcharge (or in Scotland a superiority or the interest of a creditor in a contract of ground annual) was specifically excluded from being an interest in land, so interest on a loan to purchase a rentcharge did not qualify for relief. Similarly the interest of a mortgagee was not an interest in land (*ICTA 1988, s 354(4)*).

## Interest as an Annual Payment

**4.10** The only interest on a loan to acquire property that qualifies as an annual payment after 5 April 2000 is that payable under home income plans (see 4.49). Before that date other interest (now primarily interest on a loan to acquire one's main residence) was deductible as an annual payment for income tax purposes but only if the money was borrowed for a qualifying purpose (see 4.13) and met the appropriate conditions. The interest had to be interest on a fixed loan. Overdraft interest could not qualify for relief (*ICTA 1988, s 353(3)(a)*). If the rate of interest exceeded a reasonable commercial rate the excess was not allowable (*ICTA 1988, s 353(3)(b)*). For 1993/94 and earlier years, the interest also had to be either:

(*a*) annual interest chargeable to tax under Case III of Schedule D (*ICTA 1988, s 353(1)(a)*), or

(*b*) interest payable in the UK on an advance from a bank carrying on a bona fide banking business in the UK (or from a person bona fide carrying on a business as a member of a stock exchange in the UK or bona fide carrying on the business of a discount house in the UK) (*ICTA 1988, s 353(1)(b)*).

**4.11** If the taxpayer was a resident of the Republic of Ireland, interest on a loan from an Irish building society or other lender in the Republic of Ireland was, by concession, treated as eligible for relief even if the interest was not taxable in the UK under Case III provided that the other conditions for eligibility were met (Inland Revenue Extra-Statutory Concession A28).

**4.12** The carry forward of interest in relation to rental properties (see 4.7) under the rules that applied before 1996/97 was the only circumstance in which interest paid by an individual could be carried forward. Normally, if the taxpayer's income for the year of assessment in which interest is paid was insufficient to allow full relief, no allowance was obtainable for the excess.

## Qualifying Purpose

**4.13** Assuming that care had been taken to ensure that the interest fell within *section 353* it also had to be shown to be for a qualifying purpose. The necessary conditions are contained in *ICTA 1988, ss 354–367*. Firstly, the interest had to be paid by a person for the time being owning an estate or interest in land or a caravan or houseboat, in the UK or the Republic of Ireland, on a loan to defray money applied:

(*a*) in purchasing that estate or interest – or one absorbed into the estate or interest, or given up to obtain it; or

(*b*) in improving or developing the land (or buildings on the land); or

(*c*) in paying off another loan if interest on that other loan would have been eligible for relief under *section 353* if it had not been repaid (on the assumption, if the loan was free of interest, that it carried interest).

(*ICTA 1988, s 354(1)*).

**4.14** The loan had to be made in connection with the application of money for the qualifying purpose. It had to be made on the occasion of such application or within what was in the circumstances a reasonable time after the application of the money. The funds must not have been applied for some other purpose before being used for the qualifying purpose (*ICTA 1988, s 367(2)*). The temporary deposit of the funds in a bank or building society pending their use for the qualifying purpose did not, in practice, generally debar relief. The Revenue regarded the application of the funds within six months before or after the borrowing as reasonable (MIRAS 30 para 72). A longer period might be reasonable depending on the circumstances.

**4.15** An exception to this was where a person purchased a property and a security substitution was made, i.e. the new property was substituted as security for an existing loan in place of a previous property (*ICTA 1988, s 357A* introduced by *FA 1993, s 56*). This was introduced because the then Chancellor believed – it is not clear why – that owner-occupiers with 'negative equity' (i.e. where the value of the property has fallen to such an extent that the mortgage exceeds that value) who wished to move were unable to do so because they would not be able to redeem the mortgage, and that a lender who would not permit the old house to be sold would be willing to do so if he could transfer his charge to the new house. The proceeds of the old house could then be used to buy the new one. *Section 357A* continued interest relief in such circumstances, within the £30,000 overall limit and, if less, up to the cost of the new house only, albeit that the loan on which the interest was paid was used to buy the old house which had been sold. In practice such transactions are rare. The lender will normally make a fresh 100% advance to buy the new house, the proceeds of the old being used to repay its loan as far as possible.

**4.16** Borrowing to meet revenue expenditure, i.e. items which are deductible for Schedule A purposes or would be so deductible if the building were let, was not eligible for relief, but the cost of maintenance or repairs attributable to a period before the estate or interest was acquired (which does not qualify as a Schedule A deduction) is regarded as improvements, so that borrowing in this respect qualified for relief (*ICTA 1988, s 354(2)(a)*).

**4.17** Expenditure in respect of street works for a highway or road (or in Scotland any right of way) adjoining or serving the land could be treated as expenditure in improving the land (*ICTA 1988, s 354(2)(b)*). Street works for this purpose means any works for the sewering, levelling, paving, metalling, flagging, channelling and making good of a road and includes the provision of street lighting (*ICTA 1988, s 367(1)*). Costs of maintenance or repair of such a road obviously did not qualify (*ICTA 1988, s 354(2)(b)*).

### Connected persons

**4.18** Interest on a loan applied in purchasing an estate, interest in land or a caravan or houseboat (i.e. one coming within 4.13 (*a*) above) was, however, debarred from relief if either:

(*a*) the seller and purchaser were husband and wife (living together);

(*b*) the purchaser (or his spouse) previously disposed of an estate or interest in the land, or a caravan or houseboat after 15 April 1969 and it appeared that the main purpose of the disposal and purchase was to obtain relief for interest on the loan;

(*c*) the purchasers were the trustees of a settlement, the seller was the settlor (or his spouse), and it appeared that the main purpose of the purchase was to obtain relief for interest on the loan; or

(*d*) the purchaser was directly or indirectly purchasing from a person with whom he was connected (within *ICTA 1988, s 839* – see Appendix 1) and the purchase price substantially exceeded the value of what was acquired.

(*ICTA 1988, s 355(5)*).

**4.19** A purchase from a connected person (other than one's spouse) did not result in loss of relief provided that the transaction was at around (or below) market value.

**4.20** Interest on a loan that was expended in improving or developing land or buildings was similarly disqualified from relief if the person spending the money was connected (within *ICTA 1988, s 839* – see Appendix 1) with the person who directly or indirectly received it and the money substantially exceeded the value of the work done (*ICTA 1988, s 355(5)*).

## Other Matters

**4.21** It should particularly be noted that the land had to be in the UK or Ireland for the interest to qualify for relief. Interest on a loan to acquire overseas property was not allowable up to 1994/95 even against rents from that property and from that date is allowable only against overseas rental income (see 2.150).

**4.22** If an occupier of property paid money to a landlord under an arrangement whereby money advanced at interest by the landlord was applied by the tenant in purchasing the landlord's estate or interest, but that estate was not to pass to the tenant until a later date, the tenant was treated as owning the landlord's estate or interest in the property for the purpose of determining whether the loan interest was eligible for relief (*ICTA 1988, s 354(7)*). This was aimed at arrangements where, instead of paying rent, the tenant was purchasing the property from the landlord by way of monthly payments of capital and interest but the purchase was conditional on the payments being duly made, so that he would not legally become the owner until all of the payments had been made.

**4.23** The second qualifying condition was that the land either:

(*a*) had to be used as the only or main residence of the person by whom it was paid (or, in relation to interest paid prior to 5 April 1988, of a dependent relative or former or separated spouse of his)

  (i) at the time the interest was paid, or

  (ii) if the interest was paid within twelve months of the date on which the loan was made, within that twelve-month period (*ICTA 1988, s 355(1)(a)*); or

(*b*) previously came within (*a*) above and the borrower had raised another loan in relation to another property with a view to the use of that other property as his only or main residence and to the disposal of the first property (*ICTA 1988, s 354(5)*); or

(*c*) if at the time the interest was paid the taxpayer resided in another property which was job-related accommodation, it had to be used by the borrower as a residence (even though not his main residence) or, if the interest was paid within twelve months of the date on which the loan was made, had to be so used within that twelve-month period or, at the time the interest was paid, was intended to be used in due course as his only or main residence (*ICTA 1988, s 356*).

**4.24** The relief was restricted to interest on the first £30,000 of borrowings and was given at the rate of 10% only for 1998/99 and 1999/00. For 1991/92 to 1993/94 relief was allowed at the basic rate (*ICTA 1988, s 353(4)(5)*, repealed by *FA 1994, Sch 9*). For 1994/95 it was limited to 20% and a 15% rate applied for 1995/96 to 1997/98 (*ICTA 1988, s 353(1F)(1G)*). For 1991/92 onward the interest ceased to be deducted in calculating taxable income. Instead the relief was a credit against the tax payable – and relief was limited to the amount of the payer's overall tax liability (before double tax relief and the credit for the married couples allowance, and ignoring basic rate tax retained in charge against annual payments, etc.) (*ICTA 1988, s 353(1A)(1F)(1H)*). If a borrowing was partly to acquire property and partly for some other qualifying purpose the interest had to be apportioned (*s 353(1E)*).

**4.25** The relief ceased entirely in relation to payments after 5 April 2000 (even if the amount fell due before that date) (*FA 1999, s 38(1)((3)(a)*). Relief for interest due after 1999/2000 could not be preserved by prepaying it unless the payment was made before 9 March 1999 (*FA 1999, s 38(1)(3)(b)*). Relief was also denied for any other payment of interest between 9 March 1999 and 6 April 2000 if it was paid under or in accordance with a scheme made for a tax avoidance purpose. This is a scheme the main purpose (or one of the main purposes) of which was to obtain tax relief under *section 359* (or *369(1)* – see 4.48) for a payment which discharges (or replaces, directly or indirectly) an obligation to make an interest payment that would not itself have qualified for such relief, or which is made in pursuance of an obligation that might have been expected to take the form of an obligation to make such an interest payment (*FA 1999, s 38(4)–(7)*).

## Bridging Loans

**4.26** The relief for interest on a bridging loan under 4.23(*b*) above applied only to interest payable (although not necessarily actually paid) within twelve months of the making of the loan relating to the new residence – or such longer period as the Revenue may in a particular case allow. It is the interest on the old loan, not the new, which qualified for relief under this head, the interest on the new loan being allowable by virtue of head (*a*). It should be noted that there had to be an intention to dispose of the first property; if the new house was bought with a view to refurbishing the old house and then letting it, the interest on the old loan could not fall within (*b*).

**4.27** Interest on the loan to acquire the new property had itself to be allowable. In *Hughes v Viner (58 TC 437)* the taxpayer bought a new property with the intention of occupying it as his residence, but never in fact occupied it. It was held that it was a necessary condition of relief for a bridging loan under head (*b*) that a loan on another property should already qualify for relief under head (*a*). As the loan for the new property did not come within head (*a*) (as the property was not used as a private residence), head (*b*) could not preserve interest relief on the old.

**4.28** This rule was relaxed for payments of interest made after 15 March 1993. If a property was a person's main residence but ceased to be so at a time when he intended to take steps to dispose of it within the following twelve months, interest on a loan to acquire it (or other qualifying interest in relation to it) continued to be eligible for relief for that twelve-month period or, if earlier, until the taxpayer abandoned his intentions to sell the house, e.g. he decided to take it off the market for a year until the market improved (*ICTA 1988, s 355(1A)*).

**4.29** Where on a marriage both bride and groom already owned houses, the couple may well have moved into one of the existing houses as the matrimonial home, the other one being sold. In such circumstances the bridging loan provisions did not apply, as the spouse owning the house that was put up for sale did not raise a loan on another house with a view to it being used as his main residence (as the other spouse already has an existing loan on the matrimonial residence). Relief for interest on the mortgage was, however, allowed by concession, provided that the property was sold within twelve months from the date that it was vacated and the other spouse had an existing allowable borrowing on the matrimonial home (Inland Revenue Extra-Statutory Concession A35).

## Qualifying Limit

**4.30** The relief was restricted to interest on the first £30,000 of borrowings (or sometimes less) as mentioned at 4.24. From 6 April 1991 it was given at the basic rate only, reducing to 20% for 1994/95, 15% for 1995/96 and 1996/97 and 10% thereafter. To be precise, interest was eligible for relief only to the extent that the amount of the loan did not exceed £30,000 reduced by the amount on which interest was payable on any earlier loan within heads (*a*) or (*c*) at 4.23 (*ICTA 1988, s 357*). This means that, where there were several loans, relief was given in the order in which the loans were taken out.

*Example 15*

Joe borrowed £20,000 from a building society at 6%, plus a further £40,000 from an insurance company at 8%, to buy a new main residence.

If the £20,000 loan was taken first, relief would be given each year on

| | | |
|---|---|---|
| (i) | £20,000 @ 6% p.a. | 1,200 |
| (ii) | £10,000 @ 8% p.a. | 800 |
| | | £2,000 |

If the £40,000 loan had been taken first, relief would have been given on three-quarters of that loan with no relief being due on the building society loan. The relief would then have been on

| | |
|---|---|
| £30,000 @ 8% | £2,400 |

If the two loans were made simultaneously they had to be treated as a single loan (*ICTA 1988, s 357(3)(b)*). The relief would therefore be on

$$\frac{30{,}000}{60{,}000} \times £(1{,}200 + 3{,}200) \qquad £2{,}200$$

**4.31** If a loan was made jointly to the borrower and some other person (other than the borrower's spouse) who paid part of the interest and occupied the property as his only or main residence (or the property was the only or main residence of a dependent relative, etc. of his or it qualified for relief under head (*c*) at 4.23) and owned an interest in it, then in determining the restriction on the borrower's relief the amount of the borrower's loan was treated as the proportion of the total loan which the interest he paid bore to the total interest (*ICTA 1988, s 357(2)*). It should be particularly noted that if a person actually paid more than his proportionate share of the interest, he could obtain more than a proportionate share of the relief.

*Example 16*

Jack and Jill bought a house jointly with a building society loan for £70,000. In 1998/99 they each pay 50% of the mortgage interest of £5,000. In June 1999 Jack loses his job and Jill has to pay the full interest as the loan was a joint liability. In 1999/2000 Jack actually pays £1,200 and Jill £3,800.

The split for 1998/99 was:

| | | |
|---|---|---|
| *Jack* | $£70{,}000 \times \frac{2{,}500}{5{,}000} =$ | £35,000 deemed loan |
| *Jill* | $£70{,}000 \times \frac{2{,}500}{5{,}000} =$ | £35,000 deemed loan |

The split for 1999/2000 was:

*Jack* $£70{,}000 \times \frac{1{,}200}{5{,}000} =$ £16,800

*Jill* $£70{,}000 \times \frac{3{,}800}{5{,}000} =$ £53,200

It is not clear what, if anything, happens if Jack subsequently reimbursed to Jill his share of the mortgage interest payments that she has had to make. It does not appear that the relief could be adjusted.

**4.32** In calculating the limitation on the amount eligible for relief any interest on a loan made to the taxpayer's spouse had to be treated as if it were interest on a loan made to the taxpayer himself, unless they were separated (*ICTA 1988, s 357(3)(a)(5)*) – i.e. loans to the spouse had to be taken into account to determine whether the £30,000 limit was exceeded.

**4.33** In determining whether the £30,000 limit was exceeded in relation to a loan no account was to be taken of interest added to capital to the extent that it did not exceed £1,000 (*ICTA 1988, s 357(6)*). This avoided any restriction where a loan was taken out for £30,000 but an increase in the rate of interest caused the interest debited to the loan during a year to exceed the loan repayments. Where a person had several loans it appears that the £1,000 figure applied only to the loan that caused the £30,000 limit to be breached and that no *de minimis* figure applied to interest on the earlier loans.

**4.34** Where a person had a bridging loan eligible for relief (i.e. one within head (*b*) at 4.23) its existence was ignored for the purpose of determining whether the loan for the new property breached the £30,000 limit (*ICTA 1988, s 354(5)(b)*). The £30,000 ceiling also continued to apply to the loan for the old property in the same way as before the new loan was taken out (*ICTA 1988, s 357(4)*).

**4.35** Whether or not a house was used as the only or main residence of the owner (or of a dependent relative or former or separated spouse of his), so that the interest qualified for relief under head (*a*) at 4.23, was a question of fact. It was not possible for the taxpayer to elect which of two or more properties should be regarded as his principal residence for this purpose. In *Frost v Feltham (55 TC 10)* it was held that the question as to which is a person's principal – or more important – residence could not be determined solely by the time he spends in each. In that case the taxpayer lived in tied premises, and bought a house elsewhere which he and his wife regarded as their home and where they spent a few days each month. It was held that the Commissioners were entitled to find that the house was their main residence.

**4.36** Temporary absences of up to a year are in practice ignored in determining whether a property was used as a person's main residence. So was a period when a person's employment took him away from his home, provided that this was not expected to exceed four years and he could reasonably be expected to re-occupy the residence on his return. Reoccupation for three months or more started a new four-year period (Inland Revenue Extra-Statutory Concession A27). If the property was let while the individual was away in these circumstances, he would normally have wanted to claim relief against the rental income, as this would allow relief at the higher rate as well as basic rate and the £30,000 limit would not apply. However, he was entitled to claim relief instead under the private residence rules and Concession A27 if this was more favourable as in the case of available unused allowances or losses arising on the letting income (Inland Revenue Extra-Statutory Concession A27).

**4.37** Where a property was used as the sole or main residence of more than one borrower (other than husband and wife) the £30,000 limit applied to the property and had to be apportioned equally amongst the borrowers unless the loan was taken out before 1 August 1988 (*ICTA 1988, ss 356A* to *356D*). If the amount borrowed by any of them was less than his share of the £30,000 figure the excess was divided amongst the others.

Thus in the above *Example 16*, Jack's limit was £15,000 for both 1998/99 and 1999/2000 so although Jill was deemed to have borrowed the bulk of the money her relief was restricted to a greater degree than Jack's. If Jack had paid only £600 of interest in 1999/00, so that his deemed loan was only £21,600, his limit for 1999/2000 would have been £8,400 and Jill's £21,600 (half of £30,000 plus Jack's shortfall of £6,600).

**4.38** If a married couple shared a property with other borrowers, the married couple was treated as two persons for the purpose of making this apportionment but their combined borrowings were looked at to see if they could use their full share of the relief.

Thus, if in the above example Jack's wife Judy also lived in the property, Jack's limit would have been £20,000 for 1998/99 and £16,800 for 1999/2000 and Jill's therefore £10,000 and £13,200 respectively. It does not appear to matter that Judy may not have paid any of the interest or, indeed, may not have been liable under the mortgage.

A loan made after 31 July 1988 was treated as made before that date if it was proved by written evidence both that it was made in pursuance of a written offer or memorandum made by the lender before that date and a binding contract to acquire the property had been made before that date.

**4.39** It should be noted that a loan taken out after 31 July 1988 to replace one in existence at that date was a new loan and interest on it suffered these restrictions. If an unmarried couple moved house after 31 July 1988 and preserve a pre 1 August 1988 loan, giving the new property as security instead of the old, the interest still ceased to qualify for relief when the old property was sold. The provision was aimed at unmarried couples living together as husband and wife.

However, it also applied to single people sharing a starter property. Where a large house was converted into flats each flat was normally a separate residence attracting its own £30,000 limit.

**Home Improvement Loans**

**4.40** Interest on a loan within head (*b*) in 4.13 above (for improving or developing the land) was not eligible for relief if it was a home improvement loan, i.e.

(*a*) a loan to defray money applied in improving or developing land or buildings on land, other than by the erection of a new building (which was not part of an existing residence) on land that immediately before the development began had no building on it, or

(*b*) a loan replacing (whether directly or indirectly) one within (*a*) (including one taken out before 6 April 1988).

(*ICTA 1988, s 355(2A)(2B)*).

This restriction did not apply to a loan taken out before 6 April 1988. A loan made after 5 April 1988 was regarded as having been in existence at that date if it was proved by written evidence that it was made in pursuance of an offer made by the lender before that date and that such offer was either in writing or evidenced by a written memorandum by the lender (*ICTA 1988, s 355(2C)*).

**4.41** Where land was bought bearing a derelict building, care needed to be taken. If the building was completely demolished and money borrowed to fund the erection of a new house, that would not be a home improvement loan, as there was no building on the land immediately before the development of the new house began. Accordingly, the interest would qualify for relief. If the money was borrowed to restore the existing house, the loan was a home improvement loan no matter how extensive the building work might have been. It should not be assumed that the Revenue's view of what is a new building is the same as Customs' (see 8.35 below). The indications are that the Revenue considered the incorporation of any part of the existing building, other than its foundations, as a home improvement, not the construction of a new building. Whether the courts will support this is another question. It seems very unlikely!

**Accommodation for a Dependent Relative**

**4.42** A loan for the purchase of a property used as the main residence of a dependent relative also qualified for relief up to 1987/88 provided that the accommodation was provided rent free and without any other consideration (*ICTA 1988, s 355(3)*). Payments by the relative of rates and other outgoings which are liabilities of the occupier do not constitute consideration for the use of the property. Payment of landlord's outgoings such as ground rent would do so if the occupation is conditional on the relative making such payments. A dependent relative for this purpose is a relative of the taxpayer or his spouse who is incapacitated by old age or infirmity from maintaining himself, or the mother of the taxpayer or his spouse if she is widowed, divorced, or living apart from her husband (*ICTA 1988, s 367(1)*). It should be noted that an unmarried mother cannot qualify under the test unless incapacitated. A separated spouse is one separated under an order of a court of competent jurisdiction or by deed of separation, or separated in such circumstances that the separation is likely to be permanent (*ICTA 1988, s 367(1)*).

**4.43** Where interest was eligible for relief at 5 April 1988 because the property was occupied as the main residence of a dependent relative or of a former or separated spouse, the interest continued to qualify for relief up to 1999/2000 so long as that same relative continued to occupy the property. The last interest payment on the loan made before 5 April 1988 must have attracted relief under *section 353*, or if no interest was paid on it prior to 5 April 1988 the first interest payment attracting relief must have been made within twelve months of the loan being made and the property must not have been used for any purpose other than as the only or main residence of the dependent relative (*FA 1988, s 44*). This transitional relief also applied to a loan made after 5 April 1988 if it was proved by written evidence that it was made in pursuance of a written offer (or other memorandum made by the lender) made before that date (*section 44(5)*). It should particularly be noted that if the property was remortgaged, so that the loan was replaced by a new loan, the transitional relief did not apply to the new loan. It is not clear what happens where part only of the interest qualified for relief. For example, if at 5 April 1988 the taxpayer had a £20,000 mortgage on his own house and a £25,000 mortgage on a house for a dependent relative, only the first £10,000 of which qualified for relief, and he repays his own mortgage, would the whole of the loan for the relative's house then qualify for relief or only the first £10,000? It appears that the whole of the £25,000 will qualify. On the other hand, if the mortgage on the taxpayer's house exceeded £30,000 it appears that no relief at all would be due for the interest on the loan on the relative's house following a repayment of the taxpayer's own mortgage. As with the mortgage interest relief generally, this transitional relief ceased from 6 April 2000.

## Deceased Persons

**4.44** Interest paid by personal representatives of a deceased person (within *ICTA 1988, s 701*), or by trustees of a trust created in his will, qualified for relief if:

(*a*) had the deceased survived and been the borrower the interest would have qualified for relief, assuming, if the land, caravan or houseboat concerned was used as the deceased's only or main residence at the time of his death (or it was used as a residence or was intended in due course to be used as his main residence and, in either case, he lived in job-related accommodation), that it had continued to be so used (*ICTA 1988, s 358(1)(2)*); and

(*b*) at the time the interest was paid the property was used as the main residence of the deceased's widow or widower or of any dependent relative of the deceased (or presumably, his spouse) or it would have been qualified under head (*c*) at 4.23 if that person resided in job-related accommodation (*ICTA 1988, s 358(4)*).

Interest paid after 5 April 1988 in relation to a property used as a main residence of a dependent relative of the deceased was eligible for relief only if both the deceased died before that date and the property was the only or main residence of the relative before that date (*FA 1988, s 44(4)*).

**Job-related Accommodation**

**4.45** For the purpose of head (*c*) in 4.23 above a person resided in job-related accommodation if either:

(*a*) it was provided for him (or his spouse) by reason of his or her employment and either

  (i) it was necessary for the proper performance of his or her job that he or she should reside in it, or

  (ii) the accommodation was provided for the better performance of his or her job and the employment was of the kind in which it was customary for employers to provide such accommodation, or

  (iii) special security arrangements were in force because of a special threat to the employee's security and the employee resided in the accommodation as part of those arrangements (*ICTA 1988, s 356(3)(a)*); or

(*b*) under a contract made at arm's length and requiring him or his spouse to carry on a particular trade, profession or vocation, he or she was bound to carry on that trade, etc. on premises provided by another person (not being a company in which the borrower or his spouse had a material interest or a person with whom the borrower or his spouse carried on a business in partnership) and to live on those premises or on other premises provided by that same person (*ICTA 1988, s 356(3)(b)*).

**4.46** However, accommodation was not job-related (unless (*a*)(iii) above applied) if it was provided by a company and the employee was a director of that company or of an associated company (i.e. under common control). This restriction did not apply if he did not have a material interest in the company (the one of which he was a director) and either he was a full-time working director, or the company was non-profit making (i.e. it did not carry on a trade and its functions did not consist wholly or mainly in the holding of investments or other property), or it was established for charitable purposes only (*ICTA 1988, s 356(4)(5)*).

## MIRAS

**4.47** When a loan to buy a principal private residence in the UK (but not the Republic of Ireland) was taken from a bank or building society, tax relief for the interest was normally given by deduction at source under the MIRAS (Mortgage Interest Relief At Source) scheme. For a loan to be included in the MIRAS scheme the whole of the interest had to be eligible for relief under *ICTA 1988, s 354(1)* (see 4.13 above), or would have been eligible if the £30,000 limit did not apply, and the loan must have related to the payer's principal residence (*ICTA 1988, s 369(1)*). As with mortgage interest relief on private residences MIRAS does not applied to payments after 5 April 2000 (*FA 1999, s 38(2)*). The anti-avoidance rules described at 4.25 also apply to MIRAS. A loan partly in connection with the taxpayer's residence and partly for some other purpose – whether the interest qualified for tax relief or not – was completely excluded from MIRAS (*ICTA 1988, s 370(2)(b)* and *R v HMIT (ex parte Kelly) (1991 STC 566)*). If two loans were taken out on the same day to acquire the principal private residence, neither of them could be brought into the MIRAS scheme unless they were both by the same lender (*ICTA 1988, s 373(4)*). If the two loans were made on different days, both could be within MIRAS provided that the first was less than £30,000. A joint loan could be within MIRAS only if the property qualified as the principal residence of all of the borrowers or they were husband and wife (and living together) (*ICTA 1988, s 373(6)(7)*).

**4.48** If a loan within MIRAS ceased to be eligible for inclusion within the scheme, the borrower had to notify the lender, who had to take it out of MIRAS (*ICTA 1988, s 375*). The Inland Revenue's MIRAS guidance notes to lenders required the lender to notify them as and when the lender knew the loan no longer qualified. The most common situation was where a property ceased to be used as the borrower's main residence without being sold – and where the bridging loan rules did not apply. Where a property within MIRAS was let in circumstances where Inland Revenue Extra-Statutory Concession A27 (see 4.36 above) applied, the borrowing exceeded £30,000 and it is clear that the assessable rents would exceed the interest on £30,000, the Revenue expected the taxpayer to take the loan out of MIRAS. If he did not do so they would refuse him all relief for the interest in excess of that on £30,000 and higher rate relief on the first £30,000. If the assessable rents are likely to fluctuate, 'It is administratively inconvenient to have the loan taken in and out of MIRAS. So . . . the Revenue is prepared to leave the loan in MIRAS but to grant any additional relief that would have been due on the statutory basis.' (See Revenue letter quoted in Taxation, 18 July 1991, p 410.)

## Home Income Plans

**4.49** Relief for interest on a mortgage is still given as an annual payment where the loan was taken as part of a home annuity or home income plan where at least 90% of the amount borrowed was used by the borrower to buy a life annuity on his own life or on the life of the survivor of himself and some other person or persons. The loan must have been made before 9 March 1999, the borrower or the annuitants must have been 65 or over at the time the loan was made; it must be secured on land in the UK or Eire; the borrower or one of the annuitants must own an interest in that land; the borrower or each of the annuitants must use the land as his only or main residence at the time the interest is paid; and the interest must be payable by the borrower or by one of the annuitants (*ICTA 1988, s 365* as amended by *FA 1999, s 39(1)*). For interest payments after 15 March 1993 the requirement that the property must be the main residence does not apply if, at the time it ceased to be the main residence, the intention of the borrower, or of each of the annuitants owning an interest in the land, was to take steps within the following twelve months with a view to disposing of his interest. Relief for the interest continues for the shorter of either that twelve-month period or until the intention to dispose of the interest is abandoned (*ICTA 1988, s 365(1A)*). The restriction in the rate of tax relief described at 4.23 above applies to such interest with the exception that for 1994/95 to 1999/2000 the relief continued to be given at the basic rate; it is not limited to the 10% rate (*ICTA 1988, s 353(1A)(1G)(b)*). For 2000/01 onwards the relief is no longer tied to the basic rate of tax. Instead it is given at a fixed rate of 23%. It continues to be given for interest on the first £30,000 of borrowings (*ICTA 1988, ss 365(3), 353(1G)* as substituted by *FA 2000, s 83*). MIRAS (see 4.48) continues to apply to such loans where the borrowing is from a qualifying lender.

**4.50** Relief is also given if the loan was made after 9 March 1999 in pursuance of a written offer by the lender before that date (or one evidenced by a note or memorandum made by the lender before that date) (*ICTA 1988, s 365(1AA)* inserted by *FA 1999, s 39(2)*). An interest payment made after 26 July 1999 under a pre 9 March 1999 home income plan will also qualify for relief if it is on a replacement loan made after 26 July 1999 as part of a scheme to replace a previous qualifying loan (*ICTA 1988, s 365(1AB)* inserted by *FA 1999, s 40(3)*).

If the whole of a replacement loan is not used to replace the old one at least 90% of the non-qualifying amount must be used to buy an annuity on the life of the taxpayer or of the survivor of him and some other person, such as his spouse (*ICTA 1988, s 365(1AC)(1AD)*). This will allow the annuitant to top up both the loan and the annuity if his existing loan is under £30,000. If more than 10% of the extra borrowing is used for some other purpose no relief is given at all for the replacement borrowing – even up to the amount of the old loan.

**4.51** Interest paid after 26 July 1999 continues to qualify for relief even if the annuitant ceases to occupy the property provided that he had a qualifying home income plan at 9 March 1999 (*ICTA 1988, s 365(1)(d)* as amended by *FA 1999, s 40(2)*). This will allow relief to continue if the annuitant has to go into a nursing home or decides to move to a smaller house. This relaxation also applies if although the borrower (or one of the annuitants) did not occupy the property at 9 March 1999 he did so at some time in the previous year and at 8 March 1999 it was intended to take steps to sell the property within 12 months of its ceasing to be used as the principal residence (*ICTA 1988, s 365(1A)* substituted by *FA 1999, s 40(4)*).

## Corporation Tax

### The Rules from 1 April 1996

**4.52** For accounting periods ending after 31 March 1996 interest paid by a company qualifies for relief as a debit on loan relationships. This normally means that relief will be given for it on an accruals basis but there are major exceptions. The tax provisions on loan relationships apply both to interest paid (which is a debit on a loan relationship) and to interest received (which is a credit on a loan relationship). This makes the definitions a little difficult to follow as they are intended to embrace both borrower and lender. These rules also apply to other debits in respect of loans such as bad debts and financing costs and to other credits such as loan waivers.

### What is a Loan Relationship?

**4.53** A company has a loan relationship wherever:

(*a*) it stands in the position of a creditor or debtor as regards any money debt, and

(*b*) that debt is one arising from a transaction for the lending of money (*FA 1996, s 81(1)*).

**4.54** Broadly speaking, a money debt is one which falls to be settled either by the payment of money or by the transfer of a right to settlement under a debt which is itself a money debt (*FA 1996, s 81(2)*). Money is not restricted to sterling but covers any currency (*FA 1996, s 81(6)*).

**4.55** A loan will almost always be a loan relationship. Unpaid purchase consideration is not a loan relationship, but could probably become one if the parties agreed to convert it into a loan (although this is not wholly clear). A money debt which is not a loan relationship – such as unpaid purchase consideration – is treated as a loan relationship if an instrument is issued by any person for the purpose of representing security for a money debt (*FA 1996, s 81(3)*). Therefore a mortgage will always be a loan relationship. So will a money debt represented by a debenture or loan stock, e.g. where a property is transferred to a company in consideration of the issue of loan stock in the company.

**4.56** Conversely a loan will not be a loan relationship to the extent that it arises from rights conferred by shares in a company. If company A acquires company B in consideration for issuing loan stock in itself in exchange for shares in company B, that loan stock will not be a loan relationship (*FA 1996, s 81(3)(4)*).

**4.57** Where interest on a money debt (see 4.53) is payable by a company which is (or has been) the creditor in respect of it, but the debt did not arise from a loan relationship, e.g. it arose from unpaid consideration, that interest is to be treated as if it were payable under a loan relationship (*FA 1996, s 100(1)(2)*). Other debits in respect of such a debt, such as writing it off if it proves bad, or any costs of creating the debt, are not brought within the loan relationship rules. This provision will grant relief for interest on delayed completions – and tax interest received on such transactions or interest on compensation on a compulsory acquisition – on an accruals basis.

## Taxation of Loan Relationships

### Trading Companies

**4.58** Debits and credits (e.g. interest paid and received) are ascertained separately for trading and non-trading loan relationships. A trading loan relationship for this purpose is, of course, one to which the company is a party for the purpose of a trade which it carries on (*FA 1996, s 82(2)*). Interest and other debits on trading loan relationships are treated as trading expenses and credits on trading loan relationships as trade receipts (*FA 1996, ss 80(2), 82(2)*). Although taxable rental income is calculated on trading principles, interest on a loan to acquire a property investment is on a non-trading loan relationship.

**Investment and Other Company**

**4.59** Debits and credits on non-trading loan relationships are netted off. If there is a net credit (e.g. interest received in excess of interest paid) it is taxed under Case III of Schedule D as a profit arising from the company's loan relationships (*FA 1996, ss 80(3), 82(3)–(5)*). If there is a net debit (called a deficit on loan relationships) a claim can be made to treat the whole or any part of it in the following ways:

(*a*) set against profits of the company for the same accounting period;

(*b*) treated as eligible for group relief (unless the company is a charity – *s 83(5)*);

(*c*) carried back for up to three years; or

(*d*) carried forward against non-trading profits (which expression includes capital gains).

(*FA 1996, s 83(2)* and *Sch 8 paras 2, 4*)

This effectively gives very similar treatment to loan interest paid as applied before 1 April 1996 when the interest constituted a charge on income.

**4.60** The claim must be made within two years after the end of the accounting period in which the deficit occurs (or the following accounting period if the claim is to carry forward under head (*d*)) or such longer period as the Revenue may allow (*FA 1996, s 83(6)(7)*). Different claims can be made for different parts of the deficit but two claims obviously cannot be made in relation to the same amount (*FA 1996, s 83(8)*).

**4.61** In the case of a claim under head (*a*) the profits against which the deficit is to be relieved must be identified in the claim (*FA 1996, Sch 8 para 1(2)*). In most cases it will not matter what profits are utilised. Any brought forward trading losses must be relieved in priority to setting a non-trading deficit on loan relationships against trading profits, but set-off of the non-trading deficit has priority to a claim to set off a trading loss of the same accounting period or to carry back a trading loss or a non-trading deficit on loan relationships of a later accounting period (*FA 1996, Sch 8 para 1(3)*).

**4.62** If a non-trading deficit is carried back under head (*c*) it can be set only against profits and gains on loan relationships (*FA 1996, Sch 8 para 3(4)*). The charges on income rules did not allow a carry back at all so this limited relief against past interest receipts is a little more generous than the old rules. The carry back is against income of the three years preceding the beginning of the accounting period in which the deficit arises but the deficit cannot be carried back to any period falling before 31 March 1996. For this purpose the profits (i.e. interest received) for an accounting period straddling 31 March 1996 or falling only partly within the three-year period are apportioned on a time basis (*FA 1996, Sch 8 para 3(5)(7)*). Relief is given first against profits of the latest accounting period (*FA 1996, Sch 8 para 3(3)*). Brought forward losses or non-trading deficits, charges on income (both brought forward and for the accounting period), trading losses (both of the same accounting period and carried back from a later one), non-trading deficits of the same accounting period, and, in the case of an investment company, capital allowances under *CAA 1990, s 28* (see 10.3), management expenses and charges on income (in both cases of the same or any other accounting period) must all be relieved in priority to the carried-back deficit on loan relationships (*FA 1996, Sch 8 para 3(3)(b)*).

**4.63** If no claim is made the deficit is carried forward and treated as a non-trading debit of the next accounting period, but cannot be either utilised in that next period by set-off against income other than from non-trading loan relationships or used in a group relief claim (*FA 1996, s 83(3)(4)*).

## Calculation

**4.64** For both trading and investment companies the credits and debits in respect of loan relationships for an accounting period are the amounts which in accordance with an 'authorised accounting method' (see 4.62) when taken together fairly represent all profits, gains and losses of the company (including those of a capital nature) which arise from its loan relationships and related transactions and all interest under the company's loan relationships and all charges and expenses incurred by it for the purpose of its loan relationships and related transactions (*FA 1996, s 84(1)*). This includes interest, bad debts, financing costs and loan waivers. Amounts carried to reserve are brought into account but any amount required to be transferred to a company's share premium account are ignored (*FA 1996, s 84(2)*). The Revenue view is that guarantee fees incurred in connection with a loan relationship do not fall within *section 84* unless the loan would not have been made without the guarantee (Tax Bulletin 26, December 1996).

**4.65** The charges and expenses to be brought into account are those incurred:

(*a*) in bringing any loan relationship into existence (e.g. the costs of raising loan finance),

(*b*) in entering into (or giving effect to) loan relationships or related transactions (e.g. stamp duty on a mortgage), (*c*) in making payments under loan relationships or in pursuance of loan relationships or related transactions (e.g. bank charges on interest payments or loan repayments), or

(*d*) in taking steps for ensuring the receipt of payment under loan relationships or in accordance with loan relationships or related transactions (e.g. debt enforcement costs).

(*FA 1996, s 84(3)*).

**4.66** The above expenses are allowable even where the proposed relationship proves abortive (*FA 1996, s 84(4)*). A related transaction means a disposal or acquisition (which includes a sale, gift, exchange, surrender, redemption or release) of rights or liabilities under the loan relationship (*FA 1996, s 84(5)(6)*).

**4.67** There are two alternate authorised accounting methods, the accruals basis and a mark to market basis (*FA 1996, s 85(1)*). Mark to market (i.e. revaluation to market price) cannot normally be used where the parties are connected (*FA 1996, ss 87, 88*). In any event it is not normally appropriate to property transactions. Accordingly interest payable by property companies (except perhaps in relation to hedging transactions) must be accounted for on an accruals basis. The accruals basis used must:

(*a*) conform to generally accepted accountancy practice (see 2.158),

(*b*) not incorporate changes in valuations of loan relationships,

(*c*) allocate payments to the period to which they relate without regard to either the time of payment or receipt or the date the amount becomes due and payable,

(*d*) apportion payments between periods on a just and reasonable basis,

(*e*) assume (subject to authorised arrangements for bad debts (see 4.74)) that every amount receivable under the loan relationship will be received in full as it becomes due,

(*f*) secure the making of adjustments for bad debts, and

(*g*) provide for the crediting of any debt released in the accounting period in which the release takes place.

(*FA 1996, s 85(2)(3)* as amended by *FA 2002, Sch 25 para 5*).

**4.68** Different authorised accounting methods can be used either as respects different loan relationships or in respect of the same loan relationship for different accounting periods or even different parts of the same accounting period (*FA 1996, s 86(2)*). In practice it is unlikely that a change in method during an accounting period will satisfy the condition of conforming to generally accepted accountancy practice (see 2.158). The accounting method used must be the same as that used in the company's statutory accounts unless that is not an authorised accounting method (*FA 1996, s 86(3)*).

**4.69** If there is any inconsistency or other material difference in the application of an authorised accounting method in respect of the same loan relationships for different accounting periods the debit or credit for earlier periods must be recomputed on the new basis and the difference treated as a debit or credit of the accounting period in which the change is made (*FA 1996, s 89*). A similar adjustment is made on a change of accounting method (*FA 1996, s 90*).

## Special Computational Provisions

**4.70** A payment that constitutes a distribution (see 4.111) obviously is not a debit on a loan relationship (*FA 1996, Sch 9 para 1*).

**4.71** If interest is paid more than 12 months after the end of the accounting period in which it accrues it is not dealt with on an accruals basis but is allowed when paid. This does not apply if the lender is a UK company which has brought the full accrued amount into account as a credit on its loan relationships (*FA 1996, Sch 9 para 2*).

**4.72** If the answer to the question whether any amount will become due under a loan relationship after the end of an accounting period, or the amount which will become due, or the time it will become due, depends on the exercise of an option by one of the parties to the relationship (or his associate within *ICTA 1988, s 417(3)(4)*) or is otherwise under the control of such a person, it must be assumed that he will exercise the option in the manner which (apart from taxation) is most advantageous to himself (*FA 1996, Sch 9 para 3*).

**4.73** Where a borrowing is in a foreign currency exchange gains and losses are excluded from the calculation of gains or losses on loan relationships and dealt with under the rules relating to exchange gains and losses in *FA 1993, ss 125–170* (*FA 1996, Sch 9 para 4*).

**4.74** The assumption under the accruals basis that an amount will be received in full as it becomes due (see 4.67(*e*)) is modified in relation to bad and doubtful debts provided that the accounting method requires the writing back of the debt or provision should it subsequently cease to be appropriate (*FA 1996, Sch 9 para 5*).

**4.75** This does not apply if the parties are connected. Persons are connected for this purpose if either:

(*a*) they are companies under common control (within *ICTA 1988, s 416*) or one of which controls the other, or were in such a relationship at any time in the two years preceding the start of the relevant accounting period (there is an exception if the controller is the Crown, a government department, a foreign government or an international organisation), or

(*b*) the company is a close company and the other party to the loan relationship is a participator or an associate of a participator (or was so at some time within the two years preceding the start of the relevant accounting period), and is not one solely by reason of being a loan creditor (*FA 1996, s 87*).

In such circumstances no relief is given for the bad debt even if it is a bona fide commercial loss (*FA 1996, Sch 9 para 6(3)*). The only exception is if the creditor accepts shares in the debtor company in consideration of discharging the debt and the two companies would not have been connected had it not done so, i.e. if the debt was between unconnected persons but they become connected because the creditor agrees to take shares in satisfaction of the debt (*FA 1996, Sch 9 para 6(4)(5)*). Even if the debt ceases to exist, e.g. it is waived, the debits brought into account in relation to it must be calculated as if it had continued in being, so no loss arises – but the notional continuation of the debt is not to give rise to a deduction for a notional continuing liability to pay interest on it (*FA 1996, Sch 9 para 6(6)(7)*). Not all debts constitute loan relationships so this rule will not necessarily disallow a bad debt if it arises other than by way of loan.

**4.76** Conversely, where a liability to pay a sum is released, the amount released is a credit on the loan relationship for the accounting period in which the release takes place – except where the release arises from a voluntary arrangement under the *Insolvency Act* or the debtor and creditor are connected (within 4.75 above) (*FA 1996, Sch 9 para 5(1)(3)*).

**4.77** Where the loan is not an arm's length one the debits and credits on the loan relationship must be calculated as though the transaction had been entered into on arm's length terms except where either:

(*a*) a deduction is being claimed for the acquisition at an undervalue of rights under a loan relationship, or

(*b*) the parties are members of the same group of companies (as defined in *TCGA 1992, s 170*).

(*FA 1996, Sch 9 para 11*).

**4.78** If a loan relationship is assigned within a group the transferor and transferee company are treated as if they were the same company (except for the purpose of determining which is to account for debits or credits (e.g. interest payments) not related to the assignment) (*FA 1996, Sch 9 para 12*).

**4.79** If a loan relationship is for an unallowable purpose no deduction is allowed for interest payable or other debits which (on a just and reasonable apportionment) are attributable to that unallowable purpose. A loan relationship has an unallowable purpose if one of its purposes is not amongst the business or other commercial purposes of the company. Any activities of the company that are not within the charge to corporation tax are also for unallowable purposes. The Revenue give an example of a golf club borrowing to finance a new club house where income from members is non-taxable (as mutual trading). The interest would need to be apportioned to disallow the part attributable to the mutual activity (Company Tax Manual CT 12671). A transaction which has a tax avoidance purpose is also for an unallowable purpose unless that is not one of the main purposes for which the company entered into the transaction. Any purpose that consists in securing a tax advantage (within *ICTA 1988, s 709*) is a tax avoidance purpose (*FA 1996, Sch 9 para 13*).

**4.80** This is likely to deny relief for some interest payments that were allowed under the old rules. For example, if a close company buys a house for occupation by its director that may well be an unallowable purpose – although there is a reasonable argument that it is simply a method of remunerating the director, provided of course that as a result his total remuneration package is still a fair reward for his services. Money borrowed to be lent interest free to another company may well be for an unallowable purpose. Where a company is likely to enter into such transactions it may be sensible to amend the Articles of Association to give specific power to enter into that type of transaction to assist a contention that it forms one of the business purposes of the company.

**4.81** If interest (or another debit on a loan relationship) is capitalised it is nevertheless allowed as a debit against profits, to be recognised under the normal accrual basis rules in the accounting period in which it would have fallen had it been a revenue item (*FA 1996, Sch 9 para 14*).

**4.82** Special rules apply to discounted securities. These are contained in *FA 1996, Sch 9 paras 17, 18*.

## The Rules up to 31 March 1996

**4.83** Prior to 1 April 1996, interest paid by a company could be deductible either as a trading expense or as a charge on income. Where it could be deducted as a trading expense this had to be done rather than treating it as a charge on income (*Wilcock v Frigate Investments Ltd (55 TC 530)*). Even where interest constituted a trading expense, *ICTA 1988, s 337(2)(3)* prevented a deduction if it was annual interest unless it was UK bank interest (see 6.6).

**4.84** Interest could qualify as a charge on income only if it was

(*a*) annual interest, **or**

(*b*) any other interest payable in the UK on an advance from a bank carrying on a bona fide banking business in the UK (or from a person carrying on business as a member of a UK stock exchange or as a UK discount house),

**and either**

(i) the company existed wholly or mainly for the purpose of carrying on a trade, or

(ii) the interest was wholly and exclusively expended for the purposes of a trade carried on by the company, or

(iii) the company was an investment company (one whose business consisted wholly or mainly in the making of investments and the principal part of whose income was derived therefrom), or

(iv) the payment of interest would have been eligible for income tax relief by virtue of being a loan for the purchase or improvement of property (or the replacement of a previous such qualifying loan) if it had been paid by an individual. (If the property was occupied by the company it had to be assumed for this purpose that interest was eligible for relief if the loan was to acquire a property other than a private residence, or if the loan was to acquire a residence that was used as an individual's main residence, but in the latter case the £30,000 limit applied.)

(*ICTA 1988, s 338(3)(6)*).

It will be seen that there was no bar on interest which was capitalised nevertheless being deducted from income as a charge for tax purposes. The income tax restrictions on the deductibility of interest did not, in general, apply for corporation tax.

**4.85** Following the abolition of the special rules for interest in respect of loans on let properties head (iv) above was amended for 1995/96. Interest for that year came within that head if:

(*a*) at the time it was paid the company owned an estate or interest in land (or a caravan or houseboat) in the UK or the Republic of Ireland;

(*b*) the loan was to defray money applied in purchasing that estate or interest (or one absorbed into, or given up to obtain it), in improving or developing the land or buildings on it, or in paying off another loan the interest on which would have qualified for relief under *ICTA 1988, s 338A* had it continued (and borne interest);

(*c*) the land, caravan or houseboat was either:

(i) occupied by the company and used as the only or main residence of an individual;

(ii) occupied by the company and used otherwise than as a residence; or

(iii) in any period of 52 weeks comprising the interest payment date, let at a commercial rent for over 26 weeks and when not so let either available for such letting or occupied and used within (i) or (ii) above; and

(*d*) the interest was not incurred by overdrawing an account or by debiting the account of any person as the holder of a credit card or under similar arrangements.

(*ICTA 1988, s 338A(1)* inserted by *FA 1995, Sch 7 para 2*).

**4.86** *ICTA 1988, s 354(2)* and *(7)* (see 4.16, 4.17 and 4.22) also apply for the purpose of *section 338A* (*ICTA 1988, s 338A(2)*). Where head (*c*)(i) above applies, relief was allowed only to the extent the loan did not exceed £30,000 reduced by the amount of any earlier loans in relation to the same land, caravan or houseboat within *section 338A*. *ICTA 1988, s 355(1A)* (see 4.23 and 4.28) applies for this purpose (*ICTA 1988, s 338A(3)–(5)*). If head (*c*)(i) applies and the interest was on a home improvement loan (within *ICTA 1988, s 355(2B)* – see 4.40) relief was due only if the loan was made before 6 April 1988 (or *ICTA 1988, s 355(2C)* applies – see 4.40).

**4.87** If the loan was used to purchase the estate or interest (or one absorbed into it or given up to obtain it) within head (*b*) in 4.84 the interest did not qualify for relief if either:

(*a*) the company had disposed of an estate or interest in the same land since 15 April 1969, and it appeared that the main purpose of the disposal and purchase was to obtain relief in respect of interest on the loan or to allow such interest to be treated as a charge on income; or (*b*) the company directly or indirectly purchased from a person who was connected with it and the price substantially exceeded the value of what was acquired.

**4.88** Similarly interest on a loan to improve the land, or buildings on it, did not qualify for relief if the money spent was received directly or indirectly by a person connected with the company and substantially exceeded the value of the work done (*ICTA 1988, s 338A(7)*). The definition of connected persons in *ICTA 1988, s 839* applies (see Appendix 1).

**4.89** *ICTA 1988, s 367(2)* to *(4)* applied for the purposes of *section 338A* (*ICTA 1988, s 338A(9)*). A rentcharge or a mortgage is not an interest in land for the purpose of the section (*ICTA 1988, s 338A(10)*).

**4.90** Interest is annual interest if it is on a loan that is for a period capable of exceeding twelve months. In general all interest qualifies as annual interest unless the loan is for a fixed period of under twelve months. Interest on such a fixed loan, called 'short interest', could not qualify as a charge on income unless it was paid to a UK bank. A trading company could normally obtain relief for short interest as a trading expense. Interest falling within head (iv) in 4.84 could only be relieved against income of the same accounting period (Tax Bulletin, Issue 11, May 1994, p 129).

**4.91** Relief for charges on income is given in the accounting period in which the charge is paid, not that to which it relates. Interest is deemed to be paid at the time it is debited in the company's accounts in the books of the person to whom it is payable (*ICTA 1988, s 338(3)*). It was decided in *MacArthur v Greycoat Estates Mayfair Ltd (1966 STC 1)* that this applies to both annual interest and bank interest. In *Minsham Properties Ltd v Price (1990 STC 718)* it was, however, held that charging interest to the lender's account in the taxpayer's books did not constitute payment if this merely served to increase an existing debit balance. Where interest qualified for deduction as a trading expense it was dealt with on an accruals basis like any other trading expense. If relief could not be given for a charge on income in the accounting period in which it was paid because of an insufficiency of income, then to the extent to which it was paid wholly and exclusively for the purpose of a trade carried on by the company, the excess could be carried forward and set against future trading profits (*ICTA 1988, s 393(9)*). If the company is an investment company the excess could be carried forward as a management expense provided that it was paid wholly and exclusively for the purposes of the company's business (*ICTA 1988, s 75(3)*). A charge on income cannot be carried back against profits of an earlier year, even in a trading company.

**Interest Payable to Non-residents**

**4.92** Interest paid by a company to a person not resident in the UK could be treated as a charge on income only if the company was UK resident and either

(*a*) the company deducted income tax and accounted for it to the Inland Revenue (or such a deduction would have been made but for relieving provisions of a double taxation agreement), or

(*b*) there was no obligation to deduct income tax because the interest was payable on quoted Eurobonds (within *ICTA 1988, s 124*), or

(*c*) the company was carrying on a trade and under the terms of the loan agreement the interest was to be paid, or could be required to be paid, outside the UK and was in fact paid outside the UK, and either the liability was incurred wholly or mainly for the purposes of activities of the company's trade carried on outside the UK, or, if the interest was payable in a currency other than sterling, either in or outside the UK, or

(*d*) the interest was payable out of income brought into charge to tax under Case IV or V of Schedule D, i.e. overseas source income.

(*ICTA 1988, ss 338(4), 340(1)*).

**4.93** Interest payable in a foreign currency on a loan for the purpose of UK activities of the company's trade was excluded from relief under head (*c*) in 4.92 above if either

(i) the trade was carried on by a body of persons (which expression includes a partnership) over whom the person entitled to the interest had control, or

(ii) the person entitled to the interest was a body of persons (including a partnership) over whom the person carrying on the trade had control, or

(iii) the person carrying on the trade and the person entitled to the interest were both bodies of persons and some other person had control over both of them.

(*ICTA 1988, s 340(2)*).

**4.94** The definition of control in *ICTA 1988, s 840* applied. Also, for the purpose of (*c*) in 4.92 above, the company that paid the interest was treated as carrying on any trade carried on by its 75% subsidiaries provided that both were UK companies and the shares in the subsidiary were not held as trading stock of the parent or held indirectly through a non-UK company (*ICTA 1988, s 340(3)(4)*).

## Non-UK Companies

**4.95** A non-UK company which is trading in the UK through a branch or agency is within the charge to corporation tax in respect of the income from that trade, and of investment income from property or rights held by or on behalf of the UK branch or agency (*ICTA 1988, ss 6(2)(b), 11*). Trading of course includes property dealing. Other UK income of a non-UK company is chargeable to income tax. Accordingly if a non-UK company not trading in the UK owns property in the UK, interest paid is deductible from its UK rental income only if it meets the income tax tests set out in 4.3–4.51 above.

### Withholding Tax – UK Source Loans

**4.96** Since 5 April 1994 interest payable to a non-UK resident has been deductible in the normal way provided that the loan meets the necessary conditions. However such interest will attract UK withholding tax at 20% if it is taxable on the recipient under Case III of Schedule D thus effectively eliminating the benefit of the deduction (*ICTA 1988, s 349(2)(c)*). Prior to 5 April 1994 interest paid to a non-UK resident by an individual generally had to be brought within (*a*) in 4.10 above to attract relief – and thus gave rise to the liability to deduct tax from the interest payments. Case III of Schedule D taxes, *inter alia*, 'any interest of money, whether yearly or otherwise'. However, under general principles of territoriality, the UK can tax a non-resident only on income arising in the UK. A non-resident will accordingly be chargeable to tax under Case III only if the source of the interest is a UK source loan.

**4.97** Unfortunately the rules as to what is and is not a UK source loan are not at all clear. It used to be generally accepted that a loan is a UK source loan if the borrower is resident in the UK, except where it is made under a specialty contract (i.e. under seal) and is executed abroad and governed by foreign law. A loan was in any event a UK source loan if it was secured on land in the UK. Following the abolition of exchange control the Revenue were concerned at the ease with which UK companies could borrow overseas. They announced in 1982 that they had been reviewing the treatment of interest paid to non-residents and had taken fresh legal advice. This was to the effect that in the changed circumstances there could be no confidence that the courts would attach sufficient significance to the foreign speciality contract in itself as being a decisive factor. They therefore intended to contend in future that all borrowings by UK companies are UK source loans.

**4.98** In 1970 the House of Lords in *Westminster Bank Executor and Trustee Company (Channel Islands) Ltd v National Bank of Greece SA (46 TC 472)* held that the debt between the two companies had a non-UK source. Following this, albeit somewhat belatedly, the Revenue have said that they regard the most important factors which would support a loan having a UK source as

(*a*) the residence of the debtor, i.e. the place in which the debt will be enforced,

(*b*) the source from which the interest is paid,

(*c*) the place where the interest is paid, and

(*d*) the nature and location of the security for the debt.

Unfortunately they go on to say that they are not prepared to comment in advance on where the source might be 'since the precise tax treatment depends on all the factors and on exactly how the transactions are in fact carried out' (Tax Bulletin, Issue 9, Nov 1993, p 100). Accordingly little comfort can be drawn from this statement. The Revenue (FICO) have, however, told the author that they do not consider that a loan from one non-UK resident to another will have a UK source merely because it is secured on a UK property.

**4.99** Because of the uncertainty as to the withholding tax position, the cautious are likely to continue to borrow from UK lenders. If money is borrowed outside the UK, the loan agreement is specifically made enforceable in a country other than the UK, the interest is paid outside the UK and funded other than from the UK rents (or other UK income), and the loan is not secured on the UK property but is secured by non-UK assets, the interest is unlikely to have a UK source so no withholding obligation will arise. If it is secured by a mortgage on the UK property and the interest is paid out of the rents – as will normally be the case – there may be a risk that the loan will have a UK source, in spite of the Revenue's current relaxed position, even if the borrower is non-UK resident and the rents are paid direct into his overseas bank account.

**4.100** In practice in the past the Revenue did not normally seek to contend that a loan to a UK resident individual from a non-UK resident had a UK source and that income tax ought to have been accounted for – although they have taken the point in relation to borrowings by UK companies. It is understood that this is not their current position and it would be unwise to assume that this practice will continue where UK tax relief is claimed for the interest.

**4.101** Where an obligation to deduct tax from the interest arises it is likely that the non-UK recipient will resist it. Indeed loans to acquire UK properties normally contain a provision that if an obligation to deduct tax arises the interest rate specified is to be deemed to be a net rate after deduction of the withholding tax. This grossing up will significantly increase the cost of the loan.

**4.102** The obligation under *ICTA 1988, s 349(2)(c)* to deduct and pay over to the Inland Revenue tax at the basic rate on the loan interest does not apply where the interest is payable in the UK and is an advance from a bank carrying on a bona fide banking business in the UK (*s 349(3)*). It is also not a problem if the lender is resident in a country with which the UK has a double taxation agreement exempting the resident of the other country from UK tax on interest – provided that the lender is prepared to claim the benefit of the double tax agreement (which is not always the case, even with banks) and that the claim for exemption is made to the Inspector of Foreign Dividends before the first interest payment falls due.

**4.103** For payments of interest after 31 March 2001 the obligation to deduct tax does not apply to a payment by a company (or by a partnership of which any member is a company) if the company reasonably believes that the person beneficially entitled to the interest is either:

(*a*) a UK resident company or a partnership all of the partners of which are UK companies, or

(*b*) a non-UK company which carries on a trade in the UK through a branch or agency where the interest will be deductible in computing the UK taxable profits of that branch.

(*ICTA 1988, ss 349A, 349B* inserted by *FA 2001, s 85*).

**4.104** The Revenue have power to require the deduction of tax in relation to a specified payee from payments made subsequent to their direction if they do not believe that either of the above qualifying conditions are met (*ICTA 1988, s 349C* inserted by *FA 2001, s 85*). If neither of the above conditions is in fact satisfied the payer of the interest becomes liable for the tax that ought to have been deducted notwithstanding his reasonable belief that there was no obligation (and thus no right) to do so (*ICTA 1988, s 349D*). *Section 349A* has been extended to payments by local authorities for payments of interest after 30 September 2002 (*ICTA 1988, s 349A* as amended by *FA 2002, s 94(1)*). From the same date the scope of *sections 349A–349D* is extended to cover payments to local authorities, charities, approved pension schemes, personal equity plans, TESSA managers and government departments and certain statutory bodies (*ICTA 1988, s 349B(3)–(8)* inserted by *FA 2002, s 94(2)*).

**4.105** The obligation to deduct tax applies only to payments of annual interest. It is generally accepted that interest is annual if it is on a loan for a period that is capable of exceeding 365 days (whether or not it in fact does so). Interest on late completions is annual interest, even though it is normally very short term, as it is theoretically possible, although obviously highly improbable (except as part of a tax avoidance scheme), that the delay could extend to more than a year. Prior to

6 April 1994 if interest paid by an individual was not annual interest it could not qualify for a deduction from rental income under head (*a*) in 4.10 above but this restriction no longer applies from that date.

## Capital Gains Tax

**4.106** Interest paid by an individual or a settlement cannot be claimed as a deduction against a capital gain (*TCGA 1992, s 38(3)*). Where the interest is substantial and exceeds the rental income it may sometimes be better to seek to establish that a property transaction is a trading transaction rather than a capital gain.

**4.107** Interest paid by a company can be claimed as a deduction in calculating its capital gains (or rather chargeable gains subject to corporation tax) in very limited circumstances, namely where:

(*a*) the loan was borrowed to defray expenditure on the construction of any building, structure or works;

(*b*) that expenditure is itself deductible as allowable expenditure in calculating the chargeable gain;

(*c*) the interest is referable to a period or part of a period ending on or before the disposal of the property;

(*d*) the interest is not a charge on income; and

(*e*) the interest would not constitute a trading expense – assuming that the company were carrying on a trade if it does not in fact do so.

(*TCGA 1992, s 40*).

**4.108** It is unlikely that much interest will qualify for relief under this provision. It was introduced because, prior to 1 April 1981, interest which was capitalised could not qualify as a charge on income. The repeal of that restriction largely removed the need for *section 40*. It should in any event be noted that *section 40* can only apply to interest on borrowings to meet construction costs. It does not apply where the loan was to acquire the site or an existing building.

## Interest under Development Agreements

**4.109** Where a property development is financed by an institution, the development agreement sometimes provides that interest is to be calculated on the money advanced by the institution and that for the purpose of calculating the institution's interest in the property such interest is to be added to the development costs. Where this occurs the amount involved is not interest and does not qualify for tax relief. It is a mere arithmetical figure. The easiest way to recognise whether interest is real or notional is to ascertain whether the institution has made a loan to the developer or whether it has undertaken to finance the building costs. If there is no loan the 'interest' figure will not normally be real interest.

**4.110** Where interest is physically paid under a development agreement it may be 'rolled up', i.e. it is not payable until the development is completed or sold. As prior to 1 April 1996 a deduction for interest was given when it was paid and from that date interest paid more than 12 months after the accounting period to which it relates will in many cases also not be allowed until it is paid (see 4.71), the effect may well be to bunch the deduction into a single year, and care may sometimes need to be taken to ensure that the company has income available to obtain relief for the interest in that single year. This particularly applies to investment companies, where the disposal of the property is deemed to take place on the signing of the contract but the rolled-up interest would normally be paid out of the completion monies. It may be desirable to ensure that both dates fall into the same accounting period if there is any possibility that there will be insufficient income arising in the period when the interest would otherwise be paid to attract all the relief potentially available. In many cases rolled-up interest is not interest at all; it is notional interest as described in 4.109 above.

## Interest as a Distribution

**4.111** Interest paid by a company may be required to be treated as a distribution. Such interest will not be deductible for corporation tax purposes. In effect Parliament has decided that it should be treated as a dividend and not as interest at all. Interest – or other distributions out of assets of a company in respect of securities (which can include a simple loan) of the company – must be treated as a distribution if it is payable on securities under which the consideration given by the company for the use of the principal secured is to any extent dependent on the result of the company's business (or any part of it), or under which the consideration so given represents more than a reasonable commercial return for the use of the principal (*ICTA 1988, s 209(2)(d)(e)(iii)*). There are a number of exceptions.

**4.112** The interest need not be treated as a distribution if:

(*a*) the recipient of the interest is itself chargeable to corporation tax (*ICTA 1988, s 212(1)*); and

(*b*) the consideration does not represent more than a reasonable commercial return for the use of the principal (if it does, only the excess is a distribution) (*ICTA 1988, s 209(2)(d)(e)*).

The exemption does not apply if the recipient is entitled to an exemption from tax in respect of the interest, e.g. it is a pension fund (a non-resident company is not exempt from tax) (*ICTA 1988, s 212(3)*). There was also an exemption for pre 9 March 1982 loans but this ceased on or before 9 March 1987 (as the loan had to be for a term of under five years).

**4.113** There used to be a problem if the value of the property fell and the principal of the loan, not merely the return, was dependent on the value of the property as could happen with a non-recourse loan secured on the property, i.e. one where the lender agreed to look only to the sale proceeds of the property for repayment of the loan. The Revenue sometimes took the view that as the value of the property could in theory fall to a negligible amount, the principal secured was a negligible amount and a reasonable return on that negligible amount was itself a negligible figure. For distributions after 16 April 2002 in such cases the amount of the principal secured is treated for the purpose of *section 209(2)(d)* as equal to the consideration received by the company for the issue of the security, i.e. the amount of the loan (*ICTA 1988, s 209(3AA)*, inserted by *FA 2002, s 102(1)*). This relief does not apply if the security is one which to a significant extent reflects dividends on other distributions in respect of shares in one or more of the issuing company or any associated company (or reflects fluctuations in the value of such shares) (*ICTA 1988, s 209A* inserted by *FA 2002, s 102(2)*). Nor does it normally apply if hedging arrangements have been entered into that relate to some or all of the company's liabilities under the security (*ICTA 1988, s 209B* inserted by *FA 2002, s 102(2)*).

**4.114** Where a loan agreement includes a provision under which the lender is entitled to a share of the profit on a property development, the interest will fall within *section 209(2)(e)(iii)* unless it is taken out by the above exception. This provision is accordingly of particular importance to property companies, especially as they are frequently tempted to borrow from overseas lenders.

**4.115** Interest can also constitute a distribution if it is payable on redeemable securities issued in respect of shares in the company; on securities convertible directly or indirectly into shares in the company (unless issued on terms reasonably comparable with quoted securities); on securities held by a non-UK resident company of which the borrower is a 75% subsidiary or where a non-UK company owns at least 75% of both borrower and lender; or on securities the terms of which are such that it is necessary or advantageous for a person who holds any of the securities to also have a proportionate holding of the shares of the issuing company (*ICTA 1988, s 209(2)(e)*). In the case of securities held by a non-UK company, this provision is sometimes overridden by the non-discrimination provision of the UK's many double taxation agreements.

*Chapter 5*

# Investment or Dealing?

**5.1** The tax treatment of a property transaction depends on whether it is an investment or a trading (dealing) transaction. It is therefore vital to determine what type of transaction is being entered into. Unfortunately this is by no means easy. It depends, in theory, on the motive for the acquisition of the property. This is not always clear. Worse, in practice it often depends on the taxpayer's ability to evidence what his motive was. Very few people naturally evidence their intentions in any sphere of activity. However, the tax differences between an investment and a dealing transaction are of such moment that it is important to seek to ensure that the necessary evidence is available. In particular, in the case of a company, the courts tend to expect the directors to minute all of their decisions. Many companies, particularly family companies, do not hold regular board meetings and tend to minute only formal transactions such as the approval of the annual accounts. This attitude is very dangerous for a property company.

**5.2** Many people use three categories for property transactions – investment, dealing, and development. However, development is not really a separate category from a tax point of view as development by itself is not an end; it is a means to an end. One either develops to generate income, in which case the motive for the acquisition of the property is investment, or develops to sell the completed building, in which case it is dealing. There is also a concept of an adventure in the nature of trade, but as this is taxed as if it were a trade (*ICTA 1988, s 832(1)*) the distinction is irrelevant.

**5.3** Broadly speaking, a property is bought as an investment if it is acquired in order to generate rental income. It will be bought as trading stock – and the transaction will be a dealing transaction – if it is acquired in order to make a profit from reselling it. Unfortunately this distinction is rarely clear cut. A purchaser hopes that an investment will increase in value. Accordingly (to some extent) every property can be said to have been bought with a view to reselling it at a profit. The purchase will nevertheless be as an investment if the main object was to generate income. A person who develops a building with the intention of selling it to produce a dealing profit may well let it before sale as he may be able to obtain a better price by selling it as a let building. Such a letting would not, however, transform it into an investment.

**5.4** Some people believe that a single transaction cannot be a dealing transaction. This is a myth (see 5.30). The conversion of a house into flats will normally be a dealing transaction even if the owner intends to occupy one of the flats as his residence. In such a case the way the transaction is structured can affect the tax position. Consideration needs to be given to separating out the owner's flat before the building work is done rather than after. Indeed the fact that a property is occupied as the owner's principal private residence does not prevent it having been acquired with a dealing motive. Where a person moves house frequently, making a significant gain on each transaction, it is not unknown for the Revenue to seek to show that he is dealing in the properties and living in them only incidentally to his dealing motive.

## The Basic Tests

**5.5** There are a number of basic tests that the Inland Revenue and the Courts will apply to determine whether a transaction is dealing or investment.

1 — *The motive for the acquisition of the property*. This is the fundamental test. If it was to generate income the transaction is an investment; if it was to generate a profit on sale it is dealing. The remaining tests are needed because the motive is not always clear, or there is no evidence available to substantiate the professed motive, or the professed motive is not accepted by the Revenue as the true motive. If a taxpayer claims that a property was bought as an investment – which in most, but not all, cases will produce a lower tax charge – but most of the remaining tests are indicative of dealing, the Revenue will be unlikely to accept that the professed investment motive was the true intention in purchasing the property. The remaining tests are therefore important as either reinforcing or calling into question the professed motive on acquisition. The principles to be applied where there is more than one motive are set out at 5.27.

2 — *The evidence that is available to substantiate the claimed motive.* In general the Revenue are unlikely to contend that a transaction which the taxpayer claims to be dealing is, in reality, investment. It is the purported investment transactions that they challenge. Accordingly where a property is bought as an investment it is sensible to seek to ensure that evidence is available to substantiate that investment intention. In the absence of such evidence the courts will have to infer the intention from the remaining tests. Where a person purchases a property as an investment he might be expected to calculate the yield on letting and the yield after the first rent review. A calculation showing the capital value of the property on completion of development might suggest an intention to dispose of the completed development rather

than to retain it. On the other hand the valuation may have been done to establish the mortgageability of the property for retention as an investment.

3 — *The method of finance.* Property is by its nature a long-term investment. Accordingly if the funds to acquire or develop it are borrowed on a short-term basis this is normally indicative of an intention to dispose of the property rather than retain it. It should be borne in mind that an investor may well borrow short-term on a temporary basis if he feels that interest rates are likely to fall over the following year or so, with a view to replacing this with long-term borrowings later. A developer may borrow short-term to finance the development with a view to replacing this with long-term finance secured on the completed development.

4 — *Whether the property is income producing.* If a property produces no income during the taxpayer's period of ownership it will be difficult to show that it was bought as an investment – unless of course it was bought for use as a private residence or for some other personal use where the return on the investment is the enjoyment of the property. If a property produces income but this merely equals (or is less than) the outgoings and interest on money used to acquire it, the Revenue will look on it as non-income producing. If, although a property produces no income on acquisition, it is bought in the course of putting together a development site, the generation of income after the development could well have been the initial intention.

5 — *The period of ownership.* Property investments are normally held for a period of several years. There is no hard and fast rule as to how long a property needs to be held to stamp it as an investment. A period of six years can normally be regarded as relatively safe. Four or five years is unlikely to provoke attack in most cases. If a property is held for less than about three years there is a significant risk that this will prompt the Revenue to contend that it was bought for resale. It should be borne in mind, however, that length of ownership is only one of several factors to be looked at from which to draw an inference as to what the taxpayer's motive was at the time of his acquisition of the property. Where a property is developed the period of ownership after completion of the development is what needs to be looked at – unless the property was clearly held as an investment prior to redevelopment and the redevelopment was to enhance the price obtainable on its sale. If a property produces no net income up to the first rent review, a sale shortly after that rent review could well be regarded as indicative of a dealing intention even though the property is retained for five or seven years after the letting.

6 — *The reason for the disposal.* This is not nearly as important as the reason for the acquisition. Indeed it is not really an independent test at all. It can, however, be important to displace a dealing inference where a property which is claimed to be an investment is held for a relatively

short period. If it can be shown that the reason for the sale is that the taxpayer can obtain a far better yield on an alternative investment, or he is being forced to raise money to reduce bank borrowings or to meet a specific requirement for a substantial cash sum, this is likely to displace the dealing inference that might otherwise be drawn from the short period of ownership.

7 — *The expertise of the owner.* The Inland Revenue generally contend that a builder or a property developer is more likely to acquire property for dealing than as an investment. The logic of this is hard to discern. The expertise of a builder is just as likely to enable him to recognise attractive investments as attractive trading situations.

8 — *Application for planning consent.* An application for planning consent prior to a sale may be indicative of a dealing intention particularly if the property was held for a relatively short period. On the other hand an application for planning consent may merely be a way of maximising the price obtained for an investment.

9 — *A company's objects clause.* If the taxpayer is a company its objects clause is a major factor to look at. The directors can hardly contend that they were deliberately acting *ultra vires*. Accordingly the directors will find it difficult to show that they acquired a property as an investment if the company had no powers of investment. The Revenue are under no such inhibition. Even if the company had such powers their existence will of course be neutral if it also had power to deal. Where the evidence as to the nature of a transaction is conflicting the courts will generally lean towards finding that the directors have done what they were empowered to do rather than acting outside the scope of their authority. Accordingly if the objects clause makes it clear that the company is an investment company the onus will effectively be on the Revenue to demonstrate that a purported investment transaction was in fact a dealing transaction carried out in breach of the company's powers. Where the taxpayer is a trust the powers contained in the trust deed might similarly be a pointer to the nature of a transaction.

10 — *The presentation in the owner's accounts.* Investments constitute fixed assets for accounting purposes. Dealing properties constitute current assets and are normally shown in the accounts as trading stock. Whilst the treatment in the accounts is not conclusive it is difficult for the directors of a company to contend that a property is an investment if for many years they have approved accounts which have shown it in the balance sheet as trading stock.

## Decided Cases

**5.6** The question as to whether a particular transaction is investment or dealing has spawned much litigation. Unfortunately about the only conclusions that can safely be drawn from the decided cases are that every case depends on its own individual set of facts and, possibly, that no matter how clear cut a case may seem, there is always the chance that the Commissioners will come to a different conclusion. Nevertheless an examination of some of the decided cases may be helpful as they at least indicate some of the factors to which the courts have attached significance.

**5.7** In *California Copper Syndicate Ltd v Harris (5 TC 159)* a company bought copper-bearing land in 1901 and resold it in two lots in 1902 and 1903 in exchange for the issue of shares in the purchaser company. It contended that the acceptance of shares rather than cash evidenced an initial investment intention. It was held that this was not a relevant factor. The Commissioners were entitled to find, as they had done, that the purchase of non-income producing land and its sale a year or two later was by its nature a dealing transaction. The receipt of the consideration otherwise than in cash could not change the nature of the transaction.

**5.8** In *Tempest Estates Ltd v Walmsley (51 TC 305)* land forming part of a family estate was sold to a company as part of an estate duty planning exercise. The land was on the outskirts of Bolton and thought likely to have development value at some future date. Between 1946, when the land was bought by the company from the trustees of the estate, and 1956 there were minor sales, but in 1958 a significant part of the land was sold for development. This sale appears to have been treated as the realisation of an investment. There were further comparatively small sales but the general policy was not to sell land. In 1963 the company decided to pursue a more active development policy and purported to transfer three blocks of land from investment to dealing stock. It then sold that land. It was held that the initial purchase of the land in 1946 was a trading venture. The company's directors must have known that it was only a matter of time before the land would be disposed of or developed. The fact that the company was formed for the purpose of estate duty saving was not necessarily inconsistent with an acquisition of the land for trading purposes. It should particularly be noted that the bulk of the land was held for about 17 years. Normally, once land has been held for more than about six years – particularly if it has produced rental income, as happened with *Tempest Estates* – one would feel fairly confident that the sale is the realisation of an investment. This case illustrates that all of the circumstances must be looked at. Furthermore the court had no hesitation in drawing an inference from letters written in 1958 as to the directors' intentions in 1946. This indicates that it is important not only to evidence one's intention on acquisition but also to take care that later correspondence does nothing to cast doubt on the initial professed intention.

**5.9** This decision can be contrasted with that in *Rand v Alberni Land Co Ltd (7 TC 629)*, an earlier case. A company was formed to acquire land in Vancouver in order to develop and manage it with a view to ultimate sale, the land being held in trust for various people with different interests in it. Thus the company had a clear dealing purpose. It was held that the sales of land were capital gains as the real purpose of the company was to realise the full capital value of the respective interests in the land under the trust. Whilst this was undoubtedly the motive of the shareholders in forming the company it is difficult to ascribe such a motive to the directors as such. The motive of the major shareholder was also important in the *Simmons Properties* case (see 5.21 below), a later case than *Tempest Estates* (5.8 above). It accordingly appears permissible to look at the circumstances surrounding the formation of a company to ascertain the true motive for the acquisition of the property. These can suggest that the directors' role was merely to put into effect a plan conceived by the shareholders so that the directors themselves had no motive in relation to the acquisition.

**5.10** A word of warning. In *Balgownie Land Trust Ltd v CIR (14 TC 684)* the executors of a deceased estate held land with a direction under the will to realise it. They formed the company, transferred the land to it in exchange for shares, and distributed the shares to the beneficiaries. The company borrowed money to acquire further land. Some years later it sold most of the land. It was held to be dealing. Another company formed to acquire settled land, part of which it developed as building sites and sold as the opportunity arose, was similarly held to be dealing (*St Aubyn Estates Ltd v Strick (17 TC 412)*). These can be distinguished from *Alberni Land* (5.9 above) insofar as the purchase and resale of further land in the *Balgownie* case stands as a trading transaction apart from the original land, and the development and splitting of land in the *St Aubyn* case could well have been deemed to be an appropriation of the land as trading stock if it had not been put into the company.

**5.11** The importance of the motive at the time of acquisition is exemplified by the case of *Tebrau (Johore) Rubber Syndicate v Farmer (5 TC 658)*. A company was formed to acquire land for development as a rubber plantation. It bought two estates but found that it had inadequate finance to develop them. It therefore sold them to a second company mainly for shares. It was held, reversing the decision of the Commissioners, that there was no evidence that the land had been bought for resale, and that the profit was therefore capital. On the facts it is clear that the property was bought as a fixed asset. The decision illustrates that the subsequent frustration of the initial intention cannot change the nature of the transaction.

**5.12** In February 1942 a company purchased three tenement properties in Glasgow for £20. At the time they were partly condemned as dangerous. The directors thought that a profit could be made out of the properties some day but were looking some years ahead. The company carried out some alterations and was then able to let the properties at rents fluctuating between £50 and £100 p.a. In 1949 the properties were sold and the company liquidated. It was held that the only reasonable conclusion was that the purchase was made with the intention of a resale at a profit when a suitable opportunity arose. It was therefore an adventure in the nature of trade. It did not matter that there was only a single transaction. Nor apparently did it make any difference that the rents represented a return of between 20% and 45% on the investment consistently for a period of six years – a factor which would normally be indicative that the property was bought as an investment (*CIR v Toll Property Co Ltd (34 TC 13)*).

**5.13** By contrast, in *CIR v The Hyndland Investment Co Ltd (14 TC 694)* a company was formed in 1898 to acquire certain building land in Hyndland from its three shareholders, one of whom was a builder. It erected five tenements, which were completed and let by mid-1900. The investment turned out to be a poor one and the company had to raise additional finance. After the war, in 1920, the housing shortage created a demand for vacant houses and individual flats. Taking advantage of this demand the company sold a number of flats and houses – five in 1920, three in 1921, three in 1922, four in 1923 and one in 1926 – to improve its financial position. It was left with 24 flats, all in poor repair. It was held the company had not traded in disposing of the 16 flats. Significance was attached to the facts that the company had purchased one single block of property, so if it were trading it must have done so with regard to that block, that it continued after the sales to hold a large part of that investment, and that because of the company's circumstances it was expedient to sell part of the property to ease its financial position. This shows that evidence of an alternative reason for a sale can displace a dealing inference.

**5.14** A company was incorporated in October 1933 to purchase 70 acres of land on the outskirts of Hull which the proprietor intended to develop as a garden suburb. It was accepted that this land was bought as trading stock. In 1934 it bought two further parcels of adjoining land. In 1935 it emerged that there were insoluble drainage difficulties and the garden suburb concept was abandoned in late 1936. There were a few small sales of land in 1936 and 1956 – the profits on which were treated as income. The land was shown as an investment in the company's accounts. It produced rental income but this was generally less than the expenses. In 1961 the land was compulsorily purchased by Hull Corporation. From 1952/53 onwards the company had been taxed as a property investment company and had submitted management expenses claims.

The company contended that although the land had initially been purchased as trading stock it had ceased to be held as such when the intention to develop was abandoned in 1936. It was held that the main question to be asked was what was the proper inference to be drawn from the way in which the company conducted its affairs in the 25 years from 1936 to 1961. The abandonment of a particular project of development does not involve abandoning altogether any idea of developing or otherwise dealing in land. There was accordingly no evidence that the land had ever ceased to be trading stock. The sale in 1961 was therefore made in the course of the company's trade (*Orchard Parks Ltd v Pogson (42 TC 442)*).

**5.15** It should particularly be noted that no weight was given to the fact that the Revenue had treated the company as an investment company for nine years, and little weight was given to the treatment in the company's accounts. The clear trading motive on acquisition seems to have been the prime influencing factor. This case should be contrasted with the later, non-property, one of *British-Borneo Petroleum Syndicate Ltd v Cropper (45 TC 201)*. In that case a company acquired an oil concession as trading stock. From 1935 onwards its principal source of income was royalties from this concession. There was no evidence of an appropriation from trading stock to investment. It surrendered its rights in 1964 for £900,000. It was held that this was a capital receipt. At some stage the concession had ceased to be held as trading stock. It did not matter when, as this was clearly more than six years before 1964, and the Revenue were therefore out of time to raise an assessment.

**5.16** In *Mitchell Bros v Tomlinson (37 TC 224)* two brothers decided to build houses for letting as an investment to make provision for their old age. By 1939 they had built or purchased some 60 houses, none of which were sold before 1947. Between 1942 and 1948 they bought a further 239 houses which they were able to purchase very cheaply because of wartime conditions. They sold 58 of these latter houses between 1946 and 1952. It was held that the brothers were carrying on a trade as property dealers. Although they originally had an investment intention it subsequently altered when conditions changed. It is not clear from the judgment if this change of intention applied so as to make the pre-1939 acquisitions trading stock or if it only affected the later acquisitions. It is probable that the Commissioners had in mind the later acquisitions only, i.e. they were holding that the fact that a person enters into property investment transactions does not frank all future property transactions with an investment intent.

**5.17** *CIR v Reinhold (34 TC 389)* is an interesting decision. Mr Reinhold bought four houses in January 1945 and sold them in December 1947. He bought the properties for resale and had instructed his agent to sell whenever a suitable opportunity arose. The properties had produced no net income. His only previous property transaction was ten years earlier when he had bought a hotel and resold it at a profit before he completed the purchase. It is perhaps difficult to imagine anything more clearly trading. The property was bought for resale, was held for a short period only, and produced no net income. Nevertheless, it was held to be an investment.

Relevant factors were that the taxpayer was not a property agent and his business was not associated with the purchase and sale of land; and that the transaction was an isolated transaction. A transaction does not require to be unique in the life experience of a businessman to be treated as isolated so the transaction ten years earlier did not prevent it being so. So what? As the judgment makes clear, an isolated transaction can constitute a trade, particularly if it is entered into by a company where intention can be shown from the terms of its objects. However, Lord Keith felt that where an individual enters into an isolated transaction in a subject that is normally used for investment – land, houses, stocks and shares – the inference of trading is not to be so readily drawn in regard to a single transaction from an admitted intention to sell on the arrival of a certain pre-selected time.

'It is not, in my opinion, enough for the Revenue to show that the subjects were purchased with the intention of realising them some day at a profit. This is the expectation of most, if not all, people who make investments. Heritable property is a not uncommon subject of investment and generally has the feature, expected of investments, of yielding an income while it is being held. In the present case the property yielded an income from rents. It is said that it yielded no profit . . . the intention to resell at some date at a profit is not per se sufficient in this case to attract tax . . . Here the facts in my opinion are insufficient to establish that this is an adventure in the nature of trade' (Lord Keith at p 397).

This decision is hard to understand, but is worth remembering where an individual enters into an isolated transaction.

**5.18** Another interesting case that the taxpayer was perhaps lucky to win is *Taylor v Good (49 TC 277)*. The taxpayer bought a property on impulse at an auction in July 1959 for £5,100. It was a large country house at which his mother had once worked. He had not decided what to do with it but had in mind the possibility of going to live in it. When he told his wife she refused to do this. Accordingly in September 1959, before completion of the purchase, he applied for planning permission for redevelopment. This was refused but granted on appeal in 1962. In 1963 he sold the land to a developer for £54,000. In the High Court Megarry J said that part of the gain was capital and part income and remitted the case to the Commissioners to determine when trading commenced. The Court of Appeal held that the whole of the gain was capital as there was no evidence of an appropriation to dealing stock.

**5.19** This case illustrates the supreme importance of the motive on acquisition. If the taxpayer had not been able to show that he did not start with a trading motive he would undoubtedly have lost as everything else pointed to a dealing transaction. He seems to have had no real motive on acquisition, which indicates that it is not necessary to demonstrate an investment motive, one merely needs to negate a trading one. The case also makes clear that one is not wholly safe by establishing that the property was not acquired with a dealing motive. It is still possible for there to be an appropriation to trading stock at a later date (although the *Simmons Properties* case (see 5.21 below) indicates that there must be a positive intention to appropriate).

**5.20** *Marshall's Executors & Others v Joly (20 TC 256)* similarly illustrates that it is sufficient to demonstrate the absence of any motive. One of the three partners in a property dealing partnership died and his executors required the surviving partners to realise the unsold land, which they did over the following three years. It was held that there was no evidence to support a finding that the executors had carried on a trade. They were merely collecting in the assets of the estate. By contrast, in *Newbarns Syndicate v Hay (22 TC 461)* a member of a property dealing syndicate died and his executor took his place in the syndicate. It was held that on the particular facts of the case the executor was trading. Sales continued for many years after the death, the executor participated in annual meetings of the syndicate, and he had not pressed for the land to be sold and the deceased's share paid over to him.

**5.21** *Lionel Simmons Properties Ltd (in liquidation) v CIR (53 TC 461)* is probably the most important case on the distinction between dealing and investment. It is one of the few to be heard by the House of Lords, it reversed the decision of the Commissioners on what is on the face of it primarily a question of fact, and Lord Wilberforce gives a lucid analysis of the principles involved. Mr Simmons, a surveyor and thus a property expert, sought to build up, through his companies, a property investment portfolio which he ultimately intended to float as a public group. He formed a number of companies over a period of about eight years, each to develop and retain one or two properties. On occasions he sold properties, sometimes fairly shortly after development. However, such sales were in pursuance of a policy of trading up, i.e. he would sell one property to provide funds to acquire a larger one. The profits on such sales were credited to capital reserve. He later entered into arrangements with a quoted investment trust with the object of getting the financial backing to grow to a floatable size. In 1966, following the passing of the *Rent Act 1965* and the *Finance Act 1965*, he decided that there was no future for a property investment group, sold the properties, and liquidated all of the companies.

**5.22** The Commissioners decided that some of the properties were trading stock and some investments. This was on the basis that they felt that as Mr Simmons was prepared to realise one development in order to find funds for another it was not until after completion of lettings that he could be in a position to decide finally whether to retain the property or not. Until the decision to hold was made the Commissioners regarded the property as trading stock. This is difficult to reconcile with the Court of Appeal decision in *Taylor v Good* (5.18 above) where it was made clear that no intention on acquisition is not equivalent to a possible trading motive. Nevertheless, the Court of Appeal in *Simmons* dismissed this because, in *Taylor v Good*, the Crown had accepted at Court of Appeal level that the purchase was not made for trading purposes whereas in *Simmons* the Commissioners were not satisfied that the properties were bought as investments. As the two do not seem inconsistent this distinction is somewhat obscure. The House of Lords (Lord Scarman dissenting) reversed the decision of both the Commissioners and the Court of Appeal, holding that a decision that any of the properties were trading stock was inconsistent with the primary facts found.

'One must ask, first, what the Commissioners were required or entitled to find. Trading requires an intention to trade: normally the question to be asked is whether this intention existed at the time of the acquisition of the asset. Was it acquired with the intention of disposing of it at a profit, or was it acquired as a permanent investment? Often it is necessary to ask further questions: a permanent investment may be sold in order to acquire another investment thought to be more satisfactory; that does not involve an operation of trade, whether the first investment is sold at a profit or at a loss. Intentions may be changed. What was first an investment may be put into the trading stock – and, I suppose, vice versa. If findings of this kind are to be made precision is required, since a shift of an asset from one category to another will involve changes in the company's accounts, and, possibly, a liability to tax . . . What I think is not possible is for an asset to be both trading stock and permanent investment at the same time, nor to possess an indeterminate status – neither trading stock nor permanent asset. It must be one or other, even though, and this seems to me legitimate and intelligible, the company, in whatever character it acquires the asset, may reserve an intention to change its character. To do so would, in fact, amount to little more than making explicit what is necessarily implicit in all commercial operations, namely that situations are open to review' (Lord Wilberforce).

It is interesting to note that at all levels the general investment motive of Mr Simmons was looked at to determine the motive of an individual company in acquiring an individual property. Also the decision to liquidate could not give rise to an inference of a trading motive as this did nothing more than put an end to Mr Simmons's investment plans. Frustration of a plan for investment, which compels realisation, even if foreseen as a possibility, cannot give rise to an intention to trade.

**5.23** However, a Privy Council case, *Richfield International Land & Investment Co Ltd v Inland Revenue Commissioner (1989 STC 820)*, does need to be borne in mind. In 1972 the company acquired a number of properties which it let out and showed as investments in its accounts. In 1973 it sold a small property and treated the surplus as a capital gain. The Revenue challenged this (presumably because of the short period of ownership) and the company agreed that it could be taxed as income. In 1978 it sold another fairly small property and treated the surplus as a trading profit – an indication that that particular property must have been appropriated to trading stock. In 1980 it sold the major property and treated the surplus as a capital gain. It was held that the property had become trading stock even though it was accepted that it had been acquired as an investment, had always been shown as an investment in the accounts, had been held for eight years, and had produced significant rental income throughout. The justification was that the company had accepted that the surpluses on the two small properties were taxable as trading profits. It is difficult to see how this shows evidence of an intention to appropriate the larger to trading stock, particularly in the face of the contrary treatment in the accounts. It is to be hoped that this case is merely an extreme example of the *Edwards v Bairstow & Harrison (36 TC 207)* principle, i.e. that the courts will not disturb a finding of fact unless it is so perverse that no reasonable tribunal could properly have arrived at it, rather than an undermining of the *Simmons* decision.

**5.24** It is also worth mentioning a non-property case *Waylee Investment Ltd v Commissioner of Inland Revenue for Hong Kong (1990 STC 780)*. In that case a large Hong Kong listed company was in danger of collapse, which would have damaged public confidence in the economy of Hong Kong. Its bankers, believing that its fortunes could be restored with new management, subscribed for new shares which gave them effective control. The shares were acquired by Waylee, a subsidiary of the bank. In due course the company prospered. A little over two years later the company merged with another and in September 1979, four years after the acquisition of the shares, Waylee received an unsolicited offer for the shares, which it accepted. The Revenue claimed that the shares had been acquired as trading stock. They had been held for a relatively short period. The bank had in its annual report after acquiring the shares expressed an intention to sell them as soon as conditions permitted. The rescue operation had taken place in the normal course of the bank's business. The Board of Review (the Hong Kong equivalent of the Special Commissioners) held that the shares had been acquired as a capital asset. The Privy Council affirmed this decision. The shares did not have the nature of trading stock; any attempt to sell them to meet depositor's demands would defeat the objective of showing the bank's confidence in the listed company, so they could not be regarded as circulating capital. The intention to sell as soon as conditions permitted did not necessarily label the shares as trading stock as this intention could be looked on merely as an expression of the bank's concern not to be seen to be involving itself in the management of the listed company on a long-term basis. It is also interesting to note that the court was prepared to attribute to the subsidiary the intentions of the bank itself.

**5.25** Another recent Privy Council decision worth remembering is *Beautiland Co Ltd v Commissioner of Inland Revenue for Hong Kong (1991 STC 467)*. Two companies, Cheung Kong and Wheelock Marden, reached agreement in principle for the development of a number of properties owned by one or other of their groups. They incorporated Beautiland as a joint venture company for the purpose. One of the assets contributed to Beautiland by Cheung Kong was a 30% holding in Rostock Enterprises Ltd, which itself controlled a land-owning company. Two months later an offer to acquire 81% of Rostock was received by Cheung Kong from an unconnected third party and Beautiland sold most of its 30% holding to the third party in consequence of this offer. The Revenue assessed Beautiland as a share dealer. The Privy Council held that, in spite of the fact that it was clearly intended that Beautiland might trade in land, there was nothing in the joint venture agreement to indicate that the parties had in contemplation trading in the shares of subsidiary or associated companies. It followed that there could be no question of a separate contemplation of trading in land via shares. The shares acquired by Beautiland constituted its capital structure and there were no grounds for concluding that they were acquired as trading stock.

**5.26** One particular area of difficulty is the tax treatment where, in order to obtain a particular piece of land, one has to acquire a package including other land that one does not want. In *Snell v Rosser, Thomas & Co Ltd (44 TC 343)* a building contractor wanted to buy a large house for conversion into flats for sale – clearly a trading venture. In order to obtain the house he also had to buy 5¾ acres of surrounding land. He resold this land at the first available opportunity. The profit on sale of the land was held to be trading as its acquisition was incidental to the acquisition of the stock in trade. By contrast, in a Privy Council decision (which carries the full weight of a decision of the Law Lords) three years earlier (*Iswera v Ceylon Commissioner of Inland Revenue (1965 1 WLR 663)*), it was held that where a taxpayer who wanted a particular piece of land on which to build a private residence had to buy a larger site and resell what she did not want, the sale of the surplus land was a transaction in the nature of trade, not an acquisition incidental to the acquisition of an investment.

**5.27** The principles that must be applied where a person has more than one motive in acquiring land were reviewed recently by the Court of Appeal in *Kirkham v Williams (1991 STC 342)*.

(*a*) If on an objective analysis the transaction has all the characteristics of trading, that analysis must prevail.

(*b*) If the transaction is equivocal, the subjective intention of the taxpayer must be taken into account in weighing up whether the transaction is trading or not.

(*c*) If in an equivocal case the taxpayer's sole objective is non-commercial the transaction will not be a trading transaction.

(*d*) In all other cases the overall nature of the transaction is a question of fact to be determined by the Commissioners.

In *Kirkham v Williams*, Mr Kirkham contracted to buy land in Summer 1977 and in October 1977 applied for planning permission for redevelopment. Completion of the purchase was May 1978. The land was used by Mr Kirkham partly as offices and partly for storage in connection with his business. He also carried out some limited farming activities on the land. Planning permission for the erection of a dwelling house on the land was eventually obtained in August 1980. This was built by the taxpayer. It was never his intention to purchase the property as a residence for himself and his family. The land was sold in October 1982 and the Revenue contended that it must, *inter alia*, have been acquired with the intention of disposing of it at a profit. Mr Kirkham contended that he had acquired it as a capital asset for use in his business. The General Commissioners found that the site was acquired principally to provide office and storage space for the taxpayer's business. They nevertheless held that it was a trading transaction. The Court of Appeal accepted that if the Commissioners had found that the subsidiary purpose for the acquisition of the site was trading they might be entitled to hold that the overall intention was trading. However they were silent on what that purpose was; it seemed most likely that it was farming. Furthermore, even if it was trading the subsidiary purpose could not have been implemented concurrently with the primary purpose of providing office and storage space. Mr Kirkham could not develop the site unless he obtained planning permission and even then could not do so until he had been able to provide himself with storage and office space elsewhere. Accordingly the trading purpose was severely circumscribed and its implementation indefinite in point of time. In these circumstances, 'It was not open to the Commissioners, having made a finding which was apt to characterise the transaction as an acquisition of a capital asset, to deny it that character by reason of an intention thus circumscribed and indefinite' (Nourse LJ).

**5.28** Although the production of income has long been regarded as one of the prime hallmarks of an investment, the absence of income is not necessarily fatal. In *Marson v Morton (59 TC 381)* Sir Nicholas Browne-Wilkinson, the Vice-Chancellor, was not deterred by the lack of income.

'It is true in the Reinhold case the Court of Session did rely on the fact that there would be income in rents as a relevant factor, and in my judgment it plainly is a relevant factor. But in my judgment in 1986 it is not any longer self-evident that unless land is producing income it cannot be an investment. The legal principle of course cannot change with the passage of time: but life does. Since the arrival of inflation and high rates of tax on income new approaches to investment have emerged putting the emphasis in investment on the making of capital profit at the expense of income yield. For example, the purchase of short-dated stocks giving a capital yield on redemption but no income has become commonplace . . . I can see no reason why land should be any different and the mere fact that land is not income-producing should not be decisive or even virtually decisive on the question whether it was bought as an investment.'

The facts of this case were somewhat strange. The taxpayer told an intermediary that he would be interested in investing in land. The intermediary subsequently introduced to him an opportunity to buy a site for £35,000. The taxpayer had no idea of the time-scale involved in property investment but thought it might be one or two years. He took no legal advice. He took no steps to sell the land but a few months later the intermediary said that he had a potential buyer and if the taxpayer sold he might double his money. He duly sold the land and received a cheque for £70,000. It was not until the Revenue raised questions that he discovered that he had in fact bought the land not for £35,000 but for £65,000 with a £30,000 mortgage, and had sold it for £100,000 – or indeed that both vendor and purchaser were companies associated with the intermediary. The transaction has all the signs of trading; the land was bought with borrowed money, was held for a very short period, was always intended to be held for a fairly short period, and produced no income during the period of ownership. Nevertheless it was held by the General Commissioners to be an investment, a decision that the judge upheld as one which they were entitled to make.

**5.29** There are a number of other decisions that are at least worthy of mention. *Emro Investments Ltd v Aller (35 TC 305)* illustrates that the accounting treatment adopted and a company's objects clause, although relevant, are not conclusive – the company, albeit ostensibly an investment company, was held to be trading. *Parkstone Estates Ltd v Blair (43 TC 246)* exemplifies the dangers of a company carrying on both dealing and investment activities. The company developed an industrial estate of twelve factories, one of which it let on a ten-year lease to an associated company and the remainder of which it sold. It was held that the company was trading and the let property was trading stock. If the let factory had been developed by another group company it would probably have been an investment. The fact that a property produces net rents in excess of borrowings is not necessarily conclusive of investment status. In *Parkin v Cattell (48 TC 462)* the taxpayer purchased a number of houses over a period of about eight years with controlled tenants and sold them as they became vacant. Although the Revenue initially accepted these as investments they later had second thoughts. The transactions were held to be trading, the course of dealings indicating that the prime motive for the purchases was to obtain a profit on resale, not to reap the rental income. This decision needs to be borne in mind when considering the purchase of such controlled properties or the purchase of ground rents, although the Revenue do not in practice challenge most such purchases and in many cases it will be possible to substantiate an investment intention.

*Sugarwhite v Budd (1987 STC 491)*, which is considered in more detail in 14.42 below, emphasises that it is up to the taxpayer to prove his case. In that case a company contracted to buy a property but sub-sold it within a matter of weeks, so it never completed. The Commissioners, the High Court, and the Court of Appeal all held that there was no evidence before them to show that this was not a dealing transaction – even though it is difficult to envisage any set of circumstances which on the face of it gives such an indication of dealing.

**5.30** There are a number of decisions that make clear that a single purchase and sale can constitute a trade or an adventure in the nature of trade (which is taxed as a trade), e.g. *Reynolds' Executors v Bennett (25 TC 401)*; *Gray & Gillitt v Tiley (26 TC 80)*; *Burrell & Others v Davis (38 TC 307)*; *Turner v Last (42 TC 517)* – a single purchase sold in two lots; *Johnston v Heath (46 TC 463)*; and *Clark v Follett (48 TC 677)*. In all of these cases there was a clear intention at the time of purchase to sell at a profit. Where a property is purchased jointly there is often a greater risk that the Revenue will contend that it is bought for resale. Except within families or partnerships it is relatively unusual for people to want to enter into long-term investment relationships with a co-venturer.

**5.31** Most people try to avoid being labelled as a property dealer in their own names for fear that this will mean that all future property transactions are also dealing. Whilst caution makes this a sensible approach, this worry is not wholly justified. It is perfectly possible for an individual to enter into investment transactions at the same time as he is dealing. In *Cooksey & Bibby v Rednall (30 TC 514)* two individuals jointly bought a farm in 1924 which they let. Between 1930 and 1940 they entered into a number of joint property transactions which were admitted to be dealing. The farm was sold in 1938. It was held that the Commissioner's finding that the profit on the farm was part of their trading profits could not be supported. This decision is of especial interest as it is a joint ownership case where the dealing inference might be expected to be strong. In *CIR v Dean Property Co (22 TC 706)* a partnership agreement recited that the partnership was being formed to acquire land for investment. It feued most of it in lots to an associated company. The use of the description 'partnership' normally implies a trading intent – as partnership is the carrying on of business in common 'with a view of profit'. (It is safer to describe the relationship as being a joint investment.) Nevertheless the transactions were held to be investment. If an individual is regarded as a dealer in relation to some transactions only and he has other property that has fallen in value there may be a temptation to contend that all his property transactions are trading. Normally this temptation should be resisted. In *Hudson v Wrightson (26 TC 55)* the taxpayer's contention to this effect was accepted in part, the judge remitting the case to the Commissioners for them to determine which of his other properties were trading stock. In the event they decided that none of them were.

**5.32** Particular problems arise with builders. Both the Revenue and the courts seem reluctant to accept that a builder can ever invest in property – on the rather spurious ground that his expertise of itself implies an intention to resell at a profit rather than to generate income. The Revenue tend to take a similar approach to other people in the property business such as estate agents, surveyors, architects, and developers. In *Spiers & Son Ltd v Ogden (17 TC 117)* a construction company acquired land on which it erected buildings which it let and subsequently sold. The sales were held to be part of its building trade. In *Sharpless v Rees (23 TC 361)* a builder bought land to run as a poultry farm as his health precluded his continuing as a builder. His health deteriorated further and he abandoned the idea and sold the land. The surplus on sale was held to be part of his building profits. Similarly in *Shadford v H Fairweather & Co Ltd (43 TC 291)* a building company abandoned a project to erect flats for letting and the surplus on selling the site was held to be part of its building profits. Even relatives of builders can be looked on with suspicion. In *Smart v Lowndes (52 TC 436)* a builder contracted to buy land but passed the benefit to his wife. The conveyance was in her name. The land had building potential and was sold six years later at a profit. The Revenue successfully contended that the surplus was part of the husband's trading profit and that the wife was a nominee.

**5.33** Even the generation of rental income over a number of years is not conclusive where the investor is a builder. In *J & C Oliver v Farnsworth (37 TC 51)* the surplus on a house built in 1929 and let for 24 years until its sale in 1953 was held to be part of the builder's trading profits. A similar decision applied where a building company built and let houses before the war and sold them over a period after the war as they became vacant (*James Hobson & Sons Ltd v Newall (37 TC 609)*). In *W M Robb Ltd v Page (47 TC 465)* a building company erected a factory in 1951 for occupation by another group company to which it let it. In 1962 the factory became unsuitable for the occupier's needs and a new one was built by the building company. The surplus on sale of the original factory was held to be part of the builder's trading profits.

**5.34** Even after a builder has given up building, future profits on the sale of rented properties that he built in his active days are likely to be regarded as trading profits. This is exemplified by *Gladstone Development Co Ltd v Strick (30 TC 131)* – houses sold in 1945 but building ceased in 1939; *Speck v Morton (48 TC 476)* – houses sold in 1964 but building ceased in 1949; *Granville Building Co Ltd v Oxby (35 TC 245)* – house sold in 1950 shown as an investment in the accounts since 1942; and *Andrew v Taylor (42 TC 557)* – although here the taxpayer had a partial victory, it being held that sales between 1957 (when building ceased) and 1961 were trading but later sales were investments. The only clear victory for the taxpayer was *Harvey v Caulcott (33 TC 159)* where shops that had been let by the builder for around 30 years were held to be investments. There was also a partial victory in *West v Phillips (38 TC 203)* where the builder had initially split the properties he built between trading stock and investment. It was held that those originally designated as investments were not trading stock but those originally designated as stock retained that status when sold ten years after the taxpayer had ceased building. It must of course be realised that on a cessation of a trade stock which is not sold needs to be brought into account at market value. It is likely that this was not done in the builders' cases that went to appeal and that the Revenue contended that the trade had not ceased because they were out of time to make the cessation adjustment. If a builder who contends that his trade has ceased brings his closing stock into account at market value the Revenue are unlikely to attack subsequent sales of the properties. If he does not do so he ought not to be surprised that the Revenue regard the trade as continuing after active building has ceased.

**5.35** If it can be shown that the purchase and resale of land is not a trading transaction then, unless *ICTA 1988, s 776* (see chapter 14) applies, it will not normally be taxable as income. In *Leeming v Jones (15 TC 333)* four people jointly purchased land with the intention of floating a company to which they would transfer it. The Commissioners decided that this did not amount to trading. The Revenue claimed in the alternative that if the profit was not within Case I of Schedule D it was taxable under Case VI. It was held by the House of Lords that Case VI 'sweeps up all sorts of annual profits and gains . . . but it has been settled again and again that that does not mean that anything that is a profit or gain falls to be taxed'. It must be an annual profit. Lawrence LJ in the Court of Appeal stated: 'In the case of an isolated transaction . . . there is really no middle course open. It is either an adventure in the nature of trade, or else it is simply a case of sale and resale of property.' These words were quoted with approval in the House of Lords.

*Chapter 6*

# Tax Aspects of Property Dealing Companies

**6.1** A property dealing company is one that buys properties with a view to generating profits by reselling them. It is carrying on a trade. The profits that it makes on buying and selling properties are taxed in the same way as the profits of any other trading company.

## Computation of Profits

**6.2** Like any other trading company its profits are computed in accordance with generally accepted accounting practice subject to the proviso that an expense is deductible as a trading expense only if:

(*a*) it is wholly and exclusively laid out or expended for the purposes of the trade,

(*b*) it is not of a capital nature, and

(*c*) it does not fall within any of the other specific exclusions set out in *ICTA 1988, s 74*.

### Date of Disposal or Acquisition

**6.3** In particular there are no special rules to determine the dates of disposal or acquisition of properties. This is not necessarily the contract date, which is the rule that applies for capital gains tax. Indeed, there is no compelling reason why a company should not adopt the date of the purchase contract as the acquisition date and the date of completion of a sale as the disposal date. Many companies adopt such a policy. Clearly it would need to be followed consistently. Whilst some Inspectors of Taxes may challenge such a policy it is in accordance with the accounting concepts of prudence and not anticipating profits which underlies the concept of the reliability of the reported profits. The company is under an obligation to complete the purchase of a property immediately it has contracted to buy it. It is therefore proper to recognise that liability in the company's accounts, which a policy of treating the purchase as taking place at the date of the contract does. When the company sells a property all it obtains by entering into a sale contract is a right to enforce completion subject of course to its establishing its title to the property. Unless the purchaser has the necessary funds that right is not worth very much. The tax cases, if not exactly littered with instances of things going wrong between contract and completion, certainly contain several examples of what can go wrong. For example, in *Magnavox Electronics Co Ltd (in liquidation) v Hall (59 TC 610)*, the purchaser was not able to raise the funds to complete the sale and the company took 13 months to find a new purchaser, and even then at a much reduced price. In *Zim Properties Ltd v Proctor (58 TC 371)*, the vendor was unable to demonstrate good title to the property and the purchasers accordingly refused to complete the transaction. It is also not unheard of for the parties to a contract to change their minds for one reason or another and for the contract to be discharged by mutual agreement. There are accordingly risks that accounts may reflect profits on 'sales' that never in fact take place if the disposal of a property is recognised immediately a contract is signed. In such circumstances it is more prudent to wait until completion has taken place before recognising the sale.

**6.4** This is not to say that it would not be equally proper and in accordance with generally accepted accounting practice to recognise a disposal when a contract is entered into. In the vast majority of cases the sale will have taken place before the accounts are finalised and if anything has gone wrong with the sale an appropriate adjustment can be made in the accounts to eliminate the false sale. It is, however, up to the taxpayer, not the Inland Revenue, to decide the accounting principles which he opts to adopt. Provided that these are generally accepted by the accounting profession as appropriate to the taxpayer's circumstances and that they are applied consistently it is well established that the Revenue cannot require the taxpayer to prepare his accounts on some other basis (see, for example, *Symons v Weeks and Others (56 TC 630)* and *Heather v P-E Consulting Group Ltd (48 TC 293)*).

**6.5** In a Privy Council case, *Eckel v Board of Inland Revenue (1989 STC 305)*, which was concerned with similar legislation of Trinidad and Tobago, it was held that a property trading disposal did not take place on the contract date, but rather at the time of completion, as money can only be treated as a trade debt when the trader has done all that is required to earn it. The facts were somewhat special. The taxpayer had contracted to sell land to a company controlled by herself in 1970. The conveyances were in 1973 and 1974 and the Revenue raised assessments for those years. She initially claimed that she was not trading but before the Privy Council abandoned that claim and instead contended that the sale had taken place in 1970, which was by then out of time for assessment. In 1970 the taxpayer did not have legal title to the land; she obtained that later. It seems doubtful whether this decision can be used to require a trader to adopt completion rather than contract date if he chooses not to do so.

**Stock in Trade**

**6.6** The land or properties owned by a dealing company at the end of its accounting year represent its stock in trade and work in progress. If the company is developing its sites the building costs are of course part of the cost of the stock in trade at the year end insofar as they relate to completed buildings, or part of the cost of work in progress on buildings still in the course of construction. Accordingly, such expenditure will not be deductible for tax purposes until the property is sold. Where money is borrowed for the construction of specific properties, some Inspectors contend that the interest on that borrowing is part of the cost of the building work and ought similarly to be added to the work in progress and not treated as an overhead expense of the company. This defers the obtaining of tax relief until the property is disposed of. The rules on loan relationships require the accruals basis to be used in respect of interest to allocate payments to the period to which they relate (see 4.67(*c*)), which may well support a claim that the interest needs to be treated as a cost of acquisition of the stock of properties. Prior to 1 April 1996 this problem did not arise if the interest was a charge on income (see 4.83) as a company was statutorily entitled to relief for charges when it paid them. Unfortunately, a company was not entitled to choose whether to treat interest as a charge or a trading expense. No payment which was deductible in computing profits, or any description of profits, for purposes of corporation tax could be treated as a charge on income (*ICTA 1988, s 338(2)*). It was held in *Wilcock v Frigate Investments Limited (55 TC 530)* that the word 'deductible' does not import a requirement for a formal claim for a deduction. Bank interest paid by a property dealing company is properly deductible in calculating its trading profits in accordance with normal principles of commercial accounting and is thus excluded from the possibility of being a charge on income. It is difficult in most cases to rebut a contention that where interest on a project-related loan constitutes a trading expense it should be treated as part of the cost of the stock. Where interest is not on a borrowing for a specific development but is an overhead of the business the deduction is normally claimable on an accruals basis like any other business expense.

**6.7** If a dealing company erects houses on its land and grants long leases of them at a premium it will have made a part disposal of items that it holds as trading stock. It was held in *B G Utting & Co Ltd v Hughes (23 TC 174)* that to calculate its profits it must treat the premiums as income and must bring into account the reversionary interest retained at the lower of its cost or net realisable value, which is the normal method of valuing stock in trade. The cost of the reversionary interest was arrived at by adopting the formula:

$$\text{cost of reversion} = \begin{array}{c}\text{expenditure}\\ \text{on house}\end{array} \times \frac{\text{market value of the reversion}}{\begin{array}{c}\text{premium}\\ \text{received}\end{array} + \begin{array}{c}\text{market value of}\\ \text{the reversion}\end{array}}$$

**6.8** Where builders sell houses subject to the creation of ground annuals or feu duties, by contrast, the Courts have required the market value of the ground annuals to be brought into account as income (*CIR v John Emery & Sons (20 TC 213)*; *McMillan v CIR (24 TC 417)*). The logic is that in the *Utting* case (6.7 above) the entire interest in the house was not disposed of whereas in the *Emery* case the entire interest was disposed of for a consideration consisting of an immediate cash sum plus the right to a stream of annual payments. To arrive at the true profit the market value of that right needs to be brought into account.

## Capital Allowances

**6.9** A dealing company is not entitled to claim capital allowances in respect of expenditure on properties held as trading stock. This is because *CAA 2001, s 4(2)* provides that capital expenditure – which is what attracts allowances – does not include any sum which is allowed to be deducted in computing trading profits.

**6.10** Where a property dealer lets a property which is held as trading stock the tenant may be entitled to claim capital allowances to the extent that he pays a premium for his lease. In relation to industrial buildings allowance an election can be made under *CAA 2001, s 290* to treat the grant of the lease as if it were a sale of the relevant interest for the amount of the premium. Where a building incorporates equipment that has become a landlord's fixture and neither the landlord nor any other person is entitled to claim capital allowances in respect of it, the lessee is deemed to have incurred expenditure on the fixture equal to the part of the premium that is attributable to the fixture (*CAA 2001, s 184*) (see 10.51 onwards).

## Losses

**6.11** A loss incurred by a dealing company can be dealt with in the same way as any other trading loss. It can be carried forward and set against future profits from the trade. Alternatively it can be set against general income of the accounting period in which the loss is incurred or, if this is insufficient, of the prior 12 months (the three prior years for accounting periods ended before 3 July 1997) (*ICTA 1988, s 393A(2)*). If the dealing company is a member of a group its trading loss can be surrendered to another group company under the group relief provisions. The loss cannot, however, be set against profits of other group companies for an earlier or later accounting period. If the accounting period of the dealing company is not identical to that of the other group company to which it wishes to surrender its loss, the loss can only be set against the profits of the other company for its corresponding accounting period.

If the expenses of a property dealer in relation to a let property exceed the income the excess can be treated as a trading expense; it need not be carried forward to later years as a Schedule A loss (Inspector's Manual, IM 1959).

## Section 776 (formerly ICTA 1970, s 488)

**6.12** A sale of the shares of a property dealing company attracts exemption from *ICTA 1988, s 776* provided that the company sells the whole of its trading stock (as at the date of the sale) in the normal course of its trade and so as to procure that all opportunity of profit in respect of the land arises to it (*ICTA 1988, s 776(10)*). It is usual to obtain a warranty from the purchaser of a controlling interest in the company that he will procure that this will happen. Such a warranty is not, of course, proof that the conditions of *section 776(10)* are fulfilled as far as the Revenue are concerned but, provided that the person giving it is a person of substance, it transfers the risk of an attack under the *section* to the purchaser. The exemption does not operate if an arrangement or scheme is effected as respects the land. A sale of a controlling interest of shares in a dealing company will automatically be caught by *section 776* if it does not come within this exemption even if it can be demonstrated that there was no tax avoidance motive. This is because *section 776(2)(b)* does not contain a motive test. The mere fact that the company holds land as trading stock is sufficient to trigger a charge. As the effect of *section 776* applying is likely to be that the profit on the disposal of the shares will be taxed as income it is clearly vital to seek to obtain the protection of *section 776(10)*. Unfortunately what the company does after it has been sold is not under the control of the vendor, but it is this that will determine the vendor's tax liability. *Section 776* is considered in detail in chapter 14.

## Other Matters

**6.13** The Inland Revenue rarely challenge the salaries drawn by the directors of trading companies (unless they do very little work in the business). A property dealing company is normally treated no differently to any other trading company in this respect, although the author has experienced cases where the Revenue have questioned salary payments by property dealing companies where these are extremely large, particularly if they are accompanied by large pension contributions. Accordingly, the profits of a property dealing company can normally be withdrawn from the company by this route without difficulty. Furthermore, if high salaries are drawn the company can also set up a director's pension scheme and make substantial contributions to it. Except where a pension scheme was set up before 14 March 1989, this is now less significant because of the 'cap' on new schemes which prevents pensions being funded in relation to earnings in excess of

£97,200 *per annum*. By contrast, it is very difficult to obtain tax relief for substantial salaries from an investment company and even more difficult for such a company to operate a pension scheme other than one paying very restricted benefits.

**6.14** Following the abolition of advance corporation tax, the removal of the cut-off point for employees' national insurance contributions, the increase in the rate of employers' national insurance to 11.8% and the introduction of the 20% savings rate for basic rate taxpayers, it can sometimes be more attractive to extract profits from a family company by way of dividend rather than as salary. This applies where the company pays the small companies rate of tax, which is comparatively unusual for property dealing companies, which tend to realise large amounts of profit at irregular intervals. Following the significant reduction in corporation tax rates from 1 April 1997 the effective rate on dividends for a basic rate taxpayer is 20% whereas that on remuneration is 30.23% (ignoring employees' national insurance). For a higher rate taxpayer the figures are 40% on dividends and 46.33% on remuneration. Where the full corporation tax rate applies the figures swing the other way, a dividend attracting tax of 47.5% for a higher rate taxpayer compared with 46.33% on remuneration (assuming no further employees' national insurance). Even where the small companies rate applies, it should be borne in mind that pension provision cannot be made against dividends, although from 6 April 2001 £3,600 p.a. can be paid into a stakeholder pension scheme even if the individual has no earnings. Pensions are generally a highly attractive form of tax shelter.

**6.15** Where a company paid a dividend prior to 6 April 1999 it also had to pay advance corporation tax (ACT) to the Inland Revenue. The ACT could be set against the corporation tax liability of the company for the accounting period in which the dividend is paid. In a dealing company, as all of its profits on its property transactions are trading profits, relief for ACT was normally obtainable very speedily. If the income of the accounting period was insufficient to allow full relief for the ACT, the excess ACT could be carried back and set against corporation tax in the six prior years. Alternatively it could be carried forward and set against corporation tax liabilities in subsequent years, including years after 6 April 1999 subject to a 'shadow ACT' restriction.

**6.16** There are a few special provisions that affect the computations of property dealing profits both for companies and individuals. These are considered at 22.43.

## Transactions Between a Dealing Company and an Associated Company

**6.17** If a property dealing company (one dealing in land or buildings or one whose profits on the sale of land or buildings are part of its trading profits) becomes entitled to a deduction in computing its trading profits in respect of the depreciation in value of any right subsisting against an associated non-dealing company, and that depreciation is not brought into account in computing the trading profits of the associated company, the associated company must be deemed to have received (on the last day of the period for which the dealing company claimed the deduction) income chargeable under Case VI of Schedule D of an amount equal to that deduction (*ICTA 1988, s 774(1)(a)(4)*).

**6.18** Similarly, if a dealing company makes to an associated non-dealing company any payment in respect of which it is entitled to a deduction in computing its trading profits, the non-dealing company must be treated as receiving Case VI income equal to that payment if it does not form part of its trading profits (*ICTA 1988, s 774(1)(b)*).

**6.19** If the non-dealing company is carrying on a trade it can elect to treat the deemed receipt as trading income rather than Case VI income (*ICTA 1988, s 774(2)*). If it carries on more than one trade it can choose the trade which is to be deemed to be in receipt of the trading income.

**6.20** The *section* does not apply to the writing off of a loan to the non-dealing company if it is carrying on a trade (or was formed to do so) and the loan was to meet expenditure which has proved abortive and for which the company is not entitled to claim tax relief. Nor does it apply to a payment to the non-dealing company to meet such expenditure (*ICTA 1988, s 774(3)*). It appears that a charge will still arise if the company is entitled to claim relief for the expenditure but has no income against which to set such relief – although in most cases the relief can then be given against the deemed income created by the section, thus negating the charge.

**6.21** The sort of circumstance at which the *section* is probably aimed is where a dealing company owns shares in an associated company as part of its trading stock and writes down the value of that stock, or where a dealing company lends money to an associated company which it writes off as a bad debt (although it would be very rare that a property dealing company could establish a trading deduction for it). However, the wording of *subsection (1)(b)* is very wide. It would seem to impose a charge on the purchase price of a property where a dealing company buys the property at market value from an associated investment company – although the author has never known the Revenue to seek to apply the *section* in such circumstances and it would clearly be unreasonable for them to do so. It could also apply if an investment company grants a lease at a premium to an associated dealing company.

**6.22** Two companies are associated for this purpose if one has control of the other or any person has control of both of them. A company has control of another if it has control either by itself or in conjunction with any person having control over it itself (*ICTA 1988, s 774(4)(d)(e)*). Control for this purpose means the power of a person to secure

(*a*) by means of the holding of shares or the possession of voting power in or in relation to that or any other body corporate, or

(*b*) by virtue of any powers conferred by the articles of association or other document regulating that or any other body corporate,

that the affairs of the first-mentioned body corporate are conducted in accordance with the wishes of that person (*ICTA 1988, s 840*).

# Tax Aspects of Property Investment Companies

**7.1** A property investment company is one that buys properties with a view to generating income from the rents that they produce. Although it may well hope to be able to sell its properties at some stage for more than their cost this expectation is incidental to the income generated from them. Its properties are not trading stock to be bought and sold. They are capital assets held to generate a yield. The profits on disposal of such properties are regarded as capital gains.

## Computation of Income

**7.2** An investment company is not carrying on a trade. Accordingly for tax purposes it does not calculate profits; it calculates its total income from all sources and sets against that its management expenses, charges on income and debits on loan relationships. The main source of income of a property investment company will of course be its rents. It calculates the taxable rental income in accordance with the normal Schedule A rules (see chapter 2), by reference to income earned in its accounting period. If the company has other types of income, such as bank interest, it similarly calculates the taxable amount in accordance with the rules appropriate to that income – Case III of Schedule D in the case of bank interest. Having calculated the taxable income from each source these are then aggregated, together with capital gains, to form total profits. From this the company is entitled to deduct its management expenses.

## Management Expenses

**7.3** The legislation gives little guidance as to what is covered by management expenses, other than that it includes commissions and excludes expenses that are deductible in computing income for the purposes of Schedule A (*ICTA 1988, s 75(1)*). The amount of any income, other than franked investment income and group income, 'derived from sources not charged to tax' must be deducted. It is not clear what this is intended to cover although, if pushed, the Revenue instance fees for clerical work in making entries in the share register! This seems questionable. Such a receipt is probably chargeable to tax under either Case I or Case VI of Schedule D. A company is chargeable to corporation tax 'on all its profits wherever arising' (*ICTA 1988, s 8(1)*), profits meaning income and chargeable gains (*ICTA 1988, s 6(4)(a)*). It is accordingly difficult to envisage how a company can receive income from sources not charged to tax. Only a UK-resident company can claim a deduction for management expenses. Accordingly it cannot be aimed at non-UK companies who would have income not subject to UK tax.

**7.4** The only helpful cases on what is a management expense are *London and Northern Estates Co Ltd v Harris (21 TC 197)*, in which it was held that surveyor's fees paid by a property owning company were not an expense of management, and *Southern v Aldwych Property Trust Ltd (23 TC 707)* in which the costs of advertising for tenants was similarly disallowed. In both cases the disputed expenditure would be deductible under Schedule A, i.e. they were expenses of managing the properties rather than of managing the company. The Inland Revenue invariably insist that all of the expenses of a property investment company should be analysed between expenses of managing its properties and expenses of managing the company itself, apportioning items such as directors' remuneration which relates to both functions. The property management expenses element is allowed as a Schedule A deduction. In the past if such expenses exceeded the rental income the excess had to be treated as a Schedule A loss which, unlike management expenses, could not be relieved against non-Schedule A income. However, the current Schedule A system allows such a set-off for companies (but not individuals or trusts) (see 2.48) so the distinction no longer seems important.

**7.5** In order to claim a deduction for management expenses a company must show not only that it is resident in the UK but also that it satisfies the definition of an investment company in *ICTA 1988, s 130* – a company 'whose business consists wholly or mainly in the making of investments and the principal part of whose income is derived therefrom'. A company which never has any income may not be able to satisfy this definition. A property investment company will normally have no trouble in meeting these tests. However, it is possible for a company to be neither an investment or a dealing company. Such a company cannot normally obtain tax relief for its expenses. Until recently there was no UK case law on what is an investment company although there were two Irish cases (where the definition is almost identical), *Howth Estate Company v Davies (2 ITC 74)* and *Casey v The Monteagle Estate Company Ltd (3 ITC 313)*. The question has now been considered by the UK courts in *Cook v Medway Housing Society Ltd (1997 STC 90)*. The company was a non-profit making company formed to acquire the housing stock of Rochester-upon-Medway City Council. The Revenue disputed whether the Society's business consisted wholly or mainly in the making of investments. It was conceded by both sides that 'making investments' includes holding them and that the principal part of the company's income was derived from its property portfolio. It was held that 'the term "investment" means the laying out of moneys in anticipation of a profitable capital or income return'. The fact that the company was a not-for-profit one did not conflict with such an objective as the company could generate a profit to plough back into achieving the company's overriding objective. Accordingly the purpose and nature of the business was in principle that of holding investments. The judge went on to say 'In determining what is the business of a company for the purpose of *s 130* , it is necessary to have regard to the quality, purpose and nature of the company and its activities, and this includes the objects clause in the Memorandum of Association of the company . . . It is relevant to have regard to the actual activities carried on by the taxpayer at the relevant date, but if these are viewed without regard to the taxpayer's past history or future plans they may give only a partial and incomplete picture. The critical question is whether the holding of assets to produce a profitable return is merely incidental to the carrying on of some other business, or is the very business carried on by the taxpayer . . . The very business of the society is the provision of housing at a return below the market return, but none the less a return producing a profit'. Another aspect was dealt with by Special Commissioners in *Tintern Close Residents Society Ltd v Winter (1995 Sp C 7)* and 12 similar cases. The company was incorporated 'to acquire, hold, manage, maintain and deal' with the Tintern Close estate. The Special Commissioner held that in looking at whether the business of a company consists wholly or mainly in the making of investments it is necessary to look at why the company was incorporated (was this to acquire assets in order to turn them into account for the purpose of profit so that it could be distributed to the shareholders), what its activities are, if it holds investments whether the purpose of doing so is to make money from them, and whether the purpose and motive of the operations indicate that its main business is to make investments. Applying these tests she decided that although the company held land (the common areas and the freehold reversion to the houses) it does not do so to make money and that its business, in the sense of its functions and activities, is to manage and administer Tintern Close not to make investments. It was accordingly not an investment company. The Revenue have said that they agree with the Special Commissioner's approach and seek to explain it as confirming that the holding of investments incidental to the real purpose of a company does not necessarily involve it in carrying on a business of holding investments (Tax Bulletin Number 19, October 1995). By contrast it was held in *CIR v Tyre Investment Trust Ltd (12 TC 646)* that a company can make investments, and thus be an investment company, even though it never has any intention of turning them over.

The Special Commissioners have also held that the management company for the grounds of a residential development was not an investment company and in any event the principal part of its income was derived from members' annual subscriptions not from the making of investments (*White House Drive Residents Association v Worsley (1997*

*STC (SCD) 63)*). The annual subscriptions of such a company would normally be exempt from tax under either the mutual trading principle or the Revenue's interpretation of the *Landlord and Tenant Act 1987* (see 2.108), but in this case the company sought to deduct its management expenses from interest received, which is taxable.

**7.6** An interesting case is that of *Macniven v Westmoreland Investments Ltd (1998 STC 1131)*. The company had been incorporated in 1968 as a property holding company and was clearly an investment company from 1968 to 1988. It sold its last property in 1988 and used most of the proceeds to pay accrued interest on loans. It also purchased gilts with a comparatively small part of the proceeds in order to maintain its investment status. In January 1990 it bought a property from its shareholder as an investment as it was felt it would be more satisfactory for it to hold property investments. The Revenue accepted that the company was an investment company from 1990 but challenged its status in the interim – so as to disallow brought forward management expenses. They contended that the acquisition of the gilts and the new property were to display an investment activity when the company could have no main purpose of investment – as it had no funds to invest. The Special Commissioners held that the company made investments throughout and that as bank deposits were made in the course of its investment business the objectives of the company had never changed. The judge thought that the Commissioners were correct and this was upheld in both the High Court and the House of Lords.

## Charges on Income and Debits on Loan Relationships

**7.7** As indicated above a deduction can be claimed for charges on income, namely annuities and other annual payments (including royalties and excluding payments in respect of loan relationships and any sums which are or, but for any exemption would be, chargeable under Schedule A (e.g. rent payable)). (*ICTA 1988, s 338(3)*). The most common type of annual payment by a property investment company is now a payment under deed of covenant.

**7.8** A deduction can also be claimed for deficits on loan relationships (see 4.52), which will give relief for most interest payments. Prior to 1 April 1996 annual interest and bank interest constituted charges on income. Short interest (see 4.90) did not qualify as a charge on income unless it was bank interest. The Revenue generally took the view – which in most cases is almost certainly correct – that short interest is not an expense of managing the company; it is a cost of raising finance, and thus cannot qualify as a management expense. An investment company may also have greater difficulty than a dealing company in obtaining relief for interest paid to non-UK residents, as *ICTA 1988, s 340* (head (*c*) in 4.92 above) applies only to trading companies, such as a property dealing company.

## Capital Allowances

**7.9** A property investment company will be entitled to claim capital allowances on qualifying expenditure. Allowances are given, *inter alia*, for capital expenditure on:

(*a*) plant and machinery;

(*b*) industrial buildings;

(*c*) commercial or industrial buildings in enterprise zones;

(*d*) qualifying hotels;

(*e*) agricultural buildings and works;

(*f*) cemeteries and crematoria;

(*g*) dwelling-houses let on secured tenancies;

(*h*) mines and oil wells;

(*i*) research and development;

(*j*) certain fire safety works;

(*k*) certain works at sports grounds; and

(*l*) certain expenditure on security.

**7.10** The legislation on capital allowances is considered in chapter 10. It must be realised that much of the work on the construction of a modern building can constitute plant and machinery for capital allowance purposes. Where a building will not itself qualify for allowances under one of the above heads, such expenditure should be identified and the appropriate allowances claimed. Even if a building qualifies under a different head, e.g. it is an industrial building, it may still beneficial to segregate the expenditure on plant and machinery as this frequently attracts a higher rate of allowances. Indeed the Revenue have expressed the view that, strictly speaking, expenditure on plant that becomes an integral part of a building is not expenditure on the construction of the building and therefore cannot qualify for industrial buildings allowances even if the taxpayer wants to claim them (Inland Revenue Extra-Statutory Concession B31). Plant in an industrial building is often a long-life asset (see 10.81) in which case it is unlikely to be worthwhile to segregate it. Whilst most people now realise that allowances can be claimed in relation to a new building it is still frequently not appreciated that allowances are often also available on the purchase of a second-hand building.

## Surplus Management Expenses

**7.11** An investment company does not make 'losses' for tax purposes, although it can of course incur Schedule A losses, which can be set against general income, and Case VI losses, which can be used only against future income of that same type and cannot be set against other income of the company, even for the accounting period in which the loss was incurred. Clearly, however, an investment company's management expenses can exceed its profits (which is income plus taxable capital gains), so that in commercial terms it has a loss. Such a surplus of management expenses is carried forward and treated as if it were management expenses of the next accounting period. If the brought-forward surplus serves to increase a surplus in the next period it will also increase the amount carried forward in that year (*ICTA 1988, s 75(3)*). In effect, a surplus of management expenses can be carried forward indefinitely until it is relieved. This is subject to the proviso that if the company were to cease to be an investment company, such as, for example, by becoming a trading company or by ceasing its business, any unrelieved management expenses at that stage would be lost. They could not be carried forward to a subsequent period in which the company might revert to being an investment company. Where an investment company has charges on income which it has paid wholly and exclusively for purposes of its business, or capital allowances which cannot be relieved in the accounting period to which they relate, they can be added to the surplus management expenses and treated as management expenses of the next accounting period (*ICTA 1988, s 75(3)(4)*).

**7.12** Unlike the loss of a dealing company, surplus management expenses cannot be carried back to an earlier accounting period. It should not be forgotten, though, that the capital allowances rules may allow unrelieved allowances to be carried back. In particular *CAA 2001, s 260(3)* allows capital allowances to be carried back to the extent that they cannot be relieved in the year to which they relate, and set against profits of any description of the preceding accounting period (or a part equal in length to the length of the current accounting period).

## Capital Gains

**7.13** Capital gains (or chargeable gains as they are statutorily termed) of an investment company are calculated separately from its income, but added to the income to arrive at the taxable profits of the accounting period. The differences in the calculation rules – in particular rebasing to 31 March 1982, which will eliminate from tax most gains accruing prior to that date, and indexation (and in the case of an individual or trust, tapering relief from 6 April 1998) – are likely to mean that capital gains will attract a lower effective rate of tax than income.

**7.14** If an investment company enters into a sale and leaseback transaction to raise finance, the Revenue are unlikely, in most cases, to claim that the sale is an indication that the property was bought for dealing purposes. They may well do so if the sale realises a substantial profit and the value of the lease taken back is low, so that the reality of the transaction is that the company has disposed of substantially the whole of its interest in the property. It would be difficult for them to establish a dealing motive if the company is left with the ability to generate a substantial profit rental under its leaseback.

**7.15** For the purposes of taxation of capital gains, a sale and leaseback is regarded by the Revenue as a part disposal even though the legal form of the transaction may be a complete sale combined with the grant of a lease. There is a part disposal of an asset where an interest or right is created by the disposal or where on making the disposal any description of the property remains undisposed of (*TCGA 1992, s 21(2)(b)*). It is not wholly clear that a sale and leaseback falls into either of these categories if the form of the transaction is looked on alone. The substance of the transaction is undoubtedly that the right to the leaseback is a right created by the disposal. It is in any event normally in the taxpayer's interest to accept that the transaction is a part disposal as this reduces the immediate capital gain. It must not, however, be overlooked that by applying the part disposal rules a sale and leaseback will give rise to a capital gain even if, as is often the case, the sale price does not exceed the cost. This is because it is necessary to value the leaseback, being the part of the asset deemed to be undisposed of. If the rent payable under the lease is less than the open market rent for the property, or the rent review pattern under the lease is less burdensome than is normal in the market, the lease will have a value. The capital gains tax base cost of the asset is then apportioned between the sale price of the interest sold and the value of the lease retained using the formula:

$$\text{base cost of interest sold} = \text{cost of entire interest} \times \frac{\text{sale}}{\text{price}}$$

## Close Investment-holding Companies

**7.16** *FA 1989, s 105(2)* introduced a new class of investment company, the close investment-holding company. Fortunately, most of the teeth of this animal were drawn prior to enactment, whereas the Chancellor's original concept of a close investment company would have included all close property companies and would have subjected them to a very harsh tax regime.

**Definition**

**7.17** A close investment-holding company is a close company that does not fall within a number of exceptions. Fortunately the exceptions are sufficiently widely drawn that very few property companies are likely to be close investment-holding companies. A company will not be such a company during an accounting period if it exists wholly or mainly (see 7.18 below) for any one or more of the following purposes.

(*a*) Carrying on a trade on a commercial basis.

(*b*) Making investments in land or estates or interests in land where the land is (or is intended to be) let to anyone other than

(i) a person who is connected with the company (within *ICTA 1988, s 839* – see Appendix 1), or

(ii) a person who is the spouse of an individual who is connected with the company, or who is a relative (brother, sister, ancestor or lineal descendant) or the spouse of a relative of such an individual – or of the spouse of such an individual.

(*c*) Holding shares in (or securities of, or making loans to) one or more companies each of which is either

(i) a 'qualifying company', i.e. one which is under the control of the relevant company or of another company that also controls the relevant company and which exists wholly or mainly for the purpose of carrying on a trade on a commercial basis or of making investments in land that fall within (*b*) above (or both), or

(ii) a company which is under the control of the relevant company or under common control with it and which itself exists wholly or mainly for the purpose of holding shares in (or securities of, or making loans to) one or more qualifying companies.

(*d*) Co-ordinating the administration of two or more qualifying companies.

(*e*) Existing for the purpose of a trade or trades carried on on a commercial basis by either

(i) one or more qualifying companies, or

(ii) a company that controls the relevant company.

(*f*) The making by one or more qualifying companies (or by a company that controls the relevant company) of property investments falling within (*b*) above.

Control for this purpose is as defined in *ICTA 1988, s 416*. A company in liquidation will not be a close investment-holding company in the accounting period immediately following the winding-up if it was not one in the last accounting period prior to the winding-up, although it can be one in subsequent accounting periods if the liquidation extends over more than a year. 'Where a trading company ceases to trade prior to commencement of winding up, it is the view of the Revenue that the company will be a close investment holding company for the accounting period immediately before commencement of winding up and thus also immediately thereafter' (Revenue Tax Bulletin, Issue 3). Thus, care will need to be taken to ensure that the company continues to trade, if at all possible, until it is wound up in order that *ICTA 1988, s 13A(2)* will apply.

**7.18** The Revenue usually regard the expression 'wholly or mainly' as meaning more than 50%. Accordingly it is likely that a property company will be a close investment-holding company only if more than 50% of its properties fall within categories (i) and (ii) in head (*b*) above. This of course assumes that the properties are similar. If they are not, the 50% test may need to be applied to the overall rents or the overall value of the portfolio. It needs to be borne in mind that the status of a close company has to be determined accounting period by accounting period. Accordingly if a company acquires any such proscribed properties it will be necessary to check in each accounting period whether such properties form the major part of the assets in that accounting period. It is of course the purpose for the existence of the company as a whole that needs to be looked at though. "Exists" implies the reason why the company is currently here, not why it was set up. A company whose only asset is a property with head (b)(i) or (ii) plus a large amount of cash may well be looking to invest that cash in investments that are not excluded items. If so the main reasons for the company's existence could well be to make those projected investments even though at the present time its income may derive solely from rent from a connected person.

## Consequences of Close Investment-holding Company Status

**7.19** A close investment-holding company cannot claim the benefit of the small companies rate of corporation tax (but is still an associated company for the purpose of calculating the relief due to other companies) (*FA 1989, s 105(1)*). Prior to 6 April 1999 it also suffered from the disadvantage that in certain circumstances shareholders could not claim a refund of the tax credit attaching to a distribution by the close investment-holding company (*FA 1989, s 106*). However, refunds of tax credits have ceased generally from that date.

## Other Matters

**7.20** It is often very difficult to obtain a deduction for remuneration paid to the directors of an investment company. Whilst the Revenue rarely challenge remuneration paid to directors of a property dealing company, they frequently resist such a deduction included in the management expenses of an investment company. In the leading case, *L G Berry Investments Ltd v Attwooll (41 TC 547)*, they allowed only £600 out of remuneration (in 1961 terms) paid of £1,800. The general approach is first to insist on the remuneration being apportioned between remuneration for managing the company's properties and that for managing the company itself. The first part will then be compared with what an estate agent would charge for doing the work. This would normally be between 7½% and 15% of the gross rent, depending on the work involved. Any excess would be disallowed unless the company can convince the Revenue that the nature of the properties or the services provided to tenants are such that they involve far greater work than an estate agent would be prepared to undertake. As management of the properties is generally the major work involved in an investment company, the Revenue would generally contend that only a very small salary is justifiable for managing the company itself. It is sometimes argued that a director is entitled to be remunerated for a significant amount of time that has been spent negotiating sales of properties, searching for new properties, or supervising the company's development programme. Whilst that is clearly correct, there is a risk that such a salary might be regarded by the Revenue as capital expenditure with the result that it would be taxable on the director but would not reduce the taxable income of the company. It is accordingly dangerous to pay such remuneration – although it is by no means clear that it is not properly deductible.

**7.21** The option of paying substantial pension contributions for directors is also generally not open to an investment company, partly because of the small size of the salaries that the Revenue will permit and partly because the benefits that can be provided are poor. The legislation on pension schemes lays down very strict rules, compliance with which will as of right enable only a fairly rudimentary pension to be provided (*ICTA 1988, s 590*). The legislation also gives the Revenue discretionary power to approve schemes which provide far more valuable pension benefits (*ICTA 1988, s 591*). As a matter of policy the Revenue have opted not to exercise these discretionary powers to enable investment companies to provide greater benefits than those under *section 590*. From 6 April 2001, where a person has no other pension provision, up to £3,600 p.a. can be paid into a stakeholder pension scheme (a form of personal pension scheme) irrespective of whether or not the individual has earnings and irrespective of the source of any earnings.

*Chapter 8*

# Problems of Development

## Corporation Tax

**8.1** Development can be either a trading or an investment operation. It is not a separate category taxed on its own. What determines its nature is whether it is intended to retain or sell the property after carrying out the development. If the intention is to let it and retain it to benefit from the rental flow, it is an investment. If it is intended to sell it, it is a trading or dealing transaction.

**8.2** A sale of an interest as part of a financing operation to enable the balance to be retained as an investment will not necessarily make the transaction a trading transaction. Problems can sometimes arise where there is a mixed motive. It is 'not possible for an asset to be both trading stock and permanent investment at the same time, nor to possess an indeterminate status – neither trading stock nor permanent asset. It must be one or other' (Lord Wilberforce in *Simmons v CIR* (see 5.21 above)). Where there is a mixed motive on acquisition the dominant motive will usually determine the property's status (see *Kirkham v Williams*, 5.27 above). For example, a developer may want to create an office investment. He knows that to obtain planning permission he will need to incorporate a residential element in his scheme. He does not want to have a residential investment. He therefore buys the site with the intention that he will include flats in the development scheme which he will sell to occupiers. It is probable that the erection of the flats is a trading transaction following *Iswera v Ceylon Commissioner of Inland Revenue* (see 5.26) although this is by no means certain. In that case the taxpayer had to acquire and resell land she did not want in order to obtain land that she did. This is not necessarily the same thing as being required to use for a purpose that the owner did not intend land that is bought as an investment. It is possible that would be regarded not as having formed an intention to deal in the flats but as a premature realisation of part of the investment. However the sale of the flats is dealt with, the fact of their sale will not affect the dominant investment motive for the remainder of the development.

**8.3** Very few problems arise in practice where a property development is a trading transaction. The scope of allowable deductions under

Case I of Schedule D is very broad and it is difficult to envisage any expenditure attributable to the building or the development that will not meet the 'wholly and exclusively' requirement.

## Interest Payable

**8.4** The problems arise where the development is of an investment property. The first point to watch is the allowability of interest during the development period, especially where the development is being financed by an institution other than by way of a simple loan – as will normally be the case. Is the 'interest' really interest, i.e. is there a loan? If what is described as interest in the finance agreement is simply an arithmetical figure in a calculation it will not qualify for tax relief at all (see 4.108 above). Even if interest is genuinely payable, in some cases tax relief will be due only when it is actually paid. If it is rolled up, the relief will be deferred (see 4.71). Prior to 1 April 1996 relief on bank interest was not normally due until it was paid, although for corporation tax purposes interest paid to a bank carrying on a bona fide banking business in the UK (or to a UK stockbroker or discount house) was regarded as paid when it was debited to the company's account in the lender's books (*ICTA 1988, s 338(3)*). It was held in *MacArthur v Greycoat Estates Mayfair Ltd (1996 STC 1)* that this applied to both annual interest and to bank interest. Interest was probably not paid if it was debited to an overdrawn account though, at least if subsequent credits were not made to the account in the year to cover the charge (*Paton v CIR (21 TC 626)*). This was reaffirmed in *Minsham Properties Ltd v Price (1991 STC 718)*. The position is probably different if the lender makes a transfer from a fresh loan account to cover the interest debited to the original loan account. The Revenue may well contend that the *Furniss v Dawson* principle applies in such circumstances, though, and that the reality of the transaction is that no payment of interest has been made. Where interest is rolled up it must be borne in mind that charges on income of an investment company cannot be carried back and deficits on loan relationships carried back cannot be offset against capital gains. Accordingly, on a sale, care may be needed to ensure that the interest payment does not occur in a later accounting period than that in which the capital gain crystallises. As the capital gain arises on the date of the sale contract and the interest will normally be paid on the redemption of the mortgage at completion, this can be a major problem if the two dates straddle the company's accounting date.

## Capital Allowances

**8.5** It must also be borne in mind that the structuring of a development can significantly affect the right to capital allowances. In general, the person who is entitled to claim such allowances is the person who incurs the qualifying expenditure. However, expenditure cannot be regarded as having been incurred by a person for capital allowances purposes to the extent that it has been, or is to be, met directly or indirectly by any other person (*CAA 2001, s 532*). Furthermore, if the person who incurs capital expenditure subsequently disposes of his interest in the building, he will cease to be entitled to capital allowances and the allowances already given will be withdrawn by way of a balancing charge. If, as commonly happens, as part of a financing agreement the developer's initial interest in the property is sold to the institution, care may need to be taken to ensure that the developer retains the right to the allowances – particularly if the institution is a pension fund that cannot benefit from capital allowances. One possible route is to take advantage of *CAA 2001, s 538*. This provides that where, for the purpose of a trade carried on or to be carried on by him or by a tenant of land in which he has an interest, a person contributes a capital sum to expenditure on the provision of the asset, that contribution is to be treated as expenditure by him on the asset (with the expenditure by the person who incurred it being reduced accordingly). He will be entitled to claim allowances even though he does not own the asset. If the institution wants to own the property during the development phase for its own commercial protection, it may be possible for the developer to make a contribution to it. One point to watch is that the word 'contribution' implies part only of the cost. If the developer contributes 99% of the cost there is a risk that it would be held that he has not made a contribution to the cost but rather that he has met the expenditure on the asset. As he would not own the asset this would result in a complete loss of the right to claim capital allowances. A contribution of up to about two-thirds of the cost seems to be readily accepted by the Revenue. A significantly higher contribution could be risky.

## Site Assembly

**8.6** A development often involves a site assembly. This can raise a number of points to watch. For example, an exchange of two pieces of land, such as giving site B to the owner of site A in exchange for site A, will be a disposal and an acquisition by both parties for both capital gains tax and stamp duty purposes. The fact that no cash may change hands, or that only a small equalisation payment may be made, does not mean that tax can be ignored. Both parties may be crystallising large tax liabilities. Where the exchange involves the developer not merely swapping site B for site A but also agreeing to erect a building on site B at his own cost, the cost to him of site A is likely to depend on the exact terms of his agreement with the vendor. If the agreement is to exchange the sites and to erect a building on site B, the cost of site A is probably the value of site B plus the cost of erecting the building. If the agreement is to provide the vendor with site B with the completed building on it, the cost of site A is almost certainly the value of the land and building on site B, which may be substantially greater than the aggregate of the value of the site and the cost of erecting the building. The tax treatment of the difference between these two figures will also need to be considered. If site B was bought specifically to swap it for site A, its purchase, the erection of the building, and its swap for site A is probably a trading transaction, and the difference between the cost and the exchange value a dealing profit. If it was not bought specifically, consideration will need to be given as to whether it was initially acquired as trading stock or as an investment – and if the latter whether, when the decision to offer it in exchange for site A was taken, it may have been appropriated to trading stock.

**8.7** Site assembly frequently involves not merely the purchase of land but also the need to obtain vacant possession of it. For a dealing company, a payment to a tenant to give up his tenancy should be allowable as a Schedule D, Case I deduction when the property is sold. The investment company needs to satisfy the fairly stringent conditions of *TCGA 1992, s 38* before such an expense can be deductible. The limited expenditure allowed under this provision is set out at 11.4 onwards.

**8.8** The only one of the heads into which a payment to a tenant to secure vacant possession can fall is head (*b*)(i), enhancement expenditure. The obtaining of vacant possession certainly enhances the value of the investor's freehold; but is it reflected in the state or nature of the freehold at the time of the disposal? Often the answer to the question will be 'Yes', but by no means always, and sometimes it is by no means clear. Suppose a tenant had ten years to run on his lease and a payment is made to him to surrender it prematurely. If the developed building is sold 15 years later the payment will not be reflected in the nature of the freehold at that time as the lease would have expired in any event so that there would have been no need to make the payment to create the unencumbered freehold. However, the developed building will have a new tenant paying a significantly higher rent. The payment may well be reflected in the state of the freehold insofar as it enabled the development to be carried out and the new tenant installed. If, had the development been delayed until the original tenant's lease had expired, the new tenant could have been installed by the time of the disposal with his next rent review falling on the same date as his actual review, it is highly unlikely that the payment to the tenant can be said to be reflected in the state or nature of the developed building at the time of disposal. It may have made the development economically viable by reducing delays, but that, to the author, seems to be a different thing. If the tenant was a statutory tenant, either on a monthly tenancy or holding over on a lease that has expired, it will in many cases be unlikely that a payment to him to speed up his eviction will be reflected in the state or nature of the completed development when it is ultimately sold. To the extent that the payment represents statutory compensation that had to be paid to obtain vacant possession at all, rather than to obtain it at an earlier date than if proceedings for possession had been taken, there should be no problem.

**8.9** If a tenant is not prepared to accept a payment to move out but instead insists on being provided with alternative accommodation, the cost of providing that accommodation is probably not enhancement expenditure for capital gains tax purposes. It is difficult to contend that it is incurred wholly and exclusively *on the asset*, i.e. the property being developed. Although the need to obtain vacant possession of the asset is the cause of the expenditure in buying the new property, as a separate distinct asset is obtained the courts are likely to regard the expenditure as incurred on the new property not the development one. If instead of buying alternative accommodation the developer makes a payment to a third party (which could be its wholly owned subsidiary) in consideration of the third party undertaking to rehouse the tenant this could well constitute enhancement expenditure on the development property. Another route might be to agree with the tenant a figure of compensation with a proviso that payment is to be satisfied by the provision of accommodation at a rent at under market value. In *Chaney v Watkis (58 TC 707)* the taxpayer bought a house which was occupied by his mother-in-law, Mrs Williams. Some years later, in order to sell the house with vacant possession, he agreed to pay her a capital sum of £9,400. Before completion of the sale he decided to build an extension to his own house (at a cost far in excess of £9,400) to house his mother-in-law, and orally agreed with her that he should provide her with rent-free accommodation in his house for life in consideration of her releasing him from the obligation to pay the £9,400. It was held that, even though not paid as such, the £9,400 (or some lower figure) constituted enhancement expenditure. The basis of the decision was that the value of the new obligation undertaken (the provision of rent-free accommodation) was of equal value to the £9,400 that Mr Chaney had contracted to pay. The judge in fact remitted the case to the Commissioners to determine if this was the case. If they felt the value to be less than £9,400, only the lesser amount would be deductible as enhancement expenditure – presumably because by agreeing to accept the accommodation in lieu of the £9,400 Mrs Williams would be deemed to have waived her right to any difference between the £9,400 and the value of the accommodation.

**8.10** Another problem with site assembly is that where land is held by a company, the controlling shareholders will sometimes not be prepared to permit the company to sell its land but would be willing to transfer the land to the developer by selling him all the shares in the company. The reason, of course, is that they hope to avoid one level of capital gains tax, i.e. they will pay tax only on the gain on their shares whereas if the company sells its land it will have a tax liability on the gain it makes and the after-tax amount of that gain will also reflect an increased gain to the shareholders on the disposal of their shares. The introduction of capital gains tax taper relief for individuals but not for companies aggravates this problem. The developer needs to bear very much in mind that the price he pays for the shares will not be deductible when he comes to calculate his gain on the ultimate disposal of the development. Where, as will normally be the case, the cost of the land is very much lower than its market value, the capital gains tax base cost of the owning company will be transferred to the developer, assuming that, after purchase, he transfers the land intra-group to the company that is assembling the site. The potential increase in his capital gains tax on disposal by having to take over a low base cost is a factor that the developer will normally wish to take into account – at least to some extent – in determining the price he is prepared to pay for the shares, i.e. this is likely to be lower than the price he would have paid for the land. How much lower is a matter for negotiation. It will depend on the developer's anxiety to have the land, on the potential tax saving for the vendors, and on the likelihood or otherwise of the developer wanting to dispose of an interest in the site either at the time of commencing development or the time of its completion. Where a company is purchased in order to acquire land that it owns, other factors may need to be considered. Does the company have losses that could be set against a capital gain if the property itself were sold? If so, it may be worthwhile purchasing the company and transferring the land in such a way that the capital gains tax exemption for intra-group transfers will not apply. Has the building attracted industrial buildings allowances? If so, will its transfer to the developing company trigger a balancing charge or can its demolition trigger a balancing allowance?

## Obtaining Planning Consents

**8.11** The costs of obtaining the planning consent on which the development is based will clearly form part of the deductible costs of the development. The abortive costs of unsuccessfully seeking planning consents, or of successfully seeking a planning consent which is subsequently abandoned, will not normally qualify as a deduction in calculating a capital gain. They will, of course, qualify as a trading expense in a dealing company. Sometimes, however, a developer will apply for consent in the knowledge that it is likely to be refused in order to narrow down the options open to the local authority when he puts in a revised application or to ascertain the planning criteria that are likely to be applied if he cannot obtain a sufficiently clear indication of this from the planning officers. The expenditure in such cases can be argued to be reflected in the state of the completed development as it did, and was intended to, facilitate the obtaining of the ultimate planning consent, which may well not have been obtained without the preliminary application having been made. Similarly, where an application for consent is made and then rejected, a lot of the work on preparing detailed plans and on site investigation may be work that would have been needed for the next application which may be successful. Accordingly, it can be argued that at least the cost of these works is reflected in the nature of the developed building. It must not be overlooked, though, that to qualify for a deduction, enhancement expenditure has to be wholly and exclusively incurred on the asset for the purpose of enhancing its value. If there is a dual purpose the expenditure cannot qualify. It is arguable that expenditure on application A was for the purpose of enhancing the value of the site, even though in a different manner to the enhancement arising from application B. It is not certain that it is expenditure incurred 'on the asset' if the planning application for which it was incurred never reflects in an increase in value of the asset. Investigation of the circumstances of each individual case is needed to ascertain whether a claim for a deduction for part of the expenditure on abortive applications might be sustainable.

**8.12** There is no requirement that the enhancement in value of the property must equal or exceed the amount of the expenditure. If expenditure of £10,000 results in a £2,000 increase in the value of the property the entire £10,000 appears to qualify as enhancement expenditure. 'Appears' because it is possible that the entire £10,000 is not 'expenditure reflected in the state . . . of the asset', only £2,000 of the expenditure being so reflected. However, the author has never known the Revenue to seek to raise such a contention.

**8.13** It is nowadays commonplace for a local authority to look for some specific benefit to the community as a condition for granting planning permission for a development of any substance. A planning authority is empowered to enter into legally binding agreements with a developer under *Town and Country Planning Act 1990, s 106* (formerly *Town and Country Planning Act 1971, s 52*). If a *section 106* agreement requires the developer to incorporate, say, an open space or a roadway in his development and transfer the land to the local authority, the tax treatment of the cost of that land – and of any works that the planning authority requires the developer to do on it – may need careful consideration. It is by no means clear that the cost of that land is reflected in the state or nature of the retained land. As mentioned above expenditure probably does not need to be so reflected pound for pound. Even so it is difficult to argue that expenditure on land A is reflected in the state or nature of land B. It may well have increased the value of land B but that is not the appropriate test. Furthermore, the test of enhancement expenditure looks at the motive at the point it is incurred, and at that stage the motive would not normally have been to give the land to the local authority. It is doubtful if the gift to the local authority itself constitutes expenditure. It may, however, give rise to a capital gains tax loss which could be carried forward and set against the gain on ultimate disposal of the remainder of the land. An alternative argument is that the value of what has to be given under a *section 106* agreement is part of the price of obtaining planning consent. That value is satisfied by the work carried out or the value of the land given to the local authority, in the same way as the 'expenditure' in *Chaney v Watkis* (see 8.9 above) was the value of the consideration given in exchange for satisfying the obligation that had been entered into. There is no simple or straightforward answer. Each case needs to be looked at individually in the light of the knowledge that the problem of ensuring deductibility exists.

**8.14** If the *section 106* agreement requires a payment to be made to the local authority, or work to be carried out on land owned by the local authority, the problem is eased as the developer will have incurred expenditure. Even then, however, it is possible that it could be held that it is not incurred 'on the asset', the developer's site, even though it is incurred for the purpose of enhancing its value. Where the *section 106* agreement is clearly a condition of obtaining planning permission it would be surprising if the Revenue were to take such an argument. If the *section 106* agreement is entered into not to obtain the planning permission but to speed up its implementation there could be difficulties.

## Rent-free Periods

**8.15** A developer may well allow a tenant a rent-free period at the start of his lease. This should not give rise to tax problems provided that it is incorporated in the lease, as the landlord would never have been entitled to rent for that period. Prior to 1 April 1998 there could have been Schedule A difficulties if the lease provides for rent from its commencement and the rent-free period is contained in a side letter. This is because tax under Schedule A was normally charged on rent receivable, not rent received (see 2.58 above). If the entitlement to a rent payment is waived before it becomes due, it is arguable whether that payment has ever become receivable. It probably has not, but it is possible that all of the rent under a lease may have become receivable at the date the lease is entered into, in which case a waiver would be ineffective unless it could be shown to constitute a variation of the lease. This is no longer a problem under the new Schedule A rules. The VAT implications (see 17.300) also need to be considered.

## Appropriation from and to Trading Stock

**8.16** Although most of the problems of development affect only investment companies there is one of special significance to dealers. If a property which was acquired as trading stock is developed and a tenant found, what happens if the property is not sold? If there is a positive decision to retain the property there will be an appropriation of it from trading stock to fixed capital. On such an appropriation tax becomes chargeable as if the property had been sold at its market value as trading stock and reacquired as a fixed asset at the same price (*TCGA 1992, s 161(2)*). Accordingly, corporation tax becomes payable on the trading profit realised by the deemed disposal. If there is a large gain, this can be a major problem, as the appropriation will not of course generate any money with which to pay the tax. If the property is transferred intra-group from dealing company A to investment company B the same treatment applies. A is deemed to have appropriated the property from trading stock to investment and to have then transferred it as an investment to B.

**8.17** Many people fear that, if a property which is developed as trading stock is held for several years after development, the Revenue may contend that there has in fact been an appropriation from trading stock – and so seek to collect tax on the then value of the property – even though a positive decision to appropriate it was not taken. In practice this is a very rare occurrence. In the light of the comments of Lord Wilberforce in *Simmons v CIR* (see 5.21 above), it seems doubtful whether the status of an asset can legally alter without any positive change of intention by the owner. Accordingly, the status probably cannot accidentally be altered – although it must be remembered that a positive decision does not need to be evidenced in writing but can be inferred from a course of action. This applies in particular where there is no written evidence or the evidence that does exist is equivocal. It must also be admitted that a case exists (*British-Borneo Petroleum Syndicate Ltd v Cropper (45 TC 201)* (see 5.15 above)) where a company successfully convinced the High Court that there had been an appropriation many years earlier which the then directors had not appreciated to be such. Furthermore, there is a Privy Council case (*Richfield International Land & Investment Co Ltd v Inland Revenue Commissioner of Hong Kong* (see 5.23 above)) where the Revenue convinced the Hong Kong Commissioners that an appropriation had taken place in spite of contrary treatment in the accounts.

**8.18** Where a property held as trading stock is likely to be retained after development, consideration should be given to making an appropriation from trading stock before the development starts. Although this will crystallise a tax liability which will have to be funded from somewhere, the trading profit by reference to the value of the land prior to commencing development is likely to be substantially less than that on the completed development. The appropriation should either clearly be carried out by way of transfer to an investment company or care should be taken to evidence the decision to appropriate. At a minimum there should be a board minute resolving to appropriate the property as an investment, the company's objects clause should if necessary be changed to give it specific power to hold property as an investment, and the property should be taken out of trading stock and shown as a fixed asset in the accounts.

**8.19** It is of course equally possible that a company might want to appropriate to trading stock property that it initially acquired as an investment. For example, if a property bought to produce rents has been held for a comparatively short period when a decision to develop and sell it is taken, it may be felt that it would be difficult to demonstrate the investment intention. A specific appropriation as trading stock would reinforce this intention and might be worth considering if the increase in value up to that time is significant. The tax treatment in this instance is similar. The company has a capital gains tax disposal at market value and an acquisition as trading stock at the same price. If the property is transferred intra-group from an investment company to a dealing company (which is acquiring it as dealing stock), the latter is deemed to have acquired it as an investment and immediately appropriated it to dealing stock. However, in each case an election can be made to bring the asset into trading stock at its market value reduced by the amount of the chargeable gain that would otherwise have arisen on the appropriation, in which case no tax charge will arise at the time of the appropriation (*TCGA 1992, ss 173(1), 161(1)(3)*). This election can also be made where an individual appropriates a property from investment to trading stock.

**8.20** Now that the rate of tax on income and capital gains is the same for companies it is difficult to imagine circumstances where the election would not be beneficial. It even preserves the benefit of the indexation allowance up to the date of the appropriation. At worst it defers payment of the tax. As it is often easier to shelter income than capital gains from tax, the effect of transforming the capital gain into income in this way may well be to facilitate a reduction in the tax burden. The position is different for individuals, as taper relief can significantly reduce the effective tax rate on a capital gain and the election will forfeit that relief.

**8.21** In theory at least, the election can equally be made where the value of the property has fallen since its acquisition as an investment. The effect then is to convert a capital gains tax loss into a trading loss, which is generally far more attractive. There must, however, be a genuine appropriation. An unsuccessful attempt to do this was made in *Coates v Arndale Properties Ltd (59 TC 516)*. In that case the transfer to a dealing company took place on the same day as the dealing company resold it to a third party and for a price of exactly £10,000 less than the ultimate selling price. The House of Lords had no hesitation in holding that the dealing company did not acquire the property as dealing stock; it acquired it as a tax avoidance device. *Section 173(1)* applies only where the acquisition is as dealing stock. On the facts, that decision is not surprising. In *Reed v Nova Securities Ltd (59 TC 516)* (which concerned a transfer to a share dealing company, but the principle is the same), the assets, which consisted of shares and debts, were transferred several years before any sale and at a price that was considered to be a fair market value. The company's claim in respect of the transfer of debts succeeded in the House of Lords, although that in respect of shares failed on the basis that it was clear that they had no value at the date of transfer and as such could not have been acquired in the course of the company's trade. These cases were heard after the *Ramsay* decision, so there is a good chance that a genuine appropriation from investment to trading stock, when the property had some value and before any attempt to find a purchaser had been made, would be successful.

## Structuring Development Projects

**8.22** Most major developments require more finance than the developer can provide from his own resources. The person providing the development finance will normally have his own ideas as to how the transaction should be structured – especially to ensure that he has the best possible security over the property. Where a financing institution or other provider of funds seeks to dictate the development structure it is important to think through the tax consequences of its preferred structure. If this will involve extra tax, or bring forward the date when tax would otherwise be payable, it will increase the financing requirement. In these circumstances some sort of compromise on the structure can be in everyone's interest. For example, institutions prefer to hold the freehold interest in a site. This is better security than a lease and gives the holder the ability to take over the development if things go wrong. If the developer has contracted to acquire the site it may be relatively simple to pass over the benefit of the contract to the institution without generating a significant tax liability. If he has owned the site for several years and has fought to get planning permission for the development, a disposal of the freehold to the institution is likely to generate an immediate and large tax liability. In such circumstances the institution may well be content with a mortgage.

**8.23** If the financier takes an equity interest in the project consideration needs to be given as to how this is to be done. If he takes it as part of the loan agreement this could result in a distribution when it is paid out which may not be attractive (see 4.110 above). The most satisfactory structure is frequently a joint venture between the developer and the financier. However, if the finance is provided from an overseas source there may well be a risk that the UK developer could be regarded by the Revenue as an agent for the financier unless great care is taken. This would make him liable for the non-resident's tax on his share of the profits. It might be thought that the safest structure is a jointly-owned UK company. However, this can cause problems if the property is not sold immediately on completion of the development, as the two parties will normally have different requirements as to what is to be extracted from the company and how. It is too late to decide how the financier is to be paid out his share at the stage that the development is completed and the developer decides that he would rather like to keep the property as a long-term investment! At that stage the only way may be for the joint company to sell him the property and crystallise an unnecessary tax liability, or for him to buy in the other's shares which in the long term results in two taxable gains instead of only one. There is no 'best' structure. It will depend on the individual facts. It is, however, vital to think through the structure on day one.

# VAT

The principles of VAT are considered in Chapter 17. There are particular problems of VAT on development activity which are dealt with here.

**8.24** Most property transactions are exempt for VAT purposes. This means that VAT is not charged on the sale proceeds or rent received but no relief can be claimed for VAT borne on expenditure. Most services, including professional fees and building work, are standard-rated, i.e. VAT at the 17½% standard rate ('output tax') has to be added to the value of the services by the supplier. The effect is that, to the extent that he suffers VAT on his expenditure ('input tax') but cannot recover it from Customs, VAT is an additional cost for the property developer.

**8.25** New development – as opposed to refurbishment – is now either standard-rated or zero-rated. Zero-rating means that output tax is chargeable at the rate of nil per cent (instead of 17½%), but, because the output is thus taxable, relief can be claimed for input tax suffered on expenditure. This is an ideal situation to be in. VAT does not have to be collected on behalf of Customs but they will refund to the developer tax paid on his expenditure.

**8.26** This privileged status is restricted to residential development and development for 'relevant' charitable purposes, i.e. for use by a charity otherwise than in the course of a business. Care needs to be taken with such development as a very wide meaning has been given to 'business' for VAT purposes. It is by no means self-evident when zero-rating applies.

### Residential and Relevant Charitable Development

**8.27** The items eligible for zero-rating are as follows.

1. (*a*) The first grant (or assignment or surrender) by a person constructing a building of a major interest in (or in any part of) the building or dwelling or its site if it is either designed as a dwelling or number of dwellings or is intended for use solely for a relevant residential or relevant charitable purpose.

   (*b*) The first grant (or assignment or surrender) by a person converting a non-residential building (or a non-residential part of a building) into one designed as a dwelling or number of dwellings or intended for use solely for a relevant residential purpose, of a major interest in (or in any part of) the building or dwelling or its site.

2. The supply in the course of construction of either

   (*a*) a building designed as a dwelling or number of dwellings or intended for use solely for a relevant residential or relevant charitable purpose, or

   (*b*) any civil engineering work necessary for the development of a permanent park for residential caravans,

   of any services relating to the construction other than the services of an architect, surveyor or any person acting as a consultant or in a supervisory capacity.

3. The supply to a registered housing association (within the meaning of the *Housing Association Act 1985* or its Northern Ireland extension) in the course of conversion of a non-residential building (or part of a building) into one designed as a dwelling or number of dwellings or intended for use solely for a relevant residential purpose, of any services relating to the conversion other than the services of an architect, surveyor or any other person acting as a consultant or in a supervisory capacity.

4. The supply of building materials to a person to whom the supplier is supplying services within heads 2 or 3 above which include the incorporation of the materials into the building in question (or its site).

(*VATA 1994, Sch 8 Group 5* as substituted by *VAT (Construction of Buildings) Order 1995 (SI 1995 No 280)*).

Building materials for the purpose of head 4 means goods of a description ordinarily incorporated by builders in a building of the same description (or its site) subject to a number of specified exceptions (which are set out in 8.83) (*Group 5, Note 22*) and for this purpose the incorporation of goods in a building includes their installation as fixtures (*Note 23*).

**8.28** The eligible items from 1 April 1989 to 28 February 1995 were as follows.

1. The grant (or assignment) by a person constructing a building of a major interest in (or in any part of) the building or its site if it is either

   (*a*) designed as a dwelling or number of dwellings, or

   (*b*) intended for use for a relevant residential or charitable purpose.

2. The supply, in the course of either

   (*a*) the construction of a building designed as a dwelling or number of dwellings or intended for use for a relevant residential or charitable purpose, or

   (*b*) any civil engineering work necessary for the development of a permanent park for residential caravans,

   of any services other than the services of an architect, surveyor, or other person acting as a consultant or in a supervisory capacity.

3. The supply to a person of

   (*a*) materials, or

   (*b*) builders' hardware, sanitary ware and other articles of a kind ordinarily installed by builders as fixtures

   by a supplier who also supplies to the same person services within *item 2* above (or *item 2* of *Group 6* – see 9.19 below) which include the use of the materials or the installation of the articles.

(*VATA 1994, Sch 8 Group 5*).

**8.29** It will be seen that the main changes are as follows.

(*a*) Head 1 now applies only to the first grant – which is what Customs believe was always intended.

(*b*) Head 1 has been extended to conversions.

(*c*) The building must now be intended for use solely for the qualifying purpose.

(*d*) The supply of services must now be related to the construction.

(*e*) A new head 3 has been introduced. This is to reflect the special position of housing associations which are not normally permitted to sell their properties and so are unable to grant a major interest in their converted properties.

(*f*) The wording of the previous head 3 (now head 4) has been amended, partly because builders' hardware, etc. is now included in the definition of materials in *Note 22* and partly to relax the requirement that the services had to include the incorporation of the materials into the building, whereas now it is sufficient to merely use them in providing the services. The change also takes out of zero-rating the supply of materials in connection with the supply of services to listed buildings, etc. under *VATA 1994, Sch 8 Group 6* but only because it has been moved into *Group 6* itself.

•

The various relaxations were applied by extra-statutory concession from 21 July 1994.

**8.30** There are also some further zero-rated items in relation to 'protected buildings'. These are considered in 9.19 below. A residential developer needs to seek to bring his outputs within *item 1* above. If he cannot do so, it may be that his builder can bring his outputs – which will form a large part of the cost of the development – within *items 2* or *3* so that he does not need to charge VAT to the developer.

**8.31** The meaning of relevant residential and charitable development is considered in 17.28 and 17.34 respectively. To come within *item 1* the developer also needs to show that he is 'a person constructing a building'. This term is not defined. It obviously includes a builder constructing on his own land. Customs accept that it also includes a person who commissions someone else to construct a building for him provided that some supplies of services are made to him and he exercises some measure of control over the construction (such as control over design or planning) (C & E Notice 708, para 15.2). This would normally cover the developer where he owns the land. If, however, he does not own the land, but has sold it to an institution on terms that he will carry out the development on the institution's behalf and on completion will be granted a lease, the position needs to be looked at closely. His agreement will normally be a building lease, which is an interest in land and will probably suffice to make him the person constructing the building. If the developer is purely a project manager, with the building contract being between the builder and the institution, the developer is unlikely to be a person constructing the building.

**8.32** Even if the developer is the person constructing the building, the only outputs by him which qualify for zero-rating are grants by him of a major interest in all or part of the building. A major interest is the freehold or a lease for a term certain exceeding 21 years (*VATA 1994, s 96(1)*). In Scotland a lease of not less than 20 years is also a major interest (see 17.10). Accordingly, the sale of the freehold of a relevant building will qualify for zero-rating. So will the grant of a lease for a term of over 21 years. Zero-rating will apply only to any premium received for the lease or, if there is no premium, to the first rental payment under the lease – so as to generate a zero-rated supply and bring about the ability to reclaim input tax in relation to the development. Customs have indicated that it does not matter if the lease has a break clause, even one exercisable by either party, or terms that make it unlikely that it will in fact last for over 21 years. A lease for someone's life is not for a term certain and will not qualify for zero-rating. If a developer initially grants a lease of 21 years or less and on its expiry grants a new lease of over 21 years then, although the original lease will not qualify for zero-rating, the second ought to do so, provided that it is granted by the person who constructed the building (*C & E Commrs v Link Housing Association Ltd, 1992 STC 718* – see 17.12). This may, however, not be of great comfort. Unless the first lease is very short Customs are likely to contend that it determines whether or not the developer recovers the VAT he suffers on his development costs, even taking into account the decision in *C & E Commrs v Briararch Ltd (1992 STC 732)* – see 17.141.

**8.33** If it is not wished to grant leases to occupiers of over 21 years an overriding lease to the developer's subsidiary company for such a period might be considered, with it then granting shorter subleases to occupiers. This should at least enable VAT on the construction costs – and on the costs of subsequent refurbishments which remain the developer's liability as head landlord – to be recovered. It is possible that Customs might seek to apply the *Furniss v Dawson (55 TC 324)* principle to such a strategy although it is not clear whether this principle applies to VAT.

**8.34** Rents from residential properties are always exempt from VAT even if the option to tax (see 17.158 below) is exercised in respect of the building. The only exception is that the first rental payment under a lease can be zero-rated if there is no premium (*VAT 1994, Sch 8 Group 5, Note 14*). This is to trigger the right of recovery of VAT on the development costs. Rents for relevant charitable buildings are similarly always exempt with the exception that rents for an office building are taxable at 17½% if the landlord exercises the option to tax, even though part of the building is used for relevant charitable purposes.

## Other Development

**8.35** All other development of new buildings is now potentially chargeable to VAT at the 17½% standard rate. Where the development commenced before 1 August 1989 the VAT position depended on whether or not there was a disposal of the freehold of the building and when this took place, or on whether the transitional relief applies.

**8.36** The charge to tax arises by reason of two provisions. Although property disposals, assignments and grants of leases or licences are normally exempt from VAT unless the option to tax is exercised (see 17.95 below), there is a specific exclusion from exemption for a freehold disposal of either:

(i) a building which has not been completed and which is not a residential (or relevant charitable) one;

(ii) a new building which is not a residential one;

(iii) a civil engineering work which is in the course of being constructed; or

(iv) a new civil engineering work.

**8.37** A building or civil engineering work is new if it is disposed of within three years of completion. A disposal of a building prior to completion will always attract VAT. The detailed rules are considered in 17.65 to 17.71 below.

*Developments commencing between 1 August 1989 and 28 February 1995*

**8.38** When the government first announced their proposals for charging VAT on new commercial buildings they proposed to extend the charge to cover sales of building land. It proved impossible to devise a satisfactory definition of such land. They accordingly adopted a different approach. There would be a deemed disposal – and thus a VAT charge – on the first occasion after completion of a building (or civil engineering work) on which the developer makes an exempt supply (such as enters into a lease) or occupies the building at a time when he is not a fully taxable person. The relevant provisions are contained in *VATA 1994, Sch 10 paras 5, 6*. This charge has been abolished for construction commencing after 28 February 1995. (*VAT (Buildings and Land) Order 1995* (*SI 1995 No 279*)). This developer's self-supply charge was introduced because the *Sixth Directive* requires the UK to tax building land and no satisfactory definition of building land could be derived. The July 1993 Customs discussion paper said that 'temporary measures under EC Directives would permit us to exempt building land from VAT for the time being' but it would lead to distortion in VAT treatment between purchased and self-developed buildings, and to a loss of revenue which may have to be recovered elsewhere. This seems a clear warning that the *Buildings and Land Order* introduces a window for developers which is likely to be closed again fairly shortly.

**8.39** The provisions apply only where the construction of the building commenced between 1 August 1989 and 28 February 1995. Unfortunately the legislation gives no guidance as to when construction is to be treated as commencing for this purpose. In the passage of the *Bill* through Parliament the Minister stated that construction commences 'when on the particular facts a meaningful and ongoing start has been made to the construction process' (Hansard, Standing Committee G, 18 May 1989, Col 139). This is not particularly informative. It certainly suggests that the definition in the *Town and Country Planning Acts*, which was adopted for the purposes of betterment levy, development gains tax and development land tax, will not be applied by Customs. The Minister added that 'Customs would be looking for good evidence of such a start, and also evidence, for example, that planning permission had been obtained and building contracts let'. It appears from this that Customs will not accept that a development was commenced before 1 August 1989 if a contract merely for some foundation work had been entered into or if outline planning permission only was in force. The work done before that date must have been the start of a process leading inevitably to the construction of the building in contemplation, not merely some construction work that could be utilised at a later date when the building comes to be erected. In their Notice 742A (para 22) (which has since been withdrawn) Customs express the view that demolition and site clearance are not, in themselves, regarded as commencement of construction, but pile-driving and other foundation stage work is.

**8.40** *VATA 1994, Sch 10 para 5(1)* imposes a VAT charge on the first occasion, in the period from the day when the construction of the building 'is first planned' to ten years following completion of the building, on which a 'developer' of the building

(*a*) grants an interest in, right over, or licence to occupy, the building which is an exempt supply, or

(*b*) is in occupation of the building (or uses the work) or any part of it at a time when he is not a fully taxable person.

If the ten-year period did not expire by 1 March 1997 (which it could never do as it could not start before 1 August 1989) the charge was triggered on that date (*VATA 1994, Sch 10 para 5(1)(b)* inserted by *VAT (Buildings and Land) Order 1995* (*SI 1995 No 279, Article 6*)). In other words the charge was triggered on 1 March 1997 if it had not been triggered earlier. The original legislation did not impose a charge at all if the building was used for fully taxable purposes (or no exempt supplies were made in respect of it) for ten years, but it is not now possible to escape the charge. In theory this could impose an unexpected tax burden on many traders who have constructed their own premises. In practice it should not be a problem as the tax charge will give rise to a corresponding input tax deduction which will eliminate its effect. The only exception is if the building was no longer in use for the trade at 1 March 1997 and was empty.

**8.41** For this purpose any person who either

(*a*) constructed the building,

(*b*) ordered it to be constructed, or

(*c*) financed its construction

with a view to granting an interest in, right over, or licence to occupy it, or to occupy it for his own purposes was a developer in relation to the building (*VATA 1994, Sch 10 para 5(5)*).

**8.42** From 1 January 1992 these provisions were extended so as to create a deemed disposal not only in relation to the construction of a new building but also in respect of the following constructions, enlargements and extensions of existing buildings or works:

(*a*) One either carried out wholly or partly on land ('new building land') adjoining the curtilage of an existing building or resulting in an increase in the gross external floor area of the building of 20% or more (excluding any part of the building on new building land). An annex having internal access to the existing building is regarded as an extension for this purpose. There will, however, be no deemed disposal if the developer has an interest in at least 75% of all of the land on which the enlarged building stands for the ten years prior to the end of the VAT quarter in which the additional space becomes substantially ready for occupation or use. In the case of a 20% or over increase in the floor area of an existing building no charge will arise if there has been a previous deemed disposal in relation to all or part of the land, e.g. on the original construction of the building. The purpose of the deemed disposal provisions is to impose VAT on the cost of the land and, but for this exemption, a series of deemed disposals would duplicate that charge.

(*b*) A reconstruction of an existing building in the course of which at least 80% of its floor structures are removed. Again the charge does not apply where there has been a prior deemed disposal in relation to the building.

(*c*) A reconstruction, enlargement or extension of a civil engineering work which is carried out wholly or partly on new land adjoining that on which the original work is situated. Again there is an exemption where the developer has had an interest in at least 75% of the entire land on which the enlarged work stands for at least ten years (*Sch 10 para 5(8)–(10)*).

The reconstruction, enlargement or extension had to commence after 31 December 1991. Where the extension was only partly on new building land (or new land) and there was not also a substantial reconstruction of the existing building within (*b*), above the cost of the land was the cost of the new building land (or new land) only; nothing needed to be brought into charge in respect of the remaining land. Where the extension was not on new building land but was a 20% or greater increase in floor area of the building, the cost of the land was the proportion of the total cost that the additional gross external floor area (excluding any on new building land) bore to the total such area after the enlargement (*Sch 10 para 6(7)(8)*). The meaning of curtilage is considered in 13.4(*d*). The 75% of the total land test eliminated a charge even in respect of newly-bought land if this was less than a third of the area of the site of the original building.

**8.43** If a developer (A Ltd) which was a member of a VAT group of companies granted an interest in the building, or a licence to occupy it, to another member of its VAT group (B Ltd), both B Ltd and all of the other companies in the same VAT group (or that become members of that VAT group at a time when A Ltd, or another member of the VAT group, has an interest in the building, or that have been members of the VAT group at any time when either A Ltd or B Ltd had an interest in the building) had to be treated as also being the developer (*VATA 1994, Sch 10 para 5(6)(7)*).

**8.44** There were a number of *exceptions* designed to take outside these provisions buildings that were already within the scope of VAT. There was no deemed disposal in the following circumstances.

(*a*) There was a freehold disposal of the building within three years of its construction, and *before* the exempt supply took place, which gave rise to a charge to VAT.

(*b*) The interest was owned by a fully taxable person who occupied the entire building (or the entire part of it in which he has an interest) for the purpose of his business throughout the relevant period.

(*c*) The building was designed as a dwelling or number of dwellings or intended for use solely for a relevant residential or relevant charitable purpose (or a civil engineering work is one necessary for the development of a permanent park for residential caravans).

(*d*) The construction of the building was commenced before 1 August 1989.

(*e*) The value of the deemed supply was less than £100,000 (unless the self-supply charge arose on 1 March 1997 under *para 5(1)(b)* (see 8.40)).

(*VATA 1994, Sch 10 paras 5(1)–(3), 6(5), 6(9)* inserted by *VAT (Buildings and Land) Order 1995* (*SI 1995 No 279, Article 7*)).

**8.45** A disposal of a partially completed building, even though giving rise to VAT at 17½%, did not take the building out of charge under head (*a*). It was only the disposal of a completed new building that did so (*VATA 1994, Sch 10 para 5(3)*). A sale within three years of construction avoided the charge only if it took place before the making of any exempt supplies – such as the grant of a lease or a licence – in relation to any part of the building.

**8.46** Curiously, for the purpose of head (*b*) a person was regarded as a fully taxable person not only if he was able to recover all of the input tax that he paid on supplies to him, but also if he did not use the building in connection with making any exempt supplies; for example, if all of his supplies were outside the scope of VAT or his supplies were below the VAT registration limit and he had not voluntarily registered for VAT (*VATA 1994, Sch 10 para 5(4)*).

**8.47** Where none of these exceptions applied the taxpayer was treated as making a disposal and reacquisition of his interest in the property, as a taxable supply for the purpose of a business carried on by him. This deemed supply was treated as made on the later of

(*a*) the last day of the VAT accounting period in which the grant, occupation or use took place, or

(*b*) the last day of the VAT accounting period in which the building became substantially ready for occupation or the work became substantially ready for use.

(*VATA 1994, Sch 10 para 6(1)*).

Where the charge arose on 1 March 1997 under *para 5(1)(b)* (see 8.40) the deemed supply obviously took place on that day (*VATA 1994, Sch 10 para 6(9)* inserted by *VAT (Buildings and Land) Order 1995* (*SI 1995 No 279, Article 7*)).

**8.48** The *Act* gave no guidance as to when a building becomes substantially ready for occupation. It is probably not the date of practical completion as fitting out work will still have to be done before the building could be occupied.

**8.49** The amount of this deemed supply was the aggregate of

(*a*) the value of the grants made, or to be made, to the developer in respect of the land on which the building or work was constructed, other than rent payable the amount of which could not be ascertained at the time of the deemed supply, and

(*b*) the value of all taxable supplies of goods and services, other than any that were zero-rated, made, or to be made, for (or in connection with) the construction of the building or work.

(*VATA 1994, Sch 10 para 6(2)*).

Future supplies were ignored if the deemed supply arose on 1 March 1997 under *para 5(1)(b)* (see 8.40) (*VATA 1994, Sch 10 para 6(9)* inserted by *VAT (Buildings and Land) Order 1995* (*SI 1995 No 279, Article 7*)).

**8.50** In other words, it was the sum of

(*a*) the cost of the land (including acquisition costs), and (*b*) the cost of construction of the building (other than any part of such cost which was either exempt or zero-rated).

It should be noted that this figure bears no relationship to the value of the building at the time of the deemed disposal. Where the building does not occupy the whole area purchased, what had to be deemed to be disposed of was a question of fact. In *Drs Shutes, Robinson and Ling (LON/92/3151) (VTD 11552)* part of the land was developed as an extension to a medical centre and the rest was levelled, drained and marked out as a car park. It was held that the car park land had to be included in the deemed disposal as it was land serving the new building and contributing to its usefulness.

Customs considered that the cost of construction of a building includes professional and managerial services, demolition and site clearance, site security, hire of equipment, landscaping, the cost of related infrastructure works such as roads and sewers and works pursuant to *section 106* and similar agreements (see 8.13 above), and fitting out work.

**8.51** Prior to 1 January 1992, where the developer rented the land, the figure under (*a*) appears to have been the total of all the rent payable under the lease (not discounted to a current value) up to the first rent review following completion of the development only, as the rent after that date could not be ascertained. If the lease contained an upward only rent review clause, so that the minimum rent was ascertainable, this did not seem to make any difference as the actual rent could not be ascertained. If the lease provided that the developer had to pay any other amount, such as insurance or a service charge, as additional rent it may be that no part of the rent could be ascertained and the amount under head (*a*) was nil. It seems improbable that this was the intention.

**8.52** Where the development, etc. commenced after 1 January 1992, if the land was rented, rent (and any premium) paid prior to the demolition of any building on the land on which the new building was erected was excluded from the cost of the land in so far as it was properly attributable to that demolished building. In the case of a reconstruction, enlargement or extension, the part of the rent (and premium) paid prior to the commencement of the reconstruction, etc. that was properly attributable to the building as it existed prior to the reconstruction was similarly excluded. (*Sch 10 para 6(2)(6)*). So was the rent and any premium payable under a developmental tenancy, developmental lease, or developmental licence. A developmental tenancy (or lease or licence) was a tenancy of (or lease of or licence to occupy) a building or work whose construction, enlargement or extension commenced after 31 December 1991 and triggered these deemed disposal provisions. The lease became a developmental lease at the time of the deemed disposal. (*Sch 9 Group 1, Note 7*). The overall effect was that the cost of leased land for the purpose of the deemed disposal was the part of the rent and premium actually paid up to the time of the demolition of the old building (or the commencement of the reconstruction, etc.) that was attributable to the land itself.

**8.53** Except where the self-supply charge arose on 1 March 1997 under *para 5(1)(b)* (see 8.40), where a development or reconstruction, etc. transformed a tenancy, lease or licence under which the developer was the tenant into a developmental tenancy, lease or licence, the developer had to give written notice to his landlord of the date from which it became a developmental tenancy, etc. and, in the case of a reconstruction increasing the floor area by 20% or more, the proportion of the total rent apportioned to the extension under *Sch 10 para 6(8)*. (*Sch 10 para 7* as amended by *VAT (Buildings and Land) Order 1995* (*SI 1995 No 279*, *Article 8*)). The landlord had to then charge VAT on the rent (or in the case of such an extension, the appropriate part of the rent) for the remainder of the lease (*Sch 9 Group 1, item 1(b)* and *Sch 10 para 7(2)*). If the landlord was not VAT–registered he had to register even though the rent may have been well below the registration threshold.

**8.54** The concept was that the developer would have recovered during the construction phase all of the VAT that he had paid as he would have made no exempt supplies in relation to the building during that period. Accordingly the charge under these provisions effectively required him to hand back to Customs the VAT that he had been repaid in relation to the building and in addition to pay VAT on the cost of the land. If VAT had been paid on the acquisition of the land (because the vendor had exercised the option to tax) the charge would in theory produce no extra tax for Customs other than by returning to Customs the tax that they had previously repaid. Unfortunately the original legislation did not achieve this on a change in rate of VAT. That anomaly was rectified from 1 January 1992.

**8.55** Unfortunately it is by no means clear that relief for tax paid on acquisition or on development costs would in fact be granted if the developer was not VAT-registered when he incurred such costs. There was nothing in the legislation or the Explanatory Notes to suggest that the normal rule in *regulation 111* of the *VAT Regulations 1995* (*SI 1995 No 2518*) did not apply, namely that input tax on services supplied more than six months before registration or on goods supplied prior to registration cannot be reclaimed. For VAT purposes the granting, assignment or surrender of a major interest in land is treated as a supply of goods (*VATA 1994, Sch 4 para 4*) and lesser interests as a supply of services (*VATA 1994, s 5(2)(b)*).

**8.56** Where a building was in the course of construction at 1 March 1995 the developer had two choices. He could continue to claim relief for the input tax he incurred on the development and suffer the self-supply charge in due course in the normal way. Alternatively, if he did not claim input tax relief for expenditure after 1 March 1995, and repaid to Customs the input tax (if any) he had previously claimed, he would avoid the self-supply charge. This option ceased to be available once any post-1 March 1995 input tax was reclaimed. (*VATA 1994, Sch 10 para 5(3A)* inserted by *VAT (Buildings and Land) Order 1995* (*SI 1995 No 279*, *Article 6*)).

**Need to Register for VAT**

**8.57** The need to register timeously for VAT is, and always has been, very important. In theory VAT on development expenditure for an industrial or commercial development ought always to have been recoverable where the development commenced between 31 July 1989 and 28 February 1995, as the first supply after development was either a taxable freehold disposal or a deemed disposal under the provisions in 8.38 to 8.57 above. However, this presupposes that the developer was registered for VAT at the time the expenditure is incurred. There is no requirement to register until a person makes (or expects within the next 30 days to make) taxable supplies in excess of the registration limit.

**8.58** It might be thought in these circumstances that when the obligation to register arises the taxpayer would become entitled to recover the VAT on prior expenditure incurred in generating the taxable supply. Unfortunately this is not the case. *VATA 1994, ss 25(1), 26* allow a deduction for input tax for the VAT quarter in which the supply takes place. *Section 24(6)(b)* enables Customs by regulation to grant a deduction for tax on the supply of goods or services taking place before the recipient is VAT-registered. This they have done in the *VAT Regulations 1995* (*SI 1995 No 2518*). Unfortunately *regulation 111(2)(c)* provides that no amount can be treated as input tax in respect of services which have been supplied to the taxable person more than six months before the date of the taxable person's registration. The *regulation* does give Customs power to authorise the deduction of other input tax, and it is to be hoped that they will do so where a non-VAT registered person acquires land on which he is charged VAT and does not immediately register it. However, this is by no means certain and the best advice at present is that if a developer is not VAT-registered, for example, where a development property is acquired in a newly-formed subsidiary, application for registration should be made immediately prior to the acquisition if VAT will be payable on the acquisition of the land. At the latest, application should be made at the time that construction commences in any other case. There is no similar restriction in respect of goods (other than goods disposed of before a person's registration). However, the major part of the cost of a building is the labour element, which is the provision of a service. Indeed it is likely that the entire building contract is a composite supply of labour and materials in which case the entire cost would be a supply of services. See the case of *AJ & A Elliott (VTD 4926)*. Even then *regulation 37* is permissive, not mandatory, i.e. it empowers Customs to grant relief for earlier input tax, not requires them to do so. The three-year cap imposed by *FA 1997, s 47* also needs to be borne in mind. This normally requires input tax relief to be claimed within three years of the time the tax was incurred.

**8.59** A person who is not required to register for VAT is nevertheless entitled to be registered if he can convince Customs that he is carrying on a business and intends to make taxable supplies in the course or furtherance of that business (*VATA 1994, Sch 1 para 9*). A property developer who will make a taxable supply following completion of the building should accordingly apply to register for VAT as soon as he starts to incur input tax in relation to expenditure on the development. Not only will this avoid the loss of input tax relief for early expenditure but it will significantly assist the cash flow. This is because, once registered, the developer will be able to reclaim each quarter during the development phase (or, if he so chooses, each month) the input VAT he has suffered in that period. Customs often register an intending trader subject to the condition that he will repay the input tax previously claimed should he not subsequently make any taxable supplies. The VAT tribunal in *ACS Hordern (VTD 8941)* held that this condition breached the *Sixth Directive* and is therefore unenforceable.

**8.60** A person who intends to grant an exempt lease cannot qualify to register as an 'intending trader' as he does not intend to make taxable supplies. Accordingly in such cases it might be wise to decide whether or not to exercise the option to tax (see 17.158) immediately an interest in the site for the building is acquired so as to create a right to register. In practice Customs will not allow registration if the option to tax is not exercised and notified at the same time.

**8.61** As far as the residential developer is concerned, Customs will similarly normally register a person for VAT if he intends to make zero-rated outputs on completion of the development. In the past Customs wanted some evidence that there was a genuine intention to carry out the development, such as sight of the construction contract or of the detailed planning consent. This is no longer necessary (see 17.273 below), at least in theory. Unfortunately the practice is somewhat different; if anything they now require more information rather than less. The registration will be provisional. If, when the developer comes to make supplies, they are not zero-rated but exempt, the registration will be withdrawn and Customs will reclaim the input tax refunded in error. It is accordingly most important to ensure that the first lease is zero-rated. If a developer has other income which will arise during the construction period and which will be exempt, he will need to agree with Customs before he starts his development that the input tax he suffers should be directly attributed to the exempt and zero-rated outputs respectively. If he does not, the receipt of the exempt income will forfeit the right to reclaim input tax suffered on the development costs. Direct attribution is considered further in chapter 17. A temporary exempt letting will not necessarily be fatal provided that there is evidence of an intention to make taxable supplies (*C & E Commrs v Briararch Ltd (1992 STC 732)*) (see 17.141).

**Building Work on Residential and Relevant Charitable Developments**

**8.62** The supply of building works in the course of the construction or demolition of a relevant residential or charitable building also qualifies for zero-rating, provided an appropriate certificate is obtained (see 17.42 below). This will enable the building contractor to zero-rate his charges to the developer irrespective of whether or not the developer is the person constructing the building and able to make zero-rated supplies. It will not, however, enable the developer to recover input tax on architects' and other fees which do not qualify for zero-rating. It may be possible in some cases for the builder to engage the architect and other professionals and supply the building to the developer. However, care would need to be taken to ensure that the supply is not a mixed supply which Customs are entitled to dissect into its various elements. The contractual liability of the architect almost certainly needs to be to the contractor not to the developer, which would probably not be commercially acceptable in most cases, although the growth in the use of collateral warranties may make this acceptable where these are available.

**Exclusion of Conversion, Reconstruction, Alteration or Enlargement**

**8.63** *Note 16* to *Group 5* of *Schedule 8* provides that the construction of a building does not include –

(*a*) the conversion, reconstruction, or alteration of an existing building, or

(*b*) any enlargement of, or extension to, an existing building except to the extent that the enlargement or extension creates an additional dwelling or dwellings, or

(*c*) the construction of an annexe to an existing building (subject to an exception where it is to a relevant charitable building and is capable of functioning separately from it).

Accordingly such items are VATable. Customs say that the onus of determining whether building work is taxable at the standard or zero rate is on the supplier, i.e. the builder needs to be satisfied that he is carrying out works of construction of a relevant residential or charitable building rather than works in the course of the conversion, reconstruction, alteration or enlargement of an existing building to which he would need to add VAT at 17½% (*VATA 1994, Sch 8 Group 5, Note 9*). If he guesses wrongly they will of course hold him liable to pay the tax. They have, however, given some guidance – which of course has no legal force – as to how they interpret 'the construction of a building'.

**8.64** Customs consider that the builder or developer should ask himself 'Am I constructing an entirely new dwelling or other qualifying building (for which I have a valid certificate) or am I doing something to a building which already exists?' They have volunteered their own 'common-sense' views on some of what they presumably feel to be the more clear-cut situations.

(i) Where an existing building has been demolished to foundation level, the construction of a building making use of part or all the foundations of the former building (which can include the 'slab' of the ground floor) will continue to attract the zero-rating relief.

(ii) Where what remains of an existing building is limited to a single wall such as the front facade, the construction of a building making use of that single wall or facade (or a double facade on a corner site) will continue to attract the zero-rating relief but only if the retention of the facade is required under the planning consent.

(iii) The building on to an existing house of another house to form two separate but semi-detached houses with no inter-connecting doors would qualify for zero-rating, provided that planning permission does not prevent its separate use, letting or disposal and the new building stands on its own land.

(iv) The building of a new house within an existing terrace of houses on the site of a house that has been totally demolished ('infilling') would qualify for zero-rating.

(Notice 708, para 6.1).

Although not mentioned in Notice 708, Customs have in the past given the following as examples of things that they considered did not qualify for zero-rating:

(*a*) Where the outer walls of an existing building remain, even without floor or roof, any building operations in or around that shell.

(*b*) Where internal features are retained in addition to any part of the wall structure, as the building services involved would be supplied in the course of the reconstruction of an existing building.

(*c*) The building of an additional flat on top of an existing block.

(*d*) In the case of establishments like old people's homes, residential care homes, 'new' construction within the curtilage of the establishment may be loosely referred to as extensions or additions to the qualifying building; the test here is whether what is being built is an enlargement of any of the individual buildings on the site (the internal access test being crucial here). If it is, the work is standard-rated, if not, it is zero-rated. A walkway which is no more than a covered corridor, several metres in length, at a single floor level, whose main purpose is to provide shelter in bad weather when moving between adjacent buildings, is not regarded as internal access in such cases.

(C & E Leaflet 708/2/90, para 6 now withdrawn).

**8.65** Customs felt they could give this guidance because they think that anyone would say that the buildings resulting from (i) and (ii) were really new buildings whereas in (*a*) or (*b*) the old building was being reconstructed. The author is duly chastened but, whatever most people might say, does not think that the retention of a single facade with internal fireplaces attached to it (which falls within (*b*)) is any more a reconstruction than if the fireplaces were stripped out (to come within (ii)). The dividing line between (ii) and (*a*) has led to much litigation. Some further guidance on this area can be found at 17.51 onwards.

**8.66** In practice, the VAT tribunals seem to take a more relaxed attitude than Customs which may well be why the above guidance has been dropped. In *B M Croxford (VTD 5730)* a bungalow and garage were constructed on the site of a derelict piggery utilising part of the walls of the old building. Customs contended that the retention of more than one wall prevented the work constituting the construction of a new building but the tribunal held that the work was not the conversion of an existing building, as the greater part of the piggery had been demolished. The *London Diocesan Fund* wished to replace a church with a new one. The planning permission required the retention of the old church tower. In addition, about 10% of the old building was retained, the chancel being altered to form a chapel in the new church. The VAT tribunal held that the work on the tower was a separate project of repair, but even if it were included in the main project, that constituted the substantial demolition of the old church and the construction of a new church. This was upheld in the High Court (*C & E Commrs v London Diocesan (1993 STC 369)* – see 8.71 below). In *P S Thakkar t/a Meera Homes (VTD 6127)* a large detached house was developed as a home for the elderly. The planning permission described the work as extensions. The front wall of the house and the two inner walls supporting it were retained. So were parts of other walls which could be incorporated in the design. About 40% of the foundations were retained. The new building was much larger than the old and very different in appearance. The work was held to be the construction of a new building. The tribunal said that there could be no general rule as to how much had to survive to decide the question whether there was a new building or the alteration or enlargement of an existing one.

**8.67** The VAT tribunal in *Ochil Developments Ltd (VTD 10017)* took an unusually robust view, holding that to decide the issue it was necessary to determine whether at the commencement of construction there was an existing building in the ordinary sense of the word. Applying this test it concluded that the roofless shell of a former building was not an existing building and therefore there had not been a reconstruction of an existing building. A similar result was reached in *AJ Penn (VTD 10312)* where a barn roof supported by scaffolding was held not to be an existing building. A feature of this case is that the taxpayer had at first intended to simply add an extra storey to an existing barn. However, it was discovered that the barn had no foundation and the existing walls could not safely be built on. It is interesting that the tribunal applied the test of whether there was an existing building not when the planning permission was obtained but only after the walls had been demolished and the roof put on temporary supports. This is probably incorrect (see 8.72).

**8.68** In *Joseph Samuel Developments (VTD 7177)* the VAT tribunal held that a new block of four flats at the rear of an existing block which used one wall of the block as a party wall, had independent foundations and independent gas and water supplies, but whose entrance was through the existing building, was an enlargement of the existing building – but that the construction of a two-storey block at the rear of an existing three-storey building incorporating part of that building and built partly over its flat roof but mainly on piers at first floor level was a new building as its appearance was very different to that of the existing building and its function was different to that of the existing building (there was also no internal access to the flat from the existing building and all services to it were independent of the existing building). Such a development after 21 July 1994 should qualify for zero-rating (see 17.51). The test of whether a derelict structure constitutes a building is essentially one of fact and degree. A structure that is so derelict as to have no potential and no future as a building is not susceptible to conversion, reconstruction, alteration or enlargement and cannot properly be described as an 'existing building'. Accordingly, held the tribunal in *J C Lewis*, the construction of a farmhouse on the site of a derelict barn utilising about 26% of the old walls and about 20% in volume of the internal walls, was a new building, albeit that it was similar in appearance to the original barn. This was upheld on appeal (*C & E Commrs v Lewis (1994 STC 739)*), the judge agreeing with the tribunal's approach of asking (a) whether there was an existing building, giving the word its ordinary popular meaning; and if so (b) was it susceptible to conversion, reconstruction, alteration or enlargement. In *Mr & Mrs Truran (VTD 7312)* the taxpayers demolished all of the internal walls and the roof of an existing building but under the terms of the planning permission retained all of the outer walls and re-used some of the roofing tiles. Customs successfully argued that the shell that remained was still a building and thus the new flats constructed within that shell, and as an extension to it, constituted a reconstruction and enlargement of an existing building. In *Swan Developments (Land Co) Ltd (VTD 7394)* the external walls of an office block were demolished and new walls built. The company had then, floor by floor, replaced the offices with flats, retaining only the lift shaft, 60–70% of the floors and 60% of the pillars. The tribunal held that this amounted to a conversion of one sort of a building into another; it was not possible to say that the company had constructed a building as a whole, albeit that the part of the original building incorporated into the new building was small.

**8.69** An interesting decision that casts doubt on 8.64(*d*) is that in *Associated Nursing Services plc (VTD 11203)*. The company constructed a block of residential care units, i.e. self-contained flats for the elderly, with a communal lounge adjoining an existing nursing home. Planning consent was for an extension to the nursing home and the new block had internal access to the nursing home through the party wall. The new block was held to be a separate building qualifying for zero-rating. The tribunal looked first at its function following *C & E Commrs v Great Shelford Free Church (1987 STC 249)* and *C & E Commrs v Elliott (1993 STC 369, p 386)*. It held that this was different to the nursing home, which did not make use of the block of flats (although it is clear that the flats made use of the nursing home). It was therefore not an extension or annexation. Neither the planning permission nor the internal access could override the different nature of the two buildings. In addition it considered that a bystander observing the large size of the block relative to the nursing home would not have considered it an extension or annexation. A similar result was reached in *B A Siraj t/a Europa Builders (VTD 11742)* where a block of flats was erected adjacent to a large semi-detached house which had been converted into flats and a single external staircase gave access to both. Such a development is probably now zero-rated in any event (see 17.51).

**8.70** Unfortunately, there has been little consistency. The partial demolition of a slaughterhouse in poor condition and the creation of a dwelling-house (*M J Rasmussen (VTD 1741)*); the conversion of a barn into a house where during the conversion the barn was 'virtually flattened' in the October 1987 gale (*G Wilkins (VTD 5268)*); and the conversion of stables and outbuildings into a dwelling house retaining only one wall and part of another (*R H Gleed (VTD 2481)*), have all been held to be conversions. It does, however, appear that the trend is for VAT tribunals nowadays to give greater weight to the appearance of the finished building and the replication concept, whereas in the earlier cases they tended to concentrate on how much of the old building was incorporated into the new.

**8.71** Fortunately, judicial guidance was given by the High Court on the appeals in *C & E Commrs v London Diocesan Fund; v Elliott and* *another (1993 STC 369)* and *v Penwith Property Co Ltd*, which were heard together. The *London Diocesan* case has already been mentioned in 8.66. Mr and Mrs Elliott had carried out work on a residential nursing home. The 'new' building was almost three times the size of the old, the old building was virtually unaltered but the new one was different in appearance to the old and its dimensions made it the predominant building. The VAT tribunal held that notwithstanding internal access the work could not properly be described as an enlargement of the old building. McCullough J disagreed. Penwith constructed a house using the chimney stack and about 35% of the original outer walls of a derelict old one. The new house covered about twice the area of the old. The VAT tribunal held that reconstruction implied a degree of replication and this was more important than the question of how much of the old building was incorporated in the new one. They felt that a reasonable observer would conclude that the new building lacked the requisite degree of replication for the work to constitute a reconstruction. This was upheld.

**8.72** McCullough J felt that the right approach is firstly to consider whether there is an existing building at the time the work commences. This means before any work, whether demolition or construction, begins. If there is not, the work can be zero-rated. If there is, it becomes necessary 'to consider the end result and ask whether the work done amounts to the conversion, reconstruction, alteration or enlargement of the original building in the sense in which those words are commonly used or whether the end result is a new building. If a number of buildings existed before the work began the question will be whether the work amounted to the conversion, reconstruction, alteration or enlargement of one or more of them. The matter is one of fact and degree'. He felt that in answering this second question it will in most cases be helpful to look at the finished work and ask how much of the original building has survived. If there is a stage in the works where all of the demolition has been done and none of the new work started it might be useful to consider how the site would then have looked. It is not normally helpful to consider the four words separately as the work may include elements of more than one, e.g. the main part of a derelict house may be *reconstructed*, its scullery and coal shed *converted* into a bathroom, its principal room *enlarged* by the addition of a bay window, and its surviving windows *altered* in style.

**8.73** In the *London Diocesan* case McCullough J felt that the tower was probably part of the existing building but the tribunal had considered the position alternately on the basis that it was and was not. Although he felt that many tribunals would have reached a different conclusion, McCullough J could not say that the conclusion of the VAT tribunal was one that no tribunal, on the material before it, could properly have reached. Similarly, in the *Penwith* case McCullough J felt that, although the tribunal had asked the wrong questions, it was possible that had it asked itself the right ones it might still have held that the work was zero-rated and in that event it might have been impossible to say that such a decision was so unreasonable that it should be quashed. He felt that the tribunal in Mr and Mrs Elliot's case had misunderstood the facts. It had not realised that the planning permission required an interconnecting door; it had erred in finding that the new structure had itself all the facilities for an independent nursing home; and it had exaggerated the increase in area of the new building. On the facts the only reasonable conclusion was that there was an extension to an existing building which provided internal access to it.

**8.74** Many of the subsequent VAT tribunal decisions have favoured the taxpayer. In *St John the Evangelist Parochial Church Council (VTD 11165)* a new parish centre was constructed adjoining a church. It was used for separate purposes to the church and had a separate heating system. However, a covered area was constructed between the two buildings. This was structurally independent of the church. Customs' claim that this made the parish centre an extension or annexation to the church was rejected, but it was regarded as a borderline case. In *Ronald Jamieson (VTD 10939)* the construction of houses on the site of dilapidated farm buildings (cattle sheds, etc.) was held to be zero-rated albeit that most of the old stone walls were incorporated in the houses. What was there before – single-storey roofless buildings, without flooring, with empty openings for doors and windows, defective stonework, with no utilities, and the tops of the walls overgrown with grass – was not an existing building but a derelict ruin. In *Keep Design Ltd (VTD 11581)* two semi-derelict, boarded-up late Victorian terrace blocks of workmen's cottages were replaced by 15 modern starter homes. The party walls and brick spine of the cottages were retained. The tribunal felt that the work was more extensive than a mere alteration and was not a reconstruction of existing buildings because it did not replicate what was there before. Similarly in *Lucking Brothers (VTD 11595)* where a barn and a cattle shed were transformed into a house, retaining the timber frame of the barn and part of the walls and roof timber of the cattle shed, the tribunal considered that a casual observer who was shown the completed building and given a full explanation of the work involved would view it as a new building, not a conversion or reconstruction. It felt that the similarity in external appearance between the old and new buildings was not conclusive and the planning consent which required this of little significance. Again in *Josephine Lane (VTD 11710)* where a derelict lodge was replaced with a much larger house, retaining a facade, a gable end and chimney stack, the tribunal held that an informed layman inspecting the new building would be unlikely to connect it with the old lodge, so zero-rating applied. The incorporation of features of the original building was a requirement of the planning consent and as such was felt irrelevant as it did not reflect the taxpayer's wishes. In *C & E Commrs v Marchday Holdings Ltd (1997 STC 272)* it was accepted by the Court of Appeal (in a split decision) that the construction of an office block on the site of a former industrial building was a new building albeit that it utilised about two-thirds of the concrete frame, 85% of the concrete floor slabs, some brick party walls, and the foundations of the old building. The retention of parts of the structure of the former building was relevant but did not of itself preclude the construction being a new building. It was unrealistic to ignore the cost of the work. The work as a whole was so extensive that the resulting office block was essentially a new building. Such 'conversions' are no longer able to constitute a new building from 1 March 1995 following the changes made by the *VAT (Construction of Buildings) Order 1995* (*SI 1995 No 280*) – see 17.24.

**8.75** Where four self-contained flats were constructed in the shell of a house, the interior of which was completely gutted, it was held that the construction work amounted to a conversion or alteration of an existing building (*Davies Investments (VTD 12308)*). In *St Albans Nursing Home Ltd (VTD 13488)* two adjoining detached houses were reconstructed and joined together to form a single building. It was held that the finished building had no affinity with the two previous ones in structure or appearance. The two houses had been completely transformed and their identities did not survive the construction work. In contrast, in *Wright & Fuller Ltd (VTD 15952)*, where five separate buildings were linked together and a new building intended for use as a separate dementia unit designed to operate independently was built at one end with very limited internal access and a different appearance to the rest of the building, the tribunal thought it unrealistic to restrict the expression 'existing building' to a single edifice and held that the five together constituted an existing building which had been extended. In *A R Carter (VTD 13828)* a cottage in need of substantial repair was transformed into a larger house. The completed building covered more than twice the area of the original, only about 12% of the walls derived from the cottage and there was a marked contrast between the house and the original cottage. The fact that in his planning application the taxpayer had stated he wanted to alter the existing building was dismissed on the basis that his intention at the time of the application was not conclusive evidence of the work that was actually done. In *G M & E A Flowers t/a Soar Valley Construction (VTD 13889)* the conversion of an old forge into a dwelling was held to have resulted in the creation of a new and different building. The conversion at the same time of a dairy and hay loft into dwellings was held to be an alteration as enough of the original remained for their identity to have survived the work. In *J S Bell (VTD 13448)* it was proposed to alter and enlarge two semi-detached cottages to a dwelling-house but as work progressed the condition of the buildings were found to be worse than expected. Very little could be used. The VAT tribunal accepted that the house was the construction of a new building, the old building having effectively been demolished piecemeal as work progressed.

**8.76** On the other hand in *W J E Hurford (VTD 11422)* the tribunal held that a ruinous and unstable structure (a barn with no foundations whose roof had disintegrated and most of whose timbers had to be replaced) was an existing building as it would appear to a passer-by to be a building. In *WE Talbot & Sons (VTD 10968)* a house was regarded as a reconstruction albeit that it was over 70% larger than the old one and most of the retained features, 40% of the original external walls and of the roof, were required as a condition of planning consent. The tribunal felt that there was a recognisable house in existence at each stage of the development. It was irrelevant that the original house was uninhabitable or that the interior had been completely gutted and replaced; the test related to the principal structure of the building. This decision should be contrasted with that in *P S Thakkar* (see 8.66) where on very similar facts it was held that there was a construction of a new building. In *S & H Shroufi (t/a Morris Grange Nursing Home) (VTD 14852)* where planning permission had been obtained for an extension, the tribunal held that that was what had been constructed; the extension was not a separate building, even though it had a separate entrance, was used for a different purpose to the rest of the building and the only internal access was through fire doors. Similarly in *Bruce Pugh (VTD 17013)*, a DIY builder case, the retention of part of the front wall (as part of the inner skin of the front wall of the new house) was sufficient to make the work reconstruction rather than the erection of a new building, albeit that the tribunal accepted that by any objective standard the incidental incorporation of part of the old was inconsequential.

**8.77** Temporarily constructing a separate new building adjoining an existing one and subsequently joining them up will not necessarily prevent the new building being an extension. In *Graden Builders Ltd (VTD 12637)* the builders waited three months before constructing internal access between the two. The tribunal held that the new building was an extension as there had been throughout an intention that the two should be occupied together. In *Nidderdale Building Ltd (VTD 13158)*, a builder relying on a certificate provided by a director of his customer, following confirmation from the VAT office that construction of a new wing to a nursing home was zero-rated, did not charge VAT. After he had completed the new wing the customer engaged a different builder to construct a doorway linking the two buildings. Nidderdale was held liable to account for VAT as the new wing was an extension of the existing building. The decision may not be as harsh as it seems at first sight. The planning consent and the approved plans had included an internal access, which ought to have put Nidderdale on notice and the new wing was not capable of operating separately as a nursing home – which the customer had said he intended – as it had no kitchen and no administrative accommodation.

**8.78** On the other hand, in *D S Menzies (VTD 15733)*, a residential building that was erected without access to another a metre away and subsequently linked was held to be a separate building notwithstanding that the architect suggested that, as the work had to be phased, it should be constructed as a separate entity; the planning permission was for 'additional accommodation', the linkage was done by the same builder who constructed the building (albeit under a separate contract) and the buildings were linked a mere 28 days after the construction. The VAT tribunal accepted that there was always an intention to link the two buildings but thought that the lack of funds might have prevented that happening for a substantial period and the building was usable as it was. The tribunal commented, 'it is also dangerous and productive of much uncertainty if, after works have been completed and invoiced, an alteration to a taxable status can occur because one building becomes linked with another'.

A similar result was reached in *JMB Strowbridge (VTD 16521)* where the appellant built a second nursing home adjacent to an existing one and subsequently removed the stud walls from both buildings making them into a single home. The tribunal held that the new building was an annexe but as there was no internal access at the time of completion of the building work it qualified for zero-rating. Mr Strowbridge originally intended to have a single building but decided to operate the two separately because he could not afford the VAT! By the time the building was completed five patients had died and in those changed circumstances it had become uneconomic to run the two separately. The tribunal accepted that the decision to merge the two buildings had not existed when the building was initially completed.

**8.79** Lightman J indicated in *Cantrell & Others (t/a Foxearth Nursing Home) v C & E Commrs (2000 STC 100)* that the question whether the completed building works amounted to an enlargement, extension or annexe had to be asked as at the date of the supply. It had to be answered after an objective examination of the physical characteristics of the building or buildings before and after carrying out the works, having regard to similarities and differences in appearance, the layout, and how the buildings were equipped to function. The terms of planning permissions, the motives behind undertaking the works and the intended or subsequent actual use were irrelevant (except possibly to indicate the potential for use inherent in the building). Accordingly, in giving weight to a condition in the planning permission that the new structure was to be used only as part of the nursing home, and to the effect of the works on the nursing home enterprise as a whole and the function of the new structure, the tribunal had misdirected itself in law. It will be interesting to see if this case goes further. It seems to invalidate a large number of earlier VAT tribunal decisions.

**8.80** The question in *Colchester Sixth Form College (VTD 16252)* was whether a five-storey building constructed in an area bounded on three sides by the existing college buildings was an annexe. The new building had its own water, heating and fire alarm systems and was capable of being used separately from the remainder of the college. It had its own entrance but in practice most students did not use this but accessed it via the old building. The tribunal accepted that in architectural terms an enlargement or extension could also be an annexe but felt that the scheme of the legislation could not support such a construction. Applying the two-stage test laid down in the *London*

*Diocesan Fund* case, the tribunal decided that the new building was not an enlargement of the existing one as that remained unchanged. However, it provided an additional section to the college building with a real and substantial measure of integration with the existing building. It was accordingly an extension and did not qualify for zero-rating. The tribunal commented that even if they had classified it as an annexe it would still not have attracted zero-rating as the entrance to the new structure formed the main entrance to the college.

**8.81** A new building within a synagogue complex that replaced an existing wooden structure was held to be a reconstruction of part of the existing building complex (*Yeshurun Hebrew Congregation (VTD 16487)*). The tribunal thought that if the existing building had to be looked at after the demolition of the wooden structure the new building would be an enlargement or extension of the existing building not an annexe. Similarly work carried out in two phases at a Gurudwara (a Sikh temple) were both held to be extensions to the Gurudwara (*Guru Norak Nishkan Sewak Jatha (Birmingham) UK (VTD 17499)*). In Phase I part of the Gurudwara was demolished and replaced by a new three-storey community block with internal access to the existing building. Phase II was the construction of a grand entrance porch surmounted by a new dome, which became the main entrance to the Gurudwara. The taxpayer also unsuccessfully contended that there was a single project for the construction of the temple which began in 1991 when a former Polish club was converted into a Gurudwara, and that the work started in 1993 (Phase I) and 1995 (Phase II) was part of that construction. This was dismissed as it was clear from the evidence that none of the work on either phases I or II was conceived prior to 1991.

**8.82** The provision in issue in *M G & N Smith (VTD 17035)* was *Note 16* (see 8.63), which zero-rates an extension to the extent it creates an additional dwelling. A new dwelling was built adjacent to an existing one. However a small part of the upper floor utilised unused space within the old one with access to such space from the old building having been blocked off. In effect the works resulted in two semi-detached houses, albeit that part of the upper floor of one is carried upon part of the ground floor of the other. Customs contended that *Note 16(b)* requires the additional dwelling to be contained wholly within the enlargement. They pointed out that the *Note* contains no apportionment provision. The tribunal rejected this. The natural meaning of the wording merely requires that an additional dwelling should be created. The use of the words 'except to the extent that' imputed the apportionment rule in *Note 11* (see 17.59). Accordingly the extension was zero-rated. However the work undertaken to incorporate part of the original dwelling in the new house should be standard-rated.

### Fittings

**8.83** Even if the building work qualifies for zero-rating certain goods cannot be zero-rated by the builder (although they can still be zero-rated by the person constructing the building). These are:

(*a*) finished or prefabricated furniture other than furniture designed to be fitted in kitchens;

(*b*) materials for the construction of fitted furniture, other than kitchen furniture; and

(*c*) an electrical or gas appliance, other than

(i) one designed to heat space or water (or both) or to provide ventilation, air cooling, air purification or dust extraction, or

(ii) a door entry system, waste disposal unit or machine for compacting waste which is intended for use in a building designed as a number of dwellings, or

(iii) a burglar alarm, fire alarm, or fire safety equipment or an appliance designed solely for the purpose of enabling aid to be summoned in an emergency, or

(iv) a lift or hoist,

(*d*) carpets or carpeting material.

(*VATA 1994, Sch 8 Group 5, Note 22* inserted by *VAT (Construction of Buildings) Order 1995* (*SI 1995 No 280*)). Prior to 1 March 1995 the permitted gas or electrical appliances were those designed to provide space or water heating (or both) only.

This is intended to prevent taxable furniture being disguised as zero-rated building works.

The services supplied in conjunction with the goods must be separable from them. *D & C Hodson t/a Bordercraft Workshops (VTD 13897)* supplied fitted kitchen furniture individually manufactured to meet the precise measurements made by the client or his architect. They were usually fitted by a sub-contractor. If they did not fit Hodson took them back and made the necessary adjustments. It was held that the service of ensuring that the units fitted was an intrinsic part of the supply of goods so zero-rating could not apply (see also *C & E v Jeffs and another* at 9.31).

**8.84** Customs have indicated the sort of items they consider are 'of a kind ordinarily installed by builders as fixtures' (*item 3* in 8.28 above). These can be found in Annexes D and E to Customs Notice 708.

**Phasing the Work**

**8.85** The timing of work can affect the VAT position. In *SA Whiteley (VTD 11292)* the taxpayer bought a house in 1988. He intended to modernise it, to replace an existing garage block with a new annexe containing office and staff accommodation, and to construct an indoor swimming pool. He was advised to seek planning approval in stages. Permission to develop the house was granted in June 1989 and work started. Permission to build the annexe was granted in March 1992 and work started in August 1992, the work on the house having been completed in August 1991. Permission for the swimming pool was granted in December 1992 and work commenced in February 1993. It was held that the taxpayer had constructed three separate buildings, not a single dwelling erected in stages. Accordingly the annexe and swimming pool could not qualify for zero-rating as being work carried out in the construction of the house. In *St Mary's RC School (1996 STC 1091)* the construction of a school play area 13 years after the school opened was held by the tribunal to be the completion of the original building not an addition to it although this was reversed on appeal. There was a statutory requirement for a school to include recreation areas and these had been shown on the original plan. The construction had had to be deferred until a diversion order could be obtained in respect of a public right of way which crossed the land and further funding needed to be raised to meet the cost both of that order and of the building work. The judge felt that the tribunal had not given sufficient weight to the temporal link and that a gap of 13 years was 'far too long'. In any event, lack of funds could not justify a time interval so as to be able to show that the work was continuous.

## Other Matters

**8.86** Where other work has to be done in connection with a residential development that other work might well be supplied in the course of construction of the residential development and thus itself qualify for zero-rating. In *C & E Commrs v Rannoch School Ltd (1993 STC 389)* the company built a new accommodation block at a school. It was a condition of planning consent that the company replace the sewage treatment plant serving the existing buildings. Customs contended that the replacement sewerage system was a supply of civil engineering work and thus did not qualify for zero-rating. The High Court upheld the decision of the VAT tribunal that it was zero-rated as a supply in the course of construction of the new residential block, since it was supplied at the same time or shortly after and the new block could not be occupied until the plant was installed. In *Turner Stroud and Burley Construction Ltd (VTD 14454)* a riverside house was built with a boat dock underneath and a stairway connecting it to the living accommodation. It was held that the whole building, of which the dock was a necessary part, was designed as a dwelling; it was not designed partly as a dwelling and partly as a boat store.

**8.87** In *Lonsdale Travel Ltd (VTD 12113)* a trader entered into two contracts, one with a developer to acquire a building in course of renovation and a second with a company controlled by him to carry out the renovation work, with the land contract being conditional on completion of the building works and the obligation to pay for the building work being concurrent with completion of the land contract. Customs contended that there was no supply under the building contract as the arrangements meant that the renovation work had to be completed before either contract came into force, so the sale contract would relate to the completed building. This claim was rejected, the tribunal holding that the agreements were not shams and, except as regards the date of payment, the building agreement was wholly independent of the land contract and was in force before the works were completed.

## Relief for Expenditure on Remediation of Contaminated Land

**8.88** Where a company acquires contaminated land for the purposes of a trade or of a Schedule A business it is entitled to deduct 150% of the clean up costs in calculating its taxable profits. The relief applies to expenditure incurred after 10 May 2001 (*FA 2001, s 70* and *Sch 22 paras 13, 32*). It should be noted that it does not apply to individuals or trusts. If the relief creates a loss that loss can be used in the same way as any other trading (or Schedule A) loss.

**8.89** If it prefers it can surrender the loss in exchange for a repayable tax credit of 16% (or such other percentage as the Treasury may by Order specify, *FA 2001, Sch 22 paras 14, 15*). As the corporation tax relief would be effectively at 30% (with a 20% corporation tax rate) or 45% (with a 30% one), 16% cash in hand is a substantial discount. Assuming an interest rate of say 8% the tax credit is beneficial only if the loss is unlikely to be relievable within the next 8 years (or even longer with a 30% corporation tax rate). The administrative provisions in respect of this tax credit are dealt with at 8.99. The amount that can be surrendered is obviously the lesser of the unrelieved loss or of 150% of the qualifying land remediation expenditure (see 8.92). The unrelieved loss is the actual loss less any loss relief that the company is entitled to claim (whether or not it actually does so) under *ICTA 1988, s 392A(1)* or *s 393A(1)* (relief for a trading loss or a Schedule A loss against total profits for the same or earlier accounting periods) or *section 403(1)* (group relief) (*FA 2001, Sch 22 para 14(1)–(4)*). No account is to be taken of Schedule A losses or trading losses brought forward from an earlier accounting period or a trading loss carried back from the next one (*FA 2001, Sch 22 para 14(5)*). It is not wholly clear what this means. It is probably that the profits against which a loss is available for relief under *sections 392A, 393A(1)* or *403(1)* must not be reduced by losses of another accounting period. In the case of a Schedule A loss of an investment company the unrelieved loss is the lower of

(*a*) the Schedule A loss for the accounting period, or

(*b*) the amount which falls to be carried forward under *ICTA 1988, s 75(3)* (which is an amalgam of Schedule A losses and management expenses) but after deducting so much of that amount as is brought forward from an earlier accounting period.

**8.90** The land must be in the UK (and acquired by the company for the purpose of its trade or Schedule A business) and at the time of acquisition all or part of the land must have been in a contaminated state (*FA 2001, Sch 22 para 12(1)*). The relief is given in the accounting period in which the expenditure is deductible under the normal corporation tax rules (*FA 2001, Sch 22 para 12(2)(3)*). The relief cannot be claimed if the company itself or a person with a relevant connection was responsible wholly or partly, for the contamination (*FA 2001, Sch 22 para 12(4)*). A person has a relevant connection for this purpose if he was connected to the company (within *ICTA 1988, s 839* – see Appendix 1) either

(*a*) at the time that something that gave rise to the contamination was done (or omitted to be done),

(*b*) at the time that the land was acquired by it, or

(*c*) when the relevant land remediation work was undertaken by the company (either directly or on its behalf).

(*FA 2001, Sch 22 para 31(3)(4)*). The reason for this exclusion is not wholly apparent. Clearly a polluter ought to be expected to clean up his pollution without encouragement from the tax system as he already has a statutory obligation to do so. Nevertheless where pollution occurred in the past when there was no such obligation one would have thought that the landowner should be encouraged to clean it up irrespective of who caused it.

**8.91** The following constitutes relevant land remediation.

(*a*) The doing of any works (or taking any steps) in relation to the land in question, any controlled waters affected by that land or any adjoining or adjacent land for the purpose of:

  (i) preventing or minimising (or remedying or mitigating the effects of) any harm, or any pollution of controlled waters, by reason of which the land is in a contaminated state, or

  (ii) restoring the land or waters to its former state.

(*b*) Activities preparatory to such work which are undertaken by the company (either directly or on its behalf) for the purpose of assessing the condition of the land (or controlled waters or adjacent or adjoining land).

(*FA 2001, Sch 22 para 4(1)–(5)*). For this purpose 'harm' means harm to the health of living organisms, interference with the ecological systems of which any living organism forms part, offence to the senses of human beings, or damage to property (*FA 2001, Sch 22 para 31(1)*). Pollution of controlled waters means the entry into such waters of any poisonous, noxious or polluting matter or any solid waste matter (*FA 2001, Sch 22 para 31(1)*). Controlled waters has the same meaning as in *Part III* of the *Water Resources Act 1991* (or its Scottish or Northern Irish equivalents) (*FA 2001, Sch 22 para 31(2)*). Controlled waters are affected by land in a contaminated state if (and only if) the land is in such a condition by reason of substances in, on or under it that pollution of those waters is being caused (or likely to be caused) (*FA 2001, Sch 22 para 4(6)*). 'Substance' for this purpose means any natural or artificial substance, whether in solid or liquid form or in the form of a gas or vapour (*FA 2001, Sch 22 para 31(1)*).

**8.92** Qualifying land remediation expenditure is expenditure

(*a*) on land all or part of which is in a contaminated state (see 8.93),

(*b*) on relevant land remediation (see 8.91) directly undertaken by the company or on its behalf,

(*c*) on employee costs (see 8.94),

(*d*) on materials employed directly in that relevant land remediation (*FA 2001, Sch 22 para 6*), or

(*e*) which is expenditure on sub-contracted land remediation (see 8.95)

and would not have been incurred had the land not been in a contaminated state and which is not subsidised (see 8.95) (*FA 2001, Sch 22 para 2*).

**8.93** Land is in a contaminated state if (and only if) it is in such a condition (by reason of substances in, on or under the land) that harm is being caused (or there is a possibility of harm being caused) or pollution of controlled waters is being caused (or likely to be caused) (*FA 2001, Sch 22 para 3(1)*). But a nuclear site (one for which a nuclear site licence under the *Nuclear Installations Act 1965* is in force or previously existed and the period of responsibility of the licensee has not yet come to an end) is not land in a contaminated state (*FA 2001, Sch 22 para 3 (2)(3)*).

**8.94** The employee costs attributable to relevant land remediation are the employee costs (salaries, employer's national insurance and pension contributions, but excluding benefits in kind) paid in respect of directors or employees directly and actively engaged in that relevant land remediation (*FA 2001, Sch 22 para 5(1)(2)*). Where a director or employee is partly engaged directly and actively in relevant land remediation his costs are apportioned unless he spends less than 20% of his total working time on such work (when no part of the costs are allowed) or over 80% of his time (when the full costs are allowed) (*FA 2001, Sch 22 para 5(3)*). Employees providing support services, such as secretarial or administrative services, cannot be directly and actively employed in relevant land remediation even if the whole of their time is devoted to supporting people who work full time in such tasks (*FA 2001, Sch 22 para 5(4)*). A pension fund is defined by reference to *ICTA 1988, s 231A(4)*. Unfortunately that provision was repealed by *F(No 2)A 1997, s 30(8)*. It used to define a pension fund as any scheme, fund or other arrangements established and maintained (whether in the UK or elsewhere) for the purpose of providing pensions, retirement annuities, allowances, lump sums, gratuities or other superannuation benefits (with or without subsidiary benefits).

**8.95** Expenditure which would not have been incurred had the land not been in a contaminated state includes an increase in expenditure where the increase is incurred only by reason that the land is in a contaminated state, and also the costs of any works, operations or steps taken mainly for the purpose described in *para 3* (see 8.93) (*FA 2001, Sch 22 para 7*). *Paragraph 3* does not in fact contain a purpose. The legislation probably means for the purpose of *para 4(3)*. Expenditure is subsidised if a grant or subsidy is obtained in respect of it or it is otherwise met, directly or indirectly, by someone other than the company. A grant, subsidy or payment that is not allocated to particular items of expenditure must be allocated on a just and reasonable basis (*FA 2001, Sch 22 para 8*). Sub-contracted land remediation expenditure is of course a payment made to another person (the sub-contractor) in respect of relevant land remediation contracted out by the company to that person (*FA 2001, Sch 22 para 9*). Normally the whole of a sub-contractor payment qualifies for relief even though it includes overheads and profits that would not qualify if incurred by the company itself (*FA 2001, Sch 22 para 11*). Where the company and the sub-contractor are connected (within *s 839* – see Appendix 1) the payment is qualifying expenditure only to the extent of the sub-contractor's relevant expenditure, (i.e. expenditure incurred by the sub-contractor in carrying on the activities to which the sub-contractor payment relates which is incurred on employee costs or materials, is not of a capital nature, is not subsidised and is brought into account in determining the sub-contractor's expenditure) for a period for which accounts are drawn up and that ends not more than 12 months after the end of the paying company's period of account in which the sub-contractor payment is brought into account. Relief is also denied if the sub-contractor does not recognise the payment as income within the above period (*FA 2001, Sch 22 para 10*). This denies relief both on the part of the payment attributable to the sub-contractor's own profits and overheads and on any further amount that the sub-contractor carries forward in work in progress for over 12 months.

**8.96** If qualifying land remediation expenditure (see 8.94) is capital expenditure the company can elect for it to be allowed as a deduction in computing profits unless it qualifies for capital allowances. Such an election will trigger the 150% relief under *para 12*. The deduction is given in the accounting period in which the expenditure is incurred. If the company has not commenced its trade at that time it is given in the accounting period in which the trade commences. The election must be in writing, must specify the accounting period in which it is made and must be given within two years after the end of the accounting period to which it relates (*FA 2001, Sch 22 para 1*).

**8.97** Where a company claims a land remediation tax credit (see 8.89) the Revenue can instead of paying it set it (and interest on it) against any outstanding corporation tax liabilities. If the company owes PAYE and National Insurance for periods ending within the accounting period the Revenue are not entitled to offset it against such tax but need not pay the tax credit until the PAYE has been paid. If the company's tax return for the relevant period is enquired into they do not have to repay the credit until the enquiry is completed (*FA 2001, Sch 22 para 16*). A land remediation tax credit is of course not income for any tax purposes (*FA 2001, Sch 22 para 18*). The loss surrendered for the credit obviously cannot be carried forward; nor can expenditure included in it be claimed as a deduction in calculating a capital gain in respect of the land (*FA 2001, Sch 22 paras 17, 19*).

**8.98** No enhanced deduction (or tax credit) can be claimed to the extent that a transaction is attributable to arrangements (which includes any scheme, agreement or understanding whether or not legally enforceable) entered into wholly or mainly for a disqualifying purpose. Nor can the election to treat capital expenditure as revenue be made for such expenditure. Arrangements are for a disqualifying purpose if their main object, or one of their main objects, is to enable a company to obtain

(*a*) a deduction for capital expenditure which would not otherwise be allowed (or would otherwise have been smaller),

(*b*) land remediation relief to which the company would not otherwise be entitled, or

(*c*) a land remediation tax credit to which it would not otherwise be entitled.

(*FA 2001, Sch 22 para 29*).

**8.99** A land remediation tax credit carries the same interest as that on overpaid tax (*ICTA 1988, s 826(1)(e)* inserted by *FA 2001, Sch 22 para 3(2)*). Interest runs from the filing date (as defined in *FA 1998, Sch 18 para 14*) of the corporation tax return for the accounting period for which the credit is claimed (or from the date the return is actually filed if it is filed late) (*ICTA 1988, s 826(3B)* inserted by *FA 2001, Sch 23 para 3(3)*). A claim for the tax credit must be made by being included in a company tax return (which will include an amended return) (*ICTA 1988, Sch 18 paras 10(2A)* and *83A* inserted by *FA 2001, Sch 23 paras 4, 6*). The amount claimed must be quantified at the time the claim is made (*ICTA 1988, Sch 18 para 83I* inserted by *FA 2001, Sch 23 para 6*). A claim can be withdrawn or amended but only by amending the tax return. A claim or amendment or withdrawal must be made by the first anniversary of the filing date for the company tax return (or within such later time as the Revenue allow) (*ICTA 1988, Sch 18 paras 83J, 83K* inserted by *FA 2001, Sch 23 para 6*). A fraudulent or negligent claim for a land reclamation tax credit attracts a penalty of up to 100% of the credit (*ICTA 1988, Sch 18 para 83* inserted by *FA 2001, Sch 23 para 6*).

**8.100** Special rules apply to insurance companies. These are not considered here. They are contained in *FA 2001, Sch 22 paras 14(10), 20–28* and *29(2)(d) and (e).*

# Chapter 9

# Refurbishments

## Income and Corporation Tax

**9.1** If refurbishment work is carried out by a person who holds the building as dealing stock the expenditure will normally be revenue expenditure. It will be added to the cost of the building as stock-in-trade and will be deductible when the building is sold. Exceptionally, part may constitute repairs where the building has been let, but the costs of establishing the split will not always be justified.

### Is Expenditure Capital or Revenue?

**9.2** Where a building is held as an investment, refurbishment work can be either revenue or capital. If it is capital it will normally constitute enhancement expenditure for capital gains tax purposes. The problems lie in differentiating between the two.

**9.3** In general, works will be capital if they constitute improvements or the replacement of the entire asset. They will be revenue if they constitute repairs or the replacement of part of an asset. If by carrying out improvements the need for repairs is obviated the whole of the cost will nevertheless be capital; the notional figure of what the repairs would have cost cannot be deducted as a revenue expense (*William P Lawrie v CIR (34 TC 20)*; *Curtin v M Ltd (3 ITC 227)*). If, however, the improvements constitute the most practical way of restoring the building to its original condition they might be regarded as repairs (see 9.10 below). There used to be a concession for Schedule A purposes (ESC B4) (see 2.70 above) that effectively overrode this decision. It did not, however, apply for Schedule D purposes and has in any event been withdrawn from 1 April 2001. Unfortunately, the dividing line between improvements and repairs is often difficult to discern and the only real conclusion that can be drawn from the cases that have come before the courts seems to be that the decision in a particular case will depend upon its own individual facts. Nevertheless, it is helpful to consider the cases to try to bring out the main factors that need to be considered.

**9.4** The two leading cases on the dividing line between repair and improvement are *Law Shipping Co Ltd v CIR (12 TC 621)* and *Odeon*

*Associated Theatres Ltd v Jones (48 TC 257)*. In the *Law Shipping* case a company purchased a second-hand ship as it was about to start a voyage. When it reached port it was not allowed to leave until extensive work was carried out. It was held that the work was improvements. In effect the company had not bought a seaworthy ship; it had bought a dilapidated ship. The works were works of improvement as when they were finished the company had something of a different nature to that which it had purchased. In *Odeon Associated Theatres* the company acquired a number of cinemas during and immediately after the war. Because of wartime restrictions, repairs and redecorations, which would normally be done on a regular basis, had not been carried out. The state of disrepair on acquisition had, unlike in the *Law Shipping* case, not affected the price paid for the cinemas and the company operated them as cinemas for months to years before the repair work was carried out. It was held that the work was repairs not improvements.

**9.5** It is likely that the two cases both represent extremes. In *Law Shipping* the ship could not be used as a ship at all (or virtually at all) without carrying out the works. In the *Odeon* case the works were desirable but not essential to enable the buildings to be used as cinemas. The repaired asset was the same asset as when it was in disrepair, not something different improved out of all recognition. Where works are carried out shortly after the acquisition of a building the Revenue are likely to raise *Law Shipping* to demonstrate that they are capital. It is unlikely to be sufficient to defeat such a claim to show that the premises were usable on acquisition if subsequently the purchaser carried out refurbishment works before taking occupation. This suggests that they were not usable for the purpose for which he acquired them, which is much nearer the *Law Shipping* end of the line than the *Odeon* end. On the other hand if the purchaser actually occupies the premises for several months before carrying out the work, the Revenue claim should be resisted strongly because this demonstrates that the premises were suitable for the use for which they were acquired and is much nearer the *Odeon* end of the line. In *Jackson v Laskers Home Furnishers Ltd (37 TC 69)*, a company took a lease of dilapidated premises at a peppercorn rent for the first year but under a lease containing a covenant to reinstate the premises. Even though the premises were usable, it is not surprising that the expenditure on reinstatement was held to be capital because, as in *Law Shipping*, it is clear that the premises were acquired cheaply in contemplation of the repairs needing to be carried out. This case is not authority for regarding dilapidations as capital if the premises were in reasonable repair when the lease was taken on by the trader.

**9.6** The distinction between the two kinds of replacement is brought out by *Samuel Jones and Co (Devonvale) Ltd v CIR (32 TC 513)* and *O'Grady v Bullcroft Main Collieries Ltd (17 TC 93)*. In the *Samuel Jones* case a factory chimney became unsafe. It was demolished and replaced. It was held that the chimney was an integral part of the factory and the factory after the replacement was the same asset as before. Accordingly, the work was merely repairs. *Bullcroft* also involved a chimney. In this case it was a separate structure and not part of a building. It was demolished and a new chimney built a short distance away to replace it. It was held that the new chimney was not a repair of the old. It was a separate new asset. The cost was therefore capital.

**9.7** Again the two cases are opposite ends of a line. The test applied in both was the same though. Is the item replaced 'an entirety' or is it merely part of something larger? If it is an entirety, its replacement brings about a new asset. If it is not an entirety, its replacement is probably merely the repair of the larger asset which incorporates it. Unfortunately, it is not always easy to identify the entirety. In *Wynne-Jones v Bedale Auction Ltd (51 TC 426)* it was held that a cattle ring forming part of a large cattle mart was an entirety and could not be regarded as a mere part of the mart, and in *Brown v Burnley Football & Athletic Co Ltd (53 TC 357)* it was held that a stand at a football ground was an entirety and not a mere part of the ground. On the other hand in an Irish case, *Hodgkins v Plunder & Pollak (Ireland) Ltd (3 ITC 135)*, it was held that a weighbridge which was separate from the main factory building was not an entirety. It was a small part of the factory premises as a whole.

**9.8** In *Auckland Gas Co Ltd v CIR [of New Zealand] (2000 STC 527)* the Privy Council made clear that what is a repair is not to be found by any rigid test or description but depends on a consideration of all the circumstances. For many years Auckland Gas had a mainly low pressure network of underground cast iron pipes. These had a life of around 100 years but were prone to some major problems, leakage of gas and the entry of water, which occurred at joints in the pipes, fractures in the mains and corrosion of the pipes to individual premises. Auckland Gas developed a technique of inserting a polyethylene pipe into the existing cast iron mains and service pipes. Not only did this significantly reduce the maintenance problems but it enabled the gas to be transmitted at a much higher pressure. The courts accepted that if maintenance work had been done on the pipes the cost would have been deductible. But what had been done could not realistically be regarded merely as a repair of the network. 'For a leaky cast iron and steel low pressure system which it was not worthwhile renovating there had been substituted a system constructed of a new and different material, operating at a much higher pressure . . . . The old mains and services no longer performed any function save protecting the polyethylene pipe against vibration and ground movement. That could not fairly be described as a method of fixing the faulty joints and corrosion.' Lord Nicholls pointed out that 'the desire to solve a maintenance problem is not inconsistent with carrying out work of a capital nature. The nature and extent of the work carried out not the physical assets are what is determinative of the character of the work. The fact that the method chosen is the cheapest and most effective is neutral. It does not deprive expenditure of its capital character. Replacing an object may be cheaper and better than patching and mending.' By contrast in *Transco plc v Dyall (2002 STC*

*(SCD) 199) (SpC 310)* the similar insertion of polyethylene pipes into existing cast iron gas mains was held to be repairs. In this case the company had a policy of identifying pipes most at risk and inserting polyethylene into those pipes before a failure actually occurred. Furthermore the replacement was not of whole pipes. Nor did it enable the pipeline system to transport a different type of gas or to function at a higher pressure. Nor did it increase the useful life of the system.

**9.9** Finally, it should perhaps be mentioned that whilst alterations, particularly structural alterations, are normally regarded as capital, this is not an inviolate rule. In *Conn v Robins Bros Ltd (43 TC 266)*, a company carried on business in premises which were over 400 years old. It carried out various works including strengthening a floor and replacing the shop front having eliminated a bow front. It was held that the whole of the work was repairs. In the light of the age of the building, and modern building techniques, structural alterations may be the most efficient and effective way of restoring the building to its original condition. Support for this principle can also be found in the Revenue statement following the Docklands bombing (see 2.20) and in the decision in *Transco plc v Dyall (2002 STC (SCD) 199) (SpC 310)* (see 9.8).

**9.10** In practice, the expenditure involved in most refurbishments will not fit wholly into one or other category. It is necessary to look in detail at the work done and analyse it between capital and revenue items. In most cases part of the capital items will qualify for capital allowances as plant and machinery, so the expenditure normally has to be split into three categories: repairs, plant and machinery, and other improvement work.

## Should Landlord or Tenant Incur Expenditure?

**9.11** It is sometimes optional whether expenditure on repairs is incurred by the landlord or occupier. In particular, where property is refurbished prior to letting and certain works are required by the tenant, it can sometimes be better from a tax point of view to allow him a rent-free period – and possibly pay a reverse premium to cover the costs – and leave him to carry out the work himself. As the test of whether an item is plant is whether it performs a business function, it is often difficult for the landlord to establish items as plant whereas if the tenant installs them for the specific needs of his own business, he may have a far stronger case. If all the work does not need to be carried out immediately, the tenant may also be in a stronger position than the landlord to claim that work carried out a few months later is repairs.

**9.12** Where major works need to be carried out during the continuance of a lease, it should also be borne in mind that the tenant is likely to be in a position to claim tax relief at an earlier date than the landlord. The landlord's profit rental is more likely to be smaller, in relation to the cost of the works, than are the tenant's profits. The tenant can also carry a trading loss backwards and, if it is a member of a group, can surrender it by way of group relief, whereas the landlord can only carry a Schedule A deficiency forward unless it is a company, when it has greater flexibility.

## Effect on Time Apportionment

**9.13** Before 6 April 1988 difficulties could arise with calculating the capital gain on a refurbishment where the building was acquired before 6 April 1965. Following the rebasing of capital gains to 31 March 1982, it seems likely that most gains on properties will be calculated by reference to 31 March 1982 value, so that the old time apportionment rules, which gave rise to the problem, will now not often apply. However, it should not be overlooked that they can sometimes still do so. The difficulty was that the time apportionment rules required the gain on a pre-1965 property to be apportioned to blocks of expenditure by reference to their respective costs (*TCGA 1992, Sch 2 para 16(4)*), which could operate disadvantageously.

*Example 17*

A property cost £50,000 on 6 April 1945. A refurbishment was carried out in 1983 at a cost of £100,000 and the building was sold on 5 April 1985 for £350,000. If the refurbishment had not been carried out it would have realised £200,000. Indexation is ignored.

| | £ | £ |
|---|---|---|
| Sale proceeds | | 350,000 |
| Cost | 50,000 | |
| Enhancement expenditure | 100,000 | |
| | | 150,000 |
| | | £200,000 |
| Taxable (ignoring indexation) | | |
| 50/150 × £200,000 × 20/40ths | | 33,333 |
| 100/150 × £200,000 | | 133,334 |
| | | £166,667 |

If the refurbishment had not been carried out the position would have been

| | £ |
|---|---|
| Sale proceeds | 200,000 |
| Cost | 50,000 |
| | £150,000 |
| Taxable 20/40ths | £75,000 |

The additional profit generated by the refurbishment was £50,000 but the chargeable gain has increased by £91,667.

If the taxpayer does not claim relief for the refurbishment costs the position would be

| | £ |
|---|---|
| Sale proceeds | £350,000 |
| Cost | 50,000 |
| | £300,000 |
| Taxable 20/40ths | £150,000 |

**9.14** His ideal position would therefore be to carry out the refurbishment but not to claim relief for the costs. Can he do this? The answer is unclear. The amount of a gain accruing on a disposal must be computed in accordance with *TCGA 1992, Part II* (*TCGA 1992, s 15(1)*). Unfortunately, that *Chapter* does not say how a gain is computed. It merely lays down how to arrive at the disposal consideration and the deductions. In particular *section 38* provides that 'the sums allowable as a deduction . . . shall be restricted to' specified types of expenditure. This wording does not seem apt to force someone to deduct an amount if he opts not to do so. *Paragraph 16(4)* of *Schedule 2* refers to 'any of the expenditure which is allowable as a deduction in the computation'. If *section 38* does not force the taxpayer to claim expenditure, is it still allowable as a deduction in the computation if it is not claimed? The Revenue view is that as the *Act* does not require a claim, all expenditure falling within *section 38* must be deducted. However, the Court of Appeal has held in the case of *Elliss v BP Northern Ireland Refinery Ltd (59 TC 474)*, which deals with capital allowances – where the legislation reads 'where a person incurs capital expenditure . . . there shall be made to him . . . an allowance' – that the taxpayer did not have to accept the allowances if he did not want them, and the wording of the legislation in that case seems far more mandatory than that of *section 38*. It seems doubtful that a taxpayer could be faulted for not claiming a deduction for expenditure if he does not want to. It is difficult to believe that, if he does not know the amount of all his expenditure, the legislature should have intended that he should be forced to undertake a lot of work to ascertain such information.

**9.15** It should be remembered that the legislation provides a small measure of relief from this problem in some cases. If there is no initial expenditure (i.e. cost of the asset), or such expenditure is disproportionately small as compared with any of the items of enhancement expenditure (having regard to the value of the asset immediately before the enhancement expenditure was incurred), the gain can be apportioned to the blocks of expenditure by reference to the values at that time, and the part attributable to the initial acquisition of the asset treated as arising over the period from the time of that acquisition (*TCGA 1992, Sch 2 para 16(5)*). In practice the Revenue seem reluctant to accept that this provision can be used unless the cost is very small in comparison with enhancement expenditure. It should be particularly noted that the comparison is with cost, not the value of the building immediately before the enhancement expenditure is incurred, e.g. if a building cost £50,000 in 1950 and enhancement expenditure of £30,000 is incurred in 1986 when the value of the original building is, say, £400,000, the *section* would not apply, as although £30,000 may be small in relation to £400,000 it is not disproportionately small in relation to £50,000.

## VAT

### General Principles

**9.16** Refurbishment, however major, is not the construction of a building. Accordingly the refurbishment of residential and relevant charitable buildings cannot attract zero-rating. Equally as the finished development will not be a 'new' building the disposal or grant of leases after development will be exempt from VAT. The 17½% VAT charge that applies on the disposal of a new building (see 17.110 below) does not apply. Refurbishment for this purpose includes the extension, enlargement, or reconstruction of an existing building. The dividing line between the reconstruction of a building and the construction of a new one is not always clear. Customs' guidance on this is set out in 8.64 above.

**9.17** Accordingly a developer carrying out a refurbishment is not normally in a position to claim relief for input tax he suffers on his expenditure unless he exercises the option to tax (see 17.153). VAT on refurbishment costs is thus an additional cost of the development. Because of this, when carrying out a refurbishment consideration needs to be given to making this election to bring the building into the VAT net. In theory, if the most likely tenant or purchaser for a building will be a taxable person he should not mind paying VAT on his rent or acquisition cost as he will be able to recover this from Customs. The occasion of a major refurbishment calls for a review of an initial decision not to elect, as the tax at stake is likely to be significant. In most cases it is likely to make sense to make the election at that stage.

**9.18** From 1 January 1992 the self-supply charge outlined in 8.38 to 8.56 above was extended to certain reconstructions and enlargements of existing buildings. The types of reconstruction to which the charge applied and the detailed rules are considered at 8.42 and 8.52 above. This charge does not apply to developments commenced after 28 February 1995.

## Protected Buildings

**9.19** There is a common misconception that work on a listed building is zero-rated if the building is a residential or relevant charitable one. In fact the zero-rating is fairly limited. It applies only to the substantial reconstruction or approved alteration of such a building (*VATA 1994, Sch 8 Group 6*). A protected building is a listed building within the meaning of the *Planning (Listed Buildings and Conservation Areas) Act 1990* (formerly *Part IV* of the *Town and Country Planning Act 1971*) (or the corresponding Scottish or Northern Irish legislation) or a scheduled monument within the meaning of the *Ancient Monuments and Archaeological Areas Act 1979* (or the *Historic Monuments Act (Northern Ireland) 1971*). (*VATA 1994, Sch 8 Group 6, Note 1*). The building must be designed to remain as (or become) a dwelling (or a number of dwellings), or be intended for use for a relevant residential or relevant charitable purpose (see 17.28 and 17.34 below) after the reconstruction or alteration. A building is designed to remain as (or become) a dwelling only if each dwelling within it consists of self-contained living accommodation, there is no provision for direct internal access from the dwelling to any other dwelling (or part of one) and the separate use or disposal of the dwelling is not prohibited by a covenant, statutory planning consent or similar provision. A garage occupied with a dwelling and either constructed (or reconstructed) at the same time as the dwelling is regarded as part of it (*Note 2*). The items that qualify for zero-rating are as follows.

1. The first grant by a person substantially reconstructing (see 9.22) a protected building (or by some other person if the benefit of the consideration accrues to the reconstruction) of a major interest (see 8.32 above) in, or in any part of, the building or its site.

2. The supply, in the course of an approved alteration (see 9.20) of a protected building, of any services other than the services of an architect, surveyor or any person acting as consultant or in any supervisory capacity.

3. The supply of building materials (which has the same meaning as in 8.27) to a person by a supplier who *also supplies* to the same person *services* within *item 2* above which include the incorporation of the materials into the building.

**9.20** An approved alteration to a building is:

(*a*) works of alteration to a building used for ecclesiastical purposes (excluding use as a minister of religion's residence);

(*b*) works of alteration for which consent has been given under *Historic Monuments Act (Northern Ireland) 1971, s 10*; or (*c*) works of alteration which cannot (or could not but for a Crown or Duchy interest) be carried out without consent under *Planning (Listed Buildings and Conservation Areas) Act 1990* (or the Scottish or Irish equivalents) or *Ancient Monuments and Archaeological Areas Act 1979, Part I*, and for which consent has been duly obtained (*Notes 6* to *8*).

Works of repair or maintenance cannot be an approved alteration though. Nor since 1 March 1995 can an incidental alteration to the fabric of a building resulting from carrying out repairs or maintenance. The objective is to prevent claims that, for example, the repair of a roof is an alteration because the use of modern building methods and materials has changed the pitch of the roof (VAT Information Sheet 10/95). This did not prevent the VAT tribunal in *N F Rhodes (VTD 14533*), where 65% of a roof was in disrepair so the entire roof was replaced, from holding that the remaining 35% of the cost that had been incurred for purely aesthetic reasons to restore the appearance of the whole roof qualified for zero-rating.

**9.21** The *Planning (Listed Buildings and Conservation Areas) Act 1990, s 6(2)* prevents a local authority from serving a building preservation order for five years from the date of issue of an immunity certificate by the Secretary of State for National Heritage. This is intended to give the owner an opportunity to carry out preservation work without the added burden of planning controls. However it also means that 9.20(*c*) cannot be satisfied, so a person applying for an immunity certificate in effect forfeits the VAT relief. This makes application for an immunity certificate unwise in many cases. Where an immunity certificate was issued before 1 March 1996 Customs were by concession prepared to allow the relief as if condition (*c*) were met, but now that they have highlighted the problem they expect applicants for immunity certificates to take into account the resultant loss of VAT relief (News Release 25/96).

**9.22** A building is not to be regarded as substantially reconstructed unless either:

(*a*) at least 60% (by cost) of the work carried out (excluding the cost of an architect, surveyor, etc.), would, if supplied by an independent contractor, be within the second and third heads in 9.19 above; or

(*b*) the reconstructed building incorporates no more of the original building than the external walls, together with other external features of architectural or historic interest (*Note 4*).

**9.23** The latter suggests either that the then government felt that we have no interiors worthy of preservation or that conservation is all very well but tax maximisation is far more important. To fall within head (*a*) at least 60% of the works carried out would have had to require listed building consent. In many cases it is only the exterior of a building that is listed, whereas the bulk of the building work is likely to be the interior. Accordingly this test is not always as easy to meet as it appears at first sight. It should not be assumed that any major work on a listed building which is going to be used for a residential or relevant charitable purpose will qualify for zero-rating.

**9.24** *Notes 1, 4, 6 12–14* and *22–24* of *Group 5* (see 17.6 and 17.17–21 below) also apply for the purpose of *Group 6* (*VATA 1994, Sch 8 Group 6, Note 3*). Curiously the deemed disposal provisions where a building ceases to be used for a qualifying purpose (17.65–17.71 below) do not apply to *Group 6*. Alteration does not include repair or maintenance, and where only part of any work is an approved alteration an apportionment must be made (*VATA 1994, Sch 8 Group 6, Note 5*). Similarly an apportionment is made if a service within *item 2* is supplied partly in relation to an approved alteration and partly for some other purpose (*Note 9*). In *Dr NDF Browne (VTD 11388)* a VAT tribunal held that where the most effective repair or maintenance of an old building involved the use of modern methods or different building materials it was still a repair, not an alteration. A similar decision was reached in *C & E Commrs v Windflower Housing Association (1995 STC 860)* where a replacement roof was constructed to a higher specification and designed with a view to a possible future attic conversion. Even raising the roof pitch was held to be an integral part of the remainder of the work. In *C R Morrish (VTD 14817)* the tribunal noted that the listed buildings legislation referred to 'works for alteration or extension of the building in any manner affecting its character as a building of special architectural or historic interest' and concluded that 'in any manner' gave 'alteration' a wide meaning that is not limited to structural alteration and so was able to distinguish the case from the *Windflower* one. It held that any items that altered the building in any manner that affected its character attract zero-rating. It also felt that the reconstruction works (after a severe fire) were too extensive to be excluded as repairs or maintenance, although it did disallow repairs to the outer walls under that head. On appeal (*C & E Commrs v Windflower Housing Association (1998 STC 954)*) Moses J said that the Tribunal had applied the wrong test. The statute requires consideration of three categories, reconstruction, alteration and repair and maintenance. Only alteration is zero-rated. If what was happening, viewed as a whole, was a supply in the course of rebuilding or reconstruction, it was standard-rated. The case was remitted to a fresh tribunal to find out whether there was any building in existence at all after the fire, as if there was not there could be no alteration.

In the case of *Vicar and Parochial Church Council of St Petroc Minor* work to stop damp penetration through part of the vestry wall of a listed church was held to be maintenance. Any element of alteration was an incidental result of such maintenance.

This can be contrasted with the decision in *All Saints with St Nicholas Church, Icklesham (VTD 16321)* where the work to a church was held to be an approved alteration not repair or maintenance as it was the complete replacement of the existing lighting system. The vagaries of the legislation seem well illustrated by the decision in *C Mason (VTD 16250)*. Mr Mason replaced two lengths of boundary fence by walls. The first abutted the listed building and ran up to a hedge. The second ran from the other end of the hedge to some outbuildings. The first part of the wall was held to be part of the listed building but the second part was held to be a structure separate from the listed building so that its construction could not be an alteration of that building.

**9.25** Customs take the view that an approved alteration must amount to an alteration of the building's fabric. In *C & E Commrs v Viva Gas Appliances Ltd [1983] STC 819, [1983] 1 WLR 1445, [1984] 1 All ER 112, HL* the House of Lords held that 'alteration' included any work upon the fabric of the building except that which was so slight or trivial as to be *de minimis*. Customs accept that mains electrical wiring and lighting systems are part of the fabric of a building to the extent that they are in or on the structure of the building itself. Items that extend beyond the structure, such as wiring to floodlights in the grounds of churches will not attract zero-rating. Nor will electrical appliances that are attached to and serviced by the mains supply (Business Brief 7/00).

**9.26** When considering whether a supply in the course of an approved alteration of a protected building, and services other than the specified professional services, qualify for zero-rating (under *item 2* in 9.19 above), the construction of a building separate from, but in the curtilage of, a protected building is not to constitute an alteration of that building (*VATA 1994, Sch 8 Group 6, Note 10*). The meaning of curtilage is considered in 13.4(*d*) below. Customs state that the effect is to exclude from zero-rating such items as a new workshop in the grounds of a listed dwelling. This exclusion only prevents the new building qualifying for zero-rating under *Group 6*. It might, of course, still qualify for zero-rating in its own right under *Group 5* (residential and relevant charitable development). Customs give as an example the erection of a new dwelling in the grounds of a listed hospital. It should be borne in mind though that *Group 5* is not apposite to cover the erection of a building which is not itself a dwelling but is designed for use with a dwelling, e.g. a residents' sun lounge in the garden of an old people's home. In any event what is a separate building is a question of fact. In *Martyn Arbib (VTD 11486)* the VAT tribunal held that a swimming pool building separated from the main house by a brick wall but connected by a walkway with a roof and open sides was not a separate building but an alteration to the house. The decision was upheld in the High Court. In *Ventrolla Ltd (VTD 12045)* where a replacement window was claimed to be an improvement the tribunal held that the view of the planning authority that it was an alteration requiring listed building consent was not conclusive. There was no alteration to the fabric of the building and even if the window was an alteration it was an alteration to the window not the building.

**9.27** In *C A Orme (VTD 9975)* a VAT tribunal held that the extent of the protected building could include buildings not physically attached to the main house but so close as to form an integral part of it. This was a question of fact and degree. However, a later tribunal held in *C M Lee (VTD 10662)* held that this cannot apply after 31 December 1991. A similar decision was reached in *PVR Nicholls (VTD 11115)*, where it was held that a door in the passageway between the two buildings, thus linking the two, did not justify the conclusion that the secondary building was affixed to the existing one so as to amount to an alteration to it rather than the construction of a separate building. The tribunal in *N Hardy (VTD 12776)* felt that the *Orme* principle still applied though. In that case it was held that the outbuilding and the house together formed one dwelling which was a protected building. It was also accepted, applying *Pepper v Hart (1992 STC 898)*, that when the legislation was amended it had been Parliament's intention to preserve zero-rating for domestic buildings. A similar decision was reached in *G M Morfee (VTD 13816)* where work on a barn within the curtilage of a listed building (but not specifically mentioned in the listing) was held to be in the course of an approved alteration to the main building as the two constituted a single entity which was a protected building used as the owner's dwelling. However in a more recent case *A J & L Kernahan (VTD 15203)* where conversion work was carried out on outbuildings to a listed farmhouse, the Tribunal relied on the *Orme* decision in holding that the outbuildings were not an integral part of the dwelling constituted by the main house. In *Dr A Heijn (VTD 15562)* it was accepted that converted outbuildings were within the curtilage of the house and formed part of the listed buildings but the work was held not to be eligible for zero-rating as there was insufficient evidence to show that before the work was carried out the outbuildings had been an integral part of the house so as to 'remain' part of the dwelling after the alteration. The *Orme* decision was also followed in *D & L Clamp (VTD 16422)* where it was accepted that a converted barn was part of the main house, although as its separate use was prevented by a planning agreement the building work did not qualify for zero-rating. A curious decision was reached in *R G Powell (VTD 14520)*. Mr Powell was a metalworker specialising in architectural metalwork. He was commissioned to cast and erect iron railings and gates to enclose a churchyard in order to discourage use of the churchyard by vagrants, etc. The church was a listed building. The railings were not affixed to the church but for part of the way were affixed to an existing stone wall. The tribunal held that the stone wall was a structure within the curtilage of the church so was part of the listed building. Accordingly the part of the railings attached to the wall was entitled to zero-rating but the balance was not. This decision seems curious because if the remainder of the railings were within the curtilage of the church it would be logical to regard their erection as much an alteration to the listed building as the part that altered an existing structure within its curtilage. In *D L Wilson (VTD 15803)* where the taxpayer obtained listed building consent to reconstruct his garage the work was held to be the 'construction' of a separate building falling within *Note 10*.

**9.28** The issue finally came before the courts in *C & E Commrs v Zielinski Baker & Partners Ltd* which has resulted in a split decision in the taxpayer's favour in the Court of Appeal *(2002 STC 417, [2002] EWCA Civ 692)*. Zielenski Baker are property developers. In 1994 they were instructed to prepare and oversee a scheme for a development within the ground of a listed building. The scheme included some elements which were accepted as taxable. The disputed items were the conversion of an outbuilding into games and changing facilities and the construction of an adjoining indoor swimming pool. Zielenski Baker claimed that these should be zero-rated as approved alterations to a protected building. The outbuilding was (and always had been) linked to the house by a wall and was built at the same time as the house. Listed buildings consent was necessary for the works as the outbuilding was within the curtilage of a listed building, and this was duly obtained.

**9.29** Rex L J considered the critical issue to be 'What is the building which must be protected?' If it is the outbuilding the appeal must fail as the outbuilding is not a dwelling. If it is the house the supply must be in the course of an approved alteration of a protected building. He thought that as the *Planning (Listed Buildings and Conservation Areas) Act 1990* extends the ambit of a listed building to cover any separate structure within its curtilage, provided that it has formed part of the land since before 1 July 1948, it is not easy to see why the outbuilding should be treated as a separate building, which must on its own qualify as a protected building. If that were intended, one would expect the legislation to contain provisions talking of part of a building or which deal with the concept of a separate building within the curtilage of a protected building. He branded the two-stage approach adopted by the tribunal (is the outbuilding a protected building and if so is it designed to remain or become a dwelling?) as impermissible. Instead he started with the concept of a protected building. He said that no special provision is made in the legislation for secondary buildings (other than garages) even thought the draftsman specifically had in mind the special definition in *section 1(1)(b)* of the *Planning Act* and went out of his way in *Note 10* (see 9.26) to emphasise that the construction of a separate building within the curtilage of a protected building does not constitute the alteration of a protected building. *Note 10* does not make much sense if the protected building is the new building, as it would be constructed not altered. The reference to the protected building must be the main building and *Note 10* prevents a new building from acquiring zero-rated status that it would otherwise have – and which by inference an existing subsidiary building must have. It also seemed logical to him to apply the purposive approach that, as approved alterations are more costly because they have to be done in an approved way to blend in, the government should have given limited support to maintain their use as dwellings and to encourage the preservation of the nation's heritage.

**9.30** In *K & G Levell (VTD 6202)* an old wall enclosed a kitchen garden of a listed building. A new building was erected on the outside of the wall in the style of a cart shed. The old wall was joined to the roof and gutters of the new building and although it formed the rear of, it was not part of, the supporting structure. It was held that the construction of the new building on its own separate foundation was not an 'alteration' of the wall and thus did not qualify for zero-rating. Alteration does not apparently need to be substantial. The VAT tribunal in *Wrencon Ltd (VTD 13968)* felt that the word had to be construed in the context of the planning law which required approval for any alteration which affected the building's character. This did not imply a structural alteration. It therefore felt that the painting of the outside walls which were previously unpainted was capable of qualifying for zero-rating. In that particular case they felt the work was repair as it was carried out in the context of general repairs and maintenance. *In C N Foley (VTD 13496)* changes to the height and ridges of the roof on a 13th century house were held to be alterations even though the change in the profile of the building viewed from below was slight. In *Dodson Bros (Thatchers) Ltd (VTD 13734)* re-thatching two listed buildings with Norfolk reed was held to be alterations as the different appearance of the thatch affected the character of the building. It is probably relevant that the roof was not in need of repair; in the first case it was wished to install a fire barrier and in the second it was wished to cure leakage around windows in the thatch. In *Parochial Church Council of Holy Trinity Church, Wolverhampton (VTD 13652)* works on the installation for the first time of electrical fittings was held to be an alteration to the building but where the work merely involved the repositioning of a light or where lights were installed on fittings such as the lectern rather than the fabric of the building zero-rating did not apply.

**9.31** In *C & E Commrs v Jeffs and another t/a J & J Joinery (1995 STC 759)* the appellants carried out joinery work off site to a customer's specific requirements and delivered it to the site where it was fitted by the customer's builders. The appellant made an initial site visit to take measurements and there was an implied obligation to make further site visits if any problems arose with their handiwork. Customs' contention that the work was not entitled to zero-rating under what is now *item 2* of *Group 6* (see 9.19) as it was a supply of goods without services was upheld by the court (reversing the decision of the VAT tribunal). Whether there is only a supply of goods or separate supplies of goods and services is a question of law, the answer to which is to be obtained by the application of common sense to the substance and reality of the matter as the court perceives it. In this case the services were nothing more than the normal obligations imposed by law upon any seller of goods. In *M E J Burgess and A P Holmes (VTD 14475)* the supply and fitting of individually-made display units in a shop, none of which were free-standing, was held to be a supply of services to which the goods were incidental. The tribunal accepted Customs' views that the shop-fitting works were not dissimilar to the work of painting a room, where the paint is not a separate supply of goods!

**9.32** In *Nick Hopewell-Smith (VTD 16725)* a barn was converted for use as residential accommodation ancillary to a Grade II listed farmhouse. It was 11 metres from the house and had been used for storage. After conversion the barn was physically capable of being occupied as self-contained living accommodation and there was no provision for internal access from the barn to the house. The tribunal noted that, although the planning consent prevented separate use, it did not prohibit the separate disposal of the house. Accordingly *VATA 1994, Sch 8 Group 6, Note 2(c)* did not apply as the two tests were expressed in the alternative. The building was in fact used by the family who occupied the house. The tribunal (Stephen Oliver QC) nevertheless held that the work qualified for zero-rating either because, notwithstanding that it was separated from the house, the barn could be described as a building designed to be part of a dwelling consisting of self-contained living accommodation or because it was such a dwelling in its own right.

**9.33** The taxpayer was similarly lucky in *Hill Ash Developments (VTD 16747)*. Hill Ash carried out building work on a house and associated farm buildings purchased for use as a nursing home. The house was a listed building but the farm was not. The house was used as the nursing home. The listed building consent was for extension to the nursing home and conversion of agricultural buildings to form care flats and an administration block. The tribunal held that the disputed work was a conversion of the administration block and could not qualify for zero-rating as a supply in the course of construction of a dwelling under *VATA 1994, Sch 8 Group 5*. However it did qualify for zero-rating as supplies in the course of approved alterations to a protected building. Although the administration block did not contain sleeping accommodation its use was so intimately bound up with the residential accommodation provided by the house and a new barn block as to constitute use for a relevant residential purpose following Hardy (see 9.27). As the work did not involve the construction of a building it was unnecessary to decide whether the administration block was separate from the protected building.

**9.34** In the same way as for *Group 5*, the exclusion from zero-rating under *item 2* for services consisting of the use of an item where there is no transfer of ownership but merely a transfer of an undivided share in the item, or possession of it, and for items which are acquired for use in a business but appropriated for private use (see 17.64(*c*)), apply (*VATA 1994, Sch 8 Group 6, Note 11*).

**9.35** It should be noted that whether or not a listed building qualifies for zero-rating will depend on its intended use after conversion. For example, the conversion of a listed windmill into a house can qualify but the conversion of a listed almshouse into offices would not do so, even if it had retained its residential use up to the time of conversion. At least this seems to be the intention, but it is a somewhat odd use of English to say that a windmill built in 1690 was 'designed to . . . become a dwelling' if work is carried out on it in 1990 to adapt it for use as a dwelling. It is 'intended' to become a dwelling after the substantial reconstruction. The substantial reconstruction is designed to change the building into a dwelling. It seems doubtful if the windmill itself was designed to become a dwelling. Conversely the almshouse in the other example when built would have been designed to become a building for use for a relevant residential purpose, even though after the substantial reconstruction it would no longer be so used!

**9.36** The timing of the work can be important. In *R W Gibbs (VTD 5596)* asbestos insulation was removed from pipework in the roof of a listed building. The owner had applied for listed building consent for the work but it was completed before the consent was formally granted. The VAT tribunal held, *inter alia*, that as consent had not been obtained at the time the work was carried out the work did not satisfy the definition of 'an approved alteration'. This was followed in *Alan Roper & Sons Ltd (VTD 15260)* where the tribunal said that a retrospective planning permission is in effect consent to retention of the alterations. A similar conclusion was reached in *Mr & Mrs Wells (VTD 15169)* where as the work progressed some of the planned (and approved) work proved impractical. Listed building consent for such modifications was applied for and granted retrospectively. It was held that zero-rating could not apply as such approval did not exist at the time the work was done. This seems very harsh.

# Allowances for Capital Expenditure

**10.1** Capital allowances are granted in respect of capital expenditure incurred on qualifying assets. It is normally (although not always) necessary for the person claiming the allowances to own the asset and to have incurred the expenditure attracting the allowance. As the expenditure must be capital expenditure, allowances cannot be claimed in respect of expenditure on an asset that constitutes dealing stock (*CAA 1990, s 159(1)*). A detailed consideration of all the capital allowances rules is outside the scope of this work. This chapter deals with capital allowances only in the particular context of the ownership of property. In a property context capital allowances can be claimable under the following provisions.

(*a*) Plant and Machinery (*CAA 2001, ss 11–270*).

(*b*) Industrial Buildings (*CAA 2001, ss 271–360*).

(*c*) Agricultural Buildings and Works (*CAA 2001, ss 361–393*).

(*d*) Qualifying Hotels (*CAA 2001, ss 271(3), 285(1), 317*).

(*e*) Commercial Buildings in Enterprise Zones (*CAA 2001, ss 271(1), 281, 298, 299, 302, 303*).

(*f*) Research and Development (*CAA 2001, ss 437–451*).

(*g*) Certain Fire Safety Expenditure (*CAA 2001, ss 27, 29*).

(*h*) Thermal Insulation of Industrial Buildings (*CAA 2001, ss 27, 28*).

(*i*) Dwelling Houses let on Assured Tenancies (*CAA 2001, ss 490–531*).

(*j*) Certain Expenditure on Sports Stadia (*CAA 2001, s 27(1), 30–32*).

(*k*) Authorised Quarantine Premises (repealed *FA 1988, s 94*).

(*l*) Cemeteries & Crematoria (*ICTA 1988, s 91*).

(*m*) Dredging (*CAA 2001, ss 484–489*).

(*n*) Mines and Oil Wells (*CAA 2001, ss 394–436* but see 10.200 below).

(*o*) Certain expenditure on security (*CAA 2001, s 33*).

Capital allowances can, of course, also be claimed on equipment used in the management of property (see 2.31 above).

## Plant and Machinery

### Introduction

**10.2** Much of the expenditure in relation to a modern building relates to items that constitute plant or machinery. A taxpayer is entitled, if he wishes, to isolate such expenditure and claim the appropriate capital allowances provided, of course, that he satisfies the appropriate conditions. It is often not appreciated that this applies as much to a building that is purchased second-hand as to the construction of a new building. When a person buys the freehold of an existing building he is acquiring an amalgam of three things, the land, the building and the plant and machinery included in it. The overall cost can be apportioned between these three elements. On average around 12% of the purchase price of a non air-conditioned late 1970 office building is likely to qualify for capital allowances. In a modern air-conditioned building the eligible proportion will be far greater. An interesting article on the principles involved can be found in Taxline, February 1996. Unlike with industrial building allowances, in many cases (but not all) the allowance for plant is based solely on the price the purchaser pays for the building; the initial cost of installing the plant is irrelevant. Obviously the apportionment depends on valuation techniques and requires a knowledge of building construction, so needs to be done by an architect or quantity surveyor. There are substantial restrictions on what items in a building can constitute plant for expenditure after 29 November 1993 (see 10.44–10.50). It is believed that this statutory limitation is in response to a claim by one of the major supermarket groups before the Special Commissioners that an entire supermarket and its adjoining car park qualifies as plant. A very helpful and comprehensive check list of the items in a building that might qualify for capital allowances as plant or machinery can be found in Taxation of 18 November 1993 (pages 148–150). Although this was prepared before the *Finance Act 1994* changes, most of the items are still relevant.

**10.3** Normally, capital allowances can be claimed only where the taxpayer has incurred the capital expenditure on the plant and machinery for the purposes of a trade carried on by him (*CAA 2001, s 11(4)*). Allowances are also due where the expenditure was for the purposes of a profession, employment, vocation or office (*CAA 2001, ss 15(1)(e), 80*). They can also be claimed on plant and machinery used in connection with estate management (*ICTA 1988, s 32*) or the management of the business of an investment company (*CAA 2001, ss 15(1)(g), 253*).

**10.4** Of equal, if not greater, importance in a property context is that the leasing of plant or machinery otherwise than in the course of a trade qualifies for capital allowances – irrespective of whether or not the lessee is carrying on a trade – except where the machinery or plant is let for use in a dwelling-house (*CAA 2001, ss 15(1)(h), 19*). *Section 15(1)(h)* is not restricted to cases where the letting is solely of plant or machinery; it will accordingly equally apply where a building is let and plant and machinery is included in the building so that the letting embraces such items. Indeed, leasing of plant or machinery as such would normally constitute a trade and would not need the extension provided by *section 15(1)(h)*, so the provision in practice applies primarily to the letting of buildings. The *section* contains a specific exclusion for residential property (*CAA 2001, s 35*).

## Allowances Available

**10.5** Apart from a short period during 1992 and 1993 (see below) and a number of targeted reliefs for small businesses from 1 July 1997, the capital allowances on plant and machinery incurred after 31 March 1986 consist solely of writing-down allowances, which are given at the rate of 25% p.a. on expenditure incurred in the accounting period (or in the basis period for the relevant year of assessment). For each subsequent accounting period, etc., the writing-down allowance is given at the rate of 25% p.a. on the reducing balance, i.e. on the written-down value at the beginning of the period. Balancing charges can arise where an asset is disposed of for a price in excess of the written-down value of all of the plant and machinery in that particular building (which will normally only occur on the sale of the building) and a balancing allowance can arise where the building is sold (but only in the comparatively rare circumstance where the part of the sale proceeds attributable to the plant is below its written-down value). The writing-down allowance is reduced to 6% p.a. for some expenditure on long-life assets after 25 November 1996 (see 10.81 below). First-year allowances of up to 100% were available for expenditure incurred before 1 April 1986, but were generally abolished for expenditure incurred on or after that date. There were anti-avoidance provisions, not considered here, restricting first-year allowances for certain expenditure under contracts entered into after 13 March 1984 and before 1 April 1986 (*FA 1984, Sch 12 para 5*). First-year allowances could not be claimed if the lessee did not use the building for the purposes of a trade (*CAA 1990, ss 22(4)(c), 39(1)*). First-year allowances, at the rate of 40% were reintroduced briefly for expenditure incurred between 1 November 1992 and 31 October 1993 (but not on pre-trading expenditure where a trade commenced in that period) (*FA 1993, s 115*).

**10.6** The Labour government seems to be using first-year allowances on plant and machinery as an economic tool. It reintroduced first year allowances for 'small or medium-sized enterprises' only, at 50% on expenditure during the year to 1 July 1998 (*CAA 1990, s 22 (1AA)*) and at 40% on expenditure during the year to 1 July 1999 (*FA 1998, s 84*). It extended the 40% allowance for a further year in *Finance Act 1999* before making it permanent by *FA 2000, s 70(1)*.

**10.7** A 'small or medium-sized enterprise' for this purpose is a company or business that qualifies as a small or medium-sized company under the *Companies Act* (or if it is an unincorporated business would have done had it been a company). This means it must meet two of the three tests of turnover not exceeding £11.2m, assets not exceeding £5.6m and not more than 250 staff. Most companies are small under this test. If the company is a member of a group the test is applied to the group as a whole (*CAA 2001, s 49*). Where the parent company of a group is outside the UK the group test did not apply to expenditure before 12 May 1998.

**10.8** A first-year allowance of 100% is given on expenditure by a small or medium-sized enterprise during the four years from 12 May 1998 to 11 May 2002 on plant or machinery for use primarily in Northern Ireland (*CAA 2001, s 40*). The allowance does not apply to long-life assets though (*CAA 2001, s 41*). Nor does it apply if the plant is intended to be used partly outside Northern Ireland and the main benefit of the increased allowance could reasonably be expected to be attributable to that outside use (*CAA 2001, s 42*). If an item is intended to be used in Northern Ireland but within two years is put to a use outside that Province the allowance is withdrawn (*CAA 2001, s 43*). This will obviously rarely occur in the context of assets in a property.

Where the plant or machinery is for use primarily in agriculture, fishing or fish farming, or certain activities carried out in relation to bringing agricultural or piscine products to market, the expenditure must be authorised by the Department of Agriculture for Northern Ireland (*CAA 2001, s 41(2)*). This restriction was forced on the Government by the EC Commission as State aid for those activities is illegal under EC rules.

**10.9** A 100% first-year allowance is also given for expenditure by small enterprises (but not a medium-sized one) on information and communications technology between 1 April 2000 and 31 March 2003 (*CAA 2001, s 45*). The *Companies Act 1985, s 247* definition of a small company (two out of three tests of turnover not exceeding £2.8 million, assets not exceeding £1.4 million and no more than 50 employees) applies to a company and also by analogy to an unincorporated business (*CAA 2001, s 47(3)(4)*). The definition of information and communications technology specifically includes peripherals and also equipment (including cabling) for use primarily to provide a connection between computers (or between a computer and a data communications network) and dedicated electrical systems for computers. A computer for this purpose specifically excludes computerised control or management systems (e.g. for air conditioning) or parts of other systems whose principal function is not processing or storing information (*CAA 2001, s 45(2)*).

**10.10** If a building is sold to a connected person it may be difficult to avoid a balancing charge or allowance on the sale. An election to transfer at tax written-down value can be made only where a person succeeds to a trade that was previously carried on by a connected person within *ICTA 1988, s 839* (see Appendix 1) (*CAA 2001, s 266*). Unlike industrial buildings (see 10.127 below), an election cannot be made on the mere transfer of an asset. It may be possible to attribute a nominal sum to the plant and machinery in the sale contract and claim the protection of *CAA 2001, s 61*, but there is a risk that the Revenue might regard such an apportionment as a sham (but see 10.68(*a*)). It is doubtful whether a person could succeed to the deemed trade assumed under *CAA 1990, s 61(1)*. This was apparently also the view of the Inland Revenue (see Taxline, Issue 18, Jan 1994, p 7). This is no longer a problem, as the *Capital Allowances Act 2001* defines leasing as a qualifying activity; it does not deem it to be a trade. It should also be borne in mind that it may not matter unduly if the vendor incurs a balancing charge on a sale as the purchaser will, of course, become entitled to capital allowances.

## Notification of the Incurring of Expenditure

**10.11** For chargeable periods ending before 1 April 2000 there was a special time limit for notifying the Revenue of the incurring of qualifying expenditure on plant and machinery on which a claim might be made for writing-down allowances, balancing allowances or first-year allowances. (*FA 1994, s 118(1)(2)*). Such expenditure was not qualifying expenditure unless the necessary notification was given. For income tax purposes notice needed to be given within 12 months after 31 January following the tax year in which the accounts concerned end. For corporation tax it had to be given within two years after the end of the accounting period in which the expenditure was incurred. The Board of Inland Revenue had power to extend the notice period (*FA 1994, s 118(5)*) (see Revenue Statement of Practice 6/94 for their policy on extending time limits for notification). The circumstances for an extension to be granted will have to be exceptional, for example, when illness has prevented notification being made by the relevant person and no one else could have made the notification (HC Official Report, Standing Committee A (Eleventh Sitting, 10 March 1994, Col 644)). The Revenue also had power to prescribe the form that the notification must take, but did not do so although, unlike the *Act*, their press release did state that the notice must be in writing (IR Press Release 17.12.1993, para 15). This is an unusual procedure. It was not necessary to make the claim within the time limit, although where this was done the Revenue regarded the claim as also satisfying the notice requirement under *section 118* (IR Press Release 17.12.1993, para 15). The Revenue press release indicated that 'as a minimum the written notice must have stated the aggregate amount of expenditure incurred on which a claim for tax relief may be made' (paras 15, 16). A failure to give notice cannot constitute an error or mistake giving rise to an error or mistake claim under *TMA 1970, section 33* or *42* (*FA 1994, s 118(7)*). A claim to capital allowances incorporated in an income tax self-assessment tax return was also accepted as satisfactory notification, notwithstanding that the return does not call for details of the expenditure, provided that the return was filed within the *section 118* time limit (Tax Bulletin 35, June 1998). This requirement did not fit easily with self-assessment and was repealed by *FA 2000, s 73.*

**10.12** The Revenue have said that where notification was not given, writing-down allowances on the expenditure could still be claimed in a later period if the requisite notice is timeously given in relation to that period (IR Press Release 17.12.1993, para 14). This is because notification in a subsequent year would make the expenditure qualifying expenditure, so attracting a right to the writing-down allowance in that year under *CAA 2001, s 55*. It will not however resurrect any right to a first-year allowance, as that can be given only in the period related to the incurring of the expenditure (*CAA 2001, s 39*). However, writing-down allowances can be given for a later year only if the machinery or plant still belongs to the taxpayer at some time in that later period or the basis period (*CAA 2001, s 58(4)*). If it does not the right to allowances is lost completely.

**10.13** The notification requirement was repealed because it does not fit easily with self-assessment. However it was introduced because the government was concerned about the large number of claims for allowances that were being made several years after the tax position for the accounting period had been agreed. For companies this is no longer possible as a claim for capital allowances can no longer be made after the self-assessment has become final, unless the Revenue allow a later claim (*FA 1988, Sch 18 para 82*). There is no such restriction for individuals though.

### What is Plant and Machinery?

**10.14** Clearly, the first problem is to identify what is plant and machinery. Neither term is defined. There have been no decided cases on what is meant by machinery, probably because it is generally self-evident whether or not a particular item is a machine. In a property context it will include such things as escalators, lifts, heating installation and air-conditioning installation. There have, however, been a large number of cases before the courts on what is plant. Interestingly, most of the disputed items have been building work or parts of buildings. The first, and perhaps still most quoted, attempt at a definition was made by Lindley LJ in 1887 in *Yarmouth v France (19 QBD 647)*.

'Plant in its ordinary sense . . . includes whatever apparatus is used by a businessman for carrying on his business – not his stock-in-trade, which he buys or makes for sale; but all goods and chattels, fixed or movable, live or dead, which he keeps for permanent employment in his business.'

*Yarmouth v France* was a workman's compensation case. Applying his definition, Lindley LJ found that a horse was plant and the injured workman was thus entitled to compensation.

**10.15** This test was amplified by Uthwatt J in *J Lyons & Co Ltd v Attorney-General (1944 1 All ER 477)*.

'. . . the question at issue may, I think, be put thus: Are the lamps and fitments properly to be regarded as part of the setting in which the business is carried on or as part of the apparatus used for carrying on the business? . . . the presence of lamps in this building is not dictated by the nature of the particular trade there carried on, or by the fact that it is for trade purposes that the building is used. Lamps are required to enable the building to be used where natural light is insufficient . . . In my opinion these lamps are not, in these circumstances, properly described as "plant", but are part of the general setting in which the business is carried on.'

**10.16** The *J Lyons* case was not concerned with capital allowances – the allowances for both plant and machinery and industrial buildings were not introduced until April 1946 – but with war damage compensation. Nevertheless, Uthwatt J's distinction between the setting in which a business is carried on and apparatus used for carrying on the business has been adopted by the courts in tax cases as the correct test. During the 1960s and 1970s a functional test was applied – 'What purpose does the object in question fulfil?' – but it has been made clear in recent cases that this was simply a restatement of the 'setting' versus 'apparatus' test. In the *Wimpy* case (see 10.19 below) Hoffman J indicated that there is in reality a two-part test. Is the item apparatus or part of the setting? If it is apparatus is it nevertheless part of the premises rather than plant? It will be part of the premises if after installation it would be more appropriate to describe the item as having become part of the premises than as having retained a separate identity. This is a question of fact and degree depending on, for example, whether the item visually retains a separate identity, the degree of permanence with which it is attached, the incompleteness of the structure without it, and whether it is likely to be replaced within a relatively short period.

**10.17** The premises test has come into greater prominence in recent years as taxpayers have sought to push further and further the boundary between apparatus and setting. The test was formulated by Lord Lowry in *CIR v Scottish & Newcastle Breweries Ltd (55 TC 252)*:

'Something which becomes part of the premises, instead of merely embellishing them, is not plant, except in the rare case where the premises are themselves plant, like the dry dock in Barclay Curle.'

Vinelott J in *Hunt v Henry Quick Ltd (65 TC 108)* expressed this as 'whether it would be more appropriate to describe the item as having become part of the premises than as having retained a separate identity'. The rarity of the premises themselves being plant is reinforced by the fact that the decision of the Commissioners in favour of the taxpayer was reversed in each of *Gray v Seymours Garden Centre (Horticulture) (1995 STC 706)*, *Bradley v London Electricity plc (1996 STC 1054)* and *Attwood v Anduff Car Wash (1997 STC 1167)*. In the *Seymours Garden Centre* case Lord Lowry put the test succinctly:

'It is proper to consider the function of the item in dispute. But the question is what does it function as? If it functions as part of the premises it is not plant. The fact that the building in which a business is carried on is, by its construction, particularly well-suited to the business, or indeed was specially built for that business does not make it plant.' And later, 'the fact that the planteria provides the function of nurturing and preserving the plants while they are there cannot transform it into something other than part of the premises in which the business is carried on'.

**10.18** The list of items that have been held to be plant and those that have not is useful to demonstrate the wide range of items that people have felt might be plant. However, it must be stressed that, in applying the apparatus or setting test, it is necessary to look not only at the item itself but at the business that is being carried on. For example, in *CIR v Scottish & Newcastle Breweries Ltd (55 TC 252)*, a metal sculpture representing 'Seagulls in Flight', permanently affixed to the forecourt of a hotel in Liverpool, was held to be plant. This should certainly not be taken as an indication that all sculptures are plant. Indeed, very few sculptures are likely to meet the test of apparatus with which a business is carried on. This is not to say that the decision was wrong or anomalous, but merely that the contention put forward by the taxpayer, that the creation of the appropriate 'atmosphere' is a vital ingredient of its trade, would not be applicable to most businesses.

**10.19** With this in mind the items that have been held to be plant by the courts include the following: movable partitions in the offices of shipping agents (*Jarrold v John Good & Sons Ltd (40 TC 681)*); a dry dock constructed by a company of shipbuilders and repairers (*CIR v Barclay, Curle and Co Ltd (45 TC 221)*); a swimming pool in a caravan park (*Cooke v Beach Station Caravans Ltd (40 TC 514)*); dockside grain silos of a grain importer (*Schofield v R & H Hall Ltd (49 TC 538)*); a hulk of a former sailing ship used for bunkering coal by a coal merchant (*John Hall, Junior & Co v Rickman (1906 1 KB 311)*); transformers and switchgear to bring power from the National Grid to a department store and window lighting in the store (*Cole Brothers Ltd v Phillips (55 TC 188)*); decor and murals in hotels and licensed premises (*CIR v Scottish & Newcastle Breweries Ltd (55 TC 252)*); decorative screens in the windows of a building society (*Leeds Permanent Building Society v Proctor (56 TC 293)*); light fittings, a specially designed suspended ceiling, wall panels, and cold water piping and tanks in a fast food restaurant (*Wimpy International Ltd v Warland (61 TC 51)*); decorative brickwork, murals, wall cladding for mirrors and light fittings in a fast food restaurant (*Associated Restaurants Ltd v Warland (61 TC 51)*); and fixed storage platforms in a warehouse (*Hunt v Henry Quick Ltd & King v Bridisco Ltd (1992 STC 633)*).

**10.20** Items held not to qualify as plant are a prefabricated laboratory and gymnasium in a school (*St John's School v Ward (49 TC 524)*); the canopy over the service area of a garage (*Dixon v Fitch's Garage Ltd (50 TC 509)*); a hulk of an old ferry boat used as a floating restaurant (*Benson v Yard Arm Club Ltd (53 TC 67)*); false ceilings in a restaurant to conceal and partly to support pipes, wiring, etc. (*Hampton v Fortes Autogrill Ltd (53 TC 691)*); a stand at a football ground (*Brown v Burnley Football & Athletic Co Ltd (53 TC 357)*); light fittings and their associated wiring and cables in a department store (*Cole Brothers Ltd v Phillips (55 TC 188)*); an inflatable cover for a tennis court (*Thomas v Reynolds (59 TC 502)*); the shop front wall and floor tiles, suspended ceilings, raised floor areas, specially sited staircase and fire escape trap door in a fast food restaurant (*Wimpy International Ltd v Warland (61 TC 51)*); quarantine kennels forming a permanent structure (the Revenue accepting that movable kennels were plant) (*Carr v Sayer (1992 STC 396)*); lighting affixed to storage platforms in a warehouse, which were themselves plant, to illuminate the space underneath (*Hunt v Henry Quick Ltd & King v Bridisco Ltd (65 TC 108)*); a planteria (a form of structure to protect growing plants and maintain their quality of growth) in a garden centre (*Gray v Seymours Garden Centre (Horticulture) (1995 STC 706)*); a structure housing a car wash (*Attwood v Anduff Car Wash (1997 STC 1167)*); and an underground electricity substation (*Bradley v London Electricity plc (1996 STC 1054)*).

**10.21** At first glance it is difficult to see the reasoning for some of these decisions even with an understanding of the 'setting' or 'apparatus' test. It may therefore be useful to look a little more closely at some of them. Partitioning in an office is normally part of the setting in which a business is carried on. The fact that it may be movable is irrelevant. The reason that *John Good & Sons Ltd* succeeded is that they were able to show not merely that their partitions were movable but also that they were in fact moved regularly. The demands of their business generated a need for extra space in certain departments in part of the year. The partitions were apparatus, as their function was to enlarge or reduce that space as required. The Revenue initially applied the *John Good* decision to all movable partitions but have significantly hardened their attitude in recent years and now normally look to the reason for its being movable. The *Henry Quick* case does provide some authority for the contention that it is sufficient merely for the item to be movable. In that case storage platforms erected to form a mezzanine gallery for additional storage in a warehouse were held to be plant albeit that they were movable – in the sense that they could be demounted and re-erected elsewhere – but had in fact not been moved in the four years since installation and there was no evidence that they were installed as a temporary measure. The platforms were bolted to the floor and the wall, although it was found that this was to give them stability for safety reasons not with the intention of making them permanent structures. However, the decision that the platforms were plant was upheld on the *Edwards v Bairstow (36 TC 207)* principle, the judge expressing doubt whether he himself would have regarded them as plant.

**10.22** A dry dock is not simply a place where repairs can be carried out. It performs, at least in the case of the dock used by *Barclay, Curle & Co*, the functions of getting a ship from the river, securing it while it was under repair, and returning it to the river. Accordingly, it was not simply the setting for the trade but performed active functions in the operation of the trade.

**10.23** The grain silos in *R & H Hall* were to hold the grain in a convenient position for delivery to purchasers and were thus part of the apparatus to transfer it from ship to lorry. They were not primarily intended to provide storage. If they had been they would probably have been held to be setting.

**10.24** The swimming pool in the *Beach Station Caravan* case was not part of the setting in which the business was carried on, i.e. it was not there to enhance the appearance of the site but was one of the additional amenities provided to guests. In an Irish case *O'Grady v Roscommon Race Committee (4 ITR 425)* a stand at a race track was held to be plant as it was 'part of the means to get people to go to that racecourse for viewing horses' and was thus very much akin to the *Beach Station* swimming pool. The contrary decision in the UK *Burnley Football Club* case was relied on by the Inspector and thus was effectively distinguished by the court.

**10.25** A school gymnasium, even though movable, is part of the setting in which the business of the school is carried on; it is not itself part of the apparatus used in the business, although the equipment inside it is. The filling station canopy at *Fitch's Garage* was stated by the taxpayer to have been installed to provide shelter. It is an interesting speculation whether the taxpayer would have been more successful if its main purpose had been to attract customers. A similar canopy was held to be plant in an Irish case, *O'Culachain v McMullan Brothers (1991 1 IR 363)*, where evidence was given that, whilst the canopy undoubtedly provided shelter, the purpose of its erection was to provide an attractive setting for the sale of the company's products and to create the overall impression of efficiency and of financial solidarity and, most important of all, to attract customers.

**10.26** In *Fortes Autogrill* the false ceiling was only in the public part of the restaurant. In these circumstances it is not surprising that it was held to be part of the setting. Following the *Scottish & Newcastle* case it may be that *Fortes* should have contended that in order to keep customers in a motorway restaurant for a meal rather than a snack it is important to provide a pleasant atmosphere. This argument was unsuccessful in the *Wimpy* and *Associated Restaurants* cases, with the exception of one specially designed stepped false ceiling with voids, where it was accepted by the Commissioners that its principal function was the creation of an atmosphere and that it was apparatus used in the trade and not a mere embellishment of the premises.

**10.27** Both the *St John's School* and *Yard Arm Club* cases illustrate that the fact that something is movable does not stop it constituting part of the setting in which a business is carried on. Conversely, of course, the *Barclay, Curle* and *R & H Hall* cases illustrate that the fact that something is a fixed permanent structure does not preclude it from being plant and machinery. Such a structure might of course also qualify as an industrial building. In such a case the taxpayer would be able to choose which allowance to claim.

**10.28** On the other hand in *Carr v Sayer*, Sir Donald Nicholls made clear that plant 'does not convey a meaning wide enough to include buildings in general'. It is apt to cover equipment of any size and, 'if fixed, such equipment may readily be described as a structure, but . . . the equipment does not cease to be plant because it is so substantial that, when fixed, it attracts the label of a structure or, even, a building'. Furthermore, equipment does not cease to be plant merely because it also discharges an additional function of providing the place in which the business is carried out. 'Conversely, buildings . . . do not cease to be buildings and become plant simply because they are purpose-built for a particular trading activity . . . A purpose-built building . . . *prima facie* is no more than the premises on which the business is conducted.' He also pointed out that one of the functions of a building is to provide shelter and security for people using it and for goods inside it, so the fact that a purpose-built building performs such a function cannot make it plant. Accordingly, the quarantine kennels were not plant. He did, however, add a caveat that 'there may be cases where a structure, used for housing animals or birds, is so small or made of such ephemeral materials that, despite being fixed, it will be difficult to see clearly on which side of the boundary line the structure stands'. In *Seymours Garden Centre* Vinelott J emphasised 'It is true that a planteria fulfils the same function, the protection of plants between removal from the nursery and sale, which could be achieved without the use of any permanent structure – by glass and plastic cloches or by the use of straw bales, thermal blankets or, for that matter, bonfires during frosty nights. It does not follow that a structure erected to perform the same function must be plant.' This view was upheld by the Court of Appeal. He did not necessarily rule out glasshouses ever being plant though: 'It may be that a specialised glasshouse with integral heating, temperature and humidity controls, automatic ventilation, shade screens and other equipment could be considered to be . . . apparatus for carrying on a trade and not the premises in which the trade is carried on.' The Revenue have said that they accept that in some cases a glasshouse unit and its attendant machinery are interdependent forming a single entity which will function as plant. Such units will be of an extremely sophisticated design including extensive computer controlled equipment without which the structure cannot operate and which will have been permanently installed during the construction of the glasshouse (Tax Bulletin, Issue 5).

**10.29** The *Anduff Car Wash* case emphasises that even a structure whose only purpose is to house plant is nevertheless premises in which the business is carried on. The judge there indicated that providing housing for machinery is a typical function of a building. The *London Electricity* substation, although two metres underground, was a large structure, 12 metres × 18 metres, consisting of three levels connected by stairs. It was unmanned but personnel were required to visit it to carry out maintenance. London Electricity claimed that the substation and the equipment it housed was a single functioning entity. Alternatively it was a mere box (or series of boxes) housing the plant. In holding that the substation did not qualify as plant, and reversing the decision of the Special Commissioner, Blackburne J said 'the Special Commissioner failed to ask himself what plant-like function the structure as an entity performed in London Electricity's trading activity. If he had, the true and only reasonable conclusion he could have come to was that the structure functioned as the premises in which London Electricity's trading activity is carried on rather than the apparatus with which it was carried on. No plant-like function was identified for the structure as a whole.' This seems a harsh decision, bearing in mind that the substation was not occupied, was unsuitable for occupation, and was specially designed to house substantial apparatus. In the past the Revenue have accepted that a structure built around plant whose sole purpose was to protect it from the elements was itself plant. This decision suggests that they are unlikely to do so any longer.

**10.30** In recent years the most important cases to come before the courts have been *Cole Brothers Ltd v Phillips* (Cole Brothers were the company in the John Lewis group that wanted group relief for the expenditure on the John Lewis store at Brent Cross) and *Wimpy International Ltd v Warland*. These could well be the last major cases in this area. The Court of Appeal in *Wimpy International* gave a strong indication that litigants will be wasting their time (and money) in bringing cases before the courts in this area in future. 'So what is to be done? The answer is, I think, that in these cases the courts should be especially reluctant to upset the decisions of Commissioners, unless it can be shown not only that they have erred in law but also that their error is palpable. It is not enough to show that they may have applied the wrong test . . . or that they have not stated the test in the most precise language, or that they have omitted to refer to some factor which they ought to have taken into account. Where the judges have themselves failed to find a universal test the Commissioners are not to have their language examined too closely, or dissected line by line. So the cases will, I hope, be rare when it is held that the Commissioners have, on the face of it, applied the wrong test. Still rarer should be those cases where it is held that they must have applied the wrong test, because of their findings on the facts' (Lloyd L J at p 105). Unfortunately the courts do not seem to have followed this guidance in practice, as in all of the subsequent cases won by the Revenue the courts have reversed the decision of the Commissioners.

**10.31** The *Cole Brothers Ltd v Phillips* case is interesting partly because it contains a thorough review of the authorities and partly because of the various submissions made. The company first contended that the electrical installation, which was the subject matter of the appeal, should be looked at as a whole. As part was clearly plant and everything was interdependent, the whole should be regarded as plant. This was rejected, primarily on the basis that the multiplicity of elements in the electrical system and the different purposes that they served effectively prevented them from being treated as a single entity. It is still worth considering putting forward such a contention whenever a large amount of expenditure clearly relates to plant but there is doubt as to whether the whole qualifies, as this approach was accepted in the House of Lords as likely to be a reasonable approach in some cases.

**10.32** The second contention in the Court of Appeal, although not in the House of Lords, was that it was illogical to classify the transformers as plant but not the switchgear between those transformers and the Electricity Board's substation. In finding for the company Oliver LJ propounded the useful test that 'if the building had contained no electrical equipment other than that conceded or found to be plant, could it be argued that the switchboard which was introduced as the necessary control for that installation was not either itself plant or something the cost of which was incurred in the provision of plant?' This is a useful general test to apply to ancillary equipment.

**10.33** The main area on which the company lost – specially designed interior lighting – illustrates the importance of presenting the facts properly before the General or Special Commissioners. This is the prime tribunal of fact. A finding of fact will be reversed only if there was no evidence on which the Commissioners could have reached their decision. In this case, while they had held that window lighting was apparatus to attract customers, they had held that internal lighting was part of the setting in which the business was carried on. In the House of Lords the company put forward the *CIR v Scottish & Newcastle Breweries Ltd (55 TC 252)* argument – that the lighting was designed to provide a pleasing ambience for customers – but this does not appear to have been argued before the Special Commissioners, and was therefore not considered in detail by the House of Lords, who decided the case on the grounds that the Commissioners had not erred in reaching the decision they had made on the basis of the evidence before them.

**10.34** It is a pity that this argument was not put forward in the first instance. The Commissioners placed emphasis on the fact that the building could not be used for any business without lighting. If it could have been shown that special lighting constituted plant, as it provided a function beyond merely providing light to make the building useable at all, it is likely that it would have qualified for allowances, even though it also formed part of the setting in which the business was carried on. It is significant to note that in the later case of *Wimpy International Ltd v Warland*, Hoffman J reversed the decision of the Commissioners, and held that the light fittings there were plant. The company had given evidence that the lighting intensity was far greater than in a normal shop and was designed to create an atmosphere of brightness and efficiency to attract potential customers from outside. Similarly internal lighting was held to be plant in the *Associated Restaurants* case where the lights were specially positioned to create a specific atmosphere.

**10.35** An interesting sidelight in the *Cole Brothers* case is that the case stated contains an analysis of the electrical installation showing the items that the Revenue accepted as plant, as follows.

(*a*) Wiring, etc. to heating and ventilation equipment.

(*b*) Wiring, etc. to fire alarm.

(*c*) Wiring, etc. to clocks.

(*d*) Public address system and staff location.

(*e*) Wiring, etc. to TV workshop and cash registers.

(*f*) Trunking for telephone system.

(*g*) Wiring, etc. to lifts.

(*h*) Wiring, etc. to escalators.

(*i*) Wiring, etc. to burglar alarm.

(*j*) Wiring, etc. to smoke detectors.

(*k*) Wiring, etc. to Electrical Appliance Department compactor room, etc.

(*l*) Emergency lighting system.

(*m*) Stand-by supply system.

(*n*) The fitments for the display of fittings for sale in the Lighting Department.

(*o*) Additional sockets installed in the television sales area.

**10.36** In the *Wimpy* hamburger restaurant case – and that of *Associated Restaurants*, which operated the Pizzaland Restaurant chain, which was heard with it – the items that were held to be plant included carpets; a special stepped suspended ceiling with voids that was designed to create an environment suitable to the company's assessment of the public's current taste (a borderline item); fixed wall panels and mirrors; light fittings, where the lights were of a greater than normal intensity to create an atmosphere of brightness and efficiency; cold water piping and tanks, as fast food restaurants require a far greater water storage capacity than ordinary commercial premises; a brick built plant room, erected because the trade of providing meals made it necessary to install machinery which could only be installed in a brick housing; decorative brickwork in Pizzaland shops, as the premises were complete without that purely decorative fixture (a borderline item); and fixed clay murals (which could not be removed without breaking them).

**10.37** The categorisation of light fittings in both Wimpy and Pizzaland shops as plant should be contrasted with their treatment as premises in the *Cole Brothers* case. The distinction is that in *Cole Brothers* the evidence given was merely that they were specially designed, not that they performed a specific function in the trade, whereas in these later cases the evidence was that they were chosen and positioned in order to create a specific atmosphere. If *Cole Brothers* had conceded lighting in the aisles and contended that the lighting over the counters was intended specifically to attract customers' attention to what was on offer – as they claimed for window lighting – it is probable that the result would have been different. The categorisation in both Wimpy and Pizzaland shops of cold water tanks as plant is particularly interesting. The Revenue have generally resisted such treatment in hotels, where a similar argument for abnormal capacity seems viable.

The then Minister indicated in a parliamentary statement in 1984 that basic lighting systems are not machinery or plant but that specialised lighting may qualify as plant where it performs a specific function and is not merely part of the trade's setting (Hansard, 15 February 1984, Col 203).

**10.38** It is also interesting to see what was held not to be plant in the *Wimpy* and *Associated Restaurants* cases. The items held to form part of the premises were shop fronts; wall and floor tiles, artex on walls, and high quality ceramic tiles – even though they had a relatively short life – as the walls and floor surfaces of a shop need to be covered with something so the cladding could not be regarded as a mere embellishment; and suspended ceilings (with the one exception mentioned in 10.36 above). The Revenue consider the replacement of a shop front to be a repair (see 12.41) so this decision will apply only to the initial installation. It is also interesting to note that in the *Associated Restaurants* case engineers' and architects' fees were apportioned and capital allowances granted on the proportion of the expenditure that related to allowable items. This accords with the Revenue's normal practice, but does not seem to have been given judicial support before.

**10.39** It is important to be aware of the distinction drawn in the *Wimpy* case between 'embellishments' which attract customers to the product, or create an ambience appropriate to the product, and those 'embellishments' which become part of the premises. The point needs to be made that the mere creation of an atmosphere conducive to the successful retail of a product is not of itself sufficient to sustain a claim to capital allowances. It is also important to be sensitive to the possible dangers in the lax presentation of the details of a refurbishment as there may no longer be a 'second chance' of getting it right in court.

**10.40** It is worth considering carefully what items in a building might conceivably qualify as plant or machinery in the context of the occupier's particular trade. Where a building is not constructed for a particular occupier, none of the expenditure is likely to qualify as plant but much may qualify as machinery. In a purpose-built building anything installed especially for the needs of the trade should be examined with care. The fact that something is installed to meet the occupier's requirements does not, of course, prevent it being part of the setting in which the trade is carried on, but the fact that he has asked for it does raise a question mark over whether it might constitute apparatus. In some cases the architect may build in features that he perceives are needed for the trade without having to be specifically told to do so. It may be that the plans need to be examined with this in mind. It is also worth checking whether there was any correspondence (or notes of meetings) showing that the client asked the architect to include specific items.

**10.41** Where a person carrying on a qualifying activity incurs capital expenditure on alterations to an existing building which is incidental to the installation of machinery or plant, it is treated as part of the cost of the plant and machinery (*CAA 2001, s 25*). Installation costs and other costs ancillary to the machinery are in practice also regarded as forming part of the cost of the machinery. Many of the undisputed items in the *Cole Brothers* case (10.35 above) were wiring to machinery, and thus ancillary to the machinery. Electrical wiring is not normally accepted by the Revenue as constituting plant or machinery. It can therefore be important to break down such expenditure in great detail to separate out all amounts that are ancillary to machinery. The same applies to plumbing, where the Revenue generally accept that hot water pipes are ancillary to the heating system but contend that the cost of cold water pipes is not eligible for capital allowances. As the cold water tanks and piping were regarded as plant in the *Wimpy* case and also in the *Associated Restaurants* case on the assumption that they were of a far greater capacity than would have been installed in a shop, it may well be that cold water piping and tanks in a hotel, or any other establishment where an abnormal amount of water is used, are plant.

**10.42** Interest on money borrowed specifically to finance the acquisition of plant is not ancillary to the cost of the plant and cannot qualify for allowances (*Ben-Odeco Ltd v Powlson (52 TC 459)*). An exchange loss, where a purchase of plant from abroad is in a foreign currency, may well qualify for allowances, however, depending of course exactly on how the transaction is structured (*Van Arkadie v Sterling Coated Materials Ltd (56 TC 479)*). A payment to cancel an option granted to a third party to buy an item of equipment from the taxpayer has been held to qualify for capital allowances on the basis that the buying out of the option was an integral part of the cost to the company of continuing to provide itself with that item of equipment (*Bolton v International Drilling Co Ltd (56 TC 449)*).

**10.43** If machinery or plant is demolished and replaced, the demolition costs (less any sale proceeds received) are added to the cost of the replacement asset. If it is not replaced, the demolition costs are treated as if they were expenditure on the acquisition of machinery or plant (*CAA 2001, s 26*).

*Restriction for certain fixtures, etc.*

**10.44** For expenditure after 29 November 1993, machinery and plant does not include any expenditure on the provision of

(i) a building,

(ii) an asset in a building which is incorporated in it, or

(iii) an asset in a building which is of a kind normally incorporated into buildings – but which is not so incorporated in that particular building because it is movable for some other reason.

(*CAA 2001, s 21*).

Head (iii) is obviously an anti-avoidance provision, although the concept that developers might substantially devalue the capital value of their building by not incorporating fixtures, in order to try to avoid a restriction on capital allowances, is so far-fetched that it is difficult to take it seriously. The Revenue have expressed the view that 'a building' is anything with four walls and a roof provided that it is of a reasonably substantial size. Thus while a wooden hut large enough to contain people is likely to be a building, a small dog kennel is not (IR Press Release 17.12.1993).

**10.45** *Section 21* specifically provides that the following cannot be machinery or plant.

(*a*) Walls, floors, ceilings, doors, gates, shutters, windows and stairs.

(*b*) Mains services and systems for water, electricity and gas.

(*c*) Waste disposal systems.

(*d*) Sewerage and drainage systems.

(*e*) Shafts or other structures in which lifts, hoists, escalators and moving walkways are installed.

(*f*) Fire safety systems.

There are however a great number of exceptions to these basic exclusions. These listed exclusions do not appear to add anything to the basic rule in 10.44.

**10.46** Similarly machinery or plant does not include expenditure on the provision of:

(i) The following structures or other assets:

A. A tunnel, bridge, viaduct, aqueduct, embankment or cutting.

B. A way or hard standing (e.g. a pavement, road, railway or tramway), a park for vehicles or containers, or an airstrip or runway.

C. An inland navigation – including a canal, basin or a navigable river.

D. A dam, reservoir or barrage (including any sluices, gates, generators and other equipment associated with it).

E. A dock, harbour, wharf, pier, marina, jetty or any other structure at which vessels may be kept or merchandise or passengers shipped.

F. A dike, sea wall, weir or drainage ditch.

G. Any other structure other than an industrial structure, i.e. anything (other than a building) which is, or is to be, an industrial building or structure within *CAA 1990, s 18* (or would be if that definition included an undertaking for the extraction of gas; and the provision of telecommunication, television or radio services).

(ii) The acquisition of any interest in land – but not so as to exclude the acquisition of an interest in an asset which is so installed in, or affixed to, the land as to become in law part of it if that asset would itself constitute plant or machinery.

(iii) Any works involving the alteration of land.

(*CAA 2001, ss 22, 24*).

The Revenue say that 'any substantial man-made asset' is a structure (IR Press Release 17.12.1993).

**10.47** The exceptions to the exclusions, i.e. the items that are capable of being plant are:

1. Electrical (including lighting), cold water, gas and sewerage systems which are provided mainly to meet the particular requirements of the trade or to serve particular machinery or plant used for the purposes of the trade.

2. Space or water heating systems; powered systems of ventilation, air cooling or air purification; and any ceiling or floor comprised in such systems (unless it is intended to remain permanently in place).

3. Manufacturing or processing equipment; storage equipment (including cold rooms); display equipment; and counters, checkouts and similar equipment.

4. Cookers, washing machines, dishwashers, refrigerators and similar equipment; washbasins, sinks, baths, showers, sanitary ware and similar equipment; and furniture and furnishings.

5. Lifts, hoists, escalators and moving walkways.

6. Sound insulation provided mainly to meet the particular requirements of the trade.

7. Computer, telecommunication and surveillance systems (including their wiring and other links).

8. Refrigeration or cooling equipment.

9. Sprinkler equipment and other equipment for extinguishing or containing fire; fire alarm systems.

10. Burglar alarm systems.

11. Any machinery (including devices for providing motive power).

12. Strong rooms in bank or building society premises; safes.

13. Partition walls which are movable and intended to be moved in the course of the trade.

14. Decorative assets provided for the enjoyment of the public in the hotel, restaurant or similar trades.

15. Advertising hoardings; and signs, displays and similar assets.

16. Swimming pools (including diving boards, slides and structures on which such boards or slides are mounted).

17. A glasshouse which is constructed so that the required environment (i.e. air, heat, light, irrigation and temperature) for growing plants is provided automatically by means of devices which are an integral part of its structure. The Revenue have agreed with the NFU that such a glasshouse is not a long-life asset in relation to expenditure incurred up to 31 December 2005 (Tax Bulletin 35, June 1998).

18. Cold stores.

19. Buildings provided for testing aircraft engines within the building.

20. Caravans provided mainly for holiday lettings (the Revenue adopt the definition of 'caravan' in the *Caravan Sites and Control of Development Act 1960, s 29(1)* (i.e. any structure designed or adapted for human habitation which is capable of being moved) although they believe this goes wider than the everyday meaning of the word – ESC B50).

21. A movable building intended to be moved in the course of the trade.

22. Expenditure on the alteration of land for the purpose only of installing machinery or plant.

23. Dry docks.

24. A jetty or similar structure provided mainly to carry plant or machinery.

25. Pipelines or underground ducts or tunnels with a primary purpose of carrying utility conduits.

26. Towers provided to support floodlights.

27. The provision of any reservoir incorporated into a water treatment works or the provision of any service reservoir or treated water for supply within any housing estate or other particular locality.

28. Silos provided for temporary storage, and storage tanks.

29. Slurry pits or silage clamps.

30. Fish tanks or fish ponds.

31. Rails, sleepers and ballast for a railway or tramway.

32. Structures and other assets for providing the setting for any ride at an amusement park or exhibition.

33. Fixed zoo cages.

(*CAA 2001, s 23*).

NB. An asset cannot come within 1 to 16 above if its principal purpose is to insulate or enclose the interior of the building or provide an interior wall, a floor or a ceiling which (in each case) is intended to remain permanently in place (*CAA 2001, s 23(4)*).

**10.48** It should be stressed that if something falls within the above list it does not necessarily attract capital allowances. It is simply capable of doing so. The principles outlined in 10.2 to 10.43 above must be applied to determine whether or not the item is plant in the particular circumstances of the individual trade. The government believe that all items previously held by the courts to qualify as plant, fall within the above exceptions. Introducing the Finance Bill clause, the Minister, Stephen Dorrell, said, 'the clause's intention is to prevent further erosion of the tax base as a result of extension of entitlement to capital allowances. It will not remove entitlement to capital allowances for any taxpayer who is entitled to it under the present state of case law' (Standing Committee A 10.3.1994, Col 620). He did however also point out that 'decisions by the Special Commissioners are not case law'. He later said 'the purpose of the clause is not to rewrite capital allowance law but . . . to confirm that it is not normal for buildings, structures and works to be included as what most of us understand to be plant and machinery . . . I can give the Committee the clear undertaking that it is not our intention to change the capital treatment of any class of asset under the clause . . . Most of us would start with the proposition that plant and machinery does not include buildings, structures and works . . . Unfortunately, the Courts have ruled that many assets which would normally fall within those categories are already treated as plant and machinery' (Stephen Dorrell, SCA 10.3.1994, Col 632).

**10.49** It seems doubtful whether many will agree with Mr Dorrell's assertion that 'the new rules will result in greater certainty for both taxpayer and the Revenue' (SCA 10.3.1994, Col 603). The items listed in 10.47 are presumably a definitive statement of what in a building the Revenue believe is likely to be plant. As such they should prove helpful in formulating capital allowances claims. It is particularly surprising that the Revenue appear to accept that an industrial structure (other than a building) can attract either plant and machinery allowances or industrial buildings allowances presumably at the taxpayer's option.

**10.50** The restrictions in 10.44 to 10.46 above did not apply to expenditure incurred before 6 April 1996 in pursuance of a contract entered into before 30 November 1993 or of one entered into on or after that date for the purpose of securing that the obligations under another contract entered into before 30 November 1993 are complied with (*FA 1994, s 117(2)*). Where allowances for building work are claimed under *CAA 2001, s 25* (see 10.41) the above restrictions do not apply as it is the machinery or plant installed in the building that triggers the allowance for the building alterations. Accordingly, for example, expenditure on a lift shaft to install a lift in an existing building should qualify for allowances (see Taxline, July 1995, p 3).

## Fixtures

### Equipment which becomes Landlord's Fittings

**10.51** The Court of Appeal held in *Stokes v Costain Property Investments Ltd (57 TC 688)* that where a tenant installed plant or machinery which became landlord's fittings, no one was eligible to claim capital allowances; the landlord because he had not incurred the expenditure and the tenant because he did not own the asset. This decision has been superseded by new rules contained in *CAA 2001, ss 172–204* which are, in general, designed to allow the tenant to claim allowances in such circumstances.

**10.52** The new provisions apply to expenditure on plant which is so installed or otherwise fixed in or to a building or any other description of land as to become in law part of the building or land (*CAA 2001,* *s 173(1)*). Any question as to whether an item has become part of a building is to be determined by the Special Commissioners. All persons whose tax position could be affected by the decision will be bound by it and accordingly have a right to attend and make representations at the hearing (*CAA 2001, s 204*).

**10.53** In *Melluish v BMI (No 3) Ltd (1995 STC 964)* BMI, which leased assets to local authorities, sought to obtain capital allowances by an alternative route. It included a specific provision in its leases to local authorities that, 'As between the Lessor and the Lessee the Equipment hereby leased shall remain personal or movable property and shall continue in the ownership of the Lessor notwithstanding that the same may have been affixed to any land or building'. Although Vinelott J thought that this was effective to allow BMI to retain ownership of the assets in most cases, this was rejected by both the Court of Appeal and the House of Lords which held that 'the concept of a fixture which remained personal or movable property was a contradiction in terms and an impossibility in law'. The Court of Appeal did, however, consider that the equipment leasing rules applied irrespective of whether had the lessee acquired the assets, he would himself have been able to claim capital allowances. This was upheld by the House of Lords.

**10.54** If at any time a person has claimed capital allowances otherwise than as plant and machinery in respect of expenditure relating, in whole or in part, to the construction, acquisition or provision of an asset, e.g. he claimed industrial buildings allowances, a later owner of the asset cannot claim plant and machinery allowances under these special rules relating to fixtures (*CAA 2001, s 9(1)*). This restriction does not apply if the original owner's claim was for industrial buildings allowances or scientific research allowance and the acquisition value for the current owner is fixed under *CAA 2001, ss 186, 187* (see 10.65 and 10.66) (*CAA 2001, s 9(2)*). Similarly once someone has claimed capital allowances under these special rules relating to fittings, a subsequent purchaser can only claim plant and machinery allowances in relation to that item; he cannot claim industrial buildings allowances or some other capital allowance (*CAA 2001, s 9(3)*). This restriction did not apply for chargeable periods ending before 24 July 1996 and for later periods does not affect allowances for expenditure incurred before that date (*CAA 2001, 3 Sch 10*). This is an anti-avoidance provision that seeks to prevent allowances being claimable by different people on the same expenditure.

### *Expenditure Incurred by the Tenant, etc.*

**10.55** The basic rule is that if at the time when a person incurs capital expenditure on machinery or plant (either for the purpose of a trade carried on by him or for leasing otherwise than in the course of a trade) which becomes a fixture, he has an interest in the land (i.e. the freehold, a lease, an easement, an agreement to acquire an easement, or a licence to occupy the land), the fixture is to be treated for capital allowance purposes as belonging to him in consequence of his incurring the expenditure. This will give him an entitlement to claim capital allowances (*CAA 2001, ss 172–176*). A boiler or water-filled radiator installed in a building as part of a space or water heating system is specifically treated as a fixture for this purpose (*CAA 2001, s 176(1)*). If there are two or more persons to whom a fixture would be treated as belonging under this rule it is treated as belonging to the one, if any, who owns an easement, or if none does so, to a licensee, or if none is a licensee, to the owner of the interest which is not in reversion on any other of the interests (*CAA 2001, s 176(2)(3)*). In other words, where expenditure is incurred by two persons jointly, the asset is deemed to belong to whichever of them has the lesser interest. In *JC Decaux (UK) Ltd v Francis (Insp of Taxes) (1996 Sp C 84)*, the taxpayer company leased various items of street furniture (including automatic public conveniences, electric information boards, bus shelters, etc.) to local authorities. The Special Commissioner dismissed the company's appeal for capital allowances on fixtures under what is now *CAA 2001, s 176* because the company would need to have an interest in the relevant land, in accordance with what is now *CAA 2001, s 173(1)*. The company did not have such an interest under English law, nor did its contractual rights to clean and maintain the equipment amount to a licence to occupy the land.

The Revenue consider that a licence to occupy land 'will only arise where the claimant has an exclusive licence to occupy the land in question. A licence to occupy is a permission to enter and remain on a land for such a purpose as enables the licensee to exert control over the land. It is this level of control that suggests that a licence to occupy must be an exclusive licence' (Tax Bulletin 47, May 2000). They claim that the idea of exclusive occupation is supported in part by rating law that says that there can only be one occupier of land. For long-life assets the allowance was 12% for the first of those years and nil thereafter. The expenditure has to be actually incurred during the relevant period, i.e. the allowance is not given on earlier expenditure deemed to be incurred when the trade commenced. The Revenue make no reference to the House of Lords Decision in *Street v Mountford (1985 1 AC 809)* to the effect that an exclusive licence normally constitutes a lease. It is odd that the Revenue should choose to express this view of exclusivity so soon after Customs have abandoned exclusivity as an infallible test of when a licence exists (see 17.133).

It needs to be borne in mind that there are a number of anti-avoidance provisions that will deny or restrict relief for capital allowances where plant is leased under a finance lease. Although these are aimed at the lessor, if the right to allowances is switched to the lessee by virtue of *CAA 2001, ss 172–195* the restriction will still apply.

*Right of a Purchaser of the Interest to Claim Allowances*

**10.56** If, after an item becomes a fixture,

(*a*) a person (called a 'purchaser' although it will include a person who acquires in any other manner) acquires an interest in the land (other than one created on his purchase), and

(*b*) the consideration he gives for that interest includes a capital sum which falls wholly or partly to be treated as expenditure on the provision of the fixture,

the fixture will be treated for capital allowance purposes as thereafter belonging to the purchaser (*CAA 2001, s 181*). For example, if a lessee to whom the fixture is treated as belonging sells his lease, the purchaser is entitled to contend that the price he pays includes a payment in respect of the fixture on which he is entitled to claim capital allowances. The purchaser can also claim the allowances in such circumstances if the fixture was leased to the vendor under an equipment lease and the purchaser paid a capital sum to the lessor to discharge the lessee's obligations under the lease (*CAA 2001, s 182*). Prior to 25 July 1996 there was also a third condition, namely that at the time of the purchaser's acquisition no one had yet become entitled to allowances for the fixture (or, although the vendor had been so entitled, the sale, etc. creates a disposal value to be brought into account by him).

**10.57** It is not clear what is meant by 'falls wholly or partly to be treated as expenditure on the provision of the fixture' ((*b*) of 10.56 above). It may be that this envisages the right to allowances passing to the purchaser only where part of the price he pays for the assignment of the lease is specifically attributed to the asset. It is more likely that it envisages an apportionment of the capital sum needing to be made where there is no such attribution. Such an apportionment would normally generate a balancing charge to the vendor. It would therefore be wisest to agree an apportionment on an assignment of a lease where the assignor has previously claimed allowances under these provisions or to agree that an appropriate election should be made under *CAA 2001, s 198* (see 10.73) to prevent such a charge arising.

*Election to Transfer Right to Allowances to an Incoming Lessee who Pays a Premium*

**10.58** If, after an item has become a fixture, a person who has an interest in the land and who is entitled to claim the allowance in respect of the fixture (or would be but for not being within the charge to tax) grants a lease at a premium, the lessor and lessee can jointly elect for the fixture to be treated as belonging to the lessee for capital allowance purposes in consequence of his incurring expenditure on its provision (*CAA 2001, s 183(1)*). The election must be made in writing within two years after the lease takes effect (and *not* two years after the end of the accounting period) (*CAA 2001, s 183(2)*).

**10.59** Such an election cannot be made if the lessor and lessee are connected persons of one another (within *ICTA 1988, s 839* – see Appendix 1) (*CAA 2001, s 183(1)(d)*).

**10.60** This provision allows a sublessee who pays a premium to attribute part of that premium to the fixture and claim capital allowances on it.

*Right of an Incoming Lessee to Claim Allowances*

**10.61** If someone with an interest in the land but who is not entitled to capital allowances grants a lease at a premium, the landlord's fixtures included in the building are treated as belonging to the lessee, so that he will become entitled to claim the capital allowances. This does not apply if the asset had been used for the purpose of a trade by the lessor or a connected person of his (within *ICTA 1988, s 839* – see Appendix 1) (*CAA 2001, s 184*). Prior to 24 July 1996 it also did not apply if the lessor or any other person had previously been entitled to allowances in respect of the fixture. No election is necessary; the lessee has an automatic entitlement. This will cover the situation where a freeholder or a tenant installs equipment not for the purpose of a trade nor for letting other than in the course of a trade and grants a lease at a premium. The obvious, and perhaps only, circumstance in which a person who intends to grant a lease can incur expenditure other than for letting is where he is a property dealer. As there is no requirement for him to have incurred *capital* expenditure this is probably what the provision is aimed at, i.e. it allows a person who pays a premium to a property dealer on the grant of a lease to attribute part of that premium to fixtures and claim capital allowances. He could in any event previously have done this for industrial buildings allowance purposes in certain circumstances (*CAA 2001, s 290*). The requirement that no one must have previously been entitled to allowances must particularly be noted. In *West Somerset Railway plc v Chivers (1995 STC SCD 1 SpC 1)* the taxpayer leased from BR a railway line that had initially been built between 1862 and 1874 by the Bristol and Exeter Railway Co. It was held no allowances were due as it was for the taxpayer to show that no one had previously claimed allowances and no records existed to enable it to do so. The Special Commissioner thought the reference to claiming allowances included allowances under the *Customs and Inland Revenue Act 1878* and it was therefore probable that someone, such as BR or Great Western Railway, had become entitled to allowances at some stage!

**10.62** If after 24 July 1996 an interest in land in which the relevant land (or any part of it) is comprised is held by any person at the time that the purchaser acquires his interest in the relevant land (or the lease is granted over it) and that interest is not the one acquired by the purchaser within *CAA 2001, s 181* (see 10.56) or by the lessee within *CAA 2001, s 184* (see 10.61), for example it is one held by a superior landlord, then *section 181* or *184* as the case may be is not to apply if:

(*a*) the person holding that interest falls to be treated under these provisions as the owner of the asset (other than under *CAA 2001, s 537* by virtue of having made a contribution to its cost), and

(*b*) he is entitled to capital allowances in respect of it (*CAA 2001, ss 181(2), 184(2)*).

This prevents multiple claims to an allowance in respect of a single asset.

*Purchase of an Existing Building*

**10.63** Where machinery or plant is treated as belonging to a person ('the new claimant') under these provisions, the part (if any) of that person's expenditure in excess of the 'maximum allowable amount' does not qualify for allowances if the asset was previously treated under these rules as belonging to some other person ('the prior claimant') at a 'relevant earlier time' and the prior claimant claimed capital allowances and was required to bring a disposal value into account subsequent to 24 July 1996 (*CAA 2001, ss 185(1)(2), 3 Sch 38*). The maximum allowable amount is the sum of the disposal value brought into account by the prior claimant and any installation costs (qualifying under *CAA 2001, s 25*) incurred by the new claimant (*CAA 2001, s 185(3)*). Where there has been more than one deemed change of ownership of the asset the disposal value to be brought into account is obviously that on the latest change (*CAA 2001, s 185(4)*). The restriction applies even where the prior and new claimants are the same person (*CAA 2001, s 185(5)*).

**10.64** A relevant earlier time is any time before the new claimant incurred his expenditure. An earlier time is to be disregarded (so that the restriction will not come into play) if in consequence of an intervening sale the asset had ceased to belong to any person, the sale was not a sale of the plant or machinery as a fixture and the vendor and purchaser on that sale were not connected with one another (within *ICTA 1988, s 839*).

**10.65** If a person who claimed industrial building allowances in respect of expenditure on the construction of a building which included plant or machinery transfers (e.g. sells) the relevant interest in the building, the capital allowances claimable by the purchaser (or other transferee) or by any subsequent 'owner' of the plant under these provisions is restricted to the 'relevant amount' unless his acquisition was before 25 July 1996. This is the amount equal to the part of the consideration for the transfer (from the IBA claimant) which would have been attributable to the fixture if the IBA claimant had sold the building for an amount equal to its residue of expenditure under the IBA rules (*CAA 2001, s 186*). This effectively limits the amount eligible for plant and machinery allowances to the original cost of the relevant assets. The restriction does not apply if the fixtures have been severed from the building prior to the sale.

**10.66** Similarly, where the vendor or a previous owner has at any time claimed scientific research allowance in respect of plant and machinery which is a fixture the purchaser (or transferee) can claim plant and machinery allowances only on 'the relevant amount' if he acquires the assets after 23 July 1996. The relevant amount is the proportion of the disposal value of the asset when it ceased to be used for scientific research that is attributable to the fixture (or if less, the proportion of the expenditure on which the scientific research allowance was claimed that is attributable to the fixture) (*CAA 2001, s 187*).

*Deemed Disposal by a Person who has Claimed Allowances*

**10.67** All of these provisions are made subject to *CAA 2001, s 188*. This provides that when the person to whom a fixture is treated as belonging under the above provisions ceases to own the qualifying interest (i.e. the one that entitled him to claim capital allowances) the fixture must be treated as ceasing to belong to him at that time (*CAA 2001, s 188(1)(2)*). This will create a balancing charge or allowance if he has claimed capital allowances. It applies irrespective of whether cessation of ownership is by reason of its transfer, surrender, expiry or otherwise.

**10.68** If the qualifying interest continues in existence (or would have continued but for having become merged in another interest) the former owner is treated as having sold the fixture (*CAA 2001, ss 189, 196*). The deemed price on such a sale will be as follows.

(*a*) If the cessation of ownership arises on an actual sale of the qualifying interest, the deemed price will be the part of the sale price which is treated as the purchaser's cost price of the fixture for capital allowance purposes (*CAA 2001, s 196(1)*). If the sale is at an undervalue, (*c*) below will apply instead, unless the purchaser is itself entitled to claim capital allowances (*CAA 2001, s 196(1)*). This prevents a sale at an artificially low price to a purchaser who is not within the scope of UK tax to avoid a balancing charge on the vendor. This deemed sale price will in most cases be 'the actual consideration . . . if any, for the fixtures which passes between the parties concerned, assuming that they are acting on an arm's length basis' (Hansard, 10 July 1985, Col 1186), i.e. if the parties agree to attribute a specific portion of the sale price for the interest to the fixture that is the figure that will normally be adopted. If they do not make such an attribution, an apportionment will need to be made by a valuer as provided for by *CAA 2001, ss 562–564*.

(*b*) If the cessation of ownership is a deemed cessation arising as a result of an election under 10.58 above for a lessee to claim allowances, the deemed price will be the part of the premium paid by the lessee which is treated for capital allowance purposes as expenditure by the lessee on the fixture (see 10.69 below).

(*c*) In any other case, the deemed price will be the portion of the price which, on a sale of the qualifying interest in the open market immediately prior to the cessation of ownership (and disregarding that cessation for valuation purposes), would fall for capital allowances purposes to be treated as expenditure by the purchaser on the provision of the fixture (see 10.69 below).

(*d*) If the qualifying interest does not continue in existence, e.g. the cessation of ownership is on the expiry or termination of a lease or licence, the deemed sale price is nil unless the former owner receives a capital sum by reference to the fixture, for example by way of compensation; in such a case it will be that sum.

(*CAA 2001, s 196, Table*).

**Disposal of Fixtures**

**10.69** If the taxpayer permanently discontinues his trade while the fixture is still owned (or deemed to be owned) by him, a disposal value needs to be calculated under *CAA 2001, s 61(2)*. If in such a case the fixture is severed from the land following the cessation, the sale proceeds of the fixture are not adopted as the disposal value (*CAA 2001, s 196, Table, item 6*). This is because the act of severing it from the land is likely to mean that the fixture has a scrap value only. The effect seems to be to bring *CAA 2001, s 196, Table, item 7* into play, so that the deemed disposal value is an apportioned part of the value of the building at the time of the cessation. If, following the severance, the building itself is sold the disposal value will be an apportioned part of the sale proceeds even though at that stage the fixture does not form part of the building (*CAA 2001, s 196, Table, items 9–11*). If a disposal value arises because the fixture ceases to be used wholly for the purpose of the deemed owner's trade, that disposal value will be the proportion of the sale price which would be attributable to the fixture if the deemed owner's interest in the land were sold in the open market (*CAA 2001, s 196, Table, item 12*). In other words, where the expenditure on a fitting was incurred after 11 July 1984, the purchaser cannot claim allowances on an amount greater than the original cost of the fitting (or its cost on its first acquisition after 11 July 1984 if there has been an intermediate purchase) if the vendor – or any previous owner since 11 July 1984 – claimed capital allowances.

**10.70** The purchaser will normally be entitled to allowances under general principles on the amount of his expenditure on the asset (his cost price).

**10.71** If a fixture ceases to belong to a deemed owner on the termination of a lease or licence it is treated as beginning to belong to the person who was the lessor or licensor (*CAA 2001, s 193*). This deeming will, however, only confer a right to capital allowances on the lessor if, and to the extent that, he has paid compensation to the lessee in respect of the fixture (as otherwise he will not have incurred capital expenditure on it) (*CAA 2001, s 196, Table, item 4*).

**10.72** If there is a disposal or other event that requires a disposal value to be brought into account which would otherwise be less than the 'notional written-down value' of the machinery or plant, and that event is comprised in (or occurs in pursuance of) a scheme or arrangement which has tax avoidance as one of its main objects, the disposal value must be treated as if it were that notional written-down value (*CAA 2001, s 197(1)(2)*). The notional written-down value is arrived at by deducting from the cost the capital allowances that would have been claimable if that item were the only item of plant acquired by the owner (even if they were not in fact claimed). Tax avoidance for this purpose means obtaining a capital allowance (or greater allowance) or avoiding (or reducing) a balancing charge. This anti-avoidance provision did not apply to chargeable periods ending before 24 July 1996.

## Election to Displace Normal Rules

**10.73** Alternatively (to the rules in 10.71) the purchaser and vendor can jointly elect that the disposal value should be some other figure, but not more than the lower of:

(*a*) the capital expenditure that was treated for capital allowance purposes as incurred by the vendor when he acquired the fixture, and

(*b*) the actual sale price of the entire qualifying interest in the building (or premium for the lease where *section 183* applies (see 10.58)).

In such a case the balance of the expenditure is treated as attributable to the acquisition of the interest in the building. This obviously displaces the normal apportionment rule under *CAA 2001, ss 562–564* (see 10.68(a)) (*CAA 2001, s 200(2)*). Where *CAA 2001, s 186* (see 10.65), *187* (see 10.66) or *197* (see 10.72) applies that provision must of course be applied first. The election must be made in writing and contain the names of both parties and their tax district references and sufficient information to identify the machinery or plant concerned, the relevant land and the interest acquired by the purchaser (or particulars of the lease granted to him). The amount fixed by the election must be quantified at the time the election is made (but if later circumstances result in a reduction of the maximum permissible amount it is obviously reduced to reflect the new figure). The election must be made within two years of the purchaser acquiring his interest in the property and a copy of the election must be attached to both parties' tax returns. In the case of dispute each party is entitled to appear before the Commissioners and the Commissioners must determine the amount deemed to be the disposal value as a separate issue to any other question in the proceedings (*CAA 2001, ss 200, 201*).

**10.74** The Revenue say that since the rules on fixtures work on an asset by asset basis an election would need to be made in respect of each individual fixture. In practice they accept that the election can apply to a group of assets provided that it does not distort the tax computation. In particular they will accept an election covering all of the fixtures in a single property. They will not however accept a single election covering fixtures in more than one property (Tax Bulletin 35, June 1998).

**10.75** The following will not be treated as a cessation of the deemed owner's interest in the fixture and will therefore not give rise to a balancing adjustment or a disposal value.

(*a*) A merger of the qualifying interest (the one that entitled the former owner to claim capital allowances) with another interest owned by the owner – the merged interest must be treated as the same interest as the qualifying interest.

(*b*) If the qualifying interest is a lease, a new lease being granted to the lessee on its termination – the new lease must be treated as the same interest as the qualifying interest.

(*c*) If the qualifying interest is a licence, a new licence to occupy the land being granted on its termination – the two licences must be treated as the same interest.

(*d*) If the qualifying interest is a lease, the lessee remaining in possession of the land after its termination with the consent of the lessor but without a new lease being granted – the qualifying interest is treated as continuing to subsist as long as the lessee remains in possession.

(*CAA 2001, ss 188(2), 189*).

**10.76** If at any time a fixture is permanently severed from the land, the fixture must be treated as ceasing at that time to belong to the deemed owner, so as to generate a balancing adjustment or disposal value to him, unless he in fact retains the ownership of the item following its severance (*CAA 2001, s 191*).

## Expenditure Incurred by an Equipment Lessor

**10.77** If someone ('the equipment lessor') incurs capital expenditure on machinery or plant for leasing which becomes a fixture which would have been treated for material purposes as belonging to the lessee if he had incurred the expenditure, and an agreement is entered into for a lease, directly or indirectly from the equipment lessor to another person (the 'equipment lessee') for the purposes of a trade carried on (or to be carried on) by the equipment lessee (or for leasing other than in the course of trade), then the equipment lessor and lessee can jointly elect that the fixture should be treated for capital allowance purposes as belonging to the equipment lessor (and not to the lessee) in consequence of his having incurred the expenditure (*CAA 2001, s 177(1)*). In other words, where a tenant leases equipment which becomes a landlord's fixture, the leasing company and the tenant can elect that the leasing company should be entitled to the capital allowances so as to reflect the commercial bargain between them. The election must be in writing and made to the Inspector within two years after the end of the accounting period related to the incurring of the expenditure for corporation tax and by the normal time limit for amending a return for income tax (*CAA 2001, s 177(5)*). Such an election should always be made as the lessee cannot himself claim the allowances as he will not be the person who incurred the expenditure. The lessor and lessee must not be connected persons of one another (within *ICTA 1988, s 839* – see Appendix 1). A lease of assets which will become landlord's fixtures should accordingly never be made between connected persons as neither can become eligible to claim capital allowances. The Revenue consider that an election cannot be made before the lessee's trade has started (Tax Bulletin, Issue 13, October 1994). The election cannot be made if the lease is of plant or machinery in a dwelling house, except in chargeable periods ending before 24 July 1996 (*CAA 2001, s 178*).

**10.78** If the trade has not started by the time the lease is entered into, the election is to treat the fixture as belonging to the lessee from the later of the time the expenditure is incurred or the commencement of the trade (*CAA 2001, s 177(3)*). The requirements that the lease must be for a trade or leasing activity of the equipment lessee, that the equipment lessee must be within the scope of UK tax and that the asset would have belonged to the lessee if he had incurred the expenditure do not apply if:

(*a*) the machinery or plant is fixed to land that is not a building or part of a building,

(*b*) the equipment lessee has an interest in that land,

(*c*) the equipment lessor is entitled to sever the machinery from the land at the end of the lease and retain it,

(*d*) once severed the machinery or plant is capable of being used for the same purposes on a different set of premises, and

(*e*) the lease is an operating lease.

This recognises the reality that in such circumstances the asset belongs to the equipment lessee even though ownership may technically pass to the lessor during the period it is fixed to the land.

(*CAA 2001, s 177, 179*).

**10.79** The requirements are relaxed for expenditure between 28 July 2000 and 1 January 2008 on a boiler, heat exchanger, radiator or heating control that is installed in a building as part of a space or water heating system where the agreement for the lease is approved by the appropriate Minister under the Affordable Warmth Programme. It is not necessary for the equipment to be used in a trade; it can be installed in a dwelling house, and the equipment lessee does not have to be taxable in the UK or to be entitled to claim capital allowances (*CAA 2001, s 180(1)*). Those conditions are of course incompatible with the Affordable Warmth Programme which is aimed at residential property.

**10.80** The equipment will be treated as ceasing to belong to the equipment lessor if he at any time assigns his rights under the equipment lease, or his financial obligations under the lease are at any time discharged on payment of a capital sum or otherwise (*CAA 2001, s 192(2)*). In the case of an assignment he is treated as having sold it to the assignee at the amount of the consideration for the assignment (*CAA 2001, s 196, Table, item 7*). This will generate a balancing adjustment or a disposal value. The assignee will be treated as if an election had been made under 10.77 above for him to be the equipment owner and will thus become the person entitled to claim the allowances in the future (*CAA 2001, s 194(2)*). A capital sum received in discharge of the lessor's financial obligations under the lease, must be treated as the sale proceeds of the asset and will generate a balancing adjustment or a disposal value. If a capital sum is paid by the equipment lessee to be released from his obligations, i.e. in effect he purchases the asset from the lessor, it will be treated as further expenditure on the provision of the asset and the fixture will be treated thereafter as belonging to the equipment lessee (so that he will be entitled to claim allowances on that payment) (*CAA 2001, s 195*). If the financial obligations of the equipment lessee become vested in some other person that person stands in the equipment lessee's shoes (*CAA 2001, s 192(3)*).

*Supplementary*

**10.81** Where a person becomes the deemed owner of a fixture under any of the above provisions no other person (such as the person who actually incurred the expenditure) can claim capital allowances in respect of it (*CAA 2001, s 190(2)*). This does not affect the entitlement of a person who makes a 'contribution' to the expenditure to claim allowances (to the exclusion of the deemed owner) on the amount of that contribution under *CAA 2001, s 538*.

**10.82** If a lessee incurs capital expenditure for the purposes of his trade on machinery or plant which he is required under the terms of his lease to provide and that equipment is not so installed as to become in law part of the building (i.e. it is not a landlord's fitting), the item is deemed to belong to him (if it would not otherwise do so) so long as he continues to use it for the purpose of his trade. On the expiry of his lease it will be treated as belonging to the lessor (and the expenditure as having been incurred by him) (*CAA 2001, s 70*). The purpose of this latter assumption is to ensure that if the landlord sells the item he will suffer a balancing charge. The provision seems to be defective as it does not say what is to happen if the tenant ceases to use the item for the purpose of his trade while the lease is still subsisting.

**Long-life Assets**

**10.83** The writing-down allowance on expenditure on long-life assets after 25 November 1996 (or after 1 January 2001 if in pursuance of a pre 26 November 1996 contract) is limited to 6% p.a. Machinery or plant constitutes a long-life asset if at the time when it was new it could reasonably be expected that it would have a useful economic life of at least 25 years (*CAA 2001, ss 90, 102*). This is not the useful life to the purchaser. It is the overall expected life of the asset, e.g. if the purchaser expects to use the asset for 10 years, will then sell it to a purchaser who will use it for another 10 years and who will then resell it for use for a further six years it will be a long-life asset. Expenditure during the year to 1 July 1998 by a small company (see 10.7) attracted a 12% first-year allowance in place of the writing-down allowance for the year the expenditure was incurred.

**10.84** Where expenditure is incurred on long-life assets such assets are of course separated out into a separate pool of plant and machinery. If all of such assets are disposed of, the pool – and the allowances – continues unless the trade ceases at the same time (*CAA 2001, ss 101–103*). This is the normal rule in respect of a plant and machinery pool. If a disposal value, e.g. on the disposal of an asset, falls to be brought into account by virtue of an event which is comprised in (or occurs in pursuance of) a scheme or arrangement which has avoidance of tax as one of its main objects, and that disposal value is less than the 'notional written-down value' of that plant and machinery, the disposal value must be treated as if it were equal to the 'notional written-down value'. This is the figure which would create neither a balancing allowance or a balancing charge if the expenditure on the plant or machinery in question had been the only expenditure in the pool, the *de minimis* limits did not apply to that plant and the taxpayer had claimed all the allowance to which he was entitled. Avoidance of tax for this purpose means obtaining a capital allowance or deduction (or a greater allowance or deduction) or avoiding (or reducing) a balancing charge (*CAA 2001, s 104*). This is of course an anti-avoidance provision to prevent the allowances being accelerated by selling machinery at an undervalue, or even at its second-hand market value, to a connected person to try to trigger a balancing allowance.

**10.85** There are a number of important exclusions. In the context of property, fixtures in (or provided for use in) a building used wholly or mainly as a dwelling-house, retail shop (or similar premises where retail trade or business, including repair work, is carried on), showroom, hotel or office, or for purposes ancillary to such a use will not be long-life assets (*CAA 2001, s 93*). This effectively limits the application of *section 90* to those fixtures in factories, warehouses and in specialist buildings that will not fit into one of the above categories, i.e. mainly (but not exclusively) to those buildings which qualify for industrial buildings allowances. The then Chancellor perceived 6% p.a. writing-down allowance as roughly equivalent to the 4% straight-line IBA. The idea is to discourage taxpayers from splitting their expenditure on such buildings between plant and machinery and IBA expenditure. In fact the long-life asset allowances are less attractive than IBAs after the first seven years, the extra relief in the first seven years is clawed back in the next eight and thereafter the relief is significantly below IBAs.

**10.86** There is an exclusion for expenditure incurred before 1 January 2011 on the provision of a railway asset for use in a railway business. Apart from trains, a railway asset includes anything which is (or is to be comprised in) a railway track, railway station or light maintenance depot, and any apparatus falling to be installed in association with such an asset. A railway includes tramways and other systems of guided transport. A light maintenance depot means such a depot within *Part 1* of the *Railways Act 1993* or the equivalent of such a depot in relation to a tramway, etc. A railway business is limited to the provision of a service to the public for the carriage of goods or passengers in the UK or the Channel tunnel (*CAA 2001, s 95(3)*).

**10.87** There is a *de minimis* exclusion. An individual or a partnership does not have to treat assets as long-life ones if the total expenditure on such assets during an accounting year does not exceed £100,000 (reduced proportionately for a period of less than a year). For this exclusion to apply the individual must devote substantially the whole of his time to carrying on his trade or profession. In the case of a partnership it does not apply unless all of the partners are individuals and at least half of them devote substantially the whole of their time to the business. Even where the *de minimis* limit applies, any expenditure on the provision of a share in an asset, a contribution towards the acquisition of an asset, or expenditure on the provision of an asset for leasing (including fixtures in a rental building), will attract the 6% rate. Where expenditure under a single contract is payable by instalments it must be assumed that all of the expenditure is incurred at the time of the first instalment for the purpose of applying the limit (*CAA 2001, s 100(4)*). These last two rules also apply for corporation tax. For corporation tax purposes a single £100,000 *de minimis* limit is apportioned equally between the company and all of its associated companies. Accordingly if there are ten associated companies each would have a limit of £10,000 only (even if only one is likely to purchase long-life assets) so the *de minimis* limit will be of little practical effect (*CAA 2001, s 99(4)*).

**10.88** The long-life asset rules do not apply to expenditure incurred before 26 November 1996 or to expenditure incurred before 1 January 2001 in pursuance of a contract entered into before 26 November 1996 – but if the contract is varied on or after that date they do apply to any part of the expenditure not contracted for at 26 November 1996. Nor do they apply to second-hand plant or machinery where the seller has claimed capital allowances at the 25% rate and the asset would have been a long-life asset had these rules applied at that time. The effect of this exemption is not only to exempt pre 26 November 1996 assets; it also exempts assets which in the seller's hands were covered by *de minimis* limits. Accordingly the status of an asset is in effect determined by the first purchaser (provided that all of the purchasers in the chain are entitled to claim capital allowance for it). If it is a long-life asset in his hands it will also be a long-life asset in the hands of a subsequent purchaser (*CAA 2001, s 103(2)*). If it is not a long-life asset in his hands it will not be one in the hands of a later purchaser.

## Energy-Saving Plant and Machinery

**10.89** A 100% first year allowance can be claimed on expenditure incurred after 31 March 2001 on energy-saving plant and machinery that is unused and not second-hand (*CAA 2001, s 45A(1)*, inserted by *FA 2001, 17 Sch 2*). For income tax purposes it appears that expenditure incurred between 1 April 2001 and 5 April 2001 either does not attract relief if the taxpayer has a 5 April year-end or, possibly, attracts the allowance in the year to 5 April 2002. This is because *FA 2001, s 65* states that *Schedule 17* has effect for income tax purposes for chargeable periods ending on or after 6 April 2001.

**10.90** Plant or machinery is energy-saving if, either when the expenditure is incurred or when the contract is entered into, it is of a description specified by Treasury Order and meets the energy-saving criteria specified by the Treasury for plant and machinery of that description (*CAA 2001, s 45A(2)*). The Treasury have made such an order, the *Capital Allowances (Energy-saving Plant and Machinery) Order 2001* (*SI 2001 No 2541*). This states that plant and machinery is energy-saving if:

(*a*) it falls within a technology class specified in the Energy Technology Criteria list dated 26 March 2001 and published by the Department of the Environment, Transport and Regions (DETR) on 1 April 2001. (It is now the Department for the Environment, Food and Rural Affairs (DEFRA));

(*b*) it meets the energy-saving criteria set out in that list;

(*c*) it falls within one of the classes of:

(i) boilers,

(ii) motors and drivers,

(iii) refrigeration, or

(iv) thermal screens; and

(*d*) it is of a type that is specified in, and has not been removed from, the Energy Technology Products List (dated 30 March and published by the DETR on 1 April 2001) or has been accepted for inclusion in that list (para 2.3). As the Order did not come into force until 7 August 2001, it is not clear what happens about expenditure between 1 April and 7 August. It does not seem to satisfy the definition of energy-saving plant in the absence of an Order being in force at the time the expenditure was incurred. It seems likely that the 100% first allowance will be given in practice.

**10.91** The Energy Technology Products List is a novel concept for taxation purposes. It is not a static list, so will need to be specifically consulted at the time it is proposed to purchase an item that might be eligible. The idea is that manufacturers should send details of their products to DEFRA (except for CHP, lighting or pipe insulation). If DEFRA is satisfied that a product meets the published energy-saving criteria it will issue a letter of acceptance and add the product to the Products List from that date. If the application is rejected DEFRA will indicate why and invite modification. A potential buyer of a product can then consult the Products List. If he buys an item on it that purchase will attract the 100% allowance. As might be expected the list is very detailed. There are seven broad categories:

(*a*) Boilers (with 13 sub-headings);

(*b*) Combined Heat and Power (CHP);

(*c*) Lighting;

(*d*) Motors and Drives (with 5 sub-headings);

(*e*) Pipework Insulation;

(*f*) Refrigeration (with 7 sub-headings);

(*g*) Thermal Screens.

Within each category the manufacturer and the qualifying product (identified normally by its product number where the manufacturer makes a range of products) is shown. The Inland Revenue and DEFRA have set up a joint website, called the Enhanced Capital Allowance scheme, http://www.eca.gov.uk, which contains both the Products List and an application form for manufacturers to apply for certification of their products. It will be seen from 10.90 that CHP, lighting and pipework insulation are not specified in the Order. This is probably to allow for custom-built installations to qualify.

**10.92** The Treasury are given power by Order to specify that in some cases the allowance is dependent on there being in force a relevant certificate of energy efficiency. Again this is done in the *Capital Allowances (Energy-saving Plant and Machinery) Order 2001* (*art 4*), which requires such a certificate in relation to 'combined heat and power'. A relevant certificate of energy efficiency is issued by the Minister and certifies that the plant meets the efficiency requirements. Such a certificate can be revoked. If this is done it is treated as never having been issued. In such circumstances, if the taxpayer becomes aware that the certification has been revoked he must tell the Revenue within three months and amend his tax return accordingly (*CAA 2001, s 45B*). The concept is that because a CHP unit is usually custom built it is not practicable to certify the product as such. What needs to be certified is the entire unit. This can be done off plan, but DEFRA clearly need the right to check that the actual installation has been carried out in accordance with the plan and to withhold the certificate if it has not.

**10.93** Where plant is purchased which incorporates components, some of which are included in the Products List and some not, the Treasury is given power to require the cost to be apportioned with only the part of the cost attributable to qualifying components attracting the 100% allowance. The part of the price apportioned to such components is limited to the amount specified in the Treasury Order. If the expenditure is incurred in instalments each instalment must be apportioned pro rata (*CAA 2001, s 45C*). The Treasury has specified boilers, motors and drives, and refrigeration and specified as the allowable limit the amount specified in the Energy Technology Products List for the qualifying components (*Capital Allowances (Energy-saving Plant and Machinery) Order 2001, art 5*).

**10.94** It is common with combined heat and power units for these to be installed and operated by a supplier in return for an annual fee. In such a case the supplier will retain ownership of the equipment but will not have an interest in the building in which it is installed. Ownership of the equipment will normally pass to the client on the termination of the contract. It is of course possible for similar arrangements to be entered into in relation to other types of equipment than CHP units. The energy services agreement will not normally constitute a lease so the rules at 10.77 onwards will not apply. To encourage such service providers to use energy efficient equipment, *CAA 2001, s 180A* (inserted by *FA 2001, s 66* and *18 Sch 2*) deems the energy service provider to own the equipment as a result of incurring the expenditure on it, even though in law as the equipment is affixed to the land it is owned by the landowner (*CAA 2001, s 180A(1)*).

**10.95** Section 180A applies where:

(*a*) an 'energy services agreement' (see 10.96) is entered into;

(*b*) the 'energy services provider' (see 10.96) incurs capital expenditure under that agreement on the provision of plant or machinery;

(*c*) the plant or machinery becomes a fixture;

(*d*) at the time it becomes a fixture its client has an interest in the land but the energy services provider does not;

(*e*) the plant or machinery is not provided for leasing and is not provided in a dwelling-house;

(*f*) the operation of the plant or machinery is carried out wholly or substantially by the energy services provider (or a person connected with him);

(*g*) the energy services provider and the client are not connected persons; and

(*h*) the client and the energy services provider elect that *section 180A* should apply.

(*CAA 2001, s 180A(1)*).

**10.96** An energy services provider is a person carrying on a qualifying activity consisting wholly or mainly in the provision of energy management services (*CAA 2001, s 175A(2)* inserted by *FA 2001, 18 Sch 2*). An energy services agreement is an agreement entered into by an energy services provider and another person that makes provision, with a view to saving energy or using energy more efficiently, for:

(*a*) the design of plant or machinery (or of a system or systems incorporating plant or machinery);

(*b*) obtaining and installing it;

(*c*) operating it; and

(*d*) maintaining it,

where the amount of any payment in respect of its operation is linked (wholly or partly) to energy savings or increased energy efficiency resulting from the provision or operation of the plant or machinery (*CAA 2001, s 175A(1)*).

**10.97** If the client would not have been entitled to an allowance under *CAA 2001, s 176* (see 10.55) if he had incurred the expenditure on the equipment the above election cannot be made unless the plant belongs to a class specified by Treasury Order (*CAA 2001, s 180A (2)(3)*). The only class specified to date is the technology class 'Combined Heat and Power' specified in the Energy Technology Criteria List (*Capital Allowance (Energy-saving Plant and Machinery) Order 2001, art 5*). The Criteria List is also to be found on the website www.eca.gov.uk. *Section 176* deals only with fixtures used for a qualifying activity. The Order will therefore, for example, grant the 100% first year allowance for CHP units provided to a local authority or NHS trust, which would not itself be eligible to claim the allowance as it is not a taxable entity.

**10.98** If a person purchases a building in which plant is provided under an existing energy services agreement, and in connection with that purchase he pays a capital sum to the energy service provider to discharge the agreement, the purchaser is treated as the owner of the fixture as a result of incurring expenditure equal to the payment (unless immediately after the purchase some other person has a prior right to the fixture, and *CAA 2001, s 188* (see 10.67) will apply to the energy services provider (*CAA 2001, s 182A* inserted by *FA 2001, 18 Sch 6*). It appears that this will trigger a balancing charge on the energy services provider but will not entitle the purchaser to the 100% allowance as at that stage the plant will be second-hand.

**10.99** If the energy services provider at any time assigns his rights under the energy services agreement or the client discharges his obligations under the agreement (on payment of a capital sum or otherwise), the energy services provider is treated as ceasing to be the owner of the equipment (*CAA 2001, s 192A* inserted by *FA 2001, Sch 18 para 8*). In the case of an assignment the assignee is treated both as having incurred expenditure on the equipment for a price equal to the consideration given by him and as being an energy services provider who owns the equipment under *section 180A* (*CAA 2001, s 195A* inserted by *FA 2001, Sch 18 para 9*). If the client pays a capital sum to discharge his obligations he is treated as having purchased the equipment for that amount (*CAA 2001, s 195B* inserted by *FA 2001, Sch 18 para 9*).

### Plant or Machinery for Gas Refuelling Station

**10.100** A 100% first-year allowance can also be claimed for expenditure between 16 April 2002 and 31 March 2008 on plant or machinery for a gas refuelling station provided that the plant is unused and not second-hand (*CAA 2001, s 45E* inserted by *FA 2002, Sch 20 para 3*). This covers plant for use solely for (or in connection with) refuelling vehicles with natural gas or hydrogen fuel. It includes storage tanks, any compressor, pump, control or meter used for or in connection with refuelling vehicles with such fuels, and equipment for dispensing such fuels to the fuel tank of a vehicle.

## Industrial Buildings

### Introduction

**10.101** Expenditure on the construction of an industrial building (or, to be more precise, a building which will become an industrial building), or on the cost of improvements to such a building, attracts a writing-down allowance of 4% of the cost each year. On expenditure before 31 March 1986 an initial allowance of 25% could be claimed in the first year in addition. The total allowances cannot exceed the cost. Accordingly, writing-down allowances will continue for 25 years where no initial allowance was given or for 19 years where the initial allowance was due and claimed in full. Initial allowances at the rate of 20% were reintroduced briefly for expenditure incurred between 1 November 1992 and 31 October 1993 provided that the building was first used before 1 January 1995. Where a building was intended to be used by that date the allowance was given provisionally and withdrawn if not so used. Expenditure is incurred in the year to 31 October 1993 for this purpose if it is either contracted for during that year or is payable under a contract entered into subsequently for the purpose of securing that a contract entered into during that year is complied with (*CAA 2001, 3 Sch 77*). Where some of the vendor's expenditure falls within *para 77* and some does not, the purchaser's deemed expenditure is apportioned on a proportionate basis into a *para 77* element and a residual element, and the initial allowance given only on the *para 77* element. If the vendor trades as a property developer the restriction by reference to the vendor's cost does not apply (*CAA 2001, 3 Sch 77*). If the person incurring the expenditure traded as a property developer and owned the land at November 1992, and he sold the relevant interest in the building before it was first brought into use but under a contract entered into during the year to 31 October 1993, the purchaser could claim initial allowance on his full purchase cost (*CAA 2001, 3 Sch 77*).

**10.102** If the relevant interest is purchased before the building is brought into use but after 31 October 1993 (during a year in which the conditions of *para 77* are not met), the purchaser is deemed to have incurred expenditure equal to the lower of his cost or the vendor's expenditure on the building.

### Definition of Industrial Building or Structure

**10.103** An industrial building is a building or structure in use for the purposes of:

(*a*) a trade (or part of a trade) carried on in a mill, factory or similar premises;

(*b*) a trade (or part of a trade) which consists in the manufacture of goods or materials or the subjection of goods or materials to any process;

(*c*) a trade (or part of a trade) which consists in the storage

- (i) of goods or materials to be used in the manufacture of other goods or materials,
- (ii) of goods or materials which are to be subjected in the course of a trade to any process,
- (iii) of goods or materials which have been subjected to a process but have not yet been delivered to any purchaser, or
- (iv) of goods or materials on their arrival in any part of the UK from a place outside (prior to 1 May 1995 the storage had to be by sea or air into the UK);

(*d*) a trade (or part of a trade) which consists of the maintaining or repairing of any goods or materials (other than those employed by the trader in a trade or undertaking which itself is not a qualifying process);

(*e*) a transport, dock, inland navigation, water, sewerage, electricity or hydraulic power undertaking; a tunnel undertaking; a bridge undertaking; a toll road undertaking; the working of any mine, oil well or other source of mineral deposits or of a foreign plantation; ploughing or cultivating land, the doing of any other agricultural operation or the threshing of the crops of another person; or the catching or taking of fish or shellfish.

(*CAA 2001, ss 271(1), 274*).

**10.104** The meaning of 'part of a trade' for this purpose was considered by the High Court in *Bestway (Holdings) Ltd v Luff (70 TC 512)*. Lightman J thought that at a minimum the expression must constitute 'a significant, separate and identifiable part' of the company's trade. He thought its primary purpose is to make provision for use of a building in a composite trade; use for that trade might not qualify but if use for one of the two or more component parts did that would give a right to the allowance.

Prior to that case the Revenue used to take the view that anything done in the course of a trade was part of the trade. They now say that the activities in question need to be a 'significant, separate and identifiable part of the trade carried on'. They say that this revised view should be applied to claims for capital allowances for chargeable periods ending after 31 December 1999. They will also apply their new view to open claims for earlier periods but will not seek to re-open agreed claims for such earlier periods (unless of course there is some other change in the nature and conduct of the trade that may affect entitlement to IBA for those periods) (Tax Bulletin 44, December 1999). This is a major change. It is likely that many buildings that used to qualify for allowances will no longer do so.

**10.105** The Revenue have similarly changed their views on storage in the light of the *Bestway* case. They now consider that a building is only used for storage if the purpose of keeping goods there is their storage as an end in itself. The building will not qualify if the goods are kept there for some other purpose. 'Storage which is merely a necessary and transitory incidence of the conduct of the business is not sufficient.' They believe the main impact is likely to be on the wholesale trades. For example, it has previously been accepted that premises used by a builders' merchant for storing goods or materials that are to be used in the manufacture of other goods and materials would qualify but, depending on the facts, now think that it may no longer do so (Tax Bulletin 44, December 1999). It is not at all clear what this means. The shoes in the *Lilley & Skinner* case (see 10.113) were not stored in the company's warehouse 'as an end in itself'. They were stored there as a necessary and transitory incidence of the conduct of the company's business of selling shoes. That was a House of Lords decision which clearly cannot be overturned by the High Court. Indeed Lightman J actually said, 'The authorities make clear that there may be "storage" where goods are kept or held for a limited period ... In *Saxone* the shoes were held to be stored in a warehouse though they remained there for 10 to 13 weeks or less.' He later says:

'The determining factor must be the purpose for which the goods are kept or held. If goods are delivered for safe keeping to a depository ... so long as the goods remain in the possession of the depository they may be described as "stored", but this would not be the apt description of goods handed over in the course of his business to a repairer or pawnbroker.'

The reference to storage being an end in itself was in the context of:

'All the stock in the present case is kept in the buildings, not for storage but for sale. No goods are reserved or withheld for future use: they are all likewise available for sale and intended to be sold as soon as the turnover allows. For practical reasons only part of the stock can be made physically available for self-service by customers; but that does not alter the fact that the back-up stock is intended to be made immediately available as soon as required to meet demand . . . Far from being kept in reserve, the stock is in the process or in the course of being made available to purchasers at the buildings.'

**10.106** A building which is occupied by a person carrying on a trade and used as a sports pavilion for the welfare of all or any of the workers employed in that trade is treated as if it were an industrial building (*CAA 2001, ss 271(1)(b)(iii), 280*). There is no requirement that the trade should be an industrial trade. It does, however, have to be a trade, not a profession or vocation.

**10.107** Occupying a highway concession, embracing both the right to charge tolls and the right to receive 'rent' from the government under its Design Build Finance and Operate initiative – under which the person incurring the expenditure will never own the road; he is building it on behalf of the government – is deemed to be carrying on a trade (*CAA 2001, s 341*). This did not apply before 6 April 1995 with the exception that a right to charge road tolls was deemed to be an interest in the road from 5 April 1991.

**10.108** Even if it can be brought within one of the above heads, a building or structure in use as, or as part of, a dwelling-house, retail shop (including any premises of a similar character where retail trade or business – including repair work – is carried on), showroom, hotel, or office, or for any purpose ancillary to such a purpose, is specifically excluded from industrial buildings allowances (other than certain buildings for the welfare of employees of a mine or oil well, and certain similar activities, which will have no value when the mine is exhausted or the foreign plantation ceases to be worked) (*CAA 2001, s 277*). It should be noted that the restriction is by reference to use. Accordingly, if, for example, part of a dwelling-house is set aside to be used for a qualifying purpose, expenditure on it should still qualify for relief provided that it ceases to be used as part of the dwelling-house, even though it still physically forms part of the house.

**10.109** This exclusion was considered in *Sarsfield v Dixons Group plc (1998 STC 938)*. A warehouse was constructed by Dixons Investments Limited (DIL). It was initially occupied by a retail subsidiary but from May 1981 it was used by Dixons Group Distribution Ltd (DGDL) which the Revenue accepted carried on a transport undertaking, receiving, storing and delivering the goods purchased by the Dixons group for sale from their retail shops. The Court of Appeal, reversing the decision of the High Court, said two questions needed to be asked:

(i) Is it sufficient that the use of the warehouse was ancillary to the purposes of the Dixon Group retail shops; and

(ii) whether the use of the warehouse for the purposes of DGDL's transport undertaking constituted use for a purpose ancillary to the purposes of the Dixon Group retail shops.

They answered both questions in the affirmative. The purpose of the warehouse was exclusively that of receiving, storing and distributing to the retail shops the goods necessary for them to operate as retail shops. The use of the warehouse was subservient and subordinate, and therefore ancillary, to the purposes of the retail shops. The fact that DGDL had a separate undertaking was not inconsistent with the purpose to which it put its building being ancillary to a retail shop. If, as in the *Kilmarnock* case (see 10.109), the use of the building served the purpose both of retail shops and the company's wholesale business, the use would be merely preliminary to that of the shop, but that was not the case with Dixons.

**10.110** The drawing-office of a business of structural engineers has been held to be an industrial building and not an office or ancillary to an office (*CIR v Lambhill Ironworks Ltd (31 TC 393)*). It was predominantly used for the preparation of plans for the workshop. The screening and packing of coal in paper bags has been held to constitute a process within what is now *section 274, item 2* (see 10.103(*b*) above) and not to be ancillary to a retail shop. The process took place in a separate building but the sacks of coal were sold retail by the processor (*Kilmarnock Equitable Co-operative Society Ltd v CIR (42 TC 675)*). Where any process whatever is carried on in a building, the possibility of the building being an industrial building needs to be considered as the wording of *item 2* is very wide. *Crusabridge Investments Ltd v Casings International Ltd (54 TC 246)* is an interesting case which illustrates the need to consider all of the heads of *section 274* before deciding whether a trade qualifies. Casings' business was the purchase of used car tyre casings, examining and grading them and reselling them to remoulders. It also sold remoulds on a commission basis. Its claim that it was subjecting goods to a process within *item 2* was rejected. It was, however, held that the storage of the used casings fell within *section 274, item 3(b)* and the storage of the remoulds within *section 274, item 3(c)* (see 10.103(*c*)(ii) and (iii) above respectively). Accordingly the building was an industrial building. It does not matter for the purpose of *item 3(b)* that the trade in which the goods will be processed is not that of the storer.

**10.111** Things that have been held not to be qualifying activities are a warehouse owned by selling agents for a number of manufacturers (*Dale v Johnson Bros (32 TC 487)*); an inland warehouse for goods imported in containers (*s 274, item 3(d)*) (see 10.103(*c*)(iv) above) was held to be restricted to goods in transit and does not include goods which have reached their purchaser) (*Copol Clothing Ltd v Hindmarch (57 TC 575)*); a crematorium – bodies are not goods (*Bourne v Norwich Crematorium Ltd (44 TC 164)*); a building used for making up wage packets – money is not goods (*Buckingham v Securitas Properties Ltd (53 TC 292)*); the depot of a plant hire contractor where plant was repaired and maintained as well as being stored between hirings – process implies a substantial measure of uniformity or a system of treatment and the individual nature of the repairs to each individual item of equipment could not be regarded as a process (*Vibroplant Ltd v Holland (54 TC 658)*); quarantine kennels – although dogs and cats might possibly fall within the expression goods or materials in the context of *s 274, item 3* (see 10.103(*c*)(iv) above) and are undoubtedly taken directly to the quarantine kennels from the seaport or airport of arrival, a quarantine business exists not as part of the ordinary process of physical transportation, but because of statutory restrictions, and thus the facility does not fit 'happily' into the wording (*Carr v Sayer (65 TC 15)*); a document and data processing centre of a bank – although documents are goods and they were subjected to a process the building was an 'office' as the operations carried on at the centre were of a kind that one would expect to be carried on in or by a bank in its back office (*Girobank plc v Clarke (1998 STC 182)*); and two cash and carry warehouses (which the Revenue accepted are not retail shops) – the trade carried on was not one of storage of goods or materials, it was the sale by wholesale of groceries and other products; and the checking and sorting of goods, repackaging them, labelling them, unpacking them, and the reading of product codes on the goods did not amount to the subjection of goods to a process; they were mere preliminaries to the trade of selling (*Bestway (Holdings) Ltd v Luff (1998 STC 357)*).

**10.112** A building outside the UK can qualify for allowances only if it is used for the purpose of a trade the profits of which are 'assessable in accordance with the rules applicable to Case 1 of Schedule D', i.e. the trade is carried on in the UK (*CAA 2001, s 282*).

**10.113** It will be seen that the test as to whether a building is an industrial building is applied by reference to the use to which the building is put, not the use to which the taxpayer puts it. Accordingly a taxpayer who uses a building to generate rental income is nevertheless entitled to claim allowances provided that the occupier (who is not necessarily his tenant but could be a sub-tenant or a licensee) uses the building for a qualifying purpose. If a building is used by more than one licensee of the same person it can qualify as an industrial building only if each of those licensees uses it for a qualifying purpose (*CAA 2001, s 278*). On the other hand, where a single person uses the entire building for more than one purpose, one of which is qualifying and the other or others of which are not, the entire building is an industrial building provided that an identifiable part is not set aside for the non-qualifying use (*Saxone, Lilley & Skinner (Holdings) Ltd v CIR (44 TC 122)*). In that case a warehouse was used to store shoes, one-third of which had been manufactured by a group company (and fell within *section 274, item 3(c)* (see 10.103(*c*)(iii) above)) and two-thirds of which had been purchased from other suppliers (storage of which was not a qualifying purpose). If an identifiable part of a building is the only part used for qualifying purposes then only that part qualifies for allowances (*CAA 2001, ss 283, 571*).

**10.114** Where part of a building does not qualify as an industrial building, allowances are nevertheless given on the entire cost if the capital expenditure on the non-qualifying part does not exceed 25% of the total capital expenditure on the entire building or structure (*CAA 2001, s 283(2)*). For this purpose it is necessary to look at all the expenditure since the building was constructed. Accordingly, the cost today of, say, an office extension to a factory needs to be compared with the cost of the factory when it was built. If it was built in 1930 even a very small extension in 1999 is likely to cost more than 25% of the total.

## Allowable Expenditure

**10.115** The right to allowances crystallises at the time when the expenditure is incurred (*CAA 2001, s 309(1)*). However, it cannot be known whether the building qualifies as an industrial building until it is physically occupied. Occupation by either the owner, a tenant, or a licensee is sufficient (*CAA 2001, s 271*). In practice, allowances are always given on a provisional basis pending occupation of the building. If it were to remain unoccupied for six years they would almost certainly be withdrawn at that stage although it is not wholly clear how they would do this. They would need to make a 'discovery' that the building had not been used for the qualifying purpose. However, if the accounts or tax return for the year that the expenditure is incurred clearly show that the building was not yet occupied for the qualifying purpose it is by no means clear that they would be entitled to make a discovery.

**10.116** Where a building is bought unused, i.e. before it has been used, the purchaser is deemed to have incurred expenditure on the construction of the building equal to the lower of his purchase price or the vendor's construction cost (*CAA 2001, s 295*). If the vendor was a person carrying on a trade consisting of the construction of industrial buildings with a view to their sale, the purchaser's allowances will be based on his purchase price (which will include the vendor's profit element) (*CAA 2001, s 296*). (See 10.101 above).

**10.117** IBAs can also be claimed for capital expenditure on repairs to an industrial building if these do not qualify as a revenue deduction for tax purposes (*CAA 2001, s 272*). If capital expenditure is incurred on preparing, cutting, tunnelling, or levelling land to prepare it as a site for the installation of plant or machinery and that expenditure does not attract allowances as plant and machinery it can be treated as if it were expenditure on an industrial building (*CAA 2001, s 273*). Where a building includes plant or machinery, expenditure on the provision of such items does not qualify for industrial buildings allowance (*CAA 1990, s 21(8)*). In practice, the Revenue normally allows the taxpayer to claim allowances on such expenditure either as plant or as industrial building expenditure, as he chooses.

**10.118** Problems can sometimes arise with architects' fees and other professional fees. These are not specifically catered for in the legislation and Inspectors of Taxes have been known to contend that they do not constitute expenditure 'on the construction of a building'. The probability is that they are part of the cost of construction and that allowances are due on such fees. It is generally accepted by the Revenue that construction costs include the costs of preparing, cutting, tunnelling or levelling the land. It is interesting to note that in *Associated Restaurants Ltd v Warland (61 TC 51)* the Commissioners regarded an apportioned part of the engineers' and architects' fees as forming part of the capital expenditure incurred in the installation of plant, and of the planning fees as being in principle expenditure on plant. The Revenue did not appeal against this ruling. That case was concerned with allowances for plant and machinery rather than IBAs, but it is likely that the same principle applies. An interesting discussion on this subject can be found in Taxline, January 1996, p 4.

**10.119** IBAs cannot be claimed in respect of expenditure on the acquisition of, or of rights in or over, land (*CAA 2001, s 272(1)*). The sum paid on a sale of the relevant interest in a building (or any other sale, insurance, salvage or compensation monies payable in respect of the building) must be deemed to be reduced by the amount which on a just apportionment is attributable to items not qualifying for allowances, e.g. land (*CAA 2001, s 356*). The reference only to sales is confusing. The provision undoubtedly requires a similar apportionment to be made on purchase (which will of course be a sale by the previous owner). There is an argument that where a building is bought unused from a developer allowances are claimable on the land element. This is because *CAA 2001, s 296(2)* deems the purchaser to have incurred expenditure on the construction of the building equal to the price paid by him on the purchase from the developer. This price would include the land element. As it is a deemed construction cost, one is not claiming the cost of land as such; one is merely claiming a deemed cost of construction work which happens to be statutorily calculated as a figure equal to the purchase price of the relevant interest. Accordingly *section 21* can have no application. This argument was firmly rejected by Sir John Vinelott in *Bostock v Totham (1997 STC 764)* who held that in the context the 'relevant interest' must mean the interest relevant to the capital allowance, not the legal interest in the land, so a 'just apportionment' was required under *CAA*

*2001, s 356*. He also supported the Special Commissioner's view that the just apportionment was the part of the purchase price that the cost of the building bore to the combined cost of the land and the construction work, not the purchase price less the value of the site at the date of the construction.

**10.120** The allowances are restricted where a building is bought unused if arrangements have been entered into which contain a provision having an artificial effect on pricing (*CAA 2001, s 357*). The vendor's balancing charge is similarly restricted. The arrangements which trigger this provision are:

(*a*) any arrangements relating to, or

(*b*) any other arrangements made with respect to,

any interest in (or right over) the building concerned (whether granted by the person entitled to the relevant interest or by someone else) which were entered into between any two or more persons before the sale price of the building was agreed and the effect of which was to enhance the value of the relevant interest in the building. Such arrangements have an artificial effect on pricing to the extent that they go beyond what (at the time they were entered into) it was reasonable to regard as required by the market conditions then prevailing for persons dealing with each other at arm's length in the open market. The comparison is to be made with transactions involving interests in or rights over buildings or structures of the same or a similar description (*CAA 2001, s 357(4)(5)*).

**10.121** This is an anti-avoidance provision. It is to combat schemes similar to one devised in 1994 by Matrix Securities to seek to regenerate the London Docklands property market, but to which the government took exception. Matrix wanted to sell via an Enterprise Zone Property Trust a building at its tenanted value, which because of the recession was far in excess of its vacant possession value, and entered into a scheme to create an artificial tenant. Such a scheme will now be an arrangement having an artificial effect on pricing – at least if the arm's length value is for a vacant possession building, although it is not at all clear that that is what *section 357(4)* will require in such circumstances. Very many enterprise zone buildings have rent guarantees, often from a local authority desperate to bring employment to the area. Is such a guarantee reasonably required by the market conditions? In most cases the building could be sold without it, albeit at a lower price. What incentives is it reasonable to expect might be required by market conditions? Reverse premiums, rent-free periods, customised fitting out, etc. are very common and are all designed to create a higher value for the tenanted building than it would otherwise have. This provision is accordingly likely to be extremely difficult to apply in practice.

**Relevant Interest**

**10.122** A person is entitled to claim a writing-down allowance for a particular year only if at the end of his accounting period (or the income tax base period) the building is an industrial building, and he is entitled to 'the relevant interest in it' (*CAA 2001, s 309*). The relevant interest is the interest held by the person who incurred the expenditure at the time at which it was incurred (*CAA 2001, s 286*). If he had more than one interest in the building at that time, it is whichever of those interests is reversionary on all the others, i.e. the one nearest to the freehold (*CAA 2001, s 286(3)*). If the relevant interest is a leasehold one, and the lease is extinguished by becoming merged with its immediately superior interest, that merged interest becomes the relevant interest (*CAA 2001, s 289*). If the lease expires, the interest which is immediately reversionary to it (i.e. the landlord's interest) becomes the relevant interest.

**10.123** If, on a termination of a lease, the tenant remains in possession with the consent of the landlord but without entering into a new lease, his old lease is treated as continuing whilst he remains in possession (so that if that lease is the relevant interest he will preserve his right to allowances) (*CAA 2001, s 359(2)*). If a lease contains an option to renew which is exercised, the new lease is similarly treated as if it were a continuation of the old (*CAA 2001, s 359(3)*). If a new lease is granted to a different lessee, and in connection with the transaction the new lessee makes a payment to the old, the new lease is treated as if it were a continuation of the old and as if it had been assigned in consideration of that payment (*CAA 2001, s 359(5)*). This will pass the right to the allowance to the new lessee, not the landlord, if the old lease was the relevant interest. If, on the termination of a lease which was the relevant interest, the landlord makes a payment to the tenant in respect of a building comprised in the lease, the lease must be treated as if it had been surrendered in consideration of that payment (*CAA 2001, s 359(4)*). This of course brings *CAA 2001, s 289* (see 10.122 above) into play.

**10.124** A person who incurs expenditure on the construction of a building is deemed to have the same interest at that time as he would have had if construction had been completed (*CAA 2001, s 287*). It is not clear what this provision is intended to do. It may be intended to cover a building lease where the owner is granted his lease only after completion, but in most such cases the leasehold interest would not automatically come into existence on completion so it is doubtful whether in such circumstances this statutory presumption would have the effect of deeming the leasehold interest to have existed at the date the expenditure was incurred.

**Disposal of an Industrial Building**

**10.125** If at a time when the building is (or has in the past been) an industrial building, either

(*a*) the relevant interest is sold, or

(*b*) the relevant interest comes to an end on the expiration of a foreign concession on which it was dependent, or

(*c*) if the relevant interest is a lease, the lease comes to an end other than by the owner acquiring the immediately superior interest and merging the two, or

(*d*) the building is demolished or destroyed or ceases altogether to be used (but not if it merely ceases to be used for a qualifying purpose and begins to be used for some other purpose),

a balancing allowance or charge will be made to or on the owner at that time of the relevant interest – but only if that event occurs within 25 years of the building having been first used (50 years where the expenditure was incurred before 6 November 1962) (*CAA 2001, s 314*). Once a charge or allowance has been triggered under *section 314*, the occurrence of a subsequent event without the building having been used as an industrial building in the interim cannot, of course, generate a second charge.

**10.126** A building does not cease altogether to be used merely by falling temporarily out of use. Indeed, it is treated as remaining an industrial building during the period of temporary disuse (*CAA 2001, s 285*).

**10.127** A balancing allowance will arise if the sale, insurance, salvage or compensation monies is less than the 'residue of expenditure' – namely in most cases (see 10.133 below for the full definition) the cost less the initial expenditure (if any) and writing-down allowances given (*CAA 2001, s 318(2)(3)*). If the sale proceeds, etc. exceed the residue of expenditure, a balancing charge equal to the difference is made – but limited to the allowances given (*CAA 2001, ss 314, 318(4)(5)*). If the building was not an industrial building (nor used for scientific research nor deemed to be an industrial building under *CAA 2001, s 285* – see 10.107) throughout the whole of its period of use and the sale proceeds, etc. are less than the 'capital expenditure', i.e. the initial expenditure qualifying for allowances (the cost of construction or the residue of expenditure at the time of purchase where the taxpayer was not the original owner), the balancing allowance is restricted, and can even be transformed into a balancing charge. The 'adjusted net cost' of the building first needs to be ascertained. This is the capital expenditure minus any sale proceeds, etc., reduced in the proportion that the aggregate period for which the building was an industrial building bears to the whole of the period from its first use (or from its acquisition by the taxpayer if later). The adjusted net cost is then compared with the allowances given, the difference between the two figures being the balancing charge or allowance (*CAA 2001, s 318*).

*Example 18*

Bloggs Ltd constructed a warehouse during its accounting period to 31 March 1994, at a cost of £100,000, and first occupied it on 1 January 1994. It used it for a qualifying purpose until 30 June 1997. It was then used for a non-qualifying purpose for nine months, before being let on 1 April 1998 to a tenant who used it for a qualifying purpose. The tenant went into liquidation on 30 September 2002. The building was empty thereafter until it was relet on 19 June 2003 to a new tenant who used it for a non-qualifying purpose until 31 December 2005 when it burned down. It was not insured, and only £1,000 net salvage proceeds were received.

| | | £ |
|---|---|---|
| Allowances given | | |
| 20% initial allowance | | 20,000 |
| 4% writing-down allowance, | year to 31.3.94 | 4,000 |
| | year to 31.3.95 | 4,000 |
| | year to 31.3.96 | 4,000 |
| | year to 31.3.97 | 4,000 |
| | year to 31.3.99 | 4,000 |
| | year to 31.3.00 | 4,000 |
| | year to 31.3.01 | 4,000 |
| | | 48,000 |
| notional writing-down allowance for periods when not in use as an industrial building (see 10.131 below), i.e. 5¼ years @ £4,000 p.a. | | 21,000 |
| | | £69,000 |
| Residue of expenditure (£100,000 – £69,000) | | £31,000 |

There is therefore an apparent balancing allowance of £30,000 (i.e. £31,000 – £1,000). As the building was not used as an industrial building throughout the period of ownership an adjustment may be necessary.

| Usage | Total period (years) | Period for which an industrial building (years) |
|---|---|---|
| 1.1.94 – 30.6.97 | 3½ | 3½ |
| 1.7.97 – 31.3.98 | ¾ | – |
| 1.4.98 – 30.9.00 | 2½ | 2½ |
| 1.10.00 – 31.12.05 | 5¼ | ¾ |
| | 12 | 6¾ |

Adjusted net cost (*s 4(9)*):

| | |
|---|---|
| £100,000 (cost) less £1,000 (salvage) | £99,000 |
| 6¾/12ths thereof | £55,687 |
| Allowances given | 48,000 |
| Adjusted net cost as above | 55,687 |
| Balancing allowance | £7,687 |

*Notes.*

(i) No writing-down allowance is due for the year to 31 March 1998 as the building was not in use as an industrial building on that date.

(ii) Although the building was not actually used as an industrial building between October 2000 and June 2001, it is deemed to be one by virtue of *CAA 2001, s 285* – see 10.126 above.

(iii) Curiously it appears that notional allowances must be calculated for 5¼ years (and not 5 as might be expected) as *CAA 2001, s 336(3)* refers to amounts equal to writing-down allowances made for chargeable periods of a total length equal to the period for which the building was not in use (or deemed to be in use) as an industrial building. The effect is to bring into account allowances for 10¼ years instead of 10. This arises because *CAA 2001, s 310(1)* allowed for a full year's allowance for the year to 31.3.86 even though the building was used for only ¼ of that year, and denied any allowance for the year to 31.3.98 and for the year to 31.3.02 even though it was used as an industrial building for ¼ of both years, so that in effect allowances were given for 3 months more than the period of industrial use.

(iv) If the disposal proceeds, etc. had equalled or exceeded the capital expenditure, a balancing charge equal to the whole of the allowances given would have arisen irrespective of the proportion of the period of ownership for which the building was an industrial building (*CAA 2001, s 319(4)(5)*).

**10.128** Where an industrial building is sold to a connected person an election can be made to treat the building as having been sold for a price equal to its residue of expenditure (*CAA 2001, s 569*). Such an election overrides these special rules (*CAA 2001, s 569(5)*). It must be made within two years after the sale. This election cannot be made unless both buyer and seller are within the scope of capital allowances (*CAA 2001, s 570(2)*). There was some confusion whether this provision applied for the purpose of the application of the industrial buildings allowances rules to qualifying hotels, enterprise zone buildings and research and development expenditure, but *FA 1994, section 119* made clear that it does (and always has).

**10.129** Subject to the possibility of the *Furniss v Dawson* principle being applicable, it is relatively easy to avoid a balancing charge by selling a lesser interest than the relevant interest. For example, if the relevant interest is the freehold, a 999-year lease could be granted at a premium and a nil or nominal ground rent. If it is a lease with 56 years 1 month unexpired, a sublease for 56 years 28 days could be granted at a premium. It was held in *Woods v R M Mallen (Engineering) Ltd (45 TC 619)* that the grant of a sublease for three days less than the head lease was not equivalent to a disposal of the relevant interest. It seems doubtful whether the Revenue could substantiate a claim to apply the *Furniss v Dawson* principle on the grant of a sublease unless an agreement to sell the reversion subsequently is entered into at that time, as it is hard to discern a composite transaction – although their Lordships indicated in *McGuckian v CIR (1997 STC 908)* that a composite transaction might not be crucial to the *Furniss v Dawson* principle. Additionally, the grant of a sublease may be commercially more attractive than an assignment of the lease as the sublessor can retake possession in the event of default and has control over variations of the lease, whereas he loses such rights with an assignment whilst remaining liable to the head landlord. Accordingly, even if the Revenue could categorise the grant of the sublease as an inserted step, they may have difficulty in showing that it has no commercial purpose. Where a building contains items of plant and machinery, the carving out of a lesser interest or the retention of a nominal reversion can also be used to avoid the balancing charge under the plant and machinery rules, as there will not have been a disposal of the asset in question. It is in any event implicit in the special rules for enterprise zone buildings in *CAA 2001, ss 327–331* (see 10.165–10.169) and the Revenue press releases issued at the time that the Revenue accept that this device is effective (see 10.169).

**10.130** The balancing allowance on a sale is restricted if the relevant interest is sold subject to a subordinate interest and either

(*a*) the vendor, the purchaser and the grantee of the subordinate interest (or any two of them) are connected persons (within *ICTA 1988, s 839*, see Appendix 1), or

(*b*) it appears with respect to the sale, or the grant of the lease, or related transactions, that the sole or main benefit that might have been expected to accrue to the parties or any of them was the obtaining of an allowance (not merely the balancing allowance).

(*CAA 2001, s 325*).

The vendor must add to his net proceeds of the sale any premium received by him for the grant of the subordinate interest (or any other capital consideration he has received for its grant or variation) – and if the rent payable under the subordinate interest is below a commercial rent (bearing in mind any premium) the additional premium that could have been obtained if the transaction had been at arm's length (*CAA 2001, s 325(4)(5)*).

*Example 19*

Exwye Ltd owns a freehold industrial building. It grants a lease to its subsidiary, Wyezed Ltd, for a premium of £1 million. It then sells the freehold reversion to a second subsidiary, Exzed Ltd, for its market value of £500. Exwye's residue of expenditure at the time it sold its reversion was £600,000.

| | £ |
|---|---|
| Exwye Ltd's tax position is | |
| Sale proceeds | 500 |
| Residue of expenditure | 600,000 |
| Balancing allowance | £599,500 |
| But limited to | |
| Sale proceeds | 500 |
| Premium received on grant of lease | 1,000,000 |
| | 1,000,500 |
| Residue of expenditure | 600,000 |
| Balancing charge that would have arisen | £400,500 |
| Therefore the balancing allowance is (see 10.131 below) | £ nil |

**10.131** The adjustment under *CAA 2001, s 325* cannot give rise to a balancing charge. It merely eliminates the balancing allowance (*CAA 2001, s 325(5)*). Where the restriction operates, the vendor's residue of expenditure immediately after the sale (on which the purchaser of the relevant interest is entitled to allowances) is calculated as if the full balancing allowance had been given (*CAA 2001, s 325(7)*). This effectively results in a complete loss of allowances on the expenditure. Accordingly care should be taken to avoid being caught by this provision on intra-group transfers. It is possible that the Revenue would contend that (*b*) in 10.130 above applies if a long lease is granted to take advantage of the *Mallen Engineering* case (see 10.129 above) and the reversion is subsequently sold – although it is doubtful whether the sole or main benefit test is satisfied in such circumstances. As *section 325* cannot create a balancing charge there is no real problem if the provision does apply in such a case.

**Purchase of an Existing Building**

**10.132** Where a person purchases an existing industrial building (other than one which has not previously been used – as to which see 10.116 above) the rules are modified. His writing-down allowance is not 4% of cost. Instead his allowances are based on the vendor's 'residue of expenditure' and the age of the building.

**10.133** The vendor's residue of expenditure is his original cost (the amount on which he was entitled to claim IBAs) plus any balancing charge and less the aggregate of his initial allowance (if any), writing-down allowances or research and development allowances, a notional writing-down allowance for years when the building was not an industrial building, and any balancing allowance (*CAA 2001, s 311*). Initial allowances were given on expenditure between 6 April 1944 (when the allowances were introduced) and 31 March 1986 with the exception of that in two short periods, 6 April 1952 to 14 April 1953 and 7 April 1954 to 17 February 1956. The rate of allowance fluctuated between 5% and 75% (100% for certain small buildings – 'small workshops'). Allowances were also given at 20% for expenditure between 1 November 1992 and 31 October 1993 (see 10.101).

**10.134** The notional allowance where the building was not used as an industrial building is the writing-down allowance that would have been due if it had been so used. If a balancing charge arises under *CAA 2001, s 314* (see 10.127 above) the normal rules do not apply but the residue of expenditure is instead treated as equal to the net proceeds (*CAA 2001, s 337*). Net proceeds is not defined. It probably means the sale proceeds less any part thereof attributable to land or other non-qualifying expenditure.

**10.135** The purchaser calculates his writing-down allowance by spreading the amount of the vendor's residue of expenditure over the balance of the period of 25 years from the date that the building was first used (50 years if this was prior to 6 November 1962) (*CAA 2001, s 311*).

*Example 20*

Suppose that the building in *Example 18* had instead been sold to a purchaser with a 30 June accounting date on 31 December 1997 for £170,000, of which £60,000 was attributed to the land element.

The purchaser's writing-down allowances would be calculated as follows.

Bloggs Ltd's residue of expenditure

| | £ | £ |
|---|---|---|
| Sale proceeds (£170,000 – £60,000) | 110,000 | |
| but limited to original cost | | 100,000 |
| Less allowances given | 53,000 | |
| deduct balancing charge | 53,000 | — |
| Notional allowances as before | | 21,000 |
| Residue after sale | | £79,000 |

Period remaining from 31 December 1997 to 25th anniversary of date of first use (1 January 2011) is 13 years.

| | | |
|---|---|---|
| Annual writing-down allowances (£79,000/13) | | £6,077 |
| Allowed in year to 30.6.98 (6/12 × £6,077) | £3,038 | |
| 12 years to 30.6.2010 (12 × £6,077) | £72,924 | |
| year to 30.6.2011 | £3,038 | |

**10.136** Where additions to a building have taken place at different times, each addition is regarded as if it were a separate building and, strictly speaking, the residue of expenditure and the purchaser's writing-down allowances have to be computed separately in respect of each addition. In practice this is rarely done, the whole of the allowances normally being given over the remainder of the period from the time the building was erected.

**10.137** It will be apparent from the above example that it can be attractive from an IBA point of view to buy a building when it is approaching the end of its 25-year period, although it must be borne in mind that construction costs two decades ago were significantly lower than those of the present day.

**10.138** Normally a purchaser is entitled to claim a writing-down allowance only if he purchases the relevant interest in the property (see 10.122 above). If he purchases an interest carved out of the relevant interest – which the vendor may want to do to avoid a balancing charge – he will not be entitled to claim IBAs. Instead, the 'vendor' will continue to be entitled to claim his 4% p.a. for the balance of the 25-year period.

**10.139** Where a person pays a premium for a lease of over 50 years an election can be made for the right to allowances to be transferred to him from the landlord (*CAA 2001, s 290*). The Schedule A rules (see 3.23 above) apply to determine whether a lease exceeds 50 years (*CAA 2001, s 291(3)*). The election must be made jointly by the landlord and tenant within two years after the date on which the lease takes effect – which is not necessarily the date it is granted but will often be earlier (*CAA 2001, ss 290, 291(4)*). It should be noted that this time limit is not tied to a year of assessment or accounting period. It is therefore easily overlooked. The election should therefore normally be made immediately the lease is entered into. The landlord must, of course, himself own the relevant interest (or be deemed to own it by virtue of an election that he and his own landlord made under *section 290*). The election is to treat the relevant interest as having been sold for a price equal to the premium received (*CAA 2001, s 290(2)*). An election cannot be made in respect of part only of the expenditure incurred by the landlord (*CAA 2001, s 290(3)*). He will need to give up his right to allowances entirely.

**10.140** The election can, of course, result in a balancing charge arising on the lessor so he will generally be unwilling to make it. If he has available losses he may be prepared to do so but would no doubt want to reflect in the amount of the premium the benefit he is passing to the tenant. The landlord does not, however, have to be a person who has claimed IBAs on the building. It could be a local authority which is outside the scope of tax in relation to the building, or a pension fund which is exempt from tax on its rental income, or a property dealer who is not entitled to allowances because his expenditure on the building is not capital expenditure. In such circumstances the election should always be considered – and should usually be made as a matter of course – as there is no disadvantage to the landlord in making it.

**10.141** The election cannot be made if the lessor and lessee are connected with one another (*CAA 2001, s 291(1)*), although there is an exception for statutory bodies. Not surprisingly, it also cannot be made if the sole or main benefit which might be expected to accrue to the lessor from the grant of the lease and the making of the election is the obtaining of a balancing allowance (*CAA 2001, s 291(2)*).

## Agricultural Buildings and Works

### Introduction

**10.142** Agricultural buildings allowances are granted where the owner or tenant of agricultural land incurs capital expenditure on the construction of farmhouses, farm buildings, cottages, fences, or other works. It should particularly be noted that the allowance is not restricted to buildings. It can also be claimed on such things as estate roads, fences, drainage, shelter belts of trees, water and electricity installations, glasshouses on market garden land, and even the reclamation of former agricultural land (Inland Revenue Pamphlet CA3). For expenditure after 31 March 1986 allowances are given only to a person having a major interest in the land, i.e. the freehold (or an agreement to acquire it) or a lease (of any duration). An agreement for a lease or any tenancy or licence falling short of a lease will not carry a right to allowances (*CAA 2001, s 361(1)(b)*).

### Allowances Available

**10.143** The allowance is currently an annual allowance of 4% of the qualifying expenditure. For expenditure prior to 1 April 1986 an initial allowance of 20% of the expenditure and an annual writing-down allowance of 10% for eight years was given (*CAA 2001, s 372*). Where an agricultural building is acquired before being brought into use special rules apply on the lines of those for industrial buildings (see 10.116 above) (*CAA 2001, s 370*). Balancing adjustments do not automatically arise on the disposal of agricultural buildings – instead the right to allowances passes to a purchaser or other transferee of the land (*CAA 2001, s 375*). If the transfer takes place during a chargeable period the writing-down allowance (but not any initial allowance) for that period – including any expenditure by the new owners – is apportioned on a time basis. Accordingly in the absence of special provisions full relief for such expenditure would not be obtained unless the building – or rather the land on which it stands as there is no requirement for the building to continue to exist at the time the allowance is claimed – is retained for 25 years. An initial allowance at the rate of 20% was temporarily reintroduced for expenditure contracted for in the period 1 November 1992 to 31 October 1993 (or for later expenditure incurred for the purpose of complying with such a contract). The expenditure had to be incurred for the purposes of husbandry on the land. If it was expenditure on the construction of a building, fence or other work it had to be used before 1 January 1995. If the expenditure was on a farmhouse (or other asset used partly for use) only the business proportion qualified. The allowance could be disclaimed in whole or part. Where the initial allowance was claimed a writing-down allowance could be claimed for the same period, but only if the building or works is in use at some time in that period (*CAA 1990, s 124A*).

**10.144** If any building, fence or other works on the construction of which qualifying expenditure was incurred is destroyed or demolished the owner can elect for balancing adjustments to apply unless the expenditure was incurred before 1 April 1986 (or before 1 April 1987 under a contract entered into before 14 March 1984). He would normally do so as, except where insurance proceeds are received, such an adjustment would almost always be a balancing allowance. On the disposal of the relevant interest in an agricultural building (the interest, or the most superior interest, held by the person who incurred the expenditure at that time (*CAA 2001, s 364*), the former and the new owner can jointly elect for balancing adjustments to apply. The election must be made for corporation tax purposes within two years after the end of the chargeable period and for income tax purposes within 12 months after 31 January following the tax year in which the accounts concerned end. The period was six years for expenditure in chargeable periods ending before 30 November 1993 and for income tax purposes was two years from the end of the chargeable period up to 1995/96. An election cannot be made by a person who is not within the charge to tax in the UK, nor if the transaction is one the sole or main benefit of which is the obtaining of agricultural buildings allowances – although somewhat surprisingly it can be made if the object is to crystallise a balancing charge (*CAA 2001, ss 380–382*).

**10.145** The amount of a balancing allowance or charge is, of course, the difference between the residue of expenditure – the expenditure qualifying for allowances less the allowances given (including any given to a previous owner who did not make the election under 10.144 above) – and any sale proceeds or insurance, salvage or compensation monies

(*CAA 2001, s 385*). Where only part of the expenditure qualified for allowances only a proportionate part of the sale proceeds, etc. is taken into account (*CAA 2001, s 384(2)*). A balancing charge cannot exceed the writing-down allowances given to the person on whom it is made (*CAA 2001, s 387*). This needs to be watched. Suppose A owns an agricultural building for ten years and sells it to B who retains it for four years and sells it to C. The building cost A £10,000. B and C elect for balancing adjustments but A and B do not. There will be a clawback of the £1,600 writing-down allowances given to B but no clawback of those given to A. However C's writing-down allowances, which will be spread over the balance of the 25-year writing-down period in the same way as with IBAs, are based on the residue of expenditure at the time of the sale (£10,000 – 14 years at 4% = £4,400) less the balancing allowance or plus the balancing charge made on B (*CAA 2001, s 376*). He will therefore be entitled to allowances on £6,000 only – which will be given at the rate of £545 p.a. for eleven years. This is not unreasonable as A will have had – and kept – the allowances on the remaining £4,000. As with IBAs, market value must be substituted for the sale proceeds on a disposal between connected persons or on a transaction the main purpose of which was to obtain an agricultural buildings allowance or reduce a balancing charge (*CAA 2001, ss 567–573*). The special provisions which restrict the balancing allowance on industrial buildings in certain circumstances (see 10.130 above) are repeated in virtually identical terms for agricultural buildings allowances purposes (*CAA 2001, s 389*). As with IBAs (see 10.119 above), allowances cannot be claimed on the land element of any expenditure.

## Meaning of Agricultural Land

**10.146** Agricultural land means land, houses or other buildings in the UK occupied wholly or mainly for the purpose of husbandry (*CAA 2001, s 361*). Prior to 1968 there was no definition of husbandry. In *CIR v Cavan Central Co-operative Agricultural and Dairy Society Ltd (12 TC 10)*, Madden J defined it as tilling and cultivating the soil, the raising of livestock or poultry and sometimes extended to that of silkworms, etc. He added that the word would certainly include the conversion by a husbandman of milk produced on his farm into butter or cheese. In *Lean and Dickson v Ball (12 TC 341)*, where poultry farming was held to be husbandry, Lord Clyde felt that land is occupied for husbandry if the trade or business carried on by the occupier depends to a material extent on the industrial or commercial use of the fruits (natural or artificial) of the land so occupied. From 25 July 1986, husbandry statutorily includes any method of intensive rearing of livestock or fish on a commercial basis for the production of food for human consumption (*CAA 2001, s 362*).

### Qualifying Expenditure

**10.147** To qualify for allowances it must be shown that the expenditure is incurred for the purposes of husbandry on the land in question, e.g. that it is not for personal non-business reasons (*CAA 2001, s 361(1)(b)(ii)*). Only a third of the expenditure on a farmhouse can qualify for relief. If 'the accommodation and amenities of the farmhouse are out of due relation to the nature and extent of the farm', the one-third figure is reduced to such proportion of the expenditure as may be just (*CAA 1990, s 124(2)*). In *Lindsay v CIR (34 TC 289)* it was held that a dwelling-house occupied by the head shepherd on a sheep farm which was managed by agents was a farmhouse, so the restriction applied. On the other hand where land was farmed by a father and son in partnership and the son moved to a new house built on the farm by the partnership it was held that the house was a cottage so that the one-third restriction did not apply (the father's house being the farmhouse) (*CIR v Whiteford & Son (40 TC 379)*). Where expenditure on an asset other than the farmhouse is incurred partly for the purpose of husbandry and partly for some other purpose the expenditure must be apportioned in such manner as may be just.

### Transfer of Interest in Land

**10.148** As mentioned in 10.143 above, if, in the absence of an election, the whole of the taxpayer's interest in the land (or in any part of it) is transferred to some other person, the transferee takes over the right to the future allowances in relation to that land (or part) (*CAA 2001, s 375*). It has been held that a farmer, who after incurring considerable capital expenditure, conveyed the freehold in his farm to trustees and the following day took back a lease from them, had not disposed of his whole interest in the farm and therefore retained the right to allowances (*Sargaison v Roberts (45 TC 612)*). Megarry J there felt that he should look at the realities at the expense of the technicalities. It is difficult to reconcile this decision with that in the *Mallen Engineering* case (10.129 above) which was decided in the same year.

**10.149** If the interest in land attracting the allowance is a lease, on its expiry it will be treated as having been acquired by the incoming tenant if he makes a payment to his predecessor in respect of the expenditure, or by the landlord in any other case (*CAA 2001, s 375*).

## Qualifying Hotels

**10.150** The allowances in respect of qualifying hotels are based on the industrial buildings allowances rules. To qualify for the allowance a hotel must:

1. provide accommodation in a building or buildings of a permanent nature;

2. be open for at least four months in the period April to October ('the season') during the year for which the allowance is being claimed; and

3. when it is open in the season:

   (*a*) have at least ten letting bedrooms (i.e. private bedrooms available for letting to the public generally and not normally in the same occupation for more than one month);

   (*b*) offer sleeping accommodation consisting wholly or mainly of letting bedrooms; and

   (*c*) normally provide for guests

      (i) breakfast,

      (ii) an evening meal,

      (iii) bed-making, and

      (iv) cleaning of rooms.

(*CAA 2001, s 279*).

The Revenue regard the tests at (*c*)(i) and (ii) as satisfied if the offering of breakfast and dinner is a normal event in the running of the business. They will not regard them as met if the service of either breakfast or dinner is only available on request or in exceptional circumstances (Inland Revenue Statement of Practice SP 9/87). The hotel does not have to be in the UK but one in a different climate might have difficulty in meeting the test at (2) above if it does not open throughout the year.

**10.151** If the hotel is in use throughout the twelve months ending with the last day of the accounting period (or basis period in the case of an individual) of the person claiming the allowances, the above tests must be applied by reference to that accounting period (*CAA 2001, s 279(3)*).

**10.152** If a hotel had fewer than ten letting bedrooms until a date too late for it to qualify for relief under the normal test it can instead apply the tests by reference to the period of 12 months starting from the date from which it first qualified for relief (*CAA 2001, s 279(5)*).

*Example 21*

A company erected a hotel which it opened on 1 March 1995 as a residential hotel for long-stay (over three months) guests. It prepares accounts to 30 June. On 31 January 2003 there was a change of policy and thenceforth the hotel catered only for short-term (under a month) guests.

The hotel does not qualify for relief up to the year to 30 June 2002. The year to 30 June 2003 must be looked at to decide whether allowances are due for that year as the hotel was in use for the purpose of the trade throughout the year. It did not qualify in the months July to October 2002. It does do so in the months April to June 2003 but as this is under three months, allowances are not due under the normal test.

Under the alternative test one looks at the 12 months from 1 February 2003. In that period it meets the necessary conditions for six months, April to October 2003, and can thus claim the allowances.

**10.153** Where the hotel is first used for the purpose of the trade during the accounting period, the tests are again applied by reference to the first 12 months of use (*CAA 2001, s 279(4)*).

**10.154** Under the normal IBA rules the building must be a qualifying building on the last day of the accounting period to attract a writing-down allowance. The application of the above tests cannot be used to make a building a qualifying hotel at a time after it ceased altogether to be used (*CAA 2001, s 279(6)*). It appears, however, that if it ceases to qualify but does not cease to be used altogether it can be deemed to qualify, as once it is found that the qualifying tests are met the effect seems to be to deem it a qualifying hotel for the entire accounting period. For example, suppose a hotel company preparing accounts to 31 December qualifies until 30 September 2002 and then changes to a residential hotel for long-term residents. Allowances will still be due for the year to 31 December 2002 even though at that date it no longer had ten letting bedrooms.

**10.155** Where a hotel is a qualifying hotel allowances can also be claimed on any building provided by the hotel operator for the welfare of workers employed by the hotel (e.g. a staff hostel) (*CAA 2001, s 279(7)*). Where the hotel is operated by an individual (including as a partner) expenditure on living accommodation of the proprietor does not qualify (*CAA 2001, s 279(8)*). How this exclusion is to be done is not specified. If a hotel is constructed with 50 bedrooms, one of which is used by the owner-manager, it is not on the face of it feasible to arrive at a cost of that bedroom. This specific exclusion would appear to override the normal 25% non-qualifying rule (see 10.114 above).

**10.156** The allowance is a writing-down allowance of 4% p.a. On expenditure before 1 April 1986 an initial allowance was also given (*FA 1995, s 66*). If a hotel ceases to be a qualifying hotel (other than on sale, demolition, or expiry of lease) and does not again become one within the next two years it must be treated as having been sold at its open market value at the end of the two-year period if nothing has happened in the interim to trigger a balancing adjustment (*CAA 2001, s 317*). For chargeable periods ending before 27 July 1989, expenditure on fire and safety which qualified for allowances as plant and machinery (see 10.47 above) could not qualify for hotel allowances (*CAA 1990, s 7(1)(b), (3)*). There was no option to choose which allowances to claim.

**10.157** The definition section of the IBA rules (*CAA 2001, s 271*) does not of course apply. The provision (*CAA 2001, s 284*) allowing the whole of a building to be treated as a qualifying building if at least 75% of the expenditure qualifies will, however, apply (although this seems to be subject to *CAA 2001, s 279(8)* – see 10.155) as will the exclusion of buildings outside the UK unless they are used for the purpose of a trade assessable in accordance with the rules applicable to Case I of Schedule D (*CAA 2001, s 282*).

## Commercial Buildings in Enterprise Zones

### Introduction

**10.158** The enterprise zone allowances are also based on the IBA rules. Capital expenditure on qualifying buildings in an enterprise zone will attract an initial allowance of 100% (*CAA 2001, s 306*). If the taxpayer prefers he can take a lower initial allowance (*CAA 2001, s 306(2)*). He will then be entitled to a writing-down allowance of 25% p.a. of the cost instead of the normal 4% (*CAA 2001, s 310*). The definition of an industrial building is extended to include a qualifying hotel (within 10.150 above) and a 'commercial building'. A commercial building is any building which is used for the purposes of a trade, profession or vocation, or any building used as an office, provided that it does not form part of a dwelling-house (*CAA 2001, s 281*). The expenditure must be contracted for within ten years of the zone being designated (*CAA 2001, s 298*). There is no clawback of allowances if the building ceases to be used for a qualifying purpose without being sold. There is an anomaly where a building is destroyed outside the ten-year period. The destruction gives rise to a disposal at a price equal to the insurance proceeds or compensation. Normally the balancing charge this generates will be offset by the allowances on the rebuilding costs, but it will create a real tax liability in this case as the rebuilding will not qualify for enterprise zone building allowances; indeed if it is not an industrial building or qualifying hotel it will not qualify for allowances at all.

## Plant and Machinery Installed in Buildings

**10.159** Expenditure on the provision of plant or machinery which becomes an integral part of a building is strictly speaking not eligible for enterprise zone buildings allowance. Nevertheless, by concession, the Revenue will allow the taxpayer to elect to treat such expenditure as eligible for the enterprise zone buildings allowance instead of for capital allowances on plant and machinery (Inland Revenue Press Release 6 January 1987).

## Current List of Enterprise Zones

**10.160** A list of the enterprise zones that have been designated to date is given in Appendix 2. The then government stated in December 1985 that, apart from the proposed zone at Chatham, there were then no plans to designate further zones as they had been found to be a fairly expensive means of generating employment. Two new zones were designated in March 1990 and more have been designated recently, so they may be viewed as attractive incentives once more. On the other hand, the EC may well decide that these enterprise zones should be scrapped as constituting harmful tax competition.

## Purchase of Building in Zone

**10.161** Where expenditure is incurred on the construction of a building or structure (the actual expenditure), and at the time some of the expenditure is incurred (or contracted for) the building is in an enterprise zone, but before the building is brought into use the relevant interest in it is sold, the purchaser is deemed to have incurred expenditure on the construction of the building on the date his purchase price becomes payable equal to the lesser of his net purchase price or the actual expenditure (and the actual expenditure is ignored) (*CAA 2001, ss 295–297*). If the whole of the actual expenditure was not incurred within 10 years of the site first being included in the enterprise zone, the deemed expenditure is split into enterprise zone and non-enterprise zone elements. The enterprise zone element is:

$$\text{deemed expenditure} \times \frac{\text{part of actual expenditure incurred in the ten-year period}}{\text{total actual expenditure}}$$

(*CAA 2001, s 302*).

For the purpose of calculating capital allowances only, the enterprise zone element of the expenditure is then deemed to have been incurred at a time when the building was in the enterprise zone (*CAA 2001, s 302(2)*). If there is more than one sale before the building is first used the above modification applies only to the last sale, as the intermediate one will not have triggered a right to allowances because of *CAA 2001, s 295(4)*. If the actual expenditure was incurred by a property dealer, the actual expenditure is, as for industrial buildings allowances, treated as equal to his selling price (*CAA 2001, ss 296, 297*). The anti-avoidance rule attached to *section 295* expenditure (see 10.120) also applies for the purpose of *sections 296* and *297*.

**10.162** The Revenue take the view that where a person buys an uncompleted building with the benefit of an existing building contract the purchase price consists of two elements, the purchase of the relevant interest in relation to the construction expenditure already incurred (the *section 10A* element) and the developer's obligation to complete the building (the *section 1* element). Both elements attract the 100% allowances. The Revenue have said that they believe that some agreements they have seen may be ineffective to grant to the purchaser the *section 1* element as the terms of the contract are insufficient to enable the purchaser to 'step into' the construction contract and thereby incur the future construction expenditure. This particularly applies if the vendor agrees to complete the building at his own cost which will later be reimbursed by the purchaser or the vendor retains an interest in the property during the construction period. They therefore recommend a clear contractual separation of the purchaser's obligations to purchase the partially completed building and the purchaser's arrangements with the vendor to secure the completion of the building by the purchaser incurring construction expenditure on his own account (Tax Bulletin 35, June 1998).

## Disposal of Building in Zone

**10.163** If an enterprise zone building or structure is sold within two years after its first being used, the purchaser can also claim the 100% allowance as if the building had not been used (but only if it is the first such sale) (*CAA 2001, s 301*). This applies irrespective of whether there were previously sales of the building before it was first used. The allowances are, of course, based on the lower of his net purchase price or the actual expenditure on the construction of the building. If all of the actual expenditure on the construction was not incurred during the life of the enterprise zone, the deemed expenditure must be split into an enterprise zone element and a non-enterprise zone element as outlined in 10.161 above (*CAA 2001, s 303*). Although the allowances are calculated on the lower of the purchaser's cost or the actual construction costs, any balancing allowance or charge on the vendor is calculated in the normal way (*CAA 2001, s 301(2)*). This relaxation should be particularly useful where a building is in multi-occupation as it effectively allows a developer a two-year period in which to let tenants gradually into occupation and to sell the fully-let building to an investor. For disposals between 13 January 1994 and 31 August 1994 the two-year period was extended to 31 August 1994 if it would otherwise have expired in that period (*FA 1994, s 121*).

**10.164** Expenditure incurred under a contract entered into at a time when the site of a building was not in an enterprise zone (including a contract entered into before 16 December 1991) does not qualify for allowances unless it is actually incurred within 20 years after the site in question is first included in the enterprise zone (*CAA 2001, s 298(1)*). This is an anti-avoidance provision. Without it a developer could have contracted to incur expenditure before the ten-year enterprise period expires, and gradually carry out his development in pursuance of the contract over a very long time scale while retaining the right to the allowances. *Section 298* still enables the allowances to be preserved on expenditure for up to ten years after the enterprise zone expires by contracting for such expenditure during the ten-year enterprise zone period.

**10.165** In addition to the events set out in 10.125 above, a balancing charge (but not a balancing allowance) will also arise in relation to enterprise zone buildings if any capital value is realised in relation to the relevant interest (*CAA 2001, s 328*). This does not apply if the relevant interest in the building was acquired under a contract entered into before 13 January 1994 (other than a conditional contract which became unconditional after 25 February 1994).

**10.166** For this purpose capital value is realised if, within seven years of the expenditure having been incurred and either while the building is an industrial building or after it has ceased to be one, an amount of capital value is paid which is attributable to an interest in land (the subordinate interest) to which the relevant interest is (or will become) subject (*CAA 2001, s 328(5)–(7)*). Capital value means a capital sum (or something that would have been a capital sum if it had taken the form of a money payment). Rent or the part of a premium taxable under *ICTA 1988, s 34* (see 3.2) is excluded. If the disposal is not on arm's length terms the premium or other capital sum that could have been demanded at arm's length will be a capital sum (*CAA 2001, s 331(1)*). The amount of capital realised is, of course, the capital sum. Capital value is attributable to a subordinate interest if it is paid in consideration of the grant of such an interest (e.g. a premium for the grant of a lease or a sublease); it is paid in lieu of rent payable by the person entitled to the interest or in consideration of the assignment of such rent (e.g. a lease is granted at a market rent but such rent is then commuted into the payment of a capital sum); or it is paid in consideration of the surrender of the subordinate interest or the variation or waiver of any of the terms on which it is granted (*CAA 2001, s 329(1)*). A substantial advance payment of rent will not constitute capital value. Nor will an amount in respect of which an election is made under *section 290* (see 10.139) (*CAA 2001, s 329(6)*).

**10.167** Where the acquisition of the relevant interest included arrangements for its subsequent sale, and the subsequent grant out of it of some other interest, or any other event on which capital value attributable to the subordinate interest would be paid (or treated as paid), and those arrangements either required that subsequent sale or other transaction to take place, or made it substantially more likely to occur than if the arrangements had not been entered into, *section 4A* applies even where the disposal is more than seven years after the acquisition (*CAA 2001, s 330(3)(4)*).

**10.168** An interest in land includes a lease, an easement and a licence. Agreeing to grant an interest is equivalent to granting it. If an agreement to pay an amount of capital value is made within the seven-year period but the transaction does not take place until after seven years it is deemed to occur in the seven-year period (*CAA 2001, s 331(2)(3)*).

**10.169** This prevents the avoidance of a balancing charge on an enterprise zone building under the *Woods v RM Mallen (Engineering) Ltd* principle (see 10.129). It imposes a charge only where the long lease, etc. is disposed of within seven years or anti-avoidance arrangements are entered into, e.g. to give guaranteed exit arrangements. The then government initially intended that this provision should apply to all industrial buildings but relented on the basis that 'the weakness in the capital allowances legislation is not significant in the case of buildings eligible for normal industrial buildings allowances' (Inland Revenue Press Releases 13.1.1994 and 25.2.1994).

## Enterprise Zone Property Trusts

**10.170** An enterprise zone property trust is an authorised unit trust investing in enterprise zone properties. The assets of the trust must consist wholly of land (including buildings or structures on the land) substantially the whole of which was situated in enterprise zones when it was acquired by the trust, and any part which is not in an enterprise zone must be contiguous to land held by the trust which is in the zone. From 31 March 1992 land which was situated in an enterprise zone and the construction cost on which qualified for enterprise zone allowances when it was expended or contracted for, is treated as if it is in such a zone for this purpose. Contributions by participants must be expended on the acquisition of the land or interests in land, the construction of (or the purchase of interests in) buildings or structures on that land (eligible for enterprise zone capital allowances), and the provision of machinery and plant which is an integral part of such buildings. A temporary holding of cash or of assets held in connection with the trust property, and the use of participant's contributions for expenditure incidental to (or arising out of) the permitted expenditure is also allowed. The terms of the trust must ensure that:

(i) a contribution by all the participants is made in the same tax year;

(ii) the expenditure by the trust is incurred wholly in that same tax year;

(iii) the nature of the rights and interests of all participants is the same;

(iv) the rights and interests of participants cannot be purchased, redeemed or cancelled by the trustees in whole or part other than by way of a distribution to participants generally; and

(v) the trustees are irrevocably authorised and obliged to take responsibility for agreeing with the Revenue the amount of capital expenditure attributable to each participant, the amount of any receipt to be taken into account by each participant for calculating balancing charges or allowances, the Schedule A income from the building and any interest income attributable to each participant, and for giving each participant, within three months after the end of each accounting period, a statement showing such information.

The trustees have to submit to the Revenue every year a return showing the names, addresses, tax office reference, and, in the case of an individual who was UK resident at any time in the preceding tax year, national insurance number, and their interests in the scheme (*Income Tax (Definition of Unit Trust Scheme) Regulations 1988* (*SI 1988 No 266*) and *Income Tax (Definition of Unit Trust Scheme) (Amendment) Regulations 1992* (*SI 1992 No 571*)). As far as the investor is concerned, an investment in an enterprise zone property trust gives the same tax benefit as a direct investment in an enterprise zone building. In addition, in theory at least, investment in an enterprise zone through such a trust spreads the risk as the trust can invest in a range of properties. In practice, most do not; they invest in a single building. During the recession a number of such trusts got into financial difficulties, largely because they had invested in unlet buildings on the basis of an initial rent guarantee by the developer and the developer was unable to meet the guarantee. An enterprise zone property trust also allows small investors who cannot afford to invest large amounts to invest in enterprise zone properties and enables those that can afford to do so to take instead a share in a far more substantial building which may have an institutional value.

## Flat Conversion Allowances

**10.171** From July 2001 flat conversion allowances are given on expenditure on the conversion of parts of business premises into flats (*CAA 2001, s 393A* inserted by *FA 2001, Sch 19*). There is an initial allowance of 100% of qualifying expenditure (*CAA 2001, s 393H*). This can be disclaimed in whole or in part and the balance claimed in subsequent years as a writing-down allowance of 25% of the expenditure (which can also be disclaimed in whole or part) (*CAA 2001, ss 393J, 393K*). A writing-down allowance can be claimed only if at the end of the accounting period or year of assessment the person who incurred the expenditure remains entitled to the relevant interest in the flat and has not granted a long lease of it out of that interest for a capital sum (*CAA 2001, s 393J(1)*). A long lease for this purpose is one the duration of which exceeds 50 years (*CAA 2001, s 393J(2)*). The special rules in *ICTA 1988, s 38(1)–(4)* (see 3.23) apply to determine the length of the lease but *CAA 2001, s 393V(3)* (see 10.180), which treats a new lease granted in pursuance of an option as a continuation of the old lease, does not (*CAA 2001, s 393J(3)*). The relevant interest is the interest in the flat to which the person who incurred the expenditure was entitled when it was incurred. If the relevant interest is a lease the legislation contains similar rules to those in *CAA 2001, ss 286–289* (see 10.121) (*CAA 2001, s 393F*). If the person who incurs the expenditure becomes entitled to his interest only on completion of the conversion he is treated as having had that interest when the expenditure was incurred (*CAA 2001, s 393G*).

**10.172** There are no balancing adjustments unless a relevant balancing event occurs within seven years of the time when the flat was first suitable for letting as a dwelling. There are six such events:

(*a*) a sale of the relevant interest;

(*b*) the grant of a long lease in consideration of the payment of a capital sum;

(*c*) if the relevant interest is a lease, its coming to an end other than by the holder acquiring the headlease;

(*d*) the death of the taxpayer;

(*e*) the demolition or destruction of the flat;

(*f*) the flat ceasing to be a qualifying flat (without being demolished or destroyed).

(*CAA 2001, s 393N*).

**10.173** The balancing adjustment is of course the difference between the residue of expenditure and the proceeds. In the case of the grant of a long lease the proceeds is the premium or, if greater, the commercial premium, i.e. the amount that would have been given if the transaction had been at arm's length. Curiously there appears to be no similar need to substitute an arm's length price on a sale at an undervalue. The proceeds on the termination of a lease appears to be nil (even if compensation for its termination is received) unless the landlord (or any superior landlord) is a connected person in which case the proceeds is the market value of the relevant interest at the time the lease is terminated. This is likely to be nil unless the lease is surrendered. Logically if the parties are not connected and the lease is surrendered the proceeds ought to be any amount received on the surrender. However, *section 393O* states that the proceeds are 'the amounts received or receivable in connection with the event, as shown in the *Table*'. The *Table* does not cover the case where a lease between unconnected parties comes to an end. It is possible that the wording quoted above could be interpreted by the courts as the amount received in connection with the event even where nothing is shown in the *Table* in *section 393O*, with the words after the comma being taken to apply only where there is an entry in the *Table*. However, that would be a strained interpretation of the wording.

**10.174** If the owner dies the proceeds is the residue of expenditure immediately before the death (*CAA 2001, s 393O*). This will always result in a nil balancing adjustment. It is accordingly unclear why death should trigger an adjustment. As allowances can be claimed only by the person who incurred the expenditure, the personal representatives would not have been entitled to allowances in any event.

**10.175** In the case of demolition or destruction of the flat the proceeds are the amount received for the remains of the flat together with any insurance money received in respect of the demolition or destruction and any other capital sum received as compensation (*CAA 2001, s 393O*). If the flat is rebuilt by the owner there does not appear to be any requirement to bring in the market value of the remains. It is not clear what is meant by demolition or destruction. Is a flat demolished if the interior of two adjoining flats is gutted so that the flats can be rebuilt as a single (non-qualifying) flat within the outer shell? Is a flat destroyed if it is vandalised so as no longer to be fit for human habitation? There seems little logic in parliament rushing to grant a balancing allowance in either of such circumstances.

**10.176** If the flat ceases to be a qualifying flat the proceeds is the market value of the relevant interest at that time (*CAA 2001, s 393O*). If a flat is not a qualifying flat at the time it is first suitable for letting as a dwelling no initial allowance is due and any such allowance previously given will be withdrawn (*CAA 2001, s 393I*). Similarly a writing-down allowance cannot be claimed if it is not a qualifying flat at the end of an accounting period or year of assessment (*CAA 2001, s 393J(1)*).

**10.177** Where more than one balancing event occurs a balancing adjustment is made only on the first of them (*CAA 2001, s 393M(5)*). As with other capital allowances, a balancing charge is limited to the amount of allowances previously given (*CAA 2001, s 393P(5)*).

## Qualifying expenditure

**10.178** Qualifying expenditure is capital expenditure incurred on (or in connection with) either:

(*a*) the conversion of part of a qualifying building into a qualifying flat,

(*b*) the renovation of a flat (which is or will be a qualifying flat) in a qualifying building, or

(*c*) repairs to a qualifying building to the extent that such repairs are incidental to expenditure within (*a*) or (*b*).

(*CAA 2001, s 393B(1)*).

Head (*c*) appears on the face of it a little strange. How can repairs be capital expenditure? The answer is that repairs is deemed for this purpose to be capital expenditure if it would not be allowed to be deducted in calculating the profits of a Schedule A business (*CAA 2001, s 393B(4)*). In other words it is only 'repairs' that are capital under the *Law Shipping* principle (see 9.4) that can fall within (*c*).

**10.179** There are a large number of conditions that need to be met.

(*a*) The part of the building (or the flat) in respect of which the expenditure is incurred must have been either

 (i) unused, or

 (ii) used only for storage throughout the 12 months ending immediately before the date on which the conversion or renovation work begins (*CAA 2001, s 393B(2)*).

(*b*) The expenditure must not be on

 (i) the acquisition of land or rights in or over land,

 (ii) the extension of a qualifying building (except to the extent required for the purpose of providing a means of getting to or from a qualifying flat – such as the erection of an external stairwell or lift shaft),

 (iii) the development of land adjoining or adjacent to a qualifying building, or

 (iv) the provision of furnishings or chattels (no guidance is given as to when non-allowable furnishings become allowable fixtures).

 (*CAA 2001, s 393B(3)*).

(*c*) The building in which the flat is situated must be a qualifying building. This is one where

(i) all or most of the ground floor of the building is authorised for business use (i.e. within class *A1*, shops, *A2*, financial and professional services, *A3*, food and drink, *B1*, business (which can be carried on in a residential area) or *D1(a)*, medical or health services (not attached to the residence of the practitioner) of the *Schedule* to the *Town and Country Planning (Use Classes) Order 1987* (*SI 1987 No 764*) (or the corresponding Scottish or Northern Irish legislation),

(ii) it appears that, when the building was constructed, the storeys above the ground floor were for use primarily as one or more dwellings,

(iii) the building has no more than four storeys above the ground floor (ignoring any attic unless it is or has been in use as a dwelling or part of a dwelling),

(iv) the construction of the building must either have been

1. completed before 1 January 1980, or

2. if it was extended after 31 December 1980, the extension must have been completed before 1 January 2001.

(*CAA 2001, s 393C*).

This definition gives rise to a great many uncertainties. These are considered at 10.150.

(*d*) The flat must be suitable for letting as a dwelling (see 10.180) (*CAA 2001, s 393D(1)(b)*).

(*e*) The flat must be held for the purpose of 'short-term letting', i.e. letting as a dwelling on a lease of not more than five years (*CAA 2001, s 393D(1)(c), 2*).

(*f*) It must be possible to gain access to the flat without using the part of the ground floor of the building that is authorised for business use (see (*c*) above) (*CAA 2001, s 393D(1)(d)*).

(*g*) The flat must not have more than four rooms. For this purpose a kitchen or bathroom do not count as rooms. Nor does any closet, cloakroom or hallways not exceeding 5 square metres in area (*CAA 2001, s 393D(1)(e), 3*). It is not clear whether one of the above expressions is intended as a polite word for a toilet or if a toilet is to be regarded as a room. It is probably not.

(*h*) The flat must not be a high value flat. This means that the rent that could reasonably be expected for the flat on the date on which the first qualifying expenditure on the conversion is incurred and on the assumption that

(i) the conversion or renovation had been completed,

(ii) the flat is let furnished,

(iii) the lease does not require the tenant to pay a premium (or make any other payments (presumably other than rent although the legislation does not say so) to the landlord or a connected person),

(iv) the tenant is not connected with the taxpayer,

(v) the flat is let on an assured shorthold tenancy (a short assured tenancy in Scotland),

must not exceed the following limits:

| | **Greater London** | **Elsewhere** |
|---|---|---|
| 1 or 2 room flat | £350 | £150 |
| 3 room flat | £425 | £225 |
| 4 room flat | £480 | £300 |

The Treasury have power by regulation to amend these limits.

(*CAA 2001, s 393D(f), 393E*).

It is not clear precisely what assumption (i) requires where, as often happens with building work, the specification of the works changes during the construction period. Does one assume the conversion that was intended to be carried out at the valuation date or does one use hindsight and assume the conversion that was actually carried out? It should be noted that the actual rent is irrelevant. That will not be received until a later date (i.e. after completion) so is not necessarily of assistance in arriving at a notional rental value some months or even years earlier. There is a potential question mark over expenditure on obtaining planning consent. This appears to be qualifying expenditure as it is 'in connection with' the conversion (see *s 393B(1)* – 10.178H) but is probably not expenditure 'on' the conversion, so such expenditure would not trigger the valuation date.

(*i*) The flat must not be (or have been) created or renovated as part of a scheme involving the creation or renovation of one or more high value flats (*CAA 2001, s 393D(1)(3)*). This is an odd exclusion. Suppose that for example the space above a shop is converted into three storeys of low value flats and one high value flat on the fourth storey. This condition excludes the whole of the expenditure not merely that relating to the high value flat.

(*j*) The flat must not be let to a person connected with the taxpayer (within *ICTA 1988, s 839*) (*CAA 2001, s 393D(i)(h), 575(1)*).

**10.180** For the purpose of these allowances a dwelling is defined as a building or part of a building occupied or intended to be occupied as a separate dwelling (*CAA 2001, s 393A(4)*). A flat is a dwelling which forms part of a building, is a separate set of premises (whether or not on the same floor) and is divided horizontally from another part of the building (*CAA 2001, s 393A(3)*). A qualifying flat is one that meets all of the conditions at 10.179 (*CAA 2001, s 393D(i)*). If a qualifying flat becomes temporarily unsuitable for letting as a dwelling it is nevertheless treated as continuing to be a qualifying one during that period (*CAA 2001, s 393D(4)*).

**10.181** A lease includes a tenancy and also an agreement for a lease but only at a time when the term to be covered by the lease has begun (*CAA 2001, s 393W(1)*). If a lease is terminated with the consent of the lessor and the lessee remains in possession without a new lease being granted to him the lease is treated as continuing as long as the lessee remains in occupation (*CAA 2001, s 393V(2)*). If the lease contains an option for a new lease, the exercise of that option is treated as a continuation of the old lease (*CAA 2001, s 393V(3)*). If on the termination of a lease the landlord makes a payment to the tenant in respect of a flat comprised in the lease, it is treated as having been surrendered in consideration of that payment (*CAA 2001, s 393V(4)*). If the tenant receives a payment not from the landlord but from an incoming tenant he is treated as having assigned his lease in consideration of that payment and the new tenant's lease is treated as a continuation of the old tenant's one (*CAA 2001, s 393V(5)*).

**10.182** For a short, narrowly targeted provision a lot is left for secondary legislation. The Treasury is given power to alter the definition of qualifying expenditure (*section 393B(5)*), to alter the definition of a qualifying building (*section 393C(5)*), to alter the meaning of a qualifying flat (*section 393D*) and to alter the notional rent limits (*section 393E(6)*). That does not leave very much that the Treasury cannot touch. As can be seen from 10.179 there are a great many conditions that already have to be met before the relief applies. The thought of the Treasury coming along and adding more is depressing.

**10.183** There are also a great many potential practical problems in applying the legislation. Certainty is of especial importance in relation to a tax incentive, because taxpayers who cannot tell whether or not their particular project will qualify for that incentive are unlikely to proceed on the off chance that it might do so. The ground floor of the building must have planning permission for business use, all the other floors must have been constructed as dwellings but it does not matter what any basement is or was used for. In these circumstances identifying the ground floor is pretty crucial. There are a lot of buildings where the lowest floor (to use a neutral term) is half above ground level and half below. One goes down a flight of steps to reach that floor and up a flight of steps to reach the next. If the lower floor is a basement the next floor must have a commercial use. If the lower floor is the ground floor the next floor must have been originally for residential use. See the problem? Fortunately this is one of the issues that was raised in the Parliamentary debates. Unfortunately the Minister's answer (Dawn Primarolo – the Paymaster General) was less than helpful:

'People are reasonably sensible and understand the ground floor to be the level at which one enters the property – unless one has tunnelled one's way in.'

When it was pointed out that an awful lot of buildings are on hillsides, she added:

'In Bristol, one enters the house in which I live on the ground floor, but that has become the first floor by the time one reaches the back of the house. However capital allowances and assistance have worked perfectly well in relation to the issue. The Committee is making a meal of the proposition that people . . . cannot, when looking at a property, determine the ground floor from the first floor. The distinction is clear.'

Unfortunately no one pointed out that prior to this legislation capital allowances did not depend on identifying the ground floor. And is there not a risk that the man on the Bristol Omnibus passing the Minister's back door might regard that as on the ground floor and the other entrance as in the basement? The Minister then made the quite extraordinary statement:

'We expect people to be sensible. The tax system cannot be absolute and is not designed to be. The Schedule gives clear indicators of the type of development that we want.'

Assuming that it does, which is questionable, this seems a novel approach to tax. When the Inspector says that the development does not meet the statutory conditions, is the taxpayer really entitled to respond: 'Forget the conditions, I don't need to meet them precisely, they are only intended as an indication of the type of development that attracts allowances'?

**10.184** That is not the only area of uncertainty. An attic is not a storey unless it has been in use as part of a dwelling. What if it has been used for storing household goods? Is that use as part of a dwelling? And if the building is very old who knows what the attic was used for in 1640 or whatever. The provision appears to mean use at any time. The construction of the building must have been completed before 1 January 1980. What is meant by completed? Although the flats must be held out for letting can they be temporarily occupied by the owner? Can they be let to staff at a nominal rent? As a bathroom is not a room can it be assumed that a toilet is not one either? The notional rent limit is by reference to a notional letting furnished amount. What is meant by furnished in this context? Is the condition that a flat must have been unused for a year met if it was occupied by squatters for part of that period? The demolition or destruction of the flat is a balancing event. What is destruction? Is the flat destroyed if it is trashed by vandals? Or made uninhabitable by fire? Can one demolish a flat without demolishing the rest of the building?

**10.185** Also the reasons for many of the restrictions is not apparent, so it is hard to identify precisely what it is aimed at. For example why does the relief not apply if the original building had two floors of shops and two of dwellings? Why does it apply if the shop basement is used for storage ancillary to a shop but does not apply if the shop does not have a basement so part of the first floor was designed for use for such storage? Why does it not allow the conversion of a disused shop to residential use? If a building has four storeys above the ground floor why will it allow the conversion of all four but if it has only three will not allow the construction of a fourth? Why will it not cover the construction of garages on vacant space behind the shop so as to make the flats more readily lettable? Are fitted kitchen cupboards intended to be allowable development or non-allowable furnishings? Why cannot the flat be let to a connected person even at a full market rent? Indeed why can it not be occupied by the owner? If the idea is to increase the housing stock, that is achieved as much by releasing an existing house as by bringing a new one onto the letting market. Why can't the allowances be transferred, particularly on a transfer to the purchaser of the shop itself on the sale of the business? Why can't access to the flat be through the shop? If a conversion results in the creation of six qualifying flats and one high value penthouse why is no relief given for the qualifying flats? Why must a flat be available for letting for at least seven years but an individual lease of it cannot exceed five?

**10.186** It is also hard to work out how a person will be able to utilise the allowance if he does not already carry on a Schedule A business at the time he incurs the expenditure. He must deem the expenditure to be incurred as an expense of a notional Schedule A business. This will create a Schedule A loss. Unless he is a company all that he can do with the notional loss in his notional Schedule A business is to carry it forward and set it against future rents (*ICTA 1988, s 379A*). In other words for many people the relief is a mirage. There will be no tax relief at all unless and until the taxpayer is able to let the flats or the shop or to generate other Schedule A income and even then the 'up-front tax relief' promised by the government is actually an exemption from tax on future rents up to the amount of the expenditure. If the reason the space is currently empty is because no one wishes to live above a derelict shopping precinct, the new flat will probably be just as unlettable and no actual tax relief will ever by obtained. Indeed it is unclear whether any relief will ever be obtained even if the flats are let. This is because the rents will be receipts of an actual Schedule A trade and the new *section 393T, Capital Allowances Act 2001* does not specifically allow losses of the notional Schedule A business to be treated as losses of the subsequent real Schedule A business when it comes into existence.

## Research and Development

**10.187** Where a person, while carrying on a trade, incurs expenditure of a capital nature on research and development (scientific research prior to 1 April 2000 or 2000/01) related to the trade and directly undertaken by him or on his behalf (or incurs such expenditure while not trading and afterwards sets up a trade connected with the research), the entire expenditure can be written off against trading profits in the year it was incurred (or the year the trade commences if later) (*CAA 2001, s 441*). The allowance can be disclaimed in part but if this is done there does not appear to be an ability to claim the balance in a subsequent year (*CAA 2001, s 441(3)*). The expenditure is in effect treated as a trading expense of the year in which it is incurred. Scientific research means any activities in the fields of natural or applied science for the extension of knowledge. Research and development is defined in *ICTA 1988, s 837A*. It adopts the definition that applies in accordance with generally accepted accounting practice (see 2.158) but gives the Treasury power by Regulation to modify this (*CAA 2001, s 437(2)*).

It was held in *Gaspet Ltd v Elliss (60 TC 91)* that where a trader does not directly undertake the research there must be a contractual relationship of agency or something akin thereto between the trader and the person who carries out the research – although there is no requirement that the taxpayer must actually commission the research.

**10.188** If property is purchased for the purpose of such research, it can qualify for the allowance in the same way as any other asset. However, the allowance cannot be claimed on expenditure incurred on the acquisition of, or of rights in or over, land (unless it was incurred before 1 April 1985 or before 1 April 1987 under a contract entered into before 19 March 1985) – although it can still be claimed on building work. Where land is purchased or leased on which a building or structure (other than a dwelling) is standing, the price must be apportioned between the land and the building (including any machinery or plant forming part of the building), and allowances claimed only on the latter. Allowances can also no longer be claimed on the cost of a dwelling. Where part of a building is used as a dwelling, and part for research and development, an apportionment must be made unless the part of the cost apportionable to the dwelling does not exceed 25% of the total cost referable to the entire building (i.e. excluding the land), in which case there will be no restriction (*CAA 2001, ss 438, 440*). The clawback of allowances on a disposal is, of course, restricted to the sale proceeds of assets eligible for allowances.

**10.189** A balancing charge will arise if the asset is subsequently disposed of by the owner (whether by sale or otherwise) either during, or after the discontinuance of, the trade; in the latter event the charge relates back to the date the trade ceased (*CAA 2001, s 442*). Where the expenditure was incurred before 1 April 1985 a balancing charge cannot arise if the asset is sold without ceasing to be used by the owner, e.g. on a sale and leaseback, but that anomaly has been corrected in relation to expenditure after that date. On transfers between connected persons after 15 March 1993 the election described at 10.128 above can be made (*CAA 2001, s 569*).

**10.190** The balancing charge is on the excess of the disposal value over the written-down value of the asset (or the amount of the allowances given if this is less than that excess). This amount is treated as trading income of the trade (*CAA 2001, s 442(3)*). The disposal value depends on the event giving rise to the clawback. If this occurs on a sale at or above market value the sale proceeds are used to calculate the clawback. If it occurs by the destruction of the asset the amount of any insurance monies or other compensation plus any monies received for the remains of the asset is used. Demolition costs are treated as an addition to the cost of the asset (*CAA 2001, s 445*). If the cessation of ownership occurs in any other way the market value of the asset is used (*CAA 2001, s 443(4)*). If the disposal value is less than the written-down value a balancing allowance will of course be given on the disposal. This can obviously only occur where the full 100% allowance has not been claimed (*CAA 2001, s 441(1)(b)*).

**10.191** For accounting periods ending after 31 March 2000 a small or medium-sized company (see 10.7) (but not an unincorporated business) can deduct 150% of its expenditure on qualifying research and development if this exceeds £25,000 in an accounting period. If the accounting period is less than 12 months the £25,000 figure is reduced proportionately (*FA 2000, Sch 20, para 1*). From 1 April 2002 a large company can deduct 12.5% of such expenditure (*FA 2002, Sch 12*). However in both cases qualifying research is limited to revenue expenditure and is unlikely to be incurred in a property context.

## Fire Safety Expenditure

**10.192** Expenditure incurred by a trader on fire safety precautions in certain limited circumstances – where it is, or could be, required to be carried out by the fire safety authority and would not otherwise qualify for allowances as plant – is treated as if it were expenditure on plant and machinery (*CAA 2001, s 29*). The normal plant and machinery rules apply with the exception that the asset is to be treated as belonging to the trader and to have a nil disposal value (*CAA 2001, s 63(5)*). The expenditure in question is that spent:

(*a*) in taking steps specified in a notice served on the trader by the fire authority under the *Fire Precautions Act 1971, s 5(4)* which was issued on an application for a fire certificate in respect of premises used by him for the purposes of his trade (*CAA 2001, s 29(2)*);

(*b*) in taking steps specified in a letter or other document sent to him by or on behalf of the fire authority on an application for such a certificate, which are steps that would have to be taken to obtain a certificate and could have been specified in a *section 5(4)* notice (*CAA 2001, s 29(3)*); or

(*c*) in taking steps which had to be taken to enable the premises to be used to satisfy an order made under *Fire Precautions Act 1971, s 10* restricting or prohibiting the use of the premises (*CAA 2001, s 29(4)*).

It does not appear that this relief can apply to expenditure incurred either in the course of the construction of the building or after acquiring the building but before bringing it into use. This is because the *Act* refers to premises 'used' for the purpose of the trade and does not extend to premises 'to be used' for such purposes.

Fire precautions in nursing homes are covered by the *Residential Homes Act 1980* and fire certificates for certain factories, offices and shops are required from the Health and Safety Executives, not the local authorities. Expenditure to obtain such certificates will therefore not qualify for this special relief.

## Thermal Insulation of Industrial Buildings

**10.193** Similarly a trader who incurs expenditure on adding insulation against loss of heat to an industrial building (within the meaning of *CAA 2001, ss 271(1), 274* – see 10.103 above) occupied by him for the purpose of his trade can claim capital allowances as if the expenditure were on plant and machinery, and as if it had belonged to him in consequence of his incurring the expenditure and had a disposal value of nil (*CAA 2001, s 28*). Unlike the allowances for fire safety expenditure mentioned above, these allowances can also be claimed by a landlord who incurs expenditure on thermal insulation in respect of a let building. The machinery or plant is treated as if it had been included in the lease of the building and as if its disposal value were nil (*CAA 2001, s 63(5)*). Again the relief only applies if at the time the expenditure is incurred the building is actually occupied by the trader or let by the landlord as the case may be.

## Dwelling-Houses Let on Assured Tenancies

**10.194** This was a temporary allowance only and in general ceased to apply to expenditure after 15 March 1988. It applied to expenditure incurred between 10 March 1982 and 31 March 1992 on the construction of qualifying dwelling-houses let on assured and certain other tenancies (*CAA 2001, s 490*). The allowances could be claimed only by an 'approved body', i.e. one of a description of bodies specified for the purposes of *Housing Act 1980, Part II* in an order made by the Secretary of State (*Housing Act 1980, s 56(4)*). In practice, the Minister prescribed companies individually as qualifying. Virtually all of the approved bodies were subsidiaries of insurance companies or housing associations. The intention was that approval would be given only to a body which could convince the Minister that it would be a model landlord. The allowances are accordingly not of general interest. They apply to expenditure after 15 March 1988 only if the person incurring it was an approved body at that date and had at that date contracted to incur the expenditure. The old system of assured tenancies was abolished by the *Housing Act 1988* and replaced by a new system more favourable to the landlord. As a result the government felt that there is no longer a need for the tax system to subsidise such housing.

**10.195** The allowances were given on the capital expenditure appropriate to each approved dwelling-house but subject to a maximum expenditure of £60,000 if the dwelling-house is in Greater London or £40,000 elsewhere. Where a building consists of more than one qualifying dwelling, the expenditure attributable to each is the cost of construction of the dwelling plus a proportion of the cost of the common parts (subject to a maximum of 10% of the cost of construction of the dwelling) (*CAA 2001, s 511(2)*). The allowances are an initial allowance of 75% and a writing-down allowance of 4% p.a.

**10.196** To attract a writing-down allowance the approved body must own the relevant interest in the building and the building must be a qualifying dwelling-house at the end of its accounting period (or income tax basis period). If the approved body owning the relevant interest disposes of it to another approved body, the purchaser's writing-down allowance is based on the residue of expenditure in the same way as under the industrial buildings rules. As with industrial buildings, a balancing charge or allowance will arise if, within 25 years of the building being first used, either the relevant interest is sold, or, if it is a leasehold interest, it comes to an end, or the building is demolished or ceases altogether to be used (*CAA 2001, s 513*).

**10.197** A qualifying dwelling-house is one let on an assured tenancy within *Housing Act 1980, s 56*. To avoid the unintentional withdrawal of past allowances, the definition of assured tenancy in that *Act* is kept alive for tax purposes by *FA 1988, s 95(1)*. If the tenancy ceases to be an assured tenancy but becomes either a regulated tenancy or a housing association tenancy and the landlord either is or was formerly an approved body, the house will continue to be a qualifying dwelling-house. A property will cease to be a qualifying dwelling-house if a person who either does not hold the relevant interest or did not incur the expenditure becomes the landlord, e.g. if the relevant interest becomes owned by someone who leases the property to an approved body, the allowances will not be due unless this structure results from a leaseback transaction. A house cannot qualify if the landlord is an approved co-operative housing association or a self-build society, i.e. if the tenants can benefit from the value of the building. Nor can a house qualify if the landlord and tenant are connected persons, the tenant is a director of a company connected with the landlord, the landlord is a close company and the tenant is a participator or associate, or reciprocal arrangements exist designed to give the benefit of the allowances to someone not entitled to them (*CAA 2001, ss 504, 505*).

**10.198** Further provisions are included in *CAA 2001, ss 490–531* to define 'residue of expenditure', deal with the position where a building is bought unused, extend the allowance to expenditure on repairs, define 'relevant interest', and lay down other procedural rules. They are all based on the industrial buildings allowance legislation but reference should be made to those sections to ascertain the minor areas in which they do not exactly mirror that legislation.

## Other Capital Allowances

**10.199** Capital allowances are also given for expenditure in a number of other property-related categories. These are unlikely to affect most businesses and are not therefore considered in detail here. Expenditure by a trader on a sports stadium or sports ground used for the purpose of his trade can qualify for allowances as plant and machinery to the extent that it is carried out to comply with the terms of a safety certificate under the *Safety of Sports Grounds Act 1975*, to bring the ground up to the standards required by that *Act*, or to comply with the requirements of the local authority as to the terms that they would include in a safety certificate if it had been applied for or issued (*CAA 2001, s 30*). So can expenditure in respect of a regulated stand in taking steps to comply with either a safety certificate issued for the stand or the written requirements of the local authority on matters which would be taken into account in deciding to issue, or amend the terms of, a safety certificate (*CAA 2001, s 31*). The relief did not apply to expenditure on a regulated stand prior to 1 January 1989 or expenditure on a sports ground prior to 1 January 1988. Expenditure by a trader on altering or replacing authorised quarantine premises (under the *Diseases of Animals Act 1950*) used for the purpose of his trade to comply with requirements imposed by law for the continued use of those premises could similarly be treated as if it were expenditure on plant and machinery if it was incurred before 16 March 1988, or before 1 April 1989 in pursuance of a contract entered into before 16 March 1988 (*FA 1980, s 71*; *FA 1988, s 94*). Expenditure after 6 April 1989 on an asset to improve the personal physical security of an individual who is the proprietor of, or a partner in, a business attracts capital allowances as plant. Allowances cannot be claimed for the cost of a dwelling or its grounds, but relief is due on items which become affixed to such a building (*CAA 2001, s 33*). This relief is intended to be very restricted. It is likely to apply only where there is a serious risk of a terrorist attack on the individual because of the nature of his business. A company is entitled to allowances on such expenditure under the general law, but an individual would, in the absence of specific legislation, be excluded because of the personal element of the expenditure.

**10.200** Special schemes of allowances apply to capital expenditure on cemeteries and crematoria, including the cost of the land – they are broadly designed to write off the cost over the number of grave plots or memorial garden plots (*ICTA 1988, s 91*); to capital expenditure on dredging in the course of a trade (*CAA 2001, ss 484–489*); and to qualifying expenditure in connection with the working of a mine, oil well or other source of mineral deposits of a wasting nature, or searching for, or on discovering and testing, deposits or winning access thereto, or on the construction of works which are likely to be of little value when the source is exhausted (*CAA 2001, ss 394–436*).

## The Date Expenditure is Incurred

### Introduction

**10.201** Until 17 December 1984 the capital allowances legislation provided that expenditure was treated as incurred 'when the sums in question became payable'.

**10.202** Since the introduction of capital allowances in 1945 everyone (or, as it transpired in 1984, everyone other than the Inland Revenue) had taken this to be the date that a liability to meet the expenditure is incurred. The Revenue had apparently always understood it to mean the date when actual payment became due, i.e. normally at the expiration of the supplier's normal period of trade credit. Because they understood that some people were adopting a contrary interpretation, the government announced that they intended to clarify the law to make clear that the Revenue view was right and everyone else wrong. This caused such a furore that they were ultimately persuaded to 'change' the law to reflect the erroneous view that virtually the entire accountancy and legal professions had been mistakenly adopting for the previous 40 years. They also indicated that in view of the widespread nature of the error they would allow this practice to be adopted in earlier years also. The legislation introduced does not in fact bring the law into line with accounting practice – it seeks to do so in simple cases but like most tax legislation that is introduced nowadays is hedged around with a considerable number of anti-avoidance rules which can give rise to some unexpected results.

**General Rule**

**10.203** The date on which expenditure is incurred is the date on which the obligation to pay it becomes unconditional (whether or not there is a later date on or before which the whole or any part of it is required to be paid) which, in the view of the government, is when the expenditure has a sufficient degree of certainty to require it to be reflected in business accounts (*CAA 2001, s 5(1)*). Normally this is likely to be the delivery date or the earlier time on which a liability to pay a deposit arises (to the extent of that deposit).

**10.204** The government of the day said this is the time when 'the vendor will have completed his part of the contract and the purchaser's obligation to pay will be unconditional and absolute, although not necessarily immediate if the vendor is allowed a period of trade credit' (Mr John Moore, Hansard, Standing Committee B, 6 June 1985, Col 403). In practice, the Revenue are likely to accept the adoption of the invoice date, as the obligation to pay will normally have become unconditional on or before that date. For large items of expenditure it could, however, be worth investigating whether an earlier date might meet the test if the invoice date is near the beginning of an accounting period. Where a contract provides for the purchaser to pay for goods on or within a prescribed time of delivery the Revenue consider that the obligation to pay becomes unconditional when the asset is delivered (Tax Bulletin, Issue 8, Nov 1993, p 97).

**Modification of General Rule**

**10.205** The general rule is modified in three cases.

1. The expenditure is treated as incurred at the end of the accounting period (or basis period) in which the asset became the property of the purchaser (or is otherwise attributed to him under the contract) if the obligation to pay contractually becomes unconditional as a result of the issue of a certificate (or some other event), and this occurs within a month after the end of that accounting period or basis period (*CAA 2001, s 5(4)*). This covers building work where under general law the bricks, concrete, etc. would become the property of the landowner when they are affixed to the land but the obligation to pay does not arise until the issue of an architect's certificate. It allows relief to be obtained in the accounting period in which the work is done

where the architect's certificate is issued within the next month. It also covers test periods for plant where payment may not become due until a certificate has been issued by an engineer to the effect that it is working satisfactorily.

2. If, under (or by virtue of) any agreement, the whole or any part of an amount of capital expenditure is required to be paid on (or not later than) a date which is more than four months after that on which the obligation to pay becomes unconditional, the obligation to pay that part of the expenditure must be treated as becoming unconditional immediately before the expiration of that period – with the result that the capital allowances will not be due until that time (*CAA 2001, s 5(5)*).

3. If, under (or by virtue of) any agreement, the obligation to pay an amount became unconditional on a date earlier than that which accords with normal commercial usage, the expenditure can be treated as incurred on the date 'on or before which it is required to be paid', and *CAA 2001, s 5(5)* above is not to apply to it (*CAA 2001, s 5(6)*). This applies only where the sole or main benefit which might have been expected from the obligation becoming unconditional on the earlier date is to attribute the expenditure to an earlier accounting period than would otherwise have been the case (*CAA 2001, s 5(6)(b)*).

**10.206** An example of the operation of Case (2) in 10.205 above may be helpful.

*Example 22*

Joe Bloggs Limited purchases a large item of equipment for £100,000. The supplier agrees to accept payment –

| | £ |
|---|---|
| deposit | 10,000 |
| on delivery | 20,000 |
| 3 months after delivery | 20,000 |
| 9 months after delivery | 20,000 |
| 15 months after delivery | 30,000 |

Joe Bloggs Limited prepares its accounts to 31 March. It pays the deposit on 1 September 2002. Delivery is on 28 February 2003 and the subsequent payments are all made on the due date.

| Allowances due | £ | £ | £ |
|---|---|---|---|
| Year to 31.3.2003 on deposit | 10,000 | | |
| on payment on delivery | 20,000 | | |
| on payment on 28 May | 20,000 | 50,000 | |
| writing-down allowance 25% | | 12,500 | £12,500 |
| | | 37,500 | |

| Allowances due | £ | £ | £ |
|---|---|---|---|
| Year to 31.3.2004 on payment on 28 November 2003 | | 20,000 | |
| | | 57,500 | |
| writing-down allowance 25% | | 14,375 | £14,375 |
| | | 43,125 | |
| Year to 31.3.2005 on payment on 28 May 2004 | | 30,000 | |
| | | 73,125 | |
| writing-down allowance 25% | | 18,282 | £18,282 |
| written-down value at 31.3.2005 | | 54,843 | |

## Consideration of the Rules

**10.207** Where a purchaser cannot pay the full price immediately, and agrees long credit terms with the supplier, it might be worth considering whether it is possible to use a hire purchase or similar agreement instead. This is because *CAA 2001, s 67* treats the expenditure under a HP contract which is payable after the time when the equipment is brought into use as being incurred when it is brought into use – curiously this 'in use' provision has not been amended in spite of the general abolition of the 'in use' rules. Under normal rules of construction this specific provision will override the general rule laid down by *CAA 2001, s 5*, and the government have confirmed this – 'We do not intend *clause 53* to affect the way in which *section 60* operates and has operated for many years and we do not think that it will' (Mr John Moore, Hansard, Standing Committee B, 6 June 1985, Col 409). The four-month period is long enough to cover a 100-day credit period so will cover the vast majority of normal trade credit periods. If expenditure is contemplated which attracts a longer period of trade credit, and the effect would be to defer relief for the expenditure until a later accounting period, it may be worth considering varying the credit period to reduce it to four months or, if longer, to terminate it at the end of the accounting period. However, *section 67* does not apply to fixtures to which the legislation described at 10.51–10.69 applies. Where an asset becomes a fixture after 28 July 2000 it is treated as disposed of by the owner at that time unless he is also treated as the owner under that legislation (*CAA 2001, s 69*).

**10.208** It should be noted that although the provision applies where the expenditure is required to be paid on or not later than a specified date over four months hence, it deems the expenditure to be incurred on that specific date, not on the date of payment if earlier. Accordingly, premature payment of the amount will not normally crystallise a right to allowances. It is doubtful if this was intended. If payment is to be made before the due date to bring the expenditure into an earlier accounting period, the contract should first be varied to terminate the permitted credit period on the proposed payment date.

**10.209** Case (3) of 10.205 above is an anti-avoidance measure. It appears to be defective. It seems to proceed on the assumption that the date 'on or before which an amount is required to be paid' would be the date which accords with normal commercial usage, whereas it would normally be the date on which the obligation to pay becomes unconditional. Accordingly, the right to allowances would arise on the date of payment. It will, however, cover the situation where an agreement provides for the obligation to pay an amount to become unconditional at an early date but does not require payment until a later date, and it may be that it is merely intended to cover this limited type of case.

**10.210** Where, as in most building contracts, a contract provides for retention of part of the price against satisfactory performance, the government takes the view that the obligation to pay the retention money does not become unconditional until the agreed period following the commissioning of the asset has passed and the machinery, plant or building concerned has been proved to be satisfactory. Accordingly, the right to allowances in respect of the retention moneys does not arise until that time (Hansard, Standing Committee B, 6 June 1985, Col 407).

**10.211** If any other specific tax provision provides that expenditure eligible for capital allowances is to be treated as incurred on a date later than that determined under the above rules, *CAA 2001, s 5* obviously does not override that specific provision (*CAA 2001, s 5(7)*).

### Plant, etc. leased under a Finance Lease

**10.212** Although not directly relevant to the property owner, as it is the lessor rather than the lessee who is entitled to the capital allowances, it should be mentioned that there are a number of anti-avoidance provisions in relation to plant and machinery leased under a finance lease. Where the lease was entered into after 28 November 1996, in some cases the assets will not qualify for capital allowances, although a straightforward lease providing for regular monthly or quarterly payments should not be affected. There are also special rules where the lessor and lessee are connected persons. A detailed consideration of these provisions can be found in *Tolley's Anti-Avoidance Provisions*.

*Chapter 11*

# Tax on Chargeable Gains

## Introduction

**11.1** Capital gains tax is chargeable on gains accruing on the disposal of assets which are not taxable as income, e.g. as profits of a trade of property dealing (*TCGA 1992, ss 15, 37*). The tax has been chargeable at income tax rates since 6 April 1988 and at the savings income rate from 6 April 1999. It is important to realise that capital gains are not taxed as income. If the individual's income is sufficient to make him liable to income tax at the 40% top rate, his capital gains are effectively taxed at a flat rate of 40%, subject to a tax-free first slice which for 2002/03 is the first £7,700 of chargeable gains. If the individual is not chargeable to income tax at 40% his second slice of chargeable gains (i.e. after the £7,700 exemption) is taxed at the savings rate of 20%. This slice will be the difference between his taxable income (or nil if he has losses) and £29,900. For 2000/01 onwards if the individual has not fully utilised his 10% starting rate band (£1,920 for 2002/03) against income, he can utilise that against capital gains. Any gains in excess of £29,900 are taxed at 40%. If the individual is not chargeable to income tax at 40% his chargeable gains (i.e. after the £7,700 exemption) utilise the unused balance of his lower rates. For 2002/03 these are 10% on the first £1,920 of taxable income or gains and 20% on the next £27,980. The rate is 20%, not the 22% basic rate as capital gains attract the savings rate. Prior to 2000/01 the starting rate could not be used against capital gains, so the minimum rate was 20%. A husband and wife each have their own annual exemption. There is no similar exemption for companies and most trusts have an annual exemption of half that applicable to an individual, i.e. currently £3,850. Because of taper relief (see 11.5) the effective rate of tax is, however, normally much lower than 40%. It can be as low as 10% but is likely to be between 24% and 40% on most property transactions.

**11.2** Companies are not liable to capital gains tax, but are instead charged to corporation tax on chargeable gains, calculated as for capital gains tax purposes. Such gains are charged at the normal corporation tax rates. A company treats its chargeable gains as an additional source of income, and can offset against them trading losses, management expenses, loan relationships and charges on income.

References in this chapter to capital gains tax (or to CGT) should, where appropriate, be taken as referring also to corporation tax on chargeable gains.

**11.3** An individual can set a trading loss – but not a Schedule A loss – against net capital gains of the same year of assessment to the extent that it cannot be relieved against income of that year (*FA 1991, s 72*). Any excess trading loss can be set against capital gains of the following year if the trade is still being carried on in that year. Capital gains tax losses of earlier years must be utilised against capital gains in priority to trading losses and, unlike with brought forward capital losses, the claim for relief cannot be limited to preserve the benefit of the capital gains tax annual exemption. Furthermore, because of an anomaly in the legislation it appears to result in some loss of taper relief. If the amount of capital gain available for offset is subsequently altered, e.g. because additional capital losses are established, the excess trading loss which this releases is converted into a capital gains tax loss – but ceases to be available for any relief at all if it is not utilised against future capital gains by the end of the year of assessment in which the trade ceases. The relief must be claimed at the time that a claim is made to set the trading loss against general income under *ICTA 1988, s 380*, i.e. it cannot be claimed separately but the *section 380* claim must be expressed to extend to capital gains.

## Calculation of Chargeable Gain

**11.4** A chargeable gain is calculated by deducting from the disposal consideration (or in some cases deemed disposal consideration) the allowable deductions specified by the legislation together with, in many cases, an indexation allowance to reflect the ravages of inflation. For individuals and trusts the indexation allowance has been replaced by taper relief from 6 April 1988 (see 11.5). The allowable deductions are limited to:

(*a*) (i) the consideration (in money or money's worth) given by the taxpayer (or on his behalf) wholly and exclusively for the acquisition of the asset;

(ii) the incidental costs (see 11.6 below) to the taxpayer of the acquisition (or, if the asset was not acquired by him, e.g. he created it, any expenditure wholly and exclusively incurred by him in providing the asset);

(*b*) (i) the amount of any expenditure ('enhancement expenditure') wholly and exclusively incurred on the asset by the taxpayer (or on his behalf) for the purpose of enhancing the value of the asset, being expenditure reflected in the state or nature of the asset at the time of the disposal;

(ii) any expenditure wholly and exclusively incurred by the taxpayer in establishing, preserving or defending his title to, or to a right over, the asset; and

(*c*) the incidental costs (see 11.6 below) to the taxpayer of making the disposal.

(*TCGA 1992, s 38(1)*).

The indexation allowances can only eliminate a gain. It cannot create or enhance a loss (except on disposals prior to 30 November 1993) (*TCGA 1992, s 53(1)* as amended by *FA 1994, s 93*). There was a transitional relief for individuals and trusts created before 30 November 1993, but not for companies or, curiously, for deceased estates. This allowed indexation to be used to create a maximum of £10,000 of allowable losses in aggregate during the period 30 November 1993 to 5 April 1995 but such losses could be utilised only against gains on disposals during 1993/94 and 1994/95 (*FA 1994, Sch 12*).

**11.5** For disposals after 5 April 1998 the indexation allowance is frozen at its amount at 6 April 1998 except for companies where it continues to increase (*TCGA 1992, s 53(1A)* inserted by *FA 1998, s 122*). Individuals and trusts are compensated for inflation after that date by tapering the tax payable at yearly intervals. There are different rates of taper relief depending on whether or not the property is a business asset. On a disposal of business assets after 5 April 2002 taper relief reduces the gain by 50%, provided that the asset has been held for at least a year, and by 75% if it is held for over two years. This gives an effective tax rate of 20% if an asset is held for at least a year and 10% (40% of 25% of the gain) if it is held for over two. For disposals in the period from 6 April 2000 to 5 April 2002 the taper period was four years, the gain reducing by 12.5% where the asset was held for at least a year, 25% after two years, 50% after three and 75% once it had been held for more than four years. On disposals before 6 April 2000 the taper was less generous. It reduced the gain by 7½% per annum only. The meaning of a business asset is outside the scope of this book. Broadly speaking it is one used as a fixed asset of a trade. Curiously though, a property which is let to a close trading company (even one wholly unconnected with the landlord) is a business asset. This is probably due to an accidental error in amending the wording of the legislation rather than a deliberate policy. For non-business assets taper reduces the gain by 5% per annum for the fourth to tenth years of ownership to a maximum of 60% after ten years (nine years for assets held at 17 March 1998) (*TCGA 1992, s 2A* inserted by *FA 1998, s 121*). This gives an effective tax rate of 24% while the rate of tax is 40%. There are two snags with tapering. The first is it starts only from 1998/99; earlier periods of ownership are ignored. The second is that it is given only on the taxable gain, i.e. after deducting losses and roll-over relief and similar deferrals of recognition of the gain. Where an asset was acquired before 6 April 1998 indexation allowance is still given in calculating the gain, which is then tapered.

**11.6** The incidental costs of the acquisition ((*a*)(ii) in 11.4 above) are limited to expenditure wholly and exclusively incurred by the taxpayer for the purpose of the acquisition, being either

(i) fees, commission, or remuneration paid for the professional services of any surveyor or valuer, or auctioneer, or accountant, or agent or legal advisor,

(ii) costs of transfer or conveyance (including stamp duty), or

(iii) costs of advertising to find a seller.

**11.7** The incidental costs of the disposal ((*c*) in 11.4 above) are similarly limited to expenditure wholly and exclusively incurred by the taxpayer for the purpose of the disposal being items within (i) or (ii) in 11.6 above, or

(i) costs of advertising to find a buyer, or

(ii) costs reasonably incurred in making any valuation or apportionment required for the purposes of computing the chargeable gain, including in particular expenses reasonably incurred in ascertaining market value where required by *TCGA 1992*.

(*TCGA 1992, s 38(2)*).

Head (ii) will only allow a deduction for costs of a valuation to enable a best estimate of the gain to be calculated and returned. It will not extend to subsequent costs in negotiating the value with the District Valuer or the Shares Valuation Division, or in litigating the amount of the valuation (*Caton (dec'd) v Couch (1997 STC 970)*). Accordingly, it is sensible to ensure that as much of the work as possible is done to arrive at the initial valuation, rather than estimating this and leaving the formal valuation to be done later.

## Non-Deductible Expenditure

**11.8** If expenditure cannot be brought within one of the above heads, no relief will be obtainable for it. Furthermore there is a specific prohibition on deducting any payment of interest – other than certain interest payments by companies (see 4.58 above) (*TCGA 1992, s 38(3)*). There is also a specific prohibition on deducting

(*a*) any expenditure allowable as a deduction for income or corporation tax purposes in computing the profits or gains or losses of a trade, and (*b*) any expenditure which, if the assets to which the CGT computation relates had at all times been used as a fixed asset of a UK trade, would have been allowable as a deduction in computing the profits of that notional trade.

(*TCGA 1992, s 39*).

**11.9** In the context of property, *section 39* can, in particular, deny relief in some common circumstances.

Where a liquidator or receiver has to pay arrears of rent to obtain a licence to assign a lease, the rent arrears cannot be deducted in calculating the gain arising on the assignment (*Emmerson v Computer Time International Ltd (50 TC 628)*). If the landlord will co-operate in such circumstances, an assignment of the lease with the arrears unpaid and the assignee undertaking to pay the arrears might be worth considering. It is possible that the Revenue might contend that, as the liability to pay the rent was a liability of the assignor, the relieving him of this liability constitutes money's worth, and thus the payment of the arrears by the assignee is part of the consideration received by the assignor for the assignment. If the assignee were to enter into an agreement with the landlord under which the landlord waived the arrears in consideration of a payment to him by the assignee of the same amount, it would be difficult for the Revenue to seek to tax this on the assignor. However, the assignee might find difficulty in bringing the payment into the categories of allowable deduction on a future disposal by him. It may be that it is a payment to acquire a separate asset, a right to take an assignment of the lease, which merges with the lease when the assignment takes place – so that *TCGA 1992, s 43* (assets derived from other assets) would treat the payment as part of the cost of acquiring the lease itself.

Where a person refurbishes a property prior to its disposal, a large part of the cost is likely to be repairs which, being of a revenue nature, would be excluded from CGT relief. Where a person carries out repairs on, or shortly after, acquiring a property and the cost of such repairs is excluded from being a deductible item under the Schedule A rules (2.71 above), the amount disallowed should be claimed for CGT purposes as enhancement expenditure. However, the Schedule A test that applied before 6 April 1995 for income tax and 1 April 1998 for corporation tax differed from that laid down by the courts under Schedule D (see 9.3 above) so, in theory at least, it is possible that expenditure which is not repairs for Schedule A purposes would also be excluded from capital gains tax relief because of the different test propounded by *TCGA 1992, s 39(2)*. Where a seller would not be able to obtain a deduction for dilapidations, but the purchaser would be able to treat the cost as enhancement expenditure, it may be worth considering whether the work might be undertaken by the buyer with an appropriate adjustment being made to the price.

**Contract – Date of Acquisition and Disposal**

**11.10** A further basic point that needs to be particularly borne in mind in relation to property is that for CGT purposes the date of acquisition or disposal of an asset is the date that the contract is entered into, not the date of the conveyance (*TCGA 1992, s 28(1)*). If the contract is conditional (in particular if it is conditional on the exercise of an option) the date of acquisition or disposal is the date that the condition is satisfied (*TCGA 1992, s 28(2)*). It has been held that in law there are only two types of conditional contract: a 'subject to contract' agreement and a contract where all the liabilities under the contract are conditional upon a certain event (*Lyon v Pettigrew (58 TC 452)* and *Eastham v Leigh London & Provincial Properties Ltd (46 TC 687)*). In the *Leigh London* case, a company agreed in 1962 to erect a building on land owned by a third party in consideration of the grant to it of a 125-year lease on completion. This is, of course, a fairly common building lease arrangement. The building was completed and the lease granted in 1964. The Revenue contended that the 1962 agreement was two contracts, a building agreement and a conditional contract to grant the lease. It was held that the 1962 agreement was a single and absolute contract. The distinction is often described as a condition precedent and a condition subsequent; a condition precedent being something that has to happen before the contract can take effect at all; and a condition subsequent a condition that has to be fulfilled when carrying out the contract, i.e. something that does not strike at the root of the contract and non-compliance with which will not render the contract ineffective but will usually merely give rise to a claim for damages. The inclusion of a condition subsequent will not make a contract a conditional contract.

**11.11** If a contract is never completed it is generally accepted that there is no disposal for CGT purposes, i.e. the contract date merely fixes the date of disposal once completion has taken place. This is implicit in the judgments in *Magnavox Electronics Co Ltd (in liquidation) v Hall (59 TC 610)*. In that case a contract to dispose of a property was entered into in September 1978. The purchaser defaulted. As the company had trading losses which could be set against a capital gain arising in September 1978 but not against one in the next accounting period, the liquidator struggled to keep the contract alive. It was assigned to a new company controlled by the liquidator, varied (twice) to amend both the price and the completion date, and reassigned to a new purchaser in October 1979. It was held that the second variation was not effective to vary the contract and that the October 1979 completion was accordingly not under the September 1978 contract.

**11.12** This does not, however, appear to be the Revenue's view – notwithstanding that in the *Magnavox Electronics Co Ltd (in liquidation) v Hall (59 TC 610)* case, the Case stated records that the solicitor for the Inland Revenue put forward the view that the words of the relevant provisions 'suggest that if a contract for sale is to be regarded as a disposal clear provision is necessary. In the absence of such provision it must be that disposal takes place when a sale is completed not when the contract is entered into' (*59 TC* at p 620). Unfortunately, the author has been told by an Inspector of Taxes that the view of the Revenue's Capital and Valuation Division is that a contract creates a disposal for capital gains tax purposes, even though it may not be completed, because 'if a contract for sale is capable of specific performance an immediate equitable interest in land passes to the purchaser. The legal estate remains in the vendor until the conveyance has been executed, but meanwhile equity regards the vendor as a trustee for the purchaser and is prepared to decree specific performance at the instance of the latter.' It is hard to see the justification for this in the light of the *Magnavox* case and a contrary opinion has been expressed by leading counsel. The decision in *Jones and another (Balls' Administrators) v Inland Revenue Commissioners (1997 STC 358)*, an inheritance tax case (see 18.49), also gives support to the need for a contract to be completed before there could be a sale.

**11.13** What happens if between contract and completion the taxpayer disposes of his interest in the property? Apparently nothing. He is still taxable on the disposal made by the contract. The contract date identifies the disposal including the parties to the disposal and their interests in the property the subject of the disposal (*Jerome v Kelly, SpC 284 [2001] STC (SCD) 170*). It is to be hoped that this case goes to appeal as it seems illogical. It also raises the question as to what happens on the disposal of the beneficial interest. Is there no tax? And what if the price changes after the disposal, for example a variable element becomes quantified? It is irrational that the extra money should accrue to the transferee but the tax liability on it should be thrown on the transferor.

**11.14** The normal rule set out in 11.10 is displaced where *TCGA 1992, s 22(1)* applies. This deems there to be a disposal where a capital sum is derived from assets notwithstanding that no asset is acquired by the person paying it. The section is expressed to apply in particular to:

(*a*) capital sums received as compensation for damage, loss or destruction of an asset or for any depreciation or risk of depreciation of an asset,

(*b*) capital sums received under a policy of insurance of the risk of damage, injury, loss or depreciation of assets,

(*c*) capital sums received in return for forfeiture or surrender of rights (or refraining from exercising rights), and

(*d*) capital sums received as consideration for the use or exploitation of assets.

In these four cases the time of disposal is the time when the capital sum is received (*TCGA 1992, s 22(2)*). A payment in money's worth is a capital sum for the purpose of *section 22* (*TCGA 1992, s 22(3)*).

**11.15** It was held by the House of Lords in *Marren v Ingles (54 TC 76)* that where an asset is sold for an immediate payment plus a contingent right to future consideration that is unascertainable at the date of disposal, the value of the right to receive the contingent consideration is part of the disposal proceeds but that right is itself a separate asset, a chose in action, from which a capital sum is derived when the consideration is ascertained and paid. This decision was followed in *Marson v Marriage (54 TC 59)* where land was sold for development on terms that the vendor would receive a supplemental payment depending on how much of the land the purchasers were able to develop for residential development and the permitted density. It is not uncommon for land to be sold with an additional payment becoming due when planning permission is received for development. If the additional consideration is an amount that is fixed at the date of the contract the Revenue consider that *TCGA 1992, s 48* applies. This provides that the consideration for a disposal is to be brought into account without regard to a risk of any part of the consideration being contingent – but if any part is subsequently shown to be irrecoverable, then on a claim being made to that effect, the tax payable is to be adjusted. The Revenue did for a time consider that if a maximum figure was placed on unascertainable consideration, that took it out of the *Marren v Ingles* principle and into *section 48*. However they now accept that is incorrect (Revenue CGT Manual para 148.89). It will be apparent that the precise nature of the additional consideration can affect the tax treatment. If it is a fixed, or otherwise ascertainable amount, tax is payable on the entire amount that is due to be received by reference to the contract date but will be revised if the amount is not received. If it is unascertainable the initial charge will be on the value of the chose in action with a further charge on the balance of the additional consideration when it is actually received. If the ultimate receipt is less than the initial value no adjustment can be made to the value of the additional compensation; but there will be an allowable loss on the disposal of the chose in action. A chose in action is not an interest in land and cannot therefore qualify for roll-over relief (see 11.75) or for private residence exemption (CGT Manual para 64609) (see 13.3).

**11.16** An interesting dispute arose in *Chaloner v Pellipar Investments Ltd (1996 STC 234)*. Pellipar owned three sites. It entered into a development agreement under which it would grant leases of two of the sites to a developer in consideration partly of the payment of premiums and partly of the developer developing the third site for the benefit of Pellipar. The issue was whether the value of the development of the third site was a capital sum received for the use or exploitation of assets within *TCGA 1992, s 22(1)(d)*. If it was, the 'disposal' date was the date of receipt. If it was not, then it was the date of the development agreement by virtue of *TCGA 1992, s 28(1)*. The judge felt that there is a basic distinction between a lease and a licence. A lease gives the right to actual possession; a licence gives a right to use the land with possession remaining with the owner. *Section 22(1)(d)* is apt to cover a licence but not a lease as possession is different from use. Accordingly the disposal took place at the date of the agreement.

**11.17** A detailed consideration of all the capital gains tax rules is obviously outside the scope of this work. The object of this chapter is to look at those areas which particularly affect property. CGT in relation to private residences is considered separately in chapter 13.

## Leases

**11.18** A lease of land is a wasting asset for CGT purposes if it is for less than 50 years. A lease for a longer period becomes a wasting asset when its duration reduces to 50 years (*TCGA 1992, Sch 8 para 1(1)*). If a lease is acquired subject to a sublease not at a rack rent and its value (estimated at the time of acquisition) at the expiration of the sublease will exceed its cost, it will not be a wasting asset until the sublease has expired (*TCGA 1992, Sch 8 para 1(2)*). Such a lease is in reality an appreciating asset until that time as the passage of the sublease will increase the value of the headlease.

**11.19** In *Lewis v Walters (1992 STC 97)* the taxpayer unsuccessfully claimed that a 16-year lease of a flat should be regarded as a 66-year one, and thus not a wasting asset, as the then *Leasehold Reform Act 1967* gave the tenant a right to extend the lease for a further 50 years. The terms of the lease did not provide for the extension (see 11.27(*a*) below) and, even if the statute could be interpreted as implying an additional term of the lease, the statutory right is not to an extended lease but to the grant of a 'new' tenancy, which would be a new and separate asset (see also 11.33).

**11.20** The cost of, and enhancement expenditure on, a wasting asset (less its estimated residual value) is normally written off on a straight-line basis over the anticipated life of the asset (*TCGA 1992, s 46*). However, the legislature felt that this treatment was inappropriate for leases of land, probably because it is well known that the value of a short lease drops at a far greater annual rate than the value of a longer one. Accordingly the rate at which the expenditure on a lease is deemed to waste away must be calculated by reference to a statutory table which writes off the cost progressively (*TCGA 1992, Sch 8 para 1(3)*).

**11.21** In calculating the gain on the disposal of a lease it is necessary to exclude the proportion of cost given by the formula

$$\frac{P(1) - P(3)}{P(1)}$$

and the proportion of the enhancement expenditure given by the formula

$$\frac{P(2) - P(3)}{P(2)}$$

where

P(1) = the table figure for the duration of the lease at the time of its acquisition,

P(2) = the table figure for the duration of the lease at the time when any item of enhancement expenditure is first reflected in the nature of the lease, and

P(3) = the table figure for the duration of the lease at the time of the disposal.

**11.22** The table has yearly rests. Where the lease is not for an exact number of years, a twelfth of the difference between the figures for the number of whole years in the lease and the next higher number of complete years is added to that for the number of whole years for each extra month, any odd period of under 14 days being ignored and 14 days or more being treated as a month.

*Example 23*

On 18 June 1993 Penny took an assignment of a lease expiring on 31 December 2023 at a cost of £20,000. On 8 September 1995 she finished the building of an extension at a cost of £12,000. She sold the lease on 19 August 1999 for £30,000.

| | | | | |
|---|---|---|---|---|
| Duration of lease at 18.6.1993 | 30 years | 6 months | 12 days | |
| table figure | 87.330 + | 0.520* | + NIL | = 87.850 |
| Duration of lease at 8.9.1995 | 28 years | 3 months | 22 days | |
| table figure | 85.053 + | 0.293* | + 0.098* | = 85.444 |
| Duration of lease at 19.8.1999 | 24 years | 4 months | 12 days | |
| table figure | 79.622 + | 0.493* | + NIL | = 80.115 |

*the monthly figures are calculated as follows

| | | | | | | |
|---|---|---|---|---|---|---|
| figure for 31 years | | 88.371 | (29) | 86.226 | (25) | 81.100 |
| figure for 30 years | | 87.330 | (28) | 85.053 | (24) | 79.622 |
| | | 1.041 | | 1.173 | | 1.478 |
| 1/12th | | 0.0867 | | 0.0977 | | 0.1232 |
| | (×6) | 0.520 | (×3) | 0.293 | (×4) | 0.493 |

Penny's chargeable gain (before indexation relief) is accordingly

| | | £ | £ | £ |
|---|---|---|---|---|
| Disposal proceeds | | | | 30,000 |
| *Less* cost | | 20,000 | | |
| *Deduct* non-allowable part | $\frac{87.850 - 80.115^{*}}{87.850}$ | 1,761 | | |
| | | | 18,239 | |
| Enhancement expenditure | | 12,000 | | |
| *Deduct* non-allowable part | $\frac{85.444 - 80.115}{85.444}$ | 748 | | |
| | | | 11,252 | 29,491 |
| Chargeable gain | | | | £509 |

The same result can be arrived at more easily by simply deducting the reciprocal of the formula figure

| | | £ | £ |
|---|---|---|---|
| Disposal proceeds | | | 30,000 |
| *Less* allowable cost | $\frac{80.115}{87.850} \times £20{,}000$ | 18,239 | |
| allowable enhancement expenditure | $\frac{80.115}{85.444} \times £12{,}000$ | 11,252 | 29,491 |
| | | | £509 |

**11.23** The grant of a lease at an annual rent does not give rise to a disposal for capital gains tax purposes. The grant of a lease at a premium gives rise to a part disposal, the property undisposed of being the value, at the time of the grant of the lease, of the reversionary interest (*TCGA 1992, Sch 8 para 2*).

Strictly speaking, it is arguable that there is a part disposal – for a nil value – where no premium is received, as *paragraph 2* does not necessarily override the general wording of *section 21* which provides that there is a part disposal whenever an interest in or right over an asset is created. Whilst such an interpretation would not create a deemed gain on the grant of the lease it would terminate the time apportionment period under *TCGA 1992, Sch 2 para 11(7)* if the property was acquired before 6 April 1965. The author has never known the Revenue to adopt such an interpretation. This does not prevent a taxpayer raising it if it is in his interest to do so – which is likely to be very rare.

**11.24** If, under the terms subject to which a lease is granted, a sum becomes payable by the tenant in lieu of all or part of the rent for any period or as consideration for the surrender of the lease, the lease is deemed for CGT purposes to have required the payment of a premium to the landlord (in addition to any actual premium) of that sum, for the period in relation to which it is payable (*TCGA 1992, Sch 8 para 3(2)*). Similarly, if a sum becomes payable by the tenant other than by way of rent as consideration for the waiver or variation of any of the terms of the lease, the lease is deemed to have required the payment of a premium (or additional premium) of that sum for the period from the time the variation takes effect to the time it ceases to have effect (*TCGA 1992, Sch 8 para 3(3)*). If the transaction is not at arm's length, the amount of the deemed premium under *paragraph 3(3)* (although not the amount of a deemed premium under *paragraph 3(2)*) is the sum that could have been required at arm's length for the variation.

**11.25** Prior to 6 April 1996 a deemed premium under either *sub-paragraph (2)* or *(3)* (other than a payment for the surrender of the lease) had to be treated, from the viewpoint of both landlord and tenant, as if it were part of the consideration for the grant of the lease due at the time the lease was granted (*TCGA 1992, Sch 8 para 3(4)*). This necessitated a recomputation of the gain arising to the landlord on the grant of the lease. Strangely, the six-year period for raising assessments was not extended to allow this to be done where the receipt arose more than six years after the grant of the lease. From 6 April 1996 the deemed premium (including one on surrender) is treated as becoming due, and thus assessable, at the date it is payable by the tenant and no recomputation is made even if earlier premiums have been received (*FA 1996, s 142*). If the landlord is himself a lessee under a lease of 50 years or less it must also be assumed that he had paid a premium (equal to the amount of the premium deemed to have been received by him) for the grant of the part of the sublease covered by the period in respect of which the premium (i.e. the deemed premium received) is deemed to have been paid (and that deemed consideration is treated as if it were enhancement expenditure incurred by the sublessee and attributable to that part of the sublease) (*TCGA 1992, Sch 8 para 3(5)*).

**11.26** If a premium is deemed under *paragraph 3(2)* to have been received as consideration for the surrender of a lease, the gain on its grant is not recalculated. Instead, the 'premium' is treated as consideration for a separate transaction consisting of the disposal by the landlord of his interest in the lease (*TCGA 1992, Sch 8 para 3(4)*). This separate transaction is probably itself a part disposal of the landlord's interest in the property. From 6 April 1996 this provision is extended to any deemed premium under *sub-paragraphs (2)* or *(3)* (*FA 1996, s 142*).

### Duration of Leases

**11.27** The legislation contains a number of special rules for determining the duration of a lease of land for CGT purposes. These rules are similar, but by no means identical, to those that apply for the purpose of the income tax charge on premiums (3.23 above). They obviously need to be used in applying the wasting asset table but are not limited to this; they are of general application (*TCGA 1992, Sch 8 para 8(1)*).

(*a*) If the terms of a lease include provision for its determination by notice given by the landlord it cannot be regarded as extending beyond the earliest date on which it can be so determined (*TCGA 1992, Sch 8 para 8(2)*). This provision used to apply also for Schedule A purposes but was found to give scope for avoidance and was repealed by *FA 1972, s 81(2)(a)*. It has presumably been retained for CGT purposes because there is no reason why a taxpayer should want to artificially shorten the term of his lease.

(*b*) If any of the terms of the lease or any other circumstances render it unlikely that the lease will continue beyond a date falling before the expiration of the term of the lease, it cannot be regarded as extending beyond that date (*TCGA 1992, Sch 8 para 8(3)*). This applies in particular if the lease provides for the rent to increase (or for the tenant's obligations to become in any other respect more onerous) after a given date, but includes provision for the determination of the lease on that date by notice by the tenant, and those provisions render it unlikely that the lease will continue beyond that date (*TCGA 1992, Sch 8 para 8(4)*). Hopefully, this final phrase will leave unaffected those leases where the tenant has an option to terminate the lease on a rent review.

(*c*) If the terms of a lease include provision for its extension beyond a given date by notice given by the tenant, it must be regarded as lasting for as long as it could be extended by the tenant 'but subject to any right of the landlord by notice to determine the lease' (*TCGA 1992, Sch 8 para 8(5)*). The meaning of the words in quotation marks is unclear. They are probably intended to make clear that the operation of (*a*) above is not displaced by this provision and takes precedence over it.

(*d*) The question as to what is the duration of a lease is to be decided by reference to the facts that were known or ascertainable at the time the lease was acquired or created (*TCGA 1992, Sch 8 para 8(6)*).

## Meaning of 'Lease' and 'Premium'

**11.28** For CGT purposes (unless the context otherwise requires) references to a lease must be taken to include

(*a*) an underlease,

(*b*) a sublease,

(*c*) any tenancy or licence,

(*d*) an agreement for a lease (or for an underlease, sublease, tenancy or licence), and

(*e*) in the case of land outside the UK, any interest corresponding to a lease or to anything within (*a*) to (*d*) above.

(*TCGA 1992, Sch 8 para 10(1)(a)*).

**11.29** For the purpose of applying the rules in 11.18–11.28 above and 11.31 below (but not for any other capital gains tax purposes), a premium includes any like sum, whether payable to the intermediate or a superior landlord (and in Scotland includes a gross sum payable to any landlord or intermediate landlord on the creation of a sublease) (*TCGA 1992, Sch 8 para 10(2)(3)*). For such purposes any sum other than rent which is paid on (or in connection with) the granting of a tenancy must be presumed to have been paid by way of premium except in so far as other sufficient consideration for the payment is shown to have been given (*TCGA 1992, Sch 8 para 10(2)*), i.e. it is up to the parties to produce evidence to show that the payment is not a premium.

## Grant of Sublease out of a Short Lease

**11.30** The normal part disposal rules are modified for calculating a gain accruing on the part disposal of a lease which is a wasting asset (i.e. normally one with an unexpired term of 50 years or less) (*TCGA 1992, Sch 8 para 4(1)*). If the amount of the premium is at least that which would be obtainable if the rent payable under the sublease were the same as that payable under the lease – which will normally be the case only if both lease and sublease are entered into on arm's length terms and either the rents are the same or the rent under the sublease is lower than that under the head lease – the deductible amount of the cost and enhancement expenditure is the fraction of such expenditure which, applying the wasting asset table, is to be written off over the term of the sublease (*TCGA 1992, Sch 8, para 4(2)(a)*).

*Example 24*

Sally paid a premium of £10,000 on 1 May 2002 for the grant of a ten-year lease. She granted a sublease for five years on 1 July 2002 at a premium of £6,000 and no profit rental.

Sally's chargeable gain (ignoring indexation) is as follows

| | | £ |
|---|---|---|
| Premium received | | 6,000 |
| *Less* allowable portion of premium paid | | |
| table percentage for a 10 year lease | 46.695 | |
| table percentage for a 9 years 10 month lease (i.e. the unexpired term at the time of the grant of the sublease) | 46.105 | |
| table percentage for a 4 years 10 month lease (i.e. the unexpired term of the head lease at the expiry of the sublease) | 25.932 | |
| proportion of premium for head lease relating to period of the sublease | | |
| $\frac{46.105 - 25.932}{46.695} \times 10{,}000$ | | 4,320 |
| | | 1,680 |
| *Less* deduction for part taxed under Schedule A (see 3.41 above) | | |
| 2% × (50 – (5 – 1)) × 6,000 | £5,520 | |
| *deduct* relief for premium paid (see 3.34 above) | | |
| 5/10 × 2% × (50 – (5 – 1)) × 10,000 | 4,100 | 1,420 |
| Chargeable gain | | £260 |

**11.31** If the premium is less than that which would be obtainable if the rent payable under the sublease were the same as that payable under the headlease – as will normally be the case where the head lessee is obtaining a profit rental (i.e. the rent under the sublease exceeds that under the head lease) as well as a premium – the above fraction must be multiplied by the premium and divided by the premium that would have been obtainable had the rents been the same (*TCGA 1992, Sch 8 para 4(2)(b)*). A valuation is obviously required to ascertain this notional premium.

*Example 25*

Suppose that Sally in *Example 24* had granted the sublease at a premium of £2,000 and a profit rental, and that the £6,000 figure in that example is the arm's length premium figure.

| | | £ |
|---|---|---|
| Her chargeable gain (ignoring indexation) would become | | |
| Premium received | | 2,000 |
| *Less* allowable portion of premium paid | | |
| $\frac{46.105 - 25.932}{46.695} \times \frac{2{,}000}{6{,}000} \times 10{,}000$ | | 1,440 |
| | | 560 |
| *Less* deduction for part taxed under Schedule A | | |
| 2% × (50 – (5 – 1)) × 2,000 | £1,840 | |
| *deduct* relief for premium paid, | | |
| £4,100 but limited to | 1,840 | — |
| Chargeable gain | | £560 |

**11.32** If the sublease does not extend to the whole of the land covered by the head lease the allowable expenditure must first be apportioned between the part of the premises covered by the sublease and the remainder of the premises (on the basis of their respective values) and the above rules applied to the fraction attributed to the part covered by the sublease (*TCGA 1992, Sch 8 para 4(3)*).

### Other Points on Leases

**11.33** Where a lease expires and the tenant is granted a new lease following proceedings under the *Landlord and Tenant Act 1954*, the new lease is not derived from the old but is a separate asset (*Bayley v Rogers (53 TC 420)*) (see also 11.19).

**11.34** Where part of a premium is taxed under Schedule A, the computation is modified to grant a measure of relief for this charge. The rules are considered in detail in 3.41 *et seq.* above.

**11.35** Where a leaseholder acquires the freehold reversion or a superior lease and the two interests merge, the Revenue consider that the wasting asset rules described in 11.18–11.27 above must be applied as if the lease had been disposed of on the date of the merger. The 'unwasted' balance of the cost can then be treated as part of the cost of the merged interest in accordance with *TCGA 1992, s 43*. Whilst this is logical, it is not clear that it is right as *TCGA 1992, Sch 8*, which contains the wasting asset rules, is expressed to apply in computing the gain accruing on the disposal of a lease and it is doubtful if its merger with the freehold reversion is such a disposal. Nevertheless, the Revenue must be expected to firmly resist any claim to deduct the whole cost of the lease. If the superior interest is itself a lease of under 50 years, the unwasted part of the cost of the sublease and the cost of acquiring the head lease are aggregated and that aggregate treated as the cost of the merged asset, acquired at the date of the merger, for the purpose of applying the wasting asset rules to the merged lease.

### Extension of Leases

**11.36** It is not possible in law to vary a lease so as to extend its term. Accordingly, an extension normally takes the form of the surrender of the existing lease and the grant of a new one. In such circumstances the surrender is technically a disposal of the old lease for the sum of any payment received plus the value of the new lease (less any payment made). In practice the Revenue do not regard the surrender of the old lease as a disposal provided that:

(*a*) the transaction is between unconnected parties bargaining at arm's length (or, from June 1999, if it is not, the terms of the transaction are equivalent to those that would have been made between such persons);

(*b*) the transaction is not part of (or connected with) a larger transaction;

(*c*) no capital sum is received by the lessee;

(*d*) the extent of the property in which the lessee has an interest under the new lease does not differ in any way from that under the old lease; and

(*e*) the terms of the new lease, other than in relation to its duration and the rent payable, do not differ from those of the old lease (ignoring any trivial differences) (Inland Revenue Extra-Statutory Concession D39 and Tax Bulletin 41, June 1999).

Where any of these conditions are not met, capital gains tax needs to be considered. The safest thing may be to achieve the extension by the grant of an additional lease to take effect on the expiry of the existing one. Even where a transaction is at arm's length it should not automatically be assumed that all of the above conditions will be met. In particular the landlord may well take the opportunity to modernise some of the provisions of the lease, which would prevent (*e*) from being satisfied.

**11.37** Where such a merger occurs the indexation allowance is, strictly speaking, calculable on the aggregate of the unwasted part of the cost of the lease and the cost of the superior interest from the date of acquisition of the superior interest, i.e. the date of the merger. By concession though, the Revenue will allow indexation on the unwasted part of the cost of the lease to be calculated from the date of acquisition of that lease and on the superior interest from the date of acquisition of that interest (Inland Revenue Extra-Statutory Concession D42). For disposals prior to 29 June 1992 a more generous concession operated; the indexation allowance on the aggregate of the two items of expenditure was calculated from the date of the acquisition of the lease. Where the owner of a lease of less than 50 years buys in an inferior interest, the cost of the inferior interest would probably constitute enhancement expenditure on the lease so no special rules are needed to cater for that situation.

## Part Disposals of Land

**11.38** It is often difficult to determine whether a holding of land is a single asset or a number of separate assets. For example, if two adjoining houses are purchased together, is the sale of one the complete disposal of a house or the part disposal of the pair? The calculations could in many cases produce significantly different results. The Revenue have expressed the view that, unless it appears from the facts at the time of acquisition that more than one asset was acquired, a single acquisition of land, with or without buildings – whether obtained by purchase under one contract at an inclusive price, or by gift or inheritance as a whole – should be regarded as a single asset even though it may comprise distinguishable elements such as a house and garden, farmhouses, buildings, woodlands, cottages, etc. (CCAB Press Release, June 1968). It is debatable whether this view is correct in principle, at least where the different buildings are not within a single curtilage. If the assets are contiguous it may possibly be, but even that seems doubtful. If, however, a number of scattered parcels of land are purchased as a job lot it seems doubtful whether the mere fact that a single overall price is paid could suffice to constitute them a single combined asset. If separate prices are attributed to the different assets, the inference can be drawn from the above statement of the Revenue's views that they would regard them as a number of separate purchases even though bought under a single contract.

**11.39** This is probably an academic point as, in spite of their view of the legal position, the Revenue have stated that even where there is a single inclusive price, in practice no objection is taken to treating individual houses as separate assets and apportioning the cost of a larger unit (such as a row of terraced houses) on the basis of such evidence as is available. Similarly with a block of flats, no objection is normally taken to treating individual flats as separate assets if it appears that similar flats in the same ownership, or in the same locality, have commonly been sold singly as independent dwellings (CCAB Press Release, June 1968). The Revenue have also said that where part of an estate is disposed of, e.g. on the sale of a field, they will accept that such part can be regarded as a separate asset and any fair and reasonable method of apportioning the total cost will be accepted (Statement of Practice D1). The taxpayer is not of course precluded from treating the sale as a part disposal if he wishes and the facts support a contention that the estate was a single asset. He will normally have to make up his mind which basis he wants to adopt at the time of his first disposal out of an estate, and use the same basis on subsequent sales of future parts.

### Insurance Proceeds, etc.

**11.40** If a building is destroyed – as opposed to damaged – and the insurance proceeds (or any other compensation) are used within a year of the receipt (or such longer time as the Revenue may allow) to replace the building, an election can be made to treat the asset as having been disposed of at a no gain/no loss price with the excess of the insurance proceeds over such amount then being deducted from the cost of the new building (*TCGA 1992, s 23(4)*). If the whole of the insurance proceeds are not used to buy the replacement building but the part not reinvested is less than the amount of the gain (not the chargeable gain, i.e. before time apportionment and taper relief) the gain can be reduced to the amount not reinvested with the balance of the gain being deducted from the cost of the new property (*TCGA 1992, s 23(5)*). If a building is destroyed or irreparably damaged and all or part of any compensation or insurance proceeds is used to construct or otherwise acquire a replacement building situated elsewhere, both the old and new buildings are deemed to be assets separate from the land on which they stand or stood and the old building is regarded as destroyed (*TCGA 1992, s 23(6)* inserted by *FA 1996, Sch 39 para 3*). This ensures that relief is not lost because the land is not destroyed, but also prevents the compensation being set against the land cost of the new building. *Section 23(6)* applies to sums received after 6 April 1996. Prior to that date the same effect could be obtained under ESC D19, although that was of course at the taxpayer's option. Prior to 6 April 1996 no relief was given under *section 23(4)* or *(5)* in respect of wasting assets. Now where the money is received by a lessee under a lease which is a wasting asset the sum can be set against the expenditure on the replacement building and no gain recognised but on a subsequent disposal of the asset the expenditure is set against what the base cost would have been had the asset been disposed of immediately after the replacement works (*TCGA 1992, s 23(8)* inserted by *FA 1996, Sch 39 para 3*). Prior to 6 April 1996 wasting assets were excluded from *section 23* but ESC D1 allowed the proceeds to be used to restore the building without triggering a tax charge.

**11.41** If the building is damaged rather than destroyed and the insurance proceeds (or any other compensation received) are used to restore the building, the receipt of the compensation again need not be treated as a part disposal of the asset (*TCGA 1992, s 23*). Instead, the insurance proceeds are deducted from the base cost. This treatment can also be adopted if all except a small amount of the compensation is used to restore the building. Strictly speaking this treatment can give rise to a problem on a subsequent disposal, as the original cost of the building would no longer be reflected in the state of the asset at the time of disposal, and would thus not constitute enhancement expenditure. For example, suppose a taxpayer, who had initially bought a site on which he erected a building at a cost of £200,000, receives insurance proceeds of £90,000 after a fire, and spends £95,000 on reconstruction. Logically the £90,000 should be deducted from the cost and the £95,000 added to it, giving a new base cost of £205,000. Strictly, however, a part of the original £200,000 will relate to work which has been destroyed and replaced by the new work. As such it ceases to qualify as enhancement expenditure. In practice the Revenue are unlikely to take this point.

**11.42** If the insurance proceeds are not wholly applied in restoring the building, the part so applied can be deducted from the new expenditure with only the balance being treated as disposal proceeds (*TCGA 1992, s 23(3)*). This does not apply if the part not reinvested is small or if the entire capital sum is small (even if no part of it is used to restore the building) as compared with the value of the asset. Instead it is deducted from the base cost of the asset so that any gain is deferred. If such sum exceeds the base cost of the asset the balance is of course taxable (*TCGA 1992, s 23(2)(3)*). There is no statutory definition of small. In *O'Rourke v Binks (65 TC 165)* the Court of Appeal said it is a question of fact and degree. The Revenue have said that they regard an amount as small if either it does not exceed 5% of the total or it does not exceed £3,000 (Tax Bulletin 27, February 1997).

**11.43** If a building is destroyed but no insurance proceeds are receivable, for example because it is uninsured, consideration might be given as to whether a capital loss can be established under *TCGA 1992, s 24(2)* on the grounds that the value of the asset has become negligible. Unfortunately this will rarely apply unless the building is destroyed by a nuclear holocaust, as the site will normally still have a value. To make this rule workable *section 24(3)* allows the building and land to be regarded as separate assets so as to trigger a claim under *section 24(2)*. Unfortunately it requires both land and buildings to be deemed to be sold and reacquired, so before making the election the premature crystallisation of the increase in value of the land needs to be weighed against the value of the loss on the building.

**Small Part Disposals**

**11.44** If the consideration for the transfer or other disposal of part of a holding of land does not exceed 20% of the market value of the entire holding (as it subsisted immediately before the part disposal), the vendor can elect to deduct the disposal proceeds or other consideration from the base cost of the holding instead of calculating a gain on the disposal (*TCGA 1992, s 242(1)(2)(6)*).

**11.45** The taxpayer cannot adopt this treatment if the consideration on the transfer exceeds £20,000 or if the consideration for all disposals of land by him in the year of assessment (other than disposals within *TCGA 1992, s 243* to an authority with compulsory powers under 11.46 below) exceeds £20,000 (*TCGA 1992, s 242(3)(4)*). It should be noted that all disposals of land, not merely small part disposals, need to be taken into account in applying this £20,000 test. Where the transfer is at an undervalue the £20,000 test must be applied by reference to the market value of the land disposed of (*TCGA 1992, s 242(5)*). In addition, this treatment cannot be used where the estate or interest in land is a wasting asset (*TCGA 1992, s 242(7)*) or where the transfer is a no gain/no loss transfer between spouses or members of a group of companies (*TCGA 1992, s 242(1)(b)*).

*Part Disposal to Authority with Compulsory Powers*

**11.46** Where:

(*a*) a disposal of land forming part only of a holding is made to an authority exercising or having compulsory powers;

(*b*) the consideration for the transfer (or the market value if the transfer is not for full consideration – an unlikely event on a sale to a local authority, etc.) is small as compared with the market value of the entire holding immediately before the disposal; and

(*c*) the vendor had not taken any steps, by advertising or otherwise, to dispose of any part of the holding or to make his willingness to dispose of it known to any person,

the vendor can similarly elect to deduct the disposal proceeds from the base cost of the holding instead of calculating a gain on the part disposal (*TCGA 1992, s 243(1)(2)*).

**11.47** For this purpose, proceeds will normally be regarded as small if they either do not exceed 5% of the value of the holding, or are £3,000 or less (as under 11.42), there is no special time limit for making the claim, and a claim cannot be made if the estate or interest in land in question is a wasting asset (*TCGA 1992, s 243(4)*). An authority having compulsory powers is any body that either acquires the land compulsorily for the purpose for which it was acquired, or which had (or could have) been authorised to acquire it for that purpose. It also includes a person for whom some other body has (or could have) been authorised so to acquire it (*TCGA 1992, s 243(5)*). In other words, the relief will apply on any disposal under a compulsory purchase or under the threat of compulsory purchase, including, for example, a sale to a property developer in circumstances where, had the sale not taken place, the local authority would have been likely to acquire the land and resell it to the developer. It will also apply on many voluntary sales to local authorities even though no threat of compulsory purchase is made provided that the initial approach is from the local authority not the taxpayer. In practice *section 243* is likely to operate only where the £20,000 of proceeds limit in *section 242* is breached, as *section 242* is less restrictive.

### *Part Disposal – Consideration Exceeding Base Cost*

**11.48** If, on a transaction within either *section 242* or *243*, the base cost of the entire holding is less than the consideration received on the part disposal (or is nil) the consideration cannot be deducted from the base cost. Instead the taxpayer can elect to deduct the base cost of the entire holding from the consideration for the part disposal, the balance of that consideration then being a chargeable gain (*TCGA 1992, s 244*). There is no special time limit for such an election.

## Compulsory Acquisitions

**11.49** Apart from the above relief for small part disposals there are a number of other provisions dealing with compulsory purchase of land.

Where an interest in land is acquired (otherwise than under a contract) by an authority possessing compulsory purchase powers, the time of the disposal and acquisition is the date on which the compensation for the acquisition is agreed or otherwise determined (variations on appeal being ignored for this purpose). Prior to 1996/97 (30 June 1999 for companies) the date that the authority entered on to the land was taken instead if that was earlier (*TCGA 1992, s 246*).

**11.50** Where the land is acquired under contract the normal rules apply: the disposal takes place at the time the contract is entered into, or, if it is conditional, the date that the condition is satisfied.

**11.51** Where land (or an interest in, or right over, land) is acquired under compulsory purchase powers (or is sold voluntarily in circumstances that the acquisition could have been made under compulsory purchase powers), the fact that the acquisition is made compulsorily must be ignored when considering whether the compensation ought to be apportioned and part treated as compensation for damage to, or for the loss of, an asset under *TCGA 1992, s 22(1)(a)*. So must any statutory provision treating the purchase price, compensation or other consideration as exclusively paid in respect of the land itself (*TCGA 1992, s 245(1)*). This provision was introduced in 1969 to prevent the element of compensation for disturbance – which the Revenue generally regard as a revenue receipt – being transformed into capital because under general law it is often merely an element in arriving at the price to be paid for the land on a compulsory acquisition.

**11.52** It was held in *Stoke-on-Trent City Council v Wood Mitchell & Co Ltd (1979 STC 197)* that the effect of this provision is to treat compensation for loss of profits as a trading receipt, not as a capital sum. Accordingly, the local authority could not make a deduction for corporation tax in arriving at the amount of such compensation as that element of the compensation is itself a taxable amount. Following that case the Revenue have adopted the stance that any element of compensation received for temporary loss of profits on a compulsory acquisition, or for losses on trading stock, or to reimburse revenue expenditure such as removal expenses, is revenue and should be regarded as taxable income. They will apply the same practice in those compensation cases where no interest in land is acquired – such as where compensation is paid due to damage, injury, or exploitation of land, or to the exercise of planning control (Inland Revenue Statement of Practice SP 8/79).

**11.53** If land (or an interest in land) is, or could have been, acquired compulsorily, and the compensation or purchase price includes an amount in respect of its severance from other land in which the vendor (in the same capacity) has an interest, or in respect of injurious affection of other land, the receipt must be treated as giving rise to a part disposal of that other land (*TCGA 1992, s 245(2)*). This is normally in the interest of the taxpayer, as it allows part of the base cost of the other land to be set against the compensation received.

**Roll-over Relief on Compulsory Purchase**

**11.54** Where land is compulsorily acquired or is otherwise disposed of to an authority possessing compulsory purchase powers (i.e. a person who has been – or could be – authorised to acquire it compulsorily for the purpose for which it is acquired, or for whom another person has been – or could be – authorised so to acquire it), a claim for roll-over relief can be made in certain circumstances if the proceeds are used to acquire other land (*TCGA 1992, ss 243(5), 247(1)(8)*). The Revenue consider that *section 247* also applies to a landlord where leasehold tenants exercise their statutory rights to acquire the freehold reversion or an extension of a lease of a property under the *Leasehold Reform Act 1967, Housing and Urban Development Act 1993* or the *Housing Acts 1985–1996* – as the leaseholder is an 'Authority' within *TCGA 1992, s 243(5)*, i.e. a person with compulsory purchase powers (Inland Revenue Statement of Practice SP 13/93 and Tax Bulletin No 41, June 1999).

**11.55** The taxpayer must not have taken any steps – whether by advertising or otherwise – to dispose of the land or to make his willingness to dispose of it known to the authority or to any other person (*TCGA 1992, s 247(1)(b)*). This presumably means willingness to dispose before any approach to acquire was made, and would hopefully not deny relief where a taxpayer was 'willing' to dispose of the land to the authority by private treaty because they had intimated an intention to exercise their compulsory purchase powers if he did not do so. It is understood that any steps taken by the taxpayer more than three years prior to the disposal will be ignored for the purposes of *TCGA 1992, s 247(1)(b)* (ICAEW Technical Releases 467, 477). The consideration for the disposal must be applied by the taxpayer in acquiring the new land (*TCGA 1992, s 247(1)(c)*). It must be acquired (or an unconditional contract for its acquisition entered into) within the period beginning twelve months before and ending three years after the disposal of the old land (see 11.77 above) or such longer period as the Revenue may allow (*TCGA 1992, ss 247(5)(b), 152(3)(4)*). It is obviously sensible to approach the Revenue within the time limit if the taxpayer needs to have it extended although the comments in 11.77 need to be borne in mind.

**11.56** Where a roll-over relief claim is made, the consideration for the disposal is reduced to the CGT base cost of the old land (including indexation relief) and that for the acquisition of the new is reduced by the excess of the sale proceeds over that figure (*TCGA 1992, s 247(2)*), i.e. the gain that would otherwise have arisen on the old land is deducted from the cost of the new. If, because of time apportionment, it is not wholly chargeable gain, only the chargeable part need be deducted (*TCGA 1992, s 247(5)(a)*). If the whole of the consideration is not applied on the acquisition of the new land, the taxpayer is deemed to have reinvested the cost of the original land before reinvesting the gain realised on it, i.e. the whole of the amount not reinvested is taxable up to the amount of the gain. If it is less than the gain, roll-over relief is due on the balance of the gain (*TCGA 1992, s 247(3)*).

**11.57** The relief cannot be claimed if the new land is a dwelling-house (or part of a dwelling-house, or an interest in, or right over, a dwelling-house) which qualifies for private residence relief under *TCGA 1992, ss 222–226* (see 13.3–13.31 below) at any time during the six years following its acquisition (*TCGA 1992, s 248(1)*). If a gain is rolled over into the cost of a dwelling-house which is not initially a principal private residence, but it subsequently becomes one in the six-year period, the gain on the original disposal must be recomputed to withdraw the relief.

**11.58** If the gain is rolled over into land which is a depreciating asset, i.e. a lease of under 60 years, the gain is held over for ten years or until the earlier disposal of that lease, and will become taxable at the end of the hold-over period. If new land, which is not a depreciating asset, is acquired during the period that the gain is being held over, the gain can be switched to that new land instead. A switch cannot be made to another depreciating asset, however (*TCGA 1992, ss 154, 248(3)*).

**11.59** If a claim for roll-over relief is made on a part disposal, a claim cannot also be made under *TCGA 1992, s 243* (see 11.46 above) to deduct the proceeds from the cost of the part undisposed of (*TCGA 1992, s 248(4)*). Where compensation includes an amount in respect of injurious affection to other land, a claim under *section 247* displaces the operation of *TCGA 1992, s 245(2)* (see 11.53 above) to the extent that roll-over relief is given for such an amount (*TCGA 1992, s 247(6)*). The relationship between roll-over relief and taper relief needs to be borne in mind. The acquisition of the new asset starts a new taper relief qualifying period running. This is potentially a double whammy. Not only is the benefit of the holding period of the old asset lost but the gain on the new asset is increased by the gain held over on the old – so if the new asset is not held for the full qualifying period there may be a heavy price to pay for deferring the gain on the old. If the new asset is a business asset this may not be too much of a problem as the qualifying period is only two years, but for a non-business asset the period is ten years.

## Options

**11.60** Options are very common in relation to property. For example, a developer who is assembling a site may make payments to property owners for an option over their land which would be exercised only if he can acquire all of the interests he needs for his development or is successful in obtaining planning consent for the development. This limits the developer's exposure in the event of the projected development proving abortive – as all he will have lost will be his option payments (leaving aside his time and costs of applying for planning consent) – and avoids his having to fund purchases of land many months in advance of his being in a position to carry out his development. A potential vendor is likely to find an option arrangement more attractive than a conditional contract for sale as it usually puts some money in his hand irrespective of whether or not the scheme proceeds.

**11.61** For CGT purposes the grant of an option is regarded as the disposal of a separate asset to the land over which it is granted (*TCGA 1992, s 144(1)*). The Revenue accept that roll-over relief on replacement of business assets is available in respect of gains on the grant of an option over land by reference to the underlying land (Tax Bulletin, February 1992). If the option is exercised, the grant and exercise are instead treated as a single transaction, the option money (i.e. the payment made for the grant of the option) being treated, as far as the purchaser is concerned, as part of the cost of the land acquired in pursuance of the option (*TCGA 1992, s 144(3)(a)*), and, as far as the vendor is concerned, as part of the sale proceeds (*TCGA 1992, s 144(2)*). The date of the combined transaction is determined by the sale of the land and not the grant of the option. In effect, an exercised option is a type of conditional contract, the exercise of the option normally being the event that makes the contract unconditional and thus fixing the date of the transaction (*TCGA 1992, s 28*). This also applies for taper relief, so restricting the relief on any payment made for the grant of the option (*TCGA 1992, Sch A1 para 13*).

**11.62** Similar rules apply to a put option, i.e. one enabling the vendor to require the developer to purchase his land. On the exercise of the option the option money paid merges with the cost of the land. If the vendor pays option money to a purchaser for the right to put his land on to him – a very rare occurrence – the option money is deducted from the purchaser's cost of the land and treated as a selling expense of the vendor (*TCGA 1992, s 144(2)(b)(3)(b)*). Put options can be useful where the vendor is willing to sell his land but wishes to retain a degree of control over it when he does so. For example, he may wish to delay doing so until the next fiscal year if he has exhausted his capital gains tax annual exemption for the current year.

**11.63** If possible cross options, i.e. those where the vendor has a right to require the developer to buy his land at a specified time and the developer has a simultaneous right to require the vendor to sell it to him, should be avoided where the purpose of the option is to defer the disposal date to a later tax year. For development land tax purposes the Revenue sometimes contended that such an arrangement constituted an unconditional contract for sale as either party is able to enforce completion. Although it seems dubious whether this contention is correct as, in general, the Revenue must tax the transactions that are entered into, not ignore the form of those transactions and look only to the overall effect, the taxpayer could be faced with a contentious appeal which can be both time-consuming and costly. If the options are successive rather than simultaneous, e.g. the vendor can require the developer to buy at any time during May 2003 and, in the event of his not doing so, the developer can require the vendor to sell at any time during June 2003, this will probably defeat such a contention even if it is raised, as there would be no single date on which both parties could force the sale. If the price payable for the land in pursuance of the option is undetermined, e.g. the higher of £50,000 or 70% of the open market value of the land on the date the option is exercised, this would also make it difficult for the Revenue to say that there had been a contract for sale at the time the option was entered into as such a notional contract could well be void for uncertainty.

**11.64** If a series of options is entered into solely to obtain the benefit of several years' capital gains tax annual exemptions for the vendor, the *Ramsay* principle, as extended by *Furniss v Dawson*, needs to be borne in mind – although as the legislation itself effectively treats the grant and exercise of an option as a composite transaction, that principle may well have no practical effect in relation to options as it is difficult to envisage the courts regarding a series of, say, three annual sales of land with three separate conveyances as a single transaction. Nevertheless it is as well to consider whether any commercial benefits of a spreading arrangement are present in a particular case and if so to spell them out clearly in the agreement. For example, the developer's right to acquire the second tranche of land might be conditional on his having commenced building work or having installed an estate road so that the vendor can be satisfied that the remainder of his land will not be devalued if all of the options are not exercised. Where there is a series of options extending over several years it is difficult to avoid using put and call options while reassuring both parties that the whole of the land will be sold. It might be possible to use only call options if the price for the first part of the land is disproportionately high so that the developer is effectively forced to acquire the remainder because the price is so attractive – although this could possibly prompt a challenge as to whether the purchase price for the first tranche is wholly and exclusively incurred for the acquisition of that particular piece of land.

**11.65** If an option is not exercised the landowner is taxable on the option money he receives in the year of receipt. In practice, in the past the Revenue generally waited a reasonable time to see whether it was exercised before raising an assessment although they would not wait for several years. There is no bar on their raising an assessment before the expiry of the option period (*Strange v Openshaw, 57 TC 544*). Now that the taxpayer has to self assess he will have to declare the option receipt, pay tax on it, and recover it if the option is exercised. The developer will obtain no tax relief for the option payment (unless he is a property dealer) if it lapses. If he sells the benefit of the option to another person, the grant and sale will be the acquisition and disposal of an asset (the option). An option is a wasting asset, so the cost depreciates on a time basis over the period for which it is capable of being exercised. Accordingly the part of the cost that is deductible on such a sale may be small. Care needs to be taken where expenditure in relation to the land is incurred as part of an option arrangement as is illustrated by *Garner v Pounds Shipowners and Shipbreakers (2000 STC 420)*. The company granted a call option in September 1988 to buy land for £4m. It was paid £399,750 for the option but this was to be held by a stakeholder until the release had been secured of certain covenants over the land. The company subsequently paid £90,000 to secure the release of those covenants and the option money was paid over to it in May 1990. The option was not exercised, expiring in January 1991. The company's claim that the option was not granted until May 1990 was dismissed; the option itself was an unconditional contract with the release of the covenants being a separate agreement. The Court of Appeal, reversing the decision of the High Court, held that the £90,000 was not deductible in computing the gain on the option. It was not incurred in granting the option or in establishing, preserving or defending title to it within *TCGA 1992, s 32*. On a proper construction of the documents the option was to acquire the land subject to the covenants not free of them. That was the bargain that the parties had chosen to make. This reasoning was upheld in the House of Lords. Mention should also be made of *Randall v Plumb (50 TC 392)* where the option agreement provided for the option money to be repaid if planning permission were not obtained within ten years. It was held that the consideration for the grant of the option was not the option money, but its current value taking the contingency into account. Nourse LJ in the *Pounds Shipowners* case felt that this followed from the fact that the judge in *Randall v Plumb (1995 STC 191)* had held that the contingency on which the option money was repayable did not fall within what is now *TCGA 1992, ss 48* or *49*. It followed that the position would be different where a contingency did fall within one of those provisions.

**11.66** The abandonment of an option is specifically stated not to be the disposal of an asset (*TCGA 1992, s 144(4)*). Many people felt that this could be used to advantage by a landowner granting an option to an associated person and the developer acquiring the land subject to that option and paying the associated person a substantial sum to abandon his option. However, it was held in *Golding v Kaufman (58 TC 296)* that in the context of *section 144* the meaning of 'abandonment' is limited to the extinction of the option by lapse of time or otherwise than for valuable consideration, and it is not apt to describe the exploitation by the taxpayer of the rights conferred by the option as amounting to its abandonment. Accordingly, the receipt by the associated person would be chargeable to capital gains tax by virtue of *TCGA 1992, s 22* as a capital sum received in return for the surrender of a right.

**11.67** An option binding the grantor to grant a lease for a premium is treated in the same way as an option for a sale even though when the option is granted the interest covered by it does not exist (*TCGA 1992, s 144(6)*). Where a disposal falls through and the vendor forfeits the purchaser's deposit, the forfeited deposit is treated in the same way as option money (*TCGA 1992, s 144(7)*), i.e. there is not a part disposal of the property but the complete disposal of a deemed separate asset – which will have no base cost, so the full amount of the forfeited deposit will be chargeable to CGT.

## Land Held at 31 March 1982

**11.68** Before 6 April 1988 CGT applied to gains accruing after 5 April 1965. For disposals after that date the intention is that only the gain arising since 31 March 1982 should be taxable – and only losses accruing after that date should be deductible. To achieve this the legislation requires two calculations of the gain, one by reference to cost (or 6 April 1965 value if appropriate) and the second by reference to 31 March 1982 value.

1. If both calculations show a gain, the smaller gain is taxable.

2. If both show a loss, the smaller loss is allowable.

3. If one produces a gain and the other a loss, the transaction is treated as giving rise to neither a gain nor a loss.

4. If the sale proceeds are identical to either the cost or the 6 April 1965 value, the transaction is treated as giving rise to neither a gain nor a loss.

(*TCGA 1992, s 35*).

**11.69** As an alternative a taxpayer can make a once and for all election to treat every asset that he held at 31 March 1982 (but not some only) as having been acquired at its market value at that date. The historical cost will not then be relevant to the calculation of the gain. Such a claim could generate allowable losses where the 31 March 1982 value of the land exceeded its cost and it is sold at a loss. The claim must be made by 31 January two years after the end of the tax year in which the first disposal of pre-31 March 1982 assets takes place. For most people this time limit will have passed.

**11.70** Where an asset was disposed of between 1 April 1982 and 1 April 1988 but the gain on disposal was deferred or held over, rebasing will not apply as the asset held at the later date will not be the same asset as that owned at the former. Instead, a special relief applies. Only half of the held-over gain is taxable (*TCGA 1992, Sch 4 para 1*).

**11.71** The rebasing of capital gains tax to 31 March 1982 does not affect indexation. Where land was owned at 31 March 1982 an election could be made under the pre-1988 rules to adopt the value at that date as the basis on which to calculate the indexation allowance (*TCGA 1992, s 55(1)–(6)*). Where a property has been owned for several years this was almost always advantageous. Even where a post-5 April 1988 gain is calculated by reference to cost for the purpose of 11.68 above, the taxpayer still had the option of calculating the indexation by reference to either the 31 March 1982 value or cost if this is more beneficial. An election to adopt the 31 March 1982 value is no longer required, however (*TCGA 1992, s 55(1)(2)*). If the gain itself is calculated by reference to the value at 31 March 1982, the indexation allowance must also be calculated by reference to that value, as the legislation deems the asset to have been acquired on that date.

## Land Held at 6 April 1965

**11.72** Where a gain is calculated by reference to cost and the asset was acquired before 6 April 1965, the gain is normally apportioned on a time basis over the period of ownership, the part apportioned to the period prior to 6 April 1965, when capital gains tax was introduced, not being taxable (*TCGA 1992, Sch 2 para 16*). The taxpayer can instead elect to value the land at 6 April 1965 in which case the whole of the subsequent gain based on that value will be taxable. Such an election must be made within two years after the end of the year of assessment or accounting period in which the disposal occurs and is irrevocable (*TCGA 1992, Sch 2 para 17*). If the election produces a loss and time apportionment produces a gain, the transaction is treated as giving rise to neither a gain or a loss. If the election produces a loss and the calculation by reference to actual cost shows a smaller loss, only that lesser amount is allowable (but it is not reduced by time apportionment) (*TCGA 1992, Sch 2 para 17(2)*).

**11.73** Great care needs to be taken in connection with this election (and with the election for 31 March 1982 valuation referred to in 11.69 above) as, if the District Valuer does not agree with the taxpayer's 1965 valuation, the effect could well be to produce a larger taxable gain than under the time apportionment method – in particular it must be remembered that the asset must be valued as it stood in 1965 and if it was tenanted this could well reduce the value considerably if the tenant had a favourable lease or statutory security of tenure. In *Henderson v Karmel's Exors (58 TC 201)*, Mrs Karmel owned land which she leased under an informal arrangement to a partnership of which she was a partner. She received rent from the partnership. It was contended that the land should be valued at 6 April 1965 on the basis of vacant possession but it was held that all that she had at that date was the reversion in the land expectant on the determination of the tenancy – and as it was an agricultural tenancy this significantly devalued the land. In a Lands Tribunal Case, *Burman v Pembury Property Investment Co Ltd* (Estates Gazette, 21 September 1985), it was mentioned that, although at 6 April 1965 residential tenants had some security of tenure under the *Protection from Eviction Act 1964*, the Bill which became the *Rent Act 1965* was only published a couple of weeks before 6 April 1965 and had not then become law. As the District Valuer in that case assumed an open market rental value, this suggests that the protection to tenants was far less than under the *Rent Acts* – although it is possible that he merely overlooked the point. Where there has been a part disposal since 6 April 1965 and the time apportionment basis was adopted on that part disposal, an election to adopt a 6 April 1965 value cannot be made on a subsequent disposal of the remainder (*TCGA 1992, Sch 2 para 17(5)*).

**11.74** Time apportionment cannot be used on a disposal of land in the UK if the consideration received on the disposal exceeds the current use value at the time of disposal or if any material development of the land was carried out after 17 December 1973 (*TCGA 1992, Sch 2 para 9*). Instead a 6 April 1965 valuation must be adopted (*TCGA 1992, Sch 2 para 9(2)*). If time apportionment was used on a prior part disposal the tax on the part disposal must be recalculated on the valuation basis (*TCGA 1992, Sch 2 para 9(3)*). If the adoption of a 6 April 1965 value gives a greater gain than that over the entire period of ownership the actual gain (but without time apportionment) will be adopted as the chargeable amount instead (*TCGA 1992, Sch 2 para 9(4)*). Similarly, if it would produce a larger loss, only the actual loss is allowable. If it converts an actual gain into a loss, or vice versa, the transaction is treated as giving rise to neither a gain nor a loss. In *Morgan v Gibson (1989 STC 568)* it was held that time apportionment could not be used even if the land had 'hope value' at the time of acquisition so that the development value could not be viewed as an exceptional increase in value.

**11.75** Where time apportionment applies the indexation relief must be deducted to arrive at the gain before time apportionment (*Smith v Schofield (1993 STC 268)*). This is anomalous as the result is part of the indexation (which relates to inflation since 1982) and is deemed to fall before 6 April 1965 so reducing the relief. The House of Lords reached this decision, reversing that of both the Commissioners and the Court of Appeal, with regret!

## Special Reliefs

### Roll-over Relief

**11.76** Land is one of the types of asset that qualify for CGT roll-over relief under *TCGA 1992, s 152*. So does any building or part of a building and any permanent or semi-permanent structure in the nature of a building. In both cases the asset must be both occupied and used only for the purposes of the trade (*TCGA 1992, s 155*). A lessor of tied premises is deemed to occupy (as well as use) those premises only for the purposes of his trade (*TCGA 1992, s 156(4)*). Where the old asset was used for the purpose of the trade for part only of the period of ownership, or part only of the asset was used for the purpose of the trade, fairly common occurrences with property, relief is given on an appropriate proportion of the gain. It was held in *Richart v J Lyons & Co Ltd (1989 STC 665)* that, irrespective of whether or not the gain was calculated by reference to a 6 April 1965 valuation, in calculating the extent of this restriction the use of the properties throughout the actual period of ownership – not just the period from 6 April 1965 – needs to be taken into account. However this decision does not apply for disposals after 5 April 1988 as *TCGA 1992, s 152(9)* now provides that 'period of ownership' is not to include any period before 31 March 1982. Unfortunately claiming roll-over relief can result in a loss of taper relief. This is because it works by reducing both the gain on the old asset (and thus the taper relief on that asset) and the cost of the new. The period of ownership of the old asset is not taken into account in calculating taper relief on the new asset. Accordingly if the old asset was held long enough to achieve full taper it is likely to be preferable to pay a 10% tax charge rather than having to invest the whole proceeds in the business and take the risk that the new asset may not be held for the full taper period (although the two-year holding period is likely to mean that this latter problem will rarely occur as the new asset will normally be a business asset).

**11.77** To qualify for roll-over relief an unconditional contract for the acquisition of the replacement asset must be entered into within one year before or three years after the disposal of the old. The Board, i.e. Somerset House, have power to extend both of these time limits. If it is not possible to acquire the new asset within the statutory period it is obviously sensible to approach the Revenue before the end of the three-year period and ask them to extend the time limit. Some Inspectors of Taxes seem willing to grant an extension, although the author was told by an Inspector that, in spite of Parliament reserving their decision to the Board, they have delegated to local Inspectors the power to grant (but not to refuse) an extension, but that an Inspector can only exercise this power in retrospect. In other words it is not permissible for an Inspector to agree in advance of the purchase of the new asset that he will grant an extension of the statutory period if the purchase has not taken place by the end of that period. If the taxpayer cannot acquire a replacement asset within the three-year period, however valid his reason may be, he must take the risk that when he does acquire it the Revenue may at that stage contend that it was not bought within the statutory period. This is confirmed by the Revenue's Capital Gains Tax Manual which states at para 60644, 'No decision on a possible extension of time limit can be made until the old asset has been disposed of, the new asset has been acquired and all other conditions of relief are satisfied'. If an Inspector wishes to refuse the claim he must, however, refer it to the Board. Provided that they consider that a taxpayer has a good reason for not having met the three-year limit, the Board will normally extend the time limit if the new asset is bought within six years of the disposal of the old. Similarly, it is understood that they will normally extend the period of one year prior to the disposal to three years. It was held in the High Court in *Campbell Connelly & Co Ltd v Barnett (1992 STC 316)* that despite *TCGA 1992, s 28* the acquisition date of the new asset for roll-over relief purposes is the completion date, not the contract date, because the requirement that the asset must be brought into use immediately upon acquisition makes the contract date inappropriate. Although this was not explicitly confirmed by the Court of Appeal decision (*1994 STC 50*) it is implicit in the judgment there. It seems likely that the requirement that the disposal proceeds must be reinvested would similarly require the use of the completion date for the disposal.

**11.78** Strictly speaking, if a person sells an asset and uses the proceeds to improve an existing property, roll-over relief is not due, as he will not have used the sale proceeds to acquire an asset. By concession, the Revenue will allow roll-over relief in such circumstances (Inland Revenue Extra-Statutory Concession D22). Relief will also be given for the cost of land on which the trader intends to erect a building, even though in such circumstances the asset is not immediately brought into use for the purposes of the trade, provided that the building work is carried out expeditiously and the building is brought into use for the purposes of the trade on completion (Inland Revenue Extra-Statutory Concession D24). In *Steibelt v Paling (1999 STC 594)* Sir Richard Scott V-C questioned whether D24 is a concession at all. He felt it merely the Revenue's view of the interpretation of *TCGA 1992, s 152(1)*. Accordingly the Commissioners were entitled to substitute their own views for those of the Revenue on whether the D24 tests are met. Similarly, roll-over relief will be allowed if the proceeds from the old asset are used to acquire the freehold reversion of a property of which the trader already owns the lease (Inland Revenue Extra-Statutory Concession D25). In *Watton v Tippett (1997 STC 893)* it was held that the gain on sale of half of a building could not be rolled over on to improvements to the other half, and in *Milton v Chivers (1995 Sp C 57)*, where a property was bought in anticipation of one trade and when it proved unsuitable was used for a different trade which was started 11 months after the acquisition of the building, it was held that there was not the necessary proximity between the acquisition of the building and the commencement of its use in the trade. If land is partitioned on the dissolution of a partnership it can be treated as a new asset of an individual partner provided that the partnership is dissolved immediately after the partition (Inland Revenue Extra-Statutory Concession D23). It is understood that the Revenue look for reinvestment of the net sale proceeds only and are also prepared to treat the acquisition expenses of the new asset as part of the cost of that asset for roll-over purposes. It appears that the Revenue are prepared to treat a building as a separate asset from the land on which it stands for roll-over relief purposes (Taxline, Issue 10). This can be useful if only part of the proceeds are reinvested; the reinvested part may exceed the value of one of these elements on its own. There does not appear to be any legal basis for this treatment as *TCGA 1992, s 155* does not contain an equivalent provision to *section 24(3)* and *section 152(5)* clearly envisages a building including the land on which it stands.

*New Assets which are Depreciating Assets*

**11.79** Where the new asset is a depreciating asset, i.e. one with a predictable life of 60 years or less such as a short lease, the gain on the old asset is held over for a maximum of ten years or until earlier disposal; it does not reduce the cost of the depreciating asset (*TCGA 1992, s 154*). An effect of this provision in the case of a trade carried on by an individual is that the capital gains tax exemption on death will not apply to the gain as the asset is not deemed to be disposed of on death; that is simply the trigger for the tax charge. However, by concession, the Revenue will treat the death as eliminating the held over gain (ESC D45). The Revenue have also said that even though *TCGA 1992, s 155* treats land and buildings as separate assets they regard a building constructed on leasehold land where the lease has less than 60 years to run as a depreciating asset. Conversely, where plant or machinery has become part of a building which is itself not a depreciating asset that plant will not be a depreciating asset either. Whether machinery has become part of a building will depend on the size and nature of the item, how it has become attached to the building and whether it can be removed without damage to the fabric of the building (Tax Bulletin, Issue 7).

*Replacement of Business Assets by Members of a Group*

**11.80** In *Temperley v Visibell Ltd (49 TC 129)* a company bought a site on which to build a factory but later sold it and bought another site. It was held that relief was not due as it had never been used and occupied for the purposes of the trade. It was irrelevant that it had been bought with the intention of so using it if that intention never came to fruition. An important case is *Campbell Connelly & Co Ltd v Barnett (1994 STC 50)*. A subsidiary company sold the lease of its trading premises in 1984 and moved into its parent's trading premises. In January 1986 the company bought the freehold of another property as its new trading premises. Although the intention had been to buy the property with vacant possession, at the time of completion it was subject to a lease to A Ltd and an underlease to B Ltd. In September 1986 the parent company acquired B Ltd's underlease, and the subsidiary went into possession of the property. The contract date for both acquisitions was 13 December 1985. It was held that no roll-over relief was due. The subsidiary did not bring its freehold interest immediately into use for its trade on acquisition in January 1986; it was being used to generate rental income from it. It alternatively sought to argue that its acquisition of the freehold and its parent's acquisition of the underlease were together the acquisition of the new asset, and the eight-month gap should be ignored. The judge in the High Court felt that, although *TCGA 1992, s 175(1)* provides that for roll-over relief purposes all the trades carried on by members of a group must be treated as a single trade, as a matter of construction it could not be inferred from this that all members of a group should be treated as a single person. Accordingly, it was not permissible to treat two transactions by different legal entities as a single combined transaction. This reasoning was not referred to in the Court of Appeal decision which merely said that the acquisition by the parent was not out of the consideration obtained by the subsidiary for the disposal but presumably from its own resources. The judge probably meant no more by this than that an acquisition by one company could not be treated as having been made by another. In any event the Revenue said that if necessary retrospective legislation would be introduced to ensure that the Revenue's practice of allowing roll-over relief, where one trading company in a group makes a disposal and a different trading company makes the acquisition, continues to have effect (Inland Revenue Press Release, 15 September 1992). As there has been no such legislation one assumes that the Revenue have decided that their practice reflects the law.

*Roll-over Relief Not Available*

**11.81** Land or buildings cannot qualify for roll-over relief where the trade is a trade of dealing or developing land unless the profit on sale would not form part of the trading profits, i.e. roll-over relief is due if the property is a fixed asset but not if it is trading stock (*TCGA 1992, s 156(2)(a)(3)*). It also cannot qualify for roll-over relief where the trade is one of providing services for the occupier of land in which the person carrying on the trade has an estate or interest (*TCGA 1992, s 156(2)(b)*). However, it is understood that the Revenue accept that the relief can be claimed by the owner of a caravan site. Roll-over relief does not normally apply to non-trading companies but is extended to certain not-for-profit bodies by *TCGA 1992, s 158* and Extra-Statutory Concession D15. Where additional consideration is received on the grant of planning permission and the *Marren v Ingles* principle applies (see 11.15) that additional consideration does not derive from an interest in land and thus does not qualify for roll-over relief.

*Roll-over relief on incorporation of a business*

**11.82** A different form of roll-over relief applies where an individual, partnership, trust or other unincorporated entity transfers to a company a business as a going concern, together with the whole of the assets of the business (other than cash) wholly or partly in exchange for shares issued by the company to the person transferring the business (*TCGA 1992, s 162*). On a transfer wholly for shares the chargeable gains less allowable losses on the disposal of the assets is not charged to tax but is instead deducted from the cost of the shares, which will be their market value at the time of their issue. If the net gains exceed that cost the balance is of course taxed at the time of the incorporation. Where the transfer is partly for shares and partly for some other consideration, only the appropriate proportion of the net gains is deducted from the share element and the proportion attributed to the non-share element remains taxable. If the company takes over liabilities of the business as well as its assets the Revenue do not regard the assumption of those liabilities as constituting 'other consideration' (ESC D32).

**11.83** This treatment applied automatically up to 2001/02. This sometimes created a problem with taper relief (see 11.5). As the incorporation is treated as a disposal the acquisition of the shares starts a new taper period so the shares need to be held for two years (previously four) to obtain full business asset taper relief or for ten years to obtain non-business asset taper relief. The period of ownership of the business cannot be aggregated with that of the ownership of the shares. To avoid this problem, where the transfer of the business occurs after 5 April 2002 an election can be made to disapply *section 162*. The effect of disapplying it is to crystallise the gains on the disposal of the business but to obtain taper relief on that disposal by reference to the periods of ownership of each of the individual assets. If the two-year taper period applies to the shares it is normally not worth electing – particularly as the taxpayer can adopt a wait and see policy. The election has to be made by the second anniversary of the 31 January next, following the tax year in which the assessment takes place (*TCGA 1992, s 162A(3)(4)*). For a disposal in 2002/03, this means that the election must be made by 31 January 2006. If all of the shares are disposed of (other than to a spouse) in the year of assessment following the transfer of the business, the time limit is reduced by a year, i.e. to 31 January 2005 as in the above example. Accordingly by the time the election needs to be made the taxpayer will either have disposed of the shares or will have held them for over two years, and so will be able to calculate whether or not the election is worthwhile.

**11.84** The word 'business' is wider than 'trade' so *section 162* is not limited to the incorporation of a trading activity. The Revenue say, 'It is a question of fact whether a particular activity constitutes a business. It is not easy to draw the line, but we would resist claims that the passive holding of investments or an investment property amounted to a business' (Capital Gains Manual para 65713). In *American Leaf Blending Co Sdn Bhd v Director General of Inland Revenue (1978 STC 561)*, Lord Diplock said, 'In the case of a private individual, it may well be that the mere receipt of rents from property that he owns raises no presumption that he is carrying on a business', but as that case involved a company that was no more than an aside as the judges were not called on to address the position of an individual. The inheritance tax cases considered at 18.25 onwards are of no help as with inheritance tax, a business is not relevant business property if it consists mainly of making or holding investments – although this certainly infers that holding investments can constitute a business at least in some circumstances. The mere holding of investments has been held to constitute a business for VAT purposes, but as VAT is a European tax it is probably unwise to assume that the courts will regard those cases as relevant to capital gains tax.

**11.85** The ownership and renting of a large number of investment properties is likely to constitute a business if the proprietor (or, probably, his agent) is actively involved either in managing the properties or in searching for new properties. It is difficult to guess either the minimum number of properties that is likely to constitute a business or how much involvement is needed to constitute active involvement.

## Retirement Relief

**11.86** The existence of capital gains tax retirement relief under *TCGA 1992, s 163* and *s 164* also needs to be borne in mind in appropriate circumstances although this relief is being phased out and will cease entirely for disposals after 5 April 2003. To qualify for such relief the taxpayer must dispose of a business or part of a business, normally at a time when he is 50 or over. The *Act* gives no guidance as to the meaning of a business. However, as the relief on the disposal of shares in a personal company is limited to trading companies it seems probable that it will be interpreted to cover only trades, professions and vocations.

This was one of the issues in *Hatt v Newman (2000 STC 113)* but sadly this was a taxpayer in person who did not appreciate the issue and the judge did not address it. Indeed he simply said:

'So far as the business of letting furnished rooms is concerned . . . as Vinelott J said in *Griffiths v Jackson (1983 STC 184)* [(see 2.125)] . . . the principle that the letting of furnished rooms, while it may be a business, is not a trade, is "now too deeply embedded in the law to be altered except by legislation". In my judgment . . . Mr Hatt's appeal must fail.'

The Special Commissioners said:

'In relation to his claim for retirement relief, Mr Hatt has contended that the property was an asset of his business and that the lettings were a business activity. Whilst that may be so, there is ample authority to show that the business of letting furnished rooms is not a trade.'

As both recognised that Mr Hatt was carrying on a business, which is what is referred to in *TCGA 1992, s 163*, it is unfortunate that neither sought to address why they believed that 'business' in that section could not be given its normal meaning but must be limited to a trade.

It has been held that the sale of a field by a farmer who continued to farm on the bulk of the land was not the sale of part of a business. It was merely the sale of an asset of the business and did not qualify for relief (*McGregor v Adcock (51 TC 692)*). This decision was followed in *Mannion v Johnston (61 TC 598)* where Mr Johnston sold almost half of his farm and evidence was given that the reason was that he had become too infirm to continue the business on the same scale as before. While indicating that he did not feel the *McGregor v Adcock* decision was wholly satisfactory, the judge felt that he was bound by it. As he reversed the decision of the Commissioners it is clear that whether or not there has been a disposal of part of a business is a question of law, not one of fact or degree. If a farmer is still carrying on a business of farming after the sale he is unlikely to qualify for relief. These decisions suggest that a sale of one shop out of several would not be the sale of part of a business either – although it is worth bearing in mind in such a case that the Revenue have in the past generally sought to establish that the opening of a new shop is a separate business for Schedule D purposes, not the expansion of the existing business. In *Plumbly and others v Spencer (1999 STC 677)* the taxpayer was a full-time director and shareholder of a family business which paid him rent for the use of his land. On reaching the age of 60, the taxpayer disposed of his land and the company ceased to trade. The Court of Appeal held that full retirement relief was due as the land had been held for the purpose of a business carried on by the taxpayer's personal company. They were puzzled by the inter-relationship between what is now *TCGA 1992, ss 163* and *164* but felt that this would not affect the outcome of the appeal. *Section 164(6)* specifically grants retirement relief for assets held outside the business and sold in an associated disposal but *TCGA 1992, Sch 6 para 10(1)(c)* restricts the relief where rent was paid by the business for the use of the assets. It is odd that this restriction which would arise on a sale of a trading company can apparently be circumvented by the trading company simply becoming dormant and being retained.

**11.87** Notwithstanding the general rule that for capital gains tax purposes the disposal date is the time of the contract, the Revenue practice is to adopt the completion date for calculating retirement relief provided that there is not an undue delay between contract and completion.

**11.88** It should not be overlooked that where shares in a personal company or a partnership interest are sold retirement relief can also be given for the gain on an associated disposal of assets used for the purpose of the company or partnership business. The associated disposal must take place as part of the withdrawal of the individual concerned from participation in the company or partnership business, and immediately before the disposal of the shares or partnership interest (or the earlier cessation of the business) the asset must have been in use for the purposes of that business (*TCGA 1992, s 164(6)(7)*). This relief can apply in particular where a property used in the business is owned personally by the shareholder or partner. It was held in *Clarke v Mayo (1994 STC 570)* that the words 'immediately before' in this context can legitimately be construed as meaning 'sufficiently proximate in time to the material disposal or cessation so as to justify the conclusion that the transaction in question formed part of it'. In that case the contract for the sale of the property (the associated disposal) was ten weeks before the cessation of the business, completion was four weeks before the cessation, and the sale of the shares took place a year after the cessation. It was nevertheless accepted that the sale of the property qualified for relief.

**11.89** If there is a significant gap between sales of assets, the taxpayer will have difficulty in attracting relief – although he did so in *Jarmin v Rawlings (1994 STC 1005)*. Mr Rawlings was a dairy farmer owning 64 acres of land, farm buildings and a herd of 34 cows. He decided to give up dairy farming. In October 1988 he sold at auction his milking parlour and yard – an area of approximately 1.2 acres. Between then and completion of the sale in January 1989 he sold 14 cows. The remaining 20 were transferred to his wife's family farm for calving, and most were resold by the end of 1989. He had no financial interest in their milk after the transfer. Following the sale Mr Rawlings continued farming on the remaining land by rearing and finishing store cattle. This was far less labour-intensive. He was able to make his farm labourer redundant and halve his own working time. He retained, and leased out, his milk quota because he was advised that a sale would reduce the value of the land. The judge held that what had to be identified was the business. In this case it was the production and sale of milk. The Commissioners were entitled to hold that this was a different business to the rearing and finishing of store cattle. It made no difference that all the assets of the dairy farming business had not been sold; the key thing was that the activity had ceased. He also expressed the view that the reference in the legislation to the disposal of a business could not be intended to mean a capital gains tax disposal. Accordingly it was not necessary to look only at what had been disposed of at the time of the auction; related transactions (albeit with different people) should also be taken into account, although events subsequent to completion probably could not.

**11.90** The taxpayer was less fortunate in *Wase v Bourke (1996 STC 18)*. Mr Bourke decided to give up dairy farming. He sold his entire dairy herd at market value in March 1988. He retained a few young cattle which were fattened up and then sold. In February 1989 he sold his milk quota. He did not do so earlier as it was partly used up at the time he sold his herd whereas in 1989 it was 'clean' and therefore more valuable. The farm had become an arable farm and was being farmed by the taxpayer's wife. It was agreed that the dairy business had ceased to be carried on in March 1988. As the taxpayer was under 60 at that time relief was due only if in February 1989 he had disposed of all or part of his business. It was held that the business was the production and sale of milk and that had ceased in March 1988. Accordingly what was being sold a year later was simply an asset which had formerly been used in the business. The cessation of the farming and the later sale of the milk quota could not properly be described as amounting to a single transaction. Accordingly no relief was due.

**11.91** The decision in *Barrett v Powell (1998 STC 283)* illustrates that great care may be needed where the business will not cease immediately. Mr Powell farmed 326 acres of land, 100 of which he owned, 136 which he leased from Milton Keynes Development Corp and 90 which he licenced from the Corporation. In March 1991 the Corporation paid him to surrender his lease but allowed him to continue farming the land under licence until they needed it. They terminated the licence in September 1991. Mr Powell continued to farm his 100 acres for another year and then ceased. The surrender of the lease was held to be the disposal of an asset of the business as the farming continued unchanged before and after that date. It is likely that retirement relief would have been granted if instead of surrendering the lease in 1990 Mr Powell had agreed to do so when called upon and the surrender had taken place in September 1991. A similar result was reached in *Purves v Harrison (2001 STC 267)*. Mr Harrison wished to dispose of his coach and minibus business. He could not find a purchaser at an acceptable price. In October 1989 he was approached by MPK Garages Ltd, which owned a neighbouring site, and asked whether he was prepared to sell the premises. He did so in anticipation of selling the business to another purchaser. That sale fell through and MPK allowed the business to remain in occupation on an informal licence. Mr Harrison was eventually able to sell the business in November 1990. It was held that the two sales could not in any real sense be regarded as a single disposal of the business. 'A continuing intention to dispose of the premises along with the remainder of the assets cannot alone suffice to create a sufficient connection between the two where, as here, the two disposals are to different persons and are separated by so many months.'

**11.92** Retirement relief is being phased out and ceases on 5 April 2003. The maximum relief for 2002/03 is an exemption of the first £50,000 of gains with only half of the next £150,000 being taxed.

## Reinvestment Relief

**11.93** Capital gains realised by individuals can be rolled-over by reinvesting the gain in eligible shares in a qualifying unquoted trading company (*TCGA 1992, Sch 5B*). The relief can also be claimed by a settlement where either an interest in possession is held by an individual (or a charity) or all of the beneficiaries are individuals (or charities) (*TCGA 1992, Sch 5B para 17*). Unlike with roll-over relief it is not necessary to reinvest the entire proceeds; it is only necessary to reinvest the gain and where not all the gain is reinvested relief can be claimed proportionate to the part of the gain reinvested. The full relief does not have to be claimed; the taxpayer can roll over a lesser amount, leaving a chargeable gain to utilise losses or his annual exemption. Eligible shares means shares forming part of the company's ordinary share capital other than any which carry a present or future preferential right to dividends, to redemption or to assets on a winding-up (*TCGA 1992, s 164N*). The effect on taper relief also needs to be borne in mind. The problem is the same as with roll-over relief (see 11.76) but may be less acute as reinvestment relief can apply to gains on non-business assets whereas roll-over relief cannot do so. This does not apply where the old asset is shares that themselves qualified for EIS reinvestment relief. In that case the period of ownership of the old shares is added to that of the new to ascertain the taper relief due when the new shares are sold (*TCGA 1992, Sch 5BA para 3*).

**11.94** Initially a company could not be a qualifying company if interests in land held by it exceeded 50% of the greater of its chargeable assets or its total assets but this provision does not apply to acquisitions after 28 November 1994 (*TCGA 1992, s 164A(13)* – now repealed). However, companies whose business consists primarily of certain specified property related activities are still not qualifying companies. These proscribed activities are

(*a*) property development,

(*b*) farming and market gardening,

(*c*) holding, managing or occupying woodland and other forestry activities or timber production,

(*d*) operating or managing hotels or comparable establishments or managing property used as a hotel or comparable establishment,

(*e*) operating or managing nursing homes or residential care homes or managing property used as a nursing home or residential care home.

(*ICTA 1988, s 297(2)(fa) – (fe)* and *TCGA 1992, Sch 5B para 19*). Prior to 16 March 1998 the only property related exclusion was a company (or group) whose trade (or a substantial part of it) consisted in dealing in land. However, the Revenue did not regard a trade of property development as excluded by this provision. Unfortunately the distinction between property development (for sale of the completed buildings, as investment does not in any event qualify) and property dealing is often hard to discern. A distinction has not traditionally been drawn between the two as they are taxed in the same way. Clearly, buying a property and reselling it in the same state is dealing. Equally clearly, buying a plot of land, erecting a building on it and selling it is development. The problem is where work is done on an existing building. Carrying out redecorations before reselling will not constitute development; gutting the building and reconstructing the interior will clearly do so. But where is the dividing line to be drawn? This is undoubtedly a question of fact and degree to be considered in relation to each individual building. If there are no structural alterations there is probably no development. If there are and this results in a different building, such as building a major extension or converting a house into two flats, that is probably development. The VAT cases on what is a new building (see 8.64 onwards) may be helpful as anything that results in the creation of such a building is almost certainly development. On the other hand it needs to be remembered that for VAT purposes a conversion, reconstruction or enlargement is statutorily prevented from resulting in a new building but such operations are normally likely to constitute development for reinvestment relief purposes.

## Miscellaneous

**11.95** A grant payable to an individual by virtue of a scheme under *Agriculture Act 1967, s 27* to give up occupation of an uncommercial unit is not to be treated for CGT purposes as part of the consideration accruing on the disposal of any asset (*TCGA 1992, s 249*). It is accordingly not liable to CGT.

**11.96** It has been held by the courts that statutory compensation for disturbance under the *Agricultural Holdings Act 1948 (Davis v Powell (51 TC 492))* or on the termination of a tenancy under the *Landlord and Tenant Act 1954* (*Drummond v Austin Brown (58 TC 67)*) is not a capital sum derived from the lease or received in return for the surrender of rights. It derives from the statute, not from the lease. It is accordingly not within the scope of CGT. The dicta in the *Austin Brown* judgment make clear that the exemption applies only to the statutory compensation. If the tenant receives a capital sum to surrender his lease to his landlord this will be taxable. In *Davis v Henderson (1995 Sp C 46)* the landlord served a statutory notice to quit after which the tenant entered into negotiation with him and agreed to vacate on payment of the statutory compensation of £455,180 under the *Agricultural Holdings Act 1986* plus an amount of £520,000 additional compensation for giving early vacant possession. Mr Davis accepted that the £520,000 was taxable but disputed the £455,180, which had been calculated under the statutory formula. The Special Commissioners held that the tenancy was terminated 'by reason of' the notice to quit and he vacated the premises 'in consequence of' that notice. Accordingly the £455,180 was statutory compensation and exempt from tax. It should particularly be noted that Mr Davis insisted on service of the statutory notice to quit before starting negotiations and that he did not agree a single overall figure but accepted the statutory compensation provided he was separately compensated for early vacation. The Revenue have announced both that they do not intend to appeal this decision and that they accept that the decision in *Davis v Powell (51 TC 492)* applies to compensation for tenants' improvements under the *Agricultural Holdings Act 1986, s 64* or the *Agricultural Tenancies Act 1995, s 16*. They also accept that the surrender of a business tenancy before it comes to an end does not prevent the compensation being payable under the *Landlord and Tenant Act 1954, s 37* (Tax Bulletin Number 22, April 1996). If, following the expiry of a lease, the landlord serves a notice to quit and, to save time, the tenant agrees to accept a single payment in excess of the statutory compensation it may well be that the entire amount paid by the landlord, not merely that excess, will still be chargeable to CGT as consideration for the surrender of a right. In *Pennine Raceway Ltd v Kirklees Metropolitan Borough Council (1989 STC 122)* it was held that compensation under what is now the *Town and Country Planning Act 1990, s 107* on the revocation of planning permission was liable to capital gains tax. The value of the asset in question, Pennine's licence to use a racetrack, depreciated following the withdrawal of planning permission, and it was entitled to compensation in respect of that depreciation. Accordingly, in such circumstances the compensation derived from the asset, not from the statute and was caught under *TCGA 1992, s 22(1)*.

**11.97** In calculating the consideration for the disposal of an asset for CGT purposes any money or money's worth charged to income tax as income of the person making the disposal is normally excluded (*TCGA 1992, s 37(1)*). There are two exceptions, both of which affect property. A balancing charge or an amount brought into account as disposal value of machinery or plant is not excluded – as the taxable amount merely claws back prior income or corporation tax allowances (*TCGA 1992, s 37(2)*). Secondly, where an asset is disposed of in consideration of a rentcharge or a ground annual, the capitalised value of the rent charge or ground annual – or of any other right to a series of payments in the nature of income – must be treated as consideration for the disposal even though the income will be taxed as it is received (*TCGA 1992, s 37(3)*) It is not clear what 'charged to income tax means', i.e. whether the Revenue can choose to assess the amount to capital gains tax rather than income tax, provided that they have not previously raised an assessment, or whether they cannot include the amount in a capital gains tax computation if it is within the scope of (or charge to) income tax.

**11.98** Where capital allowances have been claimed in respect of an asset and there is a CGT loss on disposal, it is restricted by the amount of the capital allowances (less any balancing charge) (*TCGA 1992, s 41*). This is reasonable, as the taxpayer will have had relief for the loss against income by virtue of the allowances. The effect is that a CGT loss cannot in practice arise on such assets, as even if the sale price is less than the written-down value a balancing allowance will arise rather than a capital gains tax loss.

**11.99** Freehold land cannot be a wasting asset for CGT purposes whatever its nature and whatever the nature of the buildings or works on it (*TCGA 1992, s 44(1)(a)*). This is in the taxpayer's interest, as only part of the cost of a wasting asset is deductible for CGT purposes.

**11.100** If, on a sale at arm's length, the vendor grants a loan to the purchaser of all or part of the proceeds, and as a result of the purchaser's default on that loan the vendor repossesses the asset, he can elect to treat the gain on the sale as being limited to the amount actually received from the purchaser (less incidental costs of the disposal). The computation of the gain or loss on a later disposal will be made by reference to the original cost and date of acquisition of the asset (Inland Revenue Extra-Statutory Concession D18). In other words, if the part of the proceeds actually received is less than the gain calculated by reference to the full proceeds, the taxpayer can opt to be taxed on the sum received (less incidental selling expenses) with no deduction for any part of the cost, leaving the cost to be relieved when the asset is resold. Property is of course the most common example of the type of asset where, in order to facilitate a sale, the vendor may agree to leave part of the purchase price on loan secured on the asset.

**11.101** Where a mortgagee enforces his mortgage in any other circumstances, the CGT position will depend on whether or not he formally forecloses. If he does so the foreclosure results in the mortgagee taking the property in satisfaction of his debt. In such circumstances, if the mortgage debt is a chargeable asset he is treated as disposing of the debt and acquiring the property for the lesser of the amount of the mortgage outstanding and the market value of the property at the time of the foreclosure. This will be the base cost of the property on a subsequent sale. If the debt was not a chargeable asset he is (in effect) treated as acquiring the property for a sum equal to the greater of the market value of the property and the amount of the mortgage outstanding (*TCGA 1992, s 251(3)*). Foreclosure is a comparatively rare occurrence. What usually happens is that the mortgagee sells the property as agent for the borrower, accounting to him for any surplus and looking to him to make good from other sources any shortfall. In such circumstances the mortgagee is treated as selling the property as a nominee for the borrower (*TCGA 1992, s 26(2)*). The capital gains tax liability on the sale will then be a liability of the borrower, not of the mortgagee who actually sells the property to enforce his security.

**11.102** If two people own two interests in land jointly, a division of interests with one taking the entire interest in one plot and the other the entire interest in the second results in a disposal by each of his half interest in one in consideration of receiving the half interest in the other. Where such an exchange of interests takes place after

19 December 1984 the Revenue allow a form of extra-statutory roll-over relief. (Inland Revenue Extra-Statutory Concession D26). Each joint owner must become the sole owner of part of the land. If, for example, two plots of land are held jointly by three people and one takes one plot leaving the others jointly owning the second, the concession would not apply to any of them – even the one who becomes a sole owner. It will apply where there are more than two joint owners provided that each ends up as the sole owner of one of the joint interests. The relief takes the same form as that provided by *TCGA 1992, ss 247, 248* (see 11.54–11.59 above). The concession will not apply if the property of which a person becomes the sole owner is a dwelling-house which qualifies for the private residence exemption, unless one of the properties concerned is the principal residence of one of the joint owners and the second is the principal residence of the other. From 29 October 1987 the concession also applies to a parallel exchange of interests in milk or potato quotas associated with the land. For the purpose of the concession a married couple is treated as a single person.

**11.103** It may be that there is a statutory way to achieve the same result. In *Jenkins v Brown (1989 STC 577)* six individuals each owned a farm. They conveyed the farms to trustees to be held for their joint benefit. As a result of the transfer each had an undivided unequal percentage share in the trust fund equal to the value of the farm he had put in. (It had previously been held in *Booth v Ellard (53 TC 393)* that putting property into such a pooling arrangement did not give rise to a disposal of the individual assets.) Subsequently three of the individuals took their farms out of the pool. It was held that this did not give rise to a disposal either. Whilst this decision is logical it was not based on the premise that there had never been a disposal of the beneficial interest in the farms, but rather that 'the measure of the beneficial interests of the settlors remained unaffected by the trust' as it was accepted that all of the farms had increased in value at the same rate whilst they were in the trust. It seems from this decision that if A has a property, Whiteacre, worth £100,000 and B has a property, Blackacre, worth £80,000 and £20,000 in cash, and they wish to exchange the properties, there would be no capital gains tax disposal if they enter into a pooling agreement covering both properties and the cash, and then dissolve the pool by B taking out Whiteacre and A the other assets.

**11.104** The Special Commissioners decided in *Cottle v Coldicott (1995 Sp C 40)* that milk quota is a separate asset from the land so that a disposal of such quota separate from the land is not a part disposal of the land. Quota acquired on the introduction of the scheme in 1984 has a nil base cost. Significance was attached to the fact that the quota was allocated by relation to a holding not to any particular parcel of land in that holding and that to treat a holding as an asset for capital gains tax purposes would cause a great many problems. It was also relevant that the taxpayer had claimed that the asset was the land and had sold the milk quota separate from leasing the land. The Special Commissioner decided that milk quota was an incorporeal asset separate from the land although it was normally required to be transferred with the land. He also held that it did not derive from the land.

# Business Occupation of Property

**12.1** The occupier of property needs to consider tax in four main areas – he wants a deduction for rent and similar payments of consideration for the use of the property; he wants a deduction for repairs; he wants to obtain allowances in relation to any capital expenditure he incurs on the property; and he needs to know whether, and how, receipts he obtains from his landlord – for example for a surrender or a variation of his lease or to induce him to take a lease – are taxable.

**12.2** Capital allowances are considered in chapter 10. A person who occupies property for the purpose of his business obtains relief for capital allowances by treating them as a deduction in arriving at his trading profit for tax purposes. Prior to 1997/98, for income tax purposes the allowances were deducted separately from the tax-adjusted trading profits (except where the trade commenced after 5 April 1994). If the capital allowances create or enhance a loss, that loss is relievable in the same way as any other trading loss. Reverse premiums are considered at 3.51 above.

## Relief for Rent, etc

**12.3** Rent of business premises will normally satisfy the requirement of being wholly and exclusively incurred for the purposes of the tenant's trade and will be deductible in the same way as any other trading expense. There are, however, two possible problem areas. The first is where the lease is entered into in the course of a trade but at the time that a payment of rent is made the premises are no longer being used for trading purposes. The second is where there has been a sale and leaseback of the premises or some similar transaction.

**12.4** Surprisingly, quite a number of cases have come before the courts on the deductibility of rent payable for a period after the premises have ceased to be used for business purposes, and on the treatment of a payment made to get rid of a lease which is no longer needed for the lessee's trade. In *CIR v Falkirk Iron Co Ltd (17 TC 625)*, the company leased a warehouse which became surplus to requirements. It could not find anyone to take over the lease but was able to sublet part of the premises. It was held that the difference between the rent paid and the rent received under the sublease was an allowable deduction against the company's trading profits. At the time the company moved out, the lease had about 2½ years unexpired, so the obligation to continue to pay the rent was of a comparatively short duration. In *Hyett v Lennard (23 TC 346)*, a trader took a 35-year lease of a shop in Oxford Street but closed the branch down after six years because it was unprofitable. He was able to sublet the premises for the remaining 29 years of the term but at a figure £1,000 below the rent which he had contracted to pay. It was held that the £1,000 difference was an allowable business expense in computing the profits of his trade, even though that particular branch had ceased.

**12.5** The issue in *Herbert Smith v Honour (1999 STC 173)* was the timing of the deduction. The taxpayer, a firm of solicitors, occupied four separate offices. In January 1990 it leased new premises in which to house the entire firm. It moved the staff to those premises in December 1990. It was still however committed to pay rent under the four old leases. In its accounts to 30 April 1990 it made a provision for the difference between the rents payable on the old premises for the entire unexpired period of the lease (one had 16 years unexpired) less the amount that it estimated it could generate by subletting the buildings. In subsequent years it reviewed the provision and as a result increased it. The Revenue accepted that accounting principles required the provision to be made but they contended that there was a rule of tax law which prohibited the anticipation of losses. This was rejected by the court which said that the overriding legal rule is what is the full amount of the profits for the year and, in general, accounts prepared in accordance with accepted principles of commercial accountancy are the guide to the amount of such profits. A supposed rule against anticipation of liabilities would be inconsistent with that basic principle. The Revenue proposed to appeal the decision but subsequently abandoned their position and accepted that there is no tax rule against the anticipation of losses. Such a provision is probably no longer allowable following the introduction of FRS 12 (see 12.44).

**12.6** It is apparent from these cases that there is normally no difficulty where the rent continues to be paid. Problems arise, however, where a tenant who no longer requires business premises makes a payment to rid himself of the lease rather than continue paying the rent. Normally a lump sum paid to rid oneself of an onerous contract is a revenue expense if the payments which would have had to be made under the contract would have been deductible (*Anglo-Persian Oil Co Ltd v Dale (16 TC 253)*). However, the courts have been reluctant to apply this principle to rent and have striven to attribute a capital nature to such payments. Thus where a company paid its landlord a lump sum to induce him to take a surrender of its lease of a coal seam, the Court of Appeal held that the payment was capital as it was to get rid of a fixed capital asset, the lease, rather than to rid the company of the onerous burden of having to continue to make the rental payments (*Mallett v Staveley Coal & Iron Co Ltd (13 TC 772)*). In *Cowcher v Richard Mills & Co Ltd (13 TC 216)*, a retail company closed a shop in 1916. The landlord agreed to accept a surrender of the lease in consideration of the tenant paying £1,812 in annual instalments of £250 – which would take eight years to pay, a period longer than the unexpired term of the lease. After it had paid 4½ instalments the company made a single payment of £600 in satisfaction of the balance of £687 payable under the instalment arrangement. The Revenue contended that the £600 was a capital payment. Rowlatt J thought that the Revenue had been wrong to allow a deduction for the £250 p.a. and that the entire amount was capital following the *Staveley Coal* case. A payment to secure the cancellation of a 40-year lease with 10 years unexpired was similarly held to be capital (*Union Cold Storage Co Ltd v Ellerker (22 TC 547)*). A capital payment to terminate a licence of a speedway stadium was also held to be capital as the licence, which at the time had five years to run, was a capital asset (*Dain v Auto Speedways Ltd (38 TC 525)*). In *West African Drug Co Ltd v Lilley (28 TC 140)* the business premises were destroyed by an earthquake when the lease had 12 years unexpired. The lessor claimed that not only was the company obliged to pay rent for the following 12 years but it also had an obligation to restore the premises. Even without the *Staveley Coal* decision it is likely that the obligation to rebuild would have been fatal to the claim, which was rejected by the court, that the payment by the company to rid itself of the lease was revenue. The payment to surrender a 10-year lease was similarly held to be capital in *Bullrun Inc v Inspector of Taxes (2000 STC (SCD) 384) (SpC 248)*.

**12.7** The moral is clearly that a taxpayer should seek to sublet his business premises if they become surplus to requirements rather than try to surrender or assign the lease. Although no cases have come before the courts on the specific point, it would seem from the decision in *Hyett v Lennard* that the shortfall of rent paid over rent received would be a trading expense even if a premium is taken under the sublease – although part of that premium would of course be taxable under the Schedule A provisions (3.2 above). An interesting question is what happens if the tenant assigns the lease and the assignee subsequently defaults, a fairly common occurrence in recent years. The landlord will look to the assignor for the rent, under the doctrine of privity of contract. Rent payments by the assignor thereafter undoubtedly qualify for relief under the *Hyett v Lennard* principle albeit that any sum received from the assignee on the assignment was a capital receipt.

**12.8** Difficulties can also arise with service charge payments if these include a contribution to a reserve fund. The main forms that service charge arrangements can take are considered in 2.100 above. If the service charge is payable as additional rent or under a covenant in the lease there should be no problem in the business tenant obtaining a deduction. If the reserve fund element is payable to trustees (or to the landlord as trustee), that payment is probably a capital payment for which the tenant is not entitled to a deduction. This is arguable, however. The payment can be said to be wholly and exclusively incurred for the purpose of giving the tenant the right to occupy the building, as it is something that he is obliged to pay under his lease to remain in occupation of the premises. Accordingly, whilst the payment is a capital receipt of the trust, it may nevertheless be revenue expenditure from the tenant's point of view. It probably depends on whether the tenant has a solely revenue motive (to continue to occupy the premises) or if part of his motive is that the reserve fund contribution will relieve him of future expenditure. If a management company is used which is a mutual trading company the tenant is almost certainly entitled to claim a deduction for the full service charge including the reserve fund element. The allowability of payments to a mutual trading company does not seem to have come before the courts but it seems implicit in *ICTA 1988, s 491* that a trader will be entitled to a deduction for such payments.

**12.9** A premium paid to obtain a renewal of a lease is, of course, capital, even if, in theory at least although not always in practice, the lease is very short – as it is to acquire an asset (*MacTaggart v B & E Strump (10 TC 17)*) – and even if it is payable by annual instalments (*Green v Favourite Cinemas (15 TC 390)*). In that case, the company leased a theatre for 21 years for an annual rent and a premium. The premium was payable by annual instalments. The landlord had the right to terminate the lease, in which case liability to pay future instalments would cease. It was held that the premium was capital expenditure. A payment to modify the terms of a lease has also been held to be capital (*Tucker v Granada Motorway Services Ltd (53 TC 92)*). In that case, the rent under a lease was based on gross takings. A payment was made to the landlord in consideration of his agreeing to amend the lease to allow tobacco duty to be deducted from the gross takings in calculating the rent. It was held that the payment was a once and for all payment for the purpose of making an identifiable capital asset (the lease) more valuable, and that it was therefore capital. If the lease is a short lease a premium attracts a measure of tax relief though (see 12.45).

**12.10** A rent based on profits is, of course, rent, not a distribution of profits. The profit relationship is merely an element in the calculation of the quantum of one of the expenses of earning that profit. Where a lease provided for rent to abate if profits were below a certain level this did not affect the nature of the payment as rent (*Union Cold Storage Co Ltd v Adamson (16 TC 293)*).

**12.11** Where the tenant will obtain something additional to the mere use of the premises for his rental payments, these payments may well be found to constitute the purchase price of a capital asset being paid by instalments. In *Ainley v Edens (19 TC 303)*, a landlord carried out structural improvements to premises let on a 60-year lease and the tenant undertook to make 50 half-yearly payments 'by way of rent', which were expressed to represent repayment of the improvements with interest. They were held to be capital. In *CIR v Land Securities Investment Trust Ltd (45 TC 495)*, the landlord conveyed his interest in the property to the tenant in return for rentcharges of £96,000 p.a. for 10 years. These significantly exceeded the previous rent. It was held that the annual payments were not revenue but were a cost of acquiring a capital asset, the reversionary interest. A company which leased premises under a long lease at a rent of £23,444 entered into a number of transactions which resulted in its rent increasing to £42,450 p.a. (compared with a rack rent for the premises of £60,000) and one of its subsidiaries becoming entitled to the freehold subject to a 22-year lease to the company's landlord at a nominal rent. The increase in the rent payable was held to be a payment to acquire a capital asset, the freehold, even though the acquisition was by another group company (*Littlewoods Mail Order Stores Ltd v McGregor (45 TC 519)*).

**12.12** An interesting case on the deductibility of rent is *Allied Newspapers Ltd v Hindsley (21 TC 422)*. A newspaper company, through a subsidiary, bought a site adjoining its printing works and erected a building on it. The subsidiary rented the building to its parent at a rack rent. The parent sublet most of the building from time to time and only ever occupied a small part of it. The reason for the acquisition of the site was that it controlled the parent company's access to its printing works. It was held that the rent paid to the subsidiary was a trading expense, as, although the parent did not occupy the building, it had entered into the lease for the purposes of its trade.

## Sale and Leasebacks, etc.

**12.13** There are two main anti-avoidance provisions that need to be considered where a sale and leaseback or similar transaction is undertaken as a result of which a trader ends up paying a higher rent than under his original lease; *ICTA 1988, ss 779* and *780*.

### ICTA 1988, s 779 – Land sold and leased back

**12.14** *ICTA 1988, s 779* dates from 1964. It is designed to stop the owner of land from selling it and taking a leaseback at a rent that is artificially high in the early years in order to reduce his trading profit. It limits the amount of rent that is deductible by the payer.

**12.15** It applies where land (or any estate or interest in land) is transferred and as a result of

(*a*) a lease of the land (or any part of the land) granted by the transferee to the transferor, or (*b*) any other transaction or series of transactions affecting the land or any estate or interest in the land,

the transferor (or an associated person) becomes liable (either at the time of the transfer or subsequently) to pay any rent under a lease of the land (or any part of the land) (*ICTA 1988, s 779(1)*). In other words it applies not only on a sale and leaseback but also on the sale of land followed by a lease of that land to the vendor or a person who is associated with him.

**12.16** The deduction that can be made by the transferor (or the associated person as appropriate) in respect of rent under the lease is limited to 'the commercial rent' for the period for which the payment is made (*ICTA 1988, s 779(4)*). The commercial rent is the rent that might be expected to be paid under a notional lease of the land negotiated in the open market at the time when the actual lease was created. The notional lease must be deemed

(*a*) to be of the same duration as the actual lease,

(*b*) to have the same terms as to maintenance and repairs as the actual lease, and

(*c*) to provide for rent payable at uniform intervals and either

(i) at a uniform rate, or

(ii) if the rent payable under the actual lease is at a progressive rate (and such that the amount of rent payable for any year is never less than the amount payable for any previous year), a rent that increases by gradations proportionate to those provided by the actual lease (*ICTA 1988, s 779(8)*).

**12.17** Paragraph (*c*)(ii) in 12.16 above of course covers the situation where the actual lease contains a rent review clause. It enables the notional lease to contain a similar clause. It should be noted that this can only be done where the reviews are upward-only reviews. If the rent could be reduced on a review the notional lease must be deemed to provide for rent to be paid at a fixed rate throughout the term of the lease. This is probably in the taxpayer's interest. The market rent under a lease for, say, 21 years with no reviews would be enormous. Nowadays such a lease is such a rarity that a landlord would want a very high rent to induce him to enter into it.

**12.18** Where the rent deduction is restricted under *section 779(4)* the amount disallowed can be carried forward and allowed in future years to the extent that the commercial rent in a later year (or where necessary later years) exceeds the actual rent (*ICTA 1988, s 779(5), (6)(c)*). There must, however, be an actual payment of rent in the later year.

Example 26

A sells a property to X and leases it back for 15 years on terms that he will pay £50,000 p.a. rent for the first two years and £1 p.a. thereafter. The commercial rent on the basis of a 15-year lease without reviews is determined to be £9,000 p.a. The deductions claimable by A are

| | Rent paid | Brought forward | Total | Commercial rent | Deduction allowed |
|---|---|---|---|---|---|
| | £ | £ | £ | £ | £ |
| Year 1 | 50,000 | – | 50,000 | 9,000 | 9,000 |
| 2 | 50,000 | 41,000 | 91,000 | 9,000 | 9,000 |
| 3 | 1 | 82,000 | 82,001 | 9,000 | 9,000 |
| Years 4–11 | 8 | 73,001 | 73,009 | 72,000 | 72,000 |
| Year 12 | 1 | 1,009 | 1,010 | 9,000 | 1,010 |
| 13 | 1 | – | 1 | 9,000 | 1 |
| 14 | 1 | – | 1 | 9,000 | 1 |
| 15 | 1 | – | 1 | 9,000 | 1 |

If the rent in years 3 to 15 had been nil instead of £1 no deduction would have been competent for any of those years as there would not have been a subsequent payment made to which the carried forward amount could be added.

**12.19** Not only must there be a subsequent payment, but that payment must also be made by the transferor or a person who is associated with him. If the transferor assigns the lease to an associated person it appears that the associate can claim the benefit of the transferor's unrelieved payments. On a transfer to a non-associate the benefit of any unallowed payment is lost.

**12.20** The following persons are associated persons of the transferor.

(*a*) An individual is associated with his spouse and any relative (brother, sister, ancestor or lineal descendent) or spouse of a relative of either the individual or his spouse.

(*b*) A trust is associated with the settlor (provided that he is an individual) and any person who is associated with the settlor.

(*c*) A person is associated with a company (or other body of persons) of which he has control (or of which persons associated with him have control, or of which he and persons associated with him together have control).

(*d*) A company is associated with another company that is under common control (within (*c*) above).

(*e*) In relation to a disposal by joint owners, those joint owners are associated with one another and with any person associated with any of them.

(*f*) If two persons each enter into a sale they are associated with one another and with any associated person of either of them if the two are acting in concert or the two transactions are in any way reciprocal. This is designed to cover the situation where A sells his building Greenacres to X; B sells his property Blackacres to X; A takes a lease of Blackacres; and B takes a lease of Greenacres. Although A and B may not be otherwise connected both will suffer a restriction on the deductibility of their rents as they are deemed to be associated.

(*g*) A company is associated with another if they both participate in (or one or both are incorporated for the purpose of) a scheme for the reconstruction of any company or companies or for the amalgamation of any two or more companies. This covers the situation where A sells its property; an unconnected company B takes a lease of the property; and B subsequently takes over A's trade on a reconstruction or amalgamation.

(*ICTA 1988, s 779(11), 783(10)*).

**12.21** The section also applies where land (or an estate or interest in land) is transferred and, as a result of a transaction or series of transactions, the transferor or a person associated with him becomes liable to make a payment (other than rent under a lease) which is in any way connected with the land, such as a rentcharge, for which tax relief is available (*ICTA 1988, s 779(2)*). Where such a payment is made (whether or not rent is also payable) the commercial rent of the land cannot be based on an actual lease as one does not exist – or if it does, it does not reflect the whole terms of the arrangement. Instead it is the rent that might have been expected to be paid under a tenant's repairing lease (i.e. one where the lessee is under an obligation to maintain and repair the whole, or substantially the whole, of the premises comprised in the lease) negotiated in the open market at the time when the transaction under which the payments became due was effected and which is for a term equal to the term over which the payments are to be made (or which is for a term of 200 years if the payments are to be made in perpetuity or for a period in excess of 200 years) (*ICTA 1988, s 779(9)*). It is interesting to note that in this case the rent under the notional lease does not have to be assumed to be at a uniform rate. The notional lease can contain whatever rent review pattern might be encountered in the open market.

**12.22** In making the comparison between actual rent (or other payments) and the commercial rent, the following provisions apply.

(*a*) If a payment is made in respect of a future period commencing more than twelve months ahead, it must be treated as having been made for the twelve months from the date of payment (*ICTA 1988, s 779(7)*).

(*b*) If a payment is expressed to be for a period which ends more than twelve months after the date of payment the part relating to the period ending within twelve months of the date of payment is treated as a payment for that year. No part of the payment can be treated as relating to any later period. Relief for that part would therefore be lost completely (*ICTA 1988, s 779(7)*). The reason for this is not readily apparent. For example, if a payment is made on 1 January 1996 in respect of the twelve months to 31 March 1998 it is treated as being made for the year to 31 December 1996. If it was made in respect of the twelve months to 31 March 1997, three-quarters of it would be treated as being in respect of the year to 31 December 1996 and the remaining one-quarter will be ignored.

(*c*) If more than one payment is made for the same period the payments must be aggregated (*ICTA 1988, s 779(6)(a)*). This includes an amount brought forward under *section 779(5)* and deemed to have been paid at the time of the next subsequent payment (*ICTA 1988, s 779(6)(c)*). If payments are made for overlapping periods they must be apportioned and the parts apportioned to the common period then aggregated (*ICTA 1988, s 779(6)(b)*).

(*d*) If part of the rent is in respect of services, or of rates usually borne by the tenant, or of the use of an asset (e.g. furniture), the part applicable to such items is deductible in full and excluded from the rent for the purpose of comparing the actual and commercial rents. A split of the payment between rent and payments for services, etc. shown in the lease or agreement under which the payments are made is not to be regarded as conclusive of the part of the payment applicable to such items (*ICTA 1988, s 779(6)(d)*).

(*e*) If a premium was paid for the lease and the transferor is entitled to a deduction for notional rent under *ICTA 1988, s 37(4)–(6)* or *87*, that notional rent is to be treated as having been paid from day to day as it becomes due (*ICTA 1988, s 779(10)*).

**12.23** If, instead of selling or otherwise transferring land or an interest in land, the owner grants a lease or enters into any other transaction involving the creation of a new interest in land, it must be regarded as equivalent to his having transferred the land. If the original interest is a lease, a surrender or forfeiture must be treated as a transfer of the lease. Any other transaction or series of transactions affecting land (or an estate or interest in land) such that a person is the owner, or one of the owners, both before and after carrying out the transaction, but another person becomes or ceases to be a joint owner is also to be regarded as equivalent to a transfer, e.g. if A is the sole owner at step one and at the end of a series of transactions the land is owned jointly by A and B with A paying rent to B, A is regarded as having transferred an interest in land to B (*ICTA 1988, s 779(3)*).

**12.24** References to a lease in the section include an underlease, sublease, tenancy or licence. In the case of land outside the UK they include any interest over the overseas land corresponding to a lease, tenancy or licence. Rent includes any other payment made under a lease (*ICTA 1988, s 779(12)*).

### ICTA 1988, s 780 – Land sold and leased back: taxation of consideration received

**12.25** This is aimed at preventing a tenant under a short lease from selling his interest for a capital sum and taking back a lease at a market rent. It was introduced following disquiet over a decision of the Special Commissioners. Although the decision was not reported (Special Commissioners' decisions have only been publicly reported since January 1995) the aggrieved taxpayers, Austin Reed, decided to seek to generate public support for their position and accordingly publicised the decision themselves. It adopts a different approach to *ICTA 1988, s 779* insofar as instead of trying to limit the deductibility of the rent, it brings the capital sum into charge to tax.

**12.26** *Section 780* applies where a lessee under a lease of land having 50 years or less to run and who is entitled to a deduction for the rent under the lease

(*a*) either assigns his lease for a capital sum or surrenders it to his landlord in return for a capital sum, and

(*b*) takes a new lease (or an assignment of another lease) for a term not exceeding 15 years of (or including) the whole or any part of the land which was the subject of the original lease.

**12.27** It provides that the whole of the rent payable under the new lease is to be deductible but that a proportion of the capital sum received is to be taxed as income (*ICTA 1988, s 780(1)*). Where the rent is deductible as a trading expense the taxable amount is treated as trading income. In any other case it is taxed under Case VI of Schedule D (*ICTA 1988, s 780(3)*).

**12.28** The taxable amount depends on the length of the lease. It is calculated by the following formula (*ICTA 1988, s 780(3)*).

$$\text{capital sum} \times \frac{(16 - \text{length of new lease in years})}{15}$$

If the length of the lease is less than a year it is treated as a year, which leaves the recipient paying tax as income on the entire amount he receives.

*Example 27*

Lotsa Luck Ltd occupies a shop under a lease which has 30 years to run. It has no rent reviews and the rent is £4,000 p.a. The landlord would prefer a modern lease paying the market rent of £30,000 p.a. with five-yearly reviews. Lotsa Luck does not want to take on a commitment to such a rent for the full 30 years. It agrees with the landlord that it will surrender its existing lease for £450,000 provided that it is granted a new 10-year lease. The new lease is at £30,000 p.a. with a review after the fifth year.

Lotsa Luck will be treated as receiving additional trading income at the time it receives the £450,000 of

$$\text{£}45{,}000 \times \frac{16 - 10}{15} = \text{£}180{,}000$$

It will be able to deduct the full £30,000 p.a. rent that it pays under the new lease. The remaining £270,000 of the capital sum will be charged to capital gains tax.

*Example 28*

Winning Ways Ltd has a lease with 3 years 7 months unexpired. It assigns the lease to Harry Hopeful for £100,000, taking back a sublease for the full term at a market rent. Harry anticipates obtaining a new lease from the landlord when the existing lease expires.

Winning Ways will be taxed as income on

$$\text{£}100{,}000 \times \frac{16 - 3^{7}/_{12}}{15} = \text{£}82{,}777$$

The remaining £17,223 will be taxed as a capital gain.

**12.29** If the capital sum is payable by instalments the calculation is done separately for each instalment. It appears that the calculation proceeds on the basis that the new lease runs from its actual commencement date, not from the date of receipt of each instalment, so the taxable fraction will remain constant, i.e. the effect will simply be to spread the taxable amount rateably over each instalment (*ICTA 1988, s 780(3)*).

**12.30** If the aggregate of the rent payable under the new lease in respect of any rental period that ends before the 15th anniversary of the lease exceeds the aggregate of the rent payable under that lease for the next following rental period, the term of the lease must be treated as ending on that date (*ICTA 1988, s 780(2)(a)*). A rental period means a quarter, month or other period in respect of which a payment of rent falls to be made under the lease.

*Example 29*

Alpha has a 30-year lease at a rent of £4,000 p.a. He surrenders it to his landlord for £100,000 and takes a new lease for 30 years at a rent of £20,000 p.a. for the first 10 years and £4,000 p.a. thereafter.

The rent payable in the 40th quarterly rental period (£5,000) exceeds that payable in the 41st (£1,000), and accordingly the lease is treated as ending immediately after the 40th quarter, i.e. as being a 10-year lease.

Alpha is therefore taxed as income on

$$£100{,}000 \times \frac{16 - 10}{15} = £40{,}000$$

**12.31** If either the lessor or the lessee has power under the new lease to terminate it before the end of its term, or the lessee has power to vary his obligations under the lease so as to reduce the rent (or in any other manner beneficial to him), the lease must be treated as being for a term expiring on the earliest date on which such a power can be exercised (*ICTA 1988, s 780(2)(b)*). If both *paragraph 2(a)* and *paragraph 2(b)* could apply to a lease, whichever gives the shortest term takes precedence.

*Example 30*

Billy has a 25-year lease at £5,000 p.a. He surrenders it to his landlord for £100,000 and takes a new lease at the open market rental. The lease has five-yearly reviews. At any review date Billy can reduce the rent back to £5,000 on payment to the landlord of a sum of £80,000 if he exercises the right at the first review date, £60,000 at the next, £40,000 at the third or £20,000 at the final review date.

As Billy has power to reduce the rent at the end of year 5 the lease must be treated as for 5 years. Billy will thus be taxed as income on

$$£100,000 \times \frac{16 - 5}{15} = £73,333$$

He will be taxed as a capital gain on the balance of £26,667.

If Billy actually reduces the rent on the first review he will not be able to obtain any reduction in the tax for the £80,000 payment that he makes.

**12.32** Any rentcharge payable by the lessee which is secured on the whole or part of the property must be aggregated with the rent for the purpose of both *paragraphs 2(a)* and *(b)* above (*ICTA 1988, s 780(2)*).

**12.33** If the new lease does not extend to the entire property which was the subject of the original lease, the amount to be used in the calculation of the income element is limited to the proportion of the capital sum which is reasonably attributable to the part of the property which was the subject of the original lease (*ICTA 1988, s 780(4)*).

*Example 31*

Henry has a 20-year lease of 5,000 sq. ft. of office space. He surrenders it to his landlord for a payment of £80,000 and takes back a new 10-year lease of 1,000 sq. ft. of the premises.

The £80,000 is apportioned between the 4,000 sq. ft. surrendered and the 1,000 sq. ft. retained. This is a valuation exercise. Assume that the split is £65,000 for the part given up and £15,000 for the part retained (it is unlikely to be proportionate as the landlord gets vacant possession of part but not of the remainder).

Henry will be taxed as income on

$$£15,000 \times \frac{16 - 10}{15} = £6,000$$

**12.34** If instead of surrendering a lease the landlord and tenant agree to vary the terms of the original lease so that in return for a capital sum the tenant undertakes to pay a higher rent (for a period that ends within 15 years of the date on which the consideration is paid), he must be treated as having surrendered the original lease and having been granted a new lease (*ICTA 1988, s 780(6)*). If the consideration is payable by instalments the 15-year period runs from the date that the last instalment is paid. It is not clear what happens in such circumstances. For example, suppose that in return for £100,000 payable by five annual instalments the tenant agrees to pay an increased rent for the next 18 years. This 18-year period ends within 15 years after the date of payment of the last instalment. It is therefore deemed to be for a term not exceeding 15 years. Presumably it will be treated as being for a term of exactly 15 years as the increased rent is payable for 18 years. Accordingly, a fifteenth of the capital sum will presumably be taxed as income.

**12.35** *Section 780* will also apply if the new lease is granted not to the original lessee but to a partner or associate of the lessee, or to an associate of a partner of the lessee (*ICTA 1988, s 780(7)*). Associate for this purpose has the same meaning as in *section 783(10)* – see (*a*) to (*e*) (but not (*f*) and (*g*)) in 12.20 above.

**12.36** *ICTA 1988, s 24* (see 3.30), which is the interpretation section for Schedule A, also applies for the purpose of *ICTA 1988, s 780 (ICTA 1988, s 780(8))*.

## Relief for Other Payments in Respect of the Premises

**12.37** A trader can claim a deduction against his trading profits for the cost of repairs to the properties from which he operates. He cannot deduct expenditure on improvements. Nor can he deduct the cost of replacing the premises – although the replacement of part may well be deductible as constituting a repair of the whole. The court decisions on what constitutes repairs are considered in 9.3–9.10 above. The Revenue guidance on the expenditure on reinstatement of bomb damaged buildings in London Dockland and Manchester in 1996 is considered at 2.20. With the exception of the reference to ESC B4 this applies equally to owner-occupied buildings as to rented ones (Tax Bulletin 26, December 1996).

**12.38** Where a payment for dilapidations is made on the termination of a lease the payment should be deductible. The Revenue apparently consider that if the payment is not used by the landlord for 'genuine repairs', or if the expenditure 'restores the building to its original state by rebuilding or dismantling items previously altered or added by tenants', it is disallowable (Taxline, Issue 12). However this seems of doubtful validity. It looks on dilapidations as deferred repairs. The distinction between income and capital, as far as the tenant who makes the payment is concerned, is whether the tenant obtains an enduring benefit from it. It seems improbable that a tenant obtains an enduring benefit from a payment he is obliged to make on the expiry of a lease under its terms.

**12.39** Where part of a dwelling-house is used for the purposes of a trade or profession, *ICTA 1988, s 74(c)* limits the rent deductible for the business portion to a maximum of two-thirds of the total, unless in any particular case it appears that, having regard to all the circumstances, some greater sum ought to be deducted. It has been held that the two-thirds limitation applies only to rent and does not prevent the deduction of a larger proportion of rates (*Wildbore v Luker (33 TC 46)*). It would equally not apply to repairs although it is difficult to imagine circumstances in which repairs to a private house could meet the wholly and exclusively test necessary to qualify for a deduction.

**12.40** The cost to the owner of a beach cafe of erecting a barrier in front of the cafe as protection from the sea has been held to be capital expenditure (*Avon Beach & Cafe Co Ltd v Stewart (31 TC 487)*). So has the cost of constructing a new access road to a company's warehouse to meet complaints from neighbours regarding the use of the original access road (*Pitt v Castle Hill Warehousing Co Ltd (49 TC 638)*).

**12.41** Replacement of shop fronts are normally dealt with on a renewals basis, i.e. the cost of a new shop front is treated as a revenue expense except to the extent that the work contains an element of improvement, which is capital. The Revenue say this is because the replacement of a shop front is the repair of the shop (which is the entirety). The cost of adapting newly acquired premises may however be capital (Inspector's Manual, IM 993). The Revenue consider that such expenditure is not machinery or plant (Capital Allowances Manual 1715). This was confirmed in the *Wimpy* and *Associated Restaurant* cases (see 10.38) where the Court of Appeal defined a shop front as part of the premises from which the business was carried on.

**12.42** Expenditure by a tenant on making good dilapidations at the expiry of a lease is an allowable deduction if the work is of the nature of deferred repairs (Inspector's Manual, IM 677). So is a sum paid to the landlord by way of composition to the extent that it reflects deferred repairs (IM 678). Where dilapidations is incurred by a new tenant as a condition of the grant of the lease (or by an existing tenant as consideration for the grant of a new lease, not in satisfaction of his obligations under the old), the payment will be capital (IM 676). Expenditure will also be capital to the extent that it consists of rebuilding the premises, reinstatement of part of the premises previously demolished by the tenant, or demolishing a part added by the tenant (IM 676). Any element of improvement will, of course, also be capital.

**12.43** An interesting point arose in *Southern Counties Agricultural Trading Society Ltd v Blackler (1999 STC (SCD) 200)*. The taxpayer occupied office premises for the purpose of its trade. It assigned its lease and paid the assignee a 'compensation payment' to reflect its belief that it had failed to meet its repairing obligations under the lease. The assignee agreed to indemnify the taxpayer against all claims resulting from any breach of any covenant in the lease. It was agreed that had the taxpayer engaged a third party to carry out the repairs the payment for remedying the dilapidations would have been a trading expense. However the taxpayer had not paid the assignee to carry out the repairs. It had paid it to assume the taxpayer's liability to make good the dilapidations. It was also clear that the taxpayer wished to dispose of the lease and move to smaller premises. The Special Commissioners agreed with the Revenue that the payment was of a capital nature to ensure the disposal of a disadvantageous asset.

**12.44** The Revenue have always taken the view that a provision for repairs is not deductible; relief can be given only when the expenditure is actually incurred. They derive this view from *ICTA 1988, s 74(1)(d)* which disallows a deduction for repairs to premises 'beyond the sum actually expended' (Inspector's Manual, IM 605f). This view was rejected by the Special Commissioners in *Jenners Princes Street Edinburgh Ltd v CIR (SpC 166)*. The company carried on a trade of retailers from a listed building. It spent an increasing amount on repairs. In 1994 it carried out a feasibility study on the possibility of a refurbishment to restore the building to its original condition and obviate the need for constant piecemeal repairs. This was completed during its accounting period to 31 January 1995. The company resolved to carry out the work and made a provision in those accounts for the estimated expenditure of £2.25m. The work was actually done in subsequent years. The Special Commissioners felt the Revenue's position illogical. If they accepted, as they did, that 'expended' in *ICTA 1988, s 74(1)(a)* should be interpreted in the accountancy sense of including accruals, 'actually expended' in *s 74(1)(d)* must have a similar meaning. The adverb 'actually' qualifies the verb; it cannot change its meaning. The Revenue gave notice of appeal but abandoned this in mid-1999. They were probably influenced by the fact that the accountancy profession had itself cut down significantly the scope for provisions in FRS 12. This permits a provision only where a business has a present obligation (legal or constructive) as a result of a past event, it is probable that expenditure will be required to settle that obligation, and a reliable estimate can be made of the amount of the obligation. It is probable that the provision in *Jenners* would not have met these conditions.

## Deduction in Respect of Premium paid

**12.45** Where a person pays a premium for the grant of a short lease (under 50 years) of premises used in connection with his trade, profession or vocation, he is allowed a deduction against profits even though the payment is capital. The deduction is based on the sum taxable on the landlord under Schedule A (3.2 above) – or if he is exempt from tax, or not taxable on the premium because he can set it against a premium that he has himself paid, the sum on which he would otherwise have been taxable (*ICTA 1988, s 87(1)(9)*). Relief is given not only for a premium paid but also for an amount of expenditure that gives rise to a charge on the landlord (or some other person) under *ICTA 1988, s 34(2)* (3.4 above); *s 34(4)* (3.6 above); *s 34(5)* (3.8 above); or *s 35* (3.14 above).

**12.46** The amount that is taxable on the landlord is spread on a day-to-day basis over the term of the lease – or the period treated as the term for the purpose of calculating the *section 34* charge (or the period from the date of the assignment where the charge is under *section 35*) – and treated as additional rent in respect of the property. The tenant is entitled to deduct each year the proportion of the additional rent that is attributable to the days falling within his accounting period or income tax basis period (*ICTA 1988, s 87(1)(2)*). If only part of the land is used for business purposes then only the deemed additional rent in relation to that part is of course deductible (*ICTA 1988, s 87(3)*). The relief is given to the person for the time being entitled to the lease (*ICTA 1988, s 87(2)*). Accordingly, where a trader takes an assignment of a lease, he needs to check whether the original tenant paid a premium or other amount qualifying for relief, as if he did the assignee will acquire a right to a tax deduction based on that payment.

*Example 32*

The lessee in *Example 4* (3.2 above) was Tarzan Enterprises Ltd, which acquired the lease for use in its trade. On 20 June 2004 Tarzan assigned the lease to X Plorer Ltd for £10,000. Tarzan Enterprises prepares its accounts to 31 December and X Plorer has a 30 June accounting date.

The term of the lease was 10 years, 7 months from 1 July 2001.

The amount taxable on the landlord, Jane, was £41,000.

The tenant is therefore entitled to a deduction of £3,874 p.a., which will be given in the following periods:

| | | | |
|---|---|---|---|
| *To Tarzan Enterprises Ltd* | | £ | £ |
| Year to 31.12.2001 (from 1.7.00) | $\frac{184}{365}$ × £3,874 | 1,953 | |
| Year to 31.12.2002 | | 3,874 | |
| 2 years to 31.12.2004 | 2 × £3,874 | 7,748 | |
| Year to 31.12.2004 (from 20.6.04) | $\frac{171}{365}$ × £3,874 | 1,815 | 15,390 |
| *To X Plorer Ltd* | | | |
| Year to 30.6.2003 (from 21.6.03) | $\frac{10}{365}$ × £3,874 | 106 | |
| Year to 30.6.2004 | | 3,874 | |
| 5 years to 30.6.2010 | 5 × £3,874 | 19,370 | |
| Year to 30.6.2011 (to 30.1.11) | $\frac{7}{12}$ × £3,874 | 260 | 25,610 |
| | | | £41,000 |

It should particularly be noted that X Plorer Ltd's relief is not based on the payment it made to Tarzan but on Tarzan's original payment to Jane.

**12.47** No relief is due for a 'premium' paid on the assignment of a lease (except in the unusual case where the initial lease was at an undervalue so that a charge arises on the assignor under *ICTA 1988, s 35*). Accordingly, a trader who is asked to pay a premium for an assignment of a lease of less than 50 years ought to investigate the possibility of taking a sublease of the premises instead – unless, of course, he is in the lucky position of X Plorer Ltd in the above example where the relief due by taking an assignment exceeds the premium that he is paying. If the assignor is not prepared to grant a sublease it may be possible to find a third party, such as a property dealing company, who is prepared to take the assignment and grant a sublease. A property dealer is generally happy to grant a sublease as the amount on which it is taxed under Schedule A reduces its Case I assessment so that its overall tax position is unaffected.

**12.48** The relief is also given where a person is not in occupation of the land but deals with his interest in it as property employed for the purposes of his trade (*ICTA 1988, s 87(4)*). This is probably intended to cover tied houses of brewers, and similar properties. In such a case if a premium is received from a brewer's tenant, *ICTA 1988, s 37(3)* (see 3.35 above) applies to restrict the notional rent deductible by the brewer, and he cannot claim a deduction under both *section 87* and *section 37*.

**12.49** If the charge on the landlord arose under *ICTA 1988, s 34(2)* – on a deemed premium where the tenant was obliged to carry out work on the premises – no relief will be due for the deemed premium to the extent that the tenant was entitled to capital allowances on the expenditure (*ICTA 1988, s 87(8)*). This is achieved by requiring the calculation to be made as if the tenant had not had to carry out the work which attracted capital allowances. In practice, where part of the work qualified for capital allowances and part did not, it is likely in most cases that the non-capital allowances work on its own would have no value to the landlord, and thus would not generate a deemed premium to the landlord on that assumption, with the result that no relief at all would be due to the tenant.

## Relief for Property Owner-Occupied at 5 April 1963

**12.50** Prior to 1963/64 tax was payable (under a previous version of Schedule A) on the 'annual value' of land and that annual value could be treated as a trading expense where the property was used by a trader for the purpose of his trade. As at the time trading profits for both individuals and companies were assessed on a preceding year basis, the abolition of the Schedule A charge resulted in a loss of relief. Transitional relief – which is still available – was therefore introduced. It is given where a person permanently ceases to occupy premises which were occupied by him for the purpose of his trade, profession or vocation at any time before 6 April 1963 (*ICTA 1988, Sch 30 para 5(2)*). Relief is not given if the trade ceases in the period in which the trader ceases to occupy the property (*ICTA 1988, Sch 30 para 5(6)*). In other words it applies where the premises are sold but the trade continues from other premises. The relief is the aggregate of the net annual values of the premises which would have been deductible in computing the profits of the trade for 1963/64 and 1964/65 (but for the change in the law) over the aggregate of any deductions allowed under *FA 1963, s 29(2)* (deduction for certain rent paid under deduction of tax) in respect of the property for those years (*ICTA 1988, Sch 30 para 5(3)*).

**12.51** The allowance is given by treating this amount as rent becoming due from day to day in the period beginning on the date the land ceases to be occupied for the purpose of the trade and continuing for the number of months (and fractions of months) for which it was occupied for the purposes of the trade in so much of the basis period for 1963/64 as fell before the start of that year plus so much of the basis period for 1964/65 as fell before the beginning of that year (*ICTA 1988, Sch 30 para 5(5)*).

*Example 33*

A company had since 1960 occupied a property with a net annual value (NAV) of £600. It has always prepared its accounts to 31 December. It sold the property on 16 July 2003.

The basis period for 1963/64 would have been the year to 31 December 1962.

The basis period for 1964/65 would have been the year to 31 December 1963.

But for the change in law the NAV deduction would have been

| | | |
|---|---|---|
| 1963/64 | ¼ × 1961/62 NAV | £150 |
| | ¾ × 1962/63 NAV | 450 |
| 1964/65 | ¼ × 1962/63 NAV | 150 |
| | | £750 |

The part of the basis period for 1963/64 that fell before 6.4.1963 was 12 months.

The part of the basis period for 1964/65 that fell before 6.4.1963 was 3 months.

The relief will therefore be spread over the 15 months from 16 July 2003.

| | |
|---|---|
| i.e. deduction in accounting period to 31.12.2003 | |
| $5\frac{1}{2}/15 \times$ £750 | £275 |
| i.e. deduction in accounting period to 31.12.2004 | |
| $9\frac{1}{2}/15 \times$ £750 | 475 |
| | £750 |

# Private Residences

**13.1** There are three main areas in which tax considerations can arise in connection with private residences; capital gains tax, the allowability of mortgage interest up to 1999/2000 (which is dealt with at 4.10 above onwards), and the deduction of expenses against taxable income. It is also of course possible that the purchase and sale of a private residence could constitute trading. It was made clear in *Kirkham v Williams (1991 STC 342)* that where a person has more than one motive in acquiring land the subjective intention of the taxpayer must be looked at to determine whether the transaction is trading (see 5.27). The Revenue claim to have had some success before the General Commissioners in characterising a transaction as trading where a person lived in a house for a short period and carried out substantial renovations during that time, but prior to *Kirkby v Hughes (1993 STC 76)* no such case had reached the High Court. The facts in that case were far more suggestive of trading than of the house having been acquired as a residence. The taxpayer, who was a building contractor and a bachelor, lived with his parents. In August 1978 he bought a four-bedroomed house which was unfit for occupancy. He renovated it and moved in temporarily while continuing to live mainly at his parents' home. He sold it in August 1981 at a substantial profit. In April 1981 he bought a vacant plot on which he built a four-bedroomed house. He intended to use it as his residence but never did. It was sold in August 1984. Part of the proceeds were used to buy a barn which he converted into a four-bedroomed house which he lived in temporarily. It is clear that the Commissioners did not believe the taxpayer's claim that any of the three properties was intended to be his private residence. The Revenue also contended in *Goodwin v Curtis* (see 13.4) that the taxpayer was trading in private residences but this was rejected by the General Commissioners and the Revenue did not appeal against the decision.

**13.2** Where a person lets part of his private residence or lets the whole whilst he is not using it himself the rent generated is of course taxable. However, no special problems arise compared with other lettings, with the possible exception that expenditure needs to be apportioned between that attributable to the letting and that to the private occupation. Clearly the method of apportionment will depend very much on the facts. Any reasonable method is likely to be acceptable provided that it represents a genuine attempt to arrive at the proportion of the total that is applicable to the letting. Problems can arise with holiday homes (where the letting season may be short) if the owner occupies a sizeable chunk of the prime time. In some cases the easiest solution is to bring in notional rent as a receipt and to claim the whole of the expenses. It should be borne in mind, however, that a large sum of expenses needs to be at risk before one should volunteer to pay tax on non-existent income. There is also a special income tax exemption for comparatively small amounts of rent (about £82 a week) received from letting part of a person's own home. This is designed to encourage people to take in lodgers. It is dealt with at 2.115–2.122.

## Capital Gains Tax Private Residence Exemption

**13.3** A gain realised by an individual on the disposal of a dwelling-house or part of a dwelling-house which has been his only or main residence throughout his period of ownership, or throughout it except for all or part of the last 36 months, is not a chargeable gain, i.e. it is not chargeable to capital gains tax (*TCGA 1992, ss 223, 223(1)*). For disposals prior to 19 March 1991 only use in the last 24 months could be ignored. The Revenue have power by statutory instrument to reduce the figure to 24 again. The government have indicated that they will not do so without giving reasonable warning (Hansard, Standing Committee B, 13 June 1991, Col 312).

### Scope of the Dwelling-House

**13.4** Dwelling-house is not defined. It probably means any building or part of a building which is used as a dwelling. Certainly the exemption is not limited to houses but extends to flats and other types of private residence. Indeed it has been held that a caravan jacked up and resting on bricks with water, electricity and telephone installed was a dwelling-house (*Makins v Elson (51 TC 437)*). The mere jacking-up of a caravan without connecting it to other facilities such as water, electricity or telephone may not suffice (*Moore v Thompson (61 TC 15)*). A residence is not defined either. It is a question of fact. The Revenue have said that they do not attempt to impose a minimum period of occupation. They take the view that it is quality of occupation rather than the length of occupation which determines whether a dwelling-house is a person's residence (Tax Bulletin, Issue 12, August 1994). This approach was followed by the General Commissioners in *Goodwin v Curtis (1998 STC 475)*. Mr Goodwin completed his purchase of a farmhouse on 7 March 1985. At the same time he separated from his wife and he took up temporary residence there. On 11 April 1995 he advertised the property for sale and a sale was completed on 3 May 1995. In autumn 1994 a company controlled by Mr Goodwin and a Mr Sharp contracted to buy a small cottage, Ayton, with the intention that they should use it as an office. They obtained planning consent but the company could not obtain finance so the purchase was completed on 3 April 1985 by Mr Goodwin personally. When Mr Goodwin sold the farmhouse he moved to Ayton as he had nowhere else to live. He immediately looked for a larger place to live in and bought a larger property, Stoneways, completion of which was on 26 July 1985. The Commissioners held that neither the farmhouse nor Ayton qualified for private residence relief. The judge felt that the test should be whether the property had been occupied by the taxpayer as his home. The Commissioners had distinguished between permanent residence and mere temporary accommodation. The judge thought that was a correct approach. The factors to be weighed up in reaching this decision were the degree of permanence, continuity and the expectation of continuity. The Commissioners were entitled to hold that both properties had been used as mere temporary accommodation and not as a residence. The Court of Appeal noted that in *Levene v CIR (13 TC 486)* Viscount Cave had adopted the dictionary definition of 'reside' as 'to dwell permanently or for a considerable time, to have one's settled or usual abode, to live in or at a particular place', and felt the same approach is appropriate for capital gains tax (a VAT tribunal, whilst accepting this same meaning of residence, has given a more relaxed meaning to 'residential' though – see 17.28). If the owner has a residence within a purpose-built hotel or other building which cannot be regarded as a dwelling-house, the Revenue will allow the relief to be claimed for the rooms actually occupied as a residence whether or not they are self-contained (Revenue CGT Manual, para 64320). The exemption applies to the disposal of the dwelling-house itself or any interest in it (*TCGA 1992, s 222(1)*). It also extends to land which the individual has for his own occupation and enjoyment with his residence as its garden or grounds up to an area (inclusive of the house) of half a hectare (approximately 1.23 acres), or such larger area as the appeal Commissioners may determine if they are satisfied that, regard being had to the size and character of the dwelling-house, that larger area is required for the reasonable enjoyment of the dwelling-house (or the part of the house owned by the individual owning the land) as a residence (*TCGA 1992, s 222(1)(b)(2)(3)*). For disposals prior to 19 March 1991 the exempt area was one acre. If the whole of the land owned with the house does not qualify for exemption the exempt part is the part which, if the remainder were separately occupied, would be the most suitable for occupation and enjoyment with the residence (*TCGA 1992, s 222(4)*). There are a number of points to watch.

(*a*) Land occupied with a residence only qualifies for exemption if it is held for occupation as its garden or grounds. This applies even where the total area including the house does not exceed half a hectare. For example, if an individual occupies a house covering a quarter of an acre plus an adjoining half-acre plot which he has never used for any purpose that plot would not qualify for exemption. The Inland Revenue have been known to contend that if land is separated from a house by a wall or fence which does not contain a gate giving direct access from the house, it is not a garden or grounds for occupation with the residence. As a general principle this is undoubtedly wrong. However, it is probably fair to assume that, if land does not have direct access from the house, there is an inference that it is not garden or grounds of the house. In *Wakeling v Pearce (1995) Sp C 32* Mrs Wakeling owned property which comprised two non-contiguous parts about 30 feet apart. Her residence was on one. On the second she maintained a small garden, a washing line and garden shed. She allowed her grandchildren, friends and family to use it for relaxation. She sold this second part in two plots in 1987 and 1988 respectively. The Special Commissioner held that the fact that the land disposed of did not adjoin the residence was not fatal. The statutory requirement was merely that the land should be used with the residence as its garden. Mrs Wakeling had done that, albeit at a substantially reduced rate, up to the moment of sale. Accordingly, the exemption applied. The Revenue decided not to appeal but only because of Mrs Wakeling's particular circumstances (Tax Bulletin, Issue 18, August 1995).

(*b*) The test as to whether land qualifies for the exemption is applied at the time of its disposal. Accordingly, if the individual sells the house but retains the land, even for only a day or two, the subsequent sale of the land cannot qualify for exemption, as at the date of sale it will not be owned for enjoyment with the house (as the house will at that time no longer be in the same ownership) (*Varty v Lynes (51 TC 419)*). The Revenue did for a time sometimes claim that the extended relief did not apply, even on a simultaneous sale of the house and garden, after the cessation of occupation but now accept that this is misconceived (Tax Bulletin, Issue 12, August 1994). The Revenue also regard this case as confirming that the use of the land other than at the date of disposal as irrelevant (Tax Bulletin, Issue 18, August 1995). However, they accept that land which has traditionally been part of the grounds of a residence but which at the date of sale is unused or overgrown can nevertheless be included in the exemption (Revenue CGT Manual, para 64364).

(*c*) It is extremely difficult to show that an area over half a hectare qualifies for relief if that area consists of land which is sold without the house being sold simultaneously. This is because it is hard to see how one can contend that land is required for the reasonable enjoyment of a house as a residence if one will continue to occupy it as a residence after having sold that land. The foregoing contention is not, however, impossible. In *Batey v Wakefield (55 TC 550)*, the taxpayer owned a house built on 1.1 acres of land. He had a bungalow for occupation by a caretaker built on the land. This was separate from the main house and had its own access from the road. When the taxpayer subsequently occupied the house full-time he no longer needed the caretaker and sold the bungalow together with 0.2 acres of the land. He managed to convince the General Commissioners not only that the sale of the bungalow was the sale of part of the dwelling-house, but also that the land wholly qualified for exemption even though it exceeded an acre and even though he could, and intended to continue to, reasonably enjoy the house without the 0.2 acres.

(*d*) In *Lewis v Rook (1992 STC 171)* the Court of Appeal indicated that whilst, as in *Batey v Wakefield*, it is possible for a dwelling-house to consist of more than one building, this can only apply if the dwelling-house is 'appurtenant to, and within the curtilage of, the main house'. Balcombe LJ cited with approval Buckley LJ in *Methuen Campbell v Walters (1979 QB 525)*: 'For one corporeal hereditament to fall within the curtilage of another, the former must be so intimately associated with the latter as to lead to the conclusion that the former in truth forms part and parcel of the latter.' In their Tax Bulletin, Issue 12, August 1994 the Revenue opine that a wall or fence separating two buildings will normally be sufficient to establish that they are not within the same curtilage.

The meaning of curtilage was explained by the Court of Session in 1951 in the case of *Sinclair-Lockhart's Trustees v Central Land Board* (Vol 1 Planning and Compensation Reports, p 320). 'The ground which is used for the comfortable enjoyment of a house or other building may be regarded in law as being within the curtilage of that house or building and thereby as an integral part of the same although it has not been marked off or enclosed in any way. It is enough that it serves the purpose of the house or building in some necessary or reasonably useful way.' For example, the garage of a house or a shed in the yard of shop premises would be in the same curtilage but two adjacent shops or houses would not normally be so comprised. If the owner of a factory was to develop land next door to the factory, even on the existing boundary of the factory, or was to use such land for storage purposes, the land would not normally be within the curtilage of the factory as it would not have previously been required for the comfortable enjoyment of the factory.

In *Lewis v Rook*, Lady Rook unsuccessfully claimed exemption for a gardener's cottage 190 yards from the main house. In *Markey v Sanders (60 TC 245)* exemption was similarly refused for a staff bungalow 130 metres from the main house. The taxpayer also lost in *Honour v Norris (1992 STC 304)* although the facts of that case were special and the decision unsurprising. Besides *Batey v Wakefield*, the taxpayer won in *Williams v Merrylees (60 TC 297)* where the disposal was of a lodge 200 metres from the main house, but on the *Edwards v Bairstow (36 TC 207)* principle as he had convinced the General Commissioners that the lodge was appurtenant to and within the curtilage of the main house. The judge held that, whilst he might not himself have reached that conclusion, it was not so unreasonable that he could overturn it.

(*e*) If a house and grounds are sold simultaneously but to different purchasers – for example, the house to someone who intends to occupy it and the grounds to a property developer – this probably also raises an inference that the land is not required for the reasonable enjoyment of the house as a residence. If the total area is under a half hectare there is unlikely to be a problem, as *section 222(1)(b)* looks to land owned for the vendor's enjoyment. If it exceeds a half hectare the test is narrower. It is necessary to show that the land is required for 'the reasonable enjoyment' of the house as a residence, i.e. anyone's enjoyment ignoring the particular circumstances of the vendor (*TCGA 1992, s 222(3)*).

(*f*) Whether or not an area of over half a hectare is required for the reasonable enjoyment of a house is normally best dealt with by the taxpayer's surveyor and the District Valuer rather than his accountant and the Inspector of Taxes. The Revenue's demarcation line is that it is for the Inspector to determine what land is garden or grounds and for the District Valuer to then decide how much of it qualifies for relief (Revenue CGT Manual, para 64353). As the appropriate area depends very much on local considerations, if agreement cannot be reached it is worthwhile considering taking an appeal before the General Commissioners. It is curious that Parliament has imposed on the Commissioners the burden of deciding the extent of the exemption bearing in mind that they have specifically precluded them from dealing with any dispute as to the value of land by requiring it to be referred to the Lands Tribunal (*TMA 1970, s 47(1)*).

(*g*) In their Tax Bulletin, Issue 2, February 1992, the Inland Revenue explain their view of what the exemption covers and the information they like to be given when a claim is made for the exemption to extend to an area of more than half a hectare. In particular, this quotes as guidance on the meaning of 'required' the words of Du Parcq J in *re Newhill Compulsory Purchase Order 1937, Payne's application* [*1938*] *2 All ER 163*: 'Required, I think, in this section does not mean merely that the occupiers of the house would like to have it, or that they would miss it if they lost it, or that anyone proposing to buy the house would think less of the house without it . . . "Required" means, I suppose, that without it there will be such a substantial deprivation of amenities or convenience that a real injury would be done to the property owner.' When faced with such a restricted interpretation by an Inspector, the context in which Du Parcq was speaking should be borne in mind. The compulsory purchase legislation in 1937 prohibited a local authority from acquiring any 'park, garden or pleasure ground or any other land reasonably required for enjoyment with the house', and the land in question in the *Newhill* case was not garden land but 'other land'. One would expect the courts to have tried to give effect to a clear intention of Parliament that local authority compulsory purchase powers, which were given for the benefit of the community should be interpreted reasonably widely. It is not clear why the Tax Bulletin article does not mention more recent compulsory purchase cases, such as *R v Secretary of State ex parte Sharkey (1990 45 EG 113)*, where the courts have taken a far less restrictive approach to the word 'required'. It is in any event doubtful to what extent the courts will look at the compulsory purchase cases to aid the interpretation of *section 222* as the intention of Parliament in this case is almost certainly to exempt the whole of a house and its grounds but without extending that exemption to extraneous land. They did so in *Longson v Baker (2001 STC 6)* where Evans-Lombe J thought there is a sufficient analogy between the two statutory provisions that it was entirely legitimate for the Commissioner to take guidance from the *Newhill* case – but that Parcq J was emphasising that what the Commissioners are engaged in is an enquiry as to fact, namely what the permitted area of land should be.

(*h*) The Revenue take the view that there are two distinct exemptions:

(i) the dwelling-house, including the land on which it stands and, where it consists of more than one building, the land between those buildings, and

(ii) its garden or grounds including any building in such grounds (Revenue CGT Manual, para 64240).

Where there are several buildings they regard it as important to determine which buildings comprise the entity, 'the dwelling-house', partly because the extent of the dwelling-house can affect the extent of the grounds (e.g. if the dwelling-house includes a stable the paddock is probably grounds) and partly because land between buildings included in the dwelling-house qualifies for relief automatically outside the half hectare test (para 64242). Because of this distinction between house and garden, curtilage (see (*d*) above) is only relevant to determine the extent of the dwelling-house; it has no relevance to the identification of the permitted area of garden or grounds (para 64251). This is probably an oversimplification. To the extent that a garden falls within the curtilage of the house it will automatically qualify for relief even if it exceeds a half hectare. The Revenue say that the test whether or not a building is within the curtilage of the main house is whether it passes automatically on a conveyance of the house without having to be specifically mentioned (para 64248). The garden of a suburban house will normally meet this test.

However the Revenue see a distinction between the curtilage of the main house and the curtilage of an estate (para 64249) and are specifically instructed to resist the argument that because a whole estate is contained within a single boundary, the whole estate should be regarded as within the curtilage of the main house. The Revenue consider that an urban house will commonly have no curtilage beyond a small garden or yard (para 64291). The Revenue also say that if a separate building is used wholly for business, private residence relief is excluded by *TCGA 1992, s 224(1)* and as such there is no need to consider whether it is in the curtilage of the main house (para 64261). It is doubtful if this is right. If it is within the curtilage and thus part of the main house it seems more correct to value the house (including the business building and land within the curtilage) and exclude from relief under *TCGA 1992, s 224(1)* the part of the overall gain which is attributable to the business building.

(*i*) A group of flats is regarded as a single dwelling-house if they are all occupied by the owner and his family, are within the same block and contiguous (Revenue CGT Manual, para 64306). If they are in the same block but on different floors or separated by other flats, the Revenue consider they will be a single dwelling only in exceptional circumstances (para 64308) and in such cases, the Revenue consider length of occupation and use to be important factors. If access between the two is only via the street they do not accept they can constitute a single dwelling-house (para 64307). This is not necessarily correct.

(*j*) The Revenue define a 'garden' as an enclosed piece of ground devoted to the cultivation of flowers, fruit or vegetables (Revenue CGT Manual, para 64361). It seems improbable that constructing a pond, creating a patio, or even paving over the entire area as has happened with many suburban front gardens will cause the land to cease to be 'garden' as this definition suggests. Their definition of grounds is 'enclosed land surrounding or attached to a dwelling-house or other building serving chiefly for ornament or recreation', although unlike the definition of garden this is not intended as an exhaustive definition (para 64362). As a general rule, land surrounding the residence and in the same ownership is the grounds of the residence unless it is in use for some other purpose (para 64363). Paddocks and orchards are normally part of the grounds if there is no significant business use (para 64364). The land does not have to be exclusively used as garden or grounds (para 64366).

(*k*) Curiously the Revenue interpret occupation and enjoyment as legal terms, i.e. possession of the land without contested claims from third parties (Revenue CGT Manual, para 64372). Such an interpretation of enjoyment seems inconsistent with the requirement for the Commissioners, who are normally concerned with facts more than law, to determine what area is required for the reasonable enjoyment of the house as a residence (*TCGA 1992, s 222(3)*). It is unlikely that they were intended to decide how much of the land is reasonably not subject to contested claims. It is equally unlikely that 'enjoyment' in *section 222(1)(b)* and *section 222(3)* were intended to have different meanings.

(*l*) What needs to be looked at in deciding what land qualifies for relief is the area required for the reasonable enjoyment of the dwelling-house; it is not permissible to take into account the particular requirements of the owner of the dwelling-house (*Longson v Baker (2000 STC (SCD) 244 SpC 238)*). Accordingly, whilst in that case it was convenient for the taxpayer's purposes to have 7.56 hectares available to them on which to keep their horses, such a large area was not necessary or vital when stabling horses at a property.

**Two or More Residences**

**13.5** Where a person has two or more residences at the same time, so that it is necessary to determine which is his main one for any period, he can conclude that question by notice in writing to the Inspector given within two years from the beginning of that period (*TCGA 1992, s 222(5)(a)*), i.e. he can elect to which the exemption is to apply, but such an identification cannot apply for a period starting earlier than two years prior to the date of the election. The Revenue consider that the election has to be made within two years of the acquisition of the second home. This was upheld in *Griffin v Craig-Harvey (1994 STC 54)*. The reasoning in that case is difficult to follow. *Section 222(5)* previously *CGTA 1979, s 101(5)* reads: 'So far as it is necessary . . . to determine which . . . is the individual's main residence for any period –

(*a*) the individual may conclude that question by notice . . . given within two years from the beginning of that period . . .,

(*b*) subject to paragraph (*a*) above, the question shall be concluded by . . . the Inspector, which may be as respects either the whole or specified parts of the period of ownership in question.'

The Special Commissioners held that 'that period' in (*a*) must relate to 'any period' in the introductory words, which most people would think is the natural construction. Vinelott J however thought that was not even 'a possible construction', and that it must refer to the 'period of ownership' in (*b*) albeit both that the word 'that' normally refers to something that has gone before, not something that follows, and that (*b*) is in any event made subject to (*a*) so would not normally need to be even looked at where (*a*) applies. He supported his view by reference to Hansard. The Minister said in 1965 in introducing the provision, 'there is no provision for the case of a man who has one house and does not need to make any option but who later buys another house and then wishes to opt to treat the other as his principal residence. The effect of this Amendment is to keep open the option so that he can exercise a choice within two years from the time when he acquires the second house.' As the Minister talked of 'the effect' rather than 'the purpose' the taxpayer's construction would have the same effect, albeit that it would also have further effects, and the Minister gave no indication that the amendment was intended to deal solely with the circumstance he outlined. Accordingly it is not clear why Vinelott J felt that it resolves the ambiguity in the wording, a *sine qua non* for recourse to Hansard to be permissible under *Pepper v Hart (1992 STC 898)*.

**13.6** The election can be varied at any time by giving a fresh notice. Again the variation cannot apply to any period over two years before the date of the new election. Vinelott J in *Griffin v Craig-Harvey* specifically accepted that if an election is made within two years of acquisition of the second property it can be varied at any time. He also specifically accepted that:

(*a*) if a person who has two residences acquires a third, an election between all three properties can be made within two years of acquiring the third;

(*b*) if a taxpayer owns three properties and ceases to use one of them as a residence, that cessation will trigger a fresh right of election between the other two;

(*c*) if a taxpayer with two houses transfers one to a settlement of which he is the life tenant the transfer will trigger a fresh right to elect (jointly with the trustees); and

(*d*) if a taxpayer has two houses one owned by himself and the other by a trust the transfer of the trust property to the taxpayer will trigger a fresh right to elect.

He declined to comment on what happens if a taxpayer who owns a residence and a let property begins to use the let property as a residence. Logically that triggers a new right to elect. In other words it appears that where a taxpayer has more than one residence any event that results in his beginning or ceasing to use a property as a residence, or in a change of ownership of one of them, will trigger a fresh right to elect – but only with effect from the date of that event – provided that he occupies at least two properties as residences immediately after the event.

**13.7** In the past the Revenue often accepted an election made more than two years after the acquisition of a second residence as effective from two years prior to the date of the election. Such elections appear now to be invalid. It is difficult to know what to do in such a case. The safest thing is probably either to transfer one of the residences to a settlement and make a fresh election if the disposal can be achieved without triggering a capital gains tax charge, or to buy or rent a holiday home as a third residence and make a fresh election. On the other hand either of these courses will incur costs and it is likely that the Revenue will consider themselves bound to honour past statements that elections were effective. The Revenue's Capital Gains Tax Manual tells staff that an invalid notice given on or before 16 October 1994 in favour of a residence in which a legal or equitable interest is held should be accepted as valid (para 64540). It is however unclear whether this is looking at all invalid notices or only at notices which were given because it was believed that a property held under licence triggered a need for an election. A Tax Bulletin article of 16 October 1994 stated that it did not (see 13.11).

**13.8** If no such election is made by the taxpayer the choice is to be made by the Inspector – whose choice can be different for different parts of the period of ownership – but subject to a right of appeal to the General or Special Commissioners within 30 days of the service on the taxpayer of notice of his determination of the question (*TCGA 1992, s 222(5)(b)*). There is a general principle that, where an officer of the Crown is given a discretion by Parliament, the exercise of which is subject to a right of appeal, he must exercise that discretion judicially, not according to his own whim (*Padfield v Ministry of Agriculture Fisheries and Foods (1968 1 All ER 694)*). Accordingly, the Inspector is almost certainly compelled to base his choice on what appears to him on his examination of the facts to be the main residence at a particular time.

If after making an election the taxpayer acquires a further residence it is probable that the election will cease to apply as the acquisition of the new residence again makes it necessary to determine which out of all the taxpayer's residences is the principal one. Accordingly a fresh election ought to be made.

**13.9** It must be borne in mind that a person can have two residences without owning them both. Thus if a person rents a house on a monthly tenancy and also owns a holiday cottage it is important for him to elect to treat the cottage as his main residence, as he cannot realise a gain on the house (except to the extent that the landlord may make a payment to him to induce him to forego his statutory tenancy rights). If he does not elect, the determination by the Inspector would almost certainly be that the house is the main residence.

**13.10** The Revenue have stated that where in such circumstances the taxpayer was unaware that an election could be made they will extend the time limit for making the election under *section 222(5)(a)* to a reasonable time after the individual first becomes aware that he is entitled to make an election, and that they will then treat it as having effect from the date on which he acquired the second residence (Inland

Revenue Extra-Statutory Concession D21). This concession applies only if the taxpayer's interest in one of the properties has 'no more than a negligible capital value in the open market'.

**13.11** The Revenue considered at one stage that where a residence was occupied under a licence, e.g. a room in a hotel or club or a room in a relative's house, and the taxpayer owned another residence he needed to elect if he wanted the owned property to be treated (contrary to the facts) as his main residence. They no longer take this view. Where an election was made before 16 October 1994 on the basis of their earlier view it remains valid if it was to treat the owned property (or one of two or more owned properties) as the main residence. If it was to treat the property occupied under licence as the main residence, e.g. to preserve the benefit of losses on the owned properties, it ceased to be effective from 16 October 1994. Unfortunately it is not always easy to distinguish between a licence and a tenancy (which does trigger a need to elect). The Revenue's Capital Gains Tax Manual tells staff 'in most cases in which a residence is rented a tenancy exists' (para 64471). That is far too broad. The House of Lords in *Street v Mountford (1985) 1 AC 809*, probably the leading case in this area, held that a right to exclusive occupation is normally a lease (and thus a tenancy). It follows from this that payment of rent for shared premises may well be a licence to occupy – although it could in some cases be a lease. There is of course a large body of law on this area under the Landlord and Tenant legislation, as many landlords have sought to grant licences rather than leases to try to avoid the occupier gaining tenant's rights under that legislation.

**13.12** If an individual acquires land and has a house built on it the Revenue will regard the house or land as being the main residence for the period up to the date that the house is first occupied provided that this does not exceed 12 months. This concession also applies where a house is bought and is not immediately occupied because it is undergoing repairs or redecorations or the taxpayer is taking steps to dispose of his previous residence (Extra-Statutory Concession D49 – formerly Statement of Practice D4). The 12-month period can be extended to up to 24 months – but no longer – if there is a good reason for the delay, i.e. one that is outside the taxpayer's control. Where ESC D49 applies principal private residence relief is given on both houses; no *section 222(5)* election is required (Tax Bulletin, Issue 12, August 1994).

**13.13** A husband and wife can only have one main residence between them whilst they are living together. Where a private residence election affects both it must be given by both (*TCGA 1992, s 222(6)(a)*). The Revenue take the view that it does not affect both if only one has an interest in the properties concerned, i.e. they accept an election signed only by the husband where he owns both properties. Such an election could not affect the subsequent acquisition of another residence by the wife as that acquisition would make it necessary to determine anew what is the main residence and thus presumably render the election ineffective from that date. Where a couple marry and both spouses own a property, the Revenue accept that a fresh two-year period begins with the marriage, but if one owns two properties and the other none they consider that a new two-year period does not apply. If the two jointly owned two properties prior to marriage, the marriage will trigger a fresh right of election as a joint election will need to be made following the marriage (Tax Bulletin, Issue 12, August 1994).

**Period of Ownership as Main Residence**

**13.14** If a house is an individual's only or main residence for part only of his period of ownership the capital gains tax exemption will apply to part of the gain (*TCGA 1992, ss 222(1), 223(2)*). This is the part which the length of the part (or the aggregate of the parts) of the period of ownership for which it was his main residence (inclusive in any event of the last 36 or 24 months (see 13.3 above) of his ownership) bears to the total length of his period of ownership, in both cases ignoring any period prior to 6 April 1965 (*TCGA 1992, s 223(2)(7)*) and in relation to a disposal after 5 April 1988 ignoring any period prior to 31 March 1982 (*FA 1988, Sch 7*). In arriving at this fraction the house can be treated as occupied as the individual's main residence (even though factually it was not) during certain specified periods of absence provided that:

(*a*) it was his main residence at some time before the start of the period of absence and at some time subsequent to that period, i.e. it was the main residence prior (but not necessarily immediately prior) to the start of the period of absence and was reoccupied at some time between the end of that period and the time of its sale; and

(*b*) the individual had no other residence eligible for relief during that period of absence.

(*TCGA 1992, s 223(3)(7)*).

**13.15** It should particularly be noted that it is necessary for the owner to reoccupy the property after the period of absence. If he sells the house without having done so – or if he reoccupies it but has a private residence exemption in force for a different property – the period of absence cannot be treated as a qualifying period. The occupation of another residence by the individual (as of course will always be the case) during the period of absence would appear to debar relief by virtue of (*b*) above unless an election is made under *TCGA 1992, s 222(5)(a)* for the first house to be regarded as his main residence. This should particularly be borne in mind where the individual is working outside the UK. A house does not need to be in the UK to qualify for the private residence relief. Accordingly, it is arguable that in the absence of an election, the overseas house would qualify for relief and the period of absence from the UK house could not then be ignored. In practice the Inland Revenue do not seem to take this point. If the period overseas is sufficiently long for the individual to have ceased to be both resident and ordinarily resident in the UK it is in any event probable that his overseas house is not a property that is 'eligible for relief' under *section 223* of the *TCGA 1992* as it would not have been within the scope of the *Act*. In such circumstances, provided that the individual sells the overseas house before returning to the UK, there is probably no problem.

**13.16** The periods of absence in question in 13.14 above are:

(*a*) any period or periods not exceeding three years in aggregate (if they exceed three years this seems to mean that the house can be treated as the main residence for the first three); plus

(*b*) any period throughout which the individual worked in an employment or office all the duties of which were performed outside the UK (however long that period may be); plus

(*c*) any period not exceeding four years (or periods which in aggregate do not exceed four years) throughout which the individual was prevented from residing in the dwelling-house or part of the dwelling-house in consequence of the situation of his place of work or in consequence of any condition imposed by his employer requiring him to reside elsewhere which was reasonably imposed to secure the effective performance by the employee of his duties (again if the aggregate exceeds four years it appears that the first four will qualify for exemption).

(*TCGA 1992, s 223(3)*).

**13.17** Although head (*b*), unlike (*a*) and (*c*), refers only to a single period it is probable that this is because there is no maximum. Accordingly each separate period meeting the head (*b*) test would wholly qualify for relief. It does seem, though, that if an individual loses his overseas employment any period spent overseas between employments will not fall within head (*b*) – although it can of course fall within head (*a*). It should also be noted that head (*b*) covers only offices and employments, it does not apply where a person is working full-time overseas as a self-employed individual or as a partner in a business. Furthermore all of the duties of an employment must be performed outside the UK; there is no exemption where any of the duties – even if they are merely incidental to the overseas duties – are performed in the UK.

**13.18** It is curious that the relief under the second part of head (*c*) should have to depend on the reasonableness of the employer, over whom the individual of course has no control. It is probably intended to impose an objective test of whether an onlooker would consider the imposition by the employer a reasonable imposition, i.e. 'reasonably imposed' should be interpreted as 'imposed reasonably'. The reference in (*c*) to part of a dwelling-house presumably envisages that part being the entirety of the individual's residence as it is difficult to envisage it being possible for a person to occupy part of his house by reason of his work but impossible for him to occupy the rest of it. It should in any event be noted that his place of work must prevent the individual from occupying his house, not merely make it more convenient for him to live elsewhere. Fortunately, the Revenue seem to take a relaxed view of this condition and do not expect a person to commute a hundred miles a day even though it may be possible for him to do so.

**13.19** It is irrelevant whether the house was unoccupied or let during the period of absence. Provided that the necessary conditions are met it is treated as the owner's private residence even if he had let it and could not therefore use it during that period. In the case of a husband and wife living together, absence due to the spouse's employment will be treated as if it were as a result of the owner's employment (Inland Revenue Extra-Statutory Concession D3). Where an individual claims exemption for a period of absence within (*b*) or (*c*) above, i.e. where his employment prevents his residing in the house, the need for him to reoccupy the property is waived if he is unable to resume residence because the terms of his employment require him to work elsewhere (Inland Revenue Extra-Statutory Concession D4).

**13.20** Where an individual has different interests in a house at different times – for example where he first buys a lease and then buys the freehold reversion so that his interest becomes a freehold interest – his period of ownership starts from the first acquisition taken into account in arriving at the expenditure that is deductible for capital gains tax purposes (*TCGA 1992, s 222(7)*). If the initial interest is a mere tenancy which had no cost it may be worth investigating whether the taxpayer incurred legal fees or other incidental expenses on the acquisition as, if so, that would appear to enable the period of ownership to be extended to include the tenancy. In the case of a husband and wife living together, if one disposes of his interest to the other, including a disposal by way of a legacy on death (and presumably also under the statutory rules on an intestacy, although the *Act* specifically refers to a passing as legatee only), the transferee's period of ownership is treated as commencing when the transferor acquired his initial interest in the property and the property is treated as having been the transferee's main residence for any period for which it was the transferor's (*TCGA 1992, s 222(7)*). As *TCGA 1992, s 62* gives an uplifted base cost this can work unfairly where the interest in the property is inherited and the property was not the principal private residence of the deceased for his whole period of ownership. In such circumstances a deed of arrangement to put the property into an interest in possession trust for the surviving spouse may be worth considering. This has the same inheritance tax effect as a direct inheritance but avoids the capital gains tax problem.

**13.21** Where a married couple separate or are divorced and one partner (usually the husband) moves out and subsequently, as part of a financial settlement, disposes of the home (or an interest in it) to the other, it can be regarded as continuing as the husband's main residence during the period up to the date of the transfer provided that it continues to be the wife's main residence throughout that period (Inland Revenue Extra-Statutory Concession D6). It should particularly be noted that this applies only where the house (or the husband's interest in it) is ultimately transferred to the wife. If it is sold and all or part of the proceeds paid to her the concession will not operate. In such a case it may be preferable to transfer the property to the wife and allow her to sell it.

**13.22** Where a person resides in 'job-related' accommodation and also owns an interest in another property which he intends in due course to occupy as his main residence the property is regarded as his main residence during the time he is living in the job-related accommodation (but this does not apply for a period prior to 31 July 1978). The definition of job-related accommodation is the same as that which applies for interest purposes (see 4.46 above) (*TCGA 1992, s 222(8)*).

## Restriction of Relief

**13.23** Where part of a house is used exclusively for the purposes of a trade or business or of a profession or vocation, the gain on disposal must be apportioned and the exemption applied only to the non-business part (*TCGA 1992, s 224(1)*). If the house was used exclusively for business purposes for part only of the period of ownership, or if at any time in a person's period of ownership there is a change in what is occupied as his residence, for example because of a reconstruction or conversion of a building, the private residence exemption is restricted 'in such manner as the Commissioners concerned may consider to be just and reasonable' (*TCGA 1992, s 224(2)*). The Revenue consider that in the context of the section time apportionment will normally be the appropriate method to use; they do not think it is normally appropriate to take into account changes in market value in apportioning gains to different periods (Tax Bulletin, Issue 12, August 1994).

**13.24** The private residence exemption does not apply at all if the acquisition of the property was made wholly or partly for the purpose of realising a gain from disposing of it (*TCGA 1992, s 224(3)*). If, although the property was not acquired in order to realise a gain from disposing of it, any expenditure subsequent to the acquisition was incurred wholly or partly for the purpose of realising a gain from the disposal, the exemption is not to apply to the part of the gain attributable to that expenditure. The *Act* gives no guidance as to how that part is to be calculated. It is probably the difference between the gain realised and the gain that would have been realised had the expenditure not been incurred. The Revenue would in most cases probably accept an apportionment of the gain in the proportion that the tainted expenditure bears to the total expenditure using the formula in *TCGA 1992, Sch 2 para 16(4)* but there is no statutory right to this. The sort of thing the provision might apply to is where a person owning a leasehold house buys in the reversion in order to be able to sell a freehold or a person converts his house into two flats in order to obtain a higher price. The expenditure does not have to be capital expenditure. If a person redecorates his house in order to obtain a higher price on sale, that would appear, in theory at least, to bring the restriction into play. Surprisingly the Revenue do not in practice apply this restriction to expenditure incurred in obtaining planning permission for redevelopment or in obtaining the release of a restrictive covenant where that is the only relevant expenditure (Tax Bulletin, Issue 12, August 1994). Where all or part of a gain is excluded from the private residence exemption under this provision it is nevertheless outside the scope of *ICTA 1988, s 776* (formerly *ICTA 1970, s 488*) by virtue of *subsection 9* of that *section* (see 14.33). It is not, however, outside the scope of Case I of Schedule D (which could apply where the house was acquired with a view to realising a profit on its disposal but probably not where the house was acquired with other motives and enhancement expenditure was incurred for such a motive).

**House Owned by a Settlement**

**13.25** The capital gains tax private residence exemption also applies to a gain accruing to the trustees of a settlement if a house owned by the settlement was the only or main residence of a person entitled to occupy it under the terms of the settlement (*TCGA 1992, s 225*). It has been held that it is not necessary for the occupier to be specifically entitled under the trust deed to occupy the property. If the trustees of a discretionary trust, in exercise of their discretionary powers, allow a beneficiary to occupy a house owned by the trust (assuming that the trust deed gives them power to do so as will normally be the case) the exemption will apply (*Sansom & Another v Peay 52 TC 1)*. Strangely, the exemption seems to apply even if the trustees charge the beneficiary a market rent for the property. The Inland Revenue take the view that a right to occupy the house rent-free gives the beneficiary an interest in possession in the house so the inheritance tax consequences will need to be considered. It may be possible to avoid this by leasing it to him for a nominal figure for a limited period, or by the trustees acquiring the house jointly with the beneficiary so that he is entitled to occupy it in his own right, and giving the right to live in the house to the youngest child of the beneficiary.

It has been suggested that if a life interest is given to a number of beneficiaries only one of which occupies the property, the capital gains tax exemption nevertheless extends to the entire gain made by the settlement (Taxline, Issue 12, August 1994). The mere existence of a power in a will or trust deed to permit a beneficiary to occupy the house on such terms as the trustees think fit does not itself create an interest in possession in the property, but its exercise may do so. The Revenue consider that using such a power either to allow non-exclusive occupation of the property or to create a contractual tenancy for full consideration will not give rise to an interest in possession. Nor will the creation of a lease for a term, or a contractual tenancy, for less than full consideration – although it will normally trigger a charge to inheritance tax under *IHTA 1984, s 65(1)(b)* (disposition by the trustees which reduces the value of relevant property). The creation of an exclusive or joint right of residence with the intention of providing the beneficiary with a permanent home will normally create an interest in possession even though it may be revocable (SP 10/79). An interest in possession will exist if a person has a present right to the present enjoyment of the property (*Pearson v CIR (1980 STC 318)*). Accordingly what is needed is to allow occupation without the creation of a right to occupy. Some guidance of what will not work can be drawn from inheritance tax cases on this area (see 13.45).

**13.26** Where the beneficiary occupies more than one residence any election as to which is to be treated as his main residence must be made jointly by him and the trustees (*TCGA 1992, s 225*).

**13.27** Relief is also given where personal representatives dispose of a house which both before and after the deceased's death had been used as the only or main residence of an individual (or individuals) who under the deceased's will or the laws of intestacy is entitled to the whole or substantially the whole of the proceeds of the house either absolutely or for life (Inland Revenue Extra-Statutory Concession D5). 'Substantially the whole' for this purpose means 75% or more (Tax Bulletin, Issue 12, August 1994). The idea is not to deny relief to someone because the house happens to be sold by the personal representatives rather than the legatee, but the Revenue consider that there is no justification to allow the benefit of the relief to be obtained by someone who did not occupy the house as a residence.

**13.28** Where an inherited property is disposed of by a beneficiary (other than the surviving spouse) the beneficiary's period of ownership is deemed to begin on the date of death so there will be a restriction of his principal private residence relief if, as will normally be the case unless he lived with the deceased, he does not go into immediate occupation from the date of death (Tax Bulletin, Issue 12, August 1994).

## House Occupied by a Dependent Relative

**13.29** Up to 5 April 1988, the private residence exemption also applied to a gain accruing to an individual on the disposal of an interest in a house which was the sole residence of a dependent relative of his (or his wife) provided rent-free and without any other consideration. Where a house was occupied by a relative at that date the exemption continues as long as the relative continues to occupy the property (*TCGA 1992, s 226(1)*). Once the relative moves out, a later period of occupation by a dependent relative, or even by the same person, will not attract exemption. If the relative ceased to occupy the property before 5 April 1988 no period after that date can accordingly attract exemption. It should be noted that the house must have been the relative's only residence during the period for which the exemption is claimed. It is not sufficient for it to have been his main residence. The payment of outgoings such as rates or electricity which are liabilities of the occupier would not debar the relief. However, strictly speaking, the relative must not pay the ground rent as this is a liability of the landlord, the relieving of which would constitute consideration given by the relative. It would similarly be dangerous for the relative to pay for structural repairs which would normally be payable by the landlord under an arm's length lease. The Revenue have nevertheless stated that, even where the relative makes such payments, they are prepared to grant the relief by concession provided that no net income is receivable by the owner taking one year with another. Net income for this purpose will be computed in accordance with the Schedule A rules, with the exception that a deduction will be allowed for mortgage payments (including the capital element) (Inland Revenue Extra-Statutory Concession D20). This is a major concession. Nevertheless it would be sensible for the relative not to make such payments if this can be avoided as Revenue concessions can be – and sometimes are – withdrawn without warning.

**13.30** A dependent relative is the mother of the individual (or of his spouse) if she is widowed or living apart from her husband or a single woman in consequence of dissolution or annulment of her marriage, or any other relative of the taxpayer or his spouse who is incapacitated by old age or infirmity from maintaining himself (*TCGA 1992, s 226(5)(6)*). It should be particularly noted that the mother must have been married at some time to qualify under the automatic test. If she was an unmarried mother she can qualify as a dependant only if she is incapacitated by old age or infirmity from maintaining herself. In practice the Revenue do not apparently take this point but will allow the relief to an unmarried mother or mother-in-law (Revenue CGT Manual, para 65582).

**13.31** Unlike the relief for the individual's own residence or that for a house owned by a trust, the relief for a house occupied by a dependant is not automatic; it must be claimed (*TCGA 1992, s 226(2)*). The relief is additional to that for the individual's own house but not more than one house can qualify for relief as the residence of a dependant of the taxpayer or his spouse at any one time (*TCGA 1992, s 226(3)*). The Inspector of Taxes is empowered to require a person claiming the relief to prove either that his spouse did not own a property occupied by a dependent relative during the period for which the relief is claimed or, if she did, that she relinquishes her right to claim relief in respect of it for that period (*TCGA 1992, s 226(4)*). Because the relief must be claimed, if a loss arises on a house provided for a dependent relative there is no restriction on that loss as no claim for relief is competent (Revenue CGT Manual, para 65084).

## Let Properties

**13.32** Where the private residence exemption applies to a house which has been wholly or partly let as residential accommodation at any time during the period of ownership, up to £40,000 (£20,000 for disposals prior to 19 March 1991) of chargeable gain on the property, to the extent that it arises by reason of the letting, is exempt from tax (*TCGA 1992, s 223(4)*). Where a property is owned jointly by a husband and wife, it appears that each is entitled to his or her own £40,000 exemption in relation to his or her share.

**13.33** In the past the Revenue took the view that to qualify for this relief the letting must be to a person who occupies the property as a residence. However, in *Owen v Elliott (1990 STC 469)* the Court of Appeal held that there is nothing in *section 223(4)* to restrict the meaning of the words 'residential accommodation', so they must be interpreted in accordance with ordinary use of the English language. The fact that different wording is used in *TCGA 1992, s 222* to confine that relief to dwelling-houses has no bearing on *section 223(4)*. Accordingly the taxpayer was entitled to the relief. In the *Owen* case the taxpayer used his property as a guest house, living in an annex in the summer but occupying the property itself in winter. He accordingly used the whole house as his principal residence for part of each year. As during the remainder of the year the property was let to guests who used it as residential accommodation, i.e. they lived there albeit generally only for one or two weeks, he was entitled to relief under *section 223(4)*. To qualify for the exemption, the owner must be entitled to the private residence exemption under *section 222*, i.e. this extra relief applies only to the individual's own house and not to one occupied by a dependent relative. It is not clear whether this relief extends to properties owned by trustees. The section refers to a gain accruing to an individual, but the reference to *TCGA 1992, s 225* in *subsection (1)(a)* would be otiose if the *section* cannot apply to trustees. The Revenue's view is that it does apply to a house owned by a trust (Revenue CGT Manual, para 64717). The intention is to encourage an occupier to let off surplus accommodation where the house has become too large for him. As some relief is given under *section 222* if a house has been a person's main residence 'at any time in his period of ownership', an individual who acquires a residential investment property ought to consider occupying it for a short period, and electing for it to be his private residence for that period. This will not only in many cases exempt a significant fraction of the gain from tax – as both the short period of occupation and the last three years will qualify for relief under *section 223* – but will also provide this extra £40,000 exemption for the taxable part. There is no limit to the number of £40,000 exemptions that a person can claim under *section 223(4)*. If the part of the gain qualifying for private residence exemption is less than £40,000, this additional relief is limited to that exempt amount. If a loss arises on the disposal it is disallowable to the extent that the basic private residence relief would have been due in the event of a gain, but there is no further restriction under *section 223* (Revenue CGT Manual, para 65083).

## Use of an Office at Home

**13.34** One area of difficulty – on which even the experts cannot agree – is whether, by claiming a deduction against income tax for part of the running costs of one's house because a room is used as an office, this will forfeit a corresponding proportion of the private residence exemption when the house is sold.

**13.35** For expenditure to qualify as a deduction in computing trading profits it must be 'wholly and exclusively expended for the purpose of the trade, profession or vocation' (*ICTA 1988, s 74(a)*). To qualify as a deduction against salary it must be an expense which the employee is 'necessarily obliged' to expend 'wholly, exclusively and necessarily in the performance of' the duties of his employment (*ICTA 1988, s 198(1)*). The capital gains tax exemption is restricted where part of the house is 'used exclusively for the purposes of a trade or business or of a profession or vocation' (*TCGA 1992, s 224(1)*). Some people feel that if the office is also used for some other purpose, e.g. at weekends or one day a year, this will prevent *section 224(1)* from coming into operation but that such use would not prevent the expenditure on, say, rates being wholly and exclusively for business purposes as it would have needed to be incurred had the business use been exclusive. The author personally finds this argument unconvincing. The Revenue will normally only allow an income tax deduction for council tax and rates if a room is set aside for business purposes, and by claiming a deduction (which requires the expense to have been incurred wholly and exclusively for the purpose of the business) one seems to be effectively conceding that the room is used exclusively for such purposes. However, the Revenue take a more relaxed view. They tell their staff that, 'The exclusive use test is a stringent one and you should not usually seek any restriction to relief for a room which has some measure of regular residential use. But occasional and very minor residential use should be disregarded. For example, if a doctor keeps private possessions in a room used as her surgery the surgery should still be regarded as exclusively in business use' (CGT manual 64666).

**13.36** There should be no problems in claiming a deduction against trading or professional income taxed under Schedule D for expenses such as telephone and electricity that depend on usage. One uses electricity wholly and exclusively for heating and lighting the home 'office' during the period it is being occupied as an office. Accordingly, the claiming of the deduction does not imply exclusive use of the room for business purposes. This does not, however, apply to rates (up to 31 March 1990), council tax, or repairs which are incurred irrespective of the period that the room is actually occupied for a particular purpose. Indeed it is doubtful if such expenses can strictly qualify as a deduction under general principles as one does not pay council tax for individual rooms, one pays it by virtue of occupation of the house as such. Similarly, one carries out repairs to maintain the value of the house as a unit. Accordingly, in allowing a claim for such expenses the Revenue are probably making a concession. The Revenue will generally allow the deduction of a modest sum (usually £1 to £5 p.w.) for 'use of home as office' in calculating Schedule D profits in lieu of claiming specific expenses. Such a claim would not jeopardise the capital gains tax exemption as it does not imply a claim that a specific area of the home is used exclusively for business.

**13.37** In many cases, even if capital gains tax is payable, the problem is not of great practical significance. Suppose a house bought for £50,000 is sold seven years later for £90,000, one-eighth having been used for business. One-eighth of the capital gain of £40,000 is £5,000 which may well be covered by the capital gains tax annual exemption. Even if the gain were £80,000 so that £10,000 would be taxable, if the annual exemption is not used against other gains the tax (before any taper relief) would be a maximum of £920 (40% of £2,300). This is equivalent to £132 p.a. over the period of ownership, which is equivalent to the income tax saving achieved by claiming an annual deduction for council tax of £330 at 40%. These figures ignore indexation, of course.

**13.38** Curiously, *section 224(1)* does not mention use for the purpose of an employment. It may be that such use is covered as it constitutes use for the employer's trade or business (the *section* merely talks of 'a trade' not the taxpayer's trade). Alternatively, it may be that no restriction is competent where an employee has an office at his home.

**13.39** The Revenue did not regard the personal community charge (which was payable between 1 April 1990 and 31 March 1993) as a property expense, but as a personal expenditure of the taxpayer. They would not therefore allow a deduction for any part of this regardless of the extent to which a person used his home for business purposes. Where, however the 'standard community charge' was paid and the property to which it related was used partly for business purposes that part of the charge which related to the business would normally be deductible (Inland Revenue Press Release, 10 November 1989). The standard community charge, which at the discretion of the local authority could amount to twice the personal community charge, was payable in relation to property which was not the occupier's main residence. It would normally apply to second homes. It was a question of fact which of a person's homes was his main one.

**13.40** They accept however that where the duties of an employment requires an employee to work at home and he uses a room or rooms exclusively for work purposes he can deduct a proportion of the council tax (Inland Revenue Press Release, 16 March 1993).

**13.41** In practice it is difficult to obtain a deduction against salary for any expenses of working at home. The Revenue tell their staff:

'It is not enough for the employee to demonstrate that he or she works from home, or even that there is an obligation placed on them to work at home. There needs to be something more; that there is an objective requirement resulting from the nature of the employment itself that requires some or all of the duties of the employment to be carried out at home and at no other place. Many employees do some of their work at home because they do not have time to complete it during the working day. That is a matter of personal choice and no deduction should be permitted. Some employees work at home because the place at which they usually work has limited opening hours and they need to work outside those hours. No deduction should be permitted in these cases. Even though the employer does not provide an alternative place at which all of the duties could be carried out there is no obligation that the work must be carried out at home . . . A deduction can only be permitted where the nature of the employment itself requires that the duties must be carried out at home and cannot be carried out in any other place.'

Mr Ainslie was semi-retired. He was employed by a firm of surveyors. He would not have been prepared to take the job if he had to travel every day to their offices and it was agreed that he should work from home. His contract of employment specifically stated, 'You will be required to work from your home.' He sought to attribute £4,000 of his salary as a fee for the use of his home. The Commissioner accepted that the employer had a contractual licence to use, through the taxpayer, the room he used at home for his work. However they had not attributed any part of Mr Ainslie's salary to such use. The Commissioner accepted both that a room dedicated to office use was needed and this must have been obvious to the employer from the outset. Nevertheless as no sum was attributed by the parties to such use a deduction could not be made from Mr Ainslie's agreed salary to reflect it (*Ainslie v Buckley, 2002 STC (SCD) 132*).

## Inheritance Tax

**13.42** For most people the private residence forms their major asset. As it is non income-producing, a gift of an interest in the private residence appears attractive as it will not affect the donor's standard of living. Unfortunately in most cases the anti-avoidance rules on reservation of benefit (see 18.59) prevent such a gift being effective. Indeed they can increase the tax liability as the effect is to treat the property as an asset of both the donor and the donee.

**13.43** Because of the difficulties in generating an effective gift of an interest in one's principal private residence during one's lifetime, conventional planning is for the house to be owned jointly (as tenants in common) by husband and wife and for each to leave his share to the children by his will. This triggers an inheritance tax charge on that share, but in many cases, particularly where there is a mortgage on the property, this will fall within the £250,000 inheritance tax nil rate band. Accordingly if the remainder of the estate is left to the surviving spouse there will be little or no tax to pay. The surviving spouse can remain in occupation of the house by virtue of her ownership of the other half-share as joint owners are each entitled to use of the asset. The surviving spouse can make *inter vivos* gifts to the children of other assets which do not have reservation of benefit problems. In this way assets that are surplus to the surviving spouse's needs can be passed IHT-free to the children leaving only her half-share of the house and the assets she needs to meet her standard of living to suffer tax on her death to the extent that they exceed her own £250,000 nil rate band. Where the value of half of the house significantly exceeds £250,000 it is possible to limit the gift to the children to that level by providing that they are entitled to £250,000 to be satisfied by the transfer to them of such proportion of the private residence as is equal to that sum.

**13.44** The only problem with this scenario is that in law joint owners hold the property on trust for sale which means that any one of them can apply to the court for an order that the property should be sold. The planning relies on the children forebearing from doing this. Unfortunately this does not always work. There have been cases where the children have forced a sale to get their hands on their share of the proceeds leaving the mother homeless, forced to move into a smaller house or forced to move into a residential home, thus thwarting the intention of the deceased spouse. The risk can be minimised in a number of ways. The easiest is for the first half-share of the property to be left not to the children but to a trust for their benefit – although under the rule in *Saunders v Vautier ([1835–42] All ER 58)* if all the beneficiaries of a settlement are of legal capacity they can bring the settlement to an end, so the trust needs to include either infants or charities if the children are all adult. Provided that the trustees are not themselves the children and the trust deed is drafted carefully so that it would not put them in breach of trust to leave the surviving spouse undisturbed, they can normally be relied upon to respect the settlor's wishes.

**13.45** An alternative approach was used by Mr and Mrs Evans. By her Will Mrs Evans left her half-share in the private residence in trust for her daughter. Unfortunately she was not prepared to trust the trustees. She included a provision: 'While my husband . . . remains alive and desires to reside in the property and keeps the same in good repair . . . my trustees shall not make any objection to such residence and shall not disturb or restrict it in any way and shall not take any steps to enforce the trust for sale on which the property is held or to realise my share therein or to obtain any rent or profit from the property.' Furthermore she provided that only on the death of Mr Evans would the daughter become entitled to her mother's share of the property – although it was accepted that such wording did not actually postpone the interest of the daughter until her father's death. It was held that the provision preventing a sale, etc. was not merely an administrative provision. It conferred real benefit on the husband as by nullifying the rights of the trustees to exploit their half-share the Will effectively gave the husband the exclusive occupation of the property for the rest of his life. This was held to create a life interest in favour of the husband in the deceased wife's half-share. As a life tenant is treated for IHT purposes as owning the assets in which his interest subsists, the effect was that on Mr Evans' death IHT was payable on the whole value of the property not merely his half-share (*CIR v Lloyds Private Banking Ltd, 1998 STC 559*).

**13.46** In the case of *Woodhall v CIR (2000 STC (SCD) 558) (SpC 261)* the will provided that the trustees must permit all or any of the deceased's three children, Annie, Alan and Eric, to reside in the house. At the date of Alan's death he was the sole person residing there. The Revenue claimed that he had an interest in possession in the house as he had a present right to present enjoyment, the test laid down in *Pearson v CIR (1980 STC 318)*. The executors claimed that Alan did not have a right to live in the house as the executors had discretion over which of the three children could live there. Alternatively if he had such a right Alan's interest could not exceed 50% as Eric also had a right to live there (Annie having died earlier). It was held that the will did not give the executors a dispositive power to decide who should occupy the house but merely an administrative power to permit such of the children as wanted to occupy the house to do so and if more than one jointly with the other. However the Commissioner accepted that Alan had an interest in possession in only half of the house as Eric also had the right to live there. This may point to a way to reduce the IHT exposure. The larger the class of people entitled to live in the house the smaller the value passing on a death. Of course in practice no one wants to risk having to share occupation with strangers. Nevertheless instead of giving a right of occupation to A it would be sensible to give the right to A, his spouse whilst they are living together and the issue of A. Indeed if A is unmarried it might be possible also to include such other persons as A may from time to time nominate, with A having a power to revoke such nomination.

**13.47** A similar decision was reached in *Faulkner v CIR (2001 STC (SCD) 112)*. In that case the will gave Mr and Mrs Harrison or the survivor of them a right to live in the house as long as they should wish. After Mrs Harrison's death Mr Harrison continued to occupy the house. On his death the Revenue claimed IHT on the whole value of the house. The will trustees contended that he only had a licence to occupy. In the alternative they claimed that if he had an interest in possession he held it jointly with the residuary beneficiaries. The Special Commissioner held that the will did not give the trustees any dispositive power to decide whether the Harrisons should occupy the house and in what way, whether by licence or otherwise; on the contrary it directed them to permit the Harrisons to occupy the house. They were entitled to claim the right of occupation, which amounted to an interest in possession. The interest in possession was not shared with the residuary beneficiaries; they were not able to claim any interest in the house at the time when Mr Harrison had the right to occupy it.

Chapter 14

# Artificial Transactions in Land – ICTA 1988, s 776 (formerly ICTA 1970, s 488)

**14.1** *ICTA 1988, s 776* is one of the main anti-avoidance provisions. It is directed specifically at property transactions. Its purpose is to prevent property dealing profits being disguised as capital. It will not normally apply to a straight purchase and sale of a property; that is likely to be taxable already as a dealing profit if the conditions necessary to bring *section 776* into play are met, and *section 776* operates only where a profit is not taxable as income, i.e. where the gain would otherwise either be taxable as a capital gain or be outside the scope of UK tax completely.

**14.2** In practice the *section* is likely to apply primarily (but by no means exclusively) in two circumstances: on the disposal of shares in a property company and where a UK resident passes the opportunity to make a trading profit on UK land to an overseas company. The first case to come before the courts in connection with *section 776*, *Yuill v Wilson (52 TC 674)*, concerned the passing of the opportunity to make a profit to an overseas company. There the land was initially held as trading stock by a UK company and this may well have been the reason for *section 776* applying at all. If land is acquired direct from an unconnected vendor by a non-UK resident company it seems doubtful whether the section could impose a tax charge on a UK resident shareholder of the acquiring company (although an indirect charge might be sustained in relation to a gain that he makes on his shares) as the fact that the overseas company is chargeable to UK tax on its gain as income would seem to prevent the sale proceeds being a capital sum (a prerequisite for the section to apply) even though the Revenue may have no means to recover that tax liability from the company. See, however, *Sugarwhite v Budd* (14.42 below) where a tax charge was imposed on the vendor.

**14.3** A major practical problem with *section 776* is that it is not one of the provisions the operation of which is dealt with by Somerset House, but is handled by the local districts, and many Inspectors of Taxes seem unclear as to its scope. Many appear to think that any large gain from the disposal of property, or of something deriving its value from property, must be caught by the *section*. This is by no means the case. For the *section* to apply a person must realise 'a gain of a capital nature' in one of three specified circumstances. If none of those three circumstances are present the *section* cannot apply however large the gain and however short the period of ownership may be.

## When does the Section Operate?

**14.4** The three circumstances, one of which is necessary to bring the *section* into operation, are where either

(*a*) land, or property deriving its value from land, is acquired with the sole or main object of realising a gain from disposing of the land, or

(*b*) land is held as trading stock, or

(*c*) land is developed with the sole or main object of realising a gain from disposing of the land when developed.

(*ICTA 1988, s 776(2)*).

**14.5** Even where one of these circumstances is present the *section* will not apply unless, in addition, a gain of a capital nature is obtained from the disposal of the land either

(i) by the person acquiring, holding or developing the land, or by a connected person (within *ICTA 1988, s 839* – see Appendix 1), or

(ii) where any arrangement or scheme is effected as respects the land which enables a gain to be realised by any indirect method, or by any series of transactions, by a person who is a party to (or concerned in) the arrangement or scheme.

(*ICTA 1988, s 776(2)*).

**14.6** Land is defined as including buildings and any estate or interest in land or buildings (*ICTA 1988, s 776(13)(a)*). A reference to land must also be construed as including part of the land, for example if a person acquires five acres of land with the object of realising a gain from its disposal and sells one acre, he cannot claim that he did not have such a motive in acquiring the one acre as it was part of the larger area and the motive related to that larger area.

**14.7** There is no exhaustive definition of 'property deriving its value from land', but this is stated to include (*a*) any shareholding in a company (or any partnership interest or interest in a settlement) deriving its value directly or indirectly from land, and

(*b*) any option, consent or embargo affecting the disposition of land.

(*ICTA 1988, s 776(13)(b)*).

**14.8** Land is to be treated as disposed of if the property in the land or control over the land is effectively disposed of. The legislation envisages that this could take place by one or more transactions, or by means of an arrangement or scheme, concerning either the land or property deriving its value from the land, and embraces all such transactions (*ICTA 1988, s 776(4)*).

**14.9** *Section 776(2)(a)* can accordingly be restated as

'Either

(*a*) any interest in land or buildings, or

(*b*) any shareholdings in a land-owning company, or

(*c*) any option or embargo affecting the disposition of land, or

(*d*) any other asset deriving its value directly or indirectly from land

is acquired with the sole or main object of realising a gain by either

(i) disposing (directly or indirectly) of the land, or

(ii) disposing of any interest in the land or any buildings on it, or

(iii) transferring control over the land, such as disposing of over 50% of a land-owning company.'

**14.10** If a minority shareholding in a land-owning company is acquired with the object of disposing of that holding, or of an enlarged holding which is insufficient to give control, *section 776(2)(a)* will not apply, although the transaction may well be a trading transaction and thus taxable as income under different provisions. This is so even if the sale takes place on an occasion when other shareholders also sell shares so that a controlling interest passes, unless the original minority acquisition was made as part of an arrangement to transfer a controlling interest. What matters is the taxpayer's motive in acquiring his minority holding. The position is not as clear if the charge is under *section 776(2)(b)* (see 14.14 below).

**14.11** The motive test applies solely at the time of acquisition. If property is acquired as a long-term investment and the owner subsequently changes his mind and decides to sell it, the increase in value after the change of mind will not be within *section 776(2)(a)* as the property was acquired with an investment motive (although as the property would probably then become trading stock it may well be within *section 776(2)(b)*).

**14.12** *Section 776(2)(a)* is unlikely in practice to apply on a straightforward purchase and sale of land. This is because if land is acquired with the sole or main object of realising a gain from disposing of it the transaction is a trading transaction under general principles – or in the case of an isolated transaction an adventure in the nature of trade – and taxable under Case I of Schedule D. The profit on disposal will not therefore be a gain of a capital nature. Where it will apply is where land, or more likely property deriving its value from land, is acquired with the intention of transferring control over the land by some indirect means.

**14.13** It should be noted, however, that the motive of acquiring to resell need not be the motive of the taxpayer. It can be the motive of a third party (*Winterton v Edwards (52 TC 655)* – see 14.37 below).

**14.14** *Section 776(2)(b)* calls for a little explanation. It is a question of fact whether land is held as trading stock. The test in this case is applied at the time of disposal, not the date of acquisition. If land is held as trading stock it is caught even though it may have been acquired for some other purpose and appropriated as trading stock. Curiously, the *section* does not exclude the increase in value prior to appropriation as trading stock in such circumstances. It may be that the draftsman felt that such increase would automatically be excluded by the computation (see 14.21 below).

**14.15** It should particularly be noted that where land is held as trading stock the *section* automatically applies. There is no motive test. Accordingly if a controlling interest in a company owning land as trading stock (and which derives its value from that land) is disposed of (so that the land is deemed to have been disposed of) the *section* will automatically come into operation even though the sale may be the bona fide realisation of a long-term investment in the shares. Under *section 776(2)(i)* (see 14.5 above) the gain of a capital nature needs to be made by the person holding, acquiring or developing the land, or by a connected person. A person acquiring property deriving its value from land, e.g. shares in a property dealing company, accordingly cannot be taxed under that *paragraph* unless he is a connected person of the company which holds the land as trading stock. A shareholder is not automatically a connected person of the company. He will only be connected if he controls the company either alone or together with persons who are connected with him (*ICTA 1988, s 839(6)*). However, if two or more persons act together to exercise control of a company they are regarded as connected in relation to the company so that their holdings would need to be aggregated under *section 839(6) (ICTA*

*1988, s 839(7)*). Although a minority shareholder will not be within *paragraph (2)(i)* if he sells his shares in isolation, what if he joins in a sale of the entire company? He is probably again outside the scope of the *paragraph* as joining in a sale agreement would not be the exercise of control over the company. However, an agreement by all of the shareholders of a property dealing company to sell their shares in the company to a third party may well be an arrangement effected as respects the land owned by the company which enables a gain to be realised by an indirect method by a person who is a party to the arrangement, and thus within *paragraph (2)(ii)*. The courts have given a very wide interpretation to 'arrangement' in other contexts and based on this it may well be that a mere agreement to sell together could constitute an arrangement.

**14.16** There is an exemption from the charge under *paragraph 2(i)* on a disposal of shares in a company that owns land as trading stock (or a holding company that owns (directly or indirectly) at least 90% of the ordinary shares of such a company). All of the land held as trading stock at the date of the disposal of the shares must be disposed of subsequently both 'in the normal course of its trade by the company that held it' and 'so as to procure that all opportunity of profit in respect of the land arises to that company' (*ICTA 1988, s 776(10)*). It is normal when selling a property dealing company to ask the purchaser for a warranty that the trading stock will be sold in the normal course of trade by the company so as to procure that all opportunity of profit will accrue to the company. The vendor is very much in the hands of the purchaser on this. If, for example, the purchaser subsequently procures that the company transfers a site at cost to another company in its group this will deprive the vendor of his exemption under *section 776(10)* – not just in respect of the value of that site but in relation to the entire sale proceeds of the shares. This illustrates the importance not only of obtaining such a warranty but of ensuring that whoever gives it is of sufficient substance that the money will be available if a claim needs to be made under it. It is to be hoped that the requirement that 'all opportunity of profit in respect of the land' must arise to the vendor is not interpreted too literally. A purchaser would not (in most cases) exist for the land unless he saw some opportunity of profit for himself in acquiring the land! The intention is obviously to deny the exemption only where some artificial transaction is entered into to direct part of the profit due to the company to a third party. Obviously if the company owns property other than the trading stock, the exemption applies only to so much of the value of the shares as derives from the trading stock; the part deriving from the other property could give rise to a charge under the *section* if it falls within *paragraph 2(a)* or *(c)*.

**14.17** This exemption applies only where the charge is under *paragraph 2(i)*. There is no exemption where the charge is under *paragraph 2(ii)* because an arrangement or scheme has been entered into. As indicated above it is possible that a sale by all of the shareholders of a company constitutes an arrangement. Fortunately, the Revenue do not seem to take this point and accept that the *section* is not intended to catch innocent transactions. It is unfortunate that the wording is so widely drawn, as even if the Revenue do not seek to tax a bona fide commercial sale of shares held for a long time as an investment they are at liberty to change their minds at any time over the following six years.

**14.18** The motive test under *section 776(2)(c)* where land is developed is applied at the time that the intention to develop the land is formed. Any increase in value occurring before that time is specifically excluded from the scope of the *section* (unless of course it is already within *paragraph (2)(a)* or *(2)(b)*). The calculation of the amount to exclude is to take account of the 'treatment under Case I of Schedule D where a person appropriates land as trading stock' (*ICTA 1988, s 776(7)*). This is a somewhat strange wording. Why merely take account of that treatment instead of adopting it? It is also unfortunate that there is no legislation as to the treatment to adopt under Case I in such circumstances. The legislation provides for the appropriation to be at market value for capital gains tax purposes (*TCGA 1992, s 161*) but this would not automatically apply for Case I also. In *Ridge Securities Ltd v CIR (44 TC 373)* it was held that the appropriation should take place at market value by analogy with the rule in *Sharkey v Wernher (36 TC 275)*, which deals with the situation where property is appropriated from trading stock. However, the *Ridge Securities* case is a High Court decision that did not go to appeal. It should also be borne in mind that it was concerned with an artificial avoidance device which could conveniently be thwarted by deeming an appropriation to trading stock at market value. Nevertheless in practice it is likely that the Revenue will regard *section 776(7)* as requiring an appropriation at market value. If the *section 776* gain is calculated on the assumption that the land was appropriated to trading stock that assumption must also be made for capital gains tax purposes (*ICTA 1988, s 777(11)*).

## The Meaning of a 'Gain of a Capital Nature'

**14.19** As indicated earlier not only must one of the three circumstances exist but also a gain of a capital nature must be realised to bring the section into operation. A gain of a capital nature is one that, apart from *section 776*, does not fall to be included in any computation of income for the purposes of the *Tax Acts* (*ICTA 1988, s 777(13)*). Accordingly, if a gain can be taxed as income under some other provision it is to be taxed under that provision, not under *section 776*. *Section 776* can only operate if the gain would escape tax or be taxed as capital if the *section* did not exist. In many cases a transaction that the Revenue seeks to tax under *section 776* will be within the scope of Case I of Schedule D. In such a case a *section 776* assessment is not competent. As the motive test under *section 776(2)(a)* is the same as that for Case I it is difficult to envisage a circumstance where a simple purchase and sale of land can fall within *section 776*. It is either a capital gain or a trading profit depending on whether or not it was bought for resale.

## The Effect of the Section

**14.20** Where *section 776* does apply the gain must be treated as income which arises when the gain is realised and which is taxable under Case VI of Schedule D (*ICTA 1988, s 776(3)(a)*). It will normally be treated as income of the person by whom the gain is realised (*ICTA 1988, s 776(3)(b)*). A gain is not realised until the recipient can effectively enjoy or dispose of it (*ICTA 1988, s 777(13)*).

**14.21** Because the *section* will often apply to a series of transactions designed to transfer land by indirect means it is difficult to lay down rules for the calculation of the gain. The *Act* does not attempt this. It requires the adoption of 'such method of computing a gain . . . as is just and reasonable in the circumstances' (*ICTA 1988, s 776(6)*). In considering what is a just and reasonable computation it requires to be taken into account:

(*a*) the value of what is obtained for disposing of the land; and

(*b*) the need to allow as a deduction only such expenses as are attributable to the land disposed of.

**14.22** As further guidance the draftsman indicates that account should be taken of:

(*a*) the way in which profits under Case I of Schedule D are computed if the transaction is the acquisition of a freehold and the grant of a lease out of it (for Case I the reversion is treated as trading stock and a proportionate part of the cost of the land is attributed to it – see *Utting v Hughes (23 TC 174)*, 6.7 above); and

(*b*) the adjustment made for Case I of Schedule D under *ICTA 1988, s 99(2)(3)*, which allows a deduction in computing trading profits for any part of a premium taxed under Schedule A.

There is no requirement to take these two factors into consideration; it is merely permissible to do so, although the court would undoubtedly expect them to be applied unless there is a good reason for not doing so.

**14.23** In calculating the gain any necessary apportionments of income or expenditure are to be made by such method as is just and reasonable in the circumstances, and any valuations that are needed to give effect to the *section* must be made (*ICTA 1988, s 777(6)*).

## A Gain Obtained for Another Person

**14.24** A charge under *section 776* can arise where the person holding, acquiring or developing the land or a connected person, or a person who is a party to a scheme or arrangement affecting the land, obtains the gain not for himself but for some other person (*ICTA 1988, s 776(2)*). For this purpose partnerships, trusts and deceased estates can be regarded as persons distinct from the persons who are for the time being partners, trustees or personal representatives (*ICTA 1988, s 777(7)*). A gain is obtained for someone by some other person if that other person directly or indirectly transmits the opportunity of making that gain to the person who receives it, whether by a premature sale or otherwise (*ICTA 1988, s 776(5)*). This is probably not an exhaustive definition. If the gain arising to A is derived from value provided indirectly by B (e.g. if something is done to pass value out of land owned by B into that owned by A) it is likely that B has obtained the gain for A. In such circumstances the charge to tax is on the person who transmits the opportunity to make the gain (B), not on the person who received it (*ICTA 1988, s 776(8)*). If part of the gain accruing to a person is derived from value (or an opportunity to realise a gain) provided by another person that person is taxable on that part and the recipient of the gain is taxable on the balance (*ICTA 1988, s 776(8)*).

**14.25** When a person is assessed in respect of a gain that he has made for another he is given a right to recover the tax from that other person, although if, as will probably normally be the case, that other person is not resident in the UK that right may not be worth much (*ICTA 1988, s 777(8)(a)*). To enable him to do so he can require the Revenue to issue him with a certificate specifying the amount assessed and the tax paid. Such a certificate is conclusive evidence of any facts stated in it. For this purpose, but not for *section 776* generally, the tax attributable to income so assessed is calculated by treating the income as the highest part of the payer's income (*ICTA 1988, s 777(8)*), but leaving out of account any payment for compensation for loss of office, profit on insurance policies or a premium on a lease (*ICTA 1988, s 833(3)*). If the person assessed does not pay the tax within six months of its due and payable date the Revenue can recover the tax from the recipient of the gain (or at least can try to do so). This does not prejudice their right to recover it from the person assessed (*ICTA 1988, s 777(8)(b)*). Irrespective of whether or not the recipient of the gain reimburses the tax to the payer it is to be treated as having been paid by the recipient of the gain for the purpose of calculating his capital gains tax liability. This enables the amount taxed under *section 776* (and expenditure taken into account in calculating the amount assessable) to be excluded from the calculation of the capital gain by virtue of *TCGA 1992, ss 37–39* (*ICTA 1988, s 777(12)*).

## Ancillary Points

**14.26** In applying *section 776*, any number of transactions can be regarded as a single arrangement or scheme if a common purpose can be discerned in them. They can also be so regarded if, although the transactions do not themselves display a common purpose, there is sufficient other evidence of their having been carried out for a common purpose (*ICTA 1988, s 776(5)(b)*). Account is also to be taken of any method, however indirect, by which any property or right is transferred or transmitted or the value of any property or right is enhanced or diminished. Any such transaction can give rise to a charge under *section 776 (ICTA 1988, s 777(2))*. The *Act* gives the following examples of the sort of thing that the draftsman had in mind.

(*a*) A sale, contract, or other transaction at an undervalue or an overvalue.

(*b*) The transfer of (or of control over) property or a right over land by assigning share capital or other rights in a company, or by assigning rights in a partnership or an interest in settled property.

(*c*) The creation of any option, consent, or embargo affecting the disposition of any property or right, either for full value or otherwise, and any payment for the release of the embargo or the giving of the consent.

(*d*) The disposal of any property or right over land on the winding-up of a company or the termination of a partnership or trust (*ICTA 1988, s 777(3)*).

**14.27** In considering the motive or intentions of any person, the objects and powers of a company as set out in its memorandum of association, or the objects and powers of any partnership or trust as set out in the partnership or trust deed, are not conclusive (*ICTA 1988, s 777(4)*). What needs to be looked at is what in fact happens. If what happens is within the section it is taxable even though it may have been *ultra vires*. As the Revenue always adopt this approach to company objects clauses and partnership deeds it is not clear why it was felt necessary to spell it out in this instance.

**14.28** Value can be traced through any number of companies, partnerships and trusts to ascertain whether and to what extent the value of any property is derived from some other property or right. At each stage of this exercise the property held by a company, partnership or trust can be attributed to the shareholders, partners, or beneficiaries in whatever manner is appropriate in the circumstances (*ICTA 1988, s 777(5)*).

**14.29** Where, under the settlement provisions, income of a trust is treated as income of the settlor, a *section 776* gain realised by the trust is of course to be treated as income of the settlor (*ICTA 1988, s 777(10)*). This also applies in any other circumstances where income is deemed to belong to some other person.

**14.30** *Section 776* applies to non-UK residents if all or any part of the land is situated in the UK (*ICTA 1988, s 776(14)*). It is difficult to envisage only part of the land being in the UK. One instance in which this can occur is that both UK and non-UK land will be taken into account in determining whether a company derives its value from land. Where the person entitled to the consideration is not resident in the UK, the Revenue can require the payer to deduct income tax at the basic rate from the consideration and pay it over to them (*ICTA 1988, s 777(9)*). They can apparently require such a deduction even if the recipient is not the taxable person (because the gain was provided for him by another). Of course, they need to know about the transaction before the payment is made. In practice this is likely to mean that the provision will only operate where the consideration is payable by instalments such that the whole amount has not been paid over by the time the Revenue considers the transaction. The Revenue did find out in advance in *Entergy Power Development Corp v Pardoe (2000 STC 286)* but this did not help them. They issued *section 777(9)* notices to a number of different potential purchasers of a company including Entergy. It was held that a person cannot be entitled to any consideration until a contract exists. Accordingly a notice issued in advance of the contract was invalid. The court accepted that this means that it is virtually impossible for the Revenue to issue directions where contract and completion take place on the same day but felt that the wording of the section indicated that Parliament had intended to give the Revenue power to intervene only once an entitlement to a contractual receipt arose.

**14.31** It is not clear if *section 776* can apply to land situated outside the UK. The declaration in *section 776(14)* that 'this section shall apply to all persons . . . if all or any part of the land in question is situated in the UK' is intended to make clear that a non-resident is taxable in respect of UK land. The wording does not appear to prevent a charge on a UK resident in relation to non-UK land, although it could be interpreted as an exhaustive definition of the scope of the *section*, in which case a charge could not arise in respect of non-UK land.

**14.32** In the past the Revenue frequently raised a *section 776* assessment and a capital gains tax assessment – and sometimes a Case I assessment as well – in respect of the same gain. In *Lord Advocate v McKenna (1989 STC 485)* it was accepted that the Revenue are entitled to raise alternative assessments in this way. However, if no appeals are made they are not entitled to seek to enforce payment of the tax due under both assessments. They must select which assessment to pursue. An attempt to enforce payment of all three alternate assessments was described by Scott LJ in the Court of Appeal as 'vexatious and oppressive' in *CIR v Wilkinson (1992 STC 454)*.

## Exemption for Principal Private Residence

**14.33** *Section 776* cannot apply to a gain accruing to an individual on a disposal of his principal private residence if the gain on disposal would be exempt if it were a capital gain (*ICTA 1988, s 776(9)*). It is somewhat surprising that the capital gains tax definition of a principal residence – which enables the taxpayer to elect which of two or more residences should be regarded as the main one – is adopted. It is not clear what happens where the gain is partly exempt, e.g. because a property was a principal residence for part only of a person's period of ownership or because it was used partly for business purposes. Where a gain on a main residence is chargeable to capital gains tax solely by virtue of *TCGA 1992, s 224*, which denies the private residence exemption to the extent that a gain is attributable to acquisition or enhancement expenditure incurred for the purpose of realising a gain from the disposal, the exemption from *section 776* still applies. The position is unclear in relation to property held by trusts. *Section 776(9)* refers specifically to a gain accruing to an individual. However it also refers to *TCGA 1992, ss 222–226*, and *section 225* can only apply to trustees. It is anybody's guess how the courts will interpret this ambiguity if called upon to do so.

## Decided Cases

**14.34** A number of cases have reached the courts in relation to *section 776*. The first was *Yuill v Wilson (52 TC 674)*. Mr Yuill controlled two UK companies which owned land as trading stock. They sold the land to two Guernsey companies at market value. Planning consent for redevelopment was obtained and the Guernsey companies resold their land to a UK company at the enhanced market value. It was held by the House of Lords that Mr Yuill, as the guiding spirit behind the scheme, had provided the Guernsey companies with the opportunity to make a capital profit. He was therefore taxable on the gain of the Guernsey companies under *section 776(8)*. The terms on which the land was sold by the Guernsey companies were peculiar. The full price was payable on completion on 25 March 1974. However, the agreement provided that the vendors would lend back almost 95% of the consideration to the purchaser. In the event of nationalisation of the land within three years of the sale the bulk of the purchase price (approximately 70%) was to be repaid. Roughly two-thirds of that sum would be repayable on nationalisation in year four and one-third in year five. The House of Lords held that the Guernsey companies had received on completion only the £248,000 that did not have to be lent back. They set the whole of the cost of the land and selling expenses (not merely a proportionate part thereof) against that £248,000. The effect was to produce a loss for 1973/74. Accordingly, no *section 776* charge could arise in that year. A charge would however arise in 1976/77 when the possibility of having to repay the top third of the consideration no longer existed. Further charges would similarly arise in 1977/78 and 1978/79.

**14.35** This case is of interest for a number of reasons. The calculation of the gain by setting the whole of the cost against the part of the consideration actually received is surprising. It appears to be based on the concept that until it is known if part of the sale proceeds needs to be repaid it is proper to make full provision for that possibility however remote it may appear. It is interesting that Mr Yuill, who never owned the land, was taxed rather than his UK companies which transferred their land to the Guernsey companies. On the face of it they are the persons who passed the opportunity of gain to Guernsey. To tax Mr Yuill seems to be drawing aside the corporate veil with a vengeance. He may have been the guiding force behind the transactions but the potential gain was never his. The transactions were all at market value. It is surprising that a sale at full market value can be regarded as a transfer of an opportunity to make a gain simply because at some later date the market value of the land increased.

**14.36** When the Revenue raised their assessment for 1976/77 Mr Yuill somewhat cheekily returned to court (*Yuill v Fletcher (58 TC 145)*). He claimed that the House of Lords ought to have valued the rights conferred on the vendor companies under their contracts and brought this into the computation as money's worth. Alternatively, if those rights were incapable of being valued in 1973/74 they should have been valued in 1974/75. This claim was based on comments that had been made in the Court of Appeal in the earlier case. In the High Court, Mr Justice Walton held that the House of Lords had already decided the matter on the same facts in *Yuill v Wilson* and he was bound by the method of calculation that they had laid down. He also expressed scepticism as to whether the rights were capable of being valued. If they were not they could not constitute money's worth. The decision was unanimously upheld in the Court of Appeal.

**14.37** The next case was *Winterton v Edwards and Byfield v Edwards (52 TC 655)*. The major shareholder in a property company, Mr Lyon, acquired two sites outside the company. The two minority shareholders protested. Mr Lyon accordingly agreed that he would pay them a share (corresponding to their interest in the company) of the profit on the developments. He duly paid over their shares in two instalments, one in 1970/71 and the other in 1971/72. The Revenue assessed the minority shareholders, Mr Winterton and Mr Byfield, on the sums of £41,395 and £45,995 that they had respectively received from Mr Lyon. It was held that conditions *(2)(a)* and *(2)(c)* both applied – the land had been both acquired and developed with the object of realising a gain from disposing of it. It did not matter that the motive had been Mr Lyon's and that Mr Winterton and Mr Edwards never themselves had any interest in the land at the time it was acquired or when the decision to develop it was taken. A scheme had been effected which enabled a gain of a capital nature to be realised. (A complex scheme was effected by Mr Lyon who did not want to pay income tax on his share of the gain.) Mr Winterton and Mr Byfield were persons 'concerned in' the scheme insofar as they benefited from it. Accordingly, all of the conditions for *section 776(2)* to operate existed and the assessment was upheld.

**14.38** The concept enunciated in *Winterton v Edwards* that the motive does not have to be in the mind of the taxpayer was also applied in *Page v Lowther (57 TC 199)*. A substantial long-established family trust held 2.6 acres of land in Kensington. They decided that it should be redeveloped. However, they felt a social responsibility to ensure that the development was in keeping with the tone of the area and were not prepared to simply sell the land to a small developer. A major development company was interested in carrying out the development but unwilling to pay the price for the land that the trustees required. To resolve these commercial problems the trustees sold a long lease of the land to the development company. The developer undertook that when it granted underleases to occupiers it would procure that the occupier paid a premium to the trustees, calculated on a formula. It was held that land had been developed within *section 776(2)(c)*, albeit that the motive was the developer's, not the trustees', and that the agreement under which the occupiers of houses were to pay premiums constituted an arrangement to which the trustees were parties. *Section 776* accordingly applied. The trustees were simply seeking to obtain the market value for their land. They appear to have been caught because they tied the premium to the development. It is not certain that the *section* would apply if they had sold the lease initially for an agreed price payable by instalments as and when the developer himself took premiums from the occupiers. It is probable that in such a case the trustees would realise their gain before the development commenced – although *Yuill v Wilson* perhaps casts doubt on this. It may be that the trustees would not realise their gain until they receive the money in which case the gain would arise after commencement of the development and would thus still be caught. The taxpayers also put forward the alternative argument that they had not sought to avoid tax and *section 776* had to be construed in the light of *subsection (1)*, 'This section is enacted to prevent the avoidance of tax . . .'. However, Mr Justice Warner felt that this did not entitle one to treat as ambiguous words which are in themselves clear, and as the transaction fell squarely within the wording of *subsection (2)* he had to find in favour of the Revenue. He also thought it tenable to take the view that the trustees had in fact avoided tax 'albeit perhaps unwittingly'.

**14.39** There is also a Special Commissioners case, *Newman v Pepper (2000 STC (SCD) 345) (SpC 243)*. This is an oddity. Denis Newman acquired a farm in 1963. In 1982 he executed a trust deed conveying the land other than the farmhouse to bare trustees to hold it as to one-eighth for each of his five children and three-eighths for himself. Two days later on 9 July 1982 the trustees granted an option to a firm of builders, Wates, to buy the land. It was common ground that the date of the formation of the first intention to develop the land was 9 July 1982. The option was exercisable after 1 August 1983. It enabled Wates to buy either the whole of the land or such part as by that time Wates had obtained planning permission for. The option defined the purchase price as 15% of the sale price of all of the buildings to be constructed on the land (subject to certain adjustments) subject to a minimum of £50,000 per developable acre. In July 1985 Wates assigned the benefit of the option to McAlpine Homes and Canberra Developments Ltd. In November 1985 McAlpine and Canberra exercised the option in relation to part of the land which was the subject of outline planning permission. That land was duly transferred, McAlpine paying £528,483 and Canberra £186,017, a total initial consideration of £714,500. In February 1986 McAlpine and Canberra entered into a deed of partition of the land. In May 1986 the trustees released Canberra from its remaining obligations under the option agreement for a payment of £175,000.

**14.40** At some stage a purported CGT hold-over election in relation to the gift by Denis Newman on the creation of the settlement was made. Colin Newman, one of the sons and one of the trustees, did not dispute this election at a meeting with the Inspector of Taxes in September 1987. However when the case came before the Commissioners Colin denied that he had ever signed the hold-over election. He claimed that it was a forgery (and presumably as a result part of the gain should have been taxed in 1982). The Commissioner rejected this contention. He also rejected a further claim that as McAlpine had entered into a mortgage containing a standard clause that it would 'pay and discharge all future rent, rates, taxes, duties, charges, assessments, impositions and outgoings whatsoever', the CGT and section 776 tax liabilities should be assessed on McAlpines not the Newmans. He similarly rejected a claim that the tax should have been assessed on the trustees not the beneficiaries even though they were mere nominees. The only thing the Commissioner said about *section 776* in his judgement was: 'In relation to the Revenue computations of the taxpayers' liabilities . . . in relation to income tax assessable pursuant to *section 776*, I find, insofar as such computations relate to factual issues and hold, insofar as such computations relate to questions of law, that such computations by the Revenue are correct.' It does not appear that any arguments were raised (by a taxpayer in person) in relation to whether Case I rather than *section 776* ought to have applied. The Revenue did not raise *section 776* assessments for 1986/87, which suggests that they did not regard the receipts from Canberra as within *section 776*. That would be logical, as in the event those receipts were not based on the value of the land when developed; it was only the receipts from McAlpines (and possibly the interim receipts from Wates) that were.

**14.41** To date the taxpayer has won one *section 776* appeal. In *Chilcott v CIR (55 TC 446)* a property dealing company, Kolinol, agreed to sell its only property under an arrangement whereby it received shares in Minet Holdings. The shareholders then sold their shares to Trafalgar House for a consideration to be satisfied by the transfer later of shares in Minet Holdings (i.e. the shares that Kolinol, by then a subsidiary of Trafalgar, would receive from Minet). There was clearly an arrangement. However, it was held that at the time of the sale of the shares in Kolinol it did not own land as trading stock and accordingly circumstance *(2)(b)* did not apply. As neither *(2)(a)* or *(c)* was in issue the gain on the shares could not be within *section 776* even though it was clear that the gain made by the shareholders of Kolinol derived from the value of the property.

**14.42** The only other case to have reached the Courts on *section 776* (leaving aside *Entergy Power Development Corp v Pardoe* (see 14.30) which was concerned with a specific detailed aspect of the legislation) is *Sugarwhite v Budd (60 TC 679)*. Mr Sugarwhite bought a property in 1973 for £20,000. He endeavoured to sell it but was unable to find a purchaser. He mentioned his predicament to a solicitor who introduced him to a Bahamian company that was prepared to buy the property for £25,000. The Bahamian company sub-sold the property to a second Bahamian company at a profit of £6,500. It was then sold to a third Bahamian company at a profit of £1,000 and finally to a UK company at a profit of a further £1,000. Mr Sugarwhite was asked to convey the property direct to the ultimate purchaser, which he did. He had a couple of years previously sold another property to a Bahamian company introduced to him by the same solicitor. The Revenue assessed Mr Sugarwhite under *section 776(8)* as having provided the opportunity of realising a gain to the three Bahamian companies. Mr Sugarwhite claimed firstly that he was not a party to an arrangement within *section 776* as he had merely entered into an arm's length sale of the property. The Special Commissioner held, however, that there had been an arrangement to enable the Bahamian companies to make a profit from the property and that as Mr Sugarwhite had signed the conveyance he was party to this. This illustrates the dangers of becoming involved with sub-sales of property without completion. A vendor of a property who is asked to convey direct to a third party needs to be very wary, particularly if it is apparent at completion that some of the funds are going to non-UK companies.

**14.43** Mr Sugarwhite's second contention was that in any event the Bahamian companies had not made a gain 'of a capital nature' as the transactions were clearly dealing transactions. None of the Bahamian companies had held the property for more than a few weeks and they had not had to pay for the property as they never completed the sub-purchase. It was held that it was for Mr Sugarwhite to produce evidence to show the motive of the Bahamian companies in acquiring the land. He had not done so. Even if he was not in a position to demonstrate the motive of the companies he could have produced the solicitor who effected the introduction, who might have been able to throw more light on the motive. The Court of Appeal indicated that if the taxpayer 'was unwilling or unable to adduce evidence' to show that the transaction was not entered into for tax avoidance purposes it was open to the Commissioner to accept that as being a possibility. Accordingly it was impossible for him to be certain that the transaction was a trading transaction – as a transaction designed solely to avoid tax is not trading – and he was therefore entitled to find that the profits made could have been gains of a capital nature. This emphasises that, however obvious the nature of a transaction may appear to be, it is not safe to assume that it will appear so clear cut to the Commissioners, and as the onus is on the taxpayer to displace an assessment it is important to bring evidence to demonstrate what in fact occurred.

## Advance Clearance of Proposed Transactions

**14.44** There is a clearance procedure whereby a taxpayer can put details of a transaction or a proposed transaction before his Inspector of Taxes and require him to say whether he is satisfied that the section does not apply to the transaction. If the Inspector states that he is so satisfied the Revenue cannot subsequently raise an assessment on the taxpayer under the *section* in respect of the transaction unless the particulars given in the clearance application were not such as to make full and accurate disclosure of all facts and considerations that are material to be known to the Inspector in making his decision (*ICTA 1988, s 776(11)*). If the Inspector is not satisfied this does not mean that he will raise an assessment under *section 776* if the transaction goes ahead. It may merely mean that he does not understand the transaction, or that he cannot make up his mind and wants the opportunity to consider it afresh when the taxpayer submits his tax return, or that he does not have enough information to make a decision and, as Parliament has felt it proper not to provide him with power to request such information, feels that it would be wrong to ask the taxpayer to supply this voluntarily.

**14.45** The clearance procedure applies only where the gain arises by virtue of *section 776(2)(a)* or *(c)*. There is no clearance procedure where the land is held as trading stock. In practice many local Inspectors of Taxes will give a clearance on the sale of shares in a property dealing company but this has no statutory effect – and because the exemption under *section 776(10)* (see 6.12 above) depends on what happens to the company's stock after the sale the Revenue cannot be in a position to give a clearance, as this must be a major unknown factor.

**14.46** The procedure is that a person who considers that *section 776(2)(a)* or *(c)* may apply to a gain of a capital nature which he either has obtained or will obtain from a proposed transaction can supply to the Inspector to whom he submits his income tax return written particulars showing how the gain will arise (or has arisen). The Inspector must then notify him, within 30 days from his receipt of those particulars, whether he is satisfied that the *section* does not apply (*ICTA 1988, s 776 (11)*).

**14.47** This clearance procedure is very unsatisfactory. As indicated above there is no power for the Inspector to seek further information from the taxpayer. The taxpayer has to guess what information the Inspector is likely to feel he needs to arrive at a decision. If clearance is refused the taxpayer does not know whether this may merely be because he has guessed wrongly or whether the Inspector really thinks the *section* applies. The author once had a clearance refused and later learned that this was because he had not thought to tell the Inspector a company's motive for purchasing the factory that it had bought twenty years earlier and used for its manufacturing activity since then (which fact he did think to tell him) but had – incorrectly as it turned out – expected that the Inspector would assume that it was bought for the purpose for which it was in fact used. The second problem is that the Revenue do not have to tell the taxpayer why a clearance is refused, and normally will not do so. Because of both these factors it is wise to discuss the transaction informally with the Inspector first before submitting a formal clearance application.

**14.48** Another problem is that on a sale of shares in a company each shareholder is statutorily required to make his own individual application to his own tax district. This can result in delays, as the shareholder's Inspector will normally consult the company's Inspector – or perhaps simply refer the application to him for a decision. It can also lead to inconsistencies, with one shareholder being given a clearance and another refused it on the same facts. Shareholders are sometimes asked by their Inspector of Taxes to send the application to the company's Inspector instead. It may be dangerous to accede to such a request. Parliament has specifically provided that the application must be made to the Inspector to whom the taxpayer submits his tax return – a most unusual provision – and in these circumstances the courts may well hold that a taxpayer who does not follow the statutory procedure departs from it at his peril, and that the clearance is void. It is also unclear to what extent, if at all, the courts might hold an application for clearance against the taxpayer if it is refused and he nevertheless proceeds with the transaction. Unlike with the clearances under *ICTA 1988, s 703* (formerly *ICTA 1970, s 460*), which can be made by any taxpayer, and *TCGA 1992, s 138* which can be made by any company concerned in a reorganisation, the only taxpayer entitled to apply for *section 776* clearance is one 'who considers that *section 776(2)(a)* or *(c)* may apply', which appears to require the taxpayer to prejudge the issue.

**14.49** Because of these problems the decision as to whether or not to apply for clearance can be difficult. If the taxpayer would not proceed with a transaction if there were any risk of his being taxed on the sale proceeds of his shares, or the gain on his property, as income, clearance will obviously need to be sought. If a taxpayer tends to worry if he has uncertainties hanging over him, a clearance application is probably also desirable, particularly if the figures are large. However, this is not a clearance that the author personally applies for as a matter of course simply to be on the safe side where he does not feel that *section 776* applies. A refusal of clearance may well not be of significance but will create unnecessary worry for the taxpayer.

## Power to Obtain Information

**14.50** The Revenue are empowered to require any person to furnish them with such particulars as they think necessary for the purpose of *section 776*. They must allow him at least 30 days to supply the particulars (*ICTA 1988, s 778(1)*). In particular, they can ask for details of:

(*a*) transactions or arrangements with respect to which the person acted on behalf of others;

(*b*) transactions or arrangements which in the Revenue's opinion should properly be investigated (even though the person on whom the notice is served may consider that a charge under *section 776* cannot arise); and

(*c*) whether the person to whom the notice is given has taken any part in any transactions or arrangements of a description specified in the notice (*ICTA 1988, s 778(2)*).

**14.51** A solicitor is not to be deemed to have taken part in any transaction for the purposes of (*c*) by reason only that he has given professional advice to a client in connection with the transaction. Furthermore, a solicitor (acting for a client) cannot be compelled to do more than state that he was acting on behalf of a client in a transaction and give the name and address of the client (*ICTA 1988, s 778(3)*). An accountant or other professional adviser can be required to disclose full details of transactions entered into by clients. It may well be that the mere giving of professional advice does not constitute taking part in a transaction, but the information that the Revenue can ask for under *subsection (1)* is not limited to the transactions set out in *subsection (2)*. In *Essex v CIR (53 TC 720)* a notice was served under *section 778*. Mr Essex appealed on the grounds that the notice was invalid as it did not indicate the transactions as to which information was required, and that the wording was so obscure that the notice was burdensome and oppressive. It was held that the notice was valid. It did not have to specify individual transactions and there was no evidence that Mr Essex had in fact found the notice unintelligible or burdensome.

## Other Artificial Transactions

**14.52** Another way for the Revenue to attack artificial transactions is to seek to apply the what is known as the *Ramsay* or *Furniss v Dawson* principle. This is a principle of construction first enunciated by the courts in *W T Ramsay Ltd v CIR (1981 STC 174)*, significantly expanded in *Furniss v Dawson (55 TC 324)*, and broadened again in *MacNiven v Westmoreland Investments Ltd (2001 STC 237)*, three House of Lords cases. This states that when it is sought to attach a tax consequence to a transaction the courts must first identify the legal nature of the transaction. If that emerges from a series or combination of transactions intended to operate as such that series may be regarded as a whole. Having identified the legal nature of a transaction the courts must then relate this to the language of the statute. The Revenue sought to apply the *Ramsay* principle to a property transaction in *CIR v Bowater Property Developments Ltd (1988 STC 476)*. The company negotiated to sell land outside its group for £202,500. It contracted to sell the land to five group companies with the intention that they would resell it to the proposed purchaser. This would avoid development land tax (which no longer exists) as that incorporated a de minimis exemption of £50,000 for each company. The proposed sale fell through but the companies later sold the land to a different purchaser. It was held that the *Ramsay* principle did not apply as there was not a pre-ordained series of transactions as the ultimate purchaser was not known at the time of the sales to the subsidiaries. This case might well now be decided differently following the *Westmoreland Investments* case.

**14.53** An alternative approach was taken by the Revenue in *Hitch v Stone (2001 STC 214) ([2001] EWCA (Civ 63))*. The purported transactions in that case were very complex. They were designed to avoid both capital gains tax and development land tax. The Revenue claimed that some of the documents were shams and thus of no effect. If such documents were ignored the transactions became the disposal of the land realising a substantial capital gain. The Revenue took an all or nothing approach. They did not claim that if they were wrong the *Ramsay* principle in any event applied. They lost in the High Court but on appeal the documents were held to be shams.

*Chapter 15*

# Use of Overseas Companies to Acquire UK Properties

**15.1** Because of the large potential profits to be made from many property transactions, and a general aversion towards paying tax, taxpayers are often tempted to seek to avoid UK tax on property transactions by routing these through an overseas company. Unfortunately it is not as simple to avoid UK tax in this way as many people think. There are a number of tax considerations that need to be borne in mind.

(*a*) For UK tax purposes it is irrelevant where a company is incorporated (unless it is in the UK); what matters is where it is resident. This is generally the country from which central management and control is exercised. For example, a Panamanian registered company which is controlled from the UK is regarded as a UK resident company for UK tax purposes. Management and control is normally exercised by the directors but they may be mere puppets of the shareholders or may have effectively delegated their powers to one of their number (or even to somebody else). In such cases the courts are likely to hold that control is exercised not by the directors but by whoever makes the decisions. As a company is normally controlled by its directors it is normally resident in the country in which the directors usually hold their board meetings. Such meetings ought to be held regularly and proper minutes maintained. The courts generally attach considerable weight to board minutes. Clearly the minutes must demonstrate that the decisions are made at board meetings – and that these do not merely rubber stamp decisions taken elsewhere – and all major decisions need to be minuted. A company that is incorporated in the UK will always be resident in the UK even if it is controlled and managed elsewhere (*FA 1988, s 66*).

(*b*) A non-UK resident company which trades in the UK is chargeable to UK tax on its UK trading profits. The purchase and resale of a single property is in many cases a dealing transaction. Accordingly, if a non-UK company enters into such a transaction in the UK it may well have a tax liability here – although if it has no UK assets the Revenue may have difficulty in enforcing the liability unless it is resident in another EC country. The country of residence is unlikely to enforce payment, as by convention one country is not normally prepared to enforce payment of another country's tax debts. The position is different in the EC, where there is an EC Directive on the mutual enforcement of tax debts. This was introduced in 1976 in relation to VAT, extended to other indirect taxes in 1992 and to direct taxes also in 2001. It has been given effect for direct tax purposes by *FA 2002, s 134*. Previously the Revenue claimed that the *Civil Jurisdiction and Judgement Act 1982* and *Order 11* of the *Rules of the Supreme Court* enabled them to enforce direct tax debts in European Community Member States. It was not clear how, as the *Act* gives effect in the UK to a European Community Convention on the mutual enforcement of debts, and the Convention specifically states: 'It shall not extend, in particular, to Revenue, Customs or administrative matters.' It must also be borne in mind that (except in relation to rental income where special rules apply – see 2.93) an overseas company can be taxed in the name of any agent that it has in the UK and the agent will then be personally liable for the tax. Great care may need to be taken to ensure that there is no one in the UK who could be deemed to be an agent. If there is, the agent can be assessed even though he may not himself receive the sale proceeds of the property. There is an exception for a broker and for an agent who is not 'an authorised person carrying on the regular agency' of the non-resident. The phrase in quotation marks is not defined (*FA 1995, ss 126* and *127*).

Whether or not a trade of property dealing is carried on in the UK where the only properties dealt in are UK ones is not clear. It used to be thought that a trade is carried on in the place where contracts for sales are entered into. However it is nowadays accepted that this is only one of the factors that the courts should take into account, albeit an important one. It is probable that trading in land or buildings situated in the UK, and the development of such land, will be regarded as taking place in the UK, particularly where the legal title can be perfected only by registering the sale in a UK Land Registry. If a UK property is bought and split, e.g. into flats, and all the resulting parts are sold to genuine non-UK residents for use as holiday homes or *pieds-à-terre* the position is less clear cut. If the overseas resident is a company controlled by, or held for the benefit of, UK residents that would probably tip the balance back to UK trading.

Under many double taxation agreements a foreign resident company which carries on a trade in the UK is taxable here only if it carries on that trade through a permanent establishment here. We do not have double tax agreements with pure tax haven countries. It may therefore be sensible to use, say, a Guernsey company and pay Guernsey tax on the profit on a dealing transaction in order to obtain the benefit of the double taxation agreement. As the

UK small companies rate of 20% is the same as Guernsey tax there is obviously little point in using such a country unless the bulk of the profits will be taken out in a tax deductible form and in such a way that no significant tax charge will arise. The provision of (genuine) administration services through a tax haven country or the payment of salary to a person who is not liable to tax on it in his home country may be possible. A Guernsey 'exempt company' is by definition treated as not resident in Guernsey for tax purposes and would thus not be entitled to benefit from the double tax agreement, so would not be appropriate for this purpose.

(*c*) If the overseas company would be a close company if it were UK resident there are a number of anti-avoidance provisions that need to be borne in mind.

(i) UK resident shareholders can be taxed on capital gains realised by the non-UK company (*TCGA 1992, s 13*). The gain is apportioned amongst the shareholders in proportion to their interests in the company and the part apportioned to a UK resident is treated as a gain realised by him (with no relief for any losses realised by the overseas company other than those arising in the same company in the same year of assessment). It does not matter that the shareholder has not received the money and may well not be in a position to force the company to pay it to him; he must find the tax out of his own resources. (There is an exception where the gain arose before 28 November 1995 and is distributed within two years of its being realised – but such a distribution will itself normally create a tax liability.)

(ii) A UK resident who has made a transfer of assets, in consequence of which income (including property dealing profits) arises to an overseas company, can be taxed on that income if he has power to enjoy it or receives a payment representing it. 'Power to enjoy' is very widely defined (*ICTA 1988, s 739*). However, simply residing in the property does not itself generate income so this will not be a problem if the overseas company was formed solely to hold the property and does not have, and never has had, other income-producing assets.

(iii) A UK resident who has not made such a transfer can be taxed as income on anything that he receives from an overseas company or settlement if its income derives from a transfer by a third party (*ICTA 1988, s 740*).

The House of Lords indicated in *Vestey v CIR (54 TC 503)* that *section 739* can normally apply only where the person who made the transfer of assets, or his spouse, is the person who has the power to enjoy, or receives, the capital payment. If the beneficiary is, say, a child of the transferor, *section 740* rather than *section 739* will normally apply. A mere power to enjoy does not bring about a charge under that section. A detailed consideration of these provisions – which need to be considered when contemplating any overseas transaction – is outside the scope of this book but can be found in *Tolley's Anti-Avoidance Provisions* by the same author.

(*d*) It should also be remembered that:

(i) the personal tax return now contains a question (part of Question 6), 'Have you or could you have received, or enjoyed directly, or indirectly, or benefited in any way from, income of a foreign entity as a result of a transfer of assets made in this or earlier years?' A similar question first appeared in an even more widely drawn form in the 1997/98 return form: 'Have you at any time made, or been associated with, a transfer of assets which has resulted in income becoming payable to a foreign entity or have you benefited in any way from such a transfer made by someone else?' On the face of the guidance, it is virtually impossible to answer 'No' to that question if the taxpayer has an interest in any overseas entity. The question requires a 'Yes' answer even if *section 741* (which provides exemptions from *sections 739* and *740*) applies or if the only income of the overseas entity is UK income which has borne tax. Answering 'Yes' without volunteering an explanation is likely to trigger an enquiry into the return. Although the current wording is narrower, it will in most cases still be difficult to state that a taxpayer could not have received income from the foreign company. However, as the question is designed to check whether a person has properly complied with his tax obligations, the question ought to be limited to a transfer of assets made by the taxpayer and there is a respectable argument that the question should be interpreted in that spirit. The explanation to Question 6 in the Tax Return Guide states that before filling in the foreign pages 'read the notes on income received by overseas trusts, companies or other entities, or benefits received from them, on Notes pages FN10 and FN11'. Pages FN10 and FN11 make clear that where the transferor is the settlor the income of the foreign trust needs to be declared but where he is not the settlor only income or benefits actually received need to be declared. It seems logical to answer Question 6 in the context of this guidance;

(ii) the Inland Revenue have power to require a person to make a return of assets acquired by him (*TMA 1970, s 12(2)(3)*). The request for a statement of assets acquired used to form part of the income tax return but no longer does so. Nevertheless the power is still there. If a person is asked to make such a return what matters is beneficial ownership. If the shares in a Jersey company are registered in the names of Jersey residents as nominees, they have to be nominees for someone and if that someone is a UK individual he needs to declare his beneficial ownership if called upon to make a return;

(iii) the Revenue are notified by the Stamp Duty Office of most transactions in UK land and try to tie these in with taxpayer's files; and

(iv) one of the main activities of the Special Compliance Office is to ensure that tax is paid on transactions in land in the UK (particularly London) by non-UK residents where this is due.

**15.2** A non-UK resident company is not liable to UK corporation tax in respect of chargeable gains on UK land which it holds as an investment (unless it is an asset of a UK business). Accordingly, if non-UK residents wish to invest in UK land they should use an overseas company and ensure that they can demonstrate that it is controlled and managed outside the UK. They also need to be able to demonstrate that the transaction is in fact an investment and not a dealing transaction. The development of property to sell after development is normally dealing not investment. A non-UK resident could equally well from a CGT point of view enter into UK investments in his own name but this is unattractive from an inheritance tax viewpoint.

**15.3** A UK resident who sets up an overseas investment company is caught by *TCGA 1992, s 13* (see 15.1(*c*)(i) above). If the overseas company is owned by an overseas trust a deferral of UK income tax can be achieved whilst the funds remain in the trust, but only if the taxpayer, his spouse, his children and his grandchildren are not potential beneficiaries. Capital gains of a non-UK settlement (and of a company controlled by it) are treated as realised by the settlor and therefore taxable on him if he is domiciled and resident or ordinarily resident in the UK. This applies not only where the settlor and his spouse are beneficiaries but also if any child of his (including an adult child), or the spouse of such a child, or a grandchild (or spouse of a grandchild), or certain companies are potential beneficiaries. There is an exemption where the settlement was created before 17 March 1998 if the beneficiary is an infant.

**15.4** Neither of these provisions apply if the shareholder of the company or the settlor of the trust is non-UK domiciled. It has been common for a foreigner who comes to the UK to hold his UK house through a foreign company. Assuming that he retains a non-UK domicile, this has inheritance tax advantages as the shares will be a non-UK asset, and therefore outside the scope of UK inheritance tax, whereas the property itself is within the scope of that tax if owned by an individual. The Inland Revenue have indicated that in such circumstances they will seek to show that the individual is a 'shadow director' of the overseas company and accordingly taxable here in respect of the occupation of the property under *ICTA 1988, ss 145* and *146*. Whether they could succeed in such a claim obviously depends on the facts – and probably, whatever the law may be, on the common reluctance of foreigners to engage in litigation with other people's Revenue authorities. Great care accordingly needs to be taken before adopting this structure – although both of the alternative options, holding the property personally or through an overseas trust, have their own tax problems. The Revenue have won a case in the House of Lords, *R v Allen (2001 STC 1537, [2001] UKHL 45)* but it was accepted by the defendant in that case (it was a criminal case) that he was a shadow director. His argument was mainly that the benefit in kind rules did not apply to a shadow director. This was unanimously dismissed by the court.

**15.5** A non-UK resident company is liable to UK income tax (not corporation tax) on rental income from UK properties. None of the UK's double taxation agreements grant an exemption from tax on rents. A non-UK company investing in UK property should normally seek to provide the whole of the finance for the property by way of loan so that it has the largest possible amount of allowable interest to set against the UK income (see 4.4 above). The income tax rules as to what interest is allowable, not their corporation tax counterparts, need to be met. There is no reason in principle why the borrowing should not be from another non-UK associated company – or even from the shareholder if he is a non-UK resident. This overcomes the problem of security. However the Revenue can be expected to scrutinise such arrangements closely. It should also be mentioned that the Inland Revenue sometimes look closely at borrowings by non-UK companies to invest in UK properties. Where these form part of a back-to-back arrangement, e.g. where the loan is secured on a deposit of cash outside the UK, they have been known to seek to disallow the interest under the *Furniss v Dawson* principle. Whilst the author is sceptical as to the efficacy of the Revenue's case, the amounts involved are generally such that most practitioners negotiate a lesser disallowance than the Revenue contend for, rather than take the issue to appeal. If a UK borrowing is not secured but is merely guaranteed by the overseas resident this problem should not arise.

**15.6** It needs to be borne in mind that a tenant or a UK agent of the landlord who collects the rent may have an obligation to deduct tax from the rent if the landlord's usual place of abode is outside the UK. 'Usual place of abode' is primarily a factual test and is thus a little easier for the tenant to identify than the landlord's place of residence; he can in some circumstances be resident here if he spends only a day in this country during a year of assessment – or, following *Reed v Clark*

*(58 TC 528)*, possibly even if he does not visit this country at all during the year of assessment. There may also be a requirement for the tenant to deduct tax from the taxable part of any premium or deemed premium that he pays (see chapter 3). As explained at 2.98 the landlord can ask the Revenue to authorise the tenant or agent not to deduct tax, but this will mean that the landlord will have to agree to file UK tax returns.

*Chapter 16*

# Woodlands

## Income Tax Exemption

**16.1** Income from the occupation of woodlands in the UK is exempt from income tax. (*ICTA 1988, s 53(4)* excludes the occupation of woodlands (or land being prepared for forestry purposes) from Case I of Schedule D and *section 15(1)* excludes all occupation of land from Schedule A). This tax exemption applies to sales of both felled and growing timber, underwoods, thinnings and all other such receipts. The exemption extends not only to woodlands but also to land which is being prepared for use for forestry purposes (*ICTA 1988, s 53(4)*). It was held in *Jaggers (t/a Shide Trees) v Ellis (1997 STC 1417)* that a Christmas tree plantation is not woodland and therefore does not fall within the exemption. The Special Commissioner felt that what is woodland or forestry is to a large extent a matter of impression. He felt that the land was not woodland because no timber was being produced and the spacing of the trees was in accordance with Christmas tree production rather than timber production. The Special Commissioner seems to have rejected the dictionary definition of woodland, i.e. land covered with trees, and invented his own definition, which appears to be land used for timber production, but did not make clear his basis for doing so. In the High Court the judge said that the word 'woodlands' is an ordinary word of the English language. The taxpayer can upset the Commissioners' decision only if she can show that on any reasonable use of the English language a Christmas tree plantation must fall within the description 'woodlands'. He said she clearly could not do this, as for the purposes of *ICTA 1988, s 53(4)* ('the occupation of land which comprises woodlands or is being prepared for forestry purposes') woodlands and land used for forestry purposes 'are to be treated as synonymous'. Why? Because, he felt 'the subsection provides for protection for land being prepared for forestry purposes and . . . land used for forestry, i.e. woodlands'. He reinforced his view by saying that when the dictionary defines 'woodland' as 'land covered with trees' it cannot mean that, as to his mind 'woodland' denotes a wood, a sizeable area of land to a significant extent covered by growing trees of some maturity'. How much maturity? Well, he thought 'there is something to be said for the rule of thumb that their wood should be capable of being used for timber'. Ergo, if woods do not produce timber they cannot be woodlands. From 29 November 1994 the cultivation of short rotation coppice is regarded as farming not forestry and is therefore taxable (*FA 1995, s 154(1)*). Such coppicing means a perennial crop of tree species planted at high density, the stems of which are harvested above ground level at intervals of less than ten years (*FA 1995, s 154(3)*). Typically, willow or poplar is planted at high density and cut back to ground level after a year to produce shoots which are harvested every three years to be made into chips for fuel. *Section 154* is to clarify the treatment of such coppicing – which suggests that the Revenue could well contend for Schedule D Case I treatment before 29 November 1994 also.

## Property Dealers

**16.2** Special rules apply to the purchase and sale of woodlands in the UK by property dealers. So much of the cost of such land as is attributable to trees or saleable underwood growing on the land is disregarded on purchase, and on a subsequent sale the same figure (correspondingly reduced where some of those trees have been felled in the interim) is deducted from the sale proceeds (*ICTA 1988, s 99(1)*). The effect is to exclude the timber purchased and not felled from the dealer's Case I profits whilst leaving within charge to tax under Case I of Schedule D both the value of any new trees planted by the dealer during the period that he held the land as trading stock and also the increase during his ownership in the value of the original trees. It should be noted that if the property dealer fells trees, or sells the right to cut standing timber, during his ownership he will be in a disadvantageous position, as the proceeds will constitute trading income but he will obtain no relief for the cost of that timber (i.e. its value at the time of acquisition of the woodland).

## Capital Gains Tax

**16.3** The part of the cost and sale proceeds of woodlands in the UK which is attributable to trees or saleable underwood growing on the land is disregarded for capital gains tax purposes (*TCGA 1992, s 250(3)(4)*). Where woodlands are managed by the occupier on a commercial basis and with a view to the realisation of profits the proceeds of felled timber or of the right to fell standing timber, and insurance proceeds for the destruction of, or damage to, trees by fire or other hazards, is also disregarded (*TCGA 1992, s 250(1)(2)*). This provision is, of course, necessary merely to ensure that income receipts which are not taxed as such cannot be subjected to capital gains tax. It appears, however, that this relief for timber applies irrespective of whether the woodlands are in the UK.

**16.4** The effect of *section 250(4)* is that on a purchase and sale of woodlands the price needs to be apportioned between the value of the land, which is chargeable to capital gains tax, and the value of the growing timber, which is not. Where forestry land is or has been purchased since 31 March 1982 the indexation allowance is likely to eliminate most of the gain on the land in most cases.

**16.5** The Forestry Commission Bulletin 84 (formerly Leaflet 12) 'Taxation of woodlands' (HMSO) (1989 edition), compiled by the Forestry Commission with the authority of the Inland Revenue, indicates that the exclusion of the value of growing timber under *subsections 250(3)* and *250(4)* applies only where the woodlands are run on a commercial basis (para 2.4). It is not clear why, as *section 250* does not contain such a limitation. However, this booklet is highly recommended, although as it is now no longer shown on the Forestry Commission website it may now be out of print. Where woodlands are not run on a commercial basis the sale of felled timber or the grant of the right to fell and remove growing timber is not taxable as income and does not fall within *section 250(1)*. It will accordingly be chargeable to capital gains tax. However, felled trees are treated as chattels and a chargeable gain can only arise if an individual tree is sold for over £6,000 (*TCGA 1992, s 262* and Forestry Commission Bulletin 84, para 2.5).

**16.6** Although no longer taxable as a business for income tax purposes, the occupation of woodlands on a commercial basis is still accepted as a business for capital gains tax purposes. Accordingly the reinvestment of the proceeds of the sale of business assets in such woodlands still qualifies for roll-over relief. Obviously the gain on the old assets can only be rolled over against the cost of land and infrastructure work, such as drainage, roads and fences, not against the cost of growing timber. Nevertheless with planting land or a young plantation such items are likely to form a significant part of the cost of a forest.

## Inheritance Tax

**16.7** There are two specific inheritance tax reliefs for forestry. The more important of them is that the ownership and management of woodlands on a commercial basis is accepted as qualifying for IHT business relief. The normal business relief rules apply. The property must have been held for at least two years (or have replaced other business property, the two together having been held for at least two out of the five years before the transfer) and a binding contract for disposal must not have been entered into at the time of the taxpayer's death or *inter vivos* gift. The relief is 100% after 9 March 1992 thus effectively conferring total exemption. The relief for a shareholding of 25% or less in an unquoted forestry company is 50%. Prior to 10 March 1992 the relief percentages were 50% and 30% respectively.

**16.8** Secondly there is a specific relief for woodlands from IHT payable on a death although the 100% business property relief effectively renders this inoperable for deaths after 9 March 1992. An election can be made to leave the value of growing trees and underwood out of account in determining the IHT on the death. The deceased must have beneficially owned the land for at least five years or become entitled to it by gift or inheritance (*IHTA 1984, s 125*). Accordingly, the relief will not apply to any part of the value of shares in forestry owning companies. The election must be made within two years after the death (or such longer time as the Revenue may allow) (*IHTA 1984, s 125(3)*). The snag of such an election is that when the whole or any part of the trees or underwood so left out of account is disposed of (including on a sale of the land including growing timber but excluding a transfer between spouses), IHT is charged on the net disposal proceeds – if the sale is for full consideration in money or money's worth – or the net value at the time of the disposal in other cases (*IHTA 1984, s 127*). The net proceeds or net value is the proceeds or value less any expenses incurred either

(*a*) in disposing of the trees or underwood, or

(*b*) in replanting to replace the trees or underwood disposed of – to the extent that the expenditure is incurred within three years after the disposal (or such longer time as the Revenue may allow), or

(*c*) in replanting to replace trees or underwood previously disposed of to the extent that the expense was not allowable on the previous disposal, e.g. because it was incurred more than three years after that disposal,

but only to the extent that such expenditure is not allowable for income tax purposes (*IHTA 1984, s 130(1)(b)(2)*).

**16.9** The IHT charge is at the rate or rates at which it would have been charged on the death if the net disposal proceeds or net value (and any previous amount of disposal proceeds, etc.) had been included in the deceased's estate at the date of his death and had formed the highest part of the value of the estate (*IHTA 1984, s 128*). The effect is of course that more IHT may well be payable at the end of the day than if the election had not been made – although this is offset by the cash flow effect of deferring the tax until the money to pay it is generated by a sale. If the rates of IHT have reduced between the death and the sale, the rate table to be used is not that in force on death but normally that in force at the time of the disposal – it is actually the rates at the last preceding reduction (*IHTA 1984, Sch 2 para 4*).

**16.10** If more than one death of an owner of the woodlands occurs before the sale, etc. takes place, the charge under *section 128* is made only by reference to the second death (*IHTA 1984, s 126(1)*). In such circumstances there will have been a real saving of IHT on the first death. Once a charge has crystallised under *section 126* a further charge will not of course arise on a later disposal of the same trees or underwood (*IHTA 1984, s 126(3)*). The 1985 edition of the Forestry Commission booklet stated that in the case of underwood a charge to tax is made only in respect of the first cutting of underwood subsequent to the death. This is not repeated in the 1989 edition but may follow from *section 126(3)*. If the 50% business property relief applied on the death, only 50% of the net proceeds of the trees or underwood is charged (*IHTA 1984, s 127(2)*). If the disposal which gives rise to the charge under *section 126* is itself an *inter vivos* gift that is not a potentially exempt transfer, the IHT payable under *section 126* is deducted from the value of the trees to calculate the IHT on the gift (*IHTA 1984, s 129*). A disposal of an interest in trees or underwood generates a *section 126* charge in the same way as a disposal of the trees themselves (*IHTA 1984, s 130(1)(c)*). Timber cut for use on the estate will not generate a *section 126* charge as it will not have been disposed of (Forestry Commission Bulletin 84, para 3.16).

**16.11** Where woodlands transferred on death 'can be divided into clearly distinct geographic areas' the election can be made for some of the separate areas only (Forestry Commission Bulletin 84, para 3.8). The Revenue regard the election once made as irrevocable.

**16.12** In the case of hardwoods which are many years from maturity the election will in many cases be worthwhile if the 100% business property relief. Deep consideration of the pros and cons needs to be given in other cases. The election will not normally be advisable if the woodland is likely to come to maturity within the next five to ten years. Strangely, although the person eligible to make the *section 125* election is the person liable for the whole or part of the tax, which would normally be the deceased's personal representative, the only person liable for the tax payable under *section 126* is the beneficiary who is entitled to the sale proceeds (or who would have been so entitled if the *section 126* disposal were a sale) (*IHTA 1984, s 208*).

**16.13** Woodlands may well of course qualify for national heritage property relief under *IHTA 1984, s 30* (see 18.53 below).

**16.14** The IHT on woodlands can be paid by ten annual instalments in the same way as tax on other disposals of land (see 18.32) (*IHTA 1984, s 227*). Tax on an *inter vivos* gift of growing timber which was excluded on a previous death can also be paid by ten equal yearly instalments (the first payable six months after the end of the month in which the transfer is made) if the gift is a potentially exempt transfer (*IHTA 1984, s 229*). It appears that this applies only to the tax on the gift and not to the charge under *section 126* which is crystallised by the gift. It is difficult to discern the logic of this. It should not be overlooked that where an election for instalments is made the instalments attract interest on overdue tax (*IHTA 1984, s 233*) except where the woodlands constitute the asset of a business or *section 229* applies (*IHTA 1984, s 234(1)*).

## Estate Duty

**16.15** Estate duty, the forerunner of capital transfer tax, applied on deaths before 13 March 1975. Where a person's estate at the time of death included growing timber, *F(1909–10)A 1910, s 61* allowed an election to be made to defer the tax on growing timber. The value of the timber was left out of account and a subsequent sale crystallised tax – but, unlike under the IHT rules, only up to the value of the growing timber at the date of death. The rate at which tax was charged on the subsequent sale of the growing timber was the estate rate, the average rate of estate duty payable on the death. This deferred charge can still crystallise. It will be crystallised by a transfer of value for IHT purposes other than a transfer between spouses (*FA 1975, s 49(4)*) (or eliminated if that transfer is a transfer on death) as well as by a sale of the timber. A transfer which crystallises the deferred charge cannot be a PET. Strictly speaking no part of a gift can be a PET if a small part carries a deferred charge. However, for transfers after 5 December 1990, the Revenue will apportion the gift and levy tax only on the woodlands (Inland Revenue Press Release, 5 December 1990).

# Value Added Tax

## Introduction

**17.1** Value added tax (VAT) on property is possibly the most complex area of VAT law. There are two separate sets of VAT rules, one for residential and certain charitable property and the other for other types of property and land. Initially there was a single set of rules under which new buildings were either exempt or zero-rated, and repairs, refurbishments, etc. attracted VAT at the standard rate, which is currently 17½%. Zero-rating is very attractive. It means that the supply of the building or services concerned is taxable at a rate of 0%. Although this effectively exempts the supply from VAT, since the supply is nominally 'taxable' it enables input VAT incurred on expenditure in relation to the supply to be recovered, whereas input tax in respect of exempt supplies is irrecoverable and therefore an additional cost to the property owner.

**17.2** VAT is not solely a UK tax. It is a European Community tax, and as such has to comply with EC law. In particular, the UK VAT legislation has to give effect to the *EC Council Directive 77/388*, popularly known as the *Sixth Directive*, which sets out the principles of VAT. There are some permitted derogations from the Directive and also a number of later directives that amend the VAT rules. The UK was forced to drop its zero-rating of commercial and industrial development from 1 April 1989, because this was held to be in breach of the permitted derogation which allows zero-rating only for 'clearly defined social reasons and for the benefit of the final consumer'.

**17.3** In general the new rules came into effect on 1 April 1989, although some of the provisions operate from 1 August 1989 and there were transitional reliefs for those who were committed to a transaction or a development on 21 June 1988. It has been felt more appropriate to cover the particular VAT rules on property development and on refurbishment within the general review of the particular tax problems arising from such operations. The consideration of the VAT position in respect of such activities will accordingly be found at 8.24–8.87 and 9.16–9.35 respectively.

**17.4** The effect of standard-rating is that the developer either has to add 17½% to his selling price and account for that tax to Customs or treat his selling prices as VAT-inclusive and account for 14.89% of that price. In most cases, he will obviously seek to adopt the former course assuming, of course, that he realises that he has a liability. Whether this reduces the price that he can obtain for the building is likely to depend on the purchaser's VAT position.

**17.5** If the purchaser is a fully taxable person, he will be able to recover the VAT from Customs. In such circumstances there is no reason to think that the imposition of VAT will affect the price that he is prepared to pay for the building. If he is not a taxable person, or is partially exempt, all or part of the VAT will represent a real additional cost. Whether this will reflect in the price of the building is likely to depend on the building itself and other potential tenants. It is unlikely, for example, that a bank which wants a branch in a new shopping centre will decide to forego the additional custom that it perceives it can obtain there because of the imposition of the VAT. Similarly the developer is unlikely to want the bank so badly that he will accept a lower price from it than he can obtain by selling to a retailer. Accordingly the bank will have to face up to paying the market price. On the other hand the market price of an office development in the centre of the City of London is likely to be determined primarily by demand by banks and financial institutions, which are generally partially exempt and can recover only a comparatively small proportion of their input tax. There is a risk that opting in such a building could depress its market price.

## Zero-rated Supplies of Residential and Certain Charitable Buildings

**17.6** Zero-rating applies only to certain supplies of, or in connection with, residential and some charitable buildings. The eligible items are:

1. (*a*) The first grant of a major interest by a person constructing a building which is either designed as a dwelling or intended for use solely for a relevant residential or relevant charitable purpose.

   (*b*) The grant by a person converting a building from non-residential to residential use of a major interest in the building.

2. The supply in the course of construction of a dwelling (or building intended for a relevant residential or charitable use) of construction work on the building.

3. The supply to a housing association in the course of conversion of a non-residential building into a dwelling (or relevant residential building) of construction work on the building.

4. The supply of building materials in conjunction with the services supplied at (2) and (3) above.

**17.7** There are obviously a number of caveats. The detailed rules are as follows:

1. (*a*) The first grant (or assignment or surrender – *Note 1, Group 5*) by a person constructing a building of a major interest in (or in any part of) the building, dwelling or its site if it is either:

   (i) *designed as* a dwelling or number of dwellings; or

   (ii) *intended for use solely* for either a relevant residential purpose, or a relevant charitable purpose.

   (*b*) The grant (or assignment or surrender), by a person converting a building, of a major interest in any part of the building, dwelling or its site deriving from the conversion of a non-residential building (or a non-residential part of a building) into one designed as a dwelling or number of dwellings or one intended for use solely for a relevant residential purpose.

2. The supply in the course of the construction of either:

   (*a*) a building which is

   (i) designed as a dwelling or number of dwellings; or

   (ii) intended for use for a relevant residential or charitable purpose; or

   (*b*) any civil engineering work necessary for the development of a permanent park for residential caravans

   of any services related to the construction other than the services of an architect, surveyor, or other person acting as a consultant or in a supervisory capacity.

3. The supply to a relevant housing association in the course of conversion of a non-residential building (or part of a building) into one either:

   (*a*) designed as a dwelling or number of dwellings; or

(*b*) intended for use solely for a relevant residential purpose,

of any services related to the conversion other than the services of an architect, surveyor or any person acting as a consultant or in a supervisory capacity.

4. The supply of building materials to a person to whom the supplier is also supplying services within heads 2 or 3 above which include the incorporation of the materials into the building in question (or its site). For this purpose 'building materials' means goods of a description ordinarily incorporated by builders in a building of the same description (or its site) subject to a number of specified exceptions (which are set out in 8.65 above) (*Note 22, Group 5*) and the incorporation of goods in a building includes their installation as fittings (*Note 23*).

(*VATA 1994, 8 Sch, Group 5*).

The rules were slightly different prior to 1 March 1995. The previous rules are set out at 8.28 above. The main changes are that zero-rating did not previously apply to the conversion of buildings and that the definition of builders fixtures has been relaxed. The relaxations were applied from 21 July 1994 by extra-statutory concession. The addition of the word 'first' in 1(*a*) is intended to make clear that zero-rating cannot apply where, for example, the original builder takes back a house in part-exchange and then resells it. The 'first grant . . . of a major interest in . . . any part of a building' is intended only to prevent zero-rating of a second disposal of that part; it does not prevent the zero-rating of a subsequent disposal of a different part (VAT Information Sheet 10/95).

**17.8** Each of the above heads is obviously subject to a number of qualifications which are considered in detail below. Zero-rating under *item 1* applies if a person constructing the building is beneficially interested in the consideration for the grant of the major interest even though he is not the person who grants that interest (*VATA 1994, Sch 10 para 8*). This ensures that zero-rating is not lost where the land is registered in the name of joint owners (who technically have an interest not in the land, but in its sale proceeds) or a nominee. It seems odd at first sight that if such a provision is felt necessary for VAT purposes, to cater for the separation of legal from beneficial ownership, a similar rule has not been enacted for income and corporation tax purposes. The reason is probably that direct taxes are imposed on the beneficial owner of an asset, so the distinction is relatively unimportant, whereas VAT is imposed on transactions, where the identity of the owner is less important than the legal nature of the transaction. This provision will in most cases be disapplied by *VATA 1994, s 51A(2)* when, and if, that provision is brought into effect (see 17.292 below).

**17.9** *Items 2* and *3* in 17.6 do not apply to a supply of services within *VATA 1994, 4 Sch 1(1)* (the transfer of an undivided share in property or the transfer of the possession of goods (which includes the grant assignment or surrender of a major interest in land)). Nor do they apply where by (or under) the directions of a person carrying on a business goods held or used for the purpose of the business are put to private use or otherwise used for a purpose other than for the purpose of the business within *4 Sch 5(4)* (*VATA 1994, 8 Sch, Group 5, Note 20*).

**What is a Major Interest in Land?**

**17.10** For the purposes of *item 1* in 17.6 above, a major interest is the freehold or a lease for a term of over 21 years (*VATA 1994, s 96(1)*). The word 'over' should particularly be noted. A lease for 21 years exactly is not a major interest. It also needs to be borne in mind that the date from which a lease runs is frequently earlier than the date the lease is executed, e.g. a lease for 21 years and 1 month from 25 March 1996 which is executed on 30 May 1996 is not a major interest. A lease must actually be for 'a term certain exceeding 21 years'. A term certain is a fixed period. A lease for the life of the tenant would not be for a term certain and could not qualify for zero-rating – probably even if it were expressed to be for a minimum period of 21 years and a day. There are no anti-avoidance provisions to prevent a person granting a 22-year lease with an option for either party to terminate it after seven years, instead of granting a seven-year lease. Customs appear to have accepted this device (C&E Notice 742A, para 11 – now withdrawn), although the fact that this is not repeated in the current Notice 708 may cast doubt on whether they are still of that view. In theory there is no reason why both parties should not have the option to terminate it prematurely. It should, however, be borne in mind that the Inland Revenue have put forward the argument that cross-options are equivalent to a contract for sale and if this argument is valid – which seems doubtful but cannot be wholly dismissed – the use of cross-options in leases may be equally vulnerable to attack by Customs. In *C S & J M Isaac (VTD 14656)* the VAT tribunal accepted that a deed of rectification which purported to extend the leases beyond 21 years was effective to do so, but the facts were unusual. In Scotland a lease of not less than 20 years is a major interest from 1 July 1998. In practice Customs have applied this by concession in the past. Scottish land law does not permit the creation of a longer lease.

**Who is a Person Constructing a Building?**

**17.11** To qualify for zero-rating the supply, i.e. the sale or the grant of the lease, must be made by a person constructing the building. This expression is not defined in the legislation. Customs consider that it covers not only a person who himself constructs a building on his own land, such as a speculative builder, but also a landowner who commissions a builder to erect a building on land that he owns (Notice 708, para 4.5.1). In other words a property developer or other landowner who engages an architect to design a building and hires a contractor to erect it will be a person constructing a building, but one who hires another person to provide a complete package of erecting a building on his land will not – although he may be if, as would almost always be the case, he has at least a right of veto over the design. VAT tribunals seem to have taken a far more restrictive approach, however. Where a land-owning company and an associated building company jointly sold houses, the land-owning company having obtained the planning permission, designed the houses, and constructed roads and sewers, the land-owning company was held not to be 'a person constructing a building' even though the building company invoiced it for the building work (*Monsell Youell Developments Ltd (1978 VATTR 1) (VTD 538)*). A similar decision was reached in *Permacross Ltd (VTD 13251)* where infrastructure work was carried out prior to selling residential building plots. In *Hulme Educational Foundation (1978 VATTR 179) (VTD 625)* a landowner which leased its site to a developer was held not to be a person constructing a building, the tribunal holding that the construction must be physically done by the person concerned (or by his servants or agents) or that person must himself directly enter into a contract or arrangement for another to do the physical construction work. *Cameron New Homes Ltd (VTD 17309)* was also held not to be a person constructing a building. It had carried out extensive work on the land, including remediation, shuttering the site ready for foundation work, altering the vehicular access and excavating for the foundations of the houses at the time it sold the building. It was nevertheless held that these works were preparatory. There was not a building under construction but merely a building site.

**17.12** It was held in *C & E Commrs v Link Housing Association Ltd (1992 STC 718)* that 'a person constructing' should be construed to mean simply 'the constructor of a building' so that a person would be covered by the expression irrespective of whether the building had been completed or was still under construction. The phrase is purely descriptive. Indeed Customs' usual contention that the first supply after completion of a building determines whether input tax is recoverable is inconsistent with the logic of their contention that a person ceases to be the person constructing a building when construction is completed. Link was held to be entitled to zero-rate in 1989 sales of buildings that it had constructed over 20 years earlier. Customs say that the *Link* decision applies only in respect of input tax incurred in relation to disposal costs (Business Brief 15/92). This is questionable. There is no obvious reason why it should not apply, for example, to input tax on refurbishment work carried out to enable the building to be sold at a realistic price. It probably would not apply to repairs whilst a tenant is in occupation, as the work would relate to the exempt rents not the zero-rated disposal.

**17.13** Customs have also expressed the view that the disposal of, or the grant of a major interest in, a partially completed building qualifies for zero-rating provided that the work has progressed beyond foundation stage (Notice 708, August 1997 edition, para 15.5 – although para 4.1.1 of the July 2002 edition refers simply to 'a zero rated building that . . . is being constructed'). This is surprisingly generous, as most people would not describe the foundations and the first course of bricks as a building at all. Customs also say that a person who acquires a major interest in an uncompleted building and continues the construction of it will also be regarded as a person constructing the building (para 15.5). This appears to give scope for avoidance. For example, a person who intends to construct and sell a building should consider leaving a little bit of the construction work undone, as the purchaser may be prepared to pay a higher price if, by finishing it himself, he becomes entitled to zero-rate his supply. Within a group of companies there may be scope for transferring the property to another group company during the construction period to double up the value of zero-rated supplies. This would not work if a group registration exists. Obviously such devices are vulnerable to attack – although in the current state of the law, if the *Ramsay* and *Furniss v Dawson* principles apply to VAT at all, the obtaining of a higher price on a sale, albeit only because of an improvement in the purchaser's tax position, is probably a commercial motive that will prevent the principle operating.

## Fixtures

**17.14** *Article 6* of the *VAT (Input Tax) Order 1992* (*SI 1992 No 3222*), as substituted by the *VAT (Input Tax) (Amendment) Order 1995* (*SI 1995 No 281*), disallows input tax relief in relation to a disposal within *item 1* in 17.6 in respect of goods included in the building other than 'building materials', which has the same meaning as is set out at 17.6 above. Prior to 1995 this did not apply to fixtures in nursing homes and similar buildings (VAT Information Sheet 10/95). Even where goods fall within that head it disallows input tax in respect of finished or prefabricated furniture (other than where designed to be fitted in kitchens) or materials for such furniture, domestic electrical or gas appliances (other than for space and/or water heating) and carpets or carpeting material. The VAT tribunal in *Edmond Homes Ltd (VTD 11567)* held that fitted units to hold wash hand basins, which contained a door which hid the pipework beneath the basin and formed a small storage area under it, were not prefabricated furniture as their prime function was to support the basins and their use as a cupboard was purely incidental. Following this decision Customs accept that, from 1 January 1994, input tax relating to all base units incorporating a wash hand basin installed in bathrooms, cloakrooms and bedrooms of new dwellings is recoverable by the housebuilder, and where such units are installed by a building contractor in new dwellings, they are zero-rated. This includes vanity or vanitory units incorporating a work surface or shelf. They still consider that other base units are fitted furniture, as are wall units such as bathroom cabinets (Business Brief 3/94). Customs' view is that an item is incorporated in a building if it is fixed to a building or its site in such a way that its fixing or removal would either require the use of tools or result in either the need for remedial work to the fabric of the building or substantial damage to the goods themselves (VAT Information Sheet, 5/00, December 2000, para 4). Goods are ordinarily incorporated in a building if in the ordinary course of events they would normally be incorporated in the construction of a building of that generic type. They do not sub-divide generic types, e.g. a large detached house is in the same category as a small terraced house, or ask if the goods themselves are the norm, e.g. a tap would be regarded as ordinarily incorporated whether it is chromium or gold-plated (para 5).

**17.15** It should be particularly noted that, under *item 4*, the materials must be supplied to the person to whom the supply of services is made, and they must be used or installed as part of the building work. These requirements are tighter than the previous rule that they needed to be supplied 'in connection with' such work.

**17.16** Gas fires (*F Booker Builders & Contractors Ltd (1977 VATTR 203) (VTD 446)*); night storage heaters forming part of an all-electric heating system (*Robert Dale & Co (Builders) Ltd (1983 VATTR 61) (VTD 1347)*); mechanical ventilator units installed for sound-proofing (*British Airports Authority (No. 5) (VTD 447)*); a warden call system and alarm switch in sheltered housing (*Garndene Communications Systems Ltd (2253)*); and a ventilation system needed because a house had been designed to be as draughtproof as possible (*C H Wigmore (1991 VATTR 290) (VTD 6040)*) have all been held to be articles of a type ordinarily installed by builders as fittings. In the last case the tribunal held that 'ordinarily' did not mean invariably, but commonly or usually, and one had to look at the generic description to which the article belonged – in that case ventilation systems – and decide whether, when such a system was needed, it would ordinarily be installed by a builder.

Trees and shrubs planted in a landscaping scheme for new housing developments were held to qualify in *Rialto Homes plc (VTD 16340)*. Following this case Customs have expressed the view that for such 'soft landscaping' to be eligible for zero-rating:

(*a*) the work must be carried out at the same time as, or immediately after, the construction of the building; and

(*b*) the landscaping work must be connected with the construction in that it produces in its results a whole with it (they accept that all planting carried out within the plot of a house will meet this condition to the extent that it is detailed on a landscaping plan approved by a planning authority under a planning condition). They consider that:

(i) screening planted along roadside verges,

(ii) work within the plot of a specific house that is not on such a landscaping scheme,

(iii) work performed after completion of the construction such as the replacement of trees and shrubs which die or become damaged or diseased, and

(iv) work carried out outside the plot of a specific house

do not fall within *item 4* and remain standard-rated (Business Brief 7/00).

In the *Garndene* case and the later case of *McCarthy & Stone plc (VTD 7014)* the tribunal looked at the category of house, in both cases sheltered housing, and determined what a builder would normally install in such housing. In *2S Airchangers Limited (VTD 12495)* Customs argued that as the company's ventilation system was a technological innovation it could not be something 'ordinarily' installed by builders. The tribunal retorted that ventilation systems were ordinarily installed by builders in new dwellings and the company's system fell into that generic category.

**17.17** Even though they may be items of a kind ordinarily installed by builders as fixtures, *VATA 1994, Sch 8 Group 5, Note 22* disallows input tax relief – thus effectively negating the benefit of zero-rating – for finished or prefabricated furniture (other than that designed to be fitted in kitchens), materials for the construction of such furniture, electrical or gas appliances other than those designed to provide space or water heating, and carpets or carpeting material. Extractor fans (*H C Moss (Electrical) Ltd (VTD 2020)*), electrically operated venetian blinds (*Frank Haslam Milan & Co Ltd (VTD 3857)*); a two-way communications speech unit in sheltered accommodation (*Garndene Communications Systems Ltd (VTD 2253)*); door entry systems, fire alarm systems and extractor fans in sheltered accommodation (*McCarthy & Stone plc (VTD 7014)*); wet and dry bollards (units incorporating an electrical and gas supply – and a sink in the case of wet bollards, plumbed in and immovable) in a school laboratory (*Sheldon School (VTD 15300)*), and wall-mounted banks of staff lockers in a nursing home (*Birmingham Council for Old People (VTD 15437)*) have all fallen foul of this restriction.

**17.18** In *C & E Commrs v McLean Homes Midland Ltd (1993 STC 335)* it was held that built-in wardrobes utilising an outer wall and two internal walls to which were fitted shelving and a door were not fitted furniture at all; they were part of the fabric of the building. The decision in *McLean Homes Midland Ltd* does not give *carte blanche* to zero-rate all fitted furniture. It was distinguished in two more recent tribunal decisions, although in both cases the facts were somewhat out of the ordinary. In *S H Wade (VTD 13164)*, the tribunal held that wardrobes, which the supplier had originally treated as standard-rated but which accountants acting for receivers of the supplier had subsequently considered should have been zero-rated, were 'fitted furniture' and their supply did not qualify for zero-rating. In *S Leon (t/a Custom Bedrooms) (VTD 13200)*, the tribunal held that the fact that two walls of a bedroom were commonly used as part of the wardrobe did not prevent supplies of items used in the construction of the wardrobe from being materials for the construction of 'fitted furniture', within what is now *VATA 1994, Sch 8 Group 5, Note 22(a)(b)*.

**17.19** Following these cases Customs have summarised their view of what they call 'this complex area', namely:

(*a*) suppliers of zero-rated construction services can generally also zero-rate the supply of building materials incorporated into the building,

(*b*) but not if they are materials for the construction of fitted furniture, other than kitchen furniture,

(*c*) the service of incorporating finished, prefabricated and fitted furniture into qualifying buildings is zero-rated when supplied in the course of construction of that building, even though the cost of the materials themselves are not – a fair and reasonable apportionment can be made,

(*d*) free-standing items of furniture are not items incorporated into a building so will always be standard-rated,

(*e*) furniture is not defined; it is very much a matter of impression, but beds, chairs, bookcases, sideboards, dining tables, cupboards (with some exceptions), dressing tables, bedside cabinets, chests of drawers, linen chests, etc. are furniture and therefore standard-rated even if they form part of a range of matching units,

(*f*) airing cupboards, under-stair storage cupboards or other similar basic storage facilities which are formed by becoming part of the fabric of the building are not furniture and can qualify for zero-rating,

(*g*) so can baths, WCs, wash hand basins, etc. and items which provide storage capacity as an incidental result of their primary function, such as shelves formed as the result of constructing simple box work over pipes,

(*h*) simple bedroom wardrobes (as in *McLean Homes (Midland)*) installed on their own are not furniture so can qualify for zero-rating, but more elaborate wardrobes – however fitted – are furniture, as are simple bedroom wardrobes installed as part of a larger installation of furniture in a room, e.g. as part of a matching range,

(*i*) the characteristics of a simple wardrobe are that it includes a space bordered by the walls, ceilings and floor (an element to bridge over a bed or create a dressing table would disqualify the construction from being simple); the sides and back would be formed by using three walls of the room or two walls and a stub wall (but the installation of a cupboard in the corner of a room where one side is a closing end panel would not qualify); on opening the wardrobe, one should see the walls of the building which would normally be bare or painted plaster (back panelling would exclude the item); and it will have no more than a single shelf running the full length of the wardrobe, a rail for hanging clothes and a closing door or doors (i.e. internal features such as divisions, drawers, shoe racks, etc. would disqualify it),

(*j*) where wash hand basins installed in bathrooms or cloakrooms are supported by basin units rather than pedestals, the basin unit will not be furniture if it is a boxlike structure entirely below the line of the top of the basin and contains a shelf and a covering door or doors with the only storage space being directly beneath the basin itself, and

(*k*) more elaborate units, with other storage space constructed on either or both sides of the basin, are furniture, as are wall units such as bathroom cabinets.

(Business Brief 12/97).

**17.20** Six weeks after the issue of this Business Brief, the VAT tribunal in *Moores Furniture Group Ltd (VTD 15044)* held that a bedroom wardrobe where the back and sides were formed by an outside wall and two internal walls qualified for zero-rating. Customs unsuccessfully claimed that the fact that the doors were decorative and designed to blend with the rest of the room took it out of (*i*) above. It also held that a similar wardrobe, where one wall was a specially constructed stub wall, was also zero-rated. However, if a closing end panel made of chipboard was used instead of a stub wall the same wardrobe became standard-rated furniture. The tribunal took note of Business Brief 12/97 on the basis that 'although not binding on the tribunal I do not believe that the Commissioners own published guidelines . . . can be ignored' in deciding against Customs that the stub wall was acceptable. While this gives Business Briefs a status that they do not deserve, it is gratifying to see Customs held bound by their own published material.

**17.21** It should not be overlooked that fixtures which do not qualify for zero-rating under *Group 8* could qualify under some other provision. In *Softley Limited t/a Softley Kitchens (VTD 15034)* zero-rating was allowed under *Group 12, item 2(g)*, equipment and appliances designed solely for use by a handicapped person. The company sold a range of kitchens specifically for disabled persons. In designing the kitchen it took into account the design of the customer's wheelchair and particular disabilities. Customs' claim that the company was not making a supply of goods, but a composite supply of goods and services of which the services were the predominant element, was rejected by the tribunal. It was a supply of goods with the services of design and fitting being integral to that supply. The low level fittings were suitable only for use by a disabled person – although some items were held to be VATable as there was insufficient evidence to distinguish them from items that would normally be supplied to a customer who was not disabled. Some taxpayers have tried an alternative approach of seeking to at least reduce the VAT by separating the furniture from the fitting service. In *I & P Ramsey t/a Kitchen Format (VTD 12393)* the taxpayer contended that he was selling kitchen furniture and arranging for a self-employed fitter to fit it. Unfortunately, the agreement with the customer was to supply and install, and the installation was guaranteed by Kitchen Format. In the light of this agreement the tribunal felt it was clear that the entire supply was by Kitchen Format and that the fitters supplied their services to Kitchen Format and not to the customer. A similar conclusion was reached in the later case of *M Wilson and others t/a M & S Interiors (VTD 17494)*.

## Demolition

**17.22** *Item 2* in 17.6 above excludes supplies in the course of the demolition of a building (demolition previously qualified for zero-rating). However, Customs have said that 'where the contract for the construction of a zero-rated building also extends to the demolition of any building on the site', they regard the demolition as being done 'in the course of' the construction of the new zero-rated building and thus qualifying for zero-rating. This requires a single contract to cover both the demolition and construction. (Hansard, 16 May 1989, col 76). However, the Minister was quoting Customs leaflet 708/2/89, and it is noted that paragraph 3.3.1 of the latest (July 2002) edition of Notice 708, which supercedes that leaflet, states that work is.

'closely connected to the construction of the building when it ... allows the construction of the building to take place, such as if you demolish existing buildings and structures immediately prior to the commencement of construction work'.

This is work 'in the course of the construction of the building'. This seems to represent belated recognition that demolition is generally carried out by a specialist demolition contractor rather than by the builder who is to construct the new building, as a project can presumably embrace a number of distinct contracts with different contractors.

### Civil Engineering Works

**17.23** Since 1989, the only civil engineering work qualifying for zero-rating is that necessary to develop a permanent park for residential caravans. This exception is intended to zero-rate concrete pitches, roads, drains, sewers and the installation of mains water and electricity on permanent residential caravan parks to give occupiers of pitches the same benefit as occupiers of a dwelling house. Whether it achieves this is unclear, as in *Stonecliff Caravan Park (VTD 11097)* the company developed a residential caravan park by installing roads, lighting and services and constructing brick skirtings for mobile homes (which were delivered to the site in two sections and assembled there). A purchaser of a mobile home entered into a pitch agreement under which he was permitted for a weekly fee to station his mobile home on the site and enjoy certain communal facilities. The tribunal held that the sales of mobile homes were zero-rated, as sales of caravans and the brick skirtings were an integral part of the sale of the home, so that the input tax on them was attributable to a zero-rated supply. However, the rest of the work was attributable to the pitch agreement which was exempt as the grant of a licence to occupy land, albeit that the work included the construction of individual pitches and the costs of connecting water and other services to the individual homes. This decision was accepted as correct in law in *C & E Commrs v Harpcombe Ltd (1996 STC 726)* where it was held that there were two separate supplies, the zero-rated sale of a mobile home and an exempt site licence, and the expenditure on providing the concrete base to the pitch related to the latter. In *P C Eccles (VTD 13372*) a claim by the taxpayer that site preparation work related wholly to the sale of mobile homes was rejected. The tribunal held that this work was essential to the exempt letting of pitches as well as to the zero-rated sales of mobile homes. In *Tingdene Developments Ltd (VTD 16546)* the tribunal again held that the concrete bases related to the exempt supply of pitches but accepted that work such as roadside kerbs, road surfacing, tree planting and other work not immediately related to the company's contractual obligations under the pitch agreements were directly referable to the taxpayer's aim of attracting new buyers in the same way as advertising and thus attributable to the sales of caravans. The construction of a civil engineering work does not, of course, include the conversion, reconstruction, alteration or enlargement of such a work (*VATA 1994, 8 Sch, Group 5, Note 15*).

### What is a Building Designed as a Dwelling?

**17.24** A building is designed as a dwelling or a number of dwellings only if the following conditions are met in relation to each dwelling:

(*a*) it consists of self-contained living accommodation;

(*b*) there is no provision for direct internal access from the dwelling to any other dwelling or part of a dwelling;

(*c*) the separate use of the dwelling, or its separate disposal, is not prohibited by the terms of any covenant, statutory planning consent or similar provision; and

(*d*) statutory planning consent has been granted in respect of it, and its construction or conversion has been carried out in accordance with that consent.

(*Sch 8 Group 5, Note 2* inserted by *VAT (Construction of Buildings) Order 1995* (*SI 1995 No 280*)).

Condition (*c*) should be particularly noted. If a dwelling is constructed in the grounds of another it is not uncommon for the planning permission to require that the two can only be sold together. The planning condition reflects a test that has in the past been applied by Customs and accepted by the VAT tribunals. In *J K Lund (VTD 12926)* Customs refused a VAT refund on the grounds that the building had been constructed unlawfully. Evidence was produced from the planning authority that, although the extent of rebuilding had been greater than provided for in the planning permission, it had decided during the course of the works not to object to it. The tribunal therefore found that the work was lawful – a pyrrhic victory for the taxpayer as they also found it was work of reconstruction. It appears that, under the new test, such acquiescence by the planners would be insufficient. This provision is apparently to prevent 'granny flats' and similar new homes, or flatlets belonging to existing buildings, from attracting zero-rating (VAT Information Sheet 10/95). This should be contrasted with the decision in A I Davison (see 17.228) where the work was lawful but the tribunal held that head (*d*) was not met as the planning permission, although permitting the construction of the dwelling, had not been granted in respect of a dwelling.

**17.25** The tribunal in *University of Bath (VTD 14235)* held that whether a building was designed as a dwelling or number of dwellings had to be considered in relation to the building as it was originally constructed. Individual student rooms without toilets, showers or kitchen facilities were not dwellings; nor were blocks of rooms with a shared kitchen. It also held that a building could not be intended for use solely as student accommodation if it was always envisaged that the rooms would be let to other people during vacation periods. A similar decision was reached in *University Court of the University of St. Andrews (VTD 15243*). In contrast, in the later case of *Denman College (VTD 15513)* (heard by a three-man tribunal chaired by Stephen Oliver QC), student accommodation blocks each consisting of eight study-bedrooms containing a bathroom and shower unit were held to be residential accommodation even though the blocks did not contain cooking facilities.

**17.26** It is specifically provided that the construction (or conversion of) a building designed as a dwelling includes the construction of (or conversion of) a garage, provided that the dwelling and the garage are constructed (or converted) at the same time and the garage is intended to be occupied with the dwelling (or with one of them if there are more than one) (*VATA 1994, 8 Sch, Group 5, Note 3*).

**17.27** There is no statutory definition of a dwelling as such. Customs' view is that the word should be given its day-to-day meaning of a place where someone lives (see 17.48).

**Relevant Residential Purpose**

**17.28** A building *is used for a relevant residential purpose* if it is used as either:

(*a*) a home or other institution providing residential accommodation for children;

(*b*) a home or other institution providing residential accommodation with personal care for persons in need of personal care by reason of

(i) old age,

(ii) disablement,

(iii) past or present dependence on alcohol or drugs, or

(iv) past or present mental disorder;

(*c*) a hospice;

(*d*) residential accommodation for students or school pupils;

(*e*) residential accommodation for members of any of the armed forces;

(*f*) a monastery, nunnery or similar establishment; or

(*g*) an institution which is the sole or main residence of at least 90% of its residents.

(*VATA 1994, Sch 8 Group 5, Note 4*).

**17.29** A building is, however, not to be regarded as used for a relevant residential purpose if it is used as:

(i) a hospital;

(ii) a prison or similar institution (e.g. a borstal establishment would not be covered by (*a*)); or

(iii) an hotel, inn or similar establishment (*Note 4*).

**17.30** If a number of buildings are constructed simultaneously on the same site and are intended for use together as a unit solely for a relevant residential purpose each of them is to be treated as intended for use solely for such a purpose (*Note 5*). This will ensure relief for nursing homes, etc. where there are separate accommodation blocks and a communal dining or recreation room in a different building. It is important to note that the buildings must be constructed at the same time. *Note 5* will not allow zero-rating for a later addition to a nursing home which is a separate building to the main home and not of itself capable of being a dwelling. For the definition of a 'dwelling', see paragraphs 17.24 and 17.25 above. Customs will by concession treat buildings as constructed at the same time if the original planning permission covers their installation but the construction is phased over a limited period (VAT Information Sheet 10/95). No guidance is given as to what is a limited period, although the cases considered at 8.85 may give some guidance as to what is not!

**17.31** There are a number of points that should be noted.

1. A building used as a residence for children can qualify even if all that is provided is the accommodation. A home or other institution providing accommodation for the elderly, disabled, etc. will qualify only if personal care is provided in addition to the accommodation. It is not wholly clear if such personal care has to be provided in the accommodation itself, but it probably does.

2. It should be noted that (*b*) in 17.28 above requires not only that personal care be provided but also that the inmates be in need of such care. No guidance is given as to what constitutes personal care. Clearly the provision of a full cleaning and nursing service, such as in a nursing home, will qualify. It is unlikely that the mere provision of a warden with residents doing everything else themselves would do so – although in such circumstances it may well be that the residents' rooms would constitute dwellings and thus qualify for zero-rating under *item 1(a)* in 17.6 above instead of *item 1(b)*.

3. The dividing line between a hospice (qualifying for zero-rating) and a hospital (which is standard-rated) is not clear. Both provide medical care. As the intention seems to be to allow zero-rating

where an institution is a person's permanent home, but to deny it where a person may stay there for a few days only, it is likely that a hospice will be limited to an institution that provides care for those whose illness is perceived to be incurable.

4. It appears that a rooming house let to a school on a lease of over 21 years as student accommodation will qualify for zero-rating even if the school lets it out to others during the vacation period, as the test is whether the building is 'intended for use as residential accommodation for students'.

5. The wording 'hotel, inn or similar establishment' should be contrasted with that used in *VATA 1994, Sch 9 Group 1, item 1*, i.e. 'hotel, inn, boarding house or similar establishment'. This suggests that a boarding house could qualify for zero-rating provided that the 90% test in head (*g*) in 17.28 above is met – although it is debatable whether a boarding house constitutes an 'institution'. If it does not it will not come within head (*g*). A property supplying accommodation and breakfast for homeless and unemployed people has been held to be a similar establishment to a hotel (*Namecourt Ltd (1984 VATTR 22) (VTD 1560)*), as has accommodation for long-term residents in a guest house (*Mrs R I McGrath (1992 STC 371)*).

**17.32** It was held in *Urdd Gobaith Cymru (Welsh League of Youth) (VTD 14881)* that residential accommodation need not imply permanence. Urdd Gobaith is an educational establishment to foster use of the Welsh language. It built lodging accommodation to be used wholly by students and teachers attending its courses. The average stay by a student was four days. The tribunal felt that while 'a residence' implies a degree of permanence, 'residential accommodation' does not; it merely signifies lodging, sleeping or overnight accommodation. It also felt that if Parliament had intended to exclude short-term accommodation, the legislation would have said so. Customs have said that they accept this decision and have changed their policy to reflect it (Business Brief 6/98). Customs point out that a building which was not residential under their old definition, but is residential under the new, cannot be 'converted' into a residential building, so input tax on such a 'conversion' is now irrecoverable. They will, however, allow zero-rating by concession where conversion commenced (or was contracted for) before 9 June 1998 when they pointed out this fact.

**17.33** In *Derby YMCA (VTD 16918)*, the YMCA owned a hostel and youth centre consisting of a complex of three buildings. It converted part of the first floor of one of these consisting of 15 hotel-style bedrooms into ten self-contained flatlets plus the provision of a staff room and ancillary laundry and toilet facilities. Customs accepted that the YMCA was a relevant housing association within *item 3* (see 17.6) and that the building was not designed as a dwelling or a number of dwellings for the purpose of *Note 7* (see 17.47). However they contended that the test was not whether it was a dwelling but rather whether it was used as a dwelling; the living accommodation was clearly the residence of most of the recipients. Alternatively they contended that the building was not used for a relevant residential purpose because it was similar to a hotel. The tribunal held that the building was a non-residential part of a building within *Note 7*; it was not designed as a dwelling, nor physically adapted for use as a dwelling, nor used for a relevant non-residential purpose (and not as a building similar to a hotel). However it also held that the new self-catering flatlets were not used for a relevant residential purpose within *Note 4(g)* (see 17.28). Accordingly zero-rating was denied.

## Relevant Charitable Purpose

**17.34** *Use for a relevant charitable purpose* is use by a charity otherwise than in the course or furtherance of a business (*VATA 1994, Sch 8 Group 5, Note 6*). The obvious example is a church. It does not appear that the charity needs to be a UK charity – although it should be borne in mind that, for income tax purposes, an overseas charity has been held not to be within the definition of a 'body which must apply its income for charitable purposes only', on the basis that those words imply a UK charity (*Camille & Henry Dreyfus Foundation Inc v CIR (36 TC 126)*). Where a charity does not carry on a business, its office premises will also fall within this head. If some of its activities constitute the carrying on of a business for VAT purposes the appropriate part of its office premises will qualify. An apportionment needs to be made, the part that is to be used for non-business purposes qualifying for zero-rating (see 17.47 below). In many cases the problems of making such an apportionment will be awesome. In *St Dunstan's Roman Catholic Church Southborough (VTD 15472)* the VAT tribunal held that the construction of a double garage within the curtilage of the church for use by the priest was for use by the charity for a relevant charitable purpose even though the priest might use his car partly for his pastoral work and partly for personal journeys.

**17.35** The courts have held that a wide meaning needs to be given to the word business in the context of VAT (see, for example, *C & E Commrs v Royal Exchange Theatre Trust (1979 STC 728)*). In *C & E Commrs v Morrison's Academy Boarding Houses Association (1978 STC 1)*, quoted with approval in the *Royal Exchange Theatre Trust* case, it was pointed out that the words 'commerce' or 'profit' are not used in association with the word 'business' and that, if activities are 'predominantly concerned with the making of taxable supplies to consumers for a consideration', the taxpayer is in the 'business' of making taxable supplies. Neill J in the *Royal Exchange Theatre Trust* case considered that the activities must include some sort of commercial element for a business to exist, although the VAT tribunal in *Hunmanby Bowling Club* (see 17.40 below) did not follow this.

**17.36** In *C & E Commrs v Lord Fisher (1981 STC 238)*, Gibson J accepted six indicia put forward by the Crown on the basis of previous cases to determine whether activities constitute a business, namely:

(*a*) whether the activity is a 'serious undertaking earnestly pursued';

(*b*) whether it is an occupation or function actively pursued with reasonable or recognisable continuity;

(*c*) whether it has a certain measure of substance as measured by the quarterly or annual value of taxable supplies made;

(*d*) whether it is conducted in a regular manner and on sound and recognised business principles;

(*e*) whether it is predominantly concerned with the making of taxable supplies for a consideration; and

(*f*) whether the taxable supplies are of a kind which, subject to differences of detail, are commonly made by those who seek to profit by them.

Lord Fisher organised shoots on his estate for his friends who contributed to the costs. The judge thought that 'the sharing of the costs of a sporting or other pleasure activity does not by itself turn an activity of pleasure and social enjoyment into a business'.

**17.37** An interesting case on what is a business is that of *Cardiff Community Housing Association Ltd (VTD 16841)*. The Association is a charity. It provides social housing for persons in need. It is a non-profit making organisation dependent wholly on Government and public grants. It claimed the construction of an office block for its own use qualified for zero-rating. Customs contended that, as it was in receipt of rental income from its properties, the charity was carrying on a business so the office would not be used for a relevant charitable purpose. The rents represented about 20% of the charity's income. The tribunal found the decision difficult but on balance felt that the charity was carrying out a function on behalf of the state in the same way as the Institute of Chartered Accountants (*ICAEW v C & E Commrs, 1997 STC 1155*) which did not amount to an economic activity. It was therefore not carrying on a business. The tribunal also found that the charity carried out its activities as a body governed by public law so that its activities were outside the scope of VAT by virtue of *Article 4(5)* of the *EC Sixth Directive*. *Morley Retreat Conference House (VTD 17265)* is a registered charity offering facilities for retreats and conferences. It runs on a non-profit making basis and, as its supplies are exempt, is not registered for VAT. It constructed a chapel and claimed that the construction work should be zero-rated, as it was supplied in the course of the construction of a building intended solely to be used for a relevant charitable purpose. It was held that the chapel was used as part and parcel of the business run by Morley, albeit that no charge was made for its use.

**17.38** In *Yarburgh Children's Trust (2002 STC 207)* a building owned by the trust, which is a charity, was used by a playgroup run by a separate charity at a concessionary rent. The trust contended that such use was otherwise than in the course of a business. Patten J felt that the balance of authority, particularly the ECJ decision in *Wellcome Trust Ltd v C & E Commrs (Case C-155/94, 1996 STC 945)* that share disposals by trustees formed part of the normal management of trust assets and were not carried out in furtherance of any business, was against treating an activity as an economic one merely because it results in a consideration or produces income. He accepted a Customs submission that the motive of the person who makes the supply cannot dictate the tax treatment of the transaction but felt that excluding such motive does not allow the tribunal to disregard the observable terms and features of the transaction in question and the wider context in which it is carried out. He felt that the tribunal needs to ascertain such things as the nature of the activities carried on by the person alleged to be in business, the terms upon which and manner in which those activities are carried out and the nature of the relationship between the parties to the transaction. The mere fact of the letting at a rent is not sufficient in itself to render that transaction an economic activity. The playgroup's occupation of the building was not in the furtherance of a business. The overwhelming impression is that the play-school was a co-operative venture run by trained staff with the benefit of help provided by parents. The tribunal was entitled to conclude that no business user was involved.

### Use as a Village Hall, etc

**17.39** Use of a building as a village hall or similarly in providing social or recreational facilities for a local community is also a relevant charitable purpose (*VATA 1994, Sch 8 Group 5, Note 6*). In *Jubilee Hall Recreation Centre Ltd v C & E Commrs (1999 STC 381)*, the Court of Appeal interpreted the scope of this provision restrictively. It felt that its purpose was to extend the relief to the case where the local community is the final consumer in respect of the services. It would not include a building intended for economic activities unless such activities are an ordinary incidence of the use of the building by a local community for social, including recreational, purposes. This introduces considerations of scale and locality. The scale of Jubilee Hall's commercial activities went far beyond the normal activities of a village hall. The court also doubted, without deciding, whether an area covering much of Central London could aptly be described as a 'local community' or whether people who worked in an area and lived elsewhere are part of its local community. In *C & E Commrs v St Dunstan's Educational Foundation (1999 STC 381)*, heard at the same time, the

Court of Appeal held that a sports centre constructed primarily for use as one of the facilities of a fee-paying school could not be brought within the scope of zero-rating merely by allowing its use by the local community when not in use by the school. Beldam LJ also doubted whether the word 'use' in this context includes the activity of leasing the building to a third party, in this case the local authority, although it appears to have been accepted that allowing the school to occupy, for no consideration, would not of itself have denied the relief. In *Bennachie Leisure Centre Association (VTD 14276)* the tribunal held that a building which was part of a larger complex and contained a central area marked out for badminton, with changing rooms, toilets, crêche, club room, office, kitchen, tea room, craft shop, thrift shop, fitness rooms and equipment store was similar to a village hall as it was suitable for both social and recreational use and was not intended for other purposes to a material extent. The building was intended to service ten parishes within a six-mile radius, which the tribunal felt comprised a local community. However, as this case was decided before the Court of Appeal decision in *Jubilee Hall*, it needs to be approached with caution.

In *Aspex Visual Arts Trust (VTD 16419)* a former chapel which had been converted into an art gallery and artists studios was held not to be similar in character to a village hall; it did not cater for the wide range of activities associated with village halls and attracted visitors from a large geographical area. The VAT tribunal in *The London Federation of Clubs for Young People (VTD 17079)* thought that a village hall is a place where a considerable variety of activities may take place but went on to say, 'But a building to which the local community (with or without others) has access and where a variety of activities may take place is not necessarily a village hall' and would not necessarily involve use in a way similar to that of village halls. It went on to find that the charity's recreation centre was neither used solely for relevant charitable purposes nor used solely as a village hall. Its expression of regret at being compelled to dismiss the appeal was somewhat diluted by going on to indicate that it would award costs against the charity should Customs wish to apply for them!

A swimming pool was held not to be similar to a village hall in *The South Molton Swimming Pool Trustees (VTD 16495)*. The tribunal placed no relevance on the fact that a swimming pool was not similar in appearance to a village hall as the provision is concerned with use not appearance. However, it differed from a village hall in that all the activities were organised by the trustees not by the local community. In any event the pool was run as a well-organised business operation and drew custom from a much wider area than a local community. In *Southwick Community Association (VTD 16441)* a community centre was held not to be similar to a village hall because membership of the association was not limited to people living in Southwick and its immediate area but included affiliated groups which included branches of national organisations. This seems a harsh decision. A day centre for the elderly annexed to a residential care home was similarly held not to be the provision of facilities solely for a local community in *Beth Johnson Housing Association (VTD 17095)*. In Ledbury Amateur Dramatic Society a building intended as a community theatre was held to be for a use similar to a village hall in providing social or recreational facilities for the local community. Customs had argued that the theatre was not similar to a village hall because ownership and management were vested in a particular charity whose object was to provide for the needs of a limited section of the population (those interested in theatre) whereas a village hall is normally managed by local trustees; that the supplies of building work were not made to the final consumer but to the trustees who carried on an economic activity by charging entrance fees to the public; and the use of the theatre for the trustees' own purposes was substantial (24 days a year!).

The judge in *C & E Commrs v Yarburgh Children's Trust (2002 STC 207)* felt that it is not enough to show that the building in question was intended to be used for an activity which could take place in a village hall and is available to members of the local community. What needs to be shown is that the building is, or fulfils the role of, a village hall or other building designed for public use in the provision of social or recreational facilities for the local community. In that case the use of the building was restricted by the terms of the *Children's Act 1989*. Accordingly, the building was not used as a village hall. As the judge decided that the building was used by a charity otherwise than in the furtherance of a business, the village hall point was not however relevant to the decision itself.

**17.40** There have also been a number of earlier tribunal decisions in relation to sports pavilions which are probably still relevant. In *Roy Meadows (VTD 11817)*, a builder constructed a building containing changing rooms, a shower room, a referee's room and a kitchen for a junior football club. The VAT tribunal held that the building was unsuitable for business use and was used by the club in a way similar to a village hall, i.e. for providing recreational facilities for a segment of the local community. It felt that this was probably a charitable objective under the *Recreational Charities Act 1958*, albeit that the club was not a registered charity, and adjourned the case for the club to produce further evidence that the building was provided for charitable purposes. In contrast, in *Hunmanby Bowling Club (VTD 12136)* where the club erected a pavilion building, the tribunal held that even if the club was a recreational charity, it used the pavilion in the course of a business because it made charges, albeit at well below a commercial rate, to non-members. The club's total income of around £1,000 p.a. was used to maintain the bowling green, not the pavilion, so this seems a harsh decision. It illustrates that requirements for zero-rating need to be strictly complied with. VAT tribunals can sometimes interpret this provision rigidly. In *Ormiston Charitable Trust (VTD 13187)* the trust erected a sports pavilion and changing room. The facilities were aimed mainly at children aged 5–15 but there were also weekly fitness classes for mothers and occasional events for fathers. There was also use by local sports clubs. Customs successfully argued that this mix of social and recreational facilities was not such as could be expected to be carried on in a village hall and the facilities were provided only for a particular section of the local community.

**17.41** The VAT treatment of work to a village hall or similar community project can also be affected by the financing. If a local authority owns the hall and uses its own funds to carry out the work to it, it is not making a supply. If it owns the hall and receives funds from other bodies that will use the hall such funds are likely to be consideration for such use. If a person who provides the funds will not use the hall, the receipt may be a donation outside the scope of VAT but only, say Customs, if such funds are freely given and neither the donating party nor a particular third party benefits. If the local authority uses its own funds to finance the work, the normal VAT rules will apply. If it uses donated funds, it will normally be able to recover the VAT under *VATA 1994, s 33* provided that it incurs the expenditure itself. Sometimes a voluntary group will approach a local authority for assistance. The local authority will set up a project fund into which funds raised locally, grants received by the local group and any subsidy from the local authority is paid. In many such cases it will be the voluntary group that owns the hall. If the local authority carries out work to the hall and gives this work away, it can recover the VAT under *section 33*. If however it receives a benefit, that is likely to be a business supply. If it simply acts as agent for the voluntary group, the supply of building work will be to the voluntary body not to the local authority, and the local authority will not be able to recover the VAT. If it charges the voluntary group for arranging the work, its charge will be a supply taxable at the standard rate (VAT Information Sheet 1/99).

### Who can Zero-rate?

**17.42** A supply within *item 1(a)(ii)* in 17.6 above – of a building intended for use for a relevant residential or charitable purpose – can be zero-rated only if the person to whom the supply is made (i.e. the purchaser, lessee or customer) is the person who will use the building for the relevant purpose and he has given to the supplier a certificate stating that the building is intended for use for a qualifying purpose (*VATA 1994, Sch 8 Group 5, Note 12*). Similarly a supply in the course of construction of a building intended solely for relevant charitable purposes and the related supply of materials can be zero-rated under *items 2* and *4* respectively only if made to a person who intends to use the building for the charitable purpose and who certifies that fact. A subcontractor cannot zero-rate his supplies to the main contractor even if the contractor holds a certificate of intended use from the charity (see *ME Smith (Electrical Engineers) Ltd (VTD 13594)*). It should be noted that, strictly speaking, the certificate must be given *before* the supply is made. If this is not done, the building is not eligible for zero-rating. Accordingly, a failure to supply the certificate cannot be corrected later, although in practice Customs may not take the point. Normally the solicitor acting in the transaction is likely to ensure that this certificate has been given.

**17.43** The certificate must be in a form to be laid down by Customs. They have in fact laid down separate forms for residential and relevant charitable development. The requirement for this certificate is because the vendor or lessor is not himself in a position to judge to what use the purchaser or lessee intends to put the building. If Customs are to forgo tax based on some person's intention, they want that intention stated in writing so that they have some comeback if what transpires does not accord with that intention.

**17.44** If such a certificate is incorrect, the certifier lays himself open to a penalty equal to the tax undercharged as a result of the incorrect certificate (*VATA 1994, s 62*). Technically, the issue of the certificate does not appear to absolve the supplier from responsibility for getting his VAT position right. Accordingly, if he has any doubt about whether he is entitled to zero-rate the supply, it is wise to obtain an indemnity or check the position with Customs, not simply rely on the certificate. Customs have said that they will not, however, seek to recover any tax due from the certifier if he takes all reasonable steps to check the validity of the declaration and then, in good faith, zero-rates the supply (C & E Notice 748, ESC A16). In *Paul Butland t/a Harrogate Site Services (VTD 6531)* planning permission had been granted for the conversion of a listed building into a nursing home but the owner had made a fresh application to use the building as a hotel. This was granted in November 1989. The builder started work in August 1989 and zero-rated the work because he claimed that he understood that it was to be converted into a nursing home. The VAT tribunal held that he was liable to account for the tax and did not accept that he was unaware of the proposed hotel use.

**17.45** What happens if Customs do not agree that the work qualifies for zero-rating and refuse to recognise the validity of the certificate? That is what happened in *Church of Christ the King (VTD 12783)*. The church purchased a warehouse to which it intended to carry out extensive building work in three stages. Customs contended that the work was a conversion, reconstruction, alteration or enlargement of an existing building and did not qualify for zero-rating. They further contended that, although stages one and two had been completed and the building was partially in use, the VAT tribunal was not entitled to hear the charity's appeal as the work was a single project which had not yet been completed and the tribunal was not entitled to hear an appeal relating to future supplies. The tribunal agreed. It also considered that it had no jurisdiction to hear an appeal against Customs' refusal to recognise the zero-rating certificates and that, in any event, such a certificate related only to the intended use of a new building and was not apt to cover construction work which did not relate to a new building. The charity would therefore have to pay over VAT to the builder but could come back to the tribunal when it had completed stage three – assuming that the unexpected VAT bill leaves it with sufficient funds to do so – and seek to show that the work should be zero-rated.

**17.46** On 30 March 1990 Customs entered into a concordat with the Committee of Vice Chancellors and Principals of the Universities of the UK (CVCP) which contained a concession allowing a university to certify student accommodation as a relevant residential building if it is 'a new building clearly intended primarily for use as student accommodation for 10 years from the date of completion'. The concordat, and therefore presumably the concession, was subsequently unilaterally withdrawn by Customs. Customs refused to allow this concession to Greenwich Property Ltd, a wholly owned subsidiary of the University of Greenwich on two grounds, that the concession applied only if the university itself made the accommodation available in the vacation period, and that they were entitled to refuse to apply a concession where they believed it was being used for the avoidance of tax. The company applied for judicial review – *R (on the application of Greenwich Property Ltd) v C & E Commrs (2001 STC 618) ([2001] EWHC Admin 230)*. The judge thought that the purpose behind the concession was to enable the universities to make profitable use of their student accommodation in vacations and still get the benefit of zero-rating. Thus 'solely' meant solely in term time. There was nothing in the wording of the concession to indicate that the university could not use a third party. The judge also dismissed the tax avoidance point as there was nothing in the concession to stipulate that it could not be used for tax avoidance. In any event he did not regard the scheme adopted as tax avoidance albeit that it included some artificial elements.

## Conversions

**17.47** In applying *items 1(b)* and *3* in 17.6 above, a building (or part of a building) is non-residential if either –

(*a*) it is neither designed nor adapted for use as a dwelling or number of dwellings or for a relevant residential purpose, or

(*b*) it is designed or adapted for such a purpose but it was constructed more than 10 years before the grant of the major interest and no part of it has been used as a dwelling or for a relevant residential purpose in the 10 years immediately preceding the grant.

(*VATA 1994, Schedule 8 Group 5, Note 7* as substituted by the *VAT (Conversion of Buildings) Order 2001* (*SI 2001 No 2305*)). *Note 7A* applies this same test for the purpose of *item 3*. The 10-year test did not apply prior to 1 August 2001. It had to be shown that the building was constructed before 1 April 1973 and had not been used as a dwelling (or dwellings) or for a relevant residential purpose at any time since that date. It is up to the taxpayer to demonstrate that the building had not been used as a dwelling in the relevant period. This was difficult when its history had to be traced back for over 25 years, particularly where there had been a number of changes of ownership during that period. Customs have said that for the purpose of (*b*) above if a house has been illegally occupied by squatters this will not disqualify it from being treated as empty (VAT Information Sheet 5/01, July 2001, para 1.4). Where part of a house was lived in during the 10-year period zero-rating cannot apply unless that part was a self-contained dwelling (para 1.5). They also say that the charge does not enable a developer to recover input tax incurred before 1 August if the house is sold after that date as such tax was incurred in relation to an exempt supply (para 2.5). This appears questionable. The sale triggers zero-rating, so on the face of it although when he incurred the input tax the developer intended to use it in making an exempt supply he surely would have changed his intention on 1 August 2001 in which case *Regulation 109* (see 17.251) would give a right to repayment. A garage occupied with a dwelling is not a non-residential building if it is separate from the dwelling (*Note 8*). Where part of a building is residential and part is not, the conversion of the non-residential part does not fall within *item 1(b)* or *3* unless it creates an additional dwelling or dwellings (*Note 9*). For example, if a building contains a shop with a flat above, the conversion of the shop into a second flat can qualify for zero-rating. The conversion of the shop to residential use, so that the entire building is used as a single residence, will not qualify, however. Customs say that there are a small number of charities which provide accommodation for rent that cannot recover VAT on conversions because they are prevented by legal constraints from selling their converted properties (and thus cannot grant a major interest in the completed building), and do not qualify as DIY builders as the receipt of rents means that they are carrying on a business. Customs will consider refunds of VAT by concession to such bodies on an individual basis (News Release 15/96).

**17.48** Problems frequently arise with pubs. Although these contain living accommodation for the publican, that accommodation is often not self-contained but shares some facilities with the pub. Conversion of the pub to a house will not fall within *item 1(b)* because the building as a whole is not a non-residential building, and the non-residential part will not normally be converted into a dwelling but merely into part of a dwelling as the other part already exists. The problem is well illustrated by the tribunal decision in *Calam Vales Ltd (VTD 16869)*. The company converted a pub into two dwellings. The conversion involved the division of the building vertically. Accordingly each of the dwellings included both an old residential and old commercial element. The company unsuccessfully argued that no part of the pub was previously a dwelling under *Note 2* as it was not self-contained, but the tribunal agreed with Customs that a dwelling for this purpose simply means a place where someone lives. However, in *C & E Commrs v Blom-Cooper ([2002] EWHC 1421 (Ch) [2002] STC 1061)* the judge held that on the facts there was previously a non-residential part of a building. The result of the building work was that a building designed as a dwelling emerged so that relief was due. This was a do-it-yourself builder case so was concerned with the interpretation of *VATA 1994, s 35(1D)* rather than *Sch 8 Group 5* but the wording is almost identical.

**17.49** The meaning of a non-residential building was in issue in *Look Ahead Housing Association (VTD 16816)*. The Association owned two buildings which had originally been town houses but had been used as bedsits since 1946. It converted them into self-contained flats. It was not disputed that the bedsits were not self-contained. Customs contended that the buildings were not non-residential before conversion. They argued that the purpose of the legislation was to promote the creation of new housing and that this had not occurred here, the buildings having been used as dwellings both before and after the conversion. The tribunal felt that the provisions had to be construed in the context of UK law not UK social policy. It held that, giving the word its ordinary meaning, a 'dwelling' would contain facilities for all the major activities of life, particularly sleeping, cooking, eating and toilet facilities (see *University of Bath* – 17.25). The bedsits did not have the characteristics of dwellings and thus were 'non-residential' as defined in *Note 7*.

### Housing Associations

**17.50** For the purpose of *item 3* in 17.6, the following are 'relevant housing associations':

(*a*) a registered social landlord under the *Housing Act 1996*, or

(*b*) a registered housing association within the *Housing Associations Act 1985* (in Scotland) or the *Housing (Northern Ireland) Order 1992*.

(*VATA 1994, 8 Sch, Group 5, Note 21*).

### Conversion, Reconstruction and Alteration

**17.51** Unless it falls within *items 1(b)* or *3* (see 17.6 above), or relates to a listed building, building work cannot be zero-rated if it consists of the conversion, reconstruction or alteration of an existing building. Nor can the enlargement of, or extension to, an existing building, except to the extent that it creates an additional dwelling or dwellings. Similarly zero-rating does not apply to an annex to an existing building unless the whole or part of that annex is intended for use solely for a relevant charitable purpose, and (*a*) it is capable of functioning independently from the existing building, and

(*b*) the only or main access to the annex is not via the existing building (and that to the existing building is not via the annex). (*Group 5, Notes 16* and *17* as amended by the *VAT (Construction of Buildings Order 2002)* (*SI 2002 No 1101*)).

The aim is to give the same tax treatment to a discrete facility housed in an annex to the main building as to one in a separate building. The annex must be capable of functioning independently of the existing building and be capable of use even if the connection to the main building is closed. The change does not give tax-free treatment to enlargements of charity buildings by the creation of additional floor-space for a single activity (VAT Information Sheet 10/95). Nor can the enlargement of, or extension to, an existing building qualify except to the extent that it creates an additional dwelling or dwellings. This will now allow the zero-rating of additional self-contained flats on top of an existing block of flats and probably also the types of additional flats considered at 8.69 and 8.70 above (VAT Information Sheet 10/95).

**17.52** Clearly a person who carries out such operations is not a person constructing a building for the purpose of *item 1* in 17.6 above. It is not clear if a restrictive covenant is a 'similar permission' to a planning consent. It is probably not. Certainly, in normal terminology it does not seem very similar. It has sometimes been suggested that head (*b*) in 17.51 above can be circumvented by erecting the new building without internal access to the adjoining one and subsequently creating such access. This ploy failed in *Highacre Construction Co Ltd (VTD 5772)*. Highacre owned a nursing home to which it wished to add an extension. A new company, M Ltd, bought the site of the extension and contracted with Highacre for it to construct it. Although the plans envisaged connecting doors, these were bricked up. Highacre zero-rated its invoices to M Ltd. M Ltd subsequently bought the nursing home from Highacre and inserted the connecting doors between the two buildings. The tribunal held that the only purpose of blocking up the internal door spaces had been to justify zero-rating the work and that in those circumstances it was permissible to look at the terms of the planning permission, which had clearly envisaged the two buildings being operated as a single entity, to determine the nature of the building work – which they held to be an enlargement of the original building. In any event the lack of internal access did not stop the addition of a self-contained flat to an existing house from being an enlargement in *J W Cooper & Sons (VTD 2402)* or in *Assetcope Ltd (VTD 4656)*. However, such an extension would now be zero-rated (see 17.51 above).

**17.53** A similar result was reached in *Raymond Symonds (VTD 9050)* where a customer engaged a builder to build a new house adjoining an existing one. It was self-contained with its own access and services. The customer subsequently engaged another builder to break through the party wall. It was held that the customer's intention was always that the two houses should subsequently be adapted to form a single dwelling. Accordingly the work done by the first builder was not eligible for zero-rating as it was merely the first stage of a clear and declared plan to convert and enlarge an existing house. This decision seems to put a builder in an impossible position as he will not necessarily know that the customer has an intention to join the two houses in such circumstances.

**17.54** The opposite happened in *Carrophil Ltd (VTD 10190)*. The company constructed a Sunday School room for a church on the site of the former vestry. It adjoined the church on two sides. Double doors which had provided access from the church to the vestry – and therefore provided access to the schoolroom – remained in place at the time of practical completion of the work. A month later the architect gave instructions for these doors to be sealed and on the schoolroom side they were covered with plasterboard. Customs contended that the schoolroom was an extension to the church with internal access. The VAT tribunal held that there was no internal access. The closing of such access, albeit as an afterthought and albeit after practical completion, was done on the instructions of the architect and was sufficiently connected with the rest of the work to be part of the construction of the schoolroom. Looking at whether the schoolroom was a taxable enlargement of the church or a zero-rated extension, the tribunal held that an educated layperson, looking at the completed work, would conclude that the church had been extended to provide accommodation for the Sunday school.

**17.55** The VAT tribunal (Stephen Oliver QC) in *BT Macnamara (VTD 16039)* observed that the exclusion from zero-rating of enlargements, extensions and annexes was expressed in order of their degree of integration with the existing building. An enlargement is structural work which produced an overall increase in the size or capacity of the existing building, extension denotes a lesser degree of integration with the existing building, being the addition of a new section or wing, while an annexe merely adjoined the existing building with the degree of integration being tenuous. In that case a new building containing classrooms and a laboratory was constructed in a gap between parts of two existing school buildings. Although the tribunal noted that the work involved no conversion or alteration to an existing building and that there was no enlargement of any individual building, the effect of the project was to produce an additional section or part of 'the building'. The degree of integration made it an extension of the existing 'building'. Even if that were wrong it was an annexe. A collection of buildings was similarly looked on by the tribunal as a single building in *Wright & Fuller Ltd (VTD 15952)* (see 8.76).

**17.56** It is often very difficult to determine whether building work which utilises part of the fabric of an existing building is a conversion, reconstruction or alteration or the creation of a completely new building. There have been a large number of decided cases on this point. As this is a question that is primarily of concern in the context of development, these cases are considered in chapter 8 at paragraphs 8.63 onwards. Zero-rating also applies to certain alterations to listed buildings used for residential and relevant charitable purposes. These are considered in chapter 9 (Refurbishments) at paragraphs 9.19 onwards.

**What is a Building?**

**17.57** From 1 March 1995 a building ceases to be an existing building only if:

(*a*) it is demolished completely to ground level; or

(*b*) the part remaining above ground level consists of no more than a single facade (or if it is a corner site, a double facade), the retention of which is a condition or requirement of a statutory planning consent or similar permission (*Group 5, Note 18*).

This prevents the restoration of a derelict cottage being regarded as the construction of a building where the useable parts of the walls are incorporated into a new house unless *item 1(b)* or *3* (see 17.6 above) applies. It effectively overrides the test that VAT tribunals have devised in recent years of whether looking at the building an onlooker would say that it is a new building or a reconstruction of what was there before. Customs interpret 'ground level' as permitting a concrete slab to remain from the previous construction (VAT Information Sheet 10/95). It is understood that where two derelict cottages are converted into one, and one of them was occupied at some time since 1 April 1973 but the other was not, Customs do not consider that zero-rating applies. Customs have indicated that a letter from the rate office, water board, electricity board or Post Office stating that they have had no contact with the property since 1 April 1973 will be satisfactory evidence that the property has not been occupied since that date (Tolley's Practical VAT, June 1996). This change was made to 'clarify' the law pending Customs' appeal against the *Marchday* decision (see 8.76). In May 1997 they were refused leave to appeal to the House of Lords. As a result, they announced on 24 September 1997 that they would consider claims for refunds on residential conversions prior to 1 March 1995 where the building work was extensive – subject, of course, to the three-year cap and the doctrine of unjust enrichment (Business Brief 20/97).

**17.58** This provision was in issue in *R M & S L Midgley (VTD 15379)*. The appellants wished to renovate and extend a dilapidated house. They obtained the necessary planning permission and started work. If things had gone to plan the work would have been VATable. However it was discovered that with one exception all of the walls of the original house were unstable and had to be demolished. The work continued. When it was nearly finished application for planning permission for the changed work was made and granted retrospectively. The house was clearly an existing building when the work began. The tribunal held that on the demolition of the walls (but not before then) it ceased to be an existing building as it then came to satisfy 17.57(*b*) above. The effect was that work up to that time was standard-rated but thereafter it was zero-rated, so an apportionment would be required. It is interesting to note that Customs accepted that the planning consent condition was met by the retrospective consent. This contrasts with their approach to listed building consent under *Group 6* (see 9.36).

**Miscellaneous**

**17.59** There are provisions for apportionment where part of a building qualifies for zero-rating and part does not (*Group 5, Notes 10* and *11*). These are likely to give rise to immense practical problems of valuation where, for example, there is a sale as a single transaction of an office building with penthouse flats on top. Is the notional residential building to be valued as if it were floating in mid-air, or is the building to be valued as if it were wholly residential and the value of the lower floors then ignored? Whilst such problems can no doubt give valuers many pleasurable hours, it needs to be remembered that a taxpayer who resolves this valuation dilemma in a different way to Customs could find himself faced with a misdeclaration penalty. A dispute will not, in the normal course of events, arise until Customs do a VAT inspection. Clearly, in such circumstances it would be advisable to tell Customs, at the time the VAT liability arises, that a valuation has been adopted in the return, and the amount and effect of such valuation, so as to give them an early opportunity to challenge it. This should hopefully provide a reasonable excuse defence against any possible misdeclaration penalty.

**17.60** Customs accept that there will be some rough edges in these apportionment rules and have announced that they will ignore a simple office incorporated into a residential building. This will cover, for example, an office for the matron in a nursing home. It is not clear how many offices this will stretch to. One would hope that it will allow as many as necessary for the efficient running of the residential building, but it will be wise to check with Customs in each individual case.

**17.61** Furthermore Customs accept that where a building is used by a charity it will not always be possible when the building is acquired to identify which part will be used for relevant charitable purposes and which will not. They will therefore 'ignore indiscriminate business use for non-business charity buildings where it is not expected to exceed 10 per cent of the time the building is normally available for use'. (Hansard, Standing Committee G, 15 May 1989, Col 73). As an alternative to the 10% concession charities can calculate the extent of qualifying non-business use by reference to floor space or the number of people using the building. The non-qualifying use will be disregarded if 90% of the floor space is used solely for non-business activity or if 90% of the people using the building are engaged solely on non-business activity. These floor space and number of users tests must be applied to the whole building not a part and the permission of Customs is needed to adopt those methods but is not needed for the standard time method (Business Brief 8/00).The Minister also gave an assurance that where residential accommodation includes a community room it would be zero-rated along with the rest 'if it is an essential part of that accommodation' (Col 74). In this context essential means normal! (Col 75).

**17.62** Zero-rating of time-shares, or where residence in a building throughout the year (or the use of the building or part of it as the grantee's principal private residence) is prevented by the terms of a covenant, statutory planning consent or similar permission, is overridden by *VATA 1994, Sch 8 Group 5, Note 13*. This is intended to prevent holiday accommodation being brought within the scope of zero-rating by selling or leasing it, ostensibly without limitation of usage, in circumstances where there is a legal bar on it being used as a permanent residence. The scope and perhaps even the validity of this provision is questionable. In *Mrs BA Ashworth (VTD 12924)* the VAT tribunal held that, in the appellant's case, the exclusion was inconsistent with *Article 13B(b)(1)* of the *EC Sixth Directive* and the discriminatory effect was not objectively justified. It therefore decided that Mrs Ashworth's occupation of the property was exempt not standard-rated. Mrs Ashworth lived in the property for 11 months a year and stayed with her daughter for the month of February during which her lease of her lodge prohibited occupation. The tribunal was influenced partly by the fact that the lodge (at a marina) did not have the attributes of a holiday site but mainly by the fact that it was clearly occupied as the appellant's home not as holiday accommodation. A similar result was reached in *Livingstone Homes UK Ltd (VTD 16649)*. The company developed new detached dwellings on substantial plots at a holiday resort in Scotland. The feu disposition of each plot was made subject to a condition that all houses on the development were to be used only as holiday dwellings and for no other purpose. The VAT tribunal held that the effect of this provision did not preclude the house being used as a principal private residence within *VATA 1994, Sch 8 Group 5, Note 13(ii)* (residence throughout the year prevented by the terms of any permission) as there was nothing to prevent a person from living in the house throughout the year and having no other home. The principal residence is not determined solely by reference to the amount of time spent there (*Frost v Fellham* – see 4.35).

**17.63** If the major interest granted is a lease of over 21 years, zero-rating applies only to the premium paid, as the intention is that all rents of residential accommodation should be exempt from VAT. The draftsman believed that, in order to trigger the right to repayment of input VAT, the first supply after the construction of the building needs to be a zero-rated supply. An exempt supply would forfeit the relief. Accordingly, if no premium is payable the first payment of rent due under the lease is treated as consideration for a zero-rated supply so as to preserve the right to repayment of input VAT (*VATA 1994, Sch 8 Group 5, Note 14*). Following the *Briararch* decision (see 17.141 below) this provision is apparently ineffective in achieving its aim. Customs seem unlikely to take this point, however.

**17.64** Other points to note are as follows.

(*a*) The construction of a civil engineering work does not cover the conversion, alteration or enlargement of such a work (*Note 15*).

(*b*) A caravan is not a residential caravan if residence in it throughout the year is prevented by the terms of a covenant, statutory planning consent or similar permission (*Note 19*).

(*c*) The reference to services in *items 2* and *3* do not include a transfer of an undivided share in goods or the transfer of the possession of goods, which are deemed to be supplies of services by *VATA 1994, Sch 4 para 1(1)*. Nor does it include the appropriation of goods to a non-business purpose which is similarly deemed to be a supply of services under *Sch 4 para 5(4)* (*Note 20*).

(*d*) The special rule in *VATA 1994, s 30(3)*, which allows goods to be imported free of VAT if their sale will qualify for zero-rating, does not apply to VAT on goods incorporated in buildings which are zero-rated under *Group 5* (*Note 22*).

## Change of Use of Residential and Charitable Buildings

**17.65** *VATA 1994, Sch 10 para 1* imposes a VAT charge if subsequent to one of the zero-rated transactions in 17.6 above, and within ten years of the completion of the building, it is used for a non-qualifying purpose.

**17.66** The provisions apply where:

(*a*) one or more such zero-rated supplies relating to a building have been made to any person (i.e. it includes earlier supplies than the supply to the current owner) but excluding any supply which was zero-rated only under the transitional rules (in *FA 1989, Sch 3 para 13(5)*);

(*b*) within ten years from the date on which the building was completed a person grants an interest in (or right over, or licence to occupy) the building – or to be more precise any part of the building to which the intended use that gave rise to zero-rating was attributable; and

(*c*) the building (or part of a building) is not intended for use for a relevant residential or charitable purpose after the grant referred to in (*b*).

**17.67** The grant of the interest must be treated as a taxable supply (in the course or furtherance of a business) which is not zero-rated under *VATA 1994, Sch 8 Group 5*. Prior to 1 June 2002, the effect was to trigger a tax charge on that grant – which expression, of course, covers a disposal as well as a lease. From that date the charge is on a proportion of the VAT that would have been chargeable if the original supply had not been zero-rated. The proportion is 10% of such VAT for each year or part of a year unexpired in the ten-year period up to the time of the trigger event (*VAT (Construction of Buildings) Order 2002* (*SI 2002 No 1101*)). For example, if after 4¾ years the building is sold for a non-qualifying use, 60% of the VAT will be clawed back (as the use qualified for only four full years).

**17.68** Similar rules apply where the owner simply alters the use of the building within the ten-year period, such as turning an old people's home into a hotel without making a disposal. In such circumstances he is deemed to make a taxable supply to himself at the time he first uses the building for the non-qualifying purpose. A change from one qualifying use to another, such as the sale of a nursing home to a charity to be used as a non fee-paying school, will not trigger the charge. The amount on which VAT is charged is not the value of the building at the time of the change of use or the value at the date the original zero-rated supply was made. It is a notional amount, the VAT payable on which is equal to the VAT that would have been payable on the original supply had it been taxable.

**17.69** These deemed disposal provisions do not apply on a change of use where the zero-rating for protected buildings rules applied (see 9.19 to 9.38 above).

**17.70** Where a building, or part of a building, used originally entirely for non-business charitable purposes becomes used for charitable business purposes for up to 10% of total use, Customs will ignore that degree of business use (Hansard, Standing Committee G, 18 May 1989, Col 116 and C & E Leaflet 708/4/90, para 7).

**17.71** It should be noted that no relief is given for any VAT paid at the time of construction on building and other costs. In many cases such VAT will have been reclaimed as inputs of a taxable business at that stage, but it is possible to envisage circumstances in which it was not reclaimable, such as if the building was occupied by a charity which was not carrying on a business. In such circumstances the charge on change of use can be penal.

## Reduced Rate on Energy Saving Materials, etc

**17.72** From 1 April 2000 the supply of services of installing:

(*a*) insulation for walls, floors, ceilings, roofs or lofts, or for water tanks, pipes or other plumbing fittings,

(*b*) draught stripping for windows and doors,

(*c*) central heating system controls (including thermostatic radiator valves),

(*d*) hot water system controls,

(*e*) solar panels,

(*f*) wind turbines,

(*g*) water turbines

in residential accommodation or in a building intended for use solely for a relevant charitable purpose is chargeable at a reduced rate of 5%.

(*VATA 1994, Sch A1, para 1(1)(aa)* and *(ab)* as amended by *FA 2000, s 135* and *Sch 35* ).

**17.73** The reduced rate also applied to such work between 1 April 1995 and 31 March 2000 but only where the supply was made to a qualifying person (see 17.76). It now applies to all residential and relevant charitable buildings. It should be noted that the 5% rate applies to materials only if they are supplied by a person who provides a service of installation. It does not apply to the purchase of materials for DIY installation.

**17.74** The 5% reduced rate also applies from 1 April 2000 to supplies to a 'qualifying person' of services of installing:

(*a*) gas-fired room heaters that are fitted with thermostatic controls,

(*b*) electric storage heaters,

(*c*) closed solid fuel fire cassettes,

(*d*) electrical dual immersion water heaters with foam-insulated hot water tanks,

(*e*) gas-fired boilers,

(*f*) oil-fired boilers, or

(*g*) radiators

in that person's sole or main residence and the supply of the materials themselves provided that they are supplied by the person who installs them (*VATA 1994, Sch A1 para 1(1)(b)* and (*c*), *s 4(A)* as amended by *FA 2000, s 135* and *Sch 35*).

**17.75** The reduced rate only applies, however, if the consideration for the supply is funded by a grant made under a scheme which:

(*a*) has as one of its objectives the funding of the installation of energy-saving materials in the homes of qualifying persons, and

(*b*) disburses, directly or indirectly, its grants in whole or in part out of funds made available to it in order to achieve that objective by either the UK Government, the EC, a local authority or under an arrangement approved by the Director General of Electricity Supply or of Gas Supply (*VATA 1994, Sch A1 para 1(1A), 5(5)*).

**17.76** A qualifying person is one who is:

(*a*) aged 60 or over, and

(*b*) in receipt of either council tax benefit, disability living allowance, disability working allowance, family credit, housing benefit, income based Job Seeker's Allowance, income support, or disablement pension or war disablement pension at the increased rate (*VATA 1994, Sch A1 para 5(2)(3)*).

**17.77** The 5% rate also applies from 1 April 2000 to the following supplies made to a qualifying person and funded under an approved scheme (i.e. one within (*b*) in para 17.75):

(*a*) connecting or reconnecting a mains gas supply to the qualifying person's sole or main residence (together with the supply of the necessary goods),

(*b*) installing, maintaining or repairing a central heating system in the qualifying person's sole or main residence (together with the supply of the necessary goods), and (*c*) installing any of the following qualifying security goods in the qualifying person's sole or main residence (together with the supply of the necessary goods):

(i) locks or bolts for windows,

(ii) locks, bolts or security chains for doors,

(iii) spy holes, and

(iv) smoke alarms.

(*VATA 1994, Sch A1, para 1(1)(d)–(g)(j)(k)*).

**17.78** The reduced rate also applies to the leasing of goods (to anyone) that form the whole or part of a central heating system installed in the sole or main residence of a qualified person, and the supply of goods that form the whole or part of such a system if immediately before being supplied they were leased under arrangements such that the consideration for the supplies consisting in the leasing of the goods was in whole or part funded by a grant under a relevant scheme (*VATA 1994, Sch A1 para 1(1)(I)(j)*). Leasing of goods can qualify if the consideration is a payment becoming due only by reason of the termination (whether by the passage of time or otherwise) of the leasing of the goods, even apparently if that payment will not be funded by a grant under a relevant scheme (*VATA 1994, Sch A1 para 1A(b)(ii)*).

**17.79** Residential accommodation has a special meaning for the purpose of the reduced rate, namely:

(*a*) a building or part of a building that consists of a dwelling or a number of dwellings,

(*b*) a building or part of a building used for a relevant residential purpose,

(*c*) a caravan used as a place of permanent habitation, or

(*d*) a houseboat.

(*VATA 1994, Sch A1 para 5(3A)*).

**17.80** Use for a relevant charitable purpose has the same meaning as in 17.34 and 17.39. Relevant residential purpose is not defined. It seems likely that the meaning in 17.28 is intended to apply but the legislation does not appear to achieve this.

**17.81** Customs have issued guidance on these provisions. They consider that 'installation' means putting in place, which involves some process by which materials like draught stripping are permanently fixed in place although some products, such as loft insulation, may simply need to be unrolled and positioned in place to be installed. Necessary minor building works such as planing doors or enlarging loft hatches are covered by installation. If the grant does not cover the full cost it is only the part covered by the grant that qualifies. For example if the grant is £700 and the cost of the installation is £1,000, 70% of the cost is VATable at 5% and the remaining 30% at 17.5%.

## Reduced rate on Residential Conversions and Renovations

**17.82** The 5% reduced rate applies to supplies in respect of certain residential conversions made after 11 May 2001. These are:

(*a*) the supply in the course of a qualifying conversion (see 17.83) of qualifying services (see 17.85) relating to the conversion (*VATA 1994, Sch A1 para 1(6)(a)*),

(*b*) the supply of building materials by a person who is supplying qualifying services in the course of a qualifying conversion where those services include the incorporation of such materials in the building concerned or its immediate site (*VATA 1994, Sch A1 para 1(6)(b)*),

(*c*) the supply in the course of the renovation or alteration (or extension) of a single household dwelling (see 17.84) of qualifying services related to that renovation or alteration, provided that the conditions at 17.90 are met (*VATA 1994, Sch A1 para 1(7)(a)*),

(*d*) the supply of building materials by a person who is supplying qualifying services in the course of such a renovation or alteration where those services include the incorporation of such materials in the building concerned or its immediate site (*VATA 1994, Sch A1 para 1(7)(b)*).

(*VATA 1994, Sch A1 paras 6, 7* inserted by *FA 2001, s 97*).

**17.83** A qualifying conversion is any of the following:

(*a*) A conversion of premises consisting of a building (or part of a building)

(i) where after the conversion the premises contain a number of single household dwellings that is different from the number of such dwellings before the conversion (but is not less than one), and

(ii) where there is no part of the premises being converted that is a part that after the conversion contains the same number of single household dwellings as before the conversion (whether zero, one or two or more).

(*VATA 1994, Sch A1 para 10*).

This is called a changed number of dwellings conversion (*VATA 1994, Sch A1 para 9(1)(a)*).

(*b*) A conversion of premises consisting of a building or part of a building where

(i) before the conversion the premises being converted contain only a single household dwelling or two or more such dwellings,

(ii) after the conversion they contain only a multiple occupancy dwelling or two or more such dwellings, and

(iii) the use to which those premises are intended to be put after the conversion is not to any extent use for a qualifying residential purpose (which although separately defined in *Sch A1 para 17* is the same thing as a relevant residential purpose for zero rating purposes – see 17.28 and 17.29)

(*VATA 1994, Sch A1 para 11*).

This is called a house in multiple occupation conversion (*VATA 1994, Sch A1 para 9(1)(b)*).

(*c*) A conversion of premises consisting of a building or two or more buildings (or part of a building or two or more parts of buildings or a combination of a building or two or more buildings and a part of a building or two or more parts of buildings) where

(i) before the conversion the premises being converted contained only a dwelling or two or more dwellings (whether single household or multiple occupancy) together with any ancillary outbuildings occupied with the dwelling or one or more of the dwellings,

(ii) if before the conversion the premises being converted contained a multiple occupancy dwelling (or dwellings), the use to which that dwelling (or any of them) was last put before the conversion was not to any extent use for a qualifying residential purpose (see (*b*)(iii) above and 17.21 and 17.22),

(iii) the premises being converted are intended to be used after the conversion solely for a qualifying residential purpose, and

(iv) if the qualifying residential purpose is an institutional purpose (i.e. it is not residential accommodation for students or school pupils or for members of the armed forces) the premises being converted are intended to form after the conversion the entirety of an institution used for that purpose

(*VATA 1994, Sch A1 para 12*).

This is called a special residential conversion (*VATA 1994, Sch A1 para 9(1)(c)*). In the case of a special residential conversion the 5% rate applies only if the supply is made to the person who intends to use the premises for the qualifying residential purpose and before the supply is made that person has given a certificate to the supplier stating that the conversion is a special residential conversion. The certificate must be in a form to be laid down by Customs (*VATA 1994, Sch A1 para 13*). This is of course similar to the rules on zero-rating of relevant residential or charitable buildings (see 17.42–17.45). Customs are empowered to specify the form of certificate in a notice published by them. They have done so in an Annex to VAT Information Sheet 4/01 (May 2001).

In all three cases any necessary statutory planning consent and statutory building control approval needed for the conversion must also have been granted – presumably before the relevant supply takes place (*VATA 1994, Sch 1A para 15*).

**17.84** Customs give as an example of (*a*) in 17.83 the installation of a lift in a block of flats consisting of four floors each with four flats. On the first three floors the footprint of each flat is changed but on the fourth floor three penthouse flats are created from the original four. Only the work to convert the top floor will be eligible for the 5% rate because it is only in this part of the building that the number of dwellings changes. Suppose however the first floor is converted into five flats as well. The overall number of flats in the building will not have changed but the 5% rate can nevertheless apply to the conversion work done on the ground and third floor as the number of dwellings on both has changed (VAT Information Sheet 4/01, para 2.4). In other words they interpret 'premises' as being different to the building in which those premises are situated, whereas in everyday parlance most people would regard the two as synonymous. Furthermore they interpret the 'premises being converted' as meaning only the part of the premises affected by the conversion work. Whilst this is a generous interpretation it could give rise to problems. For example suppose a building consists of four flats each consisting of one maisonette flat. The top flat is converted so that it can be used as a single flat with that on the third floor. If the premises being converted is the third and fourth floor then the whole work qualifies for relief as two dwellings are converted into one. On the other hand if the third floor is not part of the premises being converted then none of the work will qualify for the 5% rate as the conversion creates only part of a dwelling.

**17.85** An example of (*b*) might be the conversion of a house into bed-sits. If a three-storey house is converted into a ground floor flat for the owner and two floors of bed-sits it does not appear that any of the work would qualify. If the entire building is the premises being converted it will not qualify as after the conversion it will contain a single household dwelling (the flat), not contain only multiple occupancy dwellings. If only the first and second floor are the premises it will not qualify as prior to conversion those two floors on their own would not have been a single household dwelling but only part of such a dwelling. Curiously if the conversion is done in two stages, first to a ground floor flat and a combined first and second floor flat, and then the conversion of the larger flat into bed-sits, the first conversion would qualify under head (*a*) and the second under (*b*). The large flat does not actually need to be used as such, as the test is whether it is "designed" for occupation by a single household, not whether it is intended that it should actually be occupied for such a purpose. Suppose at a later date the ground floor flat is converted into bed-sits. If those bed-sits are self-contained and do not share facilities with those on the other two floors that appears to be a qualifying conversion. If however they are not but create additional bedrooms that will share the facilities on the other floors the conversion will not qualify as it will simply increase the size of an existing multiple occupancy dwelling, not create a new one. Head (*b*) does not allow the reverse situation, i.e. the conversion of a multiple occupancy dwelling into flats, but this is probably because it is unnecessary to do so as such a conversion falls within head (*a*).

**17.86** It should be noted that head (*c*) will not permit the conversion of a house to create additional bedrooms for an existing care home next door. The conversion must result in a completely new home, institution or hall of residence. If a group of buildings consisting of a dwelling and outbuildings is converted to a relevant residential purpose building, Customs say that although the outbuildings are not strictly the dwelling they will accept the whole of the work as a qualifying conversion provided that it all takes place at the same time (VAT Information Sheet 4/01, para 2.19).

**17.87** A single household dwelling is one that is designed for occupation by a single household and which

(*a*) consists of self-contained living accommodation,

(*b*) has no provision for direct internal access from the dwelling to any other dwelling or part of a dwelling, (*c*) is not prohibited from being used separately by the terms of any covenant, statutory planning consent or similar provision, and

(*d*) is not prohibited from being separately disposed of by any such terms.

(*VATA 1994, Sch 1A para 8(2)(4)*). This definition is similar, but not identical to, that of a dwelling for zero-rating purposes, the only practical difference being that for zero-rating purposes planning consent must also have been granted and the construction or conversion carried out in accordance with that consent. The requirement for any necessary planning permission does also apply for the 5% rate (see 17.83) but there is no obligation to actually comply with it. There is also an obligation to obtain any necessary building control consent, which does not apply to zero-rating.

A multiple occupancy dwelling is one that is designed for occupation by persons not forming a single household and which meets conditions (*a*) to (*d*) above) (*VATA 1994, Sch 1A para 8(3)(4)*). A building is designed for occupation of a particular kind both if it was originally constructed for such occupation (and not later adapted for a different kind of occupation) and if it is so designed as a result of adaptation (*VATA 1994, Sch 1A para 8(5)*).

**17.88** Where part of a supply of services qualifies for the reduced rate and part does not, an apportionment needs to be made to determine the extent to which the 5% rate applies (*VATA 1994, Sch 1A para 1(8)(9)*). A qualifying conversion includes any garage works (the construction of a garage or a conversion of a non-residential building (i.e. one neither designed nor adapted as a dwelling or dwellings or for a qualifying residential purpose), or non-residential part of a building, that results in a garage) related to the conversion. Garage works are related if they are carried out at the same time as the conversion and the resulting garage is intended to be occupied with one of the dwellings (or the institution or other accommodation in the case of a special residential conversion) resulting from the conversion (*VATA 1994, Sch 1A para 14*).

**17.89** A supply of qualifying services consists of:

(*a*) carrying out works to the fabric of the building, or

(*b*) carrying out works within the immediate site of the building in connection with the means of providing water, power, heat, drainage, security or access for the building or in connection with the provision of means of waste disposal to the building.

(*VATA 1994, Sch A1 para 16(1)*).

In the case of the conversion of part of a building the works must of course relate to that part or to the provision of water, etc. to that part (*VATA 1994, Sch A1 para 16(2)*). The incorporation, or installation as fittings, in the building of any goods is not carrying out works to the fabric of a building unless such goods are building materials (as defined in *VATA 1994, Sch 8 Group 5, Notes 22* and *23* – see 8.84) (*VATA 1994, Sch A1 para 16(3), 22*). Customs say that supplies by architects, surveyors or any person acting in a supervisory capacity, the supply of goods on hire, landscaping and work to outbuildings that remain outbuildings do not qualify for the 5% rate (VAT Information Sheet 4/01, para 3.1). This is presumably because they do not regard them as 'the carrying out of works'.

**17.90** Services in connection with the renovation, alteration or extension of a single household dwelling (i.e. within 17.82(*c*) or (*d*)) qualify for the 5% rate only if either

(*a*) the dwelling has not been lived in during the three years ending with the commencement of the relevant works, or

(*b*) if it has, it was not lived in during an earlier period of three years, the person whose occupation brought that period to an end acquired a major interest in the dwelling for a consideration during the unoccupied period (and at a time when it had been unoccupied for at least three years) the supply was made to that person, and the relevant works are carried out during the period of 12 months from the date of the acquisition of the building (where there are joint owners only one needs to have lived in the building).

(*VATA 1994, Sch A1 para 19(2)(3)(5)*).

The relevant works for this purpose are of course the works that attract the 5% rate (*VATA 1994, Sch A1 para 19(4)*). The 5% rate applies only if any statutory planning consent or building control approval needed for the renovation or alteration has been obtained (*VATA 1994, Sch A1 para 20*). Qualifying services has the same meaning as at 17.85 (*VATA 1994, Sch A1 para 21, 22*).

**17.91** Test (*b*) above is intended to allow a person to buy an empty property, move in and refurbish it around himself. However it is very restrictive, particularly if planning permission is required for the refurbishment. The refurbishment must be 'carried out', which presumably means completed rather than started, within 12 months of acquiring the house. It should also be noted that he must acquire the property for a consideration, although not necessarily an open market consideration. Acquisition as a gift or as a dividend in specie from a company will not enable the owner to qualify for the 5% rate – although it will still qualify if the taxpayer does not move into the property prior to the refurbishment as the alternative test, (*a*), does not look at what happened on the acquisition. Curiously, as the supply must be to the owner, a subcontractor cannot use the 5% rate where test (*b*) applies although he can do so under test (a). This is confirmed by Customs in VAT Information Sheet 4/01, para 3.5. Occupation by squatters in the three-year period appears to deny relief. It is likely in practice that Customs would turn a blind eye to such occupation though.

**17.92** Customs say that the relief will cover the conversion of a house into flats or flats into a house; the conversion of relevant residential purpose buildings (such as a nursing home) or non-residential buildings into single household dwellings; the conversion of houses in multiple occupation (i.e. where the accommodation is not self-contained such as bed-sits, shared houses and flats and bed and breakfast establishments with a mix of short and long stay residents) into single household dwellings; and the conversion of a building which may have been lived in, such as a pub with staff accommodation, which does not qualify as a single household dwelling into houses or flats (VAT Information Sheet 4/01, paras 2.2 and 2.11). They also say that conversion includes all works of repair, maintenance or improvement to the fabric of the building where the work forms an intrinsic part of changing the number of dwellings (para 2.4). They also say that the relief applies even if the property was originally a dwelling but was converted to some other use and is reconverted back to a dwelling (para 2.7). Customs consider that conversion into a number of dwellings means that a building is converted into semi-detached houses, terraced housing, maisonettes or flats (para 2.9), albeit though most people would regard two semi-detached houses or a terrace of houses as made up as separate buildings.

**17.93** Customs have said that a dwelling that has been used for storage or a purpose other than living accommodation for three years will 'usually' be treated as empty for the purpose of the reduced rate (VAT Information Sheet 4/01, para 1.2). They emphasise that it is the VAT registered trader's responsibility to hold proof that the supply qualifies for the reduced rate. They will accept letters from empty property officers in local authorities or other evidence such as the electoral roll, council tax data, and other sources of reliable information which show on the balance of probabilities that the building had been unoccupied for three years prior to the commencement of the work (para 1.5). Customs also say that 'renovation' (see 17.82(*c*)) includes any work of repair, maintenance (e.g. redecoration) or improvement (e.g. an extension or the installation of double glazing) carried out to the fabric of the building (para 1.3).

## Rents

**17.94** Rents from residential properties are always exempt. The only exception is the first rental payment under a lease, which can be zero-rated if there is no premium. Rents for relevant charitable buildings are also always exempt, with the exception that rents for an office building will be taxable if the landlord elects to waive the exemption ('exercises the option to tax'). Rents for commercial buildings are normally exempt but an election can be made to bring them into the scope of VAT (see 17.153 below).

## Commercial and Industrial Buildings and Land

**17.95** Transactions in land and commercial or industrial buildings are in general exempt from VAT. There are three main exceptions.

1. The disposal of a commercial or industrial building within three years of its construction – which is taxable at the 17½% standard rate (see 17.112 below).

2. Specified, mainly leisure-related, types of property which are taxed at the 17½% standard rate (see 17.114 below).

3. A disposal where the option to bring exempt disposals of land and buildings into the charge to tax has been exercised (see 17.158 below).

There were two further exceptions in relation to developments commencing between 31 July 1989 and 28 February 1995, namely:

3. In certain limited circumstances, the grant of a lease of a building the construction of which commenced between 31 July 1989 and 28 February 1995, or the reconstruction, enlargement or extension of which commenced between 31 December 1991 and 28 February 1995 (see 8.38–8.57 above).

4. Rent or other receipts under a tenancy, lease or licence that has become a developmental tenancy, lease or licence (see 8.53 above).

**17.96** *VATA 1994, Sch 9 Group 1*, which contains the exemption for land, is intended to ensure that sales of new non-residential buildings are subjected to VAT at 17½% by excluding such sales from exemption (see 17.112).

**17.97** The exemption applies to the grant of any interest in, or right over, land, or any licence to occupy land (including an assignment of such an interest or right, or in Scotland any personal right to call for or be granted any such interest or right) other than

(*a*) a freehold disposal of

(i) a building which has not been completed and which is not a residential one, or

(ii) a new building which is not a residential one, or

(iii) a civil engineering work which is in the course of being constructed, or

(iv) a new civil engineering work; or

(*b*) the grant of certain specified, mainly leisure-related, activities (see 17.114 below).

As is usual there are a number of 'Notes' which modify these basic provisions.

**Surrender of Leases**

**17.98** The surrender of an interest in land is exempt from VAT. Before 1 March 1995, a surrender was taxable and *Note 1* excluded from the normal exemption for an assignment, an assignment to one's landlord. This was an anti-avoidance provision designed to thwart avoidance of tax on a surrender. Both of these exclusions were held by the European Court of Justice to be in breach of the *EC Sixth Directive* in *Lubbock Fine & Co v C & E Commrs (1994 STC 101)*. This was a reference to the Court by the London VAT Tribunal. *Article 13B* of the *Sixth Directive* provides that 'Member States shall exempt the following under conditions which they shall lay down for the purpose of ensuring the correct and straightforward application of the exemptions and preventing any possible evasion, avoidance or abuse: . . . (*b*) the leasing or letting of immovable property excluding [the items in 17.95(2) above]. Member States may apply further exclusions to the scope of this exemption . . . (*g*) the supply of buildings or parts thereof and of the land on which they stand . . .'. It was held that the words 'letting of immovable property' in *Article 13B* cover the case where a tenant, for consideration, surrenders his lease and returns the immovable property to his immediate landlord because 'where a given transaction, such as the letting of immovable property, which would be taxed on the basis of the rents paid, falls within the scope of an exemption provided for by the *Sixth Directive*, a change in the contractual relationship, such as termination of the lease for consideration, must also be regarded as falling within the scope of that exemption'. It was further held that the power in *Article 13B(b)* to apply further exclusions from exemption enable a country to tax other types of letting, but does not allow it to tax a transaction terminating a lease where the grant of that lease was compulsorily exempt (i.e. to break down the relations created by a lease into exempt and taxable parts). As it was not necessary for the decision, the Court declined to decide whether the surrender of a lease of buildings for consideration paid by the landlord to the tenant was a compulsorily exempt supply under *Article 13B(g)*. The opinion of the Advocate General was that it was not, as by a surrender a tenant cannot transfer to the landlord the power of disposal of the building as a landlord can sell his building even when it is let.

**17.99** Customs initially took the view that the European Court decision applied only where a payment was made by the landlord to the tenant, although the Court had said that *Article 13B(b)* does not permit the UK 'to tax the consideration paid by one party to the other in connection with the surrender of the lease' which is equally apt to cover a payment by the tenant to the landlord to accept a surrender although as indicated above they declined to specifically rule on it. Their view was that such a 'reverse surrender' was a supply made by the landlord of accepting an obligation to refrain from an act (enforcing his rights under the lease) which is not the grant of an interest in land and is thus a taxable supply (Business Brief 16/94). However in September 1994 in *Marbourne Ltd (VTD 12670)*, a VAT tribunal held that the *Lubbock Fine* principle applied to a reverse surrender, albeit to do so it had to introduce the novel concept of a supply by the tenant for a negative consideration. The tribunal in *Central Capital Corporation Ltd (VTD 13319)* declined to follow the decision in *Marbourne Ltd.* It held that the relevant supply of land was made by the landlord but that, applying the European Court of Justice's decision in *Lubbock Fine & Co*, the supply by the landlord qualified for exemption under *Article 13B(b)* of the *EC Sixth Directive*. Since the original grant of the lease was not taxable, the subsequent 'reverse surrender' of that lease was also not taxable. Customs originally intended to appeal against the *Marbourne* decision, but instead the government decided to exempt reverse surrenders from 1 March 1995. Accordingly from that date *Note 1* states that a grant 'includes an assignment or surrender and the supply made by the person to whom an interest is surrendered when there is a reverse surrender' (*VAT (Land) Order 1995* (*SI 1995 No 282*)).

**Reverse Premiums**

**17.100** The ECJ considered the VAT position on reverse premium in two cases, *C & E Commrs v Mirror Group plc (Case C-409/98, 2001 STC 1453)* and *C & E Commrs v Cantor Fitzgerald International (Case C-108/99, 2001 STC 1453)*. It would be nice to be able to say that following those cases the law is clear. Unfortunately that is not the case. Each case will need to be looked at on its individual merits. That is clearly unsatisfactory with a self-assessed tax. The only safe solution is likely to be to ask Customs to rule on each transaction, assuming of course that they are prepared to do so.

In *Cantor Fitzgerald* it was the assignor, not the landlord, that made a payment to Cantor Fitzgerald to induce it to take an assignment of the lease. The VAT tribunal held that the reverse premium fell within the

*Lubbock Fine* decision. Customs appealed to the High Court which referred the question to the ECJ *(1998 STC 948*) because it felt that the scope of the principle laid down in the *Lubbock Fine* case was unclear. The ECJ ruled in favour of Customs. It held that the relevant supply is a supply of services, namely agreeing to accept an assignment of a lease of property from a lessee. Such a supply is not the letting of immovable property. The supplier had no interest in the property at the time of the supply. This differs from the *Lubbock Fine* case. Lubbock Fine assigned its right to occupy the property back to the landlord which is why the court ruled that transaction to be exempt.

**17.101** Mirror Group plc entered into two agreements with Olympia and York Canary Wharf Ltd. The first was an agreement for lease of five floors at One Canada Square. The second granted Mirror Group an option to take an extra four floors. The agreement for lease provided for an inducement payment of approximately £12m, £6.5 million to be payable on occupation of the five floors and the completion of fitting-out work that Mirror Group plc had undertaken under the lease, and the remaining £5.5m to be put into escrow and repaid to the extent that Mirror Group plc did not take up the option space. The VAT tribunal held that 'so much of the inducement as can be ascribed to Mirror Group's undertaking to enter into the lease' was exempt and the balance taxable. From the judgment this appears to mean that the £6.5m is exempt but the £5.5m is taxable as it relates to the option not to the lease. The logic of this is not wholly clear as an option is itself an interest in land (see 17.296 below). However, Customs subsequently appealed to the High Court – see Business Brief 17/98 – so this was only an interim answer. The High Court then referred the case to the ECJ. The ECJ ruled that the *Lubbock Fine* principle does not apply as Mirror Group did not have an interest in land and has left it to the UK courts to decide if Mirror Group made a supply of anything:

'It must be noted that a taxable person who only pays the consideration in cash due in respect of a supply of services, or who undertakes to do so, does not himself make a supply of services for the purposes of *Article 2(1)* of the *Sixth Directive*. It follows that a tenant who undertakes, even in return for payment from the landlord, solely to become a tenant and to pay the rent does not, so far as that action is concerned, make a supply of services for consideration if the landlord, taking the view that the presence of an anchor tenant in the building containing the leased premises will attract other tenants, were to make a payment by way of consideration for the future tenant's undertaking to transfer it business to the building concerned. In those circumstances, the undertaking of such a tenant could be qualified as a taxable supply of advertising services.'

**17.102** The *Cantor Fitzgerald* case was not a true reverse premium, as in that case it was the assignor, not the landlord, who made a payment to Cantor Fitzgerald to induce it to take an assignment of the lease. The VAT tribunal held that the reverse premium fell within the

*Lubbock Fine* decision. Customs appealed to the High Court which referred the question to the ECJ (*1998 STC 948*) because it felt that the scope of the principle laid down in the *Lubbock Fine* case was unclear. The ECJ ruled in favour of Customs. It held that the relevant supply is a supply of services, namely agreeing to accept an assignment of a lease of property from the lessee. Such a supply is not the letting of immovable property. The supplier had no interest in the property at the time of the supply. This differs from the *Lubbock Fine* case. Lubbock Fine assigned its right to occupy the property back to the landlord, which is why the court ruled that transaction to be exempt.

**17.103** The ECJ judgement suggests that an ordinary reverse premium is, in effect, outside the scope of VAT. This leaves the recipient of a reverse premium in a dilemma, at least until the High Court has determined the Mirror Group appeal. Even then, if it decides that Mirror Group was induced to become an anchor tenant, that will not necessarily help others.

**17.104** It also leaves two important questions unanswered; namely, in what circumstances can the supply be a supply of services and what happens if one party to the transaction has exercised the option to tax? The recipient of a reverse premium could legitimately take the view that it is not VATable, and risk a misdeclaration penalty if Customs subsequently discover the receipt of the premium and find a way to tax it. The safest route is probably to tell Customs of the receipt of the premium and make the case that it is not taxable. This is likely to trigger an assessment and start the interest clock running though.

**17.105** The ECJ pointed out that it was for the UK courts to ascertain whether Mirror Group made a supply of services for consideration to the landlord and, if it did, what that supply was. Without of course wishing to 'second guess' what the UK courts may decide, it seems inherently improbable that the administrator of Olympia and York Canary Wharf Ltd would have paid Mirror Group £6.5 million purely to be an anchor tenant of Canary Wharf, occupying five floors, plus a further £4.1m if it exercised an option to take three further floors. Indeed the evidence seems to be merely that 'given its high profile, Mirror Group commanded "anchor tenant" status', which is far from indicating that it was being paid to be an anchor tenant. It is hard to see why Olympia and York Canary Wharf should need an 'anchor tenant' for Canary Wharf as the company was trying to promote Canary Wharf as a financial centre. In that context, a letting to Mirror Group was not an 'anchor' letting but seems more likely to be a desperate measure to let the building to anyone prepared to move to it. Furthermore, even if the £6.5 million was in respect of Mirror Group becoming an anchor tenant, why pay the further £4.1m when that objective had already been achieved by the initial letting?

**17.106** Be that as it may, even if part of the reason for the payment was to persuade Mirror Group to become anchor tenant, it is most improbable that this was the sole motive in the eyes of the administrator. It is likely that he also wanted simply to let the space – and would have offered at least part of the reverse premium to anyone who would take the space. This in turn raises the question of whether a dual motive suggests two separate supplies. Even if it does, can this question be looked at solely from the viewpoint of the supplier or does one need also to look at it through the customer's eyes? It is most improbable that Mirror Group thought that it was being paid partly to induce it to enter into the lease and partly for a supply of advertising services that it was making to Canary Wharf. Indeed Advocate General (Tizzane) suggested that what needs to be looked at is not motive but rather,

'The contract's economic purpose, that is to say, the precise way in which performance satisfies the interests of the parties. In the case of a lease . . . this consists in the transfer by one party to another of an exclusive right to enjoy immovable property for an agreed period. It goes without saying that this purpose is the same for all the parties to the contract and thus determines its content. On the other hand, it has no connection with the subjective reasons which have led each of the parties to enter into the contract, and which obviously are not evident from its terms.'

**17.107** If motive is irrelevant it may be that it is not possible to have a situation where a reverse premium is both to induce someone to act as anchor tenant and to induce him to enter into the lease. One or the other of these elements must predominate; i.e. the contract's economic purpose must either be letting of the property or advertising.

The ECJ in *Card Protection Plan (Case C-349/96, 1999 STC 270)* stated that,

'First . . . every supply of services must normally be regarded as distinct and independent and, second, that a supply which comprises a single service from an economic point of view should not be artificially split . . . the essential features of this transaction must be ascertained in order to determine whether the taxable person is supplying the customer, being a typical consumer, with several distinct principal services or with a single service. There is a single supply in particular in cases where one or more elements are to be regarded, by contrast, as ancillary to a principal service if it does not constitute for customers an aim in itself, but a means of better enjoying the principal service supplies.'

**17.108** Can this principle also apply where there are offsetting services, as in the Mirror Group case, i.e. if Mirror Group was obtaining negative consideration for becoming a tenant and at the same time receiving actual consideration for the advertising service of becoming 'anchor tenant'? Is it necessary to ask whether these comprise a single service from an economic point of view and, if so, which is the principal one? Alternatively, must a split always be made, as part of the receipt relates to a supply by Mirror Group and part does not? It will be interesting to see how the UK courts approach this problem. Furthermore if an undertaking to be an anchor tenant rather than merely to be a tenant, is a separate supply of services, what else can fall into this category? Might agreeing to be the tenant of most of a building be a separate supply? It seems unlikely, yet it is hard to discern any real difference between being an anchor tenant and being the main tenant. It should also be noted that the court did not actually say that such a service is a separate supply, but merely that it 'could be'. Common sense suggests that it will be fairly unusual, except perhaps in relation to shopping centres where the anchor tenant may be important to attract customers to other tenants, for the anchor tenant exception to apply. In the vast majority of cases, the primary economic purpose will be to let the building.

**17.109** The second question is perhaps easier. The crux of the Mirror Group case was the nature of the supply by Mirror Group in consideration of the reverse premium. Leaving aside the anchor tenant point, the ECJ said that Mirror Group did not make a supply at all. The receipt of the reverse premium was part of the 'consideration' that it gave for the supply of the lease to it by the tenant, albeit that it was, in effect, negative consideration. It must follow from this that, if Mirror Group had opted to tax in respect of the building but Olympia and York Canary Wharf Ltd had not done so, VAT would not have been payable on the reverse premium. Olympia and York would not have been a taxable person and Mirror Group would have made no supply. The ECJ was not concerned with the VAT position of the landlord as the appellant was Mirror Group Ltd. It is therefore not surprising that it did not address the dilemma that if there was no supply by the tenant it must follow either that there was no supply at all or that the reverse premium was negative consideration for the supply by the landlord. *Article 13(C)* of the *Sixth Directive*, the *vires* for the option to tax, is not very helpful. It merely states that 'Member States may allow taxpayers a right of option for taxation in cases of (a) letting and leasing of immovable property', which brings us to UK domestic law. *VAT Act 1994 , Sch 10 para 2(1)* states that,

'where an election under this paragraph has effect in relation to any land, if and to the extent that any grant made in relation to it at a time when the election has effect by the person who made the election . . . would . . . fall within *Group 1* of *Schedule 9*, the grant shall not fall within that group'.

It seems clear that VAT is not charged on consideration; it is charged on supplies and the consideration is merely the value placed on that supply. It seems to follow from this that if the sole supply is the grant of the lease the reverse premium must be an element in valuing that grant. It is accordingly clear that the reverse premium cannot be outside the scope of VAT. Either the reverse premium must be VATable or the value of the supply must be determined under *VATA 1994, s 19(3)*, i.e.

supplies for a consideration not wholly consisting of money. The effect of this might well be that only part of the rent under the lease is VATable as the consideration for the lease would then be the difference between the rent payable over the term of the lease and the reverse premium received. The mind boggles at the problems this would create. Accepting that the reverse premium is itself taxable would afford a pragmatic solution, although taxing part only of the rent would be a more logical, albeit fairly horrific, interpretation of the legislation.

**Freehold Disposal of New Buildings, etc**

**17.110** It is important to note that head (*a*) in 17.97 above denies exemption only on the disposal of a freehold interest in a new building. Exemption will still apply to a premium for the grant of a long lease (subject to the operation of the option to tax considered at 17.187 below). Accordingly VAT on the disposal of a building the construction of which began before 1 August 1989 can be avoided by granting a 125 or 999-year lease at a premium instead. This is not necessarily advisable, however, as it will mean that input VAT paid on the construction costs will be irrecoverable. It is worth considering in cases where the potential purchaser is an exempt trader, an overseas resident, or otherwise not in a position to recover the VAT that would have to be paid on purchase.

**17.111** The reference in (*a*)(i) and (ii) in 17.97 above to a residential building is the author's shorthand not the draftsman's. It means a building designed as a dwelling or number of dwellings or intended for use for a relevant residential purpose or relevant charitable purpose. These expressions have the same meaning as in *Group 8* (see 17.28 and 17.34 above) (*Note 3*).

**17.112** It should be noted that VAT is payable on the disposal of a building only if this takes place while the building is 'new', i.e. within three years of the building being completed (unless it was both completed and fully occupied or fully used before 1 April 1989) (*Notes 4* to *6*). A sale of a non-residential building prior to the time it is completed will always attract VAT, however.

**17.113** A building is to be taken to be completed when either an architect issues a certificate of practical completion in relation to it or it is first fully occupied (*Note 2*). The certificate of practical completion is normally issued when the structural work is finished but fitting-out work still needs to be done. Accordingly the building is not necessarily fit for occupation at that stage. A civil engineering work is completed when either an engineer issues a certificate of practical completion or it is first fully used (*Note 2*). Clearly, the earlier a building is completed the better it is likely to be, so as to start the three-year period running. If no completion certificate is issued it could be many years after completion before the building is fully let, and the three-year period would not start to run until that time. It is therefore important to ensure that the architect or engineer issues a completion certificate at the earliest practical date. It could be argued that it is better for a new building to remain taxable as long as possible to ensure the recoverability of input tax on the construction costs. However the option to tax rents will enable this to be achieved by way of the grant of a lease if the building remains unsold and unlet for longer than three years.

**Leisure-related Activities**

**17.114** The miscellaneous items that attract tax at 17½% are:

(i) the grant of any interest, right or licence consisting of a right to take game or fish except where at the same time the freehold of the land over which its right is exercisable is sold to the same purchaser (see also 17.115);

(ii) the provision in an hotel, inn, boarding house or similar establishment of sleeping accommodation, etc. or of accommodation in rooms which are provided in conjunction with sleeping accommodation, or which are provided for the purpose of a supply of catering (see also 17.116–17.117);

(iii) the grant of any interest in, right over or licence to occupy holiday accommodation (prior to 1 February 1991 this was limited to the provision of holiday accommodation in a house, flat, caravan, houseboat or tent) (see also 17.122);

(iv) the provision of seasonal pitches for caravans, and the grant of facilities at sites to persons for whom such facilities are provided (see also 17.123);

(v) the provision of pitches for tents and of camping facilities;

(vi) the grant of facilities for parking a vehicle (see also 17.124);

(vii) the grant of any right to fell and remove standing timber;

(viii) the grant of facilities for housing an aircraft or mooring a ship (which includes anchoring or berthing – *Note 15*);

(ix) the grant of a right to occupy a box, seat or other accommodation at a sports ground, theatre, concert hall or other place of entertainment; and

(x) the grant of facilities for playing any sport or participating in any physical recreation (subject to the exemption in 17.125).

**17.115** Head (i) above was amended by way of the *VAT (Buildings and Land) Order 1991* with effect from 30 November 1991, as the previous rules were in breach of European Community law. Where the land is leased, VAT continues to be chargeable on the portion of the rent attributable to the sporting rights if these are 'valuable', i.e. where the rental value of the sporting rights exceeds 10% of the total rent under the lease (Customs Press Release 59/91, 5 August 1991). It is not clear whether part of a premium for the grant of a lease also has to be apportioned to the value of sporting rights. It seems likely that it does. It should be borne in mind that the VAT charge would apply not merely to the grant of a lease over, for example, a shooting moor. It can also apply on the grant (or presumably the assignment) of a lease of a farm, if the rights to take game are of significant value. If the grant of an interest in or right over land (or a licence to occupy land) includes a valuable right to take game or fish, the consideration must be apportioned and VAT charged on the gaming or fishing element (*VATA 1994, 9 Sch, Group 1, Note 8*). No guidance is given as to what is meant by 'valuable'.

**17.116** It is specifically provided that for the purpose of head (ii) a similar establishment includes premises in which there is provided furnished sleeping accommodation, whether with or without the provision of board or facilities for the preparation of food, which are used by or held out as being suitable for use by visitors or travellers (*VATA 1994, 9 Sch, Group 1, Note 9*). In spite of this the tribunal in *International Student House (VTD 14420)* thought that the provision of sleeping accommodation did not necessarily indicate that the premises were similar to a hotel, particularly where the accommodation was not held out for use by visitors or travellers. It considered that a characteristic of a hotel, inn or boarding house was that it was concerned with the business of providing accommodation. The appellant in that case was a charity providing accommodation in London for students of different nationalities with a view to furthering international friendship and co-operation. It had a selective admissions policy which aimed to create a group of resident students from different nationalities. The tribunal regarded these as important factors to distinguish the accommodation from that provided by a hotel. It was held in *Dinaro Ltd (t/a Fairway Lodge) (VTD 17148)* that a hostel building providing accommodation for vulnerable adults requiring support and supervision was not an establishment similar to a hotel. Having regard to the hostel residents' average length of stay and their need for supervision, the residents could not be regarded as travellers. In *Acorn Management Services Ltd (VTD 17338)*, by contrast, the provision to US universities of accommodation for students and faculty members attending courses in the UK was held to be similar to and in competition with a hotel. The accommodation was paid for in full by the university before the students arrived; the average stay was 15 weeks; cleaning was carried out by contractors once a week and laundry was left to the students.

**17.117** It will be noted that head (ii) leaves the hiring of meeting rooms in a hotel exempt. In *Simon Packford (VTD 11626)* it was the practice of a hotel to make a charge for the continued use of a function room where a wedding or private party continued into the evening after the reception and meal were finished. The VAT tribunal held that the supply was neither integral nor incidental to the supply of catering as that supply had finished before the paid room hire started. It adjourned the case to allow the taxpayer to produce clear evidence of the purpose for which the room was provided, the inference being that the charge is likely to be exempt. In contrast the tribunal in the case of *Willerby Manor Hotels Ltd (VTD 16673)* on similar facts, declining to follow *Packford* on the grounds that it had been decided before the CJEC decision in *Card Protection Plan Ltd*. The tribunal held that 'the hire of a function room for an evening reception is a supply ancillary to those of wedding reception facilities and is integral to the reception arrangements: it is a means of better enjoying the principal service supplied'. Accordingly, the company 'had made a composite supply of a standard-rated package of wedding reception facilities, the main ingredient in which was a supply of catering'.

**17.118** Head (ii) reflects *Article 13(B)(b)1* of the *EC Sixth Directive* which excludes from exemption the 'provisions of accommodation, as defined in the laws of the Member States, in the hotel sector or in sectors with a similar function'. In *Blasi v Finanzant Munchen I (Case C–346/95) (1998 STC 336)* the ECJ stated that while exemptions must be construed strictly, exclusions from them were not to be, and the words 'sectors with a similar function' should be broadly construed. Their purpose is to ensure that the provision of temporary accommodation in competition with the hotel sector is subject to tax. It is likely that 'similar establishment' will similarly be given a wide meaning.

**17.119** Fortified by this decision *Colaingrove Ltd (VTD 16187)*, which operated caravan parks, sought to persuade the VAT tribunal that the exclusion of seasonal pitches from exemption was not authorised by EC law. The tribunal accepted that it was unrealistic to treat the provision of caravan pitches as having a similar function to the hotel sector but noted that some versions of the text indicated that 'accommodation' was intended to have a wider meaning than its normal one of accommodation of persons. In any event the tailpiece of *Article 13B(b)(1)* of the *Sixth Directive*, 'Member States may apply further exclusions to the scope of this exemption', gave the UK a large degree of discretion to limit the scope of the exemption and the exclusion for seasonal caravan pitches was consistent with those for camping sites and car parking sites.

**17.120** This wide discretion is emphasised by the ECJ decision in *Amengual Far v Amengual Far (Case C-12/98)* to the effect that it allows member states (in that case Spain) to subject to VAT lettings of immovable property and by way of exception to exempt only lettings of immovable property to be used as dwellings.

**17.121** Head (iii) includes the grant of an interest in a dwelling which is excluded from zero-rating under *VATA 1994, 8 Sch, Group 5, Note 13* (see 17.62) because for example the grantee is not entitled to reside in it (or part of it) throughout the year (*VATA 1994, 9 Sch, Group 1, Note 11(a)*). It also includes a supply made in pursuance of a tenancy, lease or licence under which the grantee is permitted to erect and occupy holiday accommodation (*Note 11(b)*). It does not however include a freehold disposal of a building which is not a new building or the grant of a tenancy, lease or licence which is made for a consideration in the form of a premium (*Note 12*). It is not clear if *Note 12* excludes from tax the rent payable as well as the premium. It seems likely that the intention is merely to exclude the premium.

**17.122** The rules on holiday accommodation were extended in 1989 to ensure that the provision of accommodation in a tent provided by the site operator is taxable, as well as the granting of a site on which to pitch one's own tent (as previously) – which seems to be somewhat scraping the barrel on broadening the tax base! A houseboat includes a residential houseboat (*Note 10*). In *Mrs D G Everett (VTD 11736)* Customs adopted the stance that, if a houseboat is capable of self-propulsion, it is designed or adapted for use for recreation or pleasure, but this was rejected by the tribunal, which held that the phrase does not embrace a home. It must be remembered that holiday accommodation includes any accommodation advertised or held out as such or, after 1 February 1991, as suitable for holiday or leisure use (*Note 13*). Much residential property in London has been held out as such in recent years in an attempt to thwart the *Rent Acts*. Such a device is unlikely to be successful and creates an unnecessary VAT liability. In *Poole Borough Council (VTD 7180)* it was held that 'accommodation' in this context is not confined to living accommodation and that a licence to use a beach hut which provided that the hut was not to be used for living accommodation, but for pleasure only, was standard-rated as the hut was capable of being used for cooking, eating, shelter, changing clothes, etc. and thus 'accommodated' the typical requirements of holiday makers. Prior to 1 February 1991 standard-rating did not apply to the freehold sale or long-term leasing (i.e. for a year or more) of a chalet situated at a holiday or leisure park even though it was advertised as holiday accommodation and its occupation during winter months was prohibited by the planning authority. Such lettings and sales of new buildings are now standard-rated. This provision has, however, been held to breach the *EC Sixth Directive* where in reality the accommodation was a long-term residence (see 17.62 above). The freehold sale or the receipt of a premium (but not the rent) for the lease of such a building which is not new – presumably within the definition in 17.112 above although the Order does not say so – remains exempt.

**17.123** The granting of facilities for camping in caravans has always been taxable and the wording also makes clear that the provision of seasonal pitches for caravans and the grant of facilities by a third party at a site where the pitch is licensed from someone else are taxable. A seasonal pitch is a pitch which is provided for a period of less than a year, or which although provided for a longer period cannot legally be occupied by living there in a caravan throughout the period (such as where planning consent limits use of a site to the summer months) (*Note 14*). By concession, 'where a site owner can distinguish the utilities – electricity, gas and water – going to the caravans from those which are being used elsewhere on the site for swimming pools and so on, if he divides the amount by the number of caravans and designates it separately in his bills to those caravans, no VAT will be charged on the utility charges, or on the rates for the current year' (Hansard, Standing Committee G, 16 May 1989, Cols 96–97).

**17.124** The VAT charge on the grant of facilities for parking a vehicle applies not only to the operation of a car park but, in Customs' view, also on the lease of lock-up garages separate from a residence. The validity of a similar provision of Danish law under the *Sixth Directive* was upheld by the European Court of Justice in *Skatteministeriet v Henriksen (1990 STC 768)* subject to the caveat that if the letting of a garage is 'closely linked' with the letting of residential property 'so that the two lettings constitute a single economic transaction', the letting of the garage is exempt. Customs have sometimes in the past allowed exemption only if the two lettings are contained in a single lease, but the ruling of the European Court seems to go wider than that. In *C & E Commrs v Trinity Factoring Services Ltd (1994 STC 504)* the company asked tenants whether they wished to use the garage for parking a vehicle – in which case they charged VAT – or for storage – in which case they did not. It was held that the purpose of the letting had to be determined by the terms of the lease and where a lease of a garage was silent it was a necessary implication that a grant of facilities for parking a vehicle had been made. In *G W and J A Green (VTD 9016*) the taxpayers jointly invested in lock-up garages with the aid of borrowings serviced out of rental income. They contended that they were not letting the garages in furtherance of any business. The VAT tribunal held that the activities had the characteristics of a business and that VAT was payable. It also rejected a claim that each of the taxpayers was separately registrable. The supplies were made by them as joint owners and there was no basis for dividing the value of the supplies between them. They were therefore registrable jointly. The use of land for storage of caravans on a short-term basis was held to be the grant of facilities for parking a vehicle in *A C Slot (VTD 15076*) on the basis that, although the principal purpose of a caravan might be to provide accommodation, a caravan designed to be towed on roads was a vehicle.

**17.125** The grant of facilities for sport or recreation (item x) is exempt if the grant of the facilities is for either:

(*a*) a continuous period exceeding 24 hours; or

(*b*) a series of 10 or more periods where

(i) each period is in respect of the same activity carried on at the same place,

(ii) the interval between each period is at least a day but under 15 days,

(iii) consideration is payable by reference to the whole series and is evidenced by a written agreement,

(iv) the grantee has exclusive use of the facilities, and

(v) the grantee is a school, a club, an association or an organisation representing affiliated clubs or constituent associations.

(*VATA 1994, 9 Sch, Group 1, Note 16*).

Head (*b*) will cover for example the regular use of a football pitch by a club once a week or once a fortnight for its home games or licencing a school to use a swimming pool once a week. It should, however, be noted that the use must not only be regular but also exclusive.

**17.126** *Note 3* to *Group 5, Sch 8, VATA 1994* provides that the construction of, or conversion of a non-residential building to a building designed as a dwelling or a number of dwellings (see 17.24), includes the construction of a garage provided that the dwelling and the garage are constructed at the same time and the garage is intended to be occupied with the dwelling or one of the dwellings. In *Chipping Sodbury Town Trust (VTD 16641)* the Trust demolished two cottages and replaced them with semi-detached houses. It was a condition of the planning permission that two car parking spaces be provided for each house. A certificate of practical completion in respect of the houses was issued on 22 December 1997. At that time work on pathways was in abeyance as the Trust was seeking planning permission for the construction of garages. This was duly obtained and the pathing was completed at the same time as the construction of the garages. It was held that the garage had not been constructed at the same time as the houses so did not qualify for zero-rating.

**17.127** In *Threshfield Motors Ltd (VTD 16699)* the company argued that it did not provide mooring facilities but only granted a licence to occupy bare land which would become a mooring facility only if the licensee installed mooring equipment such as pontoons, ropes, chairs and gangways. The VAT tribunal held that it was still providing mooring facilities.

## What is a Licence to Occupy?

**17.128** Customs draw a distinction between an exempt licence to occupy land and a taxable licence to do something that involves coming on to land. Thus a licence to allow someone to enter a field to see the view is not a licence to occupy land. It is a taxable supply. Examples of grants that Customs consider to be exempt are a licence to occupy a particular room or office, the grant of a trading franchise inside particular premises, the grant of a catering or trading concession within specific premises, and the grant of permission to erect and maintain advertising hoardings on specific sites (C & E Notice 742B, para 6). The provision of stand space at a UK exhibition is normally exempt (but see 17.138). In *International Trade and Exhibitions J/V Ltd (VTD 14212)*, where the ground space which the stand would occupy was not ascertained when the contract was entered into, the tribunal held that what was being provided to the exhibitor was advertising services, not the right to occupy the stand. Customs have said that they accept this decision in the specific circumstances of this case but still consider that there is an exempt supply if both parties agree a specified site for the stand (Business Brief 24/96). In a later case, *Miller Freeman World-wide plc (VTD 15452)* the tribunal accepted this view that what had been supplied was a licence to occupy land. The use of tables by dealers at an antiques fair (*Mrs W B Enever (VTD 1537)*); a non-exclusive grazing licence (*J A King (1980 VATTR 60) (VTD 933)*); payments by taxi drivers for the use of a rest room (*Ferris and Budd t/a Z Cars (VTD 412)*); payments by driving instructors for non-exclusive use of an office at a driving *school* (*C W and J A Garner (VTD 1476)*); and the use by a hairdresser of a non-specific chair in a salon (*N and J Price (VTD 1443)*) are examples of things that have been found by VAT tribunals to fall into the second category and thus be taxable. In the last instance another relevant decision is in *William Walker t/a Ziska (VTD 11825)* where a self-employed hair stylist entered into two agreements with a salon owner, one licensing her the exclusive use of two chairs in the salon and the other providing her with various services. This is a fairly common arrangement, the rent of the chair being intended to be exempt and the provision of the services VATable. The tribunal held that the reality of the arrangement was that the stylist obtained the right to carry on business using the general facilities of the salon so that, despite the separate agreements, her right to exclusive occupation of the chairs was a mere incident of the supply of business facilities and this attracted VAT. The same approach was taken by the tribunal in *Anthony Winder t/a Anthony & Patricia (VTD 11784)* and *Simon Harris Hair Design Ltd (VTD 13939)*. Following the latter case, Customs told their local offices to assess VAT where it is clear that stylists working in open-plan salons are using the facilities of the premises as a whole (Business Brief 13/96). However they will not seek tax for accounting periods ending before April 1996 where chair rentals were not taxed 'due to a genuine misunderstanding, as opposed to any tax avoidance scheme', whatever that may mean (Business Brief 22/97). This is not necessarily correct. In the later case of *Herbert of Liverpool (Hair Design) Ltd (VTD 15949)* the tribunal expressed the view that 'the provision of a reception area, juniors, gowns for customers, a provision for laundry and the sale of products would be sufficiently dissociable from a hairdressing business as to allow the licence to occupy land to stand alone and therefore be treated as an exempt supply'. Unfortunately for the company, its licence covered only a chair and mirror. The tribunal felt that without a specific licence to use a specific washbasin it would not be possible to carry on the business of hairdressing. As the supply of a washbasin is not dissociable from the supply of the chair and mirror, the use of the chair and mirror was subsumed into the hairdressing business in the general area of the salon. The decision may give a pointer as to the sort of agreement that is needed to establish the licence as exempt. The end of the line may have been reached in such chair rental cases with *Quinto & Marcelio Olivieri (VTD 16991)*. There the partnership provided very little to the stylists other than the right to use the chair. Nevertheless the tribunal held that licence of the chair was not an end in itself but was ancillary to the principal supply that it identified as 'the general right to carry on business at Quinto & Mario's salon and to make use of its business facilities'. The appeal in *Mr & Mrs Broadley (t/a Professional Haircare) (VTD 16643)* was similarly dismissed on the basis that there 'was a single supply of the right to carry on a hairdressing business and the use of a designated area in the salon was an integral part of that supply'.

An alternative method succeeded in *Catherine Hunter, Arlene Kiernan, Martine Wigglesworth and Lesley Ann Wright (t/a Blues Hairshop) (VTD 16558)*. The four individuals jointly leased the salon in which each had her own workstation. They shared many of the expenses but not their income. Customs contended that this amounted to a partnership but this was rejected by the tribunal. This arrangement does not involve a licence at all as the individuals were joint owners of the interest in land.

**17.129** Customs' contention that a licence must be exclusive to constitute an interest in land was successfully challenged in *Abbotsley Golf and Squash Club Ltd (VTD 15042)*. The company granted a non-exclusive licence to Abbotsley Country Club Ltd of the occupation of its golf course. Customs claimed that the agreement was not a licence over land but merely a contractual right for the Club's members to play golf on Abbotsley's land. The taxpayer drew to the tribunal's attention the decision of the House of Lords in *Street v Mountford (1985 1 AC 809)*, a landlord and tenant case, which held that an exclusive licence was normally a lease, claiming that exclusivity therefore could not be the test of a licence. Whilst expressing disagreement with this decision, Customs opted not to appeal against it because, on reflection, they believed that 'in substance and reality' the Club had *de facto* an exclusive licence as no one else was licenced to use the golf course. In other words, they accepted the decision but not the tribunal's reasoning (Business Brief 25/97). Customs reiterated their faith in the decision by a different tribunal in *P J Lamb t/a Footloose (VTD 15136)*. Mr Lamb was a shoe retailer. He entered into an agreement with a Mr Johnson under which Mr Johnson would sell watches from the same premises and pay Mr Lamb 12½% of his gross takings as a contribution towards the shop running costs. Mr Lamb allocated one display window to Mr Johnson who also installed a display unit in the centre of the shop and another on one wall. Mr Lamb and Mr Johnson shared the shop counter. The tribunal held that Mr Johnson had been granted the use of facilities at the premises, not a licence. It was influenced by the facts that customers of Mr Johnson had to use the other areas of the shop in order that he could conduct his business, the agreement did not refer to rent and the use of the non-exclusive areas meant that Mr Johnson did not have actual physical enjoyment of the land as land. The tribunal does not appear to have been referred to the *Abbotsley* decision, however.

**17.130** This area has recently been considered both by the House of Lords in *C & E Commrs v Sinclair Collis Ltd (2001 STC 989)* and by the ECJ briefly in *E C Commission v UK (2000 STC 777) (Case C-359/97)* and in a little more detail in *Sweden v Stockholm Lindopark AB (2001 STC 103) (Case C-150/99)*. In the *Sinclair Collis* case their Lordships were split and have referred the issue to the ECJ, which may need to give it more detailed consideration than in the earlier cases.

**17.131** The EC Commission case (see 17.311) concerned road tolls. The UK argued that providing access to roads on payment of a toll represented a letting of immovable property within the meaning of *Article 13B(b)* of the *EC Sixth Directive*, the provision from which the exemption for letting land arises. The ECJ, whilst recognised that the letting of immovable property under *article 13B* is wider than the concept of letting under some national laws, held that it 'cannot be considered to cover contracts where, as here, the parties have not agreed on any duration for the right of enjoyment of the immovable property, which is the essential element of a contract to let'. The question in *Stockholm Lindopark* was whether the operation of a golf course fell within *Article 13B(b)*. The ECJ said that was a matter for the national courts to decide in the light of the facts. It acknowledged that 'it is certainly not impossible that in certain circumstances a supply of premises for the practice of sport or physical education may constitute the letting of immovable property' but held that it was not permissible for Sweden to grant a general exemption for such supplies. It also pointed out that the running of a golf course generally entails not only the passive activity of making the course available but also a large number of commercial activities, such as supervision, management, and maintenance and that 'in the absence of quite exceptional circumstances, letting out a golf course cannot therefore constitute the main service supplied'. The Advocate-General (Jacobs) was more forceful. He felt that the exemption in *Article 13B(b)* 'cannot extend to all transactions granting access, or for any other purpose, regardless of the characteristics of such access, but must in my view be limited by certain of the characteristics inherent in a contract of leasing or letting'. He pointed out that in *E C Commission v UK* (see 17.311) the court had stressed in particular the need that the agreement between the parties should take account of the duration of the enjoyment of the property. He also pointed out that the concept and letting of immovable property is neither defined in the directive, nor comprehensively defined by the court. He felt that the type of broad definition argued for in the case by the UK government could not be accepted (which may suggest that UK jurisprudence in this area may not be wholly correct). He expressed the view that, apart from the duration of the contract, a lease or let 'necessarily involves the grant of some right to occupy the property as one's own and to exclude or admit others, a right which is, moreover, linked to a defined piece or area of property'.

**17.132** *Sinclair Collis* was concerned with the placing of cigarette machines in public houses, etc. The VAT position of such machines had previously been considered by the VAT tribunal in 1990 in *Wolverhampton & Dudley Breweries (VTD 5351)* where the tribunal, looking at the substance and reality of the matter, had concluded that the use and enjoyment of the land was not a significant factor; the real subject of the agreement was the availability of the machine to customers which was not a licence to occupy land. Despite this case, Customs had ruled that *Sinclair Collis* was granting licences to occupy land when it installed a cigarette machine. The company challenged this ruling and Customs agreed that the licences were VATable. The company promptly put in a claim for repayment of past disallowed input tax, at which point Customs changed their mind and said that the supply was of licences to occupy land. The VAT tribunal agreed with the company for the same reason as in the *Wolverhampton and Dudley* case, but both the High Court and the Court of Appeal held that the dominant element of the supply was the right to install, operate and maintain machines on the premises, which they felt amounted to a licence to occupy land.

**17.133** The House of Lords reverted to the VAT tribunal's approach. Lord Slynn of Hadley thought it plain that 'the words, licence to occupy land, in the 1994 Act cannot go wider than the words, letting of immovable property, in the Sixth Directive'. He felt that 'the essential purpose of this agreement was to enable the company to bring its machines into the club owner's premises and to have them there for two years'. He felt that the letting of immovable property includes transactions which go beyond what are leases in the ordinary sense of the term and that, on balance, 'an agreement by which a machine may be fixed to a wall or put, free standing, in a particular place in a club for a sustained period is capable of amounting to the occupation of a portion of the land. It is a right given to the exclusion of all others and an individual putting it there is occupying the land by the machine'. Lord Steyn agreed with him. An opposing view was taken by Lord Nicholls of Birkenhead. He accepted that the machine occupies space on the site owner's premises and is located there 24 hours every day, so the use made of the premises by the tobacco company is not intermittent. However he did not feel these factors conclusive. 'Occupation of space is a feature of every physical object. The grant of a right to occupy space by placing an object on the supplier's premises is not conclusive even if the right is of some duration. If it were, a licence to place any object on the licensor's property would be within the exemption; for example permission to display a picture for sale on the walls of a picture gallery. That cannot be correct.' The Sinclair Collis licence was 'more naturally to be regarded as a licence to use land rather than a licence to occupy land'. Lord Millett reached a similar conclusion by a different route, namely by construing the agreement itself. This did not contain the terms of a lease but the terms on which vending machines may be positioned on the premises. It did not specify the number of machines to be covered, leaving that to be determined by agreement. It did not identify any defined areas or even the rooms where machines were to be installed; that was left in the first instance to the site owner. Sinclair Collis was given no control over access to the machines (other than an express right to itself access them). Lord Millett thought the agreement far removed from the letting of land. 'The company cannot sensibly be described as occupying any part of the premises by its machine. Such a concept can hardly apply where the part of the premises in question has no independent existence of its own, being defined by the dimensions of the machine and its location from time to time . . . The agreement . . . is not an agreement for the letting of defined areas of land with a right to place machines on them, but a right to bring machines into the site owner's premises and place them in a suitable position there. The site owner remains in sole occupation of the whole of his premises including the areas from time to time occupied by machines.' Lord Scott of Foscote took a similar view. He thought it clear, 'as a matter of common sense as well as of authority that not all licences that transform a use of the land of another from what would otherwise have been trespass into a lawful use are to be regarded as licences to occupy land'. Whether a licence creates a relationship between the licensee and the land is a question of fact and degree. He felt that there are two characteristics that distinguish a licence to occupy from a mere licence to use, namely possession and control. If neither is present he felt it difficult to understand how a licensee can be said to 'occupy'. There is authority for this view in UK land law. He also pointed out that 'A licence to occupy is something to be enjoyed by persons, whether natural or corporate. It is people or companies who must be in possession or exercise control, not inanimate objects like tables, kiosks, cars or vending machines'. He pointed out that in this case the owner of the premises remains in possession and control of the whole of the room in which the vending machine is placed. It is unnatural to treat the room as being partly occupied by the owner and partly by Sinclair Collis. The decision of the VAT tribunal in *British Telecommunications plc (VTD 16244)* also emphasises the difficulties in the Slynn/Steyn approach. It was held there that where a payphone is affixed to premises, its occupation of the space is a licence to occupy land as the site owner supplies to BT the right to have on its premises what is in effect a vending machine. However Customs accepted that where the payphone was not attached to the premises, such as a payphone in a hotel bedroom or fixed to a hospital trolley, there is no licence to occupy land.

**17.134** In another ECJ case, *Staatssecretaris van Financien v VOF Coffeeshop Siberie (Case C-158/98) (1999 STC 742)* Advocate General Fennelly opined (albeit obiter) that he would not be inclined to regard the renting of a table in a coffee shop from which to sell soft drinks as amounting to the letting of immovable property. What might be called the Slynn/Steyn view in *Sinclair Collis* does not fit well with that decision, and the concept that Sinclair Collis is primarily renting space offends common sense.

**17.135** Customs expressed the view a few years ago that a licence to occupy land exists where it relates to a clearly defined area or piece of land which in substance and reality permits the licensee an exclusive right of occupation during the times prescribed in the licence, i.e. the exclusive occupation need not be continuous, it could for example be every Thursday afternoon. In the light of the *Abbotsley* decision they also accept that a licence can exist where the land is not occupied exclusively by the licensee provided that the licence relates to a clearly defined area or piece of land, in substance and reality it allows the licensee to physically occupy the land and the rights granted are in relation to the occupation of the land thereby providing for the licensee's physical enjoyment or exploitation for the land (Business Brief 22/98).

**17.136** They think that the following are likely to be licences to occupy land:

(*a*) granting a person a pitch in a market or at a car boot sale;

(*b*) hiring a hall to a person, e.g. for a conference or a reception;

(*c*) granting a concession to operate a shop within a shop where the concessionaire is granted an area from which to sell goods or services;

(*d*) the provision of a stand or similar space to a person at an exhibition;

(*e*) the provision to the owner of coin-operated machines of sites on which to locate his machine.

**17.137** They think the following are unlikely to amount to a licence to occupy:

(*a*) ambulatory concessions, e.g. ice-cream vans on a beach;

(*b*) hairdressers' chairs in open-plan salons;

(*c*) allowing the general public access to premises or events.

(Business Brief 22/98).

**17.138** Where an exhibition organiser supplied the use of a 'conversation' table on a stand and shared use of storage and meeting facilities, it was held that it was providing a taxable package of facilities not a licence to occupy land. The conversation table had a chair on each side, was separated from adjoining tables by a partition and had a hanging sign showing the name of the organisation. Nevertheless, the tribunal held that, although an organisation was entitled to occupation of its allocated table and chairs, it did not have exclusive occupation of any part of the exhibition stand (*Swiss National Tourist Office (VTD 13192)*).

**Other Problem Areas**

**17.139** It appears that a contract to acquire land is, in Customs' view, itself an interest in land. In *Margrie Holdings Ltd v C & E Commrs (1991 STC 80)*, a Scottish case, it was held that the equivalent right under Scottish law was not an interest in land. As a result the wording of the legislation was changed by the *VAT (Buildings and Land) Order 1991* to exempt, in relation to land in Scotland, any personal right to call for or be granted an interest in land. This suggests that Customs felt that no similar clarification was needed in relation to land in England and Wales. Nevertheless the position does not seem clear. If a contract to acquire land is entered into and the benefit of that contract sold, it might be advisable to obtain confirmation from Customs that the sale will be exempt from VAT. The VAT tribunal decision in *Higher Education Statistics Agency Ltd (VTD 15917)* also points to a contract being an interest in land (see 17.281).

**17.140** In *R H Carter t/a Protheroe Carter & Eason (VTD 12047)* the VAT tribunal held that the grant of an interest in, or right over, land was confined to the grant of a legal or equitable interest, and therefore an agreement with a developer to allow a crane jib to pass through the air space over the appellant's premises was neither a right over land nor a licence to occupy land and so was taxable.

**17.141** Customs initially considered that the first supply of a building after development determines whether input tax on the construction costs is recoverable. If that first supply was an exempt supply, no part of the input tax was recoverable. The draftsman of the 1989 legislation was presumably of the same view when he deemed the first receipt of rent from letting residential accommodation to be a zero-rated supply (see 17.63 above) in order to trigger the right to recover input tax in respect of the construction of the property. However, it was held in *C & E Commrs v Briararch Ltd* and *C & E Commrs v Curtis Henderson Ltd (1992 STC 732)* that where a person constructs a building with the intention on completion of selling it as soon as a buyer can be found, he is entitled to credit for an apportioned amount of the input tax incurred on building the house notwithstanding that he lets the house on a short let before selling it. *Briararch Ltd* converted a property into offices in 1988 intending to let them on a 25-year lease. It could not find a tenant. Badly needing money to meet its interest obligations, it let the property on a four-year lease, still intending to grant the 25-year lease on the expiry of that short lease. Curtis Henderson Ltd built a house intending to sell it. It could not find a buyer. An opportunity arose to let it for a short period and it did so to provide a contribution towards the burden of interest charges. The house was let for nine months and then remained empty for a further nine months until a buyer was found. The court held that *Article 20* of the *EC Sixth Directive*, which begins 'the initial deduction shall be adjusted according to the procedures laid down by the Member States, in particular (*a*) when that deduction was higher or lower than that to which the taxable person was entitled', gives authority for necessary adjustments according to intention. What is now *Regulation 107* of the *VAT Regulations 1995* provides the procedures for such adjustment. A taxable person had deducted input tax which had been attributed to an intended taxable supply of the building; during the following six years it had used the building in making an exempt supply; so it became necessary to determine how much of that input tax was attributable to the exempt supply. In the *Briararch* case the VAT tribunal had allowed 25/29ths of the input tax. Hutchinson J felt this was probably an incorrect basis of apportionment – it would not work if the intention had been to sell the property freehold – and that a more satisfactory basis would be 'to make a comparison between the values, adjusted if necessary, of the respective disposals'. Customs said in response to this decision that they were 'considering an amendment to the legislation to prevent intention being used as a basis for determining input tax recovery' (Business Brief 15/92). However, they have as yet taken no action over this. The Business Brief also stated that where builders or developers so let a building on a temporary basis they 'will be required to produce evidence of their intention to make taxable supplies and to give an undertaking to repay input tax to Customs if there is no taxable supply' or if the exempt letting lasts longer than anticipated.

**17.142** In *Cooper and Chapman (Builders) Ltd v C & E Commrs (1993 STC 1)* the company converted a house into ten flats which it intended to let as holiday accommodation. It let some of them but, three months after completion of the conversion, granted a one-year lease of the entire building, which was of course an exempt supply. The VAT tribunal held that the expenditure on conversion had to be apportioned between the ten flats because the taxable supply which the company had intended to make was of letting the flats singly, so that only the expenditure on an individual flat would relate to the supply of that flat. The company could recover the input tax in respect of those flats which had actually been let as holiday accommodation. It could not recover input tax in relation to the other flats as the first supply of those flats was an exempt supply. This was upheld by the High Court on appeal.

**17.143** Care may sometimes need to be taken to evidence whether a developer is acting as a principal or an agent. In *Drexlodge Ltd (VTD*

*5614)* a property development company entered into an agreement with the Cooperative Insurance Society Ltd for the development of two sites owned by the Society. Despite the fact that the invoices were addressed to Drexlodge Ltd, Customs contended that supplies by subcontractors had been made to the Society through the agency of Drexlodge and sought to disallow relief for the input tax. The VAT tribunal held that the 'flavour' of the agreement was that of a joint venture not of an agency. Provisions in it which required Drexlodge to obtain the approval of the Society's surveyor for certain works were not evidence of agency. There was no evidence that the suppliers were aware of the existence of a principal other than Drexlodge with whom they had contracted.

**17.144** This should be contrasted with the position in *Peter Anthony Estates Ltd (VTD 13250)*. In that case, the company managed the letting of properties on assured shorthold tenancies on behalf of the owner. The leases were entered into in the name of the company, not that of the owner, and contained no indication that the company was acting as an agent. The arrangement with the owner was that the company would pay him a guaranteed weekly amount and retain for its own benefit the balance of the rents. The company contended that the substance of the transaction was that the company had leased the properties from the owner for the guaranteed rent and subleased them to the tenants. It was held that, as there was a formal property management agreement between the company and the owner, the company was letting the properties as an undisclosed agent of the owner, and its share of the rents were fees for managing the properties and VAT was chargeable.

**17.145** It is also important to identify exactly what is being supplied. In *Haringey Borough Council (1994 VATTR 70) (VTD 8820, VTD 12050, VTD 12462)* the Council, as Trustees of Alexandra Palace, carried out extensive repairs to Alexandra Palace and were anxious to deduct as much of the input tax as possible. They contended that when they hired out the building in the course of a business, some of the supplies made to hirers were VATable supplies separate from the licence to use the building. The VAT tribunal held that if a service is necessary to the licence, such as heating and light and water, it has to be considered as an integral part of the supply of the licence, following *British Airways plc v C & E Commrs (1990 STC 643)*. Where, however, items could reasonably have been not supplied, or the customer would expect an extra charge to be made for them, they are a separate supply. It held that the provision of floral decorations, a courtesy bus service, off-site posters, and leaflet distribution were separate taxable supplies. So were the staffing of cloakrooms (as a separate charge could instead be made to visitors) and the cleaning of exhibition stands for which a specialist contractor was engaged. The box office, turnstiles and ticket machines and the provision of staff to run these and the car parking were integral to the supply. So was the removal of rubbish, general cleaning of common areas, the staffing and stocking of toilets, the services of a stand-by electrician, and crowd control. The tribunal observed that the lack of any rational basis for apportioning consideration could be indicative of an integral supply. The tribunal decision also covered other points. A Customs appeal against certain aspects, but not including the above basis of apportionment, was dismissed by the High Court (*1995 STC 830*). Clearly if it is intended to contend that services are separate to the right to use the land, it is advisable to charge separately for them, although the omission to do so is not necessarily fatal.

**17.146** On the other hand, in *Rayner & Keeler Ltd (1991 VATTR 532) (VTD 5803, 9349)* a contractor was required both to construct or provide goods (shop fittings) and to install them. The VAT tribunal held that it would be unrealistic to separate the obligation to provide an item from the obligation to fit it and to classify them as two separate supplies. There was therefore a single supply of services, not a composite supply of goods and services. On appeal Owen J held that the tribunal had misdirected itself (*1994 STC 724*) and remitted the case to it 'to consider and analyse first the individual supplies of goods taking into account the principles laid down in *Schedule 2* and asking the question whether each supply of goods has become an integral part of a supply of services or vice versa'. This seems to reaffirm that it is a matter of impression whether a supply of goods is separable from the service of installing them or whether there is the provision of a single service.

**17.147** In *J E Greves & Sons (VTD 9777)* the taxpayer had squatted on land and claimed possessory title. Following a consent order made in High Court proceedings it agreed to vacate the land, to remove a caution registered against the title, and to abandon its claim to the land in return for a payment of £450,000. Customs contended that it could not be inferred from the order that the taxpayer had given up a right in land; accordingly the receipt was consideration for a taxable supply. The taxpayer contended that it was exempt as being for the surrender of possession of the land. It was established that, had the proceedings continued, the taxpayer would probably have established title to the land. Accordingly the VAT tribunal held that the taxpayer could be regarded as having an interest in land which it had disposed of. It felt that a consent order needs to be examined with particular care and in its context to ascertain its effect. It differs from a contract because, in a document evidencing a compromise to settle a dispute, the supply is less likely to be described in clear terms.

**17.148** In *Cullens Holdings plc (VTD 12376)* the group licenced some of its retail food stores to operators. The licence agreement gave the operator a licence to carry on business at the store premises using the group's name and business systems. Customs contended that this was a single exempt supply, namely licences to occupy land. The company contended that there was a single composite standard-rated supply of business facilities. The tribunal held that the right to carry on business using the group's name and system was clearly an important part of the agreement. It was not a normal incident of a licence to occupy land and could not be regarded as physically or economically indissociable from the licences. Accordingly there were two supplies, albeit part of a single contract, an exempt licence to occupy and a taxable supply of business rights. This decision seems to fit uneasily with the hairdresser cases referred to at 17.128. That line of cases identified a supply of business facilities but refused to regard it as separable from the licence to occupy, instead subsuming the licence as being an integral part of the single supply of business facilities.

**17.149** In *Grantham Cricket Club (VTD 12287, VTD 12863)* the club entered into an agreement with a developer under which it would surrender its tenancy to its landlord and take a new lease of alternative premises on which it would itself prepare a cricket pitch and construct a pavilion. It was paid £110,000 by the developer and an additional £70,000 by its landlord for the surrender of the lease. The club contended that the entire payment related to a single exempt supply, the vacation of its former ground. It was held that the payment from the developer clearly imposed two requirements on the club, to vacate the old premises and adapt the alternative site. The £110,000 therefore had to be apportioned between the two, the part relating to the surrender being exempt and the balance taxable.

**17.150** The importance of identifying correctly the supply for which the consideration is paid is well illustrated by *Terard Ltd (VTD 16949)*. Terard converted a commercial property into flats, which it leased to the Hyde Housing Association (HHA). In addition to the rent payable under the lease HHA agreed to pay Terard £20,000 as 'grant funding for the conversion works on their completion and the completion of the lease'. The £20,000 grant was made to HHA by the Housing Corporation under a scheme to encourage living accommodation over shops being used for housing homeless families. Normally HHA engaged contractors to carry out such work on its own properties. Terard claimed the payment was for zero-rated conversion work. It pointed out that that was the only thing for which the Housing Corporation was prepared to make a grant. Customs contended that it was for the supply of the exempt lease. The tribunal held in favour of Customs. It was strongly influenced by the fact that none of the documents actually obliged Terard to carry out the conversion work; they merely made clear that HHA would not be willing to lease the flats until that had been done to its satisfaction. They could not find any direct link between the conversion work and the consideration received. This case also illustrates two other important facets of VAT, the need to get the documents right and the need to be able to evidence what happened where there are staff changes so that the people involved in a transaction are not available to give evidence when it reaches the VAT tribunal. A similar conclusion was reached by the tribunal in *West Devon Borough Council (VTD 17107)* on fairly similar facts.

**Variations of Leases**

**17.151** Many variations of leases involve in law the surrender of the existing lease and the grant of a new lease. Customs have agreed that, where no monetary consideration passes from the landlord to the tenant as a result of (or in connection with) the variation, they will accept that the old lease is not surrendered for a non-monetary consideration (i.e. the value of the new lease) if either:

(*a*) the new lease is for the same building but for an extended term;

(*b*) the new lease is for a greater area of the same building as the old lease and for the same or an extended term; or

(*c*) the new lease is for the same land as the old and for an extended term.

This concession does not apply to ground leases or to building leases (i.e. where the lessee will develop the land) as Customs consider that in most such cases the new lease is likely to be more valuable than the old.

**17.152** If the landlord makes a payment to the tenant for a variation, Customs will 'normally' regard that payment as the sole consideration for the surrender (i.e. they will not regard the value of the new lease as being part of the consideration for the surrender of the old). However, they reserve the right to treat the value of the new lease as additional consideration if the terms are significantly more favourable than could have been negotiated by a lessee with no existing lease to surrender.

**17.153** If the tenant pays the landlord for a variation, Customs will normally look on that payment as consideration for the grant of a new lease, and thus exempt, not as consideration for the surrender of the old lease. This will not apply if the circumstances suggest that the payment is consideration for the landlord's taxable supply of the acceptance of the surrender of an onerous lease from the tenant (Law Society Press Release 1 May 1991).

**17.154** Customs do accept that variations to leases should be treated as part of the original supply of the lease so that the VAT liability follows that of the original lease (Business Brief 16/94). They also accept that the lifting of a restrictive covenant on land is also exempt unless the person lifting the restriction has elected to waive exemption on the land. They instance the lifting of a restriction to permit development which was previously forbidden, but the exemption will apply to the lifting of any restriction (Business Brief 17/94).

**17.155** Where none of these concessional exclusions apply, consideration could be given to the landlord granting to an associated company of the tenant ('Newco') a head lease on the new terms subject to the existing lease. The tenant would remain in occupation as sub-tenant of its new 'landlord', Newco, until its lease expires, and Newco would then go into occupation. However, it is likely that this would result in loss of tax relief for Newco on the difference between the rent paid under the new headlease and that received under the sub-lease as the letting by Newco, i.e. its succession to the existing lease, would not be a lease at full rent. This corporation tax disadvantage would need to be weighed against the VAT saving. It may be possible to achieve the best of both worlds by Newco being a nominee of the existing tenant. However, particularly in the light of the decisions in *Kildrummy (Jersey) Ltd v CIR (1990 STC 657)* and *Lady Ingram's Executors v CIR (1997 STC 1234)* (see 18.62 below), care may be needed in choosing the nominee.

**17.156** The recent VAT tribunal decision in *Halifax plc, Country Wide Property Investments Ltd* and *Leeds Permanent Development Services Ltd (VTD 17124)* has caused a great deal of consternation to VAT practitioners. On appeal the case was remitted to the tribunal to make a further finding of fact and has since been referred by the tribunal to the ECJ. The tribunal seems to many people to have taken a purposive approach that comes close to applying the *Furniss v Dawson* principle (see 14.52) to VAT. Whilst the decision is in parts difficult to follow, it has probably not gone that far. Halifax makes mainly exempt supplies. It owned four sites on which it wished to construct call centres. It entered into a scheme designed to increase the recoverable VAT on its construction costs. It accepted the scheme had no other commercial purpose but was purely a tax avoidance scheme. It consisted of the following steps:

(*a*) Halifax entered into an agreement to lease the sites to Leeds Permanent Development Services (LPDS) and on the same days LPDS entered into an agreement with a third company, Halifax Property Investments Ltd (HPIL) to sell the leases to HPIL with completion to take place as and when each site had been developed.

(*b*) LPDS entered into an agreement with Country Wide Property Investments (CWPI) for CWPI to construct the call centres.

(*c*) CWPI engaged builders to carry out the work.

(*d*) During the prescribed accounting period in which LPDS entered into the contract with CWPI it made a small supply of taxable construction services to Halifax. It would therefore be able to recover the whole of the input tax charged by CWPI as its only outputs in that period were taxable outputs.

(*e*) In its next prescribed accounting period LPDS assigned its lease to HPIL in pursuance of the agreement at (*a*). This was an exempt supply, but as LPDS was undoubtedly a property dealing company this would not trigger any recovery of VAT under the capital goods scheme.

(f) Halifax provided interest free finance for the entire scheme. All of the companies were Halifax subsidiaries.

The tribunal held:

(i) The transactions carried out constituted a tax avoidance scheme and had no business or economic function other than to create a VAT recovery.

(ii) Neither LPDS or CWPI made any taxable supplies in relation to the transactions. This conclusion derived both from UK and EC law. The House of Lords held in *FA & AB Lupton (47 TC 580)*, a direct tax case, that a transaction carried out solely for tax avoidance purposes was not a trading transaction and the tribunal (Stephen Oliver QC) felt that 'a similar robust approach' should be applied to Halifax. Under EC law the transactions did not constitute an economic activity. Accordingly LPDS and CWPI were not carrying on a business and were not taxable persons in relation to those transactions (*Article 4(1)* of the *EC Sixth Directive*). Halifax's reliance on the ECJ decision in *BLP Group plc v C & E Commrs (1995 STC 424) (Case C-4/94)* was misconceived as the question of attribution of input tax could not arise if no economic activities had taken place.

(iii) The commercial reality was that the supply by the outside builders was made to Halifax. It is this third finding that is most worrying. Whilst not all people agree with the second finding, it has a logical basis. However the logical result of there being no supply by CWPI is that the input tax it incurred is completely irrecoverable. It is hard to see any logic in somehow deeming that input tax to have been incurred on a supply to Halifax. Oliver justifies the conclusion by discerning some sort of contractual relationship between the builder and Halifax on the basis that Halifax owned the sites so the benefit of the works enured to it and that the building contracts contained warranties that were made enforceable by Halifax.

**17.157** Halifax have appealed the decision. On appeal Neuberger J felt that there was real doubt as to whether the tribunal had considered the subjective reasons of LPDS and CWPI for entering into the transactions and, in particular whether the sole subjective reason was tax avoidance. He accordingly remitted the case back to the tribunal to make a finding on this point. The Halifax decision was followed in *J E & H Laurie (t/a the Peacock Montessori Nursery) (VTD 17219)* where a lease and leaseback transaction was created to generate taxable supplies and allow recovery of the VAT on building works in advance of making the exempt supply of education.

## The 'Option to Tax'

**17.158** An election can be made to bring rent and other supplies – including subsequent disposals of the building – within the VAT net (*VAT 1994, Sch 10 para 2*). Technically the election is to waive the exemption from VAT. It can be made by anyone who lets property, including a pension fund and a local authority (*Finanzamt Augsburg v Marktgemeinde Welden (Case C–247/95) (1997 STC 531)*).

**17.159** The effect of the election is that any supply made by the taxpayer in relation to the building or land at a time when the election is in force must be regarded as not falling within *VATA 1994, Sch 9 Group 1*, i.e. as not being exempt, and therefore as being taxable at the standard rate of 17½% (*VATA 1994, Sch 10 para 2(1)*). Supply, of course, covers not only rents but also the disposal proceeds when the building is sold.

**17.160** Where the person making the election is a company, the election will apply not only to rents, etc. received by the company but also to those received by any relevant associate – broadly, a member of the same VAT group – in relation to the same land or building (*VATA 1994, Sch 10 para 2(1)*). For this purpose a relevant associate is any company which is either:

(*a*) a member of the same VAT group as the electing company at the time the election was made;

(*b*) a member of the same VAT group at any subsequent time at which the electing company continues to have an interest in, right over or licence to occupy the building or land (or any part of it); or

(*c*) a member of the same VAT group as another company that is itself within (*a*) or (*b*) above at a time when that company has an interest in, right over or licence to occupy the building or land.

(*VATA 1994, Sch 10 para 3(7)*).

**17.161** An example may make head (*c*) clearer. Suppose A Ltd owns a building and has granted a lease of part to B Ltd which is in the same VAT group. An election by A Ltd will force B Ltd to charge VAT (and one by B Ltd would force A Ltd to do so). A Ltd sells its interest to C Ltd which is not a member of the VAT group (but is a wholly-owned subsidiary of B Ltd). C Ltd is not bound by A's election and this transfer does not affect B's obligation to charge VAT on its rents. A Ltd is sold and subsequently C Ltd is grouped with B Ltd for VAT purposes. C Ltd will from then on be bound by the election made by A Ltd because B Ltd, another member of the VAT group, is bound by that election.

**17.162** If the taxpayer has made, or intends to make, an exempt grant in respect of the land at any time prior to making the election (and since 1 August 1989), the prior written consent of Customs to the election is needed. Customs can permit the election only if they are satisfied that a fair and reasonable attribution of the input tax incurred since 1 August 1989 in relation to the land will be achieved between exempt and taxable supplies over the entire period of ownership of the land (or, if less, the part since 1 August 1989) (*VATA 1994, Sch 10 para 3(9)*). From 1 March 1995, Customs are empowered to specify in a Notice conditions for which automatic permission can be assumed (*VAT (Buildings and Land) Order 1995* (*SI 1995 No 279*) *Article 4*). They have done so in paragraph 5.2 of Notice 742A. Prior permission is not needed where either:

1. the development is a mixed use one and the only exempt supplies have been in relation to the dwellings;

2. the taxpayer does not wish to recover any input tax on goods, services or acquisitions received before the option to tax has effect, the consideration received for exempt supplies prior to that time has been solely by way of rent, and the only input tax the taxpayer wishes to recover after the option to tax takes effect is in relation to day-to-day overheads (which does not include a refurbishment of the building);

3. although the taxpayer wishes to recover input tax incurred before the option to tax takes effect, this relates solely to tax charged by tenants on surrender of a lease, the relevant part of the building has been unoccupied since that surrender, and there will be no further exempt supplies of the property; or

4. the exempt supplies have been incidental to the main use of the property, such as the siting of an advertising hoarding within the curtilage of a building, granting space for the erection of a radio mast or receiving income from an electrical substation.

**17.163** In *C & E Commrs v Trustees of R & R Pension Fund (1996 STC 889)*, the trustees of a pension fund had constructed a commercial building and reclaimed the whole of the input tax on the building costs. They granted a 15-year lease of the building from 1 August 1993. This triggered a self-supply charge under *VATA 1994, Sch 10 para 6(1)*. On 12 December 1994 they notified their election to waive exemption. They proposed that 99.1% of the tax on the self-supply should be allowed as input tax. This was calculated as 16 months exempt out of the expected 150-year life of the building. It was agreed that the building was within the capital goods scheme. Customs refused permission for the election on the grounds that it did not give a fair and reasonable attribution of the input tax having regard to the application of the capital goods scheme. The VAT tribunal saw no reason why Customs could not agree an initial attribution of input tax in lieu of adjustment under the capital goods scheme, but the High Court reversed this decision and held that Customs were justified in refusing the election, as *VATA 1994, Sch 10 para 3(9)* did not permit them to allow an election unless a fair and reasonable attribution could be secured. Following this decision Customs said that *para 3(9)* (which was added from 1 January 1992) was introduced 'with the primary purposes of removing the block for capital items to allow the capital goods scheme to run its course' (Business Brief 17/96).

**17.164** In *The Island Trading Co Ltd (VTD 13838)*, the company used the property partly for its own business and partly for letting, and the input tax that Customs wanted repaid as a condition of accepting the election was fully recoverable under the *de minimis* provisions. Customs claimed that the *de minimis* limit did not apply where a special method of apportionment is used in respect of partially exempt supplies. The VAT tribunal rejected this, and also held that Customs could only require an adjustment to past input tax relief if this was necessary to secure a fair and reasonable attribution, and as the input tax was fully deductible under the *de minimis* rules if no election were made, Customs could not require any adjustment in that case as a condition of consenting to the election. This ruling was given before the High Court decision in *R & R Pension Fund* and may therefore be unreliable.

**17.165** An interesting scheme was tried in *C & E Commrs v Robert Gordon's College (1995 STC 1093)*. The appellant was an educational charity. It charged fees to pupils which were exempt. It spent some £3.4 million in developing some disused land and buildings as a playing field. It formed a company to exploit the playing field commercially and rented the land to the company, retaining a non-exclusive licence to use it itself. Both the charity and the company exercised the option to tax. The charity reclaimed the VAT on the development costs as directly attributable to the generation of the VATable rent. The company entered into a charitable deed of covenant under which it paid the whole of its profits to the charity. Customs contended that the arrangement was a circular transaction within the *Furniss v Dawson* principle so that the lease to the company was not a business activity. This was rejected by the VAT tribunal on the basis that the recovery of input tax is a business purpose and also that the lease was intended to enable a particular area of the college's activities to be conducted in a more efficient manner and was therefore clearly in furtherance of a business. Customs secondly claimed that the first occasion on which the school used the playing fields constituted occupation of them by the college when not a fully taxable person within 10 years of completion of the works and therefore gave rise to a self-supply charge (see *section 5(6)(b)*). The House of Lords held that, whilst this might follow from the usual principles of construction used in the UK, it was incompatible with the *Sixth Directive*. As the use the College made of the playing field was pursuant to services (i.e. the licence) supplied to it by a third party (the company) 'there could be no room for a self-supply charge within the terms of the *Sixth Directive*'. Customs did not appeal on the *Furniss v Dawson* point. This and similar arrangements have been blocked by legislation from 29 November 1994 (see 17.170 and 17.182), so that this scheme will no longer work.

### Exclusions

**17.166** An election cannot take out of exemption a supply in relation to

(*a*) a building or part of a building intended for use as a dwelling or number of dwellings or for a relevant residential purpose;

(*b*) a building or part of a building intended for use for a relevant charitable purpose, *other than as an office*;

(*c*) a grant to a registered housing association (within the meaning of the *Housing Associations Act 1985* or *Part VII* of the *Housing (Northern Ireland) Order 1981*) where the association has given the grantor a certificate stating that the land is to be used for the construction of a dwelling or dwellings or for a relevant residential purpose;

(*d*) a grant to an individual where the land is to be used for the construction of a building intended for use by him as a dwelling; or

(*e*) in relation to supplies after 28 February 1995, a pitch for a residential caravan or facilities for mooring a residential houseboat, i.e. a boat or other floating decked structure designed or adapted for use solely as a place of permanent habitation not having means of (or capable of being readily adapted for) self-propulsion, and residence in which is not prevented throughout the year by the terms of a covenant, statutory planning consent or similar permission (*VAT (Buildings and Land) Order 1995* (*SI 1995 No 279*) *Articles 2* and *4*).

(*VATA 1994, Sch 10 para 2(2)(3), 3(8)*).

**17.167** It should particularly be noted that the determining factor under (*b*) is intention, not the use ultimately made of the building, although such use might well be evidence of the intention at the time of the supply. The case of *J Watters (VTD 13337)* illustrates the problem. Mr Watters purchased a disused public house from a brewery company which had elected to waive exemption. Customs accepted that he had always intended to use the building as a dwelling, but argued that the purchase was not exempt as he had not sufficiently communicated that intention to the company. The VAT tribunal was satisfied that the building was intended for use as a dwelling at the time the supply was made and that the brewery had been told of that fact but had disregarded it as neither party realised that it affected the VAT position. It held that it was therefore unnecessary for it to decide whether a buyer's failure to communicate his intention to the seller would render the waiver of exemption ineffective. In the light of the clear wording of the legislation, it is unclear why Customs pursued this case, as it seems clear that it is the intention of the future user, not that of the vendor, that matters.

**17.168** In *SEH Holdings Ltd (VTD 16771)* the company (through another group company) contracted to purchase a former public house and on the same day agreed to resell it to two purchasers who intended to convert the property into new dwellings. The company contended that the sale to it was an exempt supply so the vendor had not been entitled to charge input tax. *Para 2(2)(a)* (head 17.166(*a*) above) refers to the intended use of the property. On the face of it, that is not restricted to the intended use by SEH, the immediate purchaser. The tribunal decided that as VAT is a tax chargeable on each transaction the exclusion must apply only to the intended use by the immediate purchaser. A vendor is contractually in a position to determine the intention of his purchaser but might be unable to ascertain the intention of a future purchaser, which would make it impossible to ascertain the tax to be charged if the wording was intended to cover such an intention. It also held that for the exemption to apply the vendor had to be aware of the intended use of the property at the time of sale and that the appellant had to show on the balance of probabilities that the vendor knew of the intention to use the property as a dwelling. As there was no evidence before the tribunal to show this, the supply to SEH was held to have been correctly charged at the standard rate. Following this case Customs said that where the immediate purchaser of a building (which the vendor had opted to tax) does not intend to use the building himself as a dwelling nor to convert the building into dwellings for sale or rent, their policy is that the vendor must account for VAT on the sale of the building. They accept that there are particular problems with auction sale where the vendor is not aware of the identity of the purchaser prior to the auction. They are reviewing this area. In the meantime they suggest that the purchaser should discuss with the vendor any problem he is facing prior to completion (Business Brief 8/01, 2 July 2001). Presumably they mean that if the purchaser does not wish to suffer VAT he must make his intentions known to the vendor.

**17.169** For some supplies made after 18 March 1997, where an election is nullified by 17.166(*a*) above, the person making the grant and the person to whom it is made can enter into a joint written declaration at or before the time of the grant that the election is to have effect. The grantee must intend, at the time the supply to him is made, to use the land for the purpose only of making a zero-rated supply by virtue of *VATA 1994, Sch 8 Group 5, item 1(b)*, i.e. converting a non-residential building into a dwelling or dwellings or into a building intended for use solely for a relevant residential purpose (see 17.6(1)(*b*) above) (*VATA 1994, Sch 10 para 2(2A)(2B)* introduced by *FA 1997, s 36*). Customs will allow VAT to be charged (and recovered by the purchaser) where the option to tax has been exercised in respect of a commercial building and the building is sold to a person who intends to convert it to residential use and make a zero-rated supply of the building (i.e. to sell it or let it on a long lease) and this will enable the vendor to recover VAT on the selling costs. The purchaser will of course be able to recover the VAT only if he ultimately makes a zero-rated supply of the building. To benefit from this concession, a vendor needs the co-operation of the purchaser, as he cannot force him to pay VAT that is not legally due. It should not be assumed that such consent will be automatically forthcoming as the election will obviously have an adverse cash flow effect for the purchaser. This gives statutory effect to an extra-statutory concession that applied from 12 February 1996.

**17.170** From 19 March 1997 the election cannot take a supply out of exemption if the grant giving rise to it was made by a developer of the land (see 17.171below) and at the time of the grant it was the intention or expectation of either the grantor, or a person responsible for financing the grantor's development of the land for exempt use (see 17.173 below), that the land would become 'exempt land' (see 17.178 below) (either immediately or eventually and whether by reason of the grant or of some other transaction) or, if it was already exempt land, that it would continue (for a period at least) to be such land. (*VATA 1994, Sch 10 para 2(3AA)* inserted by *FA 1997, s 37(2)*, *FA 1997, s 37(4)*).

**17.171** A developer is not defined. That probably does not matter as the word does not bear its normal meaning; a grant made by any person in relation to land is regarded as a grant made by a developer of that land if:

(*a*) the land (or a building, or part of a building, on it) falls to be treated by that person as a capital item within the capital goods scheme (see 17.266 below), and

(*b*) the grant was made at a time falling within the asset's adjustment period under that scheme.

(*VATA 1994, Sch 10 para 3A(2)*).

**17.172** Accordingly *paragraph 2(3AA)* (see 17.170 above) will not apply to a grant made more than 10 years after the building was acquired or constructed by the owner or after a substantial alteration, extension or refurbishment. Where a development was initially zero-rated, the 10-year period starts only from the change of use, so in such a case the *paragraph* could apply to a grant up to 20 years after the building was constructed.

**17.173** A person is responsible for financing the grantor's development of the land for exempt use if he has provided finance for the development or has entered into any agreement, arrangement or understanding (even if not legally enforceable) to do so with the intention that (or in the expectation that) the land will become exempt land (or if it is already exempt land it will continue to be so for a period at least) (*VATA 1994, Sch 10 para 3A(3)*).

**17.174** All of the following (whether direct or indirect) constitute the provision of finance for this purpose:

(*a*) providing funds for meeting any part of the cost of the grantor's development of the land;

(*b*) procuring the provision of such funds by another;

(*c*) providing funds for discharging (in whole or part) any liability that has been incurred (or may be incurred) by any person for (or in connection with) the raising of funds to meet the costs of the grantor's development of the land; and

(*d*) procuring that any such liability will be discharged by another.

(*VATA 1994, Sch 10 para 3A(4)*).

**17.175** The provision of funds includes (but is not limited to):

(*a*) making a loan;

(*b*) guaranteeing a loan or giving security for a loan;

(*c*) providing any of the consideration for the issue of shares or securities which are issued wholly or partly to raise funds for the development; and

(*d*) a transfer of assets or value as a consequence of which any funds are made available for the purpose of the development.

(*VATA 1994, Sch 10 para 3A(5)*).

**17.176** An example of the width of this provision is given by *Winterthur Life UK Ltd (VTD 15785)*. Pension contributions by a partnership of insurance brokers were made to a Self-Invested Personal Pension Plan. It was intended that the pension plan would buy a property and lease it to the partnership. The VAT tribunal felt it obvious that the payment of pension contributions intended to provide pension benefits were 'transfers of assets' within 17.175(*d*). It made no difference that their purpose was to provide pensions or that they were not conditional on the trustees acquiring the property as 'the funds were clearly "made available" in consequence of the contributions'. It was also irrelevant that the contributions were not for the avoidance of tax in that both the contributions and the investment were planned before it was ever appreciated that there was a VAT problem.

**17.177** Reference in 17.170 above to the grantor's development of the land means the acquisition by him of an asset which consists of the land, or a building (or part of a building) on the land, and which (in relation to the grantor) is within the capital goods scheme (*VATA 1994, Sch 10 para 3A(6)*). The acquisition of an asset for this purpose includes its construction or reconstruction and the carrying out of any other works which cause it to be treated as a capital item, i.e. acquisition is used in the sense of 'comes to possess' rather than 'purchases' (*VATA 1994, Sch 10 para 3A(6)*).

**17.178** Exempt land is land which either

(*a*) the grantor, or

(*b*) a person responsible for financing the grantor's development of the land for exempt use, or

(*c*) a person connected with one within (*a*) or (*b*) above (within *ICTA 1988, s 839* – see Appendix 1)

occupies for exempt purposes (i.e. not wholly or mainly for eligible purposes) (*VATA 1994, Sch 10 para 3A(7)(14)*). It is understood that Customs interpret 'mainly' in this context as meaning at least 80%, but that is not a hard and fast rule. Occupation includes occupation jointly with one or more other persons and also occupation of part only of the land (*VATA 1994, Sch 10 para 3A(13)*). Land can be exempt land only during the owner's capital goods scheme adjustment period (*VATA 1994, Sch 10 para 3A(7)*).

**17.179** A person is only in occupation of land for eligible purposes if he is a taxable person and even then only to the extent that he uses it for the purpose of making fully taxable supplies (*VATA 1994, Sch 10 para 3A(8)(9)*). If a person occupies land in order to be able to use it for an eligible purpose at a later date, he is treated as already occupying it for that eligible purpose provided that he is not occupying it in the interim for some other purpose (*VATA 1994, Sch 10 para 3A(11)*). For example, if a fully taxable trader rents a factory to which he will move his business in six months' time, that is deemed to be use for an eligible purpose if it is left empty, but if he lets it temporarily (without opting to tax) the intended future use will not suffice to qualify the factory as being currently occupied for an eligible purpose. If the owner is not a taxable person but his supplies are treated for VAT purposes as made by someone else who is a taxable person, the owner and the taxable person are treated as a single person (*VATA 1994, Sch 10 para 3A(12)*). The most obvious (if not the only) example is where the owner is acting as a nominee for a taxable person.

**17.180** Occupation of land by a government department (or other body within *VATA 1994, s 41*, i.e. one exercising functions on behalf of a Minister of the Crown) is also occupation for an eligible purpose. So is occupation by a local authority (or another body falling within *VATA 1994, s 33*) except to the extent that it uses the land for the purposes of a business carried on by it (*VATA 1994, Sch 10 para 3A(10)*).

**17.181** There is a transitional relief. The disapplication of the option to tax does not apply to a supply arising from a relevant pre-commencement grant, namely one made before 26 November 1996, or made before 31 May 1997 in pursuance of a written agreement entered into before 26 November 1996 and on terms for which provision was made in that agreement and were fixed before 26 November 1996 (*FA 1997, s 37(5)(6)*).

**17.182** The option also did not apply to a grant to a connected person (within *ICTA 1988, s 839* – see Appendix 1) if it was made between 30 November 1994 and 26 November 1996 and both parties were not fully taxable persons (*VAT (Buildings and Land) Order 1994* (*SI 1994 No 3013*)). For this purpose a person was fully taxable if at the end of the prescribed accounting period in which the grant was made he was entitled to credit for input tax on all his supplies during that period (apart from any which was irrecoverable under *VATA 1994, s 25(7)*). This anti-avoidance provision was introduced to block 'lease and leaseback' schemes such as that used in *C & E Commrs v Robert Gordon's College* (see 17.165 above). However, its wording goes much wider. For example, it applied if a taxable property was transferred intra-group in the course of a group reorganisation made for sensible commercial reasons and the transferee company owned a number of properties not all of which have been opted in. Such transfers are not uncommon where a property investment group carries out developments. The property will frequently be owned by a separate company during the development phase but after completion, when the development risk is past, transferred to a group investment company for ease of administration.

**17.183** The Minister indicated to Parliament that there would be an extra-statutory concession to let out innocent cases from the 1994 legislation. Two concessions were in fact announced. A person could be treated as fully taxable if, at the end of the prescribed accounting period in which the grant was made, he was able to recover 80% or more of his input tax (or would have been able to do so were it not for other exempt supplies of land) (News Release 62/95). A small self-administered pension scheme could be treated as a fully taxable person irrespective of what proportion of its input tax it could recover (News Release 11/96). Both of these concessions were retrospective to 30 November 1994. It appears from the fact that Customs pursued *Winterthur Life* before the VAT tribunal (see 17.176) that by 1997 the concept of letting out the innocent had been abandoned.

**17.184** Although this was intended as an anti-avoidance provision, it had the side-effect of allowing a taxpayer to avoid an option to tax. He could grant an interest in the building to a connected person. That would be an exempt supply. There would not even be a clawback of the input tax previously claimed (Notice 742, para 8.4(b)). The connected person would not be bound by the transferor's option to tax provided that the two do not form a VAT group.

**17.185** The provisions referred to at 17.166 to 17.182 above do not mean that the election is invalid; merely that it is ineffective as far as such supplies are concerned. If the use of the building were subsequently to change, the election would take effect in relation to the new supplies. It should be noted that where part of an office building is used by a charity for relevant charitable purposes, the charity will nevertheless have to pay VAT if the landlord opts to bring the building into the VAT net. The reason for this is that it would place an undue burden on the landlord if he had to ascertain each quarter how much of the building was being used by the charity for relevant and how much for non-relevant purposes (Hansard, Standing Committee G, 16 May 1989, Col 92).

## Notification

**17.186** Notification of the election must be given to the local VAT office (see 17.188 below) and Customs must also be supplied with such other information as they may require. In *C & E Commrs v McMaster Stores (Scotland) Ltd (1995 STC 846)*, it was accepted that failure to notify the election meant that it was invalid. The London tribunal had previously taken a different line, since in both *Fencing Supplies Ltd (1993 VATTR 302) (VTD 10451)* and *Resource Maintenance Ltd (VTD 13204)* an election to waive exemption was held to be valid even though it had not been notified to the Commissioners. Prior to 1 March 1995 notification did not need to be given for any category of land or building specified in a Customs and Excise notice. Notice 742B, para 45 provides that notice need not be given where the total consideration for all the supplies for the buildings or land for which a person has opted is expected to be less than £20,000 in the next twelve months. Such an election continues in effect (without notification) after 1 March.

**17.187** In *Norbury Developments Ltd (VTD 14482)* the company bought land with planning permission for mainly residential development and resold it to a developer. It was charged VAT on its purchase but did not charge VAT on its sale. It subsequently sought to waive exemption but this was rejected by Customs. Customs refused relief for any of the input tax on the purchase as, no election having been made, the land was not used to make taxable supplies. The company contended that the land was clearly 'building land' which could not be exempted under *Article 13B(h)* of the *Sixth Directive*. The tribunal referred this point to the *European Court of Justice (Case C–136/97) (1999 STC 511)*, which held that a member state is entitled to exempt a supply of building land under *Article 28(3)(b)* of the *EC Sixth Directive* (which permits the retention of pre *Sixth Directive* exemptions) notwithstanding that since the adoption of the directive it has introduced an option to tax and has reduced the scope of that exemption. Accordingly this confirms that even supplies of building land are exempt unless the option to tax is exercised (see Business Brief 22/96).

**17.188** Notification of the election must normally be given to the local VAT office within 30 days from the date the election is made (*VATA 1994, Sch 10 para 3(6)(b)*). Customs have power to extend this period. In practice people are likely to send an election to Customs immediately it is made. Indeed, although the *Act* draws a distinction between the election and its notification, in most cases the letter to Customs is likely to be the only document brought into being to evidence the election. The election must be accompanied by such information as Customs may require. In some cases the prior written permission of Customs is needed before an election can be made (see 17.162 above). The distinction between electing and notifying the election is well illustrated by the VAT tribunal decision in *Blythe Limited Partnership (VTD 16011)*. The partnership took over 16 properties from a previous partnership. It intended to elect in respect of four of them. The solicitor to one of the parties wrongly notified Customs that the partnership had elected in respect of all 16. The tribunal found as a fact that the partnership had only elected in respect of the four properties. Customs contended that the partnership was bound by the notification but the tribunal held that such notification had no effect in relation to the other 12 properties as it was a purported notification of an election that had never been made. Customs have since said that they fully agree with the tribunal's approach (Business Brief 16/99).

**17.189** It was held in *Chalegrove Properties Ltd (VTD 17151)* that notification of an election is given at the time that it is posted to Customs. In that case the company gave notice of its option to tax on 21 August 1996 and sold its property on 30 August. The tribunal thought that the normal rule that service is effected when the letter would be delivered in the normal course of post is displaced by a contrary intention in the legislation, namely that it would require purchasers in a competitive auction to despatch notification of an election in advance of the auction (see *Higher Education Statistics Agency v C & E Commrs 2000 STC 332* – 17.281). Customs have said that they accept this decision. It is sufficient where property is purchased as a TOGC (see 17.280) that on the relevant date the buyer has properly addressed, pre-paid and posted the letter. They suggest retaining evidence of posting. Where this has been done in the last three years and TOGC treatment was refused they will now accept that the transaction was a TOGC (Business Brief 11/01 21 Aug 2001). The lack of formality required for an election is emphasised by *Classic Furniture (Newport) Ltd (VTD 10451)*. The company purchased a property with completion on 31 July 1999. On 29 July the sole director became aware that the vendor proposed to charge VAT. He contacted his professional advisors who told him that he would have to elect to waive exemption in order to recover the VAT. Based on this and the oral evidence of the professional advisor that he had given the advice and of the director that he had intended to accept it, the tribunal held that the company had opted to tax. The company had a further problem that the option had not been notified in the 30-day period. It was not until 10 November, following a VAT control visit and a resultant letter from Customs rejecting relief for the input tax, that notification was given. The tribunal held that the reasons that led Customs to reject the application to accept late notification were unjustified because they had misunderstood the facts. It effectively told Customs to accept the late notification unless it had other reasons not to do so. It is doubtful if the tribunal has power to usurp in this manner the discretion given to Customs.

**17.190** The election normally takes effect from the beginning of the day on which it is made, not from the date that it is received by Customs. The taxpayer can specify a later effective date in the election, in which case it will not take effect until that date. The election can be made at any time but cannot have retrospective effect except where it is made in the circumstances outlined in 17.202 below. It is understood that in practice Customs have allowed elections to be backdated where there has been a genuine error in not notifying Customs and where a trader initially intended to sell a standard-rated freehold but market conditions forced him to lease the property (Tolley's Practical VAT, June 1991, p 47).

**17.191** In the past it was possible to elect by accident! *Fencing Supplies Ltd (1993 VATTR 302) (VTD 10451)* charged VAT on rents, apparently due to a misunderstanding of the VAT position. Subsequently, on granting a new lease to the same tenant it confirmed that it did not propose to elect to waive exemption. It did not charge VAT on the premium it received for the new lease. The VAT tribunal held that by demanding and receiving VAT to which it would only be entitled if it had waived exemption, the company had clearly indicated a decision to waive exemption. This 'decision' was not altered by the fact that it was based on a misunderstanding. The tribunal's decision in that case was followed by a subsequent tribunal in *Resource Maintenance Ltd (VTD 13204)*, but was not followed (or even referred to) in *McMaster Stores (Scotland) Ltd* (see 17.186 above), where the CS held that an election that was not notified to Customs was invalid. In an earlier case, *Hi-Wire Ltd (VTD 6204)*, the company intended to opt to tax in 1989 but did not notify Customs until September 1990. The VAT tribunal held that the election did not become effective until September 1990. This may be because there was no evidence to establish an earlier intention to elect. The law was changed from 1 March 1995 to make the validity of the election conditional upon notification so these cases are probably no longer operative except where an election was made before that date but not notified to Customs.

**17.192** In *Euro Properties (Scotland) Ltd (VTD 15291)* the receipt by the purchaser of a tax invoice (issued after the vendor had deregistered) did not help. The tribunal firmly retorted that 'notice cannot be deemed to have been given'. To add insult to injury, it told the poor purchaser that a contract for the purchase of property would normally be exempt, so a tax invoice in relation to property 'could not be regarded as a standard tax invoice' and therefore he should have checked it. This seems harsh. If he had checked it, it is unlikely that he would have discovered that the vendor had failed to notify his election to Customs.

**17.193** One taxpayer claimed that the *EC Sixth Directive* allowed the deduction of input tax incurred before the election was made and so the bar on retrospectiveness was ineffective (*Lawson Mardon Group Pension Scheme (VTD 10231)*). The VAT tribunal disagreed. Until the election is made the property is not being used in making taxable supplies, and so earlier input tax cannot be attributed to any such supply.

**17.194** Surprisingly, no specific form of election is prescribed. Customs say that it must contain the taxpayer's name, address and VAT registration number. The *Act* says that it must specify the land or a description of the land to which it is to apply (*VATA 1994, Sch 10 para 3(2)*).

## Miscellaneous

**17.195** Prior to 1 March 1995 the election to bring rent and other supplies – including subsequent disposals of the building – within the VAT net was irrevocable (*VATA 1994, Sch 10 para 3(6)* as originally enacted). For most practical purposes it still is. Revocation is now possible in two circumstances:

(*a*) within three months of making the election, but only if no tax has become chargeable, no credit for input tax has been claimed, and no grant constituting a transfer as a going concern has taken place, i.e. the election can only be revoked if it has not yet had any effect – which is likely to be a rare occurrence; and

(*b*) more than 20 years after it has effect – which cannot occur until after 1 April 2009.

Revocation requires the consent of Customs, and in the case of (*b*) such consent cannot be given retrospectively (*VATA 1994, Sch 10 para 3(4)(5)* as substituted by *VAT (Buildings and Land) Order 1995* (*SI*

*1995 No 279) Article 4*). A Customs' consultation paper of July 1993 suggested that the option might be revocable after ten years, so this appears to be a rare instance of the bulk of consultees protesting that Customs did not want to tax them heavily enough!

**17.196** A person can make as many elections as he likes for different buildings or areas of land. However, he cannot elect in relation to part only of a building (except where his entire interest in the building is in that part only). For this purpose a building also includes all land within its curtilage (*para* 3*(3)*). Furthermore, from 1 March 1995, buildings linked internally or by a covered walkway, and all parades, precincts and complexes consisting of a number of units grouped around a fully enclosed concourse must be taken to be a single building even if they would otherwise not be (*VATA 1994, Sch 10 para 3(3)* as amended by the *VAT (Buildings & Land) Order 1995* (*SI 1995 No 279*)). Prior to that date, parades, precincts and all complexes were treated as a single building (*VATA 1994, Sch 10 para 3(3)* as originally enacted).

**17.197** This creates a large number of uncertainties which may need to be resolved in advance with Customs, or perhaps decided by a VAT tribunal. For example, do two shops on different sides of the High Street and three hundred yards apart become a single building if the local authority pedestrianises the street? If building A is linked by a walkway to building B and building B by another walkway to building C, are A and C a single building if the owner owns both A and C but not B? When does a row of shops constitute a parade? Customs have suggested that they are a parade only if they form an architectural unity. Can two buildings be regarded as a single building if they are owned by different companies which are both in the same VAT group? In *C & E Commrs v Kingfisher plc (1994 STC 63)* the QB held that *VATA 1994, s 43* intended to treat all the companies in a VAT group as a single person, so Customs may well regard the two as a single building in such circumstances, particularly because treating the two as separate buildings tends to cast doubt on the efficacy of 17.160 above.

**17.198** Prior to 1 March 1995, an election in relation to agricultural land had to extend to all adjoining agricultural land owned by the taxpayer or in which he otherwise had an interest. Again, the position where there was a group registration was unclear, as the representative member did not appear to be deemed to have an interest in land held by other group members. It did not need to extend to agricultural land which was separated from the elected land by non-agricultural land unless such non-agricultural land was simply a road, railway, river or similar passageway through the land. Nor did it need to extend to land in a different ownership provided that the owner of the elected land had no interest in, or right over, or licence to occupy it and, if the electing owner was a company, no relevant associate had any such interest, right or licence either (*VATA 1994, Sch 10 para 3(4)(5)* as originally enacted). The meaning of relevant associate is considered at

17.160 above. The repeal of this rule will not affect land brought into tax by a pre-1 March 1995 election in relation to other land.

**17.199** The VAT tribunal in *A J White (VTD 15388)* held that the election even extended to goodwill. The property for which exemption had been waived was a public house. Mrs White contracted to buy it for £140,000 of which £7,000 was allocated to goodwill, £8,000 to fixtures and fittings and the balance to the property. The business was acquired on a transfer of a going concern. The vendor had opted to waive exemption but Mrs White did not do so. The effect was that the property itself attracted VAT but none of the other assets acquired did so (see 17.280 below). It appears that the vendor had assumed – wrongly – either that Mrs White had opted to waive exemption or that the TOGC rules applied to the entire transfer. He had not charged any VAT. Nevertheless Mrs White claimed as input tax 7/47ths of the £140,000. She claimed first that, even though the agreement specifically stated that she would carry on the same kind of business as the vendor, the transaction was not a TOGC at all. Customs challenged this, also claiming that

(*a*) only 56% of the premises was given over to commercial use, the remainder (the first floor flat) being residential and thus non-business, and

(*b*) the part of the price attributed to fixtures and fittings did not attract VAT because of the TOGC rules.

The election referred to 'the premises known as the Dog and Duck'. The tribunal felt that this must mean the whole of the property comprised in the registered title. This included the flat. That was not used exclusively for residential purposes as it was a condition of the licence that there should be a live-in manager, and in any event was not a dwelling as it was not self-contained living accommodation. Most of the fittings, being trade fixtures, did not form part of the land and would thus not be covered by the election (but landlord's fixtures would be). Goodwill is capable of existing as an intangible asset. However in some cases, in the tribunal's view, it is not severable from the land. That was the position here. The goodwill is an attribute of the venue and attaches to the land. Accordingly the election to waive exemption 'covered the goodwill so long as the trade of public house was conducted from the Dog and Duck'. This decision is a potential nightmare. One man's VAT recoverability is another man's liability to Customs. If expressly attributing a separate value to goodwill in the agreement will not be recognised as establishing that it is a separate asset, and goodwill may be part of the land but equally may not, the vendor of any property-based business will be vulnerable unless he finds a way to ensure that the purchaser has properly opted to tax the premises.

**17.200** A property owner does not have to wait until he lets a property before he makes the election. He can do so immediately he acquires the building or land. If a developer expects to sell or let the building within three years of construction, he should be able to register for VAT as an intending trader (if he is not already registered) as he expects to make taxable supplies. If he is building for his own occupation he may well already be VAT-registered. In any other case, such as where the property is being developed as a long-term property investment, it appears vital to at least register, if not make the election, prior to incurring any development costs, even architects or planning fees, as input tax on services supplied more than six months prior to registration is not reclaimable (*VAT Regulations 1995, SI 1995 No 2518, Reg 111(2)(c)*). Indeed, Customs have indicated that they will not allow registration of a developer of a potentially exempt building unless the election is made at the same time.

**17.201** Customs have always taken the view that if the building is demolished the election falls away. The basis of this is that the election is in relation to the building. Although in law this includes the land on which it stands once the building ceases to exist the land is a different asset and a fresh decision as to whether or not to elect can be made. Doubt has been cast on this by the ECJ case of *Finanzamt Goslar v Breitsohl (2001 STC 355) (Case C-400/98)*. Mrs Breitsohl commissioned a construction company to construct a building on land that she owned and which she intended to use as a vehicle repair workshop. As building costs escalated she became unable to finance its completion so the building company ceased work. In November 1990 she sold the building works to a third party for a price including VAT and in December 1990 sold the land to the same purchaser without VAT. The German tax authorities claimed that Mrs Breitsohl was not a taxable person as she had not carried out any economic activity. They sought to distinguish the case from *Intercommunale voor Zeewaterontzilting* (see 17.262) on the grounds that Mrs Breitsohl had no legitimate expectation of an input tax deduction as she never had the status of a taxable person. The ECJ dismissed this, holding that 'the right to deduct the VAT paid on transactions carried out with a view to the realisation of a planned economic activity still exists even where the tax authority is aware, from the time of the first tax assessment, that the economic activity envisaged, which was to give rise to taxable transactions, will not be taken up'. The German government secondly argued that as *Article 13C* of the *Sixth Directive* expressly allows member states to fix the details of the use of the option to tax the question as to whether a taxpayer can exercise the option solely in relation to buildings, to the exclusion of the land on which they stand, is a question of national law. The ECJ rejected that concept. *Article 4(3)(a)* of the *Directive*, which refers to the 'supply . . . of buildings or parts of buildings and the land on which they stand' needs to be interpreted in a uniform manner in all member states. As that *Article* distinguishes between building land on one hand and buildings and the land on which they stand on the other the court concluded that for VAT purposes buildings (or parts of buildings) and the land on which they stand cannot be dissociated from each other. The option to tax must therefore relate inseparably to the two. It seems a logical conclusion from this that the option must apply both to the building and to the land so that the destruction of the building would leave the option still attaching to the land.

**17.202** Prior to 1 January 1992, where the election was made, input tax on supplies or importations made before the first day on which it took effect could not normally be reclaimed (*VATA 1994, Sch 10 para 2(4)*). There was an important exception. Input tax incurred on supplies in relation to the building prior to making the election could be reclaimed if the taxpayer did not make any exempt supplies in respect of the building prior to the election taking effect (*VATA 1994, Sch 10 para 2(5)(a)*). In other words, if the election was made before the building was first let or sold, input tax incurred while the building was empty or being constructed could normally be relieved – provided that the person was registered for VAT when the input tax was incurred (or within six months thereafter).

**17.203** Furthermore, for this purpose supplies (such as the receipt of exempt rents) made in the period 1 April 1989 to 31 July 1989 could be ignored if no exempt supplies were made prior to 1 April 1989 and all of the supplies in the April/July period would have been taxable (zero-rated) under the old rules (*VATA 1994, Sch 10 para 2(5)(b)*). This preserved the right to deduct input tax where rents – or, apparently, sale proceeds – would have been zero-rated as arising from the grant of a major interest by a person constructing a building. It would obviously have been unreasonable to allow a person to recover input tax under the old law up to 31 March and under the new law after 31 July, without allowing recovery in the interim period. For this transitional relief to apply, an election to tax had to take effect from 1 August 1989 and the input tax being reclaimed had to be either attributable to supplies made (or deemed to be made under the Regulations) by the taxpayer after 1 April 1989 which would have been taxable under the old rules, or to supplies in the period April to July which would have been exempt under the old rules by virtue of being the grant, etc. of an interest in land. Input tax incurred in the interim period could be recovered even though the rents up to 31 July were exempt (*VATA 1994, Sch 10 para 2(5)–(7)*).

**17.204** Customs have said that where, because of a tenant's default, the landlord collects the rent from the sub-tenant under *Law of Distress Amendment Act 1908, s 6*, this does not affect the VAT position. The supply is still made by the landlord to the tenant and a separate supply by the tenant to the sub-tenant. If the option to tax has been exercised the landlord can issue a VAT invoice only to the tenant, and the sub-tenant who wishes to reclaim VAT which he had paid to the landlord can do so only if he holds a VAT invoice from the tenant (Business Brief 17/93). This seems reasonable. Customs' approach suggests that *section 6*, in effect, merely provides a collection machinery for the money; it does not create a new legal relationship.

**17.205** Where the option to tax is exercised and a grant in relation to the land would be taken to have been made (in whole or in part) before the time the election takes effect, the election is to have effect in relation to supplies to which the grant gives rise which are treated as taking place after that time, as if the grant had been made after that time (*VAT 1994, Sch 10 para 3(5A)*). Accordingly the reference to grants being exempt or taxable must be construed as references to supplies to which a grant gives rise being exempt or taxable (*VATA 1994, Sch 10 para 3(5B)*). What this is apparently saying is merely that, in order to ensure that supplies made after the election to tax rents, etc. are taxable, the assumption must be made that the lease was entered into after that time. The reason for the clarification is that the draftsman has used the word 'grant' in *Sch 10 para 2(9)* and *3(9)* to mean a supply in pursuance of the grant. It might have been clearer to have substituted a different word for 'grant' in those two places rather than introduce this deeming to neutralise the effect of the draftsman having intended the word to have a different meaning to its normal use.

**17.206** Prior to 1 March 1995, where it was necessary to determine the time of a supply, a rent payment which related wholly to a period beginning after an election comes into force was deemed to be in respect of a supply taking place on the first day of the period to which it relates (*VATA 1994, Sch 10 para 4(3)*).

**17.207** Rent for a period which bridged the date the election took effect had to be apportioned and the taxable part treated as relating to a supply made on the date the election takes effect (*VATA 1994, Sch 10 para 4(2)*).

**17.208** If a supply took place after an election took effect but the first rent payment pursuant to it covered a period beginning prior to the election, the rent was again apportioned so that only the part attributable to the period after the election took effect was taxable (*VATA 1994, Sch 10 para 4(4)*).

**17.209** To minimise administration, it is possible to issue a single tax invoice at the beginning of each year to cover all the rental payments due in the coming year. This must show the VAT-exclusive amount of rent, the dates on which each payment is due, the rate of VAT and the VAT payable. If the rate of tax changes, a new VAT invoice must be issued for the balance of the year. Where this procedure is adopted the tax point will be the due date of each payment or the date of actual payment if earlier (*VAT Regulations 1995, Reg 85*).

## Certain Developments Commencing between 31 July 1989 and 28 February 1995

**17.210** The charge to tax in relation to developments commencing between 31 July 1989 and 28 February 1995 is considered at 8.38 to 8.57 above.

## Service Charges

**17.211** An area that frequently causes problems is service charges payable under leases. Unfortunately this is an area where the legal status of the payment is often difficult to ascertain and Customs have made a number of concessions. Whilst, in general, concessions are helpful, there is in this area a tendency for local Customs officers to want to apply them as a matter of course even where they are not necessarily in the interests of the landlord levying the service charge or the tenant paying it. It is accordingly sometimes necessary to remember that a taxpayer is entitled to be taxed in accordance with the application of the law to his particular lease, whatever Customs' normal treatment of similar transactions may be. Many of the problems that have arisen in the past in relation to service charges in relation to commercial property will disappear if the option to tax (see 17.158 above) is exercised. However, as many landlords are reluctant to exercise this option, they are likely to continue to exist in practice for some time.

**17.212** Normally a service charge will be nothing more than a method of calculating the rent payable under the lease, i.e. the rent will be the aggregate of a fixed (and normally periodically reviewed) sum plus an additional amount varying with the expenditure on providing the specific services which the lease obliges the landlord to supply. This will always be the position where the lease requires the service charge to be paid as additional rent. It may not legally always be so where it is payable under a covenant in the lease. In such cases the lease may need to be studied carefully to ascertain whether the service charge is part of the consideration for the use of the premises or if it is consideration for the covenant by the landlord to provide specific services. If it is the latter then legally it will be liable to VAT at 17½%. However, Customs, probably in an attempt to adopt a standard policy towards service charges, ignore the legal niceties and say that provided the service charge 'is connected with the external fabric or the common parts of the building or estate as opposed to the demised areas of the property of the individual occupants' and it is paid for by all the occupants through a common service charge, it attracts the same VAT status as the rent (Notice 742, paras 11.2 and 12.1). In effect they regard the service charge as additional rent regardless of how it is reserved under the lease.

**17.213** One area where this does cause problems in practice is with serviced offices, i.e. where a person lets out on a short-term basis the use of an office, normally with shared use of support staff such as a receptionist, telephonist and secretary. It might be thought that as this is very similar to a hotel, the VAT treatment would be the same. Unfortunately it is not. Instead Customs' approach is to treat it as a straightforward lease. This can result in a significant loss of input tax relief. Most of the customers are likely to be VAT-registered traders who could reclaim input tax on the fee they pay. Unfortunately such things as repairs, equipment leasing for shared equipment, reception and switchboard, and costs of the support staff are regarded by Customs as costs of the 'common parts', and the proportion of the daily charge relating to such items as part of the rent – and thus exempt from VAT (C & E Notice 742, para 5.6). In most such cases it will be attractive to exercise the option to tax rents for the future. If a separate charge is made for the services of the receptionist and telephonist, it is unlikely that Customs could deem this to be part of the consideration for the supply of the premises. This might therefore be an alternative way to turn that part of the charge into a taxable supply. The VAT tribunal in *Suffolk Heritage Housing Association Ltd (VTD 13713)* held that, where a separate charge for heating based on the estimated cost of the heating supply was made to tenants of sheltered accommodation, this was sufficient to secure zero-rating; the heating was not an integral part of the exempt rent. Customs said in February 1996 that they were appealing against this decision. The appeal has not yet been reported or, presumably, heard. In any event, Customs consider that the decision was reliant on the specific form of the tenancy agreement. All the tenants took the heating supply. Although in theory they need have not done so, Customs did not consider that this was a real option – if it had been, they would have accepted that the heating was a separate supply.

**17.214** The decision of the tribunal in *Tower Hamlets Housing Action Trust (VTD 17308)* casts doubt on the traditional Customs' approach. The issue in dispute was whether there should be an apportionment for the supply of telephone equipment and photocopying services from the supply of office accommodation under a tenancy agreement. The tribunal thought the matter to be one of impression. As far as the telephones were concerned, the payment would not depend on the amount of use by the tenant of the telephone. They therefore did not regard the provision of telephone equipment as an aim in itself but as a means of better enjoying the principal service of the provision of the property.

'As a matter of commercial reality, one would expect to find telephone equipment in a serviced office just as one would expect to find furniture. It is an essential feature of a serviced office that telephones are provided.'

The telephone was accordingly part of the exempt supply of accommodation. Photocopying on the other hand was different. It would have been paid for per copy. It is difficult to see how such a supply could be ancillary to the supply of the accommodation and is an aim in itself that has no connection with the property.

**17.215** Whilst Customs' approach is often beneficial to tenants, it gives rise to two problem areas. Firstly, if services are supplied to a tenant's individual flat or office, Customs regard that part of the service charge as a separate supply from the accommodation. The effect is that they consider that VAT at 17½% needs to be added to that part of the service charge (assuming of course that the landlord's total supplies exceed the registration limit) except to the extent that it relates to zero-rated items such as electricity when the benefit of the zero-rating can be passed on to the tenant. Where a charge to the tenant for services in his individual office is specifically linked to his usage of those services, this treatment is probably correct regardless of how the charge is described in the lease, as the landlord will either be making a separate supply of the services or will be making a mixed supply of the services and the accommodation – which for VAT purposes would need to be broken down into its component elements. Where, however, the services supplied to individual offices or flats are not based on usage, it is most probable that the landlord is making a composite supply of serviced accommodation and that the entire consideration for that supply is rent. This was accepted by the VAT tribunal in *Business Enterprises (UK) Ltd (1988 VATTR 160) (VTD 3161)* in relation to the use of furniture. In practice it would be fairly unusual for a landlord to provide services to individual offices without charging separately for them – with the exception of heating which is zero-rated in any event and would thus not generate a VAT charge. This difficulty is therefore more apparent than real, although it is a major problem in relation to the use of furniture.

**17.216** Difficulties can however still arise in apportioning the expenditure between the exempt and taxable supplies. In *Sovereign Street Workspace Ltd (VTD 9550)*, where Customs contended that maintenance of the property related wholly to the exempt licence to occupy, the VAT tribunal accepted that part could be attributed to the taxable supplies because part of the building was used to provide taxable supplies such as the telephone answering service, mail handling and an information and advice service supplied to tenants. Despite this normal approach, Customs seem to have successfully argued in *First Base Properties Ltd (VTD 11598)* that cleaning of both individual offices and common parts of a building were part of the exempt supply of the premises.

**17.217** The second problem is that whilst the tenant of residential premises is, in general, content for the service charge in respect of common parts to be treated as rent, the tenant of commercial premises may well be unenthusiastic. The tenant will be left bearing the VAT suffered on his share of the service charge expenditure – but will not be able to treat it as input tax as he would have done had he incurred the expenditure direct. Accordingly, where all of the tenants are themselves taxable persons a way needs to be found to enable the service charge to be a taxable supply. Whilst this increases the tenant's initial outlay – as it increases the payment he must make to the landlord – the recovery of the tax from Customs leaves him overall better off.

**17.218** One way that ought to achieve this is for the lease specifically to separate the charge for services from that for accommodation. However, the practice of providing for a service charge to be paid as additional rent is designed to make it easier for the landlord to enforce payment and it may be unattractive to him to forfeit this benefit. Another possibility is for the service charge not to be payable to the landlord at all but to a third party, which could be a subsidiary of the landlord. However, care would need to be taken with the wording of the relevant provision to ensure that the subsidiary is itself providing the relevant services, and not merely making arrangements for their provision. It would also probably weaken the landlord's right to enforce payment and may also cause a nuisance if the landlord sells his interest in the shopping centre, industrial estate or whatever.

**17.219** Paragraph 5.4 of Notice 742 (March 2002 edition) which relates to commercial premises states,

'if you are responsible for providing services to the occupants of a building in which you have no interest, your services will always be standard-rated as they are not part of the supply of the accommodation itself.'

The previous edition used a somewhat different wording:

'if you are the person legally responsible for the provision of services to occupants (but you are not the landlord) your supply is to the occupants. The service charges they pay you will normally be standard rated'.

If the lease provides for the service charge to be paid to a separate company which will itself provide the services, the supplies by that company should fall into this head. However paragraph 5.4 also says that,

'if you are the person legally responsible for the provision of services to occupants and your contract is to arrange for the services and collect the service charge on the landlord's behalf as a managing agent, then your supply is to the landlord'.

If the landlord covenants to provide the services under the lease this limitation will probably apply (although, as indicated at 17.212, it does not necessarily reflect the law). The tenants will of course want the landlord bound to provide the services so it may not be practicable to put the responsibility on a management company, although there is no tax reason why the landlord should not guarantee the management company's obligations. It may alternatively be possible to structure the service charge arrangements in such a way that the landlord – or more likely his managing agent – incurs the service charge expenditure as agent for the tenants. This will enable him to pass on to the tenants the right to recover the input tax paid. Customs stated in 1973 that even where such an arrangement was not spelled out in the lease, the landlord could elect to treat himself as agent for the tenants in respect of service charge expenditure provided that he maintained a separate bank account for each property and the service charge was designed solely to recover expenditure (C&E Press Release 21 March 1973). The landlord would, however, need to register himself as agent, so this method is probably only practical where the service charge expenditure is above the registration limit. As Customs do not mention this method in their Notice 742, it may no longer be acceptable and should not be adopted without the prior agreement of Customs.

**17.220** In the past little consideration has been given to this problem, particularly as there was little incentive for the landlord to seek to provide the benefit of recoverability to his tenants. However, the increase in the size of service charges in recent years and the broadening of the scope of the services that the landlord may provide in, for example, a shopping centre, resulting in a far greater proportion of the expenditure bearing VAT than before, has made tenants far more conscious of their loss of input tax relief. At the same time tenants are increasingly looking on service charges and rent together as the cost of occupying the property, so that anything that the landlord can do to reduce the cost of the service charge is likely to lessen tenant resistance to a rent increase. It is accordingly in the landlord's own interest to seek to eliminate the tenants' loss of input tax relief.

**17.221** The problem has been aggravated by the decision in *Trustees of Nell Gwynn House Maintenance Fund v C & E Commrs (1999 STC 79)* although that case was decided on the wording of the leases used. The service charge of a block of flats was payable to trustees. The dispute was whether the trustees were obliged to account for VAT on the provision by them of staff. It seems to have been accepted either that VAT was not chargeable in relation to other items or that the input tax on other items equalled the output tax leaving nothing to be assessed. In the House of Lords it was agreed that there is a distinction between the case where A pays B for services to be provided by B and the case where A puts B in funds so that B can arrange for C to provide the services. In the first it is the provision of the services which constitutes the supply. In the second it is the arranging for services to be supplied. Here the trustees were supplying the staff, as they employed them. The fact that they did so as trustees did not prevent them from contracting as employers with the staff to carry out the services and so themselves supplying those services to the tenant. The House of Lords also rejected an argument based on *Glawe Spiel und Unterhaltungsgerate Aufstellungsgesellschaft mbH & Co KG v Finanzamt Hamburg-Barmbek-Uhlenhorst (Case C–38/93) (1994 STC 543)* that the consideration for the services provided by the trustees was not the gross amount receivable by the trustees but only the fee that they were entitled to retain for themselves. It felt that the commercial reality is that when the trustees take the money from the maintenance fund to pay the staff to carry out the trustees' obligations under the lease, they receive that money beneficially in consideration of the services provided. Furthermore, once it was accepted that the trustees employed the staff, the amount received by the trustees could not be 'expenses paid out in the name and for the account of' the tenants excludable under *Article 11(3)(c)* of the *EC Sixth Directive*.

**17.222** From 1 April 1994 various mandatory service charges paid by the occupants of residential property (including the owner of a freehold interest) are, by concession, treated as exempt even though the payment is made to a separate management company or the service was otherwise not supplied by the landlord. The charges concerned are for the upkeep of the common areas of an estate or block of flats, the provision of a warden, superintendent, caretaker or people performing a similar function connected with the day-to-day running of the estate or block, and the general maintenance of the exterior – including painting or window cleaning of individual dwellings if the residents cannot refuse this. The concession does not extend to optional services supplied personally to a resident, such as carpet cleaning and shopping. Nor does it apply to non-domestic property or to holiday accommodation (Business Brief 3/94 and Notice 742, para 5.10). A taxpayer does not have to take the benefit of a concession. He is entitled to be taxed in accordance with the law.

**17.223** In the *Nell Gwynn* case, the trustees submitted as an alternative that the grant of the lease and the provision for the supply of maintenance services all formed part of a single economic transaction and the trustees, like the landlord, should be treated as the grantor so that their part of the supply would be exempt. The House of Lords rejected this argument (which was based on *Article 13(B)(b)* of the *EC Sixth Directive*) as the letting of the properties was not done by the trustees and although there was a close link between the letting of the properties and the receipt of the service charges, the supply of the services was by a different taxpayer and was quite distinct from the exclusion under the Directive for the letting of the land. In the light of the concession referred to above, introduced five years before the House of Lords hearing, it is a little surprising that Customs were so insistent on not applying that concession to earlier years.

**17.224** *Clarence Holdings Ltd (VTD 17289)* dealt with timeshares. The company had set up a trust to which it had granted a long lease. Under this the company reserved the right to require the trustees to grant weekly occupancy licenses (the timeshares). The company sells to an owner such a weekly licence to occupy. The owner automatically also becomes a member of an Owners Club. The Owners Club undertakes the maintenance and administration of the estate for which it makes an annual charge to the individual owners. It was held that the annual maintenance fee was not part of the consideration for the right to occupy. It was a separate supply of services provided by the Owners Club. It is curious that Customs took this case to the tribunal as it seems hard to distinguish from the *Nell Gwyn* case.

**17.225** In *Canary Wharf Ltd (VTD 14513)* the company was head-lessee of an office building. Most of its premises were sublet on 25-year occupational underleases. A management company (a member of Canary Wharf Ltd's VAT group) was a party to the underleases. These required the management company to provide services to the common parts and the estate and to manage the car parking. In return the under-lessees covenanted with the management company to pay service charges. The management company had its own offices and employed over 230 staff. It invoiced the under-lessees direct. Customs contended that the management services were part of a single (exempt) composite supply made by the landlord. This was rejected by the VAT tribunal which held that the management company provided a separate (taxable) supply. It also felt that the group registration did not affect the fact that the supplies were in reality by the management company to the under-lessees. The tribunal seems to have been influenced by the obvious substance of the management company, although it is unclear why that should affect the legal analysis.

## Miscellaneous

### Definitions

**17.226** Many of the definitions and caveats in the *Notes* to *Sch 8, Group 5* and *Schedule 9, Group 1* also apply in relation to *Schedule 10*. Those which do not apply in *Group 5* are *Notes 7–9* (non-residential building), *11* (apportionment), *13–18* (various caveats) and *20–24*. Those which do not apply in *Group 1* are *Notes 3–14* (*VATA 1994, 10 Sch 9*).

### Do-It-Yourself Builders

**17.227** *VATA 1994, s 35* enables tax to be refunded on the supply of goods to persons constructing new homes otherwise than in the course of a business. The work must be lawful. (*VATA 1994, s 35(1), (1A)*). The provision also applies to buildings to be used for relevant residential purposes (see 17.28 above) and relevant charitable purposes (see 17.34 above) which are built by charities and voluntary bodies. Customs sought to deny relief to *Newtonbutler Playgroup Ltd (VTD 13741)*, a charity, on the basis that the provision of playgroup facilities amounted to a business and was thus not a relevant charitable purpose. Customs' view was based on the fact that parents were invited to make a weekly contribution towards the cost of refreshments. The tribunal accepted that this was not consideration for admission to the building and allowed the refund claimed. In *Mr D L & Mrs G D Rawson (VTD 7921)*, a VAT tribunal held that the supply of a fence surrounding the house qualified for zero-rating as being in the course of constructing the dwelling house, but the supply of further fences to keep out deer did not so qualify, as the expense had to be related to the house in some way and not made for other purposes. An interesting case is that *of Shinewater Association Football Club (VTD 12938)*. The club charged a small annual membership fee to cover its administrative costs. It used a playing field owned by the National Playing Fields Association. The club arranged for a new pavilion to be constructed, funded partly by a loan from the NPFA and partly from funds raised by the club. Most of the construction work was by club members on a voluntary basis. The club, and others licenced by the NPFA to use the ground, was entitled to occupy the pavilion under a licence from the NPFA. The club claimed a refund under *VATA 1994, s 35* on the materials used for construction of the pavilion. Customs rejected this on the grounds both that the supply was made in the course of a business and that the pavilion was not intended for use solely for a relevant charitable purpose. The tribunal allowed the club's appeal. The construction was undertaken in furtherance of the ownership rights of NPFA, not as part of Shinewater's business, and the pavilion facility was substantially provided to the local community in the same way as a village hall.

**17.228** From 29 April 1996 the provisions were extended to the conversion of a non-residential building (or non-residential part of a building) into a building designed as a dwelling (or dwellings), a building intended for use solely for relevant residential purposes or something that would fall into one of those categories if different parts of the building were treated as separate buildings (*VATA 1994, s 35(1A)(c), (1D)*). The notes to *VATA 1994, Sch 8 Group 5* (see 17.6 to 17.64 above) apply for the purposes of this provision. *Mr & Mrs G D King (VTD 15961)* were denied relief for converting a derelict property into their family home. They contended that, before becoming derelict, the building had been used as a commercial guest house, but it was held that it had been used as a home for elderly guests (not a nursing home) which was held to be a relevant residential purpose (as being within 17.28(*b*)(i) above). Similarly, relief was denied for the refurbishment of a derelict croft which had not been used as a residence since before April 1973. Unfortunately the owner allowed casual use from time to time in 1975 and 1978 to young relatives although the croft lacked sanitation and was too cold to be occupied in winter. Such casual use was held to be use as a residence (*James Halcro-Johnston (VTD 17147)*).

*Mr J A Moore (VTD 15972)* acquired three barns for conversion into five dwellings. He decided instead to convert them into a single dwelling with a swimming pool and workshop. The East barn was converted into a dwelling in 1994 and Mr Moore moved in. At that time the North and West barns were in the process of conversion into the swimming pool and workshop. These formed a separate building five feet from the East barn. It was held that that gap was fatal. The two barns had been converted into a separate building which was not used as a dwelling. The tribunal held that a building designed as a dwelling house must mean a single building; it could not embrace two buildings (contrast this with 17.55; it seems that a building in VAT law can mean 'building' or 'buildings' depending on which interpretation will defeat the taxpayer!).

When is planning consent not planning consent? *Mr A I Davison (VTD 17130)* applied for planning permission to construct a double garage within the curtilage of a large house. The application was subsequently amended to increase the size of the building and add first floor living accommodation. The planning authority accepted the changes as not making a material amendment and told Mr Davison that he could proceed without needing further permission. Unfortunately, Customs and the VAT tribunal thought otherwise. The tribunal accepted that the new building was a dwelling but held that zero-rating did not apply because the planning permission has not been granted in respect of it as a dwelling.

**17.229** The provision also covers the situation where a person engages a builder to carry out the conversion provided that the conversion work is lawful and the contractor is not acting as an architect, surveyor or consultant or in a supervisory capacity (*VATA 1994, s 35(1C)*). It is not clear what the exclusion for acting as architect, etc. means. It clearly excludes the cost of engaging an architect. But what if a builder is engaged on a design and build basis? It appears to deny relief for the entire cost of the work but is probably intended merely to exclude the element that relates to the prohibited activities, assuming that these are segregable.

**17.230** This relief was given by concession on buildings completed between 21 April 1994 and 29 April 1996. Customs say that a building is completed when it has been finished in accordance with the original plans or in accordance with the Building Regulations. If in doubt the date when a certificate of completion is issued by the local authority can be used (Notice 719, para 3.9). The *VAT Regulations 1995* (*SI 1995 No 2518*), *Reg 201* requires a certificate of completion in support of the claim, so in practical terms a claim cannot be made before this is issued. Customs' insistence that such a certificate is not conclusive, however, was upheld in *C & E Commrs v Arnold (1996 STC 1271)* where the judge, reversing the decision of the VAT tribunal, held that the tribunal had no jurisdiction to review the operation of an extra-statutory concession. In that case the work was substantially completed by August 1983 when the taxpayer went into occupation. The certificate of completion was not issued until November 1994. Customs had decided that the building was completed before 21 April 1994 so that the concession did not apply. In *Dr B N Purdue (VTD 13430)* the date of the certificate was held to be conclusive that the building had been completed, work after that date being held not to be part of the conversion.

**17.231** A do-it-yourself builder cannot recover the VAT he incurs on renovating a house that has been empty for over three years because any supply he makes of the house will be exempt (VAT Information Sheet 4/01 paras 1.9 and 5.2). Any conversion services supplied to him by a builder will attract the 5% rate. The purchase of materials by the DIY convertor will remain standard-rated (para 5.1). The builder will be able to reclaim the VAT on the conversion of a non-residential building into a house (but not on a changed number of dwellings conversion) – because this was already within *VATA 1994, s 35(1)(c)* (see 17.228) – and also on the renovation of a house that has been empty for ten years – because the new *Note 7* (see 17.47) treats such a building as currently being non-residential (VAT Information Sheet 4/01, Part 5).

## Who Bears the VAT?

**17.232** *VATA 1994, s 89* provides that (unless the contract provides otherwise) on a change in the rate of VAT, or exempt items becoming taxable, the contract price under contracts then in existence must be adjusted to reflect that change. It was not originally clear that this applied where an exempt item became taxable as a result of the exercise of an option to tax. Accordingly the rule was amended in 1989 to make it clear that, if the option to tax is exercised, the provisions do apply (*VATA 1994, s 89(3)*). The landlord is thus entitled to collect the VAT from the tenant, unless the lease refers specifically to the rent being inclusive of any VAT. As *section 89* provides for the contract price to be varied, the effect seems to be that the rent is increased by 17½% and whatever remedies, such as distraint or forfeiture, are available to the landlord to recover rent will apply also to the VAT. This applies only if the lease is silent regarding VAT. If the lease provides that the rent stated is inclusive of all taxes, the landlord would have to bear the VAT if he opts to charge tax.

## The VAT (Self-supply of Construction Services) Order 1989

**17.233** Where an exempt trader does his own building work, engaging his own staff instead of using a contractor, the labour element of the work would escape VAT without special provisions. The Treasury therefore issued a statutory instrument (*SI 1989 No 472*), under their general powers to deem a self-supply to be a taxable transaction, to impose VAT on a self-supply of a building.

**17.234** This provides that if a person in the course or furtherance of his business

(*a*) constructs a building,

(*b*) extends or alters a building or constructs an annex to it such that additional floor area is created of 10% more than the original area,

(*c*) constructs any civil engineering work, or

(*d*) in connection with the above, carries out any demolition work contemporaneously or preparatory thereto

those services must be treated as supplied to him for the purpose of his business and supplied by him in the course of it.

**17.235** If he is a fully taxable person, this will not matter, as the output tax on the deemed supply by him will be cancelled out by the input tax on the deemed supply to him. If he is not VAT-registered, or is an exempt or partly exempt trader, it will create a VAT liability – and apparently an obligation to register for VAT if he is not already registered – as he will not be in a position to claim relief for the input tax.

**17.236** This provision only applies if the value of the services is £100,000 or more and the deemed supply would not have been zero-rated if made by a taxable person.

**17.237** The value of the deemed supply is the market value of the services (i.e. the labour). If the performance of the services bridged 1 April 1989, only the part arising after that date is taken into account, both for arriving at the tax charge and applying the £100,000 minimum limit. It should be noted that the charge applies only to the direct labour, as the materials will already have borne tax. As a contractor normally makes a combined charge to cover both materials and his construction services, it is likely to be difficult to establish a market value for the services alone.

**17.238** If a VAT group registration is in force, all of the companies in the group must be treated as if they were a single person for the purpose of the *Order*.

## Time of Supply

**17.239** In February 1989, Customs issued Guidance Notes on their interpretation of the time of supply rules for property and their views on prepayments. The time of supply rules are particularly important insofar as if a supply fell before 1 April 1989 it was likely to be zero-rated or exempt, whereas if it falls after that date it can be taxable. They are also of importance where the rate of tax changes, such as when it was increased from 15% to 17½% on 1 April 1991.

**17.240** The time of supply is normally the earlier of:

(*a*) the date the services are performed or goods are delivered or made available to the customer,

(*b*) the date of payment, and

(*c*) the date a tax invoice is issued.

(*VATA 1994, s 6*).

**17.241** In the view of Customs it is not possible to issue a tax invoice in respect of a zero-rated supply. This is because *Regulation 20* of the *VAT Regulations 1995* states that 'Regulations 13, 14 . . . shall not apply to any zero-rated supply'. *Regulation 13* provides that 'Save as otherwise provided in these Regulations . . . a registered taxable person making a taxable supply to a taxable person shall provide him with a tax invoice'. *Regulation 14* specifies what a tax invoice must contain. *VATA 1994, s 6(15)* defines a tax invoice as 'such an invoice as is required under *paragraph* 2*(1)* of *Schedule 11* to this Act or would be so required if the person to whom the supply is made were a taxable person'. *Paragraph* 2*(1)* states that Regulations 'may require taxable persons supplying goods or other services to other taxable persons to provide them with invoices (to be known as "tax invoices")'.

**17.242** It is by no means certain that Customs' view is correct. *Regulation 20* removes the obligation to issue a tax invoice for a zero-rated supply, but does not seem to actually prevent the issue of such an invoice.

**17.243** Customs take the view that the date a building is made available is the date of the transfer of title to the property, i.e. the completion date, not the contract date, where they are different. It could be argued that if a purchaser or lessee is allowed into occupation at an earlier date, the property should be held to have been made available at that time but the Court of Session held in *Cumbernauld Development Corporation v C&E Commrs (2002 STC 226)* that the time of supply was the date on which title was given to the purchaser, which in Scotland is the date that the feu disposition is given. In that case the corporation exchanged sites with a golf club. It gave the club occupation of the site on 1 May 1996, but it was not until 6 March 1997 that the feu dispositions for the two sites were exchanged. It was held that the legislation is concerned with the supply of goods and the 'goods' in that case was the major interest in land (see 17.245). That expression must be interpreted to mean ownership of the land and not any lesser interest such as a right or mere licence to occupy. Until exchange the club had no more than a personal right against the corporation to receive a conveyance in the form of a feu disposition. In *Leser Landau (VTD 13644)* land was acquired by compulsory purchase and was vested in the purchasing authority in March 1992. The amount of the compensation was still to be determined. The taxpayer sought to register as an intending trader in March 1993 and to waive exemption so as to recover VAT on the costs of determining the consideration. The VAT tribunal upheld Customs' refusal to register him, as the disposal had taken place in March 1992. The fact that it was impossible to calculate the tax at that date did not defer the tax point until it became ascertainable; there was no reason in principle why tax should not be accounted for on an estimated amount.

**17.244** Customs also consider that one cannot make available what does not exist. Accordingly, if title to a property is transferred before the building is completed, all that can be made available at that time is what is actually in existence on the day the title is transferred. They also say this would normally be the work which has been certified by the architect as having been completed. It is arguable that this is wrong, as there would also be materials on site, work since the architect inspected, etc. Furthermore, an architect values the work done. He does not value the building in its partially completed state. It is also of course possible to make available the right to have the building completed, which would be a standard rated supply. However the completion of the work would still be a separate taxable supply.

**17.245** The grant, assignment or surrender of a major interest in land (the freehold or a lease of over 21 years) is deemed to be a supply of goods for VAT purposes (*VATA 1994, Sch 4 para 4*). However, each receipt of rent is deemed to be a separate supply occurring at the earlier of its receipt or the issue of a tax invoice for such rent (*VAT Regulations 1995, Reg 85(1)*). The landlord can, if he wishes, at the beginning of any period issue a tax invoice for the rent due for a period of up to a year showing, in addition to the usual requirements, the dates each payment falls due for payment, the VAT-exclusive amount payable on each date and the rate of tax and VAT payable on each date. If he does so, the tax point for each payment is the earlier of the due date and the date the rent is actually received. A change in the rate of VAT after the issue of such an invoice invalidates it for subsequent due dates (*Reg 85(2)(3)*). A lease of 21 years or less is a supply of services (*VATA 1994, s 5(2)(b)*) but identical tax point rules apply as those in respect of major interests (*Reg 90*).

**17.246** If a contract provides for retention of part of the consideration pending full and satisfactory performance of the contract (or of part of it), a supply is treated as taking place at the earliest of the release of the retention money or the issue of a tax invoice (*VAT Regulations 1985, Reg 89*). This will obviously apply to retentions under building contracts. Where services, or a combination of goods and services, are supplied in the course of the construction, alteration, demolition, repair or maintenance of a building or civil engineering work under a contract which provides for payment to be made periodically or from time to time, such as on the issue of an architect's certificate, those services are treated as separately and successively supplied at the earlier of (*a*) each time a payment is received, (*b*) each time the supplier issues a tax invoice, or (*c*) in relation to certain supplies in respect of exempt land (to the extent they have not previously been treated as supplied) the day on which the services are performed. The supplies covered by head (*c*) are those where, at the time the services were (or are) performed, either

(i) it was (or is) the intention or expectation of either the supplier, or of a person responsible for financing the supplier's cost of providing the services and goods, that the relevant land (i.e. the land on which the building, etc. to which the services relate is constructed) would become or continue to be exempt land (whether immediately or eventually), or

(ii) the supplier had, or has, received (and used in making the supply) a supply of services or goods, the time of supply for which was itself determined under head (*c*) above (or but for the issue of a VAT invoice would have been).

(*VAT Regulations 1995, Reg 93(1)–(3)* inserted by the *VAT (Amendment) (No 3) Regulations 1999* (*SI 1999 No 1374*)). The regulation contains detailed rules to amplify head (*c*) (*Reg 93(4)–(14)*). These are virtually identical to the tests in *VATA 1994, Sch 10 para 3A(3)–(14)* (see 17.173–17.180) with the substitution of a reference to the 'supplier' for the 'developer'. The reference to the provision of funds obviously excludes funds made available to the supplier by paying him all or part of the consideration for the supply itself (i.e. paying for the work does not constitute making funds available to the supplier to finance his costs of making the supply) (*Reg 93(6)*). The supplier's costs of providing the services and goods is the amount payable by the supplier for supplies of goods and services to him to be used in making the supply plus his own staff and other internal costs of making the supply (*Reg 93(7)*). This definition displaces that in 17.177. For such services performed between 9 December 1997 and 8 June 1999, the time of supply under head (*c*) was 18 months after the date on which the services were performed.

**17.247** Head (*c*) is of course an anti-avoidance provision. It is intended to stop exempt taxpayers setting up an in-house construction company which would sub-contract all of the work to an arm's length builder, pay the builder out of funds provided to it by another group company and not invoice its parent company for the work for many years. The government's first attempt to combat this was to create a deemed supply after 18 months. This accidentally caught a large number of innocent situations – as arm's length building disputes can take well over 18 months to resolve with payment and invoicing being left in abeyance in the interim – and in a group situation virtually invited an 18 month delay in billing. The new *Reg 93* is far better targeted. It still suffers from the problem that it is unclear when building services 'are performed'. Customs say that this is when the work is completed. That will normally be when a certificate of practical completion is issued but in a case of 'unusual delay' they will look at when the work was actually completed. A subcontractor will need to make up his own mind when his work is completed but Customs say he should ignore the need to carry out any 'snagging' work that takes place after the main work is completed. Customs also warn that leaving a small aspect of the contracted work undone would be varying the contract and 'could be seen by the Courts as a criminal act' as all the work that the contractor had 'genuinely agreed' to do would have been completed. (VAT Information Sheet 7/99). It is questionable whether in many cases that would be a correct analysis of the position. Probably a greater worry is why the draftsman should have referred to 'the date on which those services were performed', which suggests something happening on a single day, if he meant the date that a series of continuous services extending over several months was completed. The wording of the Regulations is more appropriate to each day's work being a separate supply.

**17.248** If the supplier gives an authenticated receipt containing the particulars required by a tax invoice, such receipt can be treated as a tax invoice provided that no tax invoice is issued (*Reg 13(4)*). The authenticated receipt must be issued within 30 days after the time that the supply is deemed to take place (*Reg 13(5)*). In *Crosstyle plc (VTD 7169)* a company made a progress payment in July but the authenticated receipt was dated 1 August. The VAT tribunal left open the question whether the date on the authenticated receipt had to be treated as the date of supply even if it was incorrect as, even if it did, the company had a reasonable excuse for claiming input tax relief in the wrong period. In practice Customs generally accept claims made before a receipt is issued provided that the claimant subsequently obtains a receipt (Notice 700, para 24). Although *Regulation 29(2)* provides that a person must hold a tax invoice or a comparable document, such as an authenticated receipt, before it can claim input tax relief, it is difficult to envisage either that this can override the date fixed by *Regulation 93*, or that the general rule in *VATA 1994, s 6(6)*, that the date of issue of a tax invoice is substituted as the time of supply if it is issued within 14 days of the normal time of supply, can override the specific rule of *Regulation 93*. Indeed in *Sprowston Hall Hotel Ltd (VTD 7253)* another VAT tribunal specifically held that *Regulation 93* displaced what is now *VATA 1994, s 6(5)* – and by inference also *VATA 1994, s 6(6)* which merely modifies that provision. Customs say that where a contract is terminated early, before the terms have been fulfilled, e.g. because of the insolvency of the contractor, the supply is considered to have been completed on the day that the work ceased (Business Brief 4/96), on the basis that 'that date is the basic tax point for those supplies where *VATA 1994, s 6* applies'.

This is questionable. *Regulation 93* overrides the normal tax point rules. Once a service is identified as coming within that provision, the only possible tax points are the dates of payment and the date of issue of an invoice. The termination of the contract or completion of the services is not expressed to be a tax point.

**17.249** The receipt of a deposit will often constitute a supply. In *Jelson Holdings Ltd (VTD 6632)* a developer agreed in August 1990 to sell a plot of land and construct an industrial building on it. It required a deposit of £160,000 against the building work and this was paid to its solicitor. On 20 September 1990 it was released to the company although the work was not due to be completed until December. The VAT tribunal held that the deposit had been released with the purchaser's consent and the tax point occurred on 20 September. In the tribunal's view a deposit paid solely as security (which would not constitute a supply) would be returned to the payer on performance of the contract and would not form part of the contract price. On this analysis it would seem that the receipt of a deposit by the vendor of a property would create a tax point at the latest at the date of contract, when it ceases to be security and becomes payment of part of the price.

## Place of Supply

**17.250** *Regulation 5* of the *VAT (Place of Supply of Services) Order 1992* (*SI 1992 No 3121*) deems most services in relation to land to be supplied where the land is situated. It applies to:

(*a*) the grant, assignment or surrender of any interest in (or right over) land, a personal right to call for or be granted any interest in or right over land, or a licence to occupy land or any other contractual right exercisable over (or in relation to) land;

(*b*) any works of reconstruction, demolition, conversion, reconstruction, alteration, enlargement, repair or maintenance of a building or civil engineering work; and

(*c*) services such as are supplied by estate agents, auctioneers, architects, surveyors, engineers and others involved in matters relating to land.

This gives effect to *Article 9* of the *EC Sixth Directive*, which states that the place of supply of services connected with immovable property, including the services of estate agents and experts, and of services for preparing and co-ordinating construction works, such as the services of architects and of firms providing on-site supervision, shall be the place where the property is situated (*Article 9(2)(a)*).

**17.251** Where advice is given in relation to land outside the UK, it can be difficult to determine whether it falls within the *Order* – in which case it is outside the scope of UK VAT, but there may well be an obligation to register for VAT in the country in which the land is situated if that is another EC country – or if it is a *VATA 1994, Schedule 5* consultancy service, which is outside the scope of UK VAT but with a right to recover input tax and no obligation to register in the other country. If work within the *Order* is carried out by a non-UK person on land in the UK, and the recipient of the supply is VAT-registered, he is required to account for the VAT under the reverse charge procedure and there is no requirement for the non-resident to register for VAT in the UK (*VATA 1994, s 8(6); Sch 5 paras 9, 10*). However this reverse charge procedure is not standard throughout the EC, e.g. it does not apply in Ireland.

**17.252** The *Order* was held to apply in the case of *Mechanical Engineering Consultants Ltd (VTD 13287)*, where a UK company trading as consulting engineers was engaged by a Swiss company to manage, supervise and guarantee the commissioning of a waste incinerator complex in the UK. The UK company claimed that the incinerator, which was bolted to a cradle structure attached to the land, was not part of the land, but the VAT tribunal held that it was a fixture, and thus part of the land. The *Order* was also held to apply to accountancy and book-keeping services in *Aspen Advisory Services Ltd (VTD 13489)* although the facts there were unusual. The company entered into a contract with a Channel Islands company for management of property in the UK. It delegated day-to-day management of the property to a project manager but itself provided the accountancy and book-keeping services. The VAT tribunal held that all of the services were carried out under the terms of the property management agreement and that it would be artificial to divide the services under that contract into those relating to land and those not relating to land. There was a single composite supply. Accordingly this decision does not indicate that accountancy and book-keeping are of themselves within the *Order* solely because they are accounting for land transactions. Indeed, *W H Payne & Co (1995 VATDR 490) (VTD 13668)* suggests they are not. The appellant partnership supplied accountancy, book-keeping and taxation services to several overseas companies which owned property in the UK, in relation to agreeing and accounting for their UK tax liabilities on the rents. It was held that the UK properties were not fixed establishments of the overseas companies and that the partnership was making a supply to the overseas companies of *VATA 1994, Schedule 5* services which were deemed to be supplied outside the UK.

## Partial Exemption

**17.253** Property companies will increasingly be partly exempt for VAT purposes. Some of their turnover (such as sales of new buildings and rents and sale proceeds of opted-in properties) are standard-rated; some (such as sales of new houses) are zero-rated; and some (such as sales of 'old' buildings and rents from non opted-in properties) are exempt. In such circumstances, unless one of the *de minimis* limits applies, there is a restriction on the input tax that can be reclaimed under the *VAT Regulations 1995* (*SI 1995 No 2518*).

**17.254** There is no such restriction if the exempt input tax (i.e. the tax on purchases of exempt items) is less than £625 per month on average either for the return period or the taxpayer's tax year (*VAT Regulations 1995, Reg 106*)). Before 1 December 1994 the figure was £600 per month. Prior to 1 April 1992 full relief was given only if the exempt input tax was less than either: £100 per month on average; both £250 per month on average and 50% of total input tax; or both £500 per month on average and 25% of total input tax.

This average was normally taken over the year to 31 March, 30 April or 31 May depending on the taxpayer's VAT registration quarter.

**17.255** Where the above *de minimis* limits do not apply, the input tax must be apportioned between exempt and taxable supplies. This is normally done by direct attribution, i.e.

(*a*) expenditure that is incurred in generating taxable supplies must be attributed to such supplies – the VAT being recoverable in full;

(*b*) expenditure incurred in generating exempt supplies must similarly be attributed to such supplies – so no part of the VAT will be recoverable; and

(*c*) VAT on expenditure that cannot be specifically attributed, e.g. on general overheads, is apportioned in the ratio, rounded up to the nearest whole number, that taxable supplies made by the taxpayer bears to the value of all his supplies (*Reg 101(2)(d)(4)*). For this purpose sales of capital goods used in the business and, where they are incidental to the taxpayer's business activities, zero-rated supplies in respect of buildings, exempt supplies of land or buildings, freehold disposals of new buildings, surrenders of interests in land, or disposals taxable only by virtue of the exercise of the option to tax (see 17.158 above), are ignored, as are financial services within *Sch 9 Group 5* (*Reg 101(3)*). Prior to 1 April 1992 the apportionment was in the ratio that the VAT on taxable supplies bore to the VAT on total supplies. This often worked unfairly, particularly where a property company made mainly zero-rated supplies of buildings, as most of the inputs related to such supplies were themselves zero-rated and thus generated no input tax. Customs can permit the use of an alternative method of arriving at deductible input tax. From 1 April 1992 they can also require a taxpayer to use such special method as they may require (*Reg 102*).

**17.256** In applying the partial exemption formula input tax attributable to certain exempt supplies can be treated as relating to taxable supplies (*Reg 105*). These include the granting of a lease or licence to occupy premises provided that the input tax attributable to all such supplies in the year is less than £1,000 and the only exempt input tax incurred by the taxpayer is on supplies falling within *Reg 105*. This will rarely help property companies. It is intended to prevent a trading company becoming partly exempt solely because it sublets its premises. An interesting point fell for consideration by the European Court of Justice in *Regie-Dauphinoise-Cabinet A Forest SARL v Ministre du Budget (Case C–306/94) (1996 STC 1176)*. The company was a property management company. In the course of its business it obtained advances from property owners. It was entitled to retain the interest it generated from such funds. It contended that the interest was incidental to its business of property management and therefore, by virtue of *Article 19(2)* of the *EC Sixth Directive*, should be excluded from the partial exemption calculation. The ECJ said that the investment of the monies constituted the direct, permanent and necessary extension of the taxable activity but was not incidental to the management activity; it was a consequence of the advance made by owners. Accordingly it gave rise to an input tax restriction.

**17.257** If a property developer makes both taxable and exempt supplies, it will often not be known at the time of purchase of materials what type of supply they will be used for. Customs initially said that they wouldl allow input tax relief to be claimed on a provisional basis provided that the developer maintains sufficiently detailed records to show what the materials are used for and refunds any VAT that turns out to be non-deductible. Alternatively, he can defer claiming input tax relief until the materials are actually used and the deductibility of the VAT established (Notice 742A, para 19(b) – now withdrawn). Their current view is that if the taxpayer knows from the outset what supplies he intends to make he should attribute input tax on speculative costs to those supplies from the outset. In other cases input tax on speculative supplies should be regarded initially as residual as there is no firm intention to use them to make either taxable or exempt supplies. If a speculative project is aborted the input tax will remain residual. When the taxpayer proceeds with a development he will then have a clear intention to make one or other type of supply and the allowable input tax should be adjusted under *Reg 108* or *109* (see 17.262) (VAT Information Sheet 8/01).

**17.258** In *HDG Harbour Development Group Ltd (VTD 9386)* the company made a zero-rated grant of a lease in 1987 and subsequently received exempt rents from the building subsequent to 1 August 1989. It incurred expenditure subsequent to that date on legal fees in respect of a party wall dispute and on a claim by the builder for increased costs in respect of the construction of the building. The VAT tribunal rejected the contention that these costs related to the initial construction of the building, holding that they were 'totally new matters arising in a way unconnected with the original development' and thus could only be attributed to the exempt rents.

**17.259** In *Mr & Mrs George Vitzthum (VTD 11076)* it was held that it is implicit in the definition of input tax in what is now *VATA 1994, s 24(1)* that the use of the goods or services has to be for an authorised business purpose. Accordingly, where a double garage was constructed partly for storage of business stock and partly as office space for a business carried on from the taxpayer's home, but the planning consent limited its use to storing private motor vehicles and other domestic purposes, the tax on the construction costs could not be input tax.

**17.260** A salutary tale on apportionments between exempt and taxable supplies is to be found in *C & E Commrs v University of Wales College of Cardiff (1995 STC 611)*. The college constructed two buildings for a new engineering faculty. With the approval of Customs it entered into a lease and leaseback arrangement in order to recover VAT incurred on the construction cost from 1 April 1989. Under this it granted leases in April 1992, after completion of the building work, to a wholly-owned subsidiary and opted to tax the rents. It claimed that virtually the whole of the input tax was attributable to the taxable lease, albeit that the college had used the buildings for its own partly exempt purposes between 1990 and 1992. Customs said that the apportionment had to be based on the use when the input tax was incurred. At that date the lease had not been entered into. On the basis of the 'income' of the faculty in 1989, they considered that 51% was attributable to taxable supplies and 49% to exempt ones. The court upheld this test. Customs had power under the *VAT Regulations 1995* (*SI 1995 No 2518*), *Regulation 102* to direct an approach that gives a fair and reasonable attribution of the tax for the accounting period, and under *Regulation 107* this could be adjusted by reference to the longer period of the college's VAT year. However, nothing occurring after the end of that longer period could subsequently alter the attribution. This is the sort of case where it is vital to try to agree a special method of attribution of input tax with Customs under *Regulation 102* in advance of the first supply.

**17.261** The decision in *C & E Commrs v Wiggett Construction Ltd (2001 STC 933)* is interesting. The company targets housing associations. In December 1995 it incurred input tax on the purchase of a plot of derelict land in Manchester. In December 1996 it entered into four agreements with a housing association. The first was to sell it the land, the second to construct a building on it, the third a variation of the building contract, and the fourth an agreement for the construction of additional flats. The company accepted that the land sale was exempt. However it claimed that the four contracts formed an integral package and together formed the bargain between the parties. It would never have entered into the land sale agreement without having the building contracts. The land sale attracted roughly 20% of the total consideration. The company contended that 80% of the input tax on the purchase of the land related to the construction contract. Customs not unnaturally contended that it related solely to the land sale. The VAT tribunal found in favour of the company. It was held that it was entitled to reach that conclusion on the evidence. It had applied the correct tests that the input tax had to be objectively linked to the taxable transaction, that link must be direct and immediate, and the input must be a cost component of the taxable transaction. In *St James Court Hotel Ltd (VTD 17487)* the company constructed two restaurants in order to comply with a franchise agreement to enable it to operate as a Crowne Plaza hotel. It sublet these to restaurant operators and did not opt to waive exemption for the rents. It contended that it had used the inputs exclusively in making a taxable supply of construction services to the tenants as an inducement to them to enter into the lease or, alternatively, that it had used them both in making taxable supplies of hotel services and an exempt supply of letting. The tribunal dismissed both claims; the first on the basis that there was no evidence that an inducement had been offered to tenants, and in carrying out the work the hotel simply decided to offer its restaurant premises for lease rather than to run it themselves, and the second on the basis that the expenses were directly incurred in fulfilling its contractual obligations under the agreement for lease. The tribunal commented that if the Hotel had run the restaurant itself there would clearly have been a direct link to the supplies, but stressed that there has to be an objective link between the supplies and the taxable transactions. It is clear from *BLP Group plc v C & E Commrs (Case 4-4/94, [1995] STC 424)* that this excludes situations where the causal chain has been broken by an exempt supply.

**17.262** Where input tax has been attributed to taxable supplies because the taxpayer intended to use the item in making such supplies, and at some time within the next six years he changes his mind and uses or decides to use the item to make exempt supplies, he must account for an amount equal to that input tax on the return for the period in which the exempt use takes place or the intention to make the taxable supply is abandoned, and thus repay such input tax to Customs (*Reg 108*). There are similar provisions for adjustment if input tax which was initially treated as relating to exempt supplies subsequently becomes attributable to taxable supplies (*Reg 109*). In *Cooper & Chapman (Builders) Ltd v C & E Commrs (1993 STC 1)* the company converted a house into self-contained furnished flats which it advertised as holiday accommodation and recovered VAT on the building costs. It subsequently received an offer to take a lease of the whole block as an exempt supply. It was held that the input tax had to be apportioned between what had actually been used for making holiday lettings and what related to the exempt supply of the tenancy. In *The Really Useful Group plc (VTD 6578)* the company commenced refurbishment of office premises for its own use. It subsequently decided to sell them instead and agreed a sale on terms that required it to complete the refurbishment work. Its claim that, in fulfilling its obligation to complete the refurbishment work, it was continuing to use the supplies for the purpose of its business was rejected by the VAT tribunal, which applied *Regulation 108* to require the repayment to Customs of the whole of the input tax.

The taxpayer was more successful in *Royal and Sun Alliance Insurance Group v C & E Commrs (2001 STC 1476, [2001] EWCA Civ 1476)*. Royal & Sun Alliance (RSA) (through another member of its VAT group) rented five properties which the landlords had opted to tax. It decided to sublet the properties. It did not know whether it would be beneficial to itself opt to tax until it could identify the VAT characteristics of its future subtenants. It made no claim for input tax relief in relation to the rent paid. When it found subtenants RSA exercised the option to tax. It contended that once it made the election it became entitled to reclaim the VAT paid on the rent in the earlier years, and claimed repayment of such VAT under *Regulation 109*. It originally intended to use the inputs to make exempt supplies but being unable to do so, within the six-year period it formed an intention to use the inputs in making taxable supplies. It manifested this intention by the option to tax. Customs contended that the inputs (the rents) were consumed each quarter so that by the time the option to tax was exercised the inputs could no longer be used by RSA in making any supplies. Park J felt that the grant of a lease is one transaction and to treat the rental payment as a succession of different supplies ignored both the legal form and the commercial reality. He interpreted *Regulation 85* (see 17.279), which deems each rent payment to be a separate supply, as staggering the time of the single supply of the lease rather than creating several supplies where without that paragraph there would be only one. He was fortified in this view by the fact that *VATA 1994, s 6(14)* under which that regulation was made, was in a section dealing with the time of supply. The taxpayer won by a majority in the Court of Appeal, Aldous and Sedley LJJ agreeing with the reasoning of Park J but Arden LJ thought that *Regulation 85* created a series of distinct supplies.

### *Change of Intention*

**17.263** The statutory basis for *Reg 108* is open to question. In *Intercommunale Voor Zeewaterontzilting in Liquidation v Belgian State (Case C–110/94) (1996 STC 569)* it was held that, where the tax authority has accepted that a company which has declared an intention to commence an economic activity giving rise to taxable transactions has the status of a taxable person, the status of taxable person cannot be withdrawn retrospectively (except in cases of fraud or abuse) if as a result of a feasibility study it is decided not to move to the operational stage with the result that the economic activity envisaged has not given rise to taxable transactions. In *Belgium v Ghent Coal Terminal (Case C–37/95) (1998 STC 260)* Ghent Coal bought land in 1980 and carried out improvements to it, on which it recovered the VAT, between 1981 and 1983. In March 1983 the City of Ghent required Ghent Coal to exchange the land (that was then in the course of development) for another site owned by the city. Accordingly, the original land was never used for the purpose of Ghent Coal's business. The Belgium VAT authorities required Ghent Coal to refund the input tax it had claimed on the aborted development work. The ECJ held that *Article 17* of the *Sixth Directive* must be construed as allowing a taxable person acting as such to deduct the VAT payable by him on purchases for the purpose of development intended to be used in connection with taxable transactions. The right to deduct remains acquired where, by reason of circumstances beyond his control, the taxable person has never made use of the goods or services to carry out taxable transactions. A similar decision was reached in *Finanzamt Goslar v Breitsohl (2001 STC 355) (Case C-400/98)* (see 17.201).

**17.264** Customs contend that *Reg 108* does not concern the appellant's right to deduct input tax. It is merely an adjustment of the deductible amount under *Article 20(1)*. The VAT Tribunal in *Tremerton Ltd (VTD 15590)* accepted this. However it is questionable whether an adjustment because of a change of intention falls within *Article 20(1)*. It is also questionable whether *Article 20(1)* will allow different adjustment periods to be adopted in different circumstances. It is more apt to cover simply the annual adjustment under *Reg 107*.

**17.265** In *WEH Key (VTD 15354)* Mr Key converted some residential buildings into dwellings in 1990 at a time when a sale would have been exempt. In 1994 he let them as holiday lets – a taxable activity on which he accounted for VAT. In 1994 he sold the dwellings – now zero-rated (see 8.27 above) and at the time zero-rated by concession. Customs contended that throughout Mr Key had an intention to make exempt supplies and this was upheld by the tribunal – in the absence of Mr Key, who was not represented. It is unclear to the writer how a taxpayer can make a taxable (zero-rated) supply of his entire interest in a building without first forming an intention to make such a supply. It also seems to be unclear how he can make a taxable supply without 'using' those services which created the item being supplied in making that taxable supply, which is of itself sufficient to trigger the attribution of the input tax to the taxable supply under *Reg 109*. There seems no reason why the same principle cannot be applied in reverse. If a person initially intends to make a taxable supply and ultimately makes an exempt one within the six-year period, perhaps there is no obligation to repay the input tax initially recovered on the basis that there has not been a change of intention; circumstances have merely frustrated that intention being achieved.

### Capital Goods Scheme

**17.266** Where a taxpayer is partly exempt, the proportion of its input tax that is deductible will vary year by year. If heavy capital expenditure is incurred in a year when the deductible proportion is low the taxpayer could be unfairly penalised; if it is incurred in a year when it is high he may obtain relief for what the Government consider to be too high a proportion of the VAT.

**17.267** Accordingly the capital goods scheme was introduced by the *Value Added Tax (General) (Amendment) (No 4) Regulations 1989* (*SI 1989 No 2355*) to make the deduction more equitable. These provisions are now contained in *Regs 112–116* of the *VAT Regulations 1995*.

The capital goods scheme applies only to capital expenditure on

(*a*) computers and items of computer equipment worth £50,000 or more,

(*b*) land and buildings (or parts of buildings or from 3 July 1997 a civil engineering work) worth £250,000 or more,

(*c*) a building (or part of a building) the owner's interest in which (or right over or licence to occupy) is taxed under the rules relating to the change of use of a residential or charitable building (see 17.65) where the value taxed under those rules is £250,000 or more,

(*d*) a building (or part of a building) to which the developer's self-supply charge applied (see 8.38) and the value of that supply was £250,000 or more,

(*e*) a building not falling within (*c*) or (*d*) which was constructed by the owner and first brought into use by him after 31 March 1990 if the value of all taxable supplies of goods or services made to him after that date in connection with the construction are £250,000 or more,

(*f*) a building which the owner alters (including constructing an extension or annex) where additional floor area of 10% or more is created and the value of all taxable supplies of goods or services made to him after that date in connection with the alteration are £250,000 or more,

(*g*) a civil engineering work constructed by the owner and first brought into use by him after 2 July 1997 if the aggregate value of taxable supplies to the owner after the date relating to the land or in connection with the construction of the work is £250,000 or more, and

(*h*) a building which the owner refurbishes or fits out where the value of capital expenditure on the taxable supplies of services and goods affixed to the building made to the owner in connection with the refurbishment after 2 July 1997 is £250,000 or more.

The references to taxable supplies in each case exclude zero-rated supplies. In applying head (*b*) so much of the value of a supply as consists of rent (including charges reserved as rent) can be ignored, unless either the amount is payable more than 12 months in advance or it is invoiced for a period in excess of 12 months. The legislation is seeking to prevent capital expenditure incurred at the time of purchase from being classified as an advance payment of rent. Curiously, although a service charge is caught by this restriction if it is reserved as rent it is not caught if it is simply payable under a covenant in the lease. Head (*b*) includes freehold and leasehold interests in buildings and certain extensions and alterations to buildings, and includes buildings constructed by the owner for his own use. Costs incurred prior to 1 April 1990 are not taken into account. There is no definition of refurbishment for the purpose of head (*h*). As the expenditure needs to be capital, it is first necessary to differentiate refurbishment expenditure between capital and revenue as it is only if the capital element is at least £250,000 that the head can apply. Customs' view is that they will follow the treatment adopted in the taxpayer's accounts. Conceptually in accounting terms most refurbishment work is revenue, but any element of improvement may be capital. Where a refurbishment is carried out, the capital goods scheme implications need to be borne in mind when deciding on the accounting treatment where in accounting terms it is permissible to treat expenditure as either capital or revenue. In practice in the past the Inland Revenue have frequently challenged this apportionment for direct tax purposes. If it is agreed with the Revenue that the accounting treatment is incorrect, this could have an impact on the capital goods adjustment. Customs have indicated that they would not expect any adjustment to be made unless the agreement with the Revenue cast strong doubt on whether proper consideration had been initially given at all to the split between capital and revenue.

**17.268** The scheme requires the deductible proportion of the tax on land and buildings to be re-calculated over a ten-year adjustment period, with tax being paid or repaid each year to correct the position in relation to the 10% of the cost notionally attributed to that year. In the case of computers and computer equipment the adjustment period is five years. If the property is sold during that period by way of a taxable supply, the use for the rest of the period is deemed to be fully taxable; if it is sold by means of an exempt supply, the use for the balance of the period is deemed to be exempt use. The period can be less than 10 years if during that period there is a transfer of a business as a going concern (see 17.280 below) or the owner joins or leaves the VAT group as such transactions trigger the end of an adjustment period. Prior to 3 July 1997 it was possible to shorten the adjustment period significantly by engineering several such transactions but it is now only the first transaction that will bring an adjustment period to an end – with subsequent periods ending on each anniversary of that shortened period.

**17.269** Customs issued a Statement of Practice on 19 December 1997 setting out how they intend to operate these rules (Business Brief 30/97). This states that the disposal test will not be applied:

(*a*) to sales of computer equipment,

(*b*) where an owner disposes of an item at a loss due to market conditions (such as a general downturn in property prices),

(*c*) where the value of the item has depreciated,

(*d*) where the value of the item is reduced for other legitimate reasons (such as accepting a lower price to effect a quick sale),

(*e*) where the amount of output tax on disposal is less than the total input tax claimed due only to a reduction in the VAT rate, and

(*f*) where the item is used only for taxable (including zero-rated) purposes throughout the adjustment period (including the final disposal) (para 5.1).

They say that where there is no unjustified tax advantage a business should not apply the disposal test, but should not apply to Customs for a specific ruling either. 'A business need only apply the disposal test where it has entered into arrangements for tax mitigation affecting the particular capital item or its disposal' (para 5.2). This leaves the problem of being able to recognise tax mitigation, particularly as that seems to be a concept that looks very different through the eyes of Customs than most others perceive. Customs warn that where they think the provision ought to have been applied it will be 'vigorously enforced', which suggests that there is a heavy risk of a misdeclaration penalty for getting it wrong.

**17.270** The statement also indicates that even where the provision needs to be applied the trader will need to calculate the 'net tax advantage' (i.e. 'the overall benefit from the avoidance device') and then work out how much of it is unjustified. The net tax advantage will normally be the input tax secured by the sale less any output tax due on the sale. An apportionment will be needed to work out how much of this is unjustified. Normally this should be done by using 'the ratio' that the value of the final taxable sale bears to the value of both the exempt supply and the final taxable sale (para 5.3). Where there have been other taxable supplies the ratio of exempt to taxable supplies (including the final sale) appears more reasonable.

**17.271** Particular problems arise in relation to refurbishments. For example, if a person refurbishes one floor of a building at a cost of £150,000 and three months later refurbishes a second floor, is that two separate refurbishments each costing under £250,000 or one costing over £250,000? Customs say it depends on the facts and each case needs to be looked at on its merit. Another problem is that it is often not easy to distinguish goods affixed to a building from the value of other goods. Customs have therefore introduced a concession, which allows a business to include goods not affixed to the premises in arriving at the £250,000 figure. It applies only where the adjustment period starts after 31 December 1999 although the local VAT office can extend it to other cases. To use the concession businesses must 'keep a record of the concessionary value of the capital expenditure including full details of the supplies on which the value was determined' (Business Brief 2/00). As the purpose of the concession is to avoid the costs of distinguishing the value of affixed goods from other goods the need to keep 'full details' seems to detract somewhat from its usefulness.

**17.272** The other major change from 3 July 1997 is that, 'save as the Commissioners may otherwise allow', on a disposal of a capital goods item during the adjustment period there is a final adjustment to limit the total input tax deducted over the adjustment period to the output tax charged on the disposal. This is an anti-avoidance provision. It operates capriciously and unfairly in many cases. The intention is that it will not be applied to bona fide commercial disposals but that the taxpayer will need to ask Customs to exercise this discretion not to charge tax for each individual disposal.

*Example 34*

A company with a 30 April VAT year buys a property for £300,000 plus VAT in March 2001. It uses it 80% for taxable purposes in the period to 30 April 2001, 30% for taxable purposes in the year to 30 April 2001 and 40% for taxable purposes in the year to 30 April 2003. It sells the property on 1 May 2003 for £200,000 plus VAT, the value having slumped as the area has become blighted by a motorway proposal.

The VAT position is

| | | |
|---|---|---|
| year to 30 April 2001:<br>Input tax £300,000 × 17½% | £52,000 | |
| 80% attributable to taxable use | | £42,000 |
| year to 30 April 2002: Adjustment for the year (to restrict input tax for the year to 30% use)<br>£52,500 × 1/10th × (80–30)% | | (2,625) |
| year to 30 April 2003: Adjustment for the year<br>£52,500 × 1/10th × (80–40)% | | (2,100) |
| years 4–10: deemed fully taxable so no adjustment | | – |
| Net input tax allowed | | 37,275 |
| Final adjustment to limit input tax to<br>£200,000 × 17½% | | (2,275) |
| | | 35,000 |

In practice Customs will almost certainly agree not to require the £2,275 of 'excessive' input tax to be repaid in these circumstances.

*Example 35*

The company in *Example 34* uses the property for making fully taxable supplies throughout the period of ownership.

| | |
|---|---|
| year to 30 April 2001: Input tax £300,000 × 17½% | 52,500 |
| 2 years to 30 April 2003: No adjustment | – |
| years 4–10: deemed fully taxable so no adjustment | – |
| Final adjustment | (17,500) |
| | 35,000 |

It will be seen that the greater the taxable use the more harshly the taxpayer is treated!

*Example 36*

The company in *Example 34* uses the property in its trade for fully taxable purposes. It does not exercise the option to tax.

| | |
|---|---|
| year to 30 April 2001: Input tax as before | 52,500 |
| 2 years to 30 April 2003: No adjustment | – |
| years 4–10: deemed wholly exempt so restrict input tax by | |
| 52,500 × 7/10ths (i.e. remaining 7 years) | (36,750) |
| | 15,750 |
| Final adjustment to limit input tax to £200,000 × NIL (as no VAT on sale) | (15,750) |
| | NIL |

## Registration

**17.273** Customs initially wanted strong evidence of a future intention to make taxable supplies by way of business before registering a property owner or developer for VAT. In 1990 they stated that they will register a person if he or his professional adviser write to Customs advising them that either:

(*a*) a feasibility study has been commissioned which will have to be paid for;

(*b*) he either holds title to the land, is negotiating for its purchase, or holds an option to purchase it;

(*c*) he has commissioned an architect to seek planning permission or has instructed some other professional person with the intention of selling or letting the property;

(*d*) if a sale or lease of a residential or relevant charitable building is contemplated (see 8.27 above), he has obtained the necessary certificate from the customer; or

(*e*) if a zero-rated sale of a substantially reconstructed listed building is contemplated, he has obtained the listed building consent.

(C & E Press Release 25 September 1990). The author's experience suggests that this statement was somewhat tongue-in-cheek and that documentary evidence to back up such a statement is still required. They subsequently said that following the abolition of the self-supply charge (see 8.38 above) 'local VAT offices may require more detailed information before allowing intending trader registration' (Business Brief 8/96). In practice they normally seem to look for a signed contract to buy the property or a signed building contract before being prepared to register a property company and, where supplies will be taxable only if the option to tax is exercised, expect the notice of the exercise of the option to be submitted at the same time as the application for registration. They are worried about the risk of registering someone who has no real intention to make taxable supplies. Although the *VAT Regulations 1995, Reg 108* provides for a clawback of VAT where the intention changes, the decision of the European Court of Justice in *Intercommunale voor Zeewaterontzilting v Belgian State (1996 STC 569)* casts doubts on its validity, so they may have good reason to be concerned (see 17.262 above). Where a person intends to exercise the option to tax Customs require this to be done before they will register him if he would not otherwise be a taxable person.

## Payment of Another Party's Costs

**17.274** Agreements in relation to property frequently provide for the tenant to bear the landlord's costs, e.g. on an assignment. In such circumstances Customs consider that, as the legal advice or other supply was to the landlord, the tenant is not entitled to reclaim the VAT on such costs (Notice 742B, para 15, now withdrawn). Accordingly the tax invoice should be issued by the solicitor, etc. to the landlord so that he can reclaim the VAT, and the tenant should be required to bear only the VAT-exclusive amount (or if the landlord is partly exempt the amount not reclaimable from Customs). This concept has been upheld by a VAT tribunal in *Francis Jackson Homes Ltd (6352)*, where the company was not allowed relief for the input tax on the vendor's legal and estate agency fees which it had agreed to pay on an acquisition of land, and by the High Court in *Turner v C & E Commrs (1992 STC 621)*. Redrow Group plc successfully surmounted this problem by using a tripartite agreement between itself, its customer and an estate agent (*C & E Commrs v Redrow Group plc (1999 STC 161)*). It operated an incentive scheme under which, if a customer purchased one of its houses, it would pay the fees of estate agents instructed to sell the purchaser's existing house. Redrow chose the estate agent; it instructed the agent; the agent was required to report progress to Redrow; it had to agree the price with Redrow; the instructions could not be changed without the agreement of Redrow; and Redrow were contractually liable as principal for the agent's fees unless the house owner did not proceed with his proposed purchase of a house from Redrow. The House of Lords held that the transactions between Redrow and the estate agents were a supply of services for a consideration to Redrow. They did what Redrow instructed them to do, for which they charged a fee that was paid by Redrow. The matter has to be looked at from the standpoint of the person who is claiming an input tax deduction. Was something being done for him for which, in the course or furtherance of his business, he had to pay a consideration which attracted VAT? The fact that at the same time someone else (the purchaser) also received a service as part of the same transaction does not deprive Redrow of its right to deduct. The service supplied to a person might well consist of the right to have services rendered to a third party. The grant of such a right is itself a supply of services. It is sufficient for Redrow to be entitled to deduct input tax if it received something of value in return for the payment of the agent's fee and what it obtained was for the purposes of its business.

**17.275** The importance of the contractual relationship was emphasised by the tribunal in *Ashfield District Council v C & E Commrs (2001 STC 1706)*. The Council made housing improvement grants to home-owners. It also helped the home-owner to find a suitable contractor, supervised the contractor and paid the grant money direct to the contractor. It was held that the Redrow principle could not apply as the contractual relationship was between the home-owner and the contractor, not the Council and the contractor and that the Council paid the contractor as agent for the home-owner. Accordingly it could not reclaim the VAT on the contractor's charges.

**17.276** Customs also regard the payment of the costs as part of the consideration for an assignment, etc. (Law Society Press Release 28 October 1992). For example, suppose that a lease provides that a tenant can assign his lease subject to his landlord's consent and subject to his paying the landlord's costs which came to £300 plus £52.50 VAT. If the tenant pays the full £352.50 he cannot recover the VAT. In addition the landlord is deemed to have made a supply of services to the tenant for £352.50. If the tenant is exercising a right under the lease, which will be the case where he has an absolute right to assign or where the landlord's consent is not to be unreasonably withheld, this supply is made under the lease and will not attract VAT unless the rent under the lease is VATable. If the assignment is a result of the landlord exercising his discretion, Customs regard the supply as separate from the lease so it will attract VAT. As the solicitor supplies his services to the landlord, the landlord is presumably entitled to treat the £52.50 that the tenant has paid as input tax – and to set it against the £52.50 he owes Customs on his own deemed supply.

**17.277** Business Brief 20/93 stated that, where the mortgage supports it, Customs will regard the lender as acting as agent for the borrower and that the selling costs can be treated as both supplied to and by the lender if they are added to the existing loan. They subsequently had second thoughts and retreated a little from this position from 1 July 1994 (with what they regard as their more liberal concession applying up to that date). They are now prepared to treat the lender as agent of the borrower – for the purpose of bad debt relief only and not for any other purpose – in relation to costs relating directly to the sale of the property and which would have ordinarily been incurred by the borrower had he arranged the sale himself (Business Brief 24/94). This will allow the lender to claim bad debt relief for such costs to the extent that they are not recovered from the borrower (or the sale of the property) – as *Regulation 9(3)* of the *VAT (Bad Debt Relief) Regulations 1986* (*SI 1986 No 335*) treats the latest supply as giving rise to the bad debt. The same treatment applies to expenditure on repairs and maintenance. If the lender uses its own in-house estate agency or legal department to deal with the sale, it can treat itself as making a supply as principal to the lender – provided that it accounts for output tax on that notional supply.

**17.278** Customs are not prepared to grant similar relief for costs incurred on services provided to the lender as principal, such as legal fees for taking possession, locksmith fees for securing the property, or the cost of pursuing a claim against a valuer for negligence. The VAT on such items is input tax attributable to the exempt loan. Nor are they willing to grant relief for costs in relation to letting the property; they regard these as supplied to the borrower and nothing to do with the lender. Costs incurred by a *Law of Property Act 1925* receiver in respect of the sale are covered by the concession, but only if the VAT element of such costs has been borne by the lender, i.e. not if the borrower has claimed the VAT as input VAT. Where the lender incurs expenditure on completing the construction of a partially completed building, or on major refurbishment of a property prior to sale, they are prepared to treat the charge of such costs to the borrower as a supply by the lender to the borrower (and thus potentially eligible for bad debt relief) if the sale of the building is either a taxable supply or a transfer of a going concern or, in the case of building (but not refurbishment) costs, if the property is the subject of a taxable letting and output tax on the rents has been paid over to Customs. They are not prepared to grant bad debt relief for such costs where the sale or letting of the building is exempt (Business Brief 24/94).

## Payments by Guarantors

**17.279** A similar problem arises in respect of payments of rent by a guarantor where the option to tax has been exercised and the guarantor is called on to pay the rent. The supply under the lease is to the tenant not to the guarantor, and accordingly the guarantor is not entitled to recover the VAT as input tax. *Kenwood Appliances Ltd (13876)* was the assignee of a lease granted to M Ltd and it had itself re-assigned it to F Ltd. F Ltd became insolvent and defaulted. The landlord recovered the rent from the guarantor of M Ltd's obligations, who in turn sought indemnity from Kenwood. Kenwood argued that as each payment of rent was a separate supply which was deemed under the *VAT Regulations 1995, Reg 85* to take place at the date of payment, and M Ltd's obligation which the guarantor settled arose under its lease, the supply was a supply to M Ltd. The VAT tribunal held that the deemed separate supply was a supply to the person entitled at the relevant time to enjoyment of the rights under the lease, namely F Ltd (which it appears was not VAT-registered at the time). Payments by a vendor of property who guarantees the rent it will fetch are dealt with at 17.305 below.

**Transfer of a Business as a Going Concern**

**17.280** The transfer of a business or part of a business as a going concern is neither a supply of goods or a supply of services and thus does not attract VAT (*VAT (Special Provisions) Order 1995* (*SI 1995 No 1268*) *Article 5*) provided that certain conditions are met – one of which is that 'the transferee is already, or immediately becomes as a result of the transfer, a taxable person'. This does not apply to a VATable transfer of a building or land (whether because the option to tax has been exercised or the building is a new building) unless the transferee has exercised the option to charge VAT in respect of the building concerned with effect from the date on which his acquisition takes place, and has given written notice of his election to Customs before that date (*Article 5(2)*). It should particularly be noted that the option to tax needs to be made before the first date on which the grant would have been treated as made if the transfer were not a TOGC. Customs take the view that this is normally on completion, except where a deposit is received (other than as stakeholder) when it is the date of receipt of that deposit. However it may be dangerous to rely on this view (see 17.281 below). Curiously, a formal election under *VATA 1994, Sch 10 para 2* is required even if the purchaser is a fully taxable person who will use the building in his business or if the building is new and will be sold on by the purchaser within the three-year period, so that he will in any event be a taxable person. If the transferee does not exercise the option to tax but acquires as a going concern a business which includes a VATable property, only the property will attract VAT; the going concern exclusion will still apply to the other assets (C & E Press Release 75A/91). See 17.199 above for a salutary lesson in what can go wrong unless the vendor satisfies himself that the purchaser has done all that is required of him.

**17.281** Despite their view on time as stated above, in *Higher Education Statistics Agency Ltd (VTD 15917)*, where a property was bought at auction, Customs successfully argued that a contract for the sale of land is concluded when the final bid at the auction is accepted by the auctioneer, that the result of a binding contract for the sale of land of which specific performance would be granted (i.e. that is enforceable) is that the purchaser becomes the equitable owner of the property, and therefore at the time of the auction the company acquired a beneficial or equitable interest in the land which amounts to the grant of an interest in the land and this was at a time when it was agreed that no election was in place. The High Court upheld the decision (*2000 STC 332*) but on different grounds, namely that the receipt of the deposit was deemed by *Article 56* to be a taxable supply. Customs said subsequent to the tribunal decision that there was nothing explicit in the tribunal decision to suggest that the relevant date could be the contract date (Business Brief 16/99). The tribunal decision actually states '48 . . . It is unclear what the draftsman had in mind . . . although in property law the result of a binding contract for the sale of land of which specific performance would be granted is a transfer of an equitable interest in the land there are many reasons why such a contract might not be completed and accordingly a contract is a circumstance that a grant could be said to have been treated as having been made, if for some reason it was not completed . . . 54 . . . largely for the reason that it is the decision which gives more meaning to the words "the date of which the grant would have been treated as made" (see para 48), I have decided the matter in favour of the Respondents'. That looks fairly explicit to this author. Moses J doubted whether the draftsman ever envisaged these provisions applying in the circumstances of an auction where the auctioneer acts as agent for the vendor but felt that the words of the order could not bear any alternative construction. Although not addressed by Moses J, there is probably an inference from his judgment that no problem arises where a deposit is received as stakeholder, which is Customs' long held view.

**17.282** Customs consider that a sale of a letting building can be a transfer of a business as a going concern if:

(*a*) the property is to be used by the purchaser for carrying on the same kind of business as the vendor, i.e. he will continue to let it, not necessarily to the same tenant or tenants; and

(*b*) the 'business' transferred is capable of operation as an independent business – which will apply to virtually any letting property.

It is not clear if head (*a*) is met if the property was previously let, is empty at the time of transfer, and will be relet by the purchaser only after refurbishment. The safe course is to seek to clear the position in advance with Customs. In *Golden Oak Partnership (VTD 7212)* it was held that a sale of a development site on which the vendor had intended to build accommodation to be let on zero-rated leases and on which it had installed drainage, widened the road, and constructed electricity and gas substations, and which it sold to another developer together with a building that it had used as its administrative offices, was a transfer of a going concern and not an exempt supply of land. The VAT tribunal were influenced by the facts that at the time of the sale the land was in the course of active development, the purchaser had continued the development without a break (this was not strictly correct as he obtained and implemented a new planning consent) and on completion had granted zero-rated leases. However, in *Gulf Trading and Management Ltd (VTD 16847)*, where the only work done prior to resale was to fence the land, carry out soil inspection and prepare drawings with a view to obtaining planning consent, the tribunal said such works did not relate to active development so the appellant's ownership of the site did not constitute a business.

**17.283** They do not consider there to be a transfer of a going concern where

(*a*) the purchaser of a property rental business is a member of the same VAT group as the existing tenant (as letting to oneself cannot be a business), or

(*b*) a member of a VAT group sells to a third party a property which is being rented to another member of the group (as the letting is not a business whilst the property is within the group).

However they did not take this point in relation to transactions before 1 January 1999. Where the tenant which is a member of the VAT group is only one of a number of tenants, the presence of outside tenants will however qualify the building as a TOGC (Business Brief 26/98).

**17.284** In *ACS Hordern (VTD 8941)* the taxpayer bought and planted forestry land. He registered for VAT as an intending trader. Before making any taxable supplies he sold the land. Customs sought to recover the input tax provisionally repaid on the planting, etc. costs. They contended that a business could not be a going concern until some supplies had been made. The VAT tribunal disagreed. It thought the business had been a going concern from the time the trees were planted and that, as the business was of a continuing nature and the purchaser was able to take it over and carry it on as before, there had been a transfer of a going concern.

**17.285** There is a particular problem where the property is acquired in the name of a nominee. For example, a property acquired by a partnership of more than four members will normally be registered in the name of four of them as nominees for all the partners. Similarly, if property is held for an unincorporated association it will be registered in the name of nominees. The nominee will not be carrying on the business and therefore the transfer of a going concern rules do not technically apply. From 1 June 1996 Customs are prepared to treat the beneficial owner as the transferee (if the parties wish) if the nominee holds the land for a named beneficial owner (Business Brief 10/96).

They will not do so if the identity of the beneficial owner is not disclosed to the vendor. The vendor is expected to check that the beneficial owner is VAT-registered and, where necessary, has opted to tax the property. The concession looks only at a nominee for the purchaser. Customs interpret the *VAT (Special Provisions) Order 1995* as requiring the transferee to carry on the business but there is no specific requirement for the transferor to do so. The problems of joint ownership are considered at 17.292 below.

**17.286** Where the sale of a building constitutes the transfer of a business as a going concern VAT incurred on the legal and other costs of the transfer relates to overheads of the business. It is therefore fully deductible if the business is fully taxable and partially deductible if it is partly exempt (unless there is a direct and immediate link with a clearly defined part of the business so that the overheads relate only to that part). This was confirmed by the ECJ in *Abbey National plc v C & E Commrs (2001 STC 297) (Case C-408/98)*. The logic is that in principle the various services used by the transferor for the purpose of the transfer have a direct and immediate link with the whole economic activity of the taxable person. The court did not consider the position of the transferee but that logic seems equally applicable to the transferee. In *London & Exmoor Estates Ltd (VTD 16707)*, in contrast, legal fees on the abortive purchase of a property were held not to be a cost component of any taxable supply or intended taxable supply. This decision is questionable in the light of the Abbey National decision.

**17.287** *Scottish Homes (VTD 16644)* was established as a statutory body to take over management of residential properties in the public sector. It carried out improvement works including electrical rewiring, replacement of windows and doors, major roof repairs, new kitchens and central heating systems. It claimed that it had used the improvement work in making taxable as well as exempt supplies because it carried out the improvements partly to encourage tenants to exercise their statutory right to buy. This was accepted by the tribunal. The cost of the improvement work was part of the costs of the supplies made by the business as a whole, including both sales and lettings, and there was a sufficient and immediate link to its taxable transactions to justify apportionment of the input tax.

### Apportionments on Completions

**17.288** Customs have agreed with the Law Society that apportionments of rent on the completion of a sale of a landlord's interest in tenanted property are outside the scope of VAT (Law Society's Gazette, 1 May 1991).

**Statutory Compensation**

**17.289** Compensation paid to a tenant under the *Landlord and Tenant Act 1954* or the *Agricultural Holdings Act 1986* is outside the scope of VAT (Notice 742B, para 13). However, compensation negotiated in lieu of these statutory rights, or a top-up payment to supplement it, is a standard-rated supply of services by the tenant irrespective of the VAT status of the property.

**Payments under Planning Act agreements**

**17.290** Property developers enter into a wide variety of agreements with planning authorities and water or sewage undertakings under, for example, *Town and Country Planning Act 1990, s 106* and similar enactments to provide the authority with a 'planning gain' in connection with the grant of planning permission. Customs' view on the VAT effect of such agreements is as follows.

(*a*) If a developer vests for no monetary consideration a new road or a new sewer or ancillary works in the local authority, etc. there is not a supply to the authority (so no VAT needs to be accounted for) but input tax in relation to the construction of such works is part of the cost of the main development, and therefore deductible, unless the supplies in relation to the development will be exempt supplies. (Notice 742, para 7.11).

(*b*) Similarly, if the developer provides other building work or other services free or at a nominal charge under a *section 106* agreement, the provision of those services is not a taxable supply but the input tax in relation to them is normally recoverable as part of the cost of the main development. (Notice 742, para 7.12).

(*c*) Payments in money to the local authority under such an agreement are not consideration for taxable supplies, other than a payment to a water company to supply mains water and sewerage services. (Notice 742, para 7.13).

**Transfers of Estate Roads, etc**

**17.291** If a developer of a housing or industrial estate transfers the basic amenities of estate roads and footpaths, communal parking, and open space to a management company which will maintain them, no taxable supply is regarded as taking place but the input tax in relation to such items is regarded as attributable to the houses, warehouses or factories on the estate. (Notice 742, para 7.14). Customs have said that this does not, however, apply to any other transfer of land or buildings, such as a management office (Notice 742A, para 19F – now withdrawn). The logic behind this distinction is not readily apparent. It is not repeated in the current edition of Notice 742.

**Joint Ownership**

**17.292** Where the benefit of the consideration for the grant of a major interest accrues to the person constructing the building, but that person is not the grantor, he is deemed to be the person making the grant for the purpose of determining whether zero-rating applies (*VATA 1994, Sch 10 para 8*). This is intended to cover joint ownerships and, presumably, nominees. In law, joint ownership is normally a trust for sale with the joint owners being the beneficiaries. Accordingly, they will in legal terms grant leases as trustees but, in their capacity as trustees, would not be the person constructing the building. *Sch 10 para 7* ensures that the benefit of zero-rating is not lost because of this technicality. It was held by the VAT tribunal in *GW & JA Green (VTD 9016)* that joint owners were jointly registrable for VAT (see 17.124 above). *Schedule 10, para 8* will be disapplied when *VATA 1994, s 51A* (see 17.294 below) is brought into effect and is operative. The owners of the legal title will then be deemed to be the person making the grant.

**17.293** Prior to 1995, there were no special rules for co-owners. Customs took the view that joint ownership of property constitutes a partnership between the joint owners. Accordingly, they considered that it is not possible for one joint owner to exercise the option to tax and for the other not to do so. Conversely, if one of the joint owners is a taxable person because of his other activities, his share of the income from the jointly-owned properties need not be aggregated with his individual supplies. It will be interesting to see if a VAT tribunal is prepared to impose a late registration penalty if joint owners who ought to have registered for VAT, e.g. if they are developing the building, register individually and not as a partnership. Customs' position was upheld by the VAT tribunal in *GW & JA Green (VTD 9016)* on the basis that the supply of the building was made jointly and there was no basis for dividing the value of the supplies between them. This does not seem to justify deeming two individuals to constitute a separate 'person', however.

**17.294** Statutory backing has been given to Customs' view by *VATA 1994, s 51A* from a date that at the time of writing, some seven years after this provision was introduced by *FA 1995*, is still to be fixed. It is believed that Customs are having second thoughts about this legislation. It applies to a supply consisting in the grant, assignment or surrender of an interest in or right over land (including a licence) by more than one person. It treats those persons as a single person, 'the property-owner', distinct from the individuals in relation not only to that supply but also in relation to all other grants, assignments or surrenders of interests in, or rights over land, for which the grantors are the same persons. Curiously it does not apply to a supply to more than one person. This could be rather awkward as, when land is acquired, any input tax is apparently charged to the grantors and not to the property owner, but presumably Customs will not take this point. The grantors are not, surprisingly, jointly and severally liable in relation to the VAT obligations of the property-owner. Customs can serve assessments and other notices on any of the grantors (but addressed to the property-owner by the name by which it is registered). If there is a change in the joint owners, the original owners remain liable until Customs have been notified of the change. Where the benefit of the consideration accrues to trustees, the trustees and not the beneficiaries are to be treated as the owners.

**17.295** One effect of this appears to be that if the same persons are the trustees of a number of different trusts, they will all be covered by a single VAT registration. A joint application can be made to disapply this rule so that the beneficiaries become the property-owner. Unfortunately the application is to be made jointly between the trustees and 'all of the persons for the time being in existence' who are beneficiaries. There will be practical difficulties in this in many cases. If some beneficiaries are non-UK resident, there may be difficulties in obtaining their signatures. A discretionary beneficiary of a trust is unlikely to want to take on the potential VAT liabilities involved in being part of the property-owner when he may never benefit under the trust. If some beneficiaries are infants, the election may have to be approved by the Court to be valid. Furthermore, the application is subject to Customs' discretion, so the effort involved in making it could prove futile if, at the end of the day, Customs decide that the registration should be of the trustees.

## Options

**17.296** The grant of an option to acquire land is the exempt grant of a right over land. Accordingly, it may be possible to reduce substantially the tax on the disposal of a new building by attaching most of the price to the option and requiring a comparatively small price to be paid for the building itself.

## Domestic Accommodation

**17.297** Input tax incurred by a company in relation to goods or services in connection with the provision of accommodation to be used for domestic purposes by a director of the company (or his spouse, or a relative, or the spouse of a relative of either the director or his spouse) is treated as incurred for non-business purposes, and is accordingly not deductible (*VATA 1994, s 24(3)*). This disallowance is wider than simply domestic accommodation, as it would cover, for example, an office provided for the use of personal staff of the director who he engages for his domestic purposes. 'Relative' is not defined. There is no similar restriction on accommodation provided for employees, but it should not be assumed that input tax will be recoverable in relation to building work on a house owned by a company and occupied by an employee. Prior to the introduction of this provision in 1990 the approach of the VAT tribunals to accommodation used partly for business purposes and partly as living accommodation for a director had been to regard it as being partly for business and partly for non-business purposes and to require an apportionment of the input tax. *VATA 1994, s 24(3)* does not affect the deductibility of expenditure in relation to accommodation occupied by a sole trader or partner in a partnership, but again the practice has been to treat a portion of such expenditure as having been incurred for non-business purposes even if a primary business purpose for the expenditure could be established. Since 27 July 1993 there has been a further difficulty. On an appeal against a decision of Customs in relation to the allowance of input tax on the supply of 'something in the nature of a luxury, amusement or entertainment', the VAT tribunal is prohibited from altering the decision of Customs unless it considers it was unreasonable, or would have been unreasonable if at that time they had been aware of information that became available between the time of determination and the time of the hearing (*VATA 1994, s 84(4)*, deriving from *FA 1993, s 46*). During the course of the Finance Bill debates the Minister declined to elaborate on the words in inverted commas, saying that their meaning depends on the facts of each case.

**17.298** What happens where part of a building is used as a private residence and part as business premises? That was the question in *Finanzamt Ülzen v Armbrecht (1995 STC 997)*. The European Court of Justice held that the private part is outside the scope of VAT, as where a taxable person performs transactions in a private capacity he does not act as a taxable person, and there is nothing in the *Sixth Directive* which precludes a taxable person who wishes to retain part of an item of property amongst his private assets from excluding it from the tax system. Input tax attributable to such excluded part is of course not deductible. This principle was followed by the VAT tribunal in *Wellright Ltd (VTD 14646)*. In *Dysart Developments Ltd (VTD 17333)*, where the company, which is a property development company, occupied premises in the grounds of the residence of its managing director, Customs sought to disallow 50% of the costs of reconstructing a fountain, reducing its circumference to produce additional car parking and remodelling a pond 'to promote the Appellant's landscaping ability and its environmental concerns'. The tribunal allowed the entire input tax, finding that the goods or services which were supplied to the Appellant company were wholly for the purpose of its business. It is doubtful whether this decision is of general application. Evidence was given by the managing director that she in fact derived little personal benefit from the works. The works to the fountain were necessitated by the needs of the company to accommodate its business visitors; she had been happy to keep topping up the pond, and the work to reline it was done to protect the company's reputation.

**17.299** Customs and the National Farmers Union have agreed guidelines for the recovery of input tax on repairs, maintenance, renovation, etc. of farmhouses – although Customs say that these do not give any automatic entitlement:

(*a*) in the case of a normal working farm where the VAT-registered person is actively engaged in running it, 70% of the input tax may be recovered;

(*b*) where the building work is more associated with an alteration (e.g. building an extension) it is necessary to look at the purpose for the construction; if the dominant purpose is a business one, the 70% figure will apply, but if the dominant purpose is a personal one, then the recoverable amount is unlikely to exceed 40% and in some cases will be nil;

(*c*) where farming is not a full-time occupation for the VAT-registered person, Customs expect that the recoverable portion will be somewhere between 10% and 30% only;

(*d*) if the occupant of the farmhouse is a director of a company (or a connected person) then 17.297 above will apply and nothing will be recoverable.

**Rent-free Periods**

**17.300** There was concern for a time that where a landlord granted a tenant a rent-free period, Customs might seek to exact VAT on the rent foregone. The then Minister, Mrs Gillian Shephard, explained in a House of Commons Written Answer on 17 December 1991 (Hansard, Vol 201, Col 119) that 'rent-free periods are outside the scope of VAT unless services are performed in return by the tenant for the landlord. As this is uncommon, in practice only a few cases will lead to VAT being charged.' This probably means that for a rent-free period to give rise to a VAT liability, an obligation must be imposed on the tenant to carry out works on the premises; it would not be sufficient for it to be allowed to give a tenant time to carry out such works or for it to be negotiated as one of the terms of the lease – although it would obviously be dangerous to express the rent-free period as an inducement to take the lease.

**17.301** Where a tenant was granted a lease with a rent-free period and agreed to carry out specific works to the property, a VAT tribunal held that, in carrying out the works, the tenant had made a taxable supply of the works to the landlord for a consideration (*Ridgeons Bulk Ltd (1992 VATTR 169) (VTD 7655)*). The tenant contended that the tribunal should look only at the lease, which contained no reference to the works, and that the motives for entering into it should be disregarded, but the tribunal held that the two were directly linked in a letter from the landlord to the tenant. Although this case went to appeal *(1994 STC 427)*, the appeal was concerned solely with procedural matters and the admissibility of the landlord's letter as evidence.

**Charities**

**17.302** Where a person bequeaths a dwelling or land to a charity, Customs have expressed the view that 'any supply of the property flowing from the bequest would normally be outside the scope of VAT so a charity would not be able to claim input VAT on the expenses of the sale' (Business Brief 12/92). This is because Customs' legal advice is that such assets are not 'goods which have been donated for sale' which qualify for zero-rating under *VATA 1994, Sch 8 Group 15, Item 1*. This may be open to question if the land is specifically bequeathed with a desire that the charity should sell it, as *Schedule 2* provides that the grant, assignment or surrender of a major interest in land is a supply of goods. Customs indicate that the input tax would still be irrecoverable because the land would not have been a business asset of the charity, although it is by no means clear that such sales cannot themselves constitute a business.

**Receivers**

**17.303** It was held in *re John Willment (Ashford) Ltd (1979 STC 286)* that a receiver appointed under a debenture is obliged to account to Customs for the VAT on supplies made by him since not to do so would make the company, whose agent he was, liable for a criminal offence. In *Sargent v C & E Commrs (1995 STC 398)* it was held that, notwithstanding the de-criminalisation of VAT offences, this principle not only still applies but applies equally to a receiver appointed under a fixed mortgage of a property, i.e. a *Law of Property Act 1925* receiver. The justification is that the VAT element in rents collected by the receiver constitute 'outgoings . . . affecting the mortgaged property', which the receiver is required to discharge under *Law of Property Act 1925, s 109(8)*. The Court of Appeal rejected Customs' alternative submission that *Regulation 9* of the *VAT Regulations 1995*, which enables Customs to treat any person carrying on the business of a company in liquidation or receivership as the taxable person, is wide enough to cover a *Law of Property Act* receiver who, by collecting rents from one property, carries on part of the company's business. See 17.277 above for the VAT position on selling costs of a property incurred by a receiver.

**Building Regulation Fees**

**17.304** The *Building Act 1984* enabled the private sector to apply for approval as inspectors for the purpose of the *Building Regulations*.

NHBC (Building Control Services) Ltd was approved to carry out certain work on residential development, but in the case of flats not exceeding eight storeys in height. From 13 January 1997, other private sector bodies have been approved to cover the whole range of building control work. For applications made from those dates (i.e. 11 November 1995 for NHBC work and 13 January 1997 for other work) local authorities have had to charge VAT on building regulation fees for such work. (Business Briefs 26/95, 5/97 and News Release 10/96).

**Rent Guarantees, etc**

**17.305** If a developer, vendor or lessor of a property guarantees to the purchaser that it will pay the commercial rent until a tenant or sub-tenant is found, the guarantee (and payments under it) are regarded by Customs as outside the scope of VAT. This does not apply if the documents clearly show that it is part of the consideration for the purchaser taking on the building (Notice 742, para 4.3). In most cases such an undertaking is likely to be part of the consideration. The same practice applies when the vendor agrees to pay the purchaser's mortgage interest to the extent it exceeds an agreed cap (para 4.4).

**Dilapidations**

**17.306** Customs regard a payment for dilapidations on the expiry of a lease as outside the scope of VAT, as in their view it represents a claim for damages by the landlord against the tenant's 'want of repair' (Notice 742, para 4.12). As the dilapidations are normally payable under a specific provision in the lease and a claim for damages is not normally outside the scope of VAT if it merely quantifies the value of a supply, it is difficult to follow the logic of this, particularly where the option to tax has been exercised. Where a landlord has opted a building into the tax net and the tenant is prepared to pay an amount to terminate the lease prematurely, it is worth considering whether a reduced termination payment plus a payment for dilapidations should be demanded instead of simply a taxable termination payment.

**Exchange of Land**

**17.307** Care needs to be taken where a transaction involves an exchange of land. This occurred in *Cumbernauld Development Corporation (VTD 14630)*. Cumbernauld wished to dispose of a site, the access to which was blocked by the club house and car park of a golf club. It entered into an agreement with the golf club under which the club transferred the land to Cumbernauld and Cumbernauld provided it with a club house, leisure facilities, car parking and an enlargement of the golf course adjoining on land owned by Cumbernauld. The golf club also agreed to allow preferential use of its course by local residents. The land transferred by the golf club was worth £120,000 ignoring any ransom element. The cost to Cumbernauld of carrying out the works on the adjoining land was £3 million. The agreement was expressed to be for nil consideration but the parties accepted that there had been supplies for a consideration. The question before the tribunal was what was the value of the supply of the access land by the golf club to Cumbernauld.

**17.308** The tribunal held that the £120,000 figure could not be used, as the value of the access land to Cumbernauld was far greater. As the subjective value of the supply is the value attributed by the recipient to what is received (*Empire Stores Ltd v C & E Commrs (Case C–33/93) (1994 STC 623)*), the consideration is the value of the land to Cumbernauld. This is not necessarily £3 million. Some elements of the package, such as the need to allow local residents on the course and the increased costs of maintenance of the larger course, might have a negative value that should be deducted from the figure. The case was therefore adjourned to allow the parties to try to agree a value.

### References to 'Grant'

**17.309** The word 'grant' has given rise to difficulties. It is specifically stated to include an assignment or surrender and also the supply made by a person to whom an interest is surrendered where he is paid to accept the surrender (*VATA 1994, 9 Sch, Group 1, Notes 1 & 1A*). Customs have said that it means a transfer of title or the execution of a lease and does not cover rental payments under existing leases even though such payments are deemed to be supplies. The VAT status is normally determined at the time of a grant. However, *VATA 1996, s 96(10A)* (introduced by *FA 1997, s 35(1)*) provides that, where the grant of an interest, right, licence or facility gives rise to supplies made at different times after the making of the grant and the question whether any of those supplies is zero-rated or exempt depends on the nature of the grant, that question is to be determined at the time of the supply not by reference to the time of the grant. For example, the VAT status of rents will depend on whether the option to tax has been exercised at the time each payment of VAT fell due, not on whether it had been exercised at the time the lease was entered into. This provision has retrospective effect to the introduction of VAT.

### Work required under Statutory Powers

**17.310** Local authorities have statutory powers under various legislation to require a property-owner to carry out specified works to his premises. Where the owner does not comply with the notice, the local authority can carry out the work itself and recover the cost from the property-owner. Where they do this, the supply by the builder is to the local authority. In recovering the cost the local authority is not making a supply to the landowner; it is merely exercising a statutory power. However, the local authority, having incurred the VAT, is entitled to recover it from Customs under *VAT 1994, s 33* (Business Brief 19/98). On this basis it is probably entitled to recover only the VAT-exclusive amount from the property-owner, although that may depend on the precise wording of the statute involved. If the property-owner asks the local authority to arrange for the work to be done and send him the bill, there will in contrast be a supply to the local authority by the builder and an onward VATable supply by the local authority to the property-owner.

### Road and Bridge Tolls

**17.311** The UK believes that toll charges levied by local authorities and by bodies operating under PFI (private finance initiative) or PPP (public private partnership) concessions are not payment for a supply and are thus outside the scope of VAT and that other toll charges are exempt from VAT as the grant of a right over land (Business Brief 26/99). Unfortunately, the EC Commission and the European Court of Justice do not agree and consider tolls levied by private operators to be taxable supplies, although the ECJ accepted that tolls levied by local authorities are not (*EC Commission v United Kingdom, CJEC Case C-359/97, 2000 STC 777*). The government has asked Customs to hold urgent consultations with operators of tolled bridges and roads to devise a scheme of government support to offset the cost of VAT so that motorists do not pay more and it is as simple as possible for businesses to reclaim the VAT that they have to pay (Press Release 12 September 2000). The concept of a right to pass over a stretch of road being an exempt grant of a right over land fits uneasily with a right to go on to a tennis court being a right to make use of the facilities and with Customs' concept of a licence (see 17.133 above).

# Inheritance Tax

**18.1** Inheritance tax was introduced as a combined estate and gift tax although it does not now apply to most gifts. It is chargeable on the assets held by a person on death and on the following gifts:

(*a*) those made within seven years prior to the transferor's death;

(*b*) those where the donor reserves or enjoys a benefit; and

(*c*) gifts into settlement (with some exceptions) or to companies.

There are a number of exemptions. The most important are gifts between spouses (which includes a gift on death but does not apply to a gift from a UK domiciled person to one who is domiciled elsewhere) and gifts to individuals provided that the donor survives for at least seven years after making the gift. The inter-spouse exemption also applies to a gift in settlement which creates an interest in possession in favour of the spouse. Where a house is owned jointly by husband and wife, conventional planning is for the one who dies first to leave his interest in the house to the children (at least to the extent that this can be done within the £250,000 inheritance tax nil rate band). Such planning in relation to the private residence is considered at 13.42 onwards.

Obviously where a gift is made by one individual to another it cannot be known whether or not a charge to tax will arise in respect of the gift as the exemption is conditional upon the donor surviving for the seven-year period. Such a gift is known as a 'potentially exempt transfer'. Where the donor does die in that period, so that the gift generates an inheritance tax charge, business property relief, agricultural property relief, and the right to pay the tax by instalments will be granted only if the conditions set out in 18.2, 18.24 and 18.32 below are met.

## Agricultural Property Relief

**18.2** A gift of agricultural property is effectively either exempted from inheritance tax or taxed on only 50% of its value. This is because the legislation provides that on a gift or other transfer of agricultural property which has been either (*a*) occupied by the transferor for the purpose of agriculture throughout the two years ending with the date of the transfer (or if it replaced other agricultural property they were together so occupied for at least two out of the five years to the date of the transfer), or

(*b*) owned by the transferor throughout the seven years ending with the date of transfer and occupied throughout that period (by anyone) for the purpose of agriculture (or if it replaced other agricultural property they were together so occupied for at least seven out of the ten years to the date of transfer),

the amount of the value transferred is to be reduced by:

(1) 100% if either:

(A) the interest of the transferor immediately before the transfer carries the right to vacant possession or the right to obtain it within the next twelve months (or, if it is a joint interest or interest in common, that of the joint co-owners does so); or

(B) the transferor has been beneficially entitled to the interest since before 10 March 1981, and both

(i) if he had disposed of his interest immediately before 10 March 1981 and made the appropriate claim he would have been entitled to agricultural property relief, and such relief would not have been restricted by the old £250,000 or 1,000 acres limitation, and

(ii) at no time after 9 March 1981 has the interest conferred a right to vacant possession or to obtain vacant possession within twelve months (or could have done but for any act or omission of the transferor); or

(C) the property is let on a tenancy beginning after 31 August 1995, e.g. one under the *Agricultural Holdings Act 1995* (including in Scotland one acquired after that date by right of succession),

(2) 50% in any other case.

(*IHTA 1984, ss 116–118*). Where the transferor is a settlement the trustees (who are the legal owners of the land) are of course deemed to be the transferor (*IHTA 1994, s 115(1)(b)*).

Prior to 10 March 1992 the 100% and 50% reductions were 50% and 30% respectively. The Revenue have confirmed that head (C) covers any tenancy starting after 31 August 1995 including a statutory succession to one starting before that date (Tax Bulletin, Issue 18, August 1995).

In *Exors of G W Harrold decd v CIR (1996 Sp C 71)* the Special Commissioner held that a farmhouse which had been empty but undergoing renovations for a number of years was agricultural property (see 18.7 for the definition) but was not occupied for the purpose of agriculture – or indeed for any purpose – and thus did not qualify for the 100% relief.

**18.3** For the purpose of head (C), if the tenant dies after 31 August 1995 and a new tenancy is subsequently entered into between the landlord and a person in whom the tenancy vested under the deceased tenant's Will or intestacy (or by virtue of an enactment such as the *Agricultural Tenancies Act*), the new tenancy is treated as starting from the date of death (*IHTA 1984, s 116(5A)(5B)*). Accordingly, if the landlord also dies in the interim, the 100% relief will apply, not the 50% relief that would otherwise have been due because the property is legally subject to the old pre-September 1995 tenancy. Similarly if the tenant dies after 31 August 1995 and after having given notice of his intention to retire in favour of a new tenant, the new tenancy is related back to the date of death provided that it is entered into within 30 months of the date the notice of intention to retire was given (*IHTA 1984, s 116 (5D)*).

**18.4** Following ESC F16 the minimum period of ownership or occupation conditions in 18.2(*a*) and (*b*) are regarded as satisfied in respect of an agricultural tied cottage occupied by a retired farm employee or their surviving spouse if either:

(*a*) the occupier is a statutorily protected tenant; or

(*b*) as part of the farm employee's contract of employment, occupation of the cottage is granted under a lease for the employee for life and for the life of their surviving spouse.

**18.5** By concession (ESC F17) the 100% relief under head (B)(ii) above is also given if either:

(*a*) the interest carries a right to vacant possession within 24 months of the date of transfer; or

(*b*) notwithstanding the terms of the tenancy, the transferor's interest is valued at an amount broadly equivalent to the vacant possession value (Inland Revenue Press Release 13.2.1995).

Head (*a*) covers two common situations: *Gladstone v Bower (1960 3 All ER 353)* tenancies (i.e. one for between one and under two years) and tenancies where there is a right to terminate within twelve months but under the *Agricultural Holdings Act 1986* it may take a further twelve months to gain possession. Head (*b*) is only likely to arise where the tenant and landlord are so closely connected that the landlord could dispose of both interests, e.g. land let to a company controlled by the landlord.

**18.6** Where, because of the donor's death within the seven-year period, tax becomes payable on an *inter vivos* transfer that was a potentially exempt transfer, three further conditions need to be met. It has to be shown that:

(i) the transferee has retained the ownership of the property throughout the period from the date of the gift to the date of the donee's death; and

(ii) the property is agricultural property at the date of the donor's death and has been occupied for the purposes of agriculture (not necessarily by the transferee) throughout the period from the date of the gift to the date of the donor's death; and

(iii) if the property gifted was shares in a company, the agricultural land must have continued to be owned by the company and occupied for the purpose of agriculture throughout the period to the date of the donor's death.

If the donee predeceases the donor, the period for which the above conditions must be satisfied terminates on the donee's death. If the above conditions are met in respect of part only of the property gifted, the relief applies to that part (*IHTA 1984, s 124A*). If condition (i) is not satisfied but the donee disposed of the original property and applied the whole of the consideration in acquiring replacement agricultural property, the relief can still be claimed (*IHTA 1984, s 124B*). The replacement property must be bought within three years of the disposal of the original property or such longer period as the Revenue may allow. Where the PET crystallised before 30 November 1994 the re-acquisition period was only twelve months.

The relief is calculated on the actual value transferred before grossing up for any tax payable by the donor (*IHTA 1984, s 116(7)*). If the condition in (B)(i) above is not met because the limit is exceeded (calculated before grossing up by the tax payable), the 100% deduction will still apply on the first £250,000 or 1,000 acres but the deduction will be limited to 50% on the remainder of the land (*IHTA 1984, s 116(4)*).

**18.7** The relief applies to agricultural property in the UK, the Channel Islands and the Isle of Man (*IHTA 1984, s 115(5)*). Agricultural property means agricultural land or pasture. It includes woodland and any building used in connection with the intensive rearing of livestock or fish if such woodland or building is occupied with (and its occupation is ancillary to) agricultural land or pasture. It also includes such cottages, farm buildings and farmhouses (together with the land occupied with them) as are of a character appropriate to the property (*IHTA 1984, s 115(2)*). In *Starke v CIR (1995 STC 689)*, it was held that a 2.5 acre site containing a substantial house and a number of buildings used for egg production, for producing heavy hogs, for housing cattle and storing feed, and in connection with the rearing of cattle and sheep was not agricultural land or pasture. The site was used as part of a 171 acre mixed farm, the remainder of which was owned by a farming company. The judge felt that 'land' has to be construed with 'pasture' and must therefore be given the limited meaning of bare land without buildings on it. Any other meaning would render much of the rest of the definition – in particular, buildings of a character appropriate to the property – largely pointless. This reasoning was approved by the Court of Appeal. In *Dixon v CIR (2002 STC (SCD) 53)*, there was a small amount of sales of fruit from the orchard of a cottage, hens were kept in the garden for eggs and poultry meat, and in the summer months a neighbouring farmer was allowed to graze six ewes and lambs in the orchard. It was held that, although these activities come within the definition of agriculture, the orchard and garden were not agricultural land or pasture within the meaning of *section 115(2)*. It should be stressed that the relief applies only to the agricultural value of the property, i.e. its value on the assumption that it is subject to a perpetual covenant prohibiting its use otherwise than as agricultural property (*IHTA 1984, s 115(3)*). Any excess of the market value of the land over its agricultural value is taxed in full.

**18.8** The cultivation of short rotation coppice (see 16.1 above) is regarded as agriculture from 6 April 1995. Accordingly, land on which such coppice is cultivated is agricultural land, and buildings used in connection with such cultivation are farm buildings (*FA 1995, s 154(2)*).

**18.9** On the other hand, land used solely for grazing horses used by the grazier for leisure purposes has been held by the Special Commissioners not to be agricultural land as the horses had no connection with agriculture (*Wheatley & Anor v CIR (1998 STC (SCD 60) Sp C 149)*). The Commissioner expressed an opinion that 'grazing by draught animals, for example, might qualify'.

**18.10** For transfers of value after 25 November 1996 (and previous transfers where the liability crystallises after that date) land in a habitat scheme is treated as agricultural land, management in accordance with such a scheme is regarded as agriculture, and buildings used in connection with such management are treated as farm buildings. Land is in a habitat scheme if an application for aid under the *Habitat (Water Fringe) Regulations 1994*, the *Habitat (Former Set-Aside Land) Regulations 1994*, or the *Habitat (Salt-Marsh) Regulations 1994* (or their Scottish or Northern Irish equivalents) has been accepted in respect of the land and the undertakings given in relation to the scheme are still in force (*IHTA 1984, s 124C* inserted by *FA 1997, s 94*).

**18.11** Where land is occupied by a company and the land is owned by a person who controls the company (within the meaning of *IHTA 1984, s 269*), or it is occupied by a partnership and the land is owned by a person who controls the partnership, it will be treated as being occupied by that person to ascertain whether or not relief is due (*IHTA 1984, s 119(1)*). If land is occupied by a Scottish partnership it is to be treated as being occupied by the partners for the purposes of *section 117* (minimum period of ownership) and *section 118* (replacement property) but not for any other purpose (*IHTA 1994, s 119(2)*). In particular the Revenue do not consider that it applies for the purpose of *section 121* which provides an alternative test to *section 117* (see 18.17) (*IHTA 1984, s 119*). Where replaced property is taken into account to meet the qualifying conditions, the relief is not to exceed what it would have been if the replacement had not taken place (*IHTA 1984, s 118(3)*). This appears to require the agricultural value of the previous property to be ascertained at the date of the gift rather than at the date that the property was disposed of. If it is less than the agricultural value at the date of the gift of the new property (i.e. the one gifted) the relief will be calculated on that lower amount.

**18.12** Changes resulting from the conversion of a sole tradership to a partnership or vice versa or in the composition of a partnership are to be ignored (*IHTA 1984, s 118(4)*). This presumably means that any restriction is to be simply by reference to any difference in value between the old property and the new, and no further restriction (or relaxation of the restriction) needs to be made if the taxpayer's share of the old property differs from his share of the new.

**18.13** The concept of a working farmer that applied up to 1981 has been done away with completely. The sole tests now are whether the land is used for the purpose of agriculture and how long it has been owned. The relief is 100% of the agricultural value if the land has vacant possession at the time of disposal (or will have within twelve months), irrespective of whether it has been let out during the preceding seven years or occupied by the owner himself. If it is let land at the time of disposal the relief is only 50%. The reason for this distinction is to eliminate double relief. The tenanted value of agricultural land is well below its vacant possession value and the government felt that, as this discount already confers a substantial benefit, the full 100% relief should not be given in addition. As a transitional measure a person who owned tenanted land (as well as some land he farmed himself) prior to 10 March 1981 and who would have expected to get the old 50% deduction will keep his right to the 100% deduction for so long as the land remains tenanted (or until he is in a position to bring the tenancy to an end).

**18.14** Where the transferor became entitled to his interest in the agricultural property on the death of his spouse after 9 March 1981, in looking at whether the 100% relief is due:

(*a*) he will be treated as beneficially entitled to the interest at any time his spouse was so entitled;

(*b*) if the land qualifies as let land before 10 March 1981, it must have so qualified by virtue of the spouse's ownership; and

(*c*) if the land qualifies as let land before 10 March 1981, it must not have become vacant possession land at any time after that date whilst in the ownership of either spouse.

(*IHTA 1984, s 120(2)*).

**18.15** Where the transferor became entitled to the agricultural property on the death of another person (or on the death of his spouse before 10 March 1981) he is treated as both owning and occupying it (provided he subsequently occupies it) from the date of the death. If the deceased was his spouse he is also to be treated as having occupied it for agricultural purposes and to have owned it for any period for which his spouse so occupied or owned it (*IHTA 1984, s 120(1)*).

**18.16** If

(*a*) a transfer (the earlier transfer) was eligible for relief (or would have been had the relief existed at the time) and on that transfer the property passed to a person who makes a subsequent chargeable transfer of it (the subsequent transfer) or to his spouse, and

(*b*) at the time of the subsequent transfer it is occupied for the purposes of agriculture by either the owner or the personal representatives of the transferor on the earlier transfer, and

(*c*) either the earlier or the subsequent transfer is a transfer on death, and

(*d*) the property does not qualify for relief on the subsequent transfer only because the transferor cannot meet the requisite length of ownership,

he can be treated as having owned it (and where appropriate occupied it) for the requisite period to attract the relief (*IHTA 1984, s 121*).

**18.17** In other words, if land is transferred by A to B during A's life and B dies at a time when it is occupied for the purpose of agriculture either by B or by the personal representatives of A, but B has not held the property long enough to qualify for relief in his own right, the qualifying period for the transfer on B's death is treated as having been met provided that A's transfer itself qualified for agricultural property relief. Similarly if the property is transferred to B on A's death and B makes a subsequent transfer of the land (either during his lifetime or on death) at a time when the property is occupied for the purpose of agriculture either by B or by the personal representatives of A (e.g. because they are still in the course of administering the estate), B is again treated as having owned the property for the requisite period if the transfer on A's death attracted agricultural property relief.

*Example 37*

John, a widower, owned a farm in Sussex since 1960. It was farmed by him in partnership with his two sons. John died in December 2000. He left the land to his daughter, Jane, and the partnership interest passed to his sons. In November 2001 the daughter joined the partnership. Two months later she gifted an interest in the land to her two brothers.

The land qualified for agricultural property relief on John's death. Jane's gift in January 2002 would not normally qualify for the relief as she had owned the land for less than two years. However as she was farming the land (in partnership) in January 1999 *section 121* grants the relief. (If the partnership had been a Scottish partnership the Revenue would have denied the relief unless Jane controlled the partnership (so that *IHTA 1994, s 119(1)* – see 18.11 – deemed her to be the occupier) as she did not occupy the land.

**18.18** Relief can also be given on the disposal of shares or securities of a company to the extent that the value of those shares represents the agricultural value of agricultural property. The agricultural property must form part of the company's assets and the shares or securities must give the transferor control of the company immediately before the transfer. The definition of control in *IHTA 1984, s 269* applies with the exception that shares or securities cannot be taken into account in determining control if they are valued as separate property under *IHTA 1984, s 176* (shares disposed of within three years of death) (*IHTA 1984, s 122*).

**18.19** To qualify for relief either:

(*a*) the agricultural property must have been occupied by the company (or by a person who subsequently controls the company) for the purpose of agriculture throughout the two years ending with the date of transfer, and the shares must have been owned by the transferor for the same period; or

(*b*) the agricultural property must have been owned by the company throughout the period of seven years ending with the date of the transfer and occupied (by anyone) for the purposes of agriculture throughout that period, and the shares must also have been owned by the transferor for the same period.

(*IHTA 1984, s 123(1)*).

**18.20** The replacement property provisions set out earlier also apply for this purpose (*IHTA 1984, s 123(2)*). If the shares or securities replaced other eligible property (i.e. either agricultural property or shares or securities attracting agricultural property relief) the ownership requirements in (*a*) in 18.19 above will be satisfied if the shares and the replaced property were together owned for at least two of the last five years of ownership and those in (*b*) in 18.19 above will be satisfied if they were owned for at least seven of the last ten years of ownership (*IHTA 1984, s 123(3)*).

**18.21** The relief cannot be claimed if, at the time of the transfer, the transferor has entered into a binding contract for the sale of the property unless that sale is to a company and is wholly or mainly in consideration of the issue of shares or securities which will give the transferor control of the company. Similarly, no relief will be given on a disposal of shares or securities where a binding contract for their sale exists, unless the sale is merely for the purpose of reconstruction or amalgamation (*IHTA 1984, s 124*).

**18.22** Agricultural property relief (and also business property relief – see 18.24 below) is deducted from the value of the agricultural property if that property is the subject of a specific gift. This means that if, for example, the agricultural property is gifted to the deceased's widow the benefit of the relief will be lost. If the agricultural property is included in the residue the relief is apportioned on a pro rata basis between exempt and chargeable parts of the residue – so part of the benefit will be lost to the extent that the widow has an interest in the residue (*IHTA 1984, s 39A*). Previously the relief was given in calculating the overall liability and that liability was, in general, apportioned pro rata between the exempt and chargeable parts of the estate. Clearly assets qualifying for these reliefs are not appropriate subjects of specific gifts to the surviving spouse.

### Grant of Tenancies of Agricultural Property

**18.23** The grant of a tenancy of agricultural property in the UK, the Channel Islands or the Isle of Man (but not elsewhere) for use for agricultural purposes does not constitute a transfer of value if it is made for full consideration in money or money's worth (*IHTA 1984, s 16*). This ensures that the grant of an agricultural tenancy to a connected person even if made for full consideration, cannot give rise to a transfer of value because the reduction in value of the interest retained exceeds the consideration received.

## Business Property Relief

**18.24** Land and buildings can qualify for 100% business property relief where they form part of the assets of a business carried on, either alone or in partnership, by the transferor (*IHTA 1984, ss 104(1)(a), 105(1)(a)*). They can alternatively qualify for 50% relief in two circumstances:

(*a*) where immediately before its transfer the land was used wholly or mainly for the purposes of a business carried on by a company of which the transferor had control, or for the purposes of a business carried on by a partnership of which the transferor was a partner (*IHTA 1984, s 105(1)(d)*); or

(*b*) where immediately before its transfer the land was used wholly or mainly for the purposes of a business carried on by the transferor, and was settled property in which he was beneficially entitled to an interest in possession (*IHTA 1984, s 105(1)(e)*).

Prior to 10 March 1992 the relief was 50% and 30% respectively.

**18.25** A business of property dealing does not qualify for relief (*IHTA 1984, s 105(3)*). It is not clear if this also excludes a business of property development. It probably does not (as the two have been clearly distinguished in other legislation, e.g. EIS and EIS reinvestment relief). A business consisting wholly or mainly of the making or holding of investments does not qualify for relief either (*IHTA 1984, s 105(3)*). Where the business sells a mixture of the use of property and the provision of services it can be difficult to discern whether it amounts to the holding of investments or the carrying on of a trade. This problem is considered in an income tax context at 2.123–2.136. What is said there is equally relevant to inheritance tax – although in *Powell v CIR (1997 STC (SCD) 181; Sp C 120)* the Special Commissioner said 'the income tax status of the income of the business is irrelevant in the context of inheritance tax . . . The availability of business property relief depends entirely on the interpretation of the provisions of the *IHTA 1984* and I do not believe that the past income tax treatment of the income of the business necessarily throws any light on the inheritance tax position.' There are a number of decisions of the Special Commissioners on *section 105(3)*. In *Martin & Horsfall V CIR (1995 STC (SCD) 5; Sp C 2)* the ownership and management of a number of industrial units was held to be the making or holding of investments. So was the letting of four flats (*Burkinyoung v CIR (1995 STC (SCD) 29; Sp C 3)*). The ownership and operation of a caravan park was held to be the making and holding of investments in *Hall v CIR (1997 STC (SCD) 126; Sp C 115)* and also in *Powell v CIR (1997 STC (SCD) 181; Sp C 121)*. However in *Furness v CIR (1999 STC (SCD) 232)* the operation of a caravan park was held to qualify for relief. The taxpayer was able to show the income from caravan sales and other trading activities exceeded the site rents and a considerable amount of work (including 80% of Mr Furness's time) was undertaken in looking after the welfare of the residents of the park and maintaining the park and its structures. Such considerable activity did not suggest a business concerned wholly or mainly with the holding of investments.

This decision was distinguished fairly forceably in a later case, *Weston v CIR (2000 STC (SCD) 30)* so may be of limited application: 'The caravan park in *Furniss* was not a residential park but a holiday park . . . Unlike the company's park . . . [it] was situated in beautiful countryside and offered considerable facilities to its residents.' It was held there, looking at the matter in the round, that the pitch fees were not ancillary to caravan sales but that caravan sales were, if anything, ancillary to pitch fees. The Commissioner appears to have been influenced by a letter from the specialist valuers who, in order to compare the level of return from a residential caravan park with that from commercial property, stated: 'It would not be unreasonable to assume that the trading activities (such as commission and sales) serve to cover the running costs of the park', although the valuer seemed to envisage this statement merely as a rough and ready way to justify basing the yield on the pure pitch fees. This decision was affirmed in the *High Court (2000 STC 1064)* where Lawrence Collins J said three questions need to be asked: Does the company have investments? Is it 'holding' investments? Does its business consist 'wholly or mainly' of 'holding' investments? The cases show that the meaning of investment depends on its context but that property may be held as an investment even if the person who holds it has to take active steps in connection with it. Adopting the definition of investment in *Cook v Medway Housing Society Ltd (1997 STC 90)* (see 7.5) the Commissioners were entitled to answer the first question in the affirmative. Whether a person is holding investments and whether a business consists wholly or mainly of holding investments are questions of fact. It was clear that the Commissioners had taken all of the relevant matters into account and reached a conclusion which was justified by the evidence. The executors sought to take a fresh point in the High Court that the reality was that pitch holders were paying for the services provided rather than for the mere right to enjoy the pitch, but the judge refused to let them do so on the basis that new evidential issues would need to be explored to test this claim.

**18.26** The decision of the Commissioner in the *Weston* case was also much influenced by that in *Farmer & another v CIR (1999 STC (SCD) 321)*. That case involved a farmer who clearly carried on a farming business but also let properties on the farm which were surplus to requirements. The Revenue contended that the business at the farm consisted 'mainly' of making or holding investments, not mainly of farming. The Commissioner accepted that the farm was conducted on a business-like basis. There were 23 tenancies, mostly for a year or less. Farmer did not want to grant long-term leases, which might affect the future use of the estate. Farmer was aged about 80. The farm manager spent 90% of his time on the farm and 10% on lettings. His assistant spent 95% of his time on the farm. Farmer's son, a retired solicitor, spent one and a half days a week on the farm, 30% of which was on farming and 70% on lettings. The rents received varied between 33% and 53% of turnover (mainly because the farming income fluctuated). The Revenue argued that one should look at profits not turnover but the Commissioner thought that the test must be 'of what the business consists', which indicates that all relevant factors of what a business consists requires consideration. He identified five relevant factors: the overall context of the business, the capital employed, the time spent by the employees, the turnover and the profits, and commented, 'When these factors have been considered it will then be necessary to stand back and consider in the round whether the business consisted mainly of making or holding investments'. On doing so he held that the business consisted mainly of farming.

**18.27** The nature of a company's business is a question of fact. In *Executors of the will of Brown (deceased) v CIR (1996 Sp C 83)* the taxpayer had a 99% ordinary shareholding in an unquoted company which operated a night club. The remaining share was owned by the taxpayer's brother and co-director. In 1985 the nightclub was sold and the sale proceeds were placed in an interest-bearing short-term deposit account because the taxpayer wanted access to these funds for the purposes of the business. Neither director considered that the company should cease trading and the taxpayer was actively investigating the purchase of other night clubs. Following the taxpayer's death in 1986, business property relief was claimed but the Revenue denied the relief under *IHTA 1984, s 105(3)* arguing that the company's business since the disposal of the nightclub in 1985 consisted wholly or mainly of the holding of investments. Looking at the evidence as a whole, the Special Commissioner did not accept the Revenue's argument that the nature of the business had changed and business property relief was therefore allowed. In contrast, in *Barclays Bank Trust Co v CIR (1998 STC SCD 125 Sp C 158)* where at the time of the deceased's death in 1990 the company had £300,000 of cash which it claimed was needed to acquire a business property – and subsequently spent over that sum in buying a property although not until 1997 – the Special Commissioners decided that the cash did not qualify for business property relief. It felt that in 1990 it could not be said that there was 'some imperative that the money will fall to be used upon a given project or for some palpable business purpose'.

**18.28** For the purposes of (*a*) and (*b*) in 18.24 above the transferor's interest in the business or the company, as the case may be, must itself be relevant business property in relation to the transfer (*IHTA 1984, s 105(6)*). This may mean that the relief is given only if the land is transferred in conjunction with the business or the shares in the company. The business, or, in the case of the 50% relief, the property, must have been owned by the transferor for at least two years prior to the transfer (*IHTA 1984, s 106*). If this test is not met but the property replaced other property, relief will be given (up to the value of the former property only) if the former property had been owned for at least two years and the two together were held for an aggregate period of at least two out of the five years up to the date of the transfer (*IHTA 1984, s 107*). Where the replaced property was agricultural property of a farming business the period of ownership of such property can be taken into account, as it also constitutes business property (Tax Bulletin, Issue 14, December 1994). If the transferor inherited the property on the death of his spouse, the spouse's period of ownership can be taken into account (*IHTA 1984, s 108*).

**18.29** If part only of a building was used exclusively for the purposes of a trade or business, the value must be apportioned in such manner as may be just, and relief can be given on the business element only (*IHTA 1984, s 112(4)*). Where the 100% relief applies, a further restriction will be necessary if the property was not in business use throughout the two years up to the time of the transfer (*IHTA 1984, s 112*). The relief does not apply if a binding contract for the sale of the property has been entered into at the time of the transfer (other than on the incorporation of a business wholly or mainly for shares or securities) (*IHTA 1984, s 113*).

**18.30** As with agricultural property relief (see 18.2 above), business property relief will be given only if the property gifted (or qualifying replacement property) is retained by the donee throughout the period from the date of the gift to the date of the donor's death (or the donee's death if earlier) and it would have been relevant business property if it had been retained by the donor and gifted by him immediately before his death. Even if the original property is retained, the question as to whether the relief is 100% or 50% seems to depend on what shares are retained by the transferee at the time of his death.

An interesting point on 18.24(*a*) above arose in *Walkers Executors v CIR (2001 STC (SCD) 86) (SpC 275)*. The deceased owned land held for the business of a company in which she was a 50% shareholder and chairman of the board of directors and as such entitled to a casting vote under the company's articles. It was held that she controlled the company by virtue of her casting vote, so that the property qualified for business property relief, even though when casting that vote she owed a fiduciary duty as an officer of the company.

**18.31** If assets do not constitute business property because they are wholly or mainly held as investments this does not preclude claiming agricultural property relief where appropriate. However, if assets which constitute agricultural property can qualify for business property relief it is usually preferable to claim it. Agricultural property relief can apply only to those assets that meet the tests at 18.2 onwards whereas business property relief applies to all of the assets of the business. Agricultural property relief is given only on the agricultural value of the land but business property relief is given on the full value including any development value or hope value element.

## Payment of IHT by Instalments

**18.32** Land (wherever situated) is one of the types of assets on which IHT can be paid by ten equal annual instalments. The instalments carry interest, however, unless the property forms part of a business or an interest in a business (*IHTA 1984, ss 227(3), 234(1)*). Where the tax is payable because a potentially exempt transfer becomes a chargeable transfer, the instalment provisions apply only if the donee still owns the property at the date of the donor's death (*IHTA 1984, s 227(1A)*) or has replaced it by property that itself qualifies for business property relief or agricultural property relief (*FA 1987, Sch 8 para 15(3)*).

## Transfers of Land within Seven Years before Death

**18.33** Where property was transferred *inter vivos* and the transferor dies within the following seven years (three years in relation to transfers before 17 March 1986), the recipient becomes liable to pay IHT if the gift was a potentially exempt transfer (or additional IHT if it was not) to bring the tax charge to the rate that applies on death (subject to a tapering relief for gifts more than three years prior to the death). If the value of the property has fallen between the date of the gift, etc. and the date of death, the tax (or additional tax) is based on the lower figure only (*IHTA 1984, s 131(1)(a)*). If the transferee (or his spouse) has sold the property prior to the date of death it can be based on the sale proceeds if these are below the value at the time of the gift and the sale is an arm's length sale (at a price freely negotiated at the time of sale) to an unconnected person with no right to buy back any part of the property sold (*IHTA 1984, s 131(1)(b)(3)*).

**18.34** In the case of land or an interest in land, special rules apply if either the interest sold or held at the date of death was not the same in all respects and with the same incidents as at the date of the gift, or the land in which the interest subsists was not in the same state and with the same incidents at both dates (*IHTA 1984, s 137(1)(2)*). The market value of the property at the date of death or sale must be increased by the difference between the market value of the interest at the time of the gift and what the market value at the time would have been if the circumstances prevailing at the date of the death or sale had existed at the time of the gift (*IHTA 1984, s 137(1)*). If the change in circumstances reduced rather than increased the value of the property, the value at the date of the death or sale must obviously be reduced by the difference between the values on these two assumptions at the date of the gift (*IHTA 1984, s 137(4)*).

**18.35** If compensation became payable under any enactment to the transferee or his spouse between the two dates because of the imposition of a restriction on the use or development of the land or because the value of the interest is reduced for any other reason, the imposition of that restriction is ignored (both in deciding whether the special rules apply and, if they do, the effect of their application), but the compensation received must be added to the market value of the interest at the date of death or earlier sale (*IHTA 1984, s 137(3)*).

**18.36** If the property gifted was a lease of 50 years or less its market value at the date of death (or prior sale) must be increased by the 'appropriate fraction' of the market value of the interest at the time of the gift (*IHTA 1984, s 138(1)*). The appropriate fraction is based on the capital gains tax wasting asset table (see 11.22 above) and is

$$\frac{\text{table figure for duration of lease at date of gift} - \text{table figure for duration of lease at date of death (or prior sale)}}{\text{table figure for duration of lease at date of gift}}$$

(*IHTA 1984, s 138(2)*).

## Sale of Land from Deceased Estate

**18.37** Relief is also given where an interest in land (other than an interest by way of mortgage or other security) comprised in a person's estate immediately before his death is sold by the 'appropriate person' at less than probate value within the three years following the death (*IHTA 1984, s 191*). The 'appropriate person' will normally be the personal representative. It means the person liable for the inheritance tax attributable to the value of the interest. If there is more than one such person it is the one who in fact pays the tax. The relief must be claimed by the appropriate person (*IHTA 1984, s 191(1)(b)*). No specific time limit for making a claim is given so the normal six-year limit will apply. Property sold in the fourth year after death for a price at or below its value on death, is deemed to have been sold in the three-year period unless the sale is to an authority having compulsory purchase powers (see 18.50) (*IHTA 1984, s 197A*). In *Stonor v CIR (2001 STC (SCD) 199, SpC 288)* it was held that a claim under *section 191* is not possible where no inheritance tax is payable on the death, as there is no 'appropriate person' if there is no person liable to pay the tax because no tax is payable. In that case the bulk of the assets went to charity, leaving the balance within the nil rate band. The executors sought to substitute the sale value of the properties for their probate value in order to increase their capital gains tax base cost.

**18.38** The relief is given by reference to the aggregate sale proceeds of all the land sold (note the use of 'sold', not 'disposed of') by the appropriate person (in his capacity as personal representative) in the three-year period. It is given by reducing the aggregate value of the land at the date of death to its 'sale value', that is, the aggregate sale proceeds (or, if greater, the best consideration that could reasonably have been obtained for the land at the time of sale) adjusted in accordance with such, if any, of the provisions considered below as are appropriate (*IHTA 1984, ss 190, 191*). The sale proceeds for this purpose are the gross proceeds before deduction of commission, stamp duty or other expenses which are incidental to the sale (*IHTA 1984, s 190(4)*).

**18.39** No relief will be given for a fall in the value of an interest if the amount involved is small, that is, if it is less than £1,000 (or 5% of the probate value if that is under £20,000) (*IHTA 1984, s 191(2)*). Neither will any reduction be allowed in relation to land sold:

(*a*) by a personal representative or trustee to

- (i) a person who is (or at any time since the death had been) beneficially entitled to the property or to an interest in possession in the property (or would be when the administration of the estate is completed), or
- (ii) the spouse, child, or remoter descendant of a person within (i), or
- (iii) the trustees of a settlement under which a person in (i) or (ii) has an interest in possession in property comprising the interest sold; or

(*b*) under a transaction in connection with which either the vendor or a person within (*a*)(i) to (iii) obtains a right to acquire either the interest sold or another interest in the same land.

(*IHTA 1984, s 191(3)*).

**18.40** It should be noted that the relief will be given where land is sold to the parent of a person having an interest in possession in the property or to a brother, sister, cousin, etc. No indication is given as to whether or not 'a child' includes an adopted child, an illegitimate child or a step-child. It is safest to assume it includes all three. A sale to a discretionary beneficiary will not debar the relief. A sale to trustees of a settlement in which a person within (*a*) in 18.39 above had an interest in possession at the time of the death, but gave up that interest prior to the sale, is apparently also alright. The reason for these distinctions is not readily apparent.

**18.41** A sale to a connected person of the deceased not falling within (*a*) or (*b*) in 18.39 above, or a non-arm's length sale, will still attract the relief. If such a sale is at less than market value, though, the undervalue will be excluded from relief by the general rule substituting the best consideration that could reasonably be obtained for the land for the sale proceeds. This seems a very open-ended provision. If land is sold at arm's length by auction the Inland Revenue could apparently contend that it could have fetched a higher price if sold privately or if sold in a number of small lots, and thus reduce the relief.

**18.42** Identical rules to those in *IHTA 1984, ss 137, 138* (see 18.34–18.36 above) apply where there is a change in the interest sold or in the land in which it subsists between the death and the sale (*IHTA 1984,* *s 193*) and where the interest at the date of death was a lease with 50 years or less unexpired (*IHTA 1984, s 194*).

**18.43** If any other interests (whether or not in the same ownership) were taken into account in determining the value at the date of death of the interest sold, the sale price must be increased by the difference between the probate value and what that value would have been if no interests other than the interest sold had been taken into account (*IHTA 1984, s 195*). This will apply, for example, where another interest is related property.

*Example 38*

Mark (dec'd) owned an 80-year lease which was worth £70,000 at the date of his death. The freehold was owned by Mrs Mark and at the date of Mark's death was worth £30,000. The unencumbered freehold was worth £150,000 at the time of Mark's death. Three years after the death Mark's executors sold his lease for £60,000.

As the lease and freehold are related property the value taken into account on the death for IHT purposes will not be £70,000 but

$$\frac{£70{,}000}{£70{,}000 + £30{,}000} \times £150{,}000 = £105{,}000$$

| | | £ |
|---|---|---|
| The relief will be: | | |
| Sale proceeds | | 60,000 |
| Addition | | |
| IHT value at death | 105,000 | |
| Value at death of lease only | 70,000 | 35,000 |
| | | 95,000 |
| IHT value at death | | 105,000 |
| Relief due | | £10,000 |

**18.44** If the 'appropriate person', acting as such, either

(*a*) sells an interest which would have qualified for relief but for the fact that the transaction falls within (*a*) or (*b*) in 18.39 above (sales to certain beneficiaries or with an option to reacquire an interest in the land), or

(*b*) exchanges within three years after the death (with or without any cash adjustment) an interest in land which was comprised in the deceased's estate at the time of death, (called below, for convenience, the 'non-qualifying land') and the sale price of the interest disposed of (or its market value where (*b*) applies) is higher than the value at death, the sale price or prices of interests to which the claim relates (which will normally be interests in other land) must be increased by 'the appropriate fraction' of the rise in value of the non-qualifying land (*IHTA 1984, s 196(1)(2)*). The 'appropriate fraction' is that which the fall (or, apparently where applicable, the rise, as the legislation refers to the difference between the two figures) in value of each interest affected (after taking account of adjustments in 18.42 and 18.43 above) bears to the aggregate falls (or rises) in value of all of the interests affected (*IHTA 1984, s 196(3)*). Where there are both falls and rises these must apparently always be added, never subtracted, i.e. rises will not count as negative figures. It should be noted that although the term 'appropriate fraction' is used in both *sections 194* and *196*, its meaning is not the same in both cases. The logic of *section 196* is not readily apparent. The following examples illustrate how it appears to work, however.

*Example 39*

Rupert owned the following freehold land at the date of his death, all of which was disposed of at market value within three years of the death.

| | Value at death | Sale proceeds |
|---|---|---|
| | £ | £ |
| Whiteacre | 10,000 | 8,000 |
| Blackacre | 11,500 | 9,000 |
| Greenacre | 18,500 | 20,000 |
| Redacre | 22,000 | 21,500 |
| Blueacre | 24,000 | 26,000 |
| Yellowacre | 30,000 | – |

*Notes.* Blueacre was sold to the residuary beneficiary of the estate. Yellowacre was exchanged for land at Brownacre, which was worth £24,000 at the date of exchange.

Before applying *section 196* the relief will be as follows.

| | Sale proceeds | Value at death | Relief |
|---|---|---|---|
| | £ | £ | £ |
| Whiteacre | 8,000 | 10,000 | |
| Blackacre | 9,000 | 11,500 | |
| Greenacre | 20,000 | 18,500 | |
| | £37,000 | £40,000 | £3,000 |

Blueacre and Yellowacre do not qualify for the relief. Nor does Redacre as its fall in value is under £1,000.

An adjustment is required under *section 196* in respect of Blueacre – of £2,000 (£26,000 – £24,000). No adjustment is required in respect of Yellowacre as there had been no increase in the value of that land since Rupert's death. It would clearly have been better for Yellowacre to have been sold instead of being exchanged as no relief will be obtained for the fall in value.

The difference in value of the other land is

| | | |
|---|---|---|
| | £ | £ |
| Whiteacre | (10,000 – 8,000) = | 2,000 |
| Blackacre | (11,500 – 9,000) = | 2,500 |
| Greenacre | (20,000 – 18,500) = | 1,500 |
| | | £6,000 |

The adjustment in respect of Blueacre must be apportioned between the three sites in the above proportions, e.g. the amount by which the sale proceeds of Blackacre must be increased is

$$£2,000 \times \frac{2,500}{6,000} = £833$$

The claim will therefore now become

| | Sale proceeds £ | Adjustments £ | Adjusted Sale Proceeds £ | Value at death £ | Relief £ |
|---|---|---|---|---|---|
| Whiteacre | 8,000 | 667 | 8,667 | 10,000 | |
| Blackacre | 9,000 | 833 | 9,833 | 11,500 | |
| Greenacre | 20,000 | 500 | 20,500 | 18,500 | |
| | £37,000 | £2,000 | £39,000 | £40,000 | £1,000 |

**18.45** It is not clear why it should be necessary to apportion the £2,000 between the three interests to which the claim relates instead of merely deducting it from the total claim. It appears that if the effect had been to reduce the difference between the figures for any property to less than £1,000 (or 5% of probate value) then that property would fall out of the claim.

**18.46** If any land is purchased by the 'appropriate person' (acting as such) in the period between the date of death and four months after the date of the last sale covered by *section 191* (other than one brought in by *IHTA 1984, s 197A*), an adjustment to the relief is required. If the aggregate purchase prices of all such purchases equal or exceed the aggregate prices (adjusted in accordance with *sections 193–195* but not *section 196*) of the interest covered by *section 191*, no relief will be given. In other cases the sale proceeds of each interest affected will be increased (or reduced if the value has fallen since the death) by the fraction of the difference in the values of that interest between the dates of death and sale (the latter being adjusted in accordance with *sections 193–196*, n.b. including *section 196*) which the aggregate purchase prices bear to the aggregate sales prices. Where the value at death of any interest is less than its sale price (adjusted in accordance with *sections 193–196*, the sale price must be decreased instead of increased (*IHTA 1984, s 192*).

*Example 40*

Suppose that Rupert's executors in *Example 39* purchase land for £20,000. As this is less than the £37,000 aggregate sale prices before applying *IHTA 1984, s 196*, an adjustment must be made. This will be done by increasing or decreasing the various sale proceeds by the following amounts.

| | | | |
|---|---|---|---|
| Whiteacre | $10{,}000 - 8{,}667 = 1{,}333 \times \dfrac{20{,}000}{37{,}000}$ | = | £721 |
| Blackacre | 11,500 – 9,833 = 1,667 × 20/37 | = | £901 |
| Greenacre | 18,500 – 20,500 = (2,000) × 20/37 | = | (£1,081) |

The adjusted claim now becomes

| | Adjusted sale proceeds as before | Adjustment under *section 192* | Adjusted sale proceeds | Value at death | Relief |
|---|---|---|---|---|---|
| | £ | £ | £ | £ | £ |
| Whiteacre | 8,667 | 721 | 9,388 | 10,000 | |
| Blackacre | 9,833 | 901 | 10,734 | 11,500 | |
| Greenacre | 20,500 | (1,081) | 19,419 | 18,500 | |
| | | | 39,541 | 40,000 | |
| *Less* Greenacre | | | 19,419 | 18,500 | |
| | | | £20,122 | £21,500 | £1,378 |

**18.47** As the difference between the value at death and the adjusted sale proceeds is in the case of Greenacre less than 5% of £18,500, *section 191(2)* (see 18.39 above) will now exclude this from *section 191(1)*. It accordingly no longer affects the relief.

**18.48** It should particularly be noted that, subject to the special rules contained in *section 196*, only sales of land need to be taken into account. Other disposals, such as exchanges of land or distributions to beneficiaries, do not affect the relief.

**18.49** The date of a sale or purchase will normally be the contract date (*IHTA 1984, s 198(1)*). However, if the sale or purchase results from the exercise of an option which was granted within the previous six months, the option date must be adopted instead (*IHTA 1984, s 198(2)*). If the land is disposed of to a local authority (or other body possessing compulsory purchase powers) in pursuance of a notice to treat, the date of sale will be the earlier of the date on which compensation is agreed or the date on which the local authority enters into possession. Where the land is acquired under the vesting declaration procedure the last day of the period specified in the vesting declaration will be treated as the date of sale (*IHTA 1984, s 198(3)(4)*). The question for decision in *Jones and another (Balls' Administrators) v CIR (1997 STC 358)* was whether a contract that was not completed was nevertheless a sale for this purpose. Lightman J said that the meaning of 'sold' (like 'paid') depended on the context. It could mean 'agreed to be sold' and it could mean 'conveyed or transferred on completion of a sale'. In the context of *section 191* it clearly had the latter meaning. There was no machinery for dealing with multiple contracts in the three-year period, no guidance as to what would constitute a contract and the intention was clearly that tax should not be payable on a greater price than the amount actually received.

**18.50** Where land is acquired in pursuance of a notice to treat, served before the death or within the three-year period, these rules cannot be used to deny relief by taking the sale outside the scope of *section 191*, however. In such circumstances the three-year period will be deemed to be extended to include the date of sale to the local authority (*IHTA 1984, s 197(1)*). This only applies to bring that sale into *section 191*; it will not extend the four-month period under *section 192* within which acquisitions have to be taken into account (see 18.46) (*IHTA 1984, s 197(3)*). This provision operates in the taxpayer's favour only. If the sale proceeds exceed the probate value the normal three-year rule applies (*IHTA 1984, s 197(2)*).

## Heritage Property

**18.51** Heritage property attracts a number of exemptions from inheritance tax.

**18.52** The general exemptions from inheritance tax for gifts to charity and for gifts to specified national heritage bodies, such as The National Trust, of course also apply to heritage property in the same way as other assets.

**18.53** The Revenue can also grant conditional exemption for certain private gifts (*IHTA 1984, s 30*). A conditionally exempt gift will be treated as exempt whilst certain undertakings remain in force, but a tax charge will crystallise if the building is sold or the undertakings broken. A building for the preservation of which special steps should in the opinion of the Inland Revenue be taken by reason of its outstanding historic or architectural interest qualifies for this relief. So does land where it is essential for the preservation of the character and amenities of such a building. Such land does not have to be in the same ownership. The undertakings required are that until the death of the donee, or the property is disposed of, reasonable steps will be taken for the maintenance, repair, and preservation of the property and for securing access to it by the public (*IHTA 1984, s 31(2)(a)*). Access by prior appointment only is not adequate except where the transfer was before 1 August 1998. The Revenue can require publication of details of the undertakings and other information about the property (*IHTA 1984, s 31(4 FA)*). In the cases of land, in addition to the normal undertakings, every person owning any part of the property must agree with the Revenue what specific steps are required for the maintenance, repair, and preservation of the land and the historic building, and must give an undertaking to do such work. Such an undertaking can only be required in relation to the historic building itself and any land falling between the building and the land for which exemption is sought (*FA 1985, Sch 26 para 1, 2*).

*Example 41*

Jack's family trust owns an historic building. To the south is a field owned by Jack personally and to the south of that is another field owned by Joe. Both Jack and Joe claim exemption in respect of their land.

Jack can be required to give a repairs undertaking in respect of the historic building and his land. He cannot be required to give an undertaking in relation to Joe's land as it is not between Jack's land and the building. Joe can be required to give an undertaking in respect of the building, his own land, and Jack's land.

**18.54** The Revenue can, if they think it appropriate, require separate undertakings from different people (*IHTA 1984, s 31(4B)*). For instance, in the above *Example* they might require the trustees to give the undertaking in respect of the building, and the undertakings by Jack and Joe to be restricted to their own land, or might require the undertakings to extend to the building but place a ceiling on their financial obligations.

**18.55** An undertaking under these provisions can be varied between the Revenue and the person who gave it. If that person does not agree to a proposed variation the Revenue can appeal to the Special Commissioners who are empowered to direct that it be varied (*IHTA 1984, s 35A* inserted by *FA 1998, Sch 25 para 8*). This applies even if the undertaking was given before 31 July 1998 although in such a case the variation must be limited to greater access and publication of details of the property (*FA 1998, Sch 25 para 10*).

**18.56** Where a conditionally exempt transfer has taken place, a tax charge will arise on the first occurrence of a breach of an undertaking (unless the Revenue opt to excuse it), or a disposal of the property – other than a disposal by way of gift to a person from whom the

Revenue are prepared to accept fresh undertakings, or one by private treaty to one of the specified national heritage bodies. The government have said that where a part disposal of a conditionally exempt property results solely from leasehold enfranchisement and there is no breach of undertaking in respect of the retained property the disposal will not give rise to a review of designation of the retained property (IR Press Release 7.5.1993). They indicated that a new clause to this effect would be added to the Finance Bill but, as this was not done, presumably the government felt on reflection that it was unnecessary to legislate for this concession. The death of the donee will also crystallise a tax charge if the property is sold by his executors, but not if it is left to an heir who is prepared to give the necessary undertakings. In the latter case the exemption granted to the deceased will have become absolute. This is accordingly an effective method of passing on heritage property within a family – which is of course what it is designed to allow. Where a tax charge crystallises it will be on the value of the property at the time of the breach or the sale, not on the value at the time of the original gift. As this can produce a significantly greater liability than if the exemption had never been claimed the relief should not automatically be claimed without due consideration being given as to whether a future disposal is likely.

**18.57** If there is a breach of any of the undertakings given in relation to the building and associated land, or in relation to historic objects associated with the building, that breach will crystallise the inheritance tax liability in relation to the whole of the associated items. Similarly, the disposal of any of the associated items or the death of any of the owners (without his heirs themselves giving the appropriate undertakings or the property being sold to one of the heritage bodies (within *IHTA 1984, Sch 3*) or being given in satisfaction of the inheritance tax on death) will crystallise the deferred tax on all the items (*IHTA 1984, s 32A*). The Revenue have power to allow the conditional exemption of owners who are not in breach to continue if it appears to them that the entity consisting of the associated properties has not been materially affected by the breach or disposal (*IHTA 1984, s 32A(10)*). The Minister has given an assurance that when considering the application of the provision in individual cases the Revenue will examine all relevant factors in the light of advice from the appropriate advisory bodies. A relevant factor to which weight will be given will be whether what remains of the entity after the sale or breach of the undertaking might qualify for exemption as a viable heritage unit looked at on its own merit.

**18.58** On transfers prior to 17 March 1998 the Inland Revenue were also empowered to exempt a gift of a building for the preservation of which special steps ought to be taken by reason of its outstanding historic, architectural or aesthetic interest, where the gift was to a body not established or conducted for profit (*IHTA 1984, s 26*). The exemption also extended to land used as the grounds of the building, to funds for the preservation of the property which are given with it, and to any other property given as a source of income for that purpose. The Revenue had to approve the recipient body as suitable to be responsible for the preservation of the property, and in the case of assets given to generate income must be satisfied that the amount is not excessive. They could if they wished also require undertakings to be given to restrict the building's use or disposal or to ensure its preservation and reasonable access to it by the public. This provision was felt to be no longer necessary as such bodies invariably qualify for the exemption for gifts to charities.

## Gifts with Reservation

**18.59** If on a gift after 17 March 1986 either

(*a*) possession and enjoyment of the property is not bona fide assumed by the donee at least seven years before the donor's death (or by the date of the gift if later), or

(*b*) at any time in the seven years prior to his death (or the period from the date of the gift) the property is not enjoyed to the entire exclusion, or virtually to the entire exclusion, of the donor and of any benefit to him by contract or otherwise,

the property is treated for inheritance tax purposes as remaining part of the donor's estate (*FA 1986, s 102*). This wording is similar, but not identical, to that which used to apply for estate duty purposes, namely 'property taken under any gift, whenever made, of which property bona fide possession and enjoyment shall not have been assumed by the donee immediately upon the gift and thenceforth retained, to the entire exclusion of the donor, or of any benefit to him by contract or otherwise'. If the property ceases to be subject to the reservation subsequent to the gift but prior to the donor's death it is treated as a gift at that time.

**18.60** A gift of part of an interest in a private residence would be caught by this provision as the donor would still be entitled to occupy the property by virtue of ownership of the remainder of his interest (but see 18.64 below). Similarly, a gift of the entire property subject to a right would constitute a reservation. An understanding falling short of a right may also do so, although in *Attorney-General v Seccombe (1911) 2 KB 688*, it was held that the 1889 wording, which is identical in this respect, required some legally enforceable arrangement as opposed to a merely casual one. However, it is specifically provided that retention or assumption by the donor of an incorporeal right over land is to be disregarded if it is for full consideration in money or money's worth (*FA 1986, Sch 20 para 6(1)(a)*). A gift of a private residence subject to the retention of a right to remain in occupation at a full market rent should therefore be effective (but it must be remembered that a right of occupation for one's life is treated as a settlement in which the donor has a life interest, which would render the gift ineffective). The Revenue consider that the rent paid needs to be reviewed at appropriate intervals to reflect market changes if a gift with reservation is not to arise. They do, however, accept that full consideration can cover 'a range of values reflecting normal valuation tolerances' and that any amount within that range is acceptable (Tax Bulletin Issue 9, Nov 1993, page 98). Similarly, a gift of the property subject to the grant of a lease to the donor at a market value premium plus a nominal annual rent would suffice.

**18.61** In a 1952 case, *St Aubyn v Attorney-General (1952 AC 15)*, Lord Radcliffe said 'it is the possession and enjoyment of the actual property given that has to be taken account of, and . . . if that property is, as it may be, a limited equitable interest or an equitable interest distinct from another such interest which is not given, or an interest in property subject to an interest that is retained, it is of no consequence for this purpose that the retained interest remains in the beneficial enjoyment of the person who provides the gift'. It was also pointed out in the Privy Council in *Chick v Commissioners of Stamp Duties (1958 AC 435)* in relation to similar wording that it must often be a matter of fine distinction what is the subject matter of a gift. If the gift is of a property shorn of certain rights which appertain to complete ownership, the donor cannot be said not to have been excluded from possession and enjoyment of that which he has given, e.g. if he carves out a lease and gifts only the freehold reversion, occupation by virtue of the lease should not constitute a reservation of benefit in relation to the property gifted, namely the reversion – unless the associated operations rules catch the creation of the lease (as they may well do). *FA 1986, s 102A* (inserted by *FA 1999, s 104*) (see 18.67) is designed to prevent this in most cases where the donor wishes to contrive to reside in the property. It is still relatively easy with investment property where the donor does not wish to gift his entire interest.

**18.62** Care may need to be taken in splitting the property into a lease and a reversion. In a Scottish case *Kildrummy (Jersey) Ltd v CIR (1990 STC 657)* it was held that a person cannot grant a lease to himself and such a transaction was therefore a nullity. However in *Ingram v CIR (1999 STC 37)* the House of Lords held that the position is different under English law as splitting does not treat a nominee or trustee as an agent for his beneficiary; he contracts in his own name with a right of indemnity against the beneficiary for the liabilities he incurs. The nominee incurs real obligations so cannot be regarded as a mere puppet. In the *Ingram* case the House of Lords accepted that the *St Aubyn* principle applies for inheritance tax as well as estate duty. There was no reservation of benefit. What was comprised in the gift by Lady Ingram was the freehold shorn of her leasehold interest. The effect of the *Ingram* decision has been significantly restricted in relation to gifts after 8 March 1999 by *IHTA 1984, s 102A* (see 18.67). In Scotland it may be possible to avoid the effect of

*Kildrummy* by transferring the property jointly to a nominee for the donor and a relative who will take a small beneficial interest in the property.

**18.63** There is a statutory exemption in relation to a gift of land (such as a house) if the donor initially gives up possession but later occupies the property:

(*a*) as a result of a change in the donor's circumstances which was unforeseen at the time of the gift and which was not brought about by the donor to receive the benefit of the exemption, and

(*b*) at a time when he has become unable to maintain himself through old age, infirmity, or otherwise, and

(*c*) where such occupation represents a reasonable provision by the donee for the care and maintenance of the donor, and provided that

(*d*) the donee is a relative of the donor or his spouse ('relative' does not appear to be defined for this purpose).

(*FA 1986, Sch 20 para 6(1)(b)*).

**18.64** There is also a statutory exemption if, or to the extent that, the disposal of property by way of gift is an exempt transfer by virtue of *IHTA 1984, section 18* (transfers between spouses), *section 20* (small gifts), *section 22* (gifts in consideration of marriage), *section 23* (gifts to charities), *section 24* (gifts to political parties), *section 24A* (gifts to housing associations), *section 25* (gifts for national purposes), *section 27* (maintenance funds for historic buildings), or *section 28* (employee trusts) (*FA 1986, s 102(5)*). In *Essex (exor of Somerset decd) v CIR (2002 STC (SCD) 39)* a settlor gave a 95% interest in her house to trustees on trust to pay the income to her husband for life, and after her death to hold the capital and income on discretionary trust for a class of beneficiary including herself and her issue, and subject thereto for her issue. The husband died in 1992 and the settlor in 1998. It was held that, as the creation of the settlement was an exempt transfer within *IHTA 1984, s 18, section 102(5)* took the 95% interest out of the reservation of benefit provisions. The Commissioner also opined that if he was wrong on this point, the whole of the trust property was not enjoyed to the entire exclusion of the settlor, though not because she resided in the house until her death (he accepted that she did so by virtue of her 5% interest albeit that the trustees did not seek to enforce their right to permit one of the beneficiaries to occupy it with her) but because she was one of the class of discretionary beneficiary.

**18.65** At the time of the introduction of these rules the Minister gave an assurance that 'the gift with reservation rules will not be applied to an unconditional gift of an undivided share in land merely because the property is occupied by all the joint owners or tenants in common, including the donor'. For example 'if elderly parents and the children occupy the property as their family home, each owner bearing his or her share of the running costs . . . the parents' occupation and enjoyment of the part of the house that they have given away is in return for similar enjoyment of the children of the other part of the property. Thus the donor's occupation is for a full consideration' (Hansard, Standing Committee G, 10 June 1986, Col 425). This reasoning would seem to apply equally where the children are not living regularly in the property provided that they are not specifically excluded from the ability to do so. However, it seems likely that the Revenue would seek to challenge a gift if it does not fall squarely within the minister's wording. If the children do not occupy the property at all they would probably not have assumed possession and enjoyment of it.

**18.66** The Minister also stated that the legislation does not prevent a man giving away an asset and reserving a benefit to his wife. However, if a person does this and then shares the spouse's enjoyment or benefit of the reservation without paying her for it, the Revenue take the view that he has not been excluded from enjoyment of or benefit from the gifted property (Hansard, Standing Committee G, 10 June 1986, Col 420).

**18.67** For gifts after 8 March 1999 a gift of an interest in land is treated as giving rise to a reservation of benefit if at any time in the relevant period (the seven years before the donor's death or, if shorter, the period from the date of the gift to the date of the donor's death) the donor or his spouse enjoys a significant right or interest in relation to the land or is party to a significant arrangement in relation to the land (*FA 1986, ss 102A(1)(2), 102C(1)*, inserted by *FA 1999, s 104*). A right, interest or arrangement is significant for this purpose if (and only if) it entitles or enables the donor to occupy all or part of the land, or to enjoy some right in relation to all or part of the land, otherwise than for full consideration in money or money's worth (*FA 1986, s 102A(3)*). A right, interest or arrangement is not significant if either

(*a*) it does not (and cannot) prevent the enjoyment of the land to the entire exclusion (or virtually the entire exclusion) of the donor, or

(*b*) it does not entitle or enable the donor to occupy all or part of the land immediately after the disposal, but would do so were it not for the interest disposed of, or

(*c*) in the case of a right or interest, that right or interest was granted or acquired more than seven years prior to the date of the gift (*FA 1986, s 102A(4)(5)*).

If the donor gifts more than one interest in the land (whether or not at the same time and whether or not to the same donee) *section 102A* applies separately in relation to each interest (*s 102A(6)*).

**18.68** It will be apparent that *section 102A* goes far wider than merely to attack the creation of a lease and reversion as happened in the *Ingram* case. It will also catch variants such as the creation of a lease in favour of the beneficiary to take effect at a future date after the death of the donor (so that the value of the property at that date would be reduced by the value of the lease). It should be noted that a right for the donor's spouse to occupy will not be a significant right if it does not enable the donor himself to occupy the land. Accordingly a holiday home which the donor himself rarely visits but is used by other members of the family could still be passed on using the *St Aubyn* principle. It would be dangerous for the donor to in fact occupy the property in such a case though (unless he pays a full rent for such usage) as that might well constitute an arrangement enabling him to occupy the property.

**18.69** The exclusion where the right was granted more than seven years prior to the date of the gift is intriguing. The effect is to allow the *St Aubyn* principle to apply if after the transfer of the property to the nominee and the grant of the lease to the donor, the donor waits for seven years before gifting the reversionary interest. If the gift is a potentially exempt transfer this means that the donor will have to live for fourteen years after splitting the freehold (or long leasehold) interest. Apart from the costs, there is not normally any adverse consequence of splitting the interest into two. In particular both interests will qualify for the capital gains private residence relief during the period in which both are beneficially owned by the donor. Accordingly there may be merit in splitting the interest in a property in this way now so as to give the owner the ability to gift a reversionary interest at some future time without triggering a reservation of benefit.

**18.70** It should also be noted that the provision applies only where the donor disposes of an interest by way of gift. A sale at an undervalue does not appear to trigger the provision. It is possible that the Courts would regard the undervalue as a 'gift' but the ordinary meaning of that word is not apt to do so and it would, in any event, be a gift of the undervalue not of the interest in land. *Section 102A* would also not apply if the property is split on purchase. For example when a person moves house he could arrange with the vendor to sell him a lease for a period of 50 years at a nominal rent and at the same time to sell to the purchaser's children the reversionary interest in the property. The vendor would probably be unwilling to do this for a lease of under 50 years as that would trigger an income tax charge (see 3.2) so this is unlikely to be workable if the 'donor' is already elderly. The shift in value to the children is brought about by the reduction in the value of the lease due to the effluxion of time between creating the lease and the donor dying. It probably does not affect the position if the parent gifts cash to the child to enable him to pay for the reversion provided that the gift is not conditional on the money being used to make the purchase.

**18.71** A gift after 8 March 1999 of an undivided share of an interest in land similarly gives rise to a deemed reservation of benefit unless either

(*a*) the donor does not occupy the land at any time in the relevant period (as defined in 18.67), or

(*b*) he occupies it to the exclusion of the donee for full consideration in money or money's worth, or

(*c*) both the donor and the donee occupy the land and the donor does not receive any benefit, other than a negligible one, which is provided by or at the expense of the donee for some reason connected with the gift.

(*FA 1986, s 102* inserted by *FA 1999, s 104*).

Head (*c*) above will be satisfied if the donor simply gifts the share of the interest so that the donee receives a benefit. It is only if the donee in turn provides a benefit to the donor that *section 102B* will be triggered.

**18.72** Neither *section 102A* or *section 102B* applies

(*a*) to the extent that the disposal is an exempt transfer by virtue of any of the provisions of *section 102(5)* (transfers between spouses and other exempt transfers such as for small gifts, gifts in consideration of marriage, gifts to charity, etc.) (*FA 1986, s 102C(2)*), or

(*b*) where occupation of the land by the donor would be disregarded under *FA 1986, Sch 20 para 6(1)(b)* (change in donor's circumstances – see 18.63) (*FA 1986, s 102C(3)*).

**18.73** Overall therefore the Revenue say that neither *sections 102A* or *102B* will apply in the following circumstances

(*a*) the gift is to a spouse or covered by another IHT exemption;

(*b*) the retained right or interest is negligible so that the donor is virtually entirely excluded from any enjoyment of the land;

(*c*) the donor pays full consideration for his occupation of the land;

(*d*) the occupation of the land is effectively forced on the donor by some unforeseen downturn in his financial circumstances;

(*e*) the gift is made more than seven years after the right, interest or arrangement concerned is created or entered into;

(*f*) the donor may occupy the land or enjoy some right in relation to it only on the determination of the interest that he has given away; e.g. the donor gives away a leasehold interest and retains the freehold reversion which entitles him to re-occupy the land when the lease expires; or

(*g*) the gift is of a share in land, which the donor then occupies jointly with the other owner (the donee) provided the donor receives no other benefit at the donee's expense in connection with the gift.

**18.74** The detailed rules on reservation of benefit contained in *FA 1986, Sch 20* also apply for *sections 102A* and *102B* with the exception of *paragraph* 6 (exclusion of benefit – but similar rules apply for *sections 102A* and *102B*) (*FA 1986, s 102C(4)*). Any question which falls to be answered under *section 102A* or *102B* in relation to an interest in land is to be determined by reference to the interest which is treated as property comprised in the gift (*FA 1986, s 102C(4)*). It is not clear if this applies generally or only for the purpose of *Sch 20*. If property other than an interest in land is treated as comprised in a gift under *Sch 20 para 2* (substitutions and accretions), *section 102* (not *102A* or *102B*) applies to that property even if the original gift was of an interest in land (*FA 1986, s 102C(5)*). Where two or more of *sections 102, 102A* and *102B* potentially apply only *section 102B* will apply (*FA 1986, s 102C(6)*). Where both *section 102* and *102A* could apply the charge will be under *section 102* (*FA 1986, s 102C(7)*).

**18.75** The Inland Revenue have indicated that they consider the words 'virtually to the entire exclusion' in 18.59(*b*) as covering cases where the benefit to the donor is insignificant in relation to the gifted property. They say that they operate the provision in such a way that donors are not 'unreasonably prevented from having limited access to property they have given away and a measure of flexibility is adopted in applying the test'. Examples of the sort of things they consider will not give rise to a gift with reservation in relation to a gift of a house which becomes the donee's residence are:

(*a*) 'house-sitting' for up to two weeks a year in the donee's absence,

(*b*) staying with the donee for less than a month a year,

(*c*) social visits to the donee as his guest which are no more than might be expected had the house not been gifted to the donee,

(*d*) a temporary stay at the house for a short term purpose such as to convalesce after medical treatment, to nurse the donee after medical treatment, or while the donor's own house is undergoing redecoration, (*e*) visits to the house for domestic reasons such as to baby-sit for the donees' children,

(*f*) if the house includes a library which is included in the gift, visits of less than five times in any year to consult or borrow a book, and

(*g*) visits to the grounds or other land given away by the donor to walk his dogs or for horse riding (provided such visits do not restrict the donee's own use of the land).

It should be stressed that these examples are intended for guidance. Whether or not a gift is a gift with reservation will depend on the exact facts of each individual case.

**18.76** The sort of thing the Revenue consider does give rise to a reservation of benefit are:

(*a*) staying in the house most weekends,

(*b*) staying there for a month or more each year,

(*c*) use of the house on an occasional basis if it is a second home or a holiday home which is only used on an occasional basis by the donee,

(*d*) use of the house to keep a library that is retained by the donor, and

(*e*) use of the house on a regular basis, for example, because it is necessary for the donor's work.

(Tax Bulletin, Issue 9, Nov 93, p 98).

*Chapter 19*

# Stamp Duty

**19.1** Stamp duty is payable in respect of most land transactions. It is by far the oldest of the taxes, most of the provisions dating from the 18th century or earlier. The legislation was last consolidated in 1891. Stamp duty is not actually a tax; it is a collection of separate taxes, the most important of which from a property point of view are the Duty on Conveyance or Transfer on Sale and the Lease or Tack (a Scottish leasing contract) Duty. Because of major differences between Scottish and English law, particularly in relation to land, the provisions outlined below do not necessarily apply to transfers of Scottish land in the same way as they operate in England and Wales. The *Finance Act 1991* abolishes most of the duties (from a date to be fixed) but retains those on land, an interest in the proceeds of the sale of land held on trust for sale, and a licence to occupy land (*FA 1991, s 110(2)(5)*). In his 1993 budget speech the then Chancellor stated that the abolition of the other duties would not be implemented before 5 April 1994, and that he would review the position further in the light of the conclusions of the Securities Settlement Task Force set up by the Bank of England which reported in 1994. This review is still awaited!

**19.2** The stamp duties are a tax on documents, not a tax on transactions. If a transaction is carried out without a document coming into existence no stamp duty will normally be payable (although in the case of shares or securities there will instead be a liability to stamp duty reserve tax). Unfortunately, as the *Law of Property Act 1925* (as amended by *section 2* of the *Law of Property (Miscellaneous Provisions) Act 1989*) requires a transaction in land to be in writing and contained in a single document for it to be enforceable, it is rarely wise to carry out a property transaction without a document being created. In addition, this principle has in recent years been overriden by statute in relation to a number of specific circumstances (see 19.100).

**19.3** It must also be borne in mind that it was held in *Ingram v CIR (1985 STC 835)* that the *Furniss v Dawson* principle applies to stamp duty. In that case it was wished to convey a house for £145,500. In order to avoid the duty (at 1%) of £1,455, this was done in two steps. An agreement for a 999-year lease was entered into for a premium of £145,000 payable immediately. At the time an agreement for a lease of over 35 years was not dutiable (this exemption was removed by the

*Finance Act 1984* – see 19.57 below for the current rules). The freehold was sold, subject to the agreement, for £500 to a third party who resold it to Mr Ingram for £600. He volunteered to pay duty of £6 on the acquisition. He would not of course need to enter into the lease itself, so it was hoped that the Revenue would never collect duty on the £145,000. It was held that there was a pre-ordained series of transactions designed to transfer the unencumbered freehold to Mr Ingram and the Revenue were entitled to duty on the real transaction, a freehold sale at £145,600, of £1,456.

## Duty on Conveyance or Transfer on Sale

**19.4** This duty is charged on any instrument (which includes every written document) effecting the conveyance or transfer on sale of any property (*SA 1891, s 1, FA 1999, Sch 13*). The expression 'conveyance on sale' is defined to include every instrument and every decree or order of any court or any commissioners whereby any property, or any estate or interest in it, is upon its sale transferred to or vested in a purchaser (or any other person on his behalf or by his direction) (*SA 1891, s 54*). What is an instrument effecting a conveyance for sale is not always readily apparent. In *Parinv (Hatfield) Ltd v CIR (1998 STC 305)* an agreement to purchase UK property was executed outside the UK and the transferor executed a declaration of trust in favour of the transferee, also outside the UK. The transferee submitted for stamping a transfer to the beneficial owner executed by the transferor as trustee (expecting a 50p stamp) together with a copy of the declaration of trust. It was held that the declaration of trust was itself an instrument effecting a conveyance on sale as it was only explicable in the context of the agreement to purchase the property. As it had been brought into the UK (see 19.112) it was therefore required to be stamped with *ad valorem* duty.

**19.5** A conveyance on sale is specifically stated to include an order for foreclosure. However, the *ad valorem* duty on such an order cannot exceed duty on an amount equal to the value of the property if the debt exceeds such a sum (any value stated in the order being conclusive as to the amount of such value), and the conveyance in pursuance of the order will itself be exempt from duty (*FA 1898, s 6*).

**19.6** The duty is an *ad valorem* duty (i.e. it is a percentage of the consideration for the sale). The rates are as follows

| | |
|---|---|
| if the consideration is up to £250,000 | 1% |
| if the consideration is between £250,000 and £500,000 | 3% |
| if the consideration is in excess of £500,000 | 4% |

The appropriate rate applies to the full consideration. The duty is rounded up to the next five pounds (£1 before 1 October 1999, except where the consideration was less than £500 when it was rounded up to the next 50p) (*FA 1963, s 55* and *FA 1999, s 112(1)*). If the consideration is under £500,000 the instrument must contain a certificate stating into which bracket it falls to get the benefit of the lower rates. On conveyances or other stampable instruments executed before 8 July 1997 the 1% rate applied to all sales irrespective of the size of the consideration. It also applied to an instrument executed after that date if it was executed in pursuance of a contract made before 3 July 1997 (*F(No 2)A 1997, s 49*). This wording appears wide enough to cover not only contracts intended to be completed by a conveyance but also some contracts where the final terms are to be agreed. For example, suppose A has contracted with B that he will build two houses on B's land and on completion B will sell one to A at 50% of its open market value. The conveyance to A seems to be 'in pursuance of' the original contract. The width of this wording is borne out by the decision in *Swallow Hotels Ltd v CIR (2000 STC 45)*. Swallow entered into a 30-year lease in 1992. The lease contained an option for Swallow to require the landlord to grant it a new 999-year lease at a premium (to be calculated by a complex formula). Swallow exercised the option on 26 September 1997. It was held that this conveyance in pursuance of that option was in pursuance of the contract entered into in 1992 and therefore attracted duty at the 1% rate that applied prior to 3 July 1997.

For transfers executed between 8 July 1997 and 24 March 1998 (or a later transfer in pursuance of a pre-17 March 1998 contract) the rates were 1%, 1½% and 2% respectively. For those executed between 25 March 1998 and 16 March 1999 (or a later transfer in pursuance of a pre-9 March 1999 contract) they were 1%, 2% and 3%. And for those executed between 17 March 1999 and 27 March 2000 they were 1%, 2.5% and 3.5% respectively.

**19.7** No duty is chargeable if the value of the consideration is £60,000 or under, provided that the instrument contains a statement certifying that the transaction effected by it does not form part of a larger transaction or series of transactions in respect of which the aggregate amount or value of the consideration exceeds £60,000 (*FA 1963, s 55(1)(a)*; *FA 1958, s 34*; *FA 1993, s 201*). Prior to 15 March 1993 the threshold was £30,000. For transactions entered into (i.e. stampable documents executed) between 20 December 1991 and 19 August 1992 the exemption threshold was £250,000 (*Stamp Duty (Temporary Provisions) Act 1992*). A binding contract signed and delivered before 20 August 1992 could benefit from this increased limit provided that its delivery was unconditional. A contract would not be conditional merely because the purchaser might have been entitled to return the property to the vendor after August 1992. It is possible to transfer property in advance of a sale in which case the conveyance would normally be the stampable document (see 19.32 below). If such a transfer took place before 20 August 1992 the £250,000 limit applied even though the sale takes place after that date (Inland Revenue Press Release, 10 July 1992). If the amount of the consideration is less than the market value of the property, stamp duty is still charged on the consideration, not on the market value of the property. An instrument must be treated as executed when it is delivered or, if it is delivered subject to conditions, when the conditions are fulfilled (*SA 1891, s 122(1A)*). This rule may not apply where the instrument was signed before 6 December 1993 although the Revenue's view is that it does.

**19.8** Where the consideration is in money the amount is readily ascertainable. If it is in foreign currency it must be converted to sterling at the rate ruling on the date of the instrument (*SA 1891, s 6(1)*). If the consideration consists of the transfer of another asset special rules apply to determine how that asset is to be valued. Stock or marketable securities are valued at the average price on the date of the instrument (*SA 1891, ss 6(1)* and *55(1)*). Except for transfers before 29 July 2000, it is immaterial whether the stock or marketable security has been issued at the date of the conveyance. If it has not been issued it is also immaterial when the security is to be issued and whether the issue is certain or contingent (*SA 1891, s 55(1A)* inserted by *FA 2000, s 126*). The government say that this closes a loophole by additionally taking into account the value of rights to receive a future issue of securities. It is not clear how one can tell whether a future issue of securities will be marketable or not. It is also unclear how the securities are to be valued. Something that does not exist does not have 'an average price' within *section 6(1)*. The value of a right to a future issue is likely to be very low, particularly if the right is contingent, so without valuation rules the loophole may well have been narrowed rather than closed. The value of a non-marketable security, such as a debenture of an unlisted company, is the amount outstanding at the date of the conveyance in respect of both principal and interest (*SA 1891, s 55(2)*). If the consideration is the satisfaction of a debt its value is the amount of that debt (not its value) or, if lower, the value of the property (provided that the transfer document is sent for adjudication) (*SA 1891, s 57*; *FA 1980, s 102*).

**19.9** If property is transferred subject to the payment of any money or stock, that money or stock is deemed to be part of the consideration even if it is only contingently payable and irrespective of whether or not it is secured on the property (*SA 1891, s 57*). For example, if a piece of land is sold for £100,000 with an agreement that a further £50,000 will be paid if planning permission for a particular development is obtained within the next three years, the duty will be £1,500 (1% of £150,000) even though the extra £50,000 may never be paid. Special rules apply where the contingent amount is not quantified (see 19.11).

**19.10** Similarly if property is transferred subject to the purchaser taking over a contingent liability attaching to the property, such as a guarantee secured on the land or an obligation to maintain a right of way, and the amount (or maximum amount) of the liability is ascertainable (e.g. the guarantee is in respect of a debt of a fixed amount), stamp duty is payable on that amount. One particular point to watch is where a gift of property is made subject to the donee taking over a liability to repay the mortgage. The amount of the mortgage is consideration for the transfer and will attract *ad valorem* duty even though a gift as such is exempt. Where property is transferred subject to a debt and no chargeable consideration unrelated to the debt is given by the transferee, the stamp duty position depends on whether or not the transaction is a sale. If it is, stamp duty is chargeable on the value of the debt assumed. If it is not, no stamp duty is payable. If the transferee covenants to pay the debt (or to indemnify the transferor in respect of it) the Revenue regard that undertaking as valuable consideration, so that stamp duty is payable. If no such undertaking is given the Revenue consider that such an undertaking can be implied (except in Scotland), in which case stamp duty will be payable unless there is evidence to negate that implication. If the intention of the parties at the time of the transfer is that the transferor should remain liable for the debt (and that intention can be evidenced) no stamp duty is payable (Inland Revenue Statement of Practice SP 6/90). In other words, a gift of property subject to the donee taking over the mortgage, including a mere transfer into joint names of a husband and wife or a transfer from old partners to the new on a partnership change with the new partnership taking over the mortgage liability, will attract duty on the amount of the mortgage. A transfer subject to the mortgage with the original borrower remaining solely liable for payment of the debt will not do so.

**19.11** If any part of the consideration for either the transfer or vesting of an interest in land or the grant of a lease cannot be ascertained at the time the instrument is executed the consideration must be deemed to be equal to the market value of the land (and in the case of a lease if the rent is not ascertainable the market rent must be adopted). (*FA 1994, s 242*). Prior to 8 December 1993 if the consideration was not ascertainable at the date of execution of an instrument there was nothing on which to charge *ad valorem* duty. The Inland Revenue could not wait until the amount was quantified and then charge duty with the benefit of hindsight. If part of the consideration was not ascertainable the same principle applied. For example, if a site were sold for £100,000 plus, 50% of the amount by which the value of the land with the benefit of any planning consent granted within twelve months after completion exceeded £100,000 duty could be charged only on £100,000. In *Underground Electric Railways Company v CIR (1906) AC 21*, where part of the consideration for the sale of the company was to be based on a future dividend payable on paid-up issued share capital at that time, it was held that for stamp duty purposes the consideration should be ascertained on the amount of share capital paid up at the time of the transfer. This decision was followed in *LM Tenancies 1 plc v CIR (1998 STC 326)*. Two properties were leased to a company and under the terms of the leases the consideration payable was fixed by reference to the price of the holding of government stock at the close of business on the 25th business day following the execution of the leases. The company argued that the consideration was unascertainable for stamp duty purposes and therefore the leases should be chargeable with fixed duty of £2 only. The stamp duty office contended that the consideration was ascertainable as at the date of execution of the leases, and any subsequent variation in the price of government stock should be ignored. Applying the reasoning in *Underground Electric*, it was held that it was permissible to calculate stamp duty by reference to the price of the government stock at the date the leases were executed.

**19.12** *Section 242* does not apply if the consideration could be ascertained on the assumption that any further event mentioned in the instrument were or were not to occur (*FA 1994, s 242(3)(a)*). In other words if the contingency principle can be applied – which will almost always give a greater figure than market value – duty is assessed on that greater amount. Not surprisingly the Revenue consider that a minimum rent inserted in a lease to avoid *section 242*, or which did not represent the agreed consideration or rent, would not satisfy *section 242(3)(a)* as it would not be a minimum rent for the purpose of the contingency principle (Tax Bulletin, Issue 18, August 1995).

**19.13** One trap is that if the agreement in the example in 19.11 were to provide that the additional consideration cannot exceed £500,000 the Stamp Office will contend that they are entitled to duty on £600,000. This is because they consider that if it is possible on the face of the document (and in the light of surrounding circumstances) to determine any figure that could become payable they are entitled to duty on that figure – or the highest of such figures. In the light of the decision in the capital gains tax case *Marren v Ingles (54 TC 76)* it seems doubtful whether this approach is correct where part of the consideration is unascertainable and dependent on a contingency. It is more logical to treat the value of the chose in action (the right to the contingent sum) at the date of the instrument as the amount of the additional consideration in the same way as it is treated for capital gains tax. Nevertheless the views of the Stamp Office will need to be followed until someone is brave enough to challenge them through the courts.

**19.14** If the consideration is payable by instalments over a definite period of 20 years or less the duty is payable, at the time the instrument is executed, on the total of the instalments provided that the total amount to be paid is ascertainable. This applies whether or not the instalments are equal in amount provided that the consideration is payable 'periodically for a definite period'. If the instalment period exceeds 20 years the amount on which duty is charged is the total amount that will become payable during the first 20 years. This also applies where the period is an indefinite period not terminable with a life, in which case obviously it has to be assumed that the payments will continue for over 20 years. If the consideration consists of money payable periodically during someone's life, or two or more lives, the amount on which duty is charged is the total of the sums that will become due during the first 12 years from the date of the instrument (*SA 1891, s 56*).

**19.15** It should be noted that where the consideration is not wholly in money so that a valuation is required, this will be the value at the date of the instrument of sale, i.e. normally, the conveyance – which can of course be very different to that at the date of the contract. This particularly needs to be borne in mind if property is sold with no fixed completion date or with a completion date some months away.

**19.16** It must not be overlooked that where the consideration is not in money the transfer of the asset constituting the consideration for the property sale may itself attract stamp duty.

**19.17** If property that is contracted to be sold for a single consideration is conveyed to the purchaser in a number of separate parcels by different instruments, the overall consideration can be apportioned in any way the parties think fit, but a distinct consideration for each part must be shown on the conveyance relating to that part (*SA 1891, s 58(1)*). If any part of any of the property is in a disadvantaged area (see 19.87), the apportionment must instead be made in such manner as is just and reasonable (*FA 2001, 30 Sch 2(1)*). If two or more persons contract to buy property jointly for one overall consideration and it is conveyed by separate instruments to the individual purchasers for distinct parts of the consideration, the conveyance of each part is chargeable with duty in respect of the part of the consideration specified in the conveyance (*SA 1891, s 58(2)*). If the property includes land in a disadvantaged area and the purchasers (or beneficial purchasers) are all connected persons (within *ICTA 1988, s 839* – see Appendix 1), the duty is not chargeable by reference to the part of the consideration specified in such conveyance but for duty purposes the overall consideration must be apportioned between the parcels in such manner as is just and reasonable and each conveyance stamped by reference to such apportioned amount (*FA 2001, 30 Sch 3(2)(3)(5)*).If several instruments of conveyance are required to complete the purchaser's title to a property, *ad valorem* duty is chargeable only on the principal instrument (and the parties can choose which this is by virtue of *SA 1891, s 61*) (*SA 1891, s 58(3)*).

**19.18** If in addition to other consideration the purchaser enters into a covenant to make any substantial improvement of, or addition to, the property being conveyed (or the conveyance is made partly in consideration of his previously having done such work) no duty is payable in relation to the value of such works (*FA 1900, s 10*).

## Contracts for Sale

**19.19** A contract for the sale of land does not normally attract stamp duty. However, *SA 1891, s 59* provides that a contract or agreement for the sale of any equitable estate or interest in any property whatsoever (which will include land) is dutiable as if it were an actual conveyance on sale of the estate or interest. The duty is charged on the actual consideration at the rates current at the time of completion. It is payable by the purchaser. A contract which provides for the transfer of the legal estate is not a contract for the sale of an equitable interest. If, however, it is clear that the parties never intend to complete the transaction, the contract may be stampable as a document effecting the sale of an equitable interest (*West London Syndicate v CIR (1898 2 QB 507)*). The National Conditions of Sale of land require the vendor to deliver a duly executed conveyance or transfer, so if these are used the agreement will not fall foul of *section 59*. That section will apply in two fairly common circumstances. The first is where one of several joint owners wishes to dispose of his interest in a property. In such circumstances the property is normally held on trust for sale, and all that the 'joint owner' actually possesses – and thus can sell – is an undivided equitable interest in a share of the sale proceeds. The second is where there is no intention of transferring the legal title. For example, where an individual who has mortgaged his house decides to sell it to his company subject to the mortgage but to continue to hold the property in trust for the company to avoid having to obtain the agreement of the mortgagee; or where a landowner enters into a joint venture with a developer and agrees to transfer an interest in the property to the developer, the property remaining registered in the name of the landowner but being declared to be held in trust jointly for the developer and himself (*Chesterfield Brewery v CIR (1899 2 QB 7)*).

**19.20** In *Peter Bone Ltd v CIR (1995 STC 921)* a family partnership entered into an agreement to sell the business as a going concern to a company. The deed included a provision that the partnership was to hold the land as nominee for the company and execute such assignments, transfers or conveyances of the property to such persons as the company might require. It was intended that in due course the company would sell on the land and stamp duty would be paid by the ultimate purchasers. It was held that the agreement was stampable by reference to the value of the land either under *section 59* or under *section 54* as a conveyance on sale of the equitable estate. Following completion of the contract nothing further needed to be done so there was nothing capable of being specifically performed. Accordingly the partnership did not have the same rights as the vendor under an uncompleted contract would have of requiring the purchaser to take a conveyance and relieve it of a potentially burdensome legal title.

**19.21** *Section 59* also provides that, subject to a large number of exceptions, a contract for the sale of an estate or interest in any property is to be treated as if it were a conveyance on sale. One of the exceptions is a contract for the sale of 'lands, tenements, hereditaments, or heritages'. The exceptions take most contracts out of the scope of stamp duty other than contracts for the sale of intangible property. One type of property transaction that sometimes occurs, and that is left within this provision, is an agreement to dispose of the benefit of a contract to buy a property. For example, suppose A contracts to buy a property from B for £100,000 and sells the benefit of that contract to C for £40,000. The sale from A to C will attract *ad valorem* duty of £400. When C completes the contract and pays B the £100,000 the conveyance will attract *ad valorem* duty of £1,000. In this way the full 'price' of £140,000 paid by C to acquire the property will have become dutiable.

**19.22** In addition *FA 2002, s 115* imposes duty on a contract or agreement for the sale of an estate or interest in land in the UK executed after 24 July 2002, as if it were a conveyance if the consideration exceeds £10 million (or the instrument forms part of a larger transaction or series of transactions in respect of which the aggregate value exceeds £10 million) and a conveyance is not presented for stamping within 90 days of the execution of the contract (*FA 2002, s 115(1)(2)(8)*). This is an anti-avoidance provision. It counters sales where the consideration is paid but the transaction is left to lie in contract. It also counters an increasingly popular scheme under which the land is transferred to a nominee company, the beneficial owner contracts to sell the land with the consideration being payable immediately and the purchaser being entitled to call for completion at any subsequent time, and the nominee company is also sold to the purchaser so that it both owns the beneficial interest in the land and controls the legal title to it.

**19.23** The Revenue have power to extend the 90-day period of grace to what they think reasonable in the circumstances of the case. They cannot however do so if it appears to them that substantially the whole of the intended consideration has been paid. They can impose conditions on the extension and can require a copy of the contract and such other evidence as they may reasonably require as to the facts and circumstances relevant to making their decision (*FA 2002, s 115(2)(3)*). For interest and penalty purposes the document is treated as if it had been executed at the end of the 90-day (or extended) period (*FA 2002, s 115(5)*). If the contract is subsequently rescinded or annulled (or for any other reason not substantially performed or carried into effect) the *ad valorem* duty becomes repayable, but apparently without interest (*FA 2002, s 115(6)*). If a transaction relates both to land in the UK and to other property, *section 115* applies as if there were separate transactions. The consideration must then be apportioned in a manner which is just and reasonable (*FA 2002, Sch 36, para 8)*.

The Revenue have established a special unit, the Stamp Taxes Contracts Unit, in its Manchester Stamp Office to deal with *section 115* contracts. An application to extend the 90-day period needs to be submitted in writing to that office. The Revenue say that they will endeavour to process applications within 30 days and subsequently said that in straightforward cases they will give clearance within five working days (Estates Gazette 14.9.2002). They are likely to extend the limit readily where the time of completion is dependent on an event outside the control of the parties, such as the obtaining of planning consent and if the purchase price has not been paid prior to completion. The information that needs to accompany an application is set out in Stamp Taxes Customer Newsletter No 3 (July 2002).

**19.24** To avoid double taxation the subsequent conveyance is relieved from duty. If the conveyance is to the purchaser under the contract or to a sub-purchaser where *SA 1891, s 58(4)* applies (see 19.23), i.e. the *ad valorem* duty is charged on the consideration moving from the sub-purchaser, the conveyance is chargeable with duty only to the extent that the *ad valorem* duty exceeds that already paid on the contract (plus any further duty paid under *section 115* on an intervening sub-sale) (*FA 2002, Sch 36 para 5(1)*). If the conveyance is to different sub-purchasers in parts or parcels and *SA 1891, s 58(5)* applies, (see 19.25) the conveyance of each part is chargeable with duty only to the extent that *ad valorem* duty on that part exceeds an appropriate proportion (on a just and reasonable basis) of the duty previously paid (*FA 2002, Sch 36 para 5(2)(3)*). The Revenue can nevertheless be required to stamp the conveyance as having paid *ad valorem* duty (*FA 2002, Sch 36 para 5(4)*).

**19.25** If the duty that would otherwise be chargeable on the conveyance exceeds that paid under *section 115* the excess becomes repayable (*FA 2002, Sch 36 para 6(1)*). It needs to be shown that duty was paid under *section 115*, that one or more transfers have been executed in conformity with the contract so that the whole of the property contracted to be sold has been conveyed and that all of the conveyances are duly stamped. If duty has been paid under *section 115*, on one or more intervening sub-sales references to the duty paid on the original sale include that paid on the sub-sales (*FA 2002, Sch 36 para 6*).

**19.26** Where duty has been paid under *section 115* on a sale and before any conveyance there is an intervening sub-sale, duty is chargeable under *section 115* on the agreement for the sub-sale only to the extent that the chargeable consideration (not the duty) exceeds the chargeable consideration on the sale (or previous sub-sale). Where there has been more than one earlier transaction the comparison is with the highest amount of chargeable consideration on which duty has been paid. If the sub-sale does not relate to the whole of the property the comparison is of course with an appropriate proportion (on a just and reasonable basis) of the consideration on the previous transaction (*FA 2002, Sch 36 para 3(1)–(5)*). Where duty is chargeable only on excess consideration under this provision the rate is of course determined by reference to the entire consideration (*FA 2002, Sch 36 para 3(6)*). There is a sub-sale for this purpose if the purchaser under a contract for the sale of an estate or interest in land in the UK, or a sub-purchaser under a sub-sale of such a contract, without having obtained a conveyance of the property contracts to sell the whole or part of the property contracted to be sold by the original sale to another person so as to entitle that other person to call for a conveyance from the original purchaser (*FA 2002, Sch 36 para 2*).

**Sub-sales**

**19.27** Special rules apply to sub-sales, i.e. where a person contracts to buy a property and, before completion, contracts to sell it to a third party, the two transactions being completed by a single conveyance from the original vendor to the final purchaser. For example, if the transaction postulated in 19.21 above had been carried out by way of a sub-sale, A would have contracted to sell the property to C for £140,000.

**19.28** The general rule on sub-sales is that the conveyance is to be charged with *ad valorem* duty in respect of the consideration moving from the sub-purchaser (or the last of a series of sub-purchasers) (*SA 1891, s 58(4)*), i.e. in the above example the conveyance would have been between B and C at the price of £140,000 that C had contracted to pay to A.

**19.29** This does not apply if the chargeable consideration moving from the sub-purchaser is less than the value of the property immediately before the contract of sale to him (*SA 1891, s 58(4)(a)*). Nor would it apply if there is no consideration moving from the sub-purchaser, as the transaction would then not be a sale at all. In such circumstances the position is unclear. It appears from *Fitch Lovell v CIR (1962 3 All ER 685)* that duty may be payable in respect of all contracts in the chain, but this may well not be the case if the intermediate owners are not parties to the ultimate conveyance. This was not the intention behind the amendment to the legislation made in 1984.

**19.30** Similarly, where a purchaser contracts to sell part of the property without having obtained a conveyance, duty is payable only on the consideration moving from the sub-purchaser on the conveyance to him (and on the part of the price payable by the original purchaser under the conveyance to him of the balance of the land) unless the aggregate stampable consideration for all the parcels of land is less than the value of the whole property immediately before the first contract for the sale of any of the parcels (*SA 1891, s 58(5)*).

**19.31** If a sub-purchaser takes an actual conveyance of the interest of the person immediately selling to him, i.e. a conveyance of his beneficial interest, which is chargeable to *ad valorem* duty and is duly stamped, the subsequent conveyance of the property to him by the original seller will not attract *ad valorem* duty (*SA 1891, s 58(6)*).

**19.32** If property is conveyed to a person in advance of a sale but in contemplation thereof it must be treated as a conveyance on sale (*FA 1965, s 90*). Accordingly duty cannot be avoided by transferring the property to the prospective purchaser as nominee for the vendor and then selling the beneficial interest by delivery of the nominee document. If the sale never takes place and the property is reconveyed to the original owner (or his successor on a death or bankruptcy) – but not if it is reconveyed to any other person – or it takes place at a lower price, the excess duty will be refunded. As a claim for a refund must be made within two years after the making of the transfer a refund is only competent if the land has been reconveyed within this period. All the relevant documents must be adjudicated (see 19.114 below) (*FA 1965, s 90(3)*). This provision could be used as an insurance against an increase in stamp duty in future budgets. A conveyance to the proposed purchaser could be made at an early stage in negotiations prior to the budget so that the existing rates are payable on that conveyance, with the property being reconveyed if the sale falls through. Property owners are likely to be reluctant to transfer title in advance of receiving the sale proceeds though, so this is unlikely to be practicable in many cases.

**19.33** Where a house is sold at a discount by a local authority, or by any of various other specified bodies, on terms that all or part of the discount has to be repaid in the event of specified contingencies, such as a sale of the house within a short period, duty is payable on the discounted price only, i.e. the possibility of the discount having to be repaid is ignored (*FA 1981, s 107*).

### Options

**19.34** An option attracts stamp duty on the option money at the rates shown at 19.6. An option over shares attracts duty at the full rates, not at the 0.5% rate applicable to a sale of shares (*George Wimpey & Co Ltd v CIR, 1975 STC 248*). When the option is exercised the conveyance pursuant to the option attracts full duty. Care is needed with the drafting. In the *Wimpey* case the option was granted for a payment of £15,000 to acquire the property for £10,000 per acre but with a credit against that price being granted for the £15,000 paid. It was pointed out that duty could be payable on £15,000 on grant of the option and on the full £10,000 per acre on the conveyance, resulting in the £15,000 being effectively charged twice. If the purchase price had been expressed as £X (£10,000 an acre less £15,000) this problem would have been avoided. The Revenue said in that case that they would not put forward such a claim but it is preferable not to have to rely on the Revenue not enforcing a liability in full.

## Conveyances other than on Sale

**19.35** Any instrument or court order whereby property is transferred to or vested in any person and which is not in respect of a sale or mortgage is chargeable with duty at a flat rate of £5 (50p on documents executed before 1 October 1999) (*FA 1999, s 112(2)*) (*SA 1891, s 62, 1 Sch*). This could, for instance, apply to a transfer by a nominee to the beneficial owner, or a transfer to a new trustee on his appointment, or to distributions *in specie* by a company to its shareholders or by a liquidator during the course of the liquidation. Prior to 30 November 1993 it applied to a transfer of freehold land in exchange for the assignment of a lease of other land, or the exchange of one lease for another – which was held not to be a transfer on sale in *Littlewoods Mail Order Stores v CIR (1962 2 All ER 279)*. The duty on such transactions is now governed by *Finance Act 1994, s 241* (see 19.36).

## Exchanges and Partition or Division of Land

**19.36** Prior to 7 December 1993 the exchange of one parcel of land for another did not attract *ad valorem* duty as it was not regarded as a sale. From that date such an exchange is treated as a sale for a consideration equal to the market value of the property (*FA 1994, s 241*). There is an exception for an instrument executed in pursuance of a contract made before 30 November 1993. Where, as will normally be the case, property A is exchanged for property B, duty is chargeable on each transfer. The £60,000 threshold is applied separately to each side of the exchange. Where equality money is paid it will depend on the wording of the conveyance whether this is dutiable. If this provides that say an £80,000 property will be transferred in exchange for a £100,000 property less £20,000 equality money, duty will be charged on £80,000 and £100,000 respectively. If the conveyance provides that the consideration for the transfer of the £80,000 property consists of the £100,000 one, duty on each property will be charged on £100,000 even though £20,000 of equality money is also paid. The Revenue have stated that they will want to see the contract as well as the conveyance to ascertain the true nature of the transaction (IR Press Release 18.4.94, paras 4, 6 and 10 and Tax Bulletin, Issue 18, August 1995).

**19.37** The Revenue draw a distinction between an exchange of properties and a sale of one property with part of the consideration being satisfied by the transfer of another property. For example, if a builder offers a house for sale he may receive the price from the buyer partly in the form of money and partly in the form of a transfer of the buyer's old house. Provided that the transaction is documented throughout as a sale, the Revenue consider that *ad valorem* duty is not chargeable on the transfer of the buyer's old house; it will attract only a fixed duty of £5 (IR Press Release 18.4.94, para 12 and Tax Bulletin, Issue 18, August 1995). Clearly, wherever possible, exchanges of properties should be avoided, and one sold with the consideration being satisfied by the transfer of the other so as to eliminate *ad valorem* duty in relation to one. It is not clear what would happen if a £10,000 property were sold the consideration being satisfied by accepting a £100,000 house and the vendor making a payment to the purchaser of £90,000. Logically it should attract the £5 fixed duty only.

**19.38** From 28 March 2000 an instrument which transfers an estate or interest in land but which is not a conveyance or transfer on sale for stamp duty purposes must be treated as a transfer on sale of the estate or interest if that transfer is for consideration which is or includes other property (*FA 2000, s 118(1)(2)(12)*). This is aimed at, for example, a sale of a property for cash being turned into a sale of gilts (which is not stampable) in consideration of the transfer of the property. Gilts are readily acquired and readily re-convertible into cash so the parties may be prepared to go through an acquisition and disposal of the gilts provided that the dealing costs are less than the stamp duty, which would invariably be the case if the duty is at the 4% rate.

**19.39** If the other property is or includes another estate or interest in land and ad duty is chargeable on that conveyance the duty payable is reduced by the duty paid on that other property (*FA 2000, s 118(3)*).

*Example 42*

Pat sells £1m of gilts and a £200,000 property to Jill in consideration of Jill transferring to Pat two properties worth £1.2m.

The tax payable on Jill's sale is 4% of £200,000 or £8,000. *Section 118* imposes a charge on Pat on 4% of £1.2m, or £48,000 less the £8,000 payable by Jill, giving a charge of £40,000.

*Example 43*

John transfers two office buildings worth £400,000 and £600,000 respectively to Sue and pays her £100,000 in consideration of the sale by Sue to him of a building worth £1.1m.

The tax payable on Sue's sale is 4% of £1.1m or £44,000. The tax payable under *section 118* is 4% of £1m (the value of John's buildings) or £40,000 reduced by the duty payable by Sue of £44,000, leaving John's duty at nil. In other words *section 118* does not adversely affect the sort of transaction considered at 19.30.

**19.40** If the value of the other property (i.e. the gilts) exceeds the market value of the land at the time of execution of the instrument transferring or vesting it the charge under section 118 is on the market value of the land only (*FA 2000, s 118(4)*).

**19.41** There is an exemption for an instrument giving effect to a contract made before 22 March 2000 but not where the pre-22 March contract was an option, or similar right, and the transfer of the land is made in consequence of the option, right of pre-emption or similar right being exercised after 21 March. Similarly, the exemption does not apply where the transfer of the land is not to the purchaser under the pre-22 March contract but to someone who became entitled to it because of an assignment or further contract made after 21 March (*FA 2000, s 118(11)*).

**19.42** Exchanges before 7 December 1993 attracted only the then 50p fixed duty on conveyance described in 19.35 above. However, if equality money of more than £100 was paid on an exchange of freeholds the conveyance (or principal conveyance, i.e. the one that the parties chose) was chargeable with the same *ad valorem* duty as a conveyance or sale for a consideration equal to the equality money (*SA 1891, s 73*). *Section 73* also applied to the partition or division of freehold land. It continues to do so and is extended to cover a partition or division of any interest in land (*FA 1994, s 241(4)*).

## Transfer of Land to Connected Company

**19.43** If:

(*a*) an estate or interest in land is transferred or vested in a company after 27 March 2000,

(*b*) the transferor is connected with that company (within *ICTA 1988, s 839* – see Appendix 1), and

(*c*) some or all of the consideration for the transfer or vesting consists of the issue or transfer of shares in a company with which the transferor is connected,

the instrument transferring or vesting the estate must be treated as a transfer on sale of that estate (*FA 2000, s 119(2)(3)(8)(13)*). If the deemed consideration for the transfer is less than the market value of the land, the duty must be calculated on the market value of the land reduced by any part of the actual consideration that does not consist of property (*FA 2000, s 119(4)(7)*). If the transfer also falls within *FA 2000, s 118* (see 19.38) the duty is to be calculated in accordance with *section 119*, not *section 118* (*FA 2000, s 119(5)*).

**19.44** There are a number of exceptions from *section 119*:

(*a*) if a greater amount of duty would be payable if the *section* (and *FA 2000, s 118*) did not apply (*FA 2000, s 119(6)*);

(*b*) if the transfer is by a nominee or bare trustee to his principal (where that is the company to which the land is transferred) (*FA 2000, s 120(2)*);

(*c*) if the land is being transferred by the transferor (B) to the company (A) to hold it as nominee or bare trustee for B (*FA 2000, s 120(3)*);

(*d*) if B holds the land as trustee or nominee for a third party and is transferring it to A who is to become the new trustee or nominee for that third party (*FA 2000, s 120(4)*);

(*e*) if the transfer by B to A is a transfer out of a settlement in or towards satisfaction of a beneficiary's interest and constitutes a distribution of property in accordance with the provisions of that settlement – but only if the beneficiary did not acquire his interest for money or money's worth (*FA 2000, s 120(5)*);

(*f*) if the transferee company is a person carrying on a business which consists of (or includes) the management of trusts and it is acquiring the land as a trustee in the course of that business (*FA 2000, s 120(6)*);

(*g*) if the transferor (B) is a company, it acquired the land by virtue of an instrument which was duly stamped and it is transferring it to B as a distribution of assets, either on a winding-up or as a dividend *in specie* (*FA 2000, s 120(7)*);

(*h*) if the transfer gives effect to a contract made before 22 March 2000 – but not if the instrument is made in consequence of the exercise after 21 March of any option, right of pre-emption or similar right or it transfers the property in question to someone other than the original contracting party because of an assignment or further contract after that date.

**19.45** Some people have expressed concern that this provision could impose stamp duty on a gift (or sale at a nominal figure) of land to a company on the incorporation of a business. The *Finance Bill* notes on clauses stated that 'the clause does not affect situations where specific stamp duty exemptions apply'. This is not at all clear from the legislation though. Although a gift is exempt, the charge under *section 120* is imposed by deeming the instrument to be a transfer on sale of the relevant interest. On the face of it the stamp duty consequences must follow from that deemed sale, not from the actual gift. The provision is aimed at the transfer of land to a company in consideration of the issue of securities whose value is less than that of the land and the onward sale of the company. Previously stamp duty was charged only on the value of the securities, so stamp duty at the 4% rate could be avoided.

**19.46** The provision also applies in the same way where instead of transferring the interest to the company the connected person grants a lease to the company for a premium (*FA 2000, s 121*). However, exceptions (*b*) to (*g*) in 19.44 do not apply to the grant of a lease.

## Lease Duty

**19.47** The stamp duty on a lease depends on the length of the lease and the rent payable, and whether or not a premium is paid. If the lease is for a fixed term of less than a year the duty is £5 for a lease of furnished residential accommodation and 1% of a full year's rent in any other case subject to a *de minimis* exemption where the rent is £5,000 or less (£500 prior to 28 March 2000) (*FA 1999, Sch 13 para 11*). Prior to 1 October 1999 the duty was 0.5% of the rent for a full year's rent at the rate specified in the lease rounded up to the nearest 50p (plus 1% of the amount of any premium) – except in the case of furnished lettings of residential property where there was a fixed duty of £1. In both cases there was a *de minimis* limit of £500.

**19.48** For leases of a fixed term exceeding a year, or for an indefinite term, the duty is 1% of any premium or 3% if it is over £250,000 or 4% if over £500,000 (i.e. the duty that would be payable on a conveyance on sale for a consideration equal to the premium) plus a percentage of the average rent, varying between 1% and 24%. The rate of duty on the rent is normally:

| | |
|---|---|
| if the term is indefinite | 1% |
| if the term does not exceed 7 years | 1% |
| if the term does not exceed 35 years | 2% |
| if the term does not exceed 100 years | 12% |
| if the term exceeds 100 years | 24% |

Where necessary, rent is rounded up to the nearest £50. Where the average rent does not exceed £5,000 per annum the rate of duty on indefinite leases, and on leases of seven years or less, is nil (*FA 1999, Sch 13 para 12*). The exemption from duty on conveyance on sale where the consideration is less than £60,000 (see 19.6 above) does not apply to lease duty (although it does still apply to any premium), nor does it apply to the 1% on a premium on a lease if the rent payable under the lease exceeds £600 per annum (£300 prior to 15 March 1993) (*FA 1963, s 55(2)*; *FA 1993, s 201*). For leases entered into between 20 December 1991 and 19 August 1992 no duty was payable on the premium if the average rent did not exceed £2,500 and the premium itself did not exceed £250,000. The normal duty was still payable on the rent though (*Stamp Duty (Temporary Provisions) Act 1992*).

**19.49** An area of potential difficulty is sometimes the ascertainment of the average annual rent where this is to be determined by a formula. In the past where rent levels were fixed by reference to changes in an index, such as the RPI, the Revenue's practice was to base the average on increases in the index during the year ended with the date of execution of the lease. They have abandoned this practice with retrospective effect from 25 February 1995. They now take account only of changes in the index up to the date of execution of the lease (presumably this is the increase from the time of entering into an agreement for the lease or any base date specified in the lease). In most cases this will result in the average rent being similar to the initial rent. The Revenue considered on an individual basis repaying duty overpaid on documents stamped since 25 February 1995, but only where a claim for repayment was made before 14 May 2000 (Parliamentary Answer 14.5.1999).

**19.50** A lease granted for a fixed term and thereafter until determined must be treated as being for a term equal to the aggregate of the fixed period plus such further period as must elapse before the lease can be determined (normally the notice period required to determine it) (*FA 1963, s 56*). It has been held that a lease for a definite term with an option to the tenant to renew it for a further specified term must be stamped by reference to the initial term only (*Hand v Hall (2 Ex D 355)*). If the consideration does not consist of rent – a very unusual occurrence – or the amount of the rent is not ascertainable, the duty is a fixed sum of £5 (*FA 1999, Sch 13 para 13*). No duty is payable on a lease or agreement for lease of an allotment or garden if the rent does not exceed 50p p.a. and no premium is paid (*Land Settlement (Facilities) Act 1919, s 21*). It is unlikely that this exemption will ever apply in the 1990s!

## Agreements for Lease

**19.51** An agreement for a lease bears stamp duty as if it were an actual lease for the term and consideration contained in the agreement (*SA 1891, s 75(1)*). Where duty has been paid on an agreement for a lease and an actual lease is subsequently granted which either

(*a*) is in conformity with the agreement, or

(*b*) relates to substantially the same property and term as the agreement,

the amount of duty paid on the agreement can be deducted from the amount payable on the lease (*SA 1891, s 75(2)*).

**19.52** The Inland Revenue take a very strict approach to stamp duty. No relief will be granted if neither condition (*a*) nor condition (*b*) is met, even though the differences may be slight. For example, if a tenant agrees to take a lease of Unit 1 in a development and subsequently decides to take Unit 6 instead, double duty will be payable, once on the agreement for the lease of Unit 1 and again on the actual lease of Unit 6. If an agreement for lease is rescinded, or the contract is for any other reason not performed, the duty paid on the agreement cannot be reclaimed. Care accordingly needs to be taken in relation to agreements for lease, particularly if the grant of the lease or the rent payable is conditional on the completion of building works or the granting of planning permission. This could result in a substantial overpayment of duty if the condition is not met. It would be preferable from a stamp duty point of view to give an option to call for a lease on the condition being met rather than start with an agreement for lease. The duty on the option is 1% of the option money paid (*SA 1891, s 60*).

**19.53** It should also be realised that the duty on the agreement for lease could exceed the duty payable on the lease itself. If so there will be no refund of the excess. For example, an agreement for lease may provide that a developer is to be granted a lease for 125 years at a rent of the lower of £20,000 p.a. or 10% of the construction costs of the building with 5-yearly upward only rent reviews. The Revenue will demand duty of £4,800, i.e. 24% of £20,000, on the agreement for lease. If the construction cost turns out to be £150,000 the initial rent provided in the actual lease will be £15,000 on which the duty is only £3,600.

**19.54** These problems need not arise. *FA 1994, s 240* provides that if a lease and the agreement for lease are presented for stamping together and the duty due on the agreement is paid, it can be treated for penalty purposes as having been executed at the same time as the lease. Accordingly if the lease is significantly different from the initial agreement this will enable the agreement to be discharged by mutual consent and replaced by an amended agreement. However the agreement cannot simply be ignored as the lease must either:

(*a*) contain a certificate that there is no agreement to which it gives effect; or

(*b*) be stamped with a stamp denoting that there is such an agreement and either that it is not chargeable to duty or the amount of duty paid on it (*s 240(2)*).

A lease gives effect to an agreement if it is in conformity with it or relates to substantially the same property and term as the agreement (*s 240(3)*). Accordingly if there are significant differences it may be possible to give the certificate at (*a*) without having to discharge the original agreement. This is not of course the purpose of *section 240*. It was introduced because the Revenue were in practice often prepared to stamp a lease without calling for the agreement and, having convinced themselves that they had a legal duty to stamp the agreement, want to avoid the cost and time of having to look at the two documents separately.

## Structuring the Lease

**19.55** It will be apparent that the structure of a lease can significantly affect the duty payable. A lease for 50 years at an initial rent of £20,000 p.a. will attract duty of 12% of £20,000, or £2,400. A lease for 25 years, plus a further 25-year lease to start on the expiry of the first, at an initial rent of £20,000 increased in line with the retail prices index, will attract duty of twice 2% of £20,000, or £800, although for most practical purposes the rights of the tenant may well be the same.

**19.56** If a lease or agreement for lease provides for a penal rent, duty is not chargeable on that element. If it is entered into in consideration of the surrender or abandonment of an existing lease or agreement for lease relating to the same property, duty is not chargeable on the value of the existing lease (*SA 1891, s 77(1)*). As with the duty on conveyance on sale (19.17 above), *ad valorem* duty is not chargeable on the value of a covenant to carry out substantial improvements except to the extent that duty would have been payable on such consideration if it had been contained in a separate deed (*SA 1891, s 77(2)*; *Revenue Act 1909, s 8*). A document increasing the rent payable under an existing lease is chargeable to lease duty to the extent of the increase (*SA 1891, s 77(5)*).

**19.57** If an interest in land is conveyed or transferred (or a lease is granted) subject to an agreement for a lease for a term exceeding 35 years, the conveyance will not be regarded as duly stamped unless there is denoted on it the duty paid on the agreement (*FA 1984, s 111*). This ensures that the Revenue collect the full tax by obviating the risk that they will accept a reduction in value of the property to reflect the existence of the agreement for lease and find that the agreement is not presented for stamping. It does not matter whether or not the agreement for lease is referred to in the conveyance. If more than one interest in a property is subject to an agreement for lease *section 111* applies only to the most inferior interest (*FA 1984, s 111(3)*).

**19.58** Problems can arise with some types of home annuity schemes. If a house is transferred in return for an annuity and the annuitant in addition retains a right of occupation or lease back (or some other protected right to occupation), the Revenue consider that the consideration is the value of the annuity plus the value of the occupation rights. They also contend that if the annuity contains some form of index-linking they are entitled to look at past increases in the index as evidence of what is likely to happen in the future.

## Power to Vary Stamp Duties

**19.59** From 28 July 2000 the Treasury have been given power to vary stamp duties or to alter the description of documents to which a particular duty applies by statutory instrument instead of changes having to wait for the next Finance Act (*FA 2000, s 117* and *Sch 33 para 1*). They can do this only in relation to instruments that to any extent involve either land, stock or marketable securities or any estate or interest in such items (*Sch 33 para* 2). They also cannot vary the rate or rates of existing stamp duties or the rate bands for conveyances on sale or duties on leases, except where this results from changing the category into which a particular document falls (*Sch 33 para 3*).

The statutory instrument can take effect from the date it is made but must then be laid before the House of Commons, which has 28 days in which to approve it (by a motion). If it is not approved it ceases to have effect but without prejudice to anything done in reliance of it. The period for which the regulations have statutory effect can be significantly longer than 28 days as any days on which Parliament is prorogued or dissolved or adjourned for over four days is not counted towards the total (*FA 2000, Sch 33 para 4*). If the regulations are not approved by Parliament, taxpayers can claim repayment of the duty paid under them. A claim for repayment must be made within three years of the date of the instrument (although the Revenue, not the Treasury, can by regulations alter that time limit, either upwards or downwards) (*Sch 33 para* 5). The regulations cannot remain in force for more than 18 months (*Sch 33 para 7*). The intention is that the Treasury should make temporary changes pending their enactment in the next Finance Act.

## Exceptions

**19.60** There are a number of exceptions both from the duty on conveyance on sale and from lease duty. The Stamp Office adopt a strict approach to exemptions; relief will be given only if a transaction falls squarely within the wording of the exemption, however technical or slight any breach of the conditions may appear. Apart from the statutory exemptions set out below, it should be borne in mind that when a document is executed outside the UK, although it is theoretically stampable if it relates to property in the UK, there is no requirement actually to pay the duty until 30 days after the document has been brought into the UK (*SA 1891, s 15(2)*, see 19.112 below). Accordingly stamp duty can be avoided by executing the necessary documents outside the UK and leaving them overseas. This is not always easy with land transactions, as it would not be possible to register title (although it may be possible to register a caution) and it would normally be necessary in any event to bring the documents into the UK at the time of a subsequent sale in order to establish title. There is also a risk that future VAT planning might fail because if the title is not registered it is not possible to register interests granted out of it. Customs could contend that any lease is ineffective for want of registration as required by the *Land Registration Act 1997*. Executing a share transfer in respect of shares in a UK company overseas will be counterproductive, as if there is no stampable document a liability to Stamp Duty Reserve Tax at 1.5% (not 0.5%) arises. Similarly the duty on conveyance can in theory be avoided by contracting to buy and never completing (see 19.5 above) but in practice the risks are generally too great except where the parties are associated with one another.

**FA 1930, s 42: Associated Companies**

**19.61** Stamp duty under the heading 'Conveyance or Transfer on Sale' is not payable if the effect of the document is to transfer a beneficial interest in property from one body corporate to another and the two companies are associated at the time the instrument is executed. Two bodies are associated for this purpose if one is the parent of the other (i.e. it owns beneficially at least 75% of its ordinary share capital) or another body corporate is the parent of both. Ordinary share capital is all of the issued capital of a body other than capital, the holders of which have a right to a dividend at a fixed rate but no other right to share in profits (*FA 1930, s 42* as amended by *FA 1995, s 149*).

The exemption does not apply to transfers after 28 July 2000 if at the time the instrument is executed arrangements are in existence by virtue of which at that or some later time a person (or persons together) have, or could obtain, control (within *ICTA 1988, s 840*) of the transferee company but not of the transferor (*FA 1930, s 42(2)(6)(7)* as amended by *FA 2000, s 123(3)*). From the same date the two companies are associated only if at the relevant time the parent company is beneficially entitled not only to at least 75% of the ordinary share capital, but is also beneficially entitled to at least 75% of any profits available for distribution to equity holders of the other company and to at least 75% of any assets of that company available for distribution to equity holders on a winding-up (*FA 1930, s 42(2B*) as amended by *FA 2000, s 123(4*)). The complex rules for determining what is available to equity holders contained in *ICTA 1988, Sch 18* (other than *paras 5(3)* and *5B–5E*) apply for the purposes of these two new tests (*FA 1930, s 42(5)(6)* as amended by *FA 2000, s 123(6)*). The effect of these changes is broadly to bring the stamp duty definition of a group into line with the corporation tax one. Similar changes have been made to the Northern Irish legislation, *FA (Northern Ireland) 1954, s 11*, by *FA 2000, s 124*.

**19.62** For documents executed before 1 May 1995 one of the companies had to be the beneficial owner of at least 90% of the issued share capital of the other or a third company the beneficial owner of at least 90% of the issued share capital of both of them. Issued share capital looks solely at nominal value of shares. For example, if a company has £1 shares, 10 out of 100 ordinary shares plus 900 out of 900 preference shares would give 910 out of 1,000 shares and would thus qualify for relief. Ownership of 10 out of 100 fully paid ordinary shares and another 900 out of 900 ordinary shares one penny paid up would also qualify. Indirect ownership through other companies can be taken into account (*FA 1930, s 42(3)*). *Schedule 4* to the *Finance Act 1938* contains detailed attribution rules where shares are held through a series of companies. These are largely a matter of common sense. The decision in *Wood Preservation v Prior (45 TC 112)*, where it was held that for loss relief purposes a company had ceased to be beneficial owner of a subsidiary which it had contracted to sell, needs to be borne in mind in applying this relief. Although the change was designed to bring the stamp duty grouping rules into line with those for capital gains tax, the test is not identical where some of the shares are held indirectly, as *Schedule 4* does not mirror the capital gains tax rules. Accordingly it is not safe to assume that both exemptions will automatically apply on intra-group transfers.

**19.63** Prior to 1 May 1995 there was no exemption from lease duty (on either a lease or an agreement for lease) where a lease was granted from one company in a group to another. Such a transaction is now exempt if lessor and lessee are both bodies corporate and are associated at the time the document is executed (and in the case of an agreement for a lease the lease is to be granted to either the lessee or to another company which is also associated at the time the agreement is executed) (*FA 1995, s 151(1)(2)*). The exemption does not apply if an arrangement exists whereby either any part of the consideration is to be provided or received (directly or indirectly) by a third party – other than another associated company – or the companies were to cease to be associated by severing the group relationship (*FA 1995, s 151(3)(4)*). The lease needs to be presented for adjudication to attract the exemption (*FA 1995, s 151(5)*). The definition of associated companies is the same as in 19.61 (*FA 1995, s 151(7)–(10)*). The amended definition of associated company at 19.61 applies for this purpose where the instrument is executed after 28 July 2000 (*FA 2000, s 125*).

**19.64** For the exemption to apply the instrument has to be submitted to the Stamp Office to give them the opportunity to assess whether the exemption is due. If they agree that it is, the document will be stamped denoting that it is not liable to duty (*FA 1930, s 42(1)*). It also needs to be shown that the document was not executed in pursuance of, or in connection with, an arrangement under which either:

(*a*) any part of the consideration is provided or received directly or indirectly by a third party other than another associated company;

(*b*) the interest in question was previously conveyed or transferred directly or indirectly by such a person; or

(*c*) the transferor and transferee will cease to be associated by reason of a change in the percentage of the issued share capital of the transferee company held by the group, i.e. the transferee company will leave the group thus taking the property outside the group.

(*FA 1967, s 27(3)*).

**19.65** *FA 1967, s 27(2)* indicates that *section 42* applies only where the companies are limited liability companies, although there is nothing in *section 42* itself to suggest this.

**19.66** Care may need to be taken where the purchase price is borrowed. The Stamp Office have been known to contend that the borrowing constitutes an arrangement within (*a*) in 19.64 above if the lender imposes restrictions on the use of the money, which will of course often be the case.

**19.67** There is no similar exemption from duty on the grant of a lease by one associated company to another.

## FA 1986, ss 75, 76: Company Reconstructions

**19.68** There is an exemption from the duty on conveyance on sale if one company acquires the whole or part of the undertaking of another company (the target company) in pursuance of a scheme for the reconstruction of the target company (*FA 1986, s 75(1)(2)*). The document must be sent for adjudication (*FA 1986, s 75(3)*). Three conditions must be met:

(*a*) the registered office of the acquiring company must be in the UK and the consideration either consist wholly of the issue of redeemable shares in the acquiring company to *all* of the shareholders of the target company, or of such an issue plus the assumption of liabilities of the target company;

(*b*) the acquisition must be effected for bona fide commercial reasons and not form part of a scheme or arrangement of which one of the main purposes is the avoidance of stamp duty, income tax, corporation tax or capital gains tax; and

(*c*) after the acquisition each shareholder in each of the companies must be a shareholder of the other; and the proportion of shares held by any shareholder must be the same in both companies.

(*FA 1986, s 75(4)(5)* as amended by *FA 2000, s 127*).

This exemption will rarely apply as not many reconstructions take this form. The most common example which does is a spin-off of part of the business of a company to its shareholders.

**19.69** In any other case where one company acquires the undertaking of another, the duty on conveyance on sale is reduced to 0.5% instead of the normal 1% provided that condition (*a*) in 19.68 above is met (or would be met but for the inclusion in the consideration of cash not exceeding 10% of the nominal value of the shares in the acquiring company being issued). Also, in some cases the shares may be issued to the target company itself, as well as to the shareholders therein. The document must be sent for adjudication (*FA 1986, s 76*).

**19.70** For transfers executed after 23 April 2004 (other than in pursuance of a binding contract made before 18 April 2002), if the instrument transfers land in the UK it also needs to be shown that the acquiring company is not associated (under common control within *s 416, ICTA 1988*) with another company which is a party to arrangements with the target company that relate to shares of the acquiring company issued in connection with the transfer of the undertaking or part (*FA 1986 s 76(3A)*, inserted by *FA 2002, s 112*). Where an instrument transfers both land in the UK and other assets, it is treated as two separate instruments for this purpose, one relating to the UK land and the second to the other assets (*FA 1986, s 76(3B)*). The reference to arrangements includes any scheme, agreement or understanding, whether or not legally enforceable (*FA 1986, s 76(6A)*).

**19.71** There is no similar exemption for the transfer by a partnership or a sole trader of its undertaking on incorporation of the business. The condition that the shares had to be non-redeemable did not apply on reconstructions under an agreement executed before 28 July 2000.

## Claw back of section 76 relief

**19.72** The *section 76* relief is withdrawn if, within two years after the date on which the instrument was executed, control of the acquiring company changes and, at the time of that change the acquiring company holds an estate or interest in land that either was transferred to it by the relevant instrument or that is derived from an estate or interest so transferred (and was not acquired by an instrument that bore *ad valorem* stamp duty) (*FA 2002, s 113(1)(2)*). If at the time of the change of control, it holds any part of the land transferred, it is only the *section 76* relief on that part which is clawed back (*FA 2002, s 113(3)*). References in *section 113* to the transfer of land include the grant or surrender of an estate or interest in or over land. The control of a company changes if it becomes controlled (within *ICTA 1988, s 416*)

(i) by a different person,

(ii) by a different number of persons, or

(iii) by two or more persons, at least one of whom is not the person (or one of the persons) who previously controlled it.

(*FA 2002, s 113(4)*).

**19.73** There is no clawback of the relief if either

(*a*) the transfer would in any event have been exempt from duty under the Exempt Instruments Regulations (see 19.80) (*FA 2002, Sch 35 para 2*),

(*b*) the control of the acquiring company changes as a result of an intra-group transfer to which *FA 1930, s 42* (see 19.61) applies (*FA 2002, Sch 35 para 3*),

(*c*) the control of the acquiring company changes as a result of a transfer of shares in relation to which share acquisition relief applies under *FA 1986, s 77* (this confers an exemption on the acquisition of another company wholly for shares when the shareholdings of the two companies are identical, i.e. where a new holding company is put on top of an existing company without any change in ultimate ownership taking place) (*FA 2002, Sch 35 para 4*), or

(*d*) the control of the acquiring company changes as a result of a loan creditor (within *ICTA 1988, s 417(7)*) becoming (or ceasing to be) treated as having control of the company if the other persons who were previously treated as controlling the company continue to be so treated (*FA 2002, Sch 35 para 5*).

**19.74** The exemption under (*b*) and (*c*) above is itself withdrawn if, within the two-year period from the acquisition of the land, the conditions for the *section 42 or 77* relief cease to be met. For a transfer within (*b*), this is if a company holding shares in the acquiring company to which the intra-group share transfer related (the company that acquired the land under the *section 76* transfer), ceases to be a member of the same group as that company at a time when the acquiring company still owns any of the land (or an interest in land derived from it) (*FA 2002, Sch 35 para 3(3)*). For a transfer within (*c*), this is if control of the new parent company changes at a time when both that company still holds any shares transferred to it by the exempt transfer under *section 77*, and the acquiring company still owns the land (or an interest in land derived from it) (*FA 2002, Sch 35 para 4(3)*).

**19.75** Where *section 76* relief is withdrawn, the stamp duty is payable by the acquiring company within 30 days after the control of the company changes (*FA 2002, s 113(2)(b)*). If the trigger event is the withdrawal of an exemption under 19.64D it is payable within 30 days of that trigger event (*FA 2002, Sch 35 para 3(4), 4(4)*). If the duty is not paid within that 30-day period, interest runs not from that due date, but from 30 days after that date of the *section 76* transfer (*FA 2002, Sch 35 para 6*). This is because as the relief is withdrawn, the due date for interest purposes is that which would have applied if no relief had been given. The acquiring company (i.e. the one that acquired the land) is required to notify the Revenue within the 30 day period in which payment of the tax is due, of the occurrence of the trigger event and the duty and interest payable by it (*FA 2002, Sch 35 para 7*). The stamp duty reserve tax regulations in relation to the determination of duty and interest, appeals against such a determination and the collection and recovery of the duty and interest apply to duty becoming due under *section 113* (*FA 2002, Sch 35 para 8*).

**19.76** If the acquiring company does not pay the tax within six months of the date on which it becomes payable the Revenue can collect it from

(*a*) any company which at any 'relevant time' was a member of the same group as the acquiring company and was above it in the group structure, or

(*b*) any person who at any relevant time was a controlling director of either the acquiring company or of a company which controlled that company.

(*FA 2002, Sch 35 para 9(1)(2)*).

A relevant time for this purpose is any time between the execution of the relevant instrument (the one that attracted the *section 76* relief) and the change of control that triggered the withdrawal of the relief (*FA 2002, Sch 35 para 9(3)*). Two companies are in the same group if one of them has control of the other or both are under the control of the same person or persons. A company is above another in the group structure if, either it controls it, or it controls another company that is above the first company in the group structure. A controlling director is one who has control of the company. The definition of a director both in *ICTA 1988, s 168(8)* and *ICTA 1988, s 419(5)* applies, which brings in both a shadow director and a manager or other person who is not a director but is concerned in the management of the company and controls at least 30% of the ordinary share capital (*FA 2002, Sch 35 para 9(4)*).

**19.77** Before seeking to recover the duty from such a third party, the Revenue must have issued to the acquiring company a notice of determination of the amount payable (*FA 2002, Sch 35 para 9(1)(b)*). They must also serve a notice on the third party requiring him to pay the amount that remains unpaid within 30 days of the service of the notice. They can serve such a notice only within three years of the date of the notice of determination. The notice is treated as a notice of determination for the purposes of appeals and recovery of the duty and interest (*FA 2002, Sch 35 para 10(1)–(4)*). Once the third party has paid the duty he has a right of recovery against the acquiring company (*FA 2002, Sch 35 para 10(5)*). If he cannot recover it he cannot claim it as a deduction in computing his own taxable profits, even if the acquiring company could have claimed such a deduction, e.g. if it acquires the property as trading stock (*FA 2002, Sch 35 para 10(6)*).

**19.78** The Revenue have power by notice to require any person to provide them with such information (including documents and records) as they may reasonably require for the purpose of *section 113*. They must allow at least thirty days for the provision of such information. There is a penalty for non-compliance with such a notice of up to £300, plus a further penalty of up to £60 a day if the failure continues after the initial penalty is imposed. Without his client's consent, a barrister or solicitor cannot be obliged to disclose information with respect to which a claim to professional privilege could be maintained (*FA 2002, Sch 35 para 11*).

## FA 1982, s 129: Charities

**19.79** Neither the *ad valorem* duty on conveyance on sale, the fixed duty on other conveyances, nor the *ad valorem* lease duty is payable on a conveyance, transfer or lease (or agreement for lease) to a charity provided that the transfer is sent for adjudication. There is no similar exemption on a transfer by a charity, presumably because the purchaser normally pays the stamp duty and there is no logic in giving him an exemption merely because he happens to acquire the property from a charity.

## FA 1985, s 82: Gifts inter vivos

**19.80** A gift *inter vivos* is exempt from stamp duty (*FA 1985, s 82*). The deed must however be sent for adjudication except where it is exempted under the *Stamp Duty (Exempt Instruments) Regulations 1987* (*SI 1987 No 516*). This exempts an instrument executed on or after 1 May 1987 in respect of a voluntary disposition *inter vivos* for no consideration (i.e. a gift but not a sale at an undervalue or a transfer in satisfaction of a debt), an appointment of trustees, the conveyance of property from a deceased estate to a specific legatee or from an intestate estate to the statutory beneficiaries, the appropriation of property from a deceased estate to satisfy a pecuniary legacy or on a transfer to the residuary legatee, a distribution of property from a settlement to a beneficiary, the conveyance of property in consideration of marriage or in connection with a divorce, etc., a transfer from a liquidator to a shareholder, the grant of an easement otherwise than for cash, or a deed of arrangement following a death. The instrument must contain a certificate signed by the transferor, his solicitor or a duly authorised agent that one of the appropriate conditions is met.

**FA 1985, s 83: Transfers in Connection with Divorce, etc**

**19.81** *Ad valorem* stamp duty under the heading 'Conveyance or Transfer on Sale' is not chargeable on a document by which property is transferred from one party to a marriage to the other if it is executed in pursuance of a court order made on granting a decree of divorce, nullity or judicial separation; or made after the granting of such a decree and in connection with the dissolution or annulment of the marriage or the parties' judicial separation; or made in pursuance of an agreement of the parties in contemplation of, or otherwise in connection with, such a dissolution, annulment or separation. The document instead attracts a fixed duty of £5. There is no general exemption for transfers between spouses although in most such cases the exemption for gifts is likely to apply.

**FA 1985, s 84: Deeds of Arrangement**

**19.82** *Ad valorem* duty under the heading 'Conveyance or Transfer on Sale' is not chargeable on a deed of arrangement entered into by his heirs within two years of a person's death varying the disposition of property of which he was competent to dispose. This exemption does not apply if there is any consideration in money or money's worth (other than the making of a variation in respect of another of the dispositions). A similar exemption applies to the appropriation of property by a personal representative to meet a pecuniary legacy (including the statutory legacy on an intestacy). A fixed duty of £5 is in all cases chargeable instead. The deed must normally be sent for adjudication.

**Insolvency Act 1986, ss 190, 378**

**19.83** Certain documents in relation to an insolvent liquidation (including a creditors' voluntary winding-up) or bankruptcy are exempt from stamp duty if the property remains in the equitable ownership of the bankrupt or the insolvent company.

**FA 1987, s 55: Crown Exemption**

**19.84** Stamp duty is not chargeable on a conveyance, transfer or lease made (or agreed to be made) to a Minister of the Crown or the Solicitor for the affairs of Her Majesty's Treasury, i.e. to a government department.

**FA 1988, s 150: Northern Ireland**

**19.85** Where a document is required to be stamped both in Great Britain and in Northern Ireland it can be stamped in either; it does not need to be stamped twice. However if the rates are different and it is stamped with the lower rate it cannot be used in the other country without additional stamp duty being paid equal to the difference (*FA 1998, s 150*). Northern Ireland enacted stamp duty legislation of its own between 1922 and 1974 (when responsibility was transferred back to the UK Parliament) which was not identical to that in the UK. This provision is aimed at documents stamped during that period.

**FA 2000, s 130: Transfers to Registered Social Landlord**

**19.86** Stamp duty is not chargeable on a conveyance on sale of land, or a lease of land after 28 July 2000 to a qualifying landlord if either it is controlled by its tenants, the transferor is a qualifying transferor or it has purchased the estate or interest (or the lease), with the assistance of a public subsidy (*FA 2000, s 130(1)*). A qualifying landlord for this purpose is a body registered as a social landlord under the *Housing Act 1996, section 1(1)* (or the corresponding Scottish or Northern Irish enactments (*FA 2000, s 130(5)*)). A qualifying landlord is controlled by its tenant if the majority of its board members (i.e. directors, trustees or management committee members as appropriate) are tenants occupying properties owned or managed by the qualifying landlord (*FA 2000, s 130(2)(3)*). A qualifying transferor means another qualifying landlord, a Housing Action Trust, a principal council under the *Local Government Act 1972* and certain other equivalent bodies in Scotland and Northern Ireland (*FA 2000, s 130(6)*). A public subsidy is a grant or other financial assistance from the National Lottery, a social housing grant under the *Housing Act 1996, section 18*, financial assistance for regeneration and development under the *Housing Grants, Construction and Regeneration Act 1996, section 126* or certain grants under the Scottish or Northern Irish *Housing Acts* (*FA 2000, s 130(7)*). The instrument has to be adjudicated and stamped as exempt and the qualifying landlord has to certify to the Revenue that it is exempt (*FA 2000, s 130(8)(9)*). Most registered social landlords are charities and thus already exempt from duty so this levels the playing field for other transferees.

**FA 2001, s 92: Land in Disadvantaged Areas**

**19.87** In order to encourage the development of land and property in deprived areas, the Chancellor proposed in his March 1991 budget to abolish stamp duty in designated areas. The necessary legislation was introduced in *FA 2001, s 92*. Unfortunately the EC forced the Chancellor to draw in his horns somewhat. He announced in November 1991 that he would exempt both residential and commercial property transfers up to £150,000 from 30 November 2001 and intended at a later date (subject to EC clearance) to raise the limit substantially or abolish it, but only in relation to non-residential transfers (see 19.91).

**19.88** The legislation is accordingly drawn in the form of a total exemption but its scope is severely limited by statutory instrument. The legislation provides that no *ad valorem* stamp duty is chargeable on a conveyance or transfer of an interest in land, or on a lease of land, where the land is situated in a disadvantaged area and the relevant instrument is executed after the designation date (*FA 2001, s 92(1)(8)*). It is left to the Treasury to decide what are disadvantaged areas and to designate such areas by regulation. Such designation can be for a limited period and different provision can be made for different cases (*FA 2001, s 92(4)(5)(9)(10)*). The relevant Regulation provides that *section 92(1)* is not to apply to a transfer on sale or a lease of land if the value of the consideration exceeds £150,000 (or otherwise could not be certified at under £150,000) (*Regs 3 & 4, Variation of Stamp Duties Regulations 2001, SI 2001 No 3746*). The *Stamp Duty (Disadvantaged Areas) Regulations 2001* (*SI 2001 No 3747*) designated nearly 2000 disadvantaged areas with effect from 30 November 2001. It does so by reference to electoral wards in England, Wales and Northern Ireland and by reference to postcodes in Scotland. The designated areas are spread throughout the UK. The full list can be found either in the Regulations or on the Revenue's website.

**19.89** To attract the exemption, the instrument must be sent for adjudication and stamped as exempt (*FA 2001, s 92(2)(3)*). If a lease has a premium of under £150,000 the exemption applies only to the premium. The rent element is still taxable (*Reg 5, Variation of Stamp Duties Regulations 2001, SI 2001 No 3746*). The exemption also does not apply to documents liable to the £5 fixed stamp duty under *FA 1999, Sch 13 para 11* (lease of furnished dwelling – –see 19.47), *13* (lease where rent is not ascertainable – see 19.50) or *16* (conveyance or transfer of property otherwise than on sale) (*Reg 6*).

The Revenue have given the following guidance:

(*a*) If VAT is payable the exemption applies only if the VAT inclusive amount exceeds £150,000.

(*b*) Although the designation is by reference to electoral wards (except in Scotland) the Revenue want to know the postcode and they will work out the ward themselves. If a piece of land does not have a postcode they want a map pinpointing the location of the property and the ward in which it falls.

(*c*) The Revenue suggest that the document should contain a certificate stating 'I/we hereby certify that this instrument is exempt from stamp duty by virtue of the provisions of *FA 2001, s 92(2,*'. It does not require a £150,000 certificate of value but does require a £250,000 one.

(Press release 27.11.2001).

**19.90** If land is situated partly in a designated area and partly outside it the consideration must be apportioned on a just and reasonable basis and stamp duty paid on the consideration attributed to the part outside the designated area (*FA 2001, Sch 30 para 1*). The remainder is also ignored in determining whether a certificate of value can be given (*FA 2001, Sch 30 para 3*). For example suppose land is conveyed for £600,000 of which £380,000 is attributed to land in a designated area. The solicitor can certify that the value of the transaction does not exceed £250,000.

**19.91** The Chancellor announced in November 2001 that he intends to raise significantly or abolish the £150,000 limit for transactions involving non-residential property in these disadvantaged areas. *Section 110, Finance Act 2002* introduces a new *section 92A* to the *Finance Act 2001* which gives the Treasury power by regulation to do this. Differentiating between residential and non-residential property requires one of these, in this case residential property, to be defined.

**19.92** Residential property for this purpose is:

(*a*) a building that is used (or suitable for use) as a dwelling (or which is in the process of being constructed or adapted for such use,

(*b*) land that is or forms part of the garden or grounds of a building within (*a*) (including any building or structure on such land), and

(*c*) an interest in or right over land that subsists for the benefit of a building within (*a*) or land within (*b*).

(*FA 2001, s 92B(1)*, inserted by *FA 2002, s 110(3)*).

**19.93** The following uses are specifically regarded as for a residential purpose:

(*a*) residential accommodation for school pupils,

(*b*) residential accommodation for students (other than use as a hall of residence for students in further or higher education),

(*c*) residential accommodation for members of any of the armed forces, and

(*d*) an institution that is the sole or main residence of at least 90% of its residents (other than one falling within 19.91 below).

(*FA 2001, s 92B(2)*).

**19.94** Conversely the following uses are specifically regarded as not being for residential purposes:

(*a*) a home or other institution providing residential accommodation for children,

(*b*) a hall of residence for students in further or higher education,

(*c*) a home or other institution providing residential accommodation with personal care for persons in need of personal care by reason of

(i) old age,

(ii) disablement,

(iii) past or present dependence on alcohol or drugs, or

(iv) past or present mental disorder,

(*d*) a hospital or hospice,

(*e*) a prison or similar establishment, and

(*f*) a hotel, inn or similar establishment.

(*FA 2001, s 92B(3)*).

**19.95** A building within 19.91 is of course excluded from being residential even if it is suitable for use as a residence (*FA 2001 s 92B(4)*). If an empty building is suitable for use both for a purpose within 19.93 and one within 19.94, it cannot be regarded as suitable for use as a dwelling (including a deemed dwelling under 19.90) if the use for which it is most suitable falls within 19.94. However if there is no use for which it is most suited, or the use for which it is most suited falls within 19.93, it is treated as a dwelling (*FA 2001, s 92B(5)*). The Treasury are given power to change or clarify the items within 19.93 and 19.94 (*FA 2001, s 92B(7)*). They also have power by regulation to provide that, where there is a single contract for the conveyance, transfer or lease of land comprising (or including) six or more separate dwellings, none of that land is to count as residential property for the purpose of the stamp duty exemption (*FA 2001, s 92B(6)*). It is depressing to note that the list in 19.94 above does not mirror the definition of relevant residential property for VAT purposes (see 17.27). Indeed a number of items of relevant residential property are specifically excluded from qualifying as residential property for stamp duty purposes.

## Building Work

**19.96** It has been held that where land is sold or leased and at the same time related arrangements to erect a building on the land are entered into, the cost of the building works can be part of the stampable consideration for the disposal of the land or the grant of the lease (*M'Innes v CIR (1934 SC 424)*). In *Paul v CIR (1936 SC 443)* Lord Normand felt that the *M'Innes* principle could not apply unless both the vendor of the land and the building contractor are one and the same person (or one was the agent or nominee of the other) and the contracts are so interlocked that if default is made in one the other would not be enforceable by either party. In *Prudential Assurance Co Ltd v CIR (1992 STC 863)* it was held that the *M'Innes* principle could not apply unless the completion of one contract was dependent on the performance of the other. The Prudential contracted to buy a partially completed building (with the benefit of pre-lets agreements) and at the same time entered into a development agreement with the developers under which it agreed to pay the developers each month (up to a maximum) the sum the developers had already contracted to pay the builder. The conveyance of the partially completed building was executed six months later at a time when £4m of work was still to be done. The Revenue contended that there was a single contract for sale of the completed building contained in two instruments. It was held that albeit that the two were part of one transaction, of which the intended result was that the Prudential would become the owner of the land together with the new building being constructed by the developer, that was not the legal shape of the transaction; the sale agreement was, as the parties intended, completed independently of the carrying out of the building work under the development agreement.

The Revenue view following this case is that, to avoid stamp duty on the combined consideration, the two contracts must be genuinely independent of each other and capable of being completed independently. They do not regard them as being independent if in the event of default on one contract the other becomes unenforceable. In any event, even if there are two contracts the consideration for the sale of the land will include the amount payable under the second contract for any building work on the land completed at the date of execution of the land sale – the Prudential accepted that the value of such work attracted duty (SP 8/93).

## Value Added Tax

**19.97** The Stamp Office take the view that where VAT is payable on the transfer of land the VAT forms part of the consideration for the land – irrespective of whether or not it might be recoverable from Customs – and stamp duty is payable on it. This view was upheld in *Glenrothes Development Corporation v CIR (1994 STC 74)* as the words 'consideration for the sale' in *Finance Act 1963, s 55(1)* cannot reasonably be construed as excluding the part of the consideration consisting of VAT. More contentiously, the Revenue consider that stamp duty is chargeable on the price of non-residential property plus VAT (and lease duty needs to be based on the rent plus VAT) even where no VAT is actually charged, unless it is not possible for the election to waive exemption from VAT (see 17.158) still to apply to the transaction (SP 11/91). They say it will depend on the facts of each case whether that possibility exists. As the election cannot operate retrospectively, stamp duty on notional VAT should not apply on a freehold sale provided that the document is not presented for stamping on the day it is signed. The main problem arises with leases, where it is possible for the option to charge VAT to be exercised at some future time in the currency of the lease. The Revenue initially stated in SP 6/91 (which was replaced by SP 11/91) that they will not charge stamp duty on notional VAT if there is a binding agreement between the parties that the election will not be made. Although this was not repeated in SP 11/91, it is probably safe to assume that such an agreement will still suffice. Indeed this was confirmed by the Minister in a House of Lords Written Answer on 18 February 1992 (Hansard Vol 5, Col 43). Customs have also confirmed that an agreement entered into after the lease has been signed but before it is stamped will be effective to exclude stamp duty on notional VAT (Law Society Gazette, 4 March 1992). It is by no means clear that the Revenue's view is correct, particularly in relation to the rental element of lease duty, where the assumptions must be made that VAT will continue for the life of the lease (or the first 100 years thereof) and at the current rate of 17½%. This seems to breach the principle that *ad valorem* stamp duty can only be levied to the extent that it is possible to ascertain a figure from the face of the document and surrounding circumstances. It also seems of doubtful validity where a purchase price is not fixed initially but is calculated under a formula and at the time of the conveyance it is possible to ascertain a contingent figure, e.g. because the agreement refers to a maximum amount. To add hypothetical future VAT to that contingent figure by assuming that the tax will continue to be payable and the rate will remain unchanged seems to depart from the concept that a consideration must be capable of being quantified at the time the lease is entered into. SP 11/91 also states that if the lease treats VAT as part of the rent, lease duty will be charged on the VAT-inclusive amount. If it provides for the payment of the VAT otherwise than as rent, the duty on the VAT element will be chargeable under *SA 1891, s 56* (see 19.14 above) as consideration payable periodically. If a Deed of Variation is entered into to provide for payment of VAT by way of additional rent, that deed itself may well attract lease duty under *SA 1891, s 77(5)* (see 19.56 above). The Revenue say that when sending a conveyance or lease for stamping it should be stated in a covering letter whether the property is commercial or residential, if this is not apparent from the document itself. A slight consolation is that they confirm that, as stamp duty is paid to the Revenue and not to the vendor or lessor, it does not form part of the consideration for VAT purposes and thus cannot itself attract VAT. Customs & Excise have also confirmed that where a lease is entered into between two companies in a VAT group, so that the supply is ignored for VAT purposes, stamp duty is not chargeable on notional VAT. In a sub-sale notional VAT can be ignored in determining whether the consideration payable on the sub-sale is less than the value of the property (see 19.29 above) (Law Society Gazette, 4 March 1992).

## Assignments and Surrenders of Leases

**19.98** If consideration is payable for an assignment of a lease this will attract the *ad valorem* duty on conveyance or sale described in 19.4 to 19.18 above. The surrender of a lease for a consideration is also liable to *ad valorem* duty as a conveyance on sale. In any other case it attracts a fixed duty of £5 (50p before 1 October 1999). If a tenant pays his landlord to accept a surrender of the lease this is not a conveyance on sale and only the £5 duty would be payable.

**19.99** Prior to 8 December 1993 a surrender by operation of law did not attract duty provided that no document was brought into being. Accordingly a person could agree orally to sell his lease to his landlord and deliver over the lease against receipt of the sale price, with the landlord – who would at that stage own both the lease and the reversion – merging the two interests, without necessarily attracting duty. However, *Finance Act 1994, s 243* provided that if in pursuance of any agreement a lease is surrendered otherwise than by deed, the agreement (even apparently if oral) is to be treated as if it were a deed executed at the time of surrender. It is not clear how this obligation is to be enforced. There are no special penalties for non-compliance and once a surrender has taken place the landlord is unlikely to ever need to evidence it. This dilemma has been resolved in relation to a lease which is surrendered (renounced in Scotland) after 28 July 2000. Any document evidencing the surrender must be treated as if it were a deed executed at the time of the surrender (*FA 2000, s 128(1)*). This applies to a document containing a statutory declaration notwithstanding anything in the Land Registration Rules (*FA 2000, s 128(2)*). Duty is not, however, payable under this provision if the surrender is made as consideration for the grant of a new lease or agreement for lease of the same premises (*FA 2000, s 128(3)*). The new lease will of course itself be stampable in such circumstances. *Section 128* obviously does not apply to a document if another document has already been stamped as a deed evidencing the surrender (*FA 2000, s 128(4)*). However, the Land Registry must not give effect to such a document unless it bears a stamp confirming that some other document has been duly stamped (*FA 2000, s 128(6)*). An application to make or remove an entry in a land register is itself a potentially stampable document under *section 128* (*FA 2000, s 128(7)*).

## Miscellaneous

### Mortgages

**19.100** A mortgage deed is no longer liable for *ad valorem* stamp duty (*FA 1971, s 64(1)(c)*).

**Particulars Delivered Procedure**

**19.101** On a transfer on sale of freehold land, or the grant or assignment (on sale) of a lease for seven years or more, there is an obligation on the purchaser or lessee to send to the Stamp Office both the transfer and a document signed by the transferee or some person on his behalf (normally his solicitor) showing:

(*a*) the description of the document effecting the transfer;

(*b*) its date;

(*c*) the names and addresses of the transferor and transferee (or lessor and lessee);

(*d*) the situation of the land and a plan if it is needed to identify the land;

(*e*) the estate or interest transferred (including the term and rent if it is a lease);

(*f*) the consideration;

(*g*) details of any rights reserved or of any restrictions or covenants affecting the value; and

(*h*) any information provided (e.g. on searches) by the local authority relating to entries of the land in the register kept under *Town and Country Planning Act 1990, s 69(1)* or its Scottish equivalent.

(*FA 1931, s 28, Sch 2*).

**19.102** It is normal for the solicitor to do this by means of submitting a 'Particulars Delivered' form. If the above information is not submitted within 30 days after the transfer document is executed (or 30 days after it was first brought into Great Britain if it was executed overseas), the transferee is liable to a fine of up to £50 (*FA 1931, s 28(1)*). Where an agreement for lease has been produced to the Stamp Office under *section 28* it is not necessary to submit a particulars delivered form (or the lease) in respect of the lease itself unless the lease is 'inconsistent with' the agreement (*FA 1931, s 28(2)*).

**19.103** The Inland Revenue have power by statutory instrument to exempt from these requirements such class of document as they may prescribe (*FA 1985, s 89*). The relevant Order, *The Stamp Duty (Exempt Instruments) Regulations 1985* (*SI 1985 No 1688*), exempts an instrument executed on or after 1 January 1986 on a transfer on sale where the consideration is below the limit on which stamp duty is chargeable (and is appropriately so certified) and the transfer is of registered land or is a transfer that itself requires to be registered under the *Land Registration Act 1925*.

**19.104** In addition *section 28* does not apply to a document which relates solely to incorporeal hereditaments or to a grave plot (*FA 1931, s 28(3)*).

### Shared Ownership Transactions

**19.105** Special rules apply to certain leases of a dwelling-house for the exclusive use of the lessee (or joint lessees) where the lease provides for the lessee to acquire the reversion, a premium is payable which is calculated by reference either to the market value of the property or partly by reference to that value (and partly in consideration of rent), and the lease shows the market value of the property and states that the parties intend duty to be charged in accordance with these rules (*FA 1980, s 97*). They apply only if the lease is granted by a housing association, a local housing authority, or certain statutory housing bodies. In such circumstances conveyance on sale duty is chargeable on the market value of the property instead of lease duty being chargeable on the rent. Provided that the document states that it has been executed in pursuance of a lease stamped under *section 97*, the ultimate transfer of the reversion in accordance with the lease is exempt from duty (*FA 1980, s 97(1)(4)*).

**19.106** If a lease of a dwelling for the exclusive use of the lessee granted by such a body provides that the lessee may, on payment of a sum, require the rent payable under the lease to be reduced, and the lease is granted partly in consideration of rent and partly for a premium based on a market value premium for a lease at the reduced rent (or at the lowest rent which the tenant can opt to pay – or calculated by reference to such a premium), the lease can similarly be charged to duty on the amount of such market value premium (which will be higher than the actual premium). The element based on the rent will be calculated by reference to the minimum rent for which the tenant can opt (*FA 1981, s 108*).

**19.107** Both of these provisions are designed to facilitate transactions whereby a ‘sale’ (or grant of a long lease at a premium) is made to a purchaser who is unable to finance the purchase price in one sum, and the transaction is structured so that he pays ‘rent’ which is set against the purchase price, the tenant being given a right to purchase for a nominal figure when all the rental payments have been made.

**19.108** These exceptions also apply to a lease granted by a person under the right to buy legislation contained in *Part V* of the *Housing Act 1985* (*FA 1987, s 54*). Slightly different provisions apply to the ‘rent to mortgage scheme’ introduced into that *Act* by the *Housing and*

*Urban Development Act 1993*. This gives council tenants a new option to buy their homes for an initial payment plus a balance to be met by an interest free loan from the landlord (normally a local authority). The amount repayable on the loan is a percentage of the value of the property at the time the loan is redeemed. Accordingly at the time the agreement is entered into the 'purchase consideration' is not known. This has two effects. If the value is under £60,000 it is not possible to certify that the total amount payable will not exceed this figure; and if it exceeds that figure the only amount on which duty could be charged is the deposit as that is the only ascertainable amount. To resolve both of these problems *FA 1993, ss 202* and *203* provide that the consideration on such a purchase is deemed to be the price that would have been payable on a straightforward purchase under the *Housing Act 1985, s 126*, i.e. the market value less the appropriate discount.

**Transactions in Shares**

**19.109** The stamp duty rules and exemptions in relation to transfers of shares and securities are outside the scope of this book. Similarly Stamp Duty Reserve Tax, which applies virtually solely to transactions in shares and securities, and which it is proposed will be abolished when and if the stamp duty on share transfers is repealed, is not considered here. However, it should be borne in mind that the stamp duty payable on a sale of the shares in a company that owns a property is normally at a rate of 0.5%, whereas the duty on a sale by the company of the property is up to 4%. Furthermore, if the property is subject to a mortgage, the value of the shares will reflect the liability to repay the loan, whereas on a sale of the property duty would be payable on its full value ignoring the mortgage. Accordingly, from a stamp duty point of view, it is normally preferable to sell the shares rather than the property – although this decision is more likely to be influenced by capital gains tax or corporation tax or, more importantly, by commercial considerations. The increase in the rate of stamp duty to 4% on large properties has led many purchasers to consider buying the company rather than the property where the company owns a single investment property which the purchaser intends to retain as an investment. Some people feel that the government intend to increase stamp duty each year until it reaches a level of 6% or 7%, so the stamp duty could well become an increasing burden. The main commercial risk of buying a company is the possible existence of significant undisclosed liabilities. If the vendor is prepared to give the normal warranties on the sale of a company this risk may not be significant provided that the vendor is not a man of straw. However, the risk is likely to be considerably higher if the vendor is a non-UK company or trust which is outside the scope of UK capital gains tax. Such a vendor is normally indifferent as to whether he sells the property or the company and the stamp duty is generally the purchaser's liability.

**19.110** It must also be borne in mind that where an agreement for the sale of shares provides that the purchaser will procure the repayment of indebtedness the Stamp Office take the view that the stampable consideration includes the amount to be repaid.

**Administration**

**19.111** Stamp duty is largely a voluntary tax insofar as there are no specific means for the Inland Revenue to force payment or to force the submission of documents for adjudication (other than where *FA 1931, s 28* applies – see 19.102 above). The sanction for a document not being duly stamped is that it cannot be produced in evidence in any legal proceedings (including arbitration) (*SA 1891, s 14*).

**19.112** The *ad valorem* duties on conveyance on sale and on leases or agreements for leases is payable within 30 days of the execution of the document or, if it is sent for adjudication, within 14 days after the issue of the assessment. A document executed outside the UK is liable for duty. However, such duty need only be paid within 30 days of its first being brought into the UK (*SA 1891, s 15(2)*). Most documents can be stamped late on payment of the duty plus a penalty. For documents executed after 1 October 1999 the penalty is up to £300 if the document is presented up to a year late and (if greater) up to 100% of the tax if it is presented later. Prior to that date it was £10 plus 5% p.a. of the duty (if it exceeds £10) for the period from the date of its execution up to a maximum of the unpaid duty (*SA 1891, s 15(1)*). In the case of the *ad valorem* duties on conveyance on sale and on leases, the Revenue could in addition charge a further penalty of £10 plus 100% of the duty unless there was a reasonable excuse for the delay in stamping (*SA 1891, s 15(2)*). The Revenue have power to mitigate or remit penalties (*SA 1891, s 15(3)(b), 15B(4)*). Prior to the changes made by *FA 1999* they indicated that they would, in general, mitigate penalties to a level equivalent to an interest charge of

> around 10% p.a. for a delay of under 3 months
> 10%–15% p.a. for a delay of 3–12 months.

A higher mitigated penalty was charged prior to 9 June 1993 when interest rates were higher. The degree of mitigation will obviously be influenced by the reasons for, and length of, the delay. If this exceeds twelve months they may well not mitigate at all (Law Society Gazette, 29 May 1991 and 9 June 1993). The Revenue have not said whether the increase in the maximum penalty will affect this practice.

**19.113** Up to 24 July 2002, where a document was executed outside the UK a penalty could be imposed only if the document was not stamped within 30 days of its first being brought into the UK (*SA 1891, s 15B(1)(b)*). From that date a penalty is chargeable if the document is not stamped within 30 days of execution and if it relates to land in the UK (*SA 1891, s 15B(1)(a)* as amended by *FA 2002,* *s 114*). A document relates to land in the UK for this purpose if it concerns a transaction which to any extent involves land in the UK (*SA 1891, s 15B(1A)*).

**19.114** The above penalties apply not only if a document has not been stamped at all, but also if it has been stamped but on the basis of an inadequate figure. There accordingly needs to be some sort of clearance procedure. This is contained in *SA 1891, s 12*. A person is entitled to submit an executed document to the Revenue and require them to express an opinion as to whether it is chargeable to duty and if so what amount is payable. This procedure is known as adjudication. The Revenue are, of course, entitled to ask for such evidence as they deem necessary to enable them to reach a decision. There is a right of appeal to the High Court against a decision of the Commissioners to assess a particular amount of duty under this procedure (*SA 1891, s 13*). However, the duty has to be paid before the appeal can be heard (*SA 1891, s 13(1)*). If the appeal succeeds, the duty and any penalty will, of course, be repaid (*SA 1891, s 13(4)*). The court can (but need not) order it to be repaid with such interest as it may determine (*FA 1965, s 91*). The Revenue cannot require a document to be adjudicated. However, many of the exemptions and reliefs are conditional on the document being submitted for adjudication.

**19.115** All the facts and circumstances affecting the liability of a document to duty must be set out in the document. Any person who, with intent to defraud the Crown, either executes a document in which the facts are not fully set out, or is concerned in the preparation of such a document and neglects to set forth in it all such facts, is liable to a fine of up to £3,000 (*SA 1891, s 5*). In practice the Stamp Office will accept disclosure and a covering letter will satisfy this requirement.

**19.116** If a document relates to several distinct matters, the duty on each of these must be calculated separately as if it were contained in a separate document (*SA 1891, s 4*).

**19.117** Interest at the same rate as on overdue income tax is also payable on documents executed after 1 October 1999 which are presented late. No interest is payable if it amounts to less than £25. In any other case interest is rounded down to the nearest £5. The interest is not deductible for income or corporation tax purposes (*SA 1891, s 15A* inserted by *FA 1999, s 109*). Where a document executed outside the UK is brought into this country the interest runs from 30 days after the document is executed not from the time it is brought into the UK, and is payable irrespective of whether or not a penalty also arises (*SA 1891, s 15A(1)(b), (2)*).

**19.118** If an instrument within *FA 2000, s 120* (exemptions from *s 119* on a transfer of land to a connected company (see 19.44)) or *s 130* (transfer to registered social landlord (see 19.86)) was executed between 22 March 2000 and 28 July 2000 but was not stamped until after

28 July 2000, it is stampable in accordance with the law in force at the time it is stamped, i.e. it will be exempt.

## Sale of Chattels

**19.119** If the consideration for the conveyance or transfer on sale of a property includes an amount attributed by the parties as chattels that part of the consideration does not attract stamp duty provided that the chattels pass by delivery and are not conveyed in the document. The Revenue are concerned at the number of cases where the consideration attributed to chattels is more than a small part of the total consideration, particularly where this brings the consideration for the property just below £250,000 or £500,000. They have warned that in such cases they will ask for a full inventory and breakdown of the consideration for the chattels to ensure that items claimed as chattels are properly so and that the allocation of the consideration is bona fide and not in breach of *SA 1891, s 5* (see 19.115). They also say that fitted kitchen cabinets and cupboards, fitted kitchen white goods, fitted bathroom sanitary ware, central heating systems, plants growing in the soil and gas fires connected to piped supply are unlikely to be chattels but rather fixtures. The test is the degree of annexation to the building and the purpose or object of annexation (Tax Bulletin 54, August 2001). The Revenue do however say that where it would be possible for plant and machinery to be relatively easily severed from the property to which it is fixed, such as by removing some bolts securing it to the floor, they will not insist that this is done before accepting that it is not fixed plant (Stamp Taxes Bulletin 1, August 2001).

*Chapter 20*

# The Council Tax

**20.1** In addition to central government taxation local authorities impose two property taxes, the council tax and non-domestic rates (except in Northern Ireland). The council tax started on 1 April 1993, replacing the community charge, a form of local authority taxation of individuals known colloquially as the poll tax. It is imposed by the *Local Government Finance Act 1992* and section references below are to that *Act* unless otherwise stated.

**20.2** The rate of tax is fixed locally by each 'billing authority' and will vary from year to year depending on the billing authority's budget requirements and whether or not the Secretary of State for the Environment exercises his power to limit, or cap, the rate chosen by an individual authority. District councils and London borough councils are billing authorities (*section 1*). Liability to pay the tax is determined on a daily basis and is based on the facts prevailing at the end of each day (*section 2*).

**20.3** The tax is payable in respect of any dwelling that is not an exempt dwelling (*section 4*). The exemptions are set out in 20.7. In calculating the tax certain categories of people are granted discounts of either 25% or 50% (see 20.20 below). In addition a new social security benefit, council tax benefit, has been introduced to help those who cannot afford to pay the full tax.

## What is Domestic Property?

**20.4** A dwelling is defined as any property which would have been a hereditament for the purpose of the *General Rate Act 1967* had it remained in force and which is not covered by a local or central non-domestic rating list (or exempt from local non-domestic rating under *Part III* of the *Local Government Finance Act 1988*). The *Local Government Finance Act 1988, s 42* excludes from rating domestic property and *section 66* defines such property as:

(*a*) property used wholly for the purposes of living accommodation, (*b*) a yard, garden, outhouse or other appurtenance belonging to or enjoyed with property within (*a*),

(*c*) a private garage used wholly or mainly for the accommodation of a private motor vehicle,

(*d*) private storage premises used wholly or mainly for the storage of articles of domestic use,

(*e*) a caravan pitch on a protected site used as the sole or main residence of an individual,

(*f*) a mooring occupied by a boat which is the sole or main residence of an individual, or

(*g*) property not in use where it appears that its next use will be domestic.

Property which is wholly or mainly used in the course of a business for the provision of accommodation for short periods (with domestic or other services) to individuals whose sole or main residence is elsewhere is not domestic through *section 66(2)*. Nor is time-share accommodation or property wholly or mainly used in the course of a business for the provision of short-stay accommodation, i.e. (subject to exceptions) accommodation which is provided for short periods to individuals whose sole or main residence is elsewhere and which is not self-contained catering accommodation provided commercially (*Standard Community Charge and Non-Domestic Rating (Definition of Domestic Property) Order 1990* (*SI 1990 No 162*) and *Non-Domestic Rating (Definition of Domestic Property) Order 1993* (*SI 1993 No 542*)).

**20.5** A composite residence, i.e. one used partly as a dwelling and partly for some other purpose, is also included (*section 3(1)–(3)*). However the *Council Tax (Situation and Valuation of Dwellings) Regulations 1992* (*SI 1992 No 550*) provides that the value of a dwelling which is a composite hereditament is that portion of the value of the hereditament which can reasonably be attributed to domestic use of the dwelling. The balance of the value is of course liable to non-domestic rating. A yard, garden, outhouse or other appurtenance belonging to, or enjoyed with, property used wholly for the purpose of living accommodation, private garage which either has a floor area of 25 square metres or less or is used wholly or mainly for accommodation of a private motor vehicle, and private storage premises used wholly or mainly for the storage of articles of domestic use, are specifically excluded from themselves constituting dwellings (*section 3(4)*). The Minister is given power to amend the definition of a dwelling and to prescribe that one dwelling should be treated as two or more and vice versa (*section 3(5)(6)*). He has provided in the *Council Tax (Chargeable Dwellings) Order 1992* (*SI 1992 No 549*) (as amended by the *Council Tax (Chargeable Dwellings, Exempt Dwellings and Discount*

*Disregards) Amendment Order 1997* (*SI 1997 No 656*)) that where a single property contains more than one self-contained unit each such unit must be treated as a separate dwelling, and where a multiple property, i.e. one that would otherwise be two or more dwellings, consists of a single self-contained unit (or of such a unit plus premises constructed or adapted for non-domestic purposes) and is occupied as more than one unit of separate living accommodation the listing officer (see 20.31 below) can, if he thinks fit, having regard to all the circumstances including the extent if any to which the property has been structurally altered, treat the property as a single dwelling. A self-contained unit is defined as a building or part of a building, a caravan, or a boat which has been constructed or adapted for use as separate living accommodation (prior to 1 April 1997 it also covered a caravan or boat).

**20.6** A particular problem can arise with 'granny flats' and similar annexes to a house. A number of valuation tribunals have held that these are part of the main house. The Inland Revenue appealed four of these cases – *Rodd v Ritchings*, *Gilbert v Childs*, *Batty v Burfoot* and *Batty v Merriman* – on the basis that the *Chargeable Dwellings Order* required a granny flat to be treated as a separate dwelling to the main house. In each case it was held that the valuation tribunal had misdirected itself and its decision in favour of the taxpayer must be quashed and the case remitted for reconsideration (*The Times*, 21 June 1995). In *Rodd v Ritchings* the valuation tribunal's decision had been based on the fact that the granny flat could not be used as a separate unit without breaching the planning consent. In *Gilbert v Childs* the tribunal had looked not at whether the annexe was built or adapted as a separate dwelling, which is the test applied by the *Order*, but whether those living in it in fact shared access to services and shared family life with the occupants of the main house. In *Batty v Burfoot* and *Batty v Merriman* the tribunal had reasoned that it was not practical to sell the granny flat on the open market separate from the house, which ignored the statutory presumptions imposed by the *Order*. It should be stressed that these decisions do not necessarily mean that the *Chargeable Dwellings Order* prevents a granny flat from being part of the main building. That is a question of fact to be decided in the light of each individual case. They probably make it likely that in most cases it will fall to be treated as a separate building.

## Classes of Exempt Dwellings

**20.7** The *Council Tax (Exempt Dwellings) Order 1992* (*SI 1992 No 558*) as amended by the *Council Tax (Exempt Dwellings) (Amendment) Order 1992* (*SI 1992 No 2941*), the *Council Tax (Exempt Dwelling) (Amendment) Order 1993* (*SI 1993 No 150*), the *Council Tax (Exempt Dwellings) (Amendment) Order 1994* (*SI 1994 No 539*), the *Council Tax (Discount Disregards and Exempt Dwellings) (Amendment) Order 1995*

(*SI 1995 No 619*), the *Council Tax (Chargeable Dwellings, Exempt Dwellings and Discount Disregards) Amendment Order 1997* (*SI 1997 No 656*), the *Council Tax (Exempt Dwellings and Discount Disregards) (Amendment) Order 1998* (*SI 1998 No 291*), the *Council Tax (Exempt Dwellings) (Amendment) Order 1999* (*SI 1999 No 536*) and the *Council Tax (Exempt Dwellings) (Amendment) (England) Order 2000* (*SI 2000 No 424*) set out the categories of dwelling that are exempted from the council tax. These cover student and armed forces accommodation and certain unoccupied buildings. The detailed exemptions are:

Class A: A vacant dwelling (i.e. one which is unoccupied and substantially unfurnished) which either:

(*a*) requires, or is undergoing, major repair works (including structural works) to render it habitable;

(*b*) is undergoing structural alteration; or

(*c*) has been vacant for a continuous period of under six months following the substantial completion of works within (*a*) or (*b*).

but only for the first 12 continuous months (in total) in which such conditions apply.

Class B: An unoccupied dwelling owned by a charity and which was previously occupied in furtherance of the objects of the charity. Again the exemption applies only for the first six months of a period that the property is empty.

Class C: A vacant dwelling which has been empty for a continuous period of less than six months.

Class D: An unoccupied dwelling which, but for his detention, would be the sole or main residence of a person detained in a prison, hospital or any other place by virtue of an order of a UK court (or of a Standing Civilian Court under the *Armed Forces Act 1976*) or detailed under *Sch 3 para 2* of the *Immigration Act 1971* (awaiting deportation) or *ss 46–48* or *136* of the *Mental Health Act 1983* or their Scottish equivalents and who is the owner or tenant of the dwelling. Imprisonment for default in paying the council tax itself or for default in payment of a fine will not attract the exemption though. This exemption also extends to a dwelling which was previously the sole or main residence of the qualifying person provided that he has been in detention for the entire period since it was last occupied. A dwelling is unoccupied under this head only if all of its occupants are in detention.

Class E: An unoccupied dwelling which was previously the sole or main residence of a qualifying person whose current one is in a hospital (but not a private hospital), a registered residential care home, registered nursing home or registered mental care home in which he is receiving care or treatment (or both) as a patient and who is an owner or tenant of the dwelling. The person must have been in the hospital or home for the whole period since he last occupied the house as his sole or main residence.

Class F: A dwelling which has been unoccupied since the death of a person who either:

(i) owned the freehold or a lease of over six months (from the grant) and there is no other person (other than the personal representative) who is a qualifying person, i.e. a person who is liable for the council tax in respect of the dwelling as an owner, or

(ii) was a tenant under a lease of less than six months, a secure or statutory tenant, or a contractual licensee of the dwelling at the time of his death and his personal representative (acting as such) is the person liable for the rent or licence fee.

The exemption applies only until six months after probate or letters of administration have been granted. A single period of temporary occupation of up to six weeks can be ignored in determining whether the property is unoccupied.

Class G: An unoccupied dwelling, the occupation of which is prohibited by law (or which is kept unoccupied by reason of the exercise of powers under any Act of Parliament).

Class H: An unoccupied dwelling held for occupation by a minister of religion as a residence from which to perform the duties of his office.

Class I: An unoccupied dwelling which was previously the sole or main residence of a qualifying person who has his sole or main residence in another place (other than one of those listed in Class E) for the purpose of receiving personal care required by reason of old age, disablement, illness, alcohol or drug dependence, or mental disorder. He must have been in the clinic, etc. since he last occupied the house as his residence and must be the owner or tenant of the dwelling.

Class J: An unoccupied dwelling which was previously the sole or main residence of a person who currently has his sole or main residence elsewhere for the purpose of providing (or better providing) personal care for someone else who requires such care by reason of old age, disablement, illness, alcohol or drug dependence or mental disorder. This head will cover, for example, the house of someone who moves in with an elderly parent to care for him leaving his own house temporarily unoccupied. The person must have been living in the other residence since he last occupied his own house as his residence and must be an owner or tenant of the dwelling.

Class K: An unoccupied dwelling which was last occupied as their main residence by one or more students (as defined in *Sch 1 para 4*), and in relation to which every qualifying person is a student and either has been one since the last occupier ceased to occupy the building as his sole or main residence or became one within six weeks of that date.

Class L: An unoccupied dwelling where a mortgagee is in possession under the mortgage.

Class M: A dwelling comprising a hall of residence provided predominantly for the accommodation of students which is owned or managed by a prescribed educational establishment (within *Sch 1 para 5*) or a charity or is the subject of an agreement allowing such an establishment to nominate the majority of the persons to occupy the accommodation.

Class N: A dwelling which is occupied by one or more residents all of whom are students, or which is occupied only by one or more students as term-time accommodation (in which case the dwelling is deemed to also be occupied as student accommodation during any vacation in which the student has an interest in the property or licence to occupy it, provided that he has previously used or intends to use the dwelling as term-time accommodation. Student for this purpose includes a college or school leaver within Class C of *SI 1992 No 2942* – see 20.22(9)). From 1 April 1995 it also includes a spouse or dependent of a student, provided that such a person is not a British citizen, who is prevented by immigration laws from taking paid employment or claiming benefits, etc. in the UK (*Council Tax (Discount Disregards and Exempt Dwellings) (Amendment) Order 1995* (*SI 1995 No 619*)).

Class O: A dwelling owned by the Minister of Defence and held for the purposes of armed forces accommodation other than accommodation for visiting forces.

Class P: A dwelling in respect of which at least one person who otherwise would be liable to pay council tax has a relevant association under the *Visiting Forces Act 1952* with a body, contingent or detachment of the forces of a country covered by the *Act*.

Class Q: An unoccupied dwelling owned by a trustee in bankruptcy.

Class R: A dwelling consisting of a pitch or mooring but which is not occupied by a caravan or boat.

Class S: A dwelling occupied only by persons aged under 18.

Class T: An unoccupied dwelling which forms part of a single property which includes another dwelling if the two cannot be let separately without a breach of planning consent.

Class U: A dwelling occupied only by persons who are severely mentally impaired (see 20.24) and who but for this exemption would be liable to pay the council tax. From 1 April 1999 this exemption also applies if the dwelling is owned or occupied by one or more students (within Class N).

Class V: A dwelling at least one occupier of which is entitled to Diplomatic (and some similar statutory) privileges and immunities and is not a British citizen (or British Dependent Territories citizens British National (Overseas) citizen, British Overseas citizen, British subject or British protected person) nor a permanent resident of the UK. Where such a person has more than one UK dwelling the exemption applies only to his main UK residence.

Class W: A dwelling which forms part of a single property (i.e. one which would otherwise be one dwelling) consisting of more than one dwelling and which is the sole or main residence of a dependent relative of a person who resides in the other dwelling (or one of them). For this purpose, relative covers the person's spouse, 'common-law' spouse, parent, grandparent, child, stepchild, grandchild, brother, sister, uncle, aunt, nephew or niece, or a parent or child of any of these people. From 1 April 1998 it also includes a great (or great-great) grandparent, grandchild, uncle, aunt, nephew or niece. It also includes such a relative of the person's spouse or of someone living together with that person as husband and wife. It probably includes a former spouse (or live-in partner); the *Order* states a relationship by marriage shall be treated as a relationship by blood, which suggests that the relationship will survive a termination of the marriage. A relative is dependent if he is 65 or over or is severely mentally impaired or substantially and permanently disabled (whether by illness, injury, congenital deformity or otherwise).

## Valuation Bands

**20.8** For the purpose of the tax all dwellings in the local authority area have been allocated into eight categories, bands A to H. Band D represents an average property. Band A contains properties worth less than 50% of average value and Band H those worth more than 400% of the average. The values are as at 1 April 1991. In theory, the large fluctuations in house prices since then should not have an adverse effect as the tax differentials are effectively based on relative values rather than actual prices. In practice, as changes in value have not been uniform, it will probably have an effect on houses near the margin of a band. However as a taxpayer will be told only which band his house falls into, not the value placed on it, no one can be sure whether or not the arbitrary choice of 1 April 1991 as a reference date has prejudiced them.

**20.9** The council tax payable in respect of all dwellings in a billing authorities area must be allocated in the ratios 6 (band A):7:8:9:11:13:15:18 (band H) (*sections 5* and *74*). The bands are as follows.

| *Band* | *England* | *Wales* | *Scotland* |
|---|---|---|---|
| A | Up to £40,000 | Up to £30,000 | Up to £27,000 |
| B | £40,001–£52,000 | £30,001–£39,000 | £27,001–£35,000 |
| C | £52,001–£68,000 | £39,001–£51,000 | £35,001–£45,000 |
| D | £68,001–£88,000 | £51,001–£66,000 | £45,001–£58,000 |
| E | £88,001–£120,000 | £66,001–£90,000 | £58,001–£80,000 |
| F | £120,001–£160,000 | £90,001–£120,000 | £80,001–£106,000 |
| G | £160,001–£320,000 | £120,001–£240,000 | £106,001–£212,000 |
| H | Over £320,000 | Over £240,000 | Over £212,000 |

The Minister is given power to substitute other bands and to change the ratios in which the tax is allocated between the bands (*section 5(4)*). He has not yet done so. The value of a dwelling for the purpose of allocating it to a band is the value as shown in the billing authorities' valuation list (*section 5(6)*).

**20.10** It will be seen that the tax bill as percentages of those for band A and for band D (the average value) will be as follows:

| *Band* | *% of band A* | *% of band D* |
|---|---|---|
| A | 100.0 | 66.7 |
| B | 116.7 | 77.8 |
| C | 133.3 | 88.9 |
| D | 150.0 | 100.0 |
| E | 183.3 | 122.2 |
| F | 216.6 | 144.4 |
| G | 250.0 | 166.7 |
| H | 300.0 | 200.0 |

**20.11** It should be stressed that the grading is applied by reference to the values in the country as a whole. Thus if the rate of tax levied by each local authority were the same (which will not of course be the case), a £5 million property in Hampstead would attract three times the tax of a £14,000 one in Cleveland. When the tax was introduced the then government indicated that in the South East, 40% or more of the properties in Barnet, the City of Westminster and South Buckinghamshire, and 30% or more of those in Camden, Islington, Kensington and Chelsea, Richmond and Kingston-on-Thames, would fall within Bands G or H, while in the rest of the country very few houses would be in those bands. As a Band G property attracts two and a half times, and a Band H property three times, the tax produced by a Band A one, local authorities with a high proportion of Band G and Band H properties will in theory need to levy a much smaller basic charge (i.e. for Band D properties) than councils in, say, Cleveland, which apparently has no Band G or Band H properties at all, to raise the same revenue.

**20.12** The intention is that this disparity will be corrected by the allocation of government grant. It is intended that the total amount of central government general grants to local authorities will be distributed so that the local authorities in each area can finance spending at a standard level by levying the same Band D charge. It is not wholly clear what this means. Previously grants were distributed so that authorities could finance spending at a standard level by levying a common community charge, yet not only did the levels of community charge vary enormously across the country, but so did the government's March 1990 estimates of what local authorities would need to charge to provide a standard level of service. In practice Band D charges for 2000/01 vary between £728 (Runnymede) and £1,024 (Newark and Sherwood). The low and high for 1993/94 were £92 (Wandsworth) and £772 (Tameside).

## Liability

**20.13** The person who is liable to pay the tax in respect of a chargeable dwelling for a particular day is:

(*a*) the owner of the freehold (of all or any part of it) if he resides there;

(*b*) a leaseholder (of all or any part of it) who resides in the dwelling, unless another resident has a superior interest (in which case it will be that person who will be liable);

(*c*) if none of the residents holds a lease, a statutory or secure tenant (of all or part of the dwelling) who resides in it;

(*d*) if there is no such person, a resident who has a contractual licence to occupy the whole or any part of the dwelling;

(*e*) if there are none of the above, any person who is resident in the dwelling; or

(*f*) if no one is resident in the dwelling, the owner of it (*section 6(1)(2)*).

**20.14** If two or more people meet one of these tests they are jointly and severally liable for the tax unless one or more of them is severely mentally impaired (within *Sch 1 para 2* see 20.24), in which case the other or others is solely liable (*section 6(3)(4)*). A person under 18 cannot be liable for the tax as a resident (although he could be under head (*f*) as an owner). A person is resident in a property only if it is his sole or main residence (*section 6(5)*). A statutory tenancy for the purpose of head (*c*) is one under the *Rent Act 1977* or the *Rent (Agriculture) Act 1976*. A secure tenancy is one within *Part IV* of the *Housing Act 1985* (*section 6(6)*). For the purpose of head (*f*) the owner means any person who has a material interest in the whole or any part of the house (the freehold or a lease of six months or more) where at least part of that interest is not subject to a material interest that is inferior to his own (*section 6(5)(6)*).

**20.15** In the case of a pitch occupied by a caravan, or a mooring occupied by a boat, the owner of the caravan or boat is liable for the tax – other than for any day for which he is not resident in the caravan or boat but someone else is, in which case that other person is liable for the tax for that day (*section 7(1)–(3)*). Permanent holiday caravans and boats are not liable to council tax. They were instead subjected to business rates (see 20.85) by the *Rating (Caravans and Boats) Act 1996*. If two or more persons are liable for the tax on a particular day they are jointly and severally liable for it, any severely mentally impaired person again being excluded (*section 7(4)(5)*). If a caravan or boat is subject to a hire purchase or conditional sale agreement the owner is, of course, the person in possession under the agreement. If it is subject to a bill of sale or mortgage it is the person entitled to the asset apart from the bill or mortgage (*section 7(7)*).

**20.16** The above rules do not apply to five specified classes of dwellings (*section 8(1)*). These are as follows.

Class A: A residential care home, nursing home or hostel within *Sch 1 para 7*.

Class B: A dwelling inhabited by a religious community whose principal occupation consists of prayer, contemplation, education, the relief of suffering, or any combination of these.

Class C: A dwelling which is in multiple occupation, i.e. one which was constructed or adapted for occupation by persons who do not constitute a single household or ('and' prior to 1 April 1995) which is inhabited by a person (or persons) who is a tenant of part only of the dwelling, or has a licence to occupy part, or has a licence to occupy the dwelling as a whole but is not liable to pay rent or a licence fee in respect of the whole dwelling.

Class D: A dwelling in which at least one of the residents is employed in domestic service and resides in the dwelling wholly or mainly for the purpose of his employment, the other residents are all either similarly employed or are members of the family of such employee, and which is occupied from time to time by that person's employer, i.e. a dwelling occupied by resident domestic staff and their families, such as a housekeeper's flat. Domestic service is not defined. It would probably include a gardener as well as servants actually working in the house.

Class E: A dwelling which is inhabited by a minister of religion as a residence from which he performs the duties of his office.

Class F A dwelling provided to an asylum seeker under (or under arrangements made under) the *Immigration and Asylum Act 1994, s 95*.

(The *Council Tax (Liability for Owners) Regulations 1992 – SI 1992 No 551*, the *Council Tax (Liability for Owners) (Amendment) Regulations 1993 – SI 1993 No 151*, the *Council Tax (Liability for Owners and Additional Provisions for Discount Disregards) (Amendment) Regulations 1995 – SI 1995 No 620* and the *Council Tax (Liability for Owners) (Amendment) (England) Regulations 2000* (*SI 2000 No 537*).

**20.17** In these cases the owner of the dwelling is liable to pay the tax. If there are two or more such owners they are jointly and severally liable (except for one who is a severely mentally impaired person). In the case of a dwelling in multiple occupation the person liable to pay the tax is the person with the lowest interest, freehold or leasehold, extending to the entire building (*section 8(3)–(5)*). In the case of a dwelling within Class E if a minister of the Church of England is the inhabitant and the owner and is in receipt of a stipend the person liable for the tax is the Diocesan Board of Finance. The owner is also liable for the tax in respect of other dwellings of a prescribed class if the billing authority so decides in relation to all dwellings of that class situated in its area (*section 8(2)*). No regulations prescribing such classes have yet been made though.

**20.18** A husband and wife are jointly and severally liable for the tax if one is the person liable under *sections 6–8* and the other is resident in the dwelling but would not otherwise be liable (and is not a severely mentally impaired person) (*section 9(1)(2)*). This joint and several liability applies not only to married couples but also to unmarried persons living together as husband and wife (*section 9(3)*).

## Amount of Liability

**20.19** The amount for which a person is liable for any day is, of course, the annual amount fixed by the billing authority for a house in the appropriate band divided by the number of days in the financial year (to 31 March) (*section 10(1)*). In practice the authority will (and are entitled to) assume that he will remain in the house through the financial year, a retrospective adjustment being made subsequently if this assumption proves unfounded. If a billing authority fixes different rates for different parts of its area, the Minister is empowered to introduce rules for ascertaining in which part of the authority's area each dwelling is situated and he has done this in the *Council Tax (Situation and Valuation of Dwellings) Regulations 1992* (*SI 1992 No 550*) (*section 10(2)*).

## Discounts

**20.20** In some cases the taxpayer will be entitled to a discount of either 25% or 50%. This is based on the number and status of the adult occupants (i.e. over 18). The tax assumes an average of two adults per household. If there is only one adult in the household on a particular day the discount is 25% for that day. If there are no adults the discount is 50%. Certain categories of people are disregarded for this purpose (see 20.22). If all of the adults in a household fall to be disregarded the discount is accordingly 50% (i.e. as if there are no adults). If all but one fall to be disregarded the discount is 25%. The Minister is empowered to alter the 25% and 50% figures.

**20.21** The then government initially said that a 50% discount will also apply to a property which is:

(i) not the principal residence of anyone, e.g. a second home;

(ii) a property which is empty because the owner lives in job-related accommodation;

(iii) empty property which is eligible for occupation only by agricultural workers;

(iv) property which cannot be occupied throughout the year because of a planning restriction; or

(v) domestic property which is a self-contained part of a non-domestic property and which is difficult to let separately or which cannot be used as living accommodation because of a restriction in a tenancy agreement.

However they do not yet appear to have brought forward the necessary regulations. It may be that these are all regarded as examples of properties in which there are no adults in the household so that no further legislation is needed. However, as the tax is imposed on a daily basis this does not seem strictly correct as far as second homes are concerned, as such a property is the residence of the owner on the days it is occupied. The then government also indicated that where properties are in multiple occupation, e.g. hostels, they would probably be exempted from the council tax and brought within the scope of the business rates. Again the appropriate order does not appear to have been made.

**20.22** A person falls to be disregarded for days on which he meets the appropriate conditions for the purpose of determining the discount to be given if he is either:

1. a person in detention (20.23);

2. severely mentally impaired (20.24);

3. a person over 18 in respect of whom child benefit is payable (or would be payable but for *Social Security Contributions and Benefits Act 1992, Sch 9 para 1(c)* (*Sch 1 para 3*);

4. a student (20.25);

5. a hospital patient – but only if the hospital is a health service hospital within the meaning of the *National Health Service Act 1977* (or its Scottish equivalent) or a military, air-force or naval unit or establishment at which medical or surgical treatment is provided, and the hospital has become his sole or main residence (*Sch 1 para 6*);

6. a patient in a home (20.26);

7. a care worker (20.27);

8. a resident of a hostel, night shelter, etc. where the accommodation is predominantly provided otherwise than in separate and self-contained sets of premises for persons of no fixed abode and no settled way of life, and under licences to occupy which do not constitute tenancies (*Sch 1 para 10*);

9. other persons that the Minister may prescribe (*Sch 1 para 11*). By the *Council Tax (Additional Provisions for Discount Disregards) Regulations 1992* (*SI 1992 No 552*) as amended by the *Council Tax (Additional Provisions for Discount Disregards) (Amendment) Regulations 1993* (*SI 1993 No 149*) he has prescribed members of International Headquarters and Defence Organisations; members of religious communities who have no income or

capital of their own and are dependent on the community; and a school leaver who is under 20 and has ceased a qualifying or full time course of education (within *SI 1992 No 548* – see 20.25) between 1 May and 31 October in that year; by the *Council Tax (Additional Provisions for Discount Disregards) (Amendment) Regulations 1992* (*SI 1992 No 2942*) he has prescribed persons having a relevant association with a body, contingent, or detachment of the forces of a country covered by the *Visiting Forces Act 1952*; by the *Council Tax (Liability for Owners and Additional Provisions for Discount Disregards) (Amendment) Regulations 1995* (*SI 1995 No 620*) he has prescribed the spouse or dependant of a student (as defined in *Sch 1 para 4*) if that person is not a British citizen and is prevented by his immigration status from taking paid employment or from claiming benefits; and by the *Council Tax (Additional Provisions for Discount Disregards) Amendment Regulations 1997* (*SI 1997 No 657*) he has prescribed persons entitled to Diplomatic (and some similar statutory) privileges and immunities who are not British citizens (or British Dependent Territories citizens, British National (Overseas) citizens, British Overseas citizens, British subjects, nor British protected persons) nor permanent residents of the UK.

**20.23** A person in detention is one detained in a prison, a hospital, or elsewhere by order of a UK court or a Standing Civilian Court established under the *Armed Forces Act 1976*; one detained under *Immigration Act 1971, Sch 3 para 2* awaiting deportation; one detained under *Part II* or *sections 46–48* or *136* of the *Mental Health Act 1983* (or the equivalent Scottish legislation); or if the Minister so prescribes one imprisoned, detained or in custody under the *Army Act 1955*, the *Air Force Act 1955* or the *Naval Discipline Act 1957*. He has so prescribed by the *Council Tax (Discount Disregards) Order 1992* (*SI 1992 No 548*) provided that the detention is not under open arrest and forms part of a continuous period of arrest exceeding 48 hours. A person temporarily discharged or temporarily released under *section 28* or *47(5)* of the *Prison Act 1952* (or its Scottish equivalent) is treated as still detained. However, a person who is detained under Regulations made under *Sch 4 para 8*, i.e. for not paying his council tax, or for default in payment of a fine does not count as a person in detention and thus cannot attract any discount (*Sch 1 para 1*).

**20.24** To qualify as severely mentally impaired a person must be entitled to one of several specified Social Security benefits (or would be so entitled if he had not reached pensionable age) and must produce a certificate from a registered medical practitioner that he is (or is likely to be) severely mentally impaired, i.e. he has a severe impairment of intelligence and social functioning (however caused) which appears to be permanent (*Sch 1 para 2* and *Council Tax (Discount Disregards) Order 1992, Reg 3* as amended by the *Council Tax (Discount Disregards) (Amendment) Order 1994* (*SI 1994 No 543*), the *Council Tax (Discount Disregards and Exempt Dwellings) (Amendment) Order 1995*

(*SI 1995 No 619*), the *Council Tax (Discount Disregards) (Amendment) Order 1996* (*SI 1996 No 636*), the *Council Tax (Discount Disregards) (Amendment) (No 2) Order 1996* (*SI 1996 No 3143*) and the *Council Tax (Chargeable Dwellings, Exempt Dwellings and Discount Disregards) Amendment Order 1997* (*SI 1997 No 656*)).

**20.25** The disregard of students applies to a student, student nurse, apprentice or youth training trainee who meets such conditions as the Minister may impose. The Minister is also empowered to define the expressions student, etc. The term initially excluded a student nurse in full-time education but this exclusion was removed from 1 April 1994 by the *Council Tax (Discount Disregards) (Amendment) Order 1994* (*SI 1994 No 543*). The institution at which a student or student nurse is studying must, if so requested by the student, give him a certificate, containing such information as the Minister may prescribe, provided that he asks for it within a year after the completion of the course (*Sch 1 paras 4, 5*). He has prescribed all of these things by *Regulations 4, 5* of the *Council Tax (Discount Disregards) Order 1992* (*SI 1992 No 548*) as amended by the *Council Tax (Exempt Dwellings and Discount Disregards) (Amendment) Order 1998* (*SI 1998 No 291*). A student is defined as a person undertaking a full time course of education at a specified educational establishment or a person under 20 undertaking a qualifying course at such an establishment, and a foreign language assistant (i.e. an overseas student on an educational/teaching assignment). A course is not full time if any work experience component exceeds the tuition and study element. From 1 April 1995 this does not apply to an initial teacher training course (*Council Tax (Discount Disregards and Exempt Dwellings) (Amendment) Order 1995* (*SI 1995 No 619*)). A student ceases to qualify if he abandons his course or is expelled (*Council Tax (Discount Disregards) (Amendment) Order 1996* (*SI 1996 No 636*)). An apprentice qualifies only if earning less than £160 p.w. (£130 before 1 April 1998).

**20.26** The disregard for patients in homes applies to those in a residential care home (one required to be registered under *Part 1* of the *Registered Homes Act 1984* or exempted from registration under *section 1(4), (5)(j)* of that *Act*, a building in which residential accommodation is provided under *National Assistance Act 1948, s 21*, or a building run by the Abbeyfield Society); a nursing home (required to be registered under the *Registered Homes Act 1984* or exempted from registration under *section 21(3)(a)* of that *Act*); a mental nursing home (within the meaning of the *Registered Homes Act 1984*); or hostel (as defined in *Regulation 6* of the *Council Tax (Discount Disregards) Order 1992*, i.e. a bail hostel, probation hostel or hostel providing residential care) in England and Wales. The person must be receiving care or treatment at the home and it must have become his sole or main residence (*Sch 1 para 7*). Similar rules apply to Scotland (*Sch 1 para 8*).

**20.27** A person is a care worker if he is engaged in providing care or support (or both) to another person or persons, and meets the conditions contained in *Council Tax (Additional Provisions for Discount Disregards) Regulations 1992, Sch 1* as amended by the *Council Tax (Additional Provisions for Discount Disregards) (Amendment) Regulations 1994* (*SI 1994 No 540*) (*Sch 1 para 8*), the *Council Tax (Additional Provisions for Discount Disregards) (Amendment) Regulations 1996 (SI 1996 No 637*) and the *Council Tax (Discount Disregards) (Amendment) Regulations 1998 (SI 1998 No 294*).

**20.28** A Welsh billing authority (but not an English or Scottish one) can decide in relation to dwellings or classes of dwelling in their area that may be specified by the Minister, either to grant a 25% discount for empty dwellings or not to allow any discount for such dwellings in place of giving the normal 25% discount for a dwelling with only one adult resident (*section 12*). Such a decision must be advertised within 21 days of its determination in a local newspaper.

**20.29** The Minister is empowered, by regulation, to specify payment of a lower amount of council tax than that to which a person is liable under *sections 10–12* (*section 13*). The *Council Tax (Reductions for Disabilities) Regulations 1992* (*SI 1992 No 554*) as amended by the *Council Tax (Reduction for Disabilities) (Amendment) Regulations 1999* (*SI 1999 No 1004*) does so in respect of certain houses that have been adapted to meet the needs of a severely disabled resident by deeming the house to fall into the next lower valuation band (or reducing the bill proportionately for a dwelling within Band A). The *Council Tax (Transitional Reduction Scheme) (England) Regulations 1993* (*SI 1993 No 175*) and *Council Tax (Transitional Reduction Scheme) (England) (Amendment) Regulations 1993* (*SI 1993 No 253*) reduce in certain cases the council tax that a person is liable to pay for 1993/94. The reduction applies where the person continues to occupy a house that was his only or main residence on 31 March 1993. Broadly it is the amount by which the authority's council tax rate (subject to a cap) exceeds the sum of its 1992/93 community charge plus an amount which varies according to the valuation band in which the dwelling falls. The *Council Tax (Transitional Reduction Scheme) (England) Regulations 1994* (*SI 1994 No 135*) continues relief for such people for 1994/95, the *Council Tax (Transitional Reduction Scheme) (England) Regulations 1995* (*SI 1995 No 209*) continues the relief for 1995/96. The *Local Government Changes for England (Council Tax) (Transitional Reduction) Regulations 1996* (*SI 1996 No 176*) and the *Local Government Changes for England (Council Tax) (Transitional Reduction) Regulations 1997* (*SI 1997 No 215*) similarly provided for reductions for 1996/97 and 1997/98 to cap the additional tax that a person had to pay following the 1996 local government reorganisation.

## Administration

**20.30** The administrative provisions are contained in *Schedule 2* but this is little more than a series of enabling provisions. The real provisions are contained in secondary legislation, the *Council Tax (Administration and Enforcement) Regulations 1992* (*SI 1992 No 613*) as amended by the *Council Tax (Administration and Enforcement) (Amendment) Regulations 1992* (*SI 1992 No 3008*), the *Council Tax (Administration and Enforcement) (Amendment) Regulations 1993* (*SI 1993 No 196*), the *Council Tax (Administration and Enforcement) (Amendment) (No 2) Regulations 1993* (*SI 1993 No 1773*), the *Local Government Changes for England (Community Charge and Council Tax, Administration and Enforcement) Regulations 1995* (*SI 1995 No 247*) and the *Council Tax (Administration and Enforcement) (Amendment) Regulations 1998* (*SI 1998 No 295*).

**Preparation of Valuation Lists**

**20.31** The Inland Revenue are responsible for the preparation of valuation lists. They must appoint a listing officer for each billing authority (*section 20*). It appears that the listing officer must be an Inland Revenue employee (*section 26(5)*). They must also carry out such valuations as they think necessary or expedient for facilitating the compilation and maintenance of valuation lists and must furnish to listing officers information obtained in carrying out such valuations or in the exercise of their powers under *section 27* (see 20.38 below) and such information contained in particular delivered forms (which are sent to them for stamp duty purposes) as they think expedient (*section 21(1)*). The valuations must be done by reference to values at 1 April 1991 (*section 21(2)*). The Revenue can appoint people other than civil servants to assist them in carrying out valuations and can disclose to such persons any survey report obtained for the purpose of rating (including non-domestic rating) or obtained in exercise of their powers under *section 27*. If such a person uses such information for any purpose other than council tax valuation he is liable to imprisonment for up to two years or a fine or both (*section 21(3)–(5)*). To carry out the 1991 general revaluation the Inland Revenue in exercise of this power appointed a number of firms of valuers to carry out valuations under the guidance of the Revenue's own Valuation Branch.

**20.32** The listing officer compiles and maintains the valuation list. The initial list had to be compiled on 1 April 1993 and came into force on that date. The valuations were by reference to 1 April 1991. Whenever the listing officer subsequently compiles a list he must as soon as reasonably practicable send a copy to the billing authority who must deposit it at its principal office (*section 22(8)*). The valuation list must show, for each day for which it is in force, each dwelling which is situated in the billing authority's area, the valuation band applicable to the dwelling, the reference number ascribed to the dwelling by the listing officer, (where relevant) an indication that the dwelling is a composite one, and where the entry on the list has been altered an indication of the day from which (or period for which) the alteration has effect and whether the alteration was made pursuant to the order of a valuation tribunal or the High Court (but the omission of any matter required to be included will not of itself invalidate the list) (*section 23* and *Council Tax (Contents of Valuation List) Regulations 1992* (*SI 1992 No 553*)).

**Alteration of Valuation Lists**

**20.33** The Minister is empowered to make regulations to deal with the alteration of valuation lists (*section 24*). He has duly done so by the *Council Tax (Alteration of Lists and Appeals) Regulations 1993* (*SI 1993 No 290*). A proposal to alter the list can be made by either a billing authority or by an interested person such as the person liable for the tax. The proposal must be made in writing to the listing officer and must contain specified information (*Reg 6*). The listing office must acknowledge receipt within 28 days and send the proposer a statement setting out the procedure for agreeing such proposals (*Reg 7*). The grounds on which a proposal can be made are limited, namely:

(*a*) the property is not a dwelling – which would include that it should be shown as several buildings;

(*b*) a dwelling has been omitted from the list;

(*c*) the dwelling has been included in the wrong valuation band – this ground for appeal had to be made by 30 November 1993 if the dwelling was on the initial list but a person who becomes the taxpayer in relation to the dwelling after the list was initially compiled can make a proposal within six months of becoming the taxpayer (provided that he was not the taxpayer at an earlier time since the list was compiled, a proposal has not previously been determined by a valuation tribunal, the new taxpayer is not a subsidiary, fellow subsidiary or parent company of the previous one and the new taxpayer is not a 'new' partnership resulting from a partnership change);

(*d*) since the dwelling was included on the list in its current valuation band building or demolition work (other than as part of a redevelopment) has been carried out on it, and the building has become or ceased to be a composite hereditament, or there has been a change in the domestic element if it was such an hereditament; and

(*e*) account has not been taken of a decision made within the previous six months by the local valuation tribunal or the High Court (*Reg 5*).

**20.34** Following receipt of a proposal the listing officer has six weeks to send a copy of it to the taxpayer and (if so requested generally by the authority) the billing authority (*Reg 9*). If he thinks the proposal is well founded he must serve notice on the proposer and the taxpayer that he proposes to alter the list and must alter it within six weeks (*Reg 10*). A proposer may withdraw his proposal by written notice – but if he was the taxpayer and has moved, only with the consent of the current taxpayer. Any interested person who is aggrieved by the withdrawal can be substituted as proposer provided that he was competent to make the original proposal (*Reg 11*). If the listing officer, the proposer, the current taxpayer, the taxpayer at the date of the proposal and any person who has served notice on the listing officer asking to be a party to the proceedings agree how the list should be altered, the valuation officer must make the alteration and the proposal is treated as withdrawn (*Reg 12*). If the listing officer considers the proposal is not well-founded and the parties cannot reach agreement under *Reg 12* the listing officer has to refer the matter to the local valuation tribunal. This must be done within six months of the service of the initial proposal (*Reg 13*). The procedure on such a reference is considered in 20.76.

**20.35** An alteration has effect from the date of the event that gave rise to the need for it, not the date of the proposal or the date of any agreement (*Reg 14*). This does not apply where a valuation tribunal orders a valuation band to be increased; it is to be altered only with effect from the date their decision is given (*Reg 29*). The listing officer must notify the billing authority (subject to specified exemptions) and the taxpayer within six weeks of making an alteration to the list (*Reg 15*). Within six months of the service of the notice under *Reg 15* the billing authority or any interested person can make a fresh proposal to restore the list to its original state or to alter it further (*Reg 5(6)*). An alteration to a valuation band can only be made where either one of the events in 20.33(*d*) has occurred, the listing officer is satisfied that the property is in the wrong valuation band, or an order of a valuation tribunal or the High Court requires the alteration to be made (*Reg 4*).

**20.36** If the Minister makes an order changing the valuation bands such an order must specify a date by which the new valuation list is to be prepared and the date that it is to come into force, a new reference date, and new dates for the listing officer to send to the billing authority two drafts of the list (*section 25*).

**20.37** If a valuation officer (i.e. any listing officer or any other Inland Revenue officer appointed by the Revenue to carry out any of his functions – but not a private sector valuer appointed to assist him) needs to value a dwelling he (and any servant of the Crown authorised by him in writing) is empowered to enter on, survey and value the dwelling. Three clear days notice of such a visit must be given, disregarding a Saturday, Sunday, Christmas Day, Good Friday and any Bank Holiday. Any person who intentionally delays or obstructs a person in the exercise of these powers is liable, on summary conviction, to a fine up to level 2 (£500) (*section 26*).

**Requests for Information**

**20.38** A listing officer or the Inland Revenue can require a charging authority (under *section 144(1)* of the *Local Government Finance Act 1988*), a billing authority, a community charges registration officer or any other person prescribed by the Minister to supply him with such information relating to property as he reasonably believes will assist him in carrying out his council tax functions (*section 27(1)*). A valuation officer can also serve on the owner or occupier (or any former owner or occupier) of any dwelling a notice requesting him to supply any information specified in the notice which he believes will assist him in carrying out his function. Provided that the information is in the person's possession or control, such a notice must be complied with within 21 days. Failure to do so without reasonable excuse renders him liable on summary conviction to a fine of up to level 2 (£500). Knowingly or recklessly supplying false information in response to such a request can attract a term of imprisonment of up to three months, or a fine up to level 3 (£1,000) or both (*section 27(2)–(5)*). If in the course of carrying out its functions information comes to the notice of a charging or billing authority which it considers would assist a listing officer it must inform him (*section 27(6)*). A listing officer and the Inland Revenue are also empowered to use for council tax purposes any other information available to them, whatever its source, and whether or not obtained under statutory powers (*section 27(7)*).

**20.39** A billing authority will wish to satisfy itself that the valuation lists are complete and accurate and that they are kept up to date – as the greater the number of taxpayers the lower the rate of tax it needs to impose and errors in the list can lead to a shortfall in its budgeted income. An authority can require, by written notice, any person who it believes to be a resident, owner or managing agent (i.e. a person authorised to arrange lettings of the dwelling) of a particular dwelling to supply to it such information (as is in that person's possession or control) as it requests for the purpose of identifying who is liable for the council tax for any period in respect of the dwelling (The *Council Tax (Administration and Enforcement) Regulations 1992, Reg 3*). Such information must be supplied within 21 days of the request and must be in such form as the billing authority specify. An authority can also seek information from any other billing authority, a precepting authority, any levying authority or the electoral registration officer for any area of Great Britain. The information it can ask such a body for is limited to the name, address and any past or present place of residence of a person and the dates during which he is known or thought to have resided there. The request for information must be in writing and the information must be supplied within 21 days of its being requested provided, of course, that it is in the possession or control of the person asked. Such a body cannot be asked to supply information obtained by it, or by one of its committees, in its capacity as police authority (or as a constituent council of such an authority), or as an employer. It can also ask community charge registration officers for the name and any past or present address of any person, the days on which he resided at an address, the days on which he was an exempt individual, and any information relevant to his status as such a person. A billing authority can also if it wishes volunteer to another billing authority or a levying authority any information that it obtains in exercising its council tax functions and that it thinks will be useful to that other authority for collecting the council tax (*Reg 4*). Precepting authorities are county councils, metropolitan county police authorities, the Northumbria Police Authority, Metropolitan County fire and civil defence authorities, the London Fire and Civil Defence Authority, the Receiver for the Metropolitan Police District, the sub-treasurer of the Inner Temple, the under-treasurer of the Middle Temple, parish and community councils, the chairman of a parish meeting and the charter trustees (*section 39*). A levying authority is a Scottish islands authority or Scottish regional authority (*section 97*).

**20.40** A Registrar of Births and Deaths has to supply the billing authority within seven days of the registration of the death of a person aged 18 or over with the name and surname of the deceased, the date of his death and his usual address (*Reg 5*). The billing authority can, of course, also utilise for the purpose of the council tax information that it itself obtains under any other enactment other than in its capacity as a police authority or, prior to 1 April 1995, a constituent council of such an authority (*Reg 6*).

**20.41** Anyone, including a billing authority, can require a listing officer to give him access to such information as is needed to establish the state (or past state) of a list maintained by him which has been in force at any time in the previous five years (*section 28(1)*). A taxpayer can also require a billing authority to give him access to such information as will enable him to establish the state of the copy of such a list which was deposited with it under *section 22(8)* or of a proposed list that has been deposited with it under *section 22(6)* but is not yet in force (see 20.32 above) (*section 28(2)(3)*). Such requests must be complied with at a reasonable time and place and without payment being sought, but the information can be provided in such form as the listing officer or billing authority thinks fit (*section 28(8)*). If it is provided in documentary form the enquirer can, on payment of a reasonable charge, either make copies of the document or require the person having custody of it to supply him with a photographic copy. If the information is not provided in documentary form, e.g. it is provided by accessing a computer terminal, he is entitled on payment of a reasonable charge either to make a transcript of it or to require the person having control of access to the information to supply him with a copy in documentary form (*section 28(5)–(7)*). If without reasonable excuse a person having custody of the information intentionally obstructs a person exercising a right under the section he is liable to a fine of up to level 2 (£500) (*section 28(8)*).

**20.42** Any person can, similarly, at a reasonable time and without payment also inspect any proposal made or notice of appeal given under regulations made under *section 24* if they relate to a list currently in force or in force at any time within the previous five years and make, or ask to be provided with, copies of all or part of the document on payment of a reasonable charge (*section 29*).

## Exempt Dwellings

**20.43** When a billing authority received the copy of the proposed valuation list sent to it under *section 22(5)(b)* it had to notify the 'taxpayers' concerned (other than for forces accommodation) by 31 March 1993 if it considered that any of the dwellings were exempt dwellings (see 20.7) on that date.

**20.44** Every billing authority is required to take reasonable steps each year to check whether any dwellings in its area are exempt dwellings for any part of the year (*Reg 8*). Having done that it must assume for billing purposes that every dwelling that it has reason to believe is exempt is in fact exempt and that all other dwellings are chargeable dwellings (*Reg 9*). When it treats a dwelling as exempt for all or part of the year it must notify the relevant person (i.e. the one or ones who would be liable to pay the council tax if it were not exempt) of that fact. The notice must be given as soon as is reasonably practicable and must show the valuation band into which the dwelling falls and the tax that would be payable if it were not exempt (or an estimate if at the time the rate has not been fixed) ignoring council tax benefit and social security benefits; must summarise the effect of the *section 24 Regulations* for altering the list; and give a summary of the classes of dwelling that are exempt. If there is more than one relevant person the billing authority can choose to which of them to give the notice. It does not have to repeat any information that it has previously notified to that relevant person under *Regulation 7* (see 20.43) (*Reg 10*).

**20.45** If at any time during the financial year concerned or the following year a person who has been notified by the billing authority that a dwelling is exempt, has reason to believe that it is a chargeable dwelling for any part of the year, he must notify the billing authority within 21 days of forming that opinion. If two people are both jointly and severally liable for the tax notification but one satisfies the obligation of both, it appears that if the authority serves the *Regulation 10* notice on one only the other does not have any obligation to notify as he is not a person who 'has been informed' in accordance with *Regulation 10 (Reg 11)*. As the penalty for not notifying is only £50 (*Sch 3 para 1*) it seems unlikely that many people will comply with this obligation.

**20.46** The billing authority can serve notice on any person who it believes is resident in, or the owner or managing agent of, a dwelling that it believes is an exempt dwelling requesting such information as it needs to ascertain the identity of the relevant person in relation to it. If the information is in that person's possession or control he must supply it within 21 days of the request (*Reg 12*).

## Discounts

**20.47** Before calculating an individual's liability to council tax the billing authority must take reasonable steps to ascertain whether the property attracts a discount under *section 11* or *12* (see 20.20 and 20.28) (*Reg 14*). If it believes it does, it must allow that discount in calculating the tax payable (*Reg 15*). If a person is given a discount to which he is not entitled (or a larger discount than is due) he must notify the billing authority within 21 days of first having reason to believe that he is not entitled to it (*Reg 16*). Again the penalty is only £50. There is no obligation to notify the authority if too little discount has been granted but it is obviously in the taxpayer's interest to do so.

## Billing

**20.48** The Regulations contain a rigid procedure that must be followed. For each financial year the billing authority must send a demand notice to the liable person. If a person is liable for the tax in respect of more than one dwelling a separate demand note must be issued for each dwelling (*Reg 18*). The demand notice must be served as soon as is practicable after the billing authority fixes the rate of tax. The *Council Tax and Non-Domestic Rating (Demand Notices) (England) Regulations 1993* (*SI 1993 No 191*) (as amended by the *Local Government Changes for England (Council Tax and Non-Domestic Ratings Demand Notices) Regulations 1995* (*SI 1995 No 23*), the *Council Tax and Non-Domestic Rating (Demand Notices) (England) (Amendment) Regulations 1995* (*SI 1995 No 121*), the *Council Tax and Non-Domestic Rating (Demand Notices) (England) (Amendment) Regulations 1996* (*SI 1996 No 504*), the *Council Tax and Non-Domestic Rating (Demand Notices) (England) (Amendment) Regulations 1997* (*SI 1997 No 394*), the *Council Tax and Non-Domestic Rating (Demand Notices) (England) (Amendment) Regulations 2000* (*SI 2000 No 5*), the *Council Tax and Non-Domestic Rating (Demand Notices) (England) (Amendment) Regulations 2001* (*SI 2001 No 3554*) and the *Council Tax and Non-Domestic Rating (Demand Notices) (England) (Amendment) Regulations 2002* (*SI 2002 No 180*) set out very extensive information that needs to be shown in a council tax demand. However a failure to do so, if due to a mistake, does not affect the collectability of the tax. The *Council Tax (Administration and Enforcement) (Amendment) Regulations 1997* (*SI 1997 No 393*) enables a single demand notice to cover several financial years.

**20.49** Unless the demand note is issued after the end of the financial year concerned, the amount demanded must be calculated on the assumption that the chargeable person will remain liable for the tax throughout the year, the property will remain in the same valuation band, any reduction will continue to apply, the building will continue to be a chargeable dwelling, any discount will continue at the same rate and any entitlement to council tax benefit will continue (*Reg 20(1)–(3)*). If the demand notice is issued during the year and the person is not liable for the tax on the day it is issued it must only demand payment of tax up to the last day for which he was liable (*Reg 20(4)*). This obviously assumes that the demand notice will be issued only after he ceases to be liable, which seems an odd assumption. If the demand notice is issued after the end of the financial year it must be for the tax actually payable (*Reg 20(5)*).

**20.50** The tax is payable by instalments except where a demand notice is issued after 31 December in the financial year in which case it is payable 'as a single instalment' on such day as the authority specifies in the demand notices. Except where a *Part II* Scheme is operated (see below), it is normally payable in ten consecutive monthly instalments. It is up to the authority to choose which ten. It appears that if it wishes it can adopt different payment dates for different dwellings and which day in the month the amount is payable on. If the demand notice is issued after 30 April the number of instalments is one less than the number of whole months remaining. For example, if it is issued on 4 June, there are nine whole months to the following 31 March so the tax is payable by eight instalments. If the tax divided by the number of instalments does not result in an exact pound the monthly instalments other than the first are rounded up or down to the nearest pound, and the first is adjusted to the balance needed to collect the exact amount due over the year. If the total tax is less than £10 the authority can demand the whole amount in a lump sum. If it exceeds £10 but the instalments would be less than £5 per month it can require the tax to be paid by the number of £5 instalments that is necessary to collect the amount payable (*Reg 21* and *Sch 1, Part I*). From 1 April 1995 it can also require the first two instalments to be paid together, and if it revises a person's tax liability during the year must take into account any tax prepaid (*Council Tax (Administration and Enforcement) (Amendment) Regulations 1995* (*SI 1995 No 22*)).

**20.51** The authority can opt to use a *Part II* Scheme to collect the council tax from its council tenants, but not from other people – although if a house ceases to be a council house during the year it can remain in the scheme until the end of the financial year. If it adopts such a scheme it must continue to use it each year until it decides to vary or revoke it. It cannot be varied after the rate for the financial year has been fixed and cannot be revoked later than 31 December of the prior year, e.g. if the scheme is to be revoked for 1996/97 this must be done by 31 December 1995. Such a scheme must provide for the tax to be payable by between ten and 52 instalments. The first instalment cannot be due less than 14 days after the issue of the demand and they must all be payable during the financial year, but subject to this the authority has complete flexibility. The idea is of course to allow it to collect the tax at the same time as the rent (*Reg 21* and *Sch 1, Part II*).

**20.52** A taxpayer and the authority can agree that the tax should be payable in some other manner, e.g. as a single payment (*Reg 21(6)*). This will enable an authority to offer an early payment discount to speed up and simplify collection (see 20.56). If a demand note is issued after the end of the year, or during the year and after the taxpayer has ceased to own or occupy the property, the tax can be demanded either in one sum or by such instalments as the authority may decide (*Reg 21(7)*).

**20.53** No one can be required to make a payment in respect of the tax unless a formal demand notice has been issued (*Reg 22*). Assuming that this has been duly done, if a person fails to pay any instalment for which he is liable the billing authority must serve a reminder notice on him stating the instalments owing, and the effect of not paying. This is that if the outstanding instalments are not paid within seven days from the issue of the reminder, the whole of the balance for the year will become payable in a further seven days. If the notice is the second reminder notice to be issued to him in respect of the same year, late payment of any further instalment will cause the whole of the balance of the year to automatically become payable the day after that instalment fell due. The reminder notice procedure obviously does not apply after all of the instalments have fallen due or after the tax has ceased to be payable by instalments (*Reg 23*). The *Council Tax (Administration and Enforcement) (Amendment) Regulations 1997* (*SI 1997 No 393*) makes clear that this procedure also applies where tax is payable by instalments under *Reg 21* (see 20.50).

**20.54** If the tax actually due proves to be more than was estimated when the demand notice was issued, the excess is payable in one sum 14 days after the issue by the billing authority of a notice of the actual chargeable amount (*Reg 24(1)*). If the estimate was excessive the billing authority must notify the taxpayer. He can then claim repayment unless the reduction is because he moved house within the same district so that he owes tax to the same billing authority on another house – in which case the billing authority can credit the overpayment against the tax due. If the taxpayer does not claim repayment the billing authority can either repay it or credit it against any subsequent liability of the liable person to its council tax, e.g. the following year's tax (*Reg 24(2)(6)*). If after the issue of a demand notice but before the tax actually due can be calculated (which cannot be done until after the end of the financial year) it becomes apparent that the estimate was wrong, the billing authority can recalculate the tax and require an interim payment of any underpayment or make an interim refund. It must do this if the taxpayer so requires (*Reg 24(3)*). It must in any event recalculate the instalments due for the remainder of the year and serve notice of these on the taxpayer (*Sch 1 para 10*).

**20.55** If after a demand notice is served on a person he ceases to be the liable person, the authority cannot enforce subsequent instalments. It must serve a notice on him showing the actual tax due for the period that he was liable and demand payment of the balance or make a refund (if the taxpayer so required) or set off the balance owing against another council tax liability the taxpayer owes it (*Sch 1 para 9*).

**20.56** A billing authority can accept payment in one sum (and issue a demand notice for the tax in one sum) of such lesser amount as it may determine than the tax due, i.e. it can give a cash discount for prompt payment, provided that it decides on the discount not later than when it fixes the rate of tax, it makes the same offer to all its taxpayers who are entitled to pay the same number of instalments, and that the tax would otherwise have been payable by at least two instalments (*Reg 26(1)(2)*). If the estimated tax due is subsequently increased, the balance is payable as a single payment within 14 days of being calculated but subject to the same percentage discount (*Reg 25(4)(6)(9)*). If it is reduced, any repayment (if claimed) or amount set against another liability is also reduced in the same proportion (*Reg 25(5)(6)(9)*). Notice of the difference must be served on the taxpayer. A billing authority is also empowered to accept a discounted amount in satisfaction of any instalment to induce payment to be made otherwise than in coin or bank notes, e.g. it can offer a discount for payment by cheque, provided that it decides the circumstances in which it is prepared to do so not later than when it fixes the rate of tax (*Reg 26*).

**20.57** *Regulation 27* contains rules for ascertaining the amounts for which persons are jointly and severally liable if they are not so liable throughout the year – these seem merely to certify what common sense would dictate by apportioning the total tax on a daily basis. No amount can be collected from such a person unless the authority has served a notice on him showing the amount due (*Reg 28*). There are provisions for adjusting the amount thought to be due if circumstances change or the original estimate proves incorrect (*Reg 28*).

## Enforcement

**20.58** As with administration the enforcement powers are not contained in the *Act* but were left to the Minister to deal with by statutory instrument and are contained in the *Council Tax (Administration and Enforcement) Regulations 1992*. These provide a variety of methods of enforcement, namely:

(*a*) attachment of earnings orders,

(*b*) distress,

(*c*) commitment to prison, and

(*d*) charging orders.

**20.59** The billing authority first applies to a magistrates' court for a liability order. Before doing so it must serve on the taxpayer a final notice showing the amount in respect of which it proposes to make the application – unless it is seeking the order in relation to an unpaid instalment and has already served him with a reminder notice (*Reg 33*). It must allow seven days from the service of the final notice before applying for the order. This is then done by making a complaint to a Justice of the Peace, and requesting the issue of a summons directing the taxpayer to appear before the magistrates' court. The application must be made within six years of the sum in question becoming due. The authority then serves the summons on the taxpayer either by delivering it to him or leaving it at, or posting it to, his usual or last known place of abode (or the registered office of a company). If, before the application is heard, the taxpayer tenders to it the sum specified in the summons plus an amount equal to the authority's reasonable costs up to that time the authority cannot proceed with the order. Subject to that, the magistrates must make a liability order if they are satisfied that the amount demanded has become payable and it has not been paid and that the summons was served at least 14 days earlier. The order must cover both the tax and the authority's costs. If the tax has been paid before the hearing, and the billing authority so requests, the magistrates must still make an order in relation to costs. The magistrates can make separate liability orders on each individual or can deal with more than one person (e.g. all the cases they hear at a sitting) in a single order (*Regs 34, 35*).

**20.60** When a liability order has been made the debtor must supply the billing authority with the following information within 14 days of the authority requesting it, provided that it is in his possession or control:

(*a*) the name and address of his employer,

(*b*) information about his earnings or expected earnings,

(*c*) information about deductions therefrom for income tax, national insurance, and superannuation scheme payments,

(*d*) his work or identity number or other information to enable his employer to identify him,

(*e*) information as to sources of his income other than from an employer, and (*f*) whether another person is jointly and severally liable for the tax (*Reg 36*).

**Attachment of Earnings Orders**

**20.61** Based on this information the authority can then itself make an attachment of earnings order requiring the employer to make deductions in respect of the council tax from the debtor's net earnings (earnings less tax, national insurance and pension scheme contributions) and pay them over to the authority (*Reg 37*). It must send a copy of the order to the debtor (*Reg 41(3)*). It should particularly be noted that the authority does not have to return to court. The liability order triggers its right to serve an attachment of earnings order. From 1 October 1998 it cannot make an order if it already has two such orders in force against the debtor.

**20.62** Where an attachment of earnings order is made the employer must deduct the following percentage from the employee's net salary, i.e. salary less PAYE, national insurance and pension contributions (*Reg 38*).

| *Daily Earnings* | *Weekly-Earnings* | *MonthlyEarnings* | *DeductionRate* |
|---|---|---|---|
| Up to £8 | Up to £55 | Up to £220 | 0% |
| £8.01–£15 | £55.01–£100 | £220.01–£400 | 3% |
| £15.01–£20 | £100.01–£135 | £400.01–£54 | 5% |
| £20.01–£24 | £135.01–£165 | £540.01–£660 | 7% |
| £24.01–£38 | £165.01–£260 | £660.01–£1,040 | 12% |
| £38.01–£53 | £260.01–£370 | £1,040.01–£1,480 | 17% |
| Over £53 | Over £370 | Over £1,480 | 17% of first £1,480 (or £53 or £270) + 50% of the excess. |

The earnings limits were lower prior to 1 October 1998.

**20.63** Special rules apply where a person is paid at other intervals (*Reg 38(1)(c)(4)(10)*). Where he receives an advance against pay the deduction must be made from the advance as well, although not as if it were part of the salary for the period in which it is paid (*Reg 38(2)*). If the employer is entitled to recoup an earlier advance against pay from the salary this can be deducted in arriving at net earnings (*Reg 38(3)*). Prior to 1 April 1994 so could repayments of a previous loan from the employer. Such loan repayments must now be ignored, i.e. the council tax deduction is to be calculated before making the loan deduction (*Council Tax (Administration and Enforcement) (Amendment) Regulations 1995* (*SI 1995 No 22*)).

**20.64** The employer can also if he wishes add (and retain) a further pound to each deduction he makes, towards his administrative costs (*Reg 39(1)*). He must provide the employee with a statement at the same time as his payslip showing both the total deductions to date and the further deductions he is required to make. If he does not in fact employ the debtor, he must tell the billing authority within 14 days of receiving the order. He must also tell it within 14 days of ceasing to employ him (*Reg 39(2)–(6)*). The debtor is also obliged to tell the billing authority within 14 days if he changes his job or becomes re-employed (*Reg 40*). If he changes job and the new employer is aware of the existence of the order and which billing authority made it, it must notify the authority within 14 days that it has become the debtor's employer – so that the authority can then serve it with an attachment of earnings order (*Reg 39(7)*).

**20.65** Once the debt has been paid in full the billing authority must notify the employer so that he can stop deducting. It can, if it wishes, discharge the order. If it does so it must of course notify the employer (*Reg 41(1)(2)*). If two or more attachment of earnings orders for any of council tax, community charge, or under the *Attachment of Earnings Act 1971* or the *Child Support Act 1991* are served on an employer in respect of the same employee he must give effect to them in the order in which they were made. An attachment of earnings order in respect of the payment of a judgment debt or of payment under an administration order should not be dealt with until all other orders have been settled though (*Reg 42*). There is no bar to an attachment of earnings order being served on a government department (*Reg 43*). If the defaulter is a local councillor (of a billing or precepting authority) an attachment of earnings order can be made against his local authority attendance and special responsibility allowances. In such circumstances the deduction is at a flat rate of 40% (*Reg 44*).

## Distress

**20.66** Where a liability order has been made the billing authority can also distrain on the debtor's goods for both the outstanding tax and the costs of the distress (but *Schedule 5* places limits on some of those costs). If the debtor pays the full amount due (including costs) before the sale of the goods they must not be sold. They need not be returned to the debtor though; they must 'be made available for collection' by him. A distress can be levied anywhere in England and Wales, but the bailiff must produce written authorisation from the authority and must give the debtor a copy of *Regulation 45* and *Schedule 5* to the Order. Distress cannot be levied on goods which general law protects from distress (*Reg 45*). Nor can it be levied on tools, books, vehicles and equipment which are necessary to the debtor for personal use by him in his work or on clothing, bedding, furniture, household effects and provisions which are necessary for satisfying the basic domestic needs of the debtor and his family (*Reg 45*). From 1 October 1998 distress can be levied only by a certified bailiff and only if the billing authority has served at least 14 days earlier written notice on the debtor stating that a liability order has been made and its amount, and warning that distress may be levied if the amount is not paid within 14 days and that this will attract costs.

**20.67** A person aggrieved by the levy of distress (or an attempt to do so) has a right of appeal to a magistrates court. This is done by making a complaint to a Justice of the Peace requesting the issue of a summons against the billing authority. The court can order the goods to be returned or if they have been sold can order compensation to be paid. If it feels that an attempted levy was irregular it can require the authority to desist from proceeding in its proposed manner (*Reg 46*).

### Imprisonment

**20.68** If the authority has sought to levy distress but was unable to find sufficient goods, and the debtor is an individual over 18, it can apply to a magistrates court for the issue of a warrant committing the debtor to prison. The court may inquire into the debtor's means and whether the failure to pay was due to wilful default or culpable neglect. If the court decides that it was, it can issue a warrant to commit him to prison immediately, or postpone the issue of the warrant until such time and on such conditions as it thinks fit. The court must make the enquiries in the debtor's presence, so cannot proceed with the hearing if the debtor does not turn up. However a Justice of the Peace can then issue a warrant for his arrest to force him to attend. If the outstanding tax and reasonable costs (up to the limit specified by the *Council Tax (Administration and Enforcement) (Amendment) Regulations 1994* (*SI 1994 No 505*)) are paid before the debtor is imprisoned the warrant must not be executed. If it is paid while he is in prison he must be released. The term of imprisonment cannot exceed three months. If after the committal order is made part of the debt is paid, the term imposed is reduced proportionately (*Reg 47*). If the magistrates do not issue a warrant or fix a term of imprisonment they can remit all or part of the debt. If circumstances change, the billing authority can make a fresh application for imprisonment on the first application (*Reg 48*).

### Charging Order

**20.69** If the tax due under the liability order (i.e. excluding cost) is £1,000 or more, the authority can apply to the county court for a charging order on the debtor's interest in the dwelling concerned to secure the debt (*Reg 50*).

### Other Matters

**20.70** When a liability order is made, the amount is deemed to be a debt, thus entitling the authority to petition as a creditor for the debtor's bankruptcy or winding-up (*Reg 49*).

**20.71** Once a warrant committing the debtor to prison is made no further steps can be taken by way of attachment of earnings, distress, bankruptcy or a charging order or under the *Council Tax (Deductions for Income Support) Regulations 1993* (*SI 1993 No 494*) (*Reg 52(1)*). The authority can only use one of the other remedies at any one time, but can resort to attachment of earnings, distress and, from 1 April 1994, deduction under the Income Support regulations more than once and in any order it chooses (*Reg 52(2)(3)* and *Reg 7*, *Council Tax (Administration and Enforcement) (Amendment) Regulations 1994* (*SI 1994 No 505*)). An application for an order under *SI 1993 No 494* cannot be made while steps to enforce payment are being taken under this provision (*Reg 52(2A)*). If the enforcement remedy is an income support deduction, simultaneous action can, however, be taken against another person who is not a member of the other's family (*Reg 8* of the *Council Tax (Administration and Enforcement) (Amendment) Regulations 1994* (*SI 1994 No 505*)).

**20.72** Where two or more persons are jointly and severally liable for the tax a liability order can be obtained against one or both. If it is made against both, the authority does not need to choose the same enforcement remedies against both. However it cannot enforce remedies against one while it is already in the course of enforcing remedies against the other. Nor can it apply to have one imprisoned unless distress has been unsuccessfully tried against all of them and once it seeks imprisonment of one of them it cannot seek an order under *SI 1993 No 494* in relation to any of them (*Reg 54*).

## Appeals

**20.73** A person can apply to a valuation tribunal if he is aggrieved by:

(*a*) any decision of a billing authority that a dwelling is a chargeable dwelling or that he is liable to pay council tax in respect of it,

(*b*) any calculation made by the authority (including an estimate) of the tax that he is liable to pay (*section 16(1)(2)*).

A valuation tribunal is the new name for the valuation and community charge tribunals set up under *Local Government Finance Act 1988, Schedule 11* (*section 15(1)*). The procedure for alterations to the valuation list, which is not technically an appeal against the listing, is considered at 20.33. The appeals procedure where such a proposal is rejected is dealt with at 20.76.

**20.74** The Minister is empowered to prescribe matters against which no appeal can be made (*section 16(3)*). He has done so in the *Council Tax (Administration and Enforcement) Regulations 1992, Reg 30* which prevents an appeal on the grounds that an assumption as to the future that has been made in the calculation of the tax may prove to be inaccurate.

**20.75** Before appealing to the tribunal a person must serve a written notice on the billing authority stating what aggrieves him and his grounds for being upset (*section 16(4)–(6)*). He must then wait until either:

(*a*) the authority notifies him in writing that it believes his grievance is not well-founded and sets out the reasons for that belief,

(*b*) the authority notifies him in writing that steps have been taken to deal with his grievance, and what those steps are, or

(*c*) it does not give either notification within two months of being served with the notice of appeal (*section 16(4)(7)(8)*).

The idea is, of course, to give the billing authority an opportunity to try to resolve the dispute before resorting to the tribunal.

**20.76** In the absence of agreement (see 20.34) a proposal to alter the valuation list must also be referred by the listing officer to the local valuation tribunal. The tribunal must make arrangements to hear such appeals – and any preliminary appeal against the validity of the proposal (*Council Tax (Alteration of Lists and Appeals) Regulations 1993, Reg 18*). Such an appeal can be disposed of by written representation if all the parties agree (*Reg 20*). At least four weeks notice of the hearing must be given to the parties. It must also be advertised conspicuously at the tribunals office, the billing authority's office, and one other place in the area (*Reg 22*). Any party can appear in person (with assistance from any person if he wishes) or by counsel, a solicitor or any other representative (*Reg 24*). The hearing is in public before a three-man tribunal (two if the parties agree). The listing officer generally begins the hearing. Any party can call witnesses (*Reg 25*). There are detailed rules relating to evidence. The tribunal has power to order a pre-hearing review to clarify the issues (*Reg 21*). There is power in certain circumstances for the decision to be set aside by a fresh tribunal and reheard (*Reg 30*). There is power for the parties to agree to refer the dispute to arbitration instead of it being heard by the valuation tribunal (*Reg 33*). Notice of any appeal to the High Court against a decision of the tribunal must be given within four weeks of the decision. Such an appeal can be made only on a question of law (*Reg 32*). The valuation tribunal also deals with appeals in respect of the Regulations under *section 24* in relation to altering the valuation lists, and appeals against penalties for failing to supply information or supplying incorrect information under *Sch 3 para 1* (see 20.78).

**20.77** No appeals can be made against the following matters except by way of judicial review:

(*a*) the specification by the Minister of a class of 'exempt dwelling' (see 20.7),

(*b*) a determination by a billing authority under *section 8(2)* or, in Wales, *section 12(1)*,

(*c*) the calculation by a billing authority of its budget or of the rate of tax it proposes to levy,

(*d*) the calculation by a precepting authority of its budget (*section 66*).

## Penalties

**20.78** The penalty for failure to supply information when so requested, for failing without a reasonable excuse to give notice to a billing authority (or in Scotland a laying authority) or for knowingly providing inaccurate information is a fixed amount of £50. The penalty can be imposed by the authority – it does not need to take court action. It can also be quashed by the authority. Curiously an English or Welsh authority can revoke the penalty on any ground but in Scotland the taxpayer has to show that he had a reasonable excuse for his failure. If after imposing a penalty for failing to provide information or giving incorrect information, the authority again requests the person to supply the same information, the penalty for not doing so the second time is £200. It can ask for the information as many times as it likes until it is provided, each further refusal attracting another £200 penalty (*Sch 3 paras 1, 2*). An appeal against a penalty can be made to a valuation tribunal (see 20.76) or in Scotland a valuation appeal committee. This is the case even if the ground of appeal is that there was no power to impose a penalty (*Sch 3 para 3*).

**20.79** Where a person is convicted of an offence he cannot also be charged a penalty for the same default (*Sch 3 para 4*). The Treasury have power to change the £50 or £200 figure, but only to adjust for the effect of inflation (*Sch 3 para 5*). The Minister is empowered to make regulations for the collection of penalties and has done so in the *Council Tax (Administration and Enforcement) Regulations 1992*. These permit the authority to collect the penalty either by treating it as part of the tax (and thus collecting it by instalments) or by serving a notice on the taxpayer demanding payment within 14 days (*Reg 29(1)*). They cannot add it to the tax where the taxpayer is jointly liable with someone else for the tax (*Reg 27(2)(e)*).

**20.80** Penalties up to level 2 (£500) can also be imposed on a debtor who fails to supply information following the making of a liability order (see 20.60), or on the debtor or an employer who fails to notify a billing authority of a change of employment or fails to give the debtor the requisite notification in relation to an attachment of earnings order. They can be imposed up to level 3 (£1,000) on a debtor who provides false information, on an employer who fails to comply with an attachment of earnings order (unless he proves that he took all reasonable steps to do so), and on an employer who knowingly or recklessly gives a false statement in relation to an attachment of earnings order (*Reg 56*).

**20.81** Payment of a penalty cannot be demanded while any appeal or arbitration over it is outstanding, that is, until it is finally disposed of by the tribunal or is abandoned or fails for non-prosecution (*Reg 29(2)–(4)*). If a penalty is paid and subsequently quashed by the authority, or by the valuation tribunal or the High Court, the authority can use the money against any other liability of the payer to council tax or penalty but must repay the excess (*Reg 29(5)*).

**20.82** Most of the penalties are fixed by reference to the standard scale of penalties which was introduced by *section 35* of the *Criminal Justice Act 1982* as amended by *section 17* of the *Criminal Justice Act 1991*. The current penalty levels are as follows:

| | |
|---|---|
| Level 1 | £200 |
| Level 2 | £500 |
| Level 3 | £1,000 |
| Level 4 | £2,500 |
| Level 5 | £5,000 |

Level 5 is sometimes referred to as the 'statutory maximum'.

## Miscellaneous

**20.83** The Minister is empowered to make regulations to deal with what happens when a person dies owing council tax, including as the spouse of someone who owes the tax, or penalties (*section 18*). The *Council Tax (Administration and Enforcement) Regulations 1992, Reg 58* make his executors or personal representatives liable for such tax and, if the billing authority serves a notice on them requiring payment, for future tax that would have been due from the deceased but for his death. The executors are entitled to deduct the amount out of the estate. Unfortunately, their liability is not limited to assets in the estate. It may, accordingly, in future be dangerous to accept appointment as personal representative of an insolvent estate.

**20.84** *Sections 30–38* and *65* of the *Act* contain the rules billing authorities must follow in settling the level of the tax and are not considered here. *Sections 39–52* contain similar rules for precepting authorities. *Sections 53–64* deal with the Minister's capping powers. Because of the difference in land and other law in Scotland, the government have opted to enact separate legislation for Scotland. This is contained in *sections 70–99* and is broadly similar to the provisions in respect of England and Wales. A new social security benefit, council tax benefit, is introduced to shield the poorest sections of society from the impact of the tax. This is enacted in *Schedule 9* and outside the scope of this book.

## The Uniform Business Rate

**20.85** Property which is not liable to the council tax attracts non-domestic rating. The rateable value of such properties is based on their rental value on a letting from year to year (on the basis that the tenant undertook to pay all usual tenant's rates and taxes and to bear the cost of repairs and insurance and other expenses (if any) necessary to maintain the hereditament in a state to command that rent) (*Local Government Finance Act 1988, Sch 6 para 2*). In *Benjamin v Anston Properties (11.3.1998)* the Lands Tribunal held that this does not require an assumption that the property has been put into a reasonable state of repair at the valuation date and a property should therefore be valued in its existing state. The effect of this decision was reversed (with retrospect effect to 1 April 1990) by the *Rating (Valuation) Act 1999* which requires three assumptions, namely that the tenancy begins on the valuation date, immediately before that date the property was in a state of reasonable repair (other than any repairs which a reasonable landlord would regard as uneconomic) and the tenant undertakes to bear all usual tenant's rates and taxes and to bear the cost of repairs insurance and any other expenses necessary to maintain the property in a state to command the rent (*section 1*). Properties liable to the uniform business rate (UBR) were valued at 1 April 1988 by local valuation officers and are required to be revalued every five years (*LGFA 1988, s 41*). The revaluation to 1 April 1993 was duly carried out and applied for 1995/96 onwards. The next revaluation was to 1 April 1998 and applies to 2000/01 onwards.

**20.86** There is an exemption for:

(*a*) agricultural land and agricultural buildings

(*b*) fish farms

(*c*) places of religious worship

(*d*) certain property of Trinity House

(*e*) sewers

(*f*) property of drainage authorities

(*g*) parks

(*h*) property used for the disabled

(*j*) air-raid protection works

(*k*) swinging moorings

(*l*) property in enterprise zones

(*m*) such other categories as the Minister may determine.

(*LGFA 1988, Sch 3*).

(n) Unoccupied property with a rateable value of less than £1,900 (The *Non-Domestic Rating (Unoccupied Property)(England)(Amendment) Regulations 2000 – SI 2000 No 520*). Unoccupied industrial property is also exempt from empty property rate. The rate on other unoccupied property is 50% of the normal rate.

Charities are entitled to an 80 per cent relief from rates for non-domestic property which is wholly or mainly used for charitable purposes. A local authority has power to remit or reduce the rate bill of charities, clubs and certain other non-profit bodies (*LGFA 1988, s 41*). A public house, petrol filling station, general store (i.e. one wholly or mainly selling both food and general household goods), food store or post office in a rural area is entitled to a 50% reduction in its rates if it is the sole such business in a settlement and its rateable value is £6,000 or less. This relief was first introduced in 1998 and was limited to post offices and general stores, but its scope has since been broadened and the *Non-Domestic Rating (Designation of Rural Areas) (England) Order 2001* (*SI 2000 No 3916*) has designated the whole of England as rural apart from certain urban areas. The billing authority can increase this exemption to up to 100% if it wishes. A billing authority has discretion to remit all or part of the rates of any other building in such a settlement if its rateable value is £12,000 or less and the property is used for a purpose which benefits the local community (*LGFA 1988, ss 42A–43* as amended by the *Local Government Rating Act 1997*). The Minister confirmed this can cover public houses and garages.

**20.87** The rate for a building is arrived at by multiplying the rateable value of the property by a standard rate poundage which is fixed annually, not by the local authority like council tax, but by the government – which gives rise to the name of uniform business rate. In England the rate for 2002/03 is 43.7p. Following devolution the Scottish and Welsh Assemblies fix the rate in those countries. For 2002/03 it is 47.8p and 43.3p respectively. The rate poundage for subsequent years (other than revaluation years) will increase in line with inflation. It is determined by the formula:

$$\text{poundage for the preceding year} \times \frac{\text{RPI for September of the preceding year}}{\text{RPI for September of the year before the preceding year}}$$

In revaluation years the figure arrived at by this formula is adjusted by:

$$\frac{\text{total rateable values in the valuation list on the last day of the preceding financial year}}{\text{estimated rateable values in the next valuation list}}$$

**20.88** The poundage for 1990/91, the first year following the rating reform, was 34.8p in England and 36.2p in Wales. That for 1991/92 was 38.6p in England and 40.8p in Wales; for the following year 1992/93 it was 40.2p and 42.5p respectively, for 1993/94 it was 41.6p and 44.0p, for 1994/95 42.3p and 44.8p, for 1995/96 43.2p and 39p, for 1996/97 44.9p and 41.4p, for 1997/98 45.8p and 42.2p, for 1998/99 47.4p and 42.9p, for 1999/2000 48.9p and 44.3p, for 2000/01 (following the revaluation) 41.6p and 41.2p, and for 2002/03 43p and 42.6p. The City of London has power to set its own rate within specified limits, but has not to date differed from the national one. The system in Scotland was different up to 1994/95 but for 1995/96 to 1999/2000 the rate for Scotland was the same as for England. For 2000/01 it was 45.8p, and for 2002/03 47p. The 1995/96 figures follow the rating revaluation and are not therefore directly comparable with previous years.

**20.89** Business rates are allocated to local authorities (and precepting authorities) in proportion to their adult populations.

**20.90** The 1990 revaluation and the introduction of the uniform business rate brought about major changes in the rate burden for different business sectors and in different areas. Previously the poundage was fixed locally by each individual local authority and the division of the burden between properties in each local rating area was based on 1973 rental values.

**20.91** Transitional arrangements were accordingly introduced to phase in the very large increases faced by some businesses. The annual increase for buildings included on the rating list at 1 April 1990 with a rateable value of £500 or more was initially limited to 20% (increased by the percentage increase in the retail prices index) of the previous year's tax where the rateable value was £15,000 or more in Greater London or £10,000 elsewhere, and 15% where it was below that level (*Local Government and Housing Act 1989, Sch 5 para 40*, introducing a new *LGFA 1988, Sch 7A*). This phasing was subsequently relaxed by the *Non-Domestic Rating Act 1992*, *1993* or *1994*.

**20.92** If the rates were less than under the old system the reduction in liability was similarly limited in this case to 10% p.a. in real terms

(15% for properties with a rateable value under £15,000 (£10,000 outside Greater London)). The *Non-Domestic Rating Act 1992* reduced the restriction. There was no minimum for 1993/94 onwards.

**20.93** The 1995 rating valuation did not throw up any significant change in overall rateable values in England although it did give rise to major variations in respect of individual properties. For 1995/96 the government again limited the increase, this time to 10% plus inflation on the 1993/94 rate (7½% plus inflation if the rateable value is under £10,000 (£15,000 in London) and 5% plus inflation for composite hereditaments). Reductions were similarly limited to 5% plus inflation for larger properties and 10% plus inflation for smaller ones.

**20.94** The 1994 Regulations also prescribed limits to the reductions for 1996/97 to 1999/2000, but in this case they were not constant. The reduction for large properties (including composite ones) was limited to 5% plus inflation for 1995/96 and 1996/97, increasing to 15% plus inflation for 1997/98 and 30% plus inflation for 1998/99 and 1999/2000. The corresponding percentages for small properties (including composite ones) were 10%, 20% and 35%.

**20.95** Transitional arrangements were again introduced to cushion businesses from the April 2000 revaluation. These are much more simple than those which applied on previous revaluations. The increase in the amount payable, i.e. over the previous year's rates bill, is limited to the following.

| | *Small property* | *Other* |
|---|---|---|
| 2000/01 | 5% | 12.5% |
| 2001/02 | 7.5% | 15% |
| 2002/03 | 7.5% | 17.5% |
| 2003/04 | 7.5% | 17.5% |
| 2004/05 | 7.5% | 17.5% |

A small property is one with a rateable value of £18,000 or less in Greater London or £12,000 or less elsewhere.

**20.96** This relief is again partly paid for by a limit on the reduction in the rates bills for those whose bills go down. The reduction is limited to the following percentages.

| | *Small Property* | *Other* |
|---|---|---|
| 2000/01 | 5% | 2.5% |
| 2001/02 | 5% | 2.5% |
| 2002/03 | 10% | 5% |
| 2003/04 | 12.5% | 7.5% |
| 2004/05 | 25% | 15% |

*Chapter 21*

# Landfill Tax

**21.1** A special tax on landfill waste disposal was introduced from 1 October 1996. The tax applies to all waste disposal operations at landfill sites in the UK. It is imposed on the site operator. In addition VAT is payable on the landfill tax-inclusive price, i.e if the operator makes a charge for disposal of £1,000 and landfill tax is £200 he will have to charge the customer £1,410 (£1,000 + £200 + 17½% of £1,200). The customer will be able to treat the VAT as input tax in the normal way but will not be able to reclaim any part of the landfill tax – although if the waste disposal is a revenue expense the full £1,200 VAT-exclusive figure will be a business expense attracting a corporation tax deduction.

**21.2** The Inland Revenue have confirmed that where a trader generates waste and pays landfill tax on it, the landfill tax will qualify as a deductible expense in calculating profit for income or corporation tax purposes provided that the other costs of disposing of the waste, e.g. the carriage and the waste disposal charge, are themselves deductible. Where a landfill site operator makes a payment to an environmental body (see 21.35) that payment will be deductible provided that it meets the test of being wholly and exclusively for the purpose of the trade. *Prima facie* this test will normally be met (Tax Bulletin 23, June 1996).

**21.3** The tax is under the control of Customs & Excise. It applies to all forms of landfill disposal which involve the deposit of waste in or on land. There is no *de minimis* exemption. Landfill site operators will normally account for the tax quarterly by reference to deliveries to the site during the quarter.

**21.4** Although the professed objectives of the tax are to promote greater efficiency in the waste management market by ensuring landfill waste disposal is properly priced, and to encourage the production of less waste and a greater emphasis on recycling, as it does not apply to incineration there were fears that it could instead encourage that alternative method of disposal which many feel more environmentally damaging. However the government stated in 1998 that research shows that already almost a third of companies began, or were considering, waste recycling, re-use or minimisation as a result of the tax. (Business Brief 9/98).

**21.5** The tax applies to a disposal of materials as waste made by way of landfill at a landfill site on or after 1 October 1996 (*FA 1996, s 40(2)*). For this purpose material is disposed of as waste if the person disposing of it (or if the person on whose behalf or at whose request, it is being disposed of) does so with the intention of discarding it. The fact that someone else could, or does, benefit from, or make use of, the materials will not prevent there being a disposal as waste (*FA 1996, s 64*). *ICI Chemicals and Polymer Ltd* manufactures hydrogen fluoride a by-product of which is dehydrous calcium sulphate (Andricite). It discovered that Andricite can be used for encapsulating mercury waste and used it as such in its landfill site. Customs contended that the Andricite was waste, i.e. something that ICI intended to discard or throw away, and felt that the fact that it was also able to be used for site engineering purposes was irrelevant. The VAT and Duties Tribunal (*L00002*) noted that Andricite had a saleable value and that ICI did not have the intention of disposing of it as useless but intended to use it for encapsulating mercury. It was therefore not 'waste' within the meaning of *section 64*.

**21.6** A similar decision was reached by the tribunal in *Darfish Ltd (L00005)* where soil was brought onto a landfill site specifically to be used for site engineering purposes. However on appeal (20 March 2000 unreported) Moses J held that in deciding whether the material was waste the tribunal should have looked at the intention of the disposers of the material (topsoil and sub-soil), Hallamshire and Wilson Bowden, not the intention of Darfish, the site operator, and remitted the case to the tribunal to decide this point. In that case Moses J thought that disposal cannot be confined to the moment of deposit. It is a term wider than 'discarding', and wider than 'deposit'. Disposal will include, but not be confined to, any of the processes of removal, transport and deposit. It must include deposit because it is the deposit which triggers the tax and also identifies the time when the landfill site operator must be identified as such, but disposal is not limited to the process of deposit'.

In *C & E Commrs v Parkwood Landfill Ltd (2002 STC 417, [2002] EWHC 47(Ch))* Sir Andrew Morritt V-C thought it clear that Moses J treated the disposal of waste as different from the disposal by way of landfill. In the Parkwood case a joint venture company, Parkwood Recycling Ltd. acquired domestic waste from Sheffield City Council, crushed, sorted, and graded it and separated it into saleable materials and other which went to landfill (and on which tax was presumably paid). The saleable materials included aggregates and fines, which were sold to Parkwood Landfill which used them at its landfill site for road-making and landscaping. Parkwood contended that such materials were not waste of Parkwood Recycling. Customs contended that tax was due as the Council had discarded the material as waste. The judge felt that,

'on a literal construction of *s 65(1)* there was a disposal by way of landfill . . . That which must be disposed of is not waste but material subject to a disposal as waste. It matters not by whom the disposal is made . . . The disposal for the purpose of the 1996 Act is more than the legal transaction by which it is effected or property in the material passes. Provided that the material can be identified as having been subject to a disposal as waste I can see no basis on which it is possible to exclude material which was waste but has been recycled before a disposal by way of landfill.'

He concluded that tax was payable and commented,

'A disposal may be made in more than one place, at more than one time and by more than one legal transaction. In the absence of clarification in further legislation the proper application of *s 40(2)* will have to be ascertained on a case by case basis.'

This clearly leaves the law in a very unsatisfactory state!

**21.7** A disposal is by way of landfill if either:

(*a*) the material is deposited on the surface of land or on a structure set into the surface, or

(*b*) the material is deposited under the surface of land (*FA 1996, s 65(1)*).

Material means material of any kind and includes objects, substances and products of all kind (*FA 1996, s 70(1)*). Placing the material in a container before disposal will not prevent it being by way of landfill (*FA 1996, s 65(2)*). Depositing the material and later covering it with earth (or with similar matter such as sand or rocks) and depositing material in a cavity such as a cavern or mine are both caught (*FA 1996, s 65(3)(8)*). If material is deposited within (*a*) with a view to it later being covered with earth (so that it will fall within (*b*)) the charge arises under (*a*) when it is deposited, and not under (*b*) when it is later covered (*FA 1996, s 65(4)*). Land covered by water is within *section 65* if it is above the low water mark of ordinary spring tides (*FA 1996, s 65(7)*). The Treasury have power by statutory instrument to amend these rules (*FA 1996, s 65(5)(6)*). A site is a landfill site only if it has been granted a site licence under Part II of the *Environmental Protection Act 1990* (or its Scottish or Northern Ireland equivalent) (*FA 1996, s 66*). Where a company brought soil onto a landfill site and paid a tipping fee to the site operator the soil was held to be waste notwithstanding that it was set aside by the operator and later used in the site restoration, as it was material deposited on the surface of the site (*F L Gamble & Sons Ltd L00004*).

**21.8** The tax is based on weight. The standard rate is £13 per tonne (£10 before 1 April 2000, £11 before April 2001 and £12 before 1 April 2002), reduced proportionately for parts of a tonne after the first or, if less than a tonne is disposed of, a proportionately reduced sum (*FA 1996, s 42(1)*). For taxable disposals made or treated as made before 1 April 1999 the rate was £7 per tonne. The government have said that they intend to increase the rate by £1 each year until it reaches £15 from 1 April 2004. A reduced rate of £2 per tonne applies to inactive or inert waste (called 'qualifying material'). There are no proposals to amend this rate. The Treasury are given power by statutory instrument to determine what qualifies for the reduced rate. They have done so by the *Landfill Tax (Qualifying Material) Order 1996* (*SI 1996 No 1528*). This applies the reduced rate to the deposit of:

(1) Naturally occurring rocks and soils (including clay, sand, gravel, sandstone, limestone, crushed stone, china clay, construction stone, stone from the demolition of buildings or structures, slate, topsoil, peat, silt and dredgings).

(2) Glass, ceramics and concrete (including fritted enamel, bricks, tiles, clayware, pottery, china, bricks and mortar, refractory bricks, reinforced concrete, concrete blocks, breeze blocks and aircrete blocks – but not glass-fibre or glass-reinforced plastic or concrete plant washings).

(3) Unused processed or prepared minerals (namely moulding sands, clays, clay absorbents such as Fuller's earth, bentonite and other mineral absorbents, man-made mineral fibres, glass fibre, silica, mica and mineral abrasives – but not sand containing organic binders, glass-reinforced plastic or asbestos).

(4) Furnace slags (including vitrified wastes, fused and insoluble residues from thermal processing of minerals, and slag from waste incineration).

(5) Bottom ash and fly ash from wood or coal combustion (but not fly ash from municipal, clinical and hazardous waste incinerators or sewage sludge incinerators).

(6) Low-activity inorganic compounds (namely titanium dioxide, calcium carbonate, magnesium carbonate, magnesium oxide, magnesium hydroxide, iron oxide, ferric hydroxide, aluminium oxide, aluminium hydroxide, and zirconium dioxide).

(7) Calcium sulphate (including gypsum and calcium sulphate based plasters – but not plasterboard) if it is either disposed of at a site licenced to take only non-putrescible (inactive) waste or is land-filled in a separate containment cell within a mixed site.

(8) Calcium hydroxide and brine which is deposited in brine cavity.

(9) Water which contains any of the above qualifying materials in suspension.

Customs announced on 18 September 1996 that the £2 rate would also apply to foundry sand, at least initially (News Release 48/96). This appears to be an extra-statutory concession, the necessary Regulation not having been laid. To qualify for the lower rate the transfer note (as defined in the *Environmental Protection (Duty of Care) Regulations 1991* (*SI 1991 No 2839*) must describe the materials in accordance with the above list and in the case of water must also describe the material held in suspension (*Article 6*). The waste must not contain or be contaminated with other unqualifying material subject to a (yet to be announced) *de minimis* limit where that material does not lead to any potential for pollution. Where a load contains some incidental active waste this will in general be ignored if it is ignored for environmental regulatory purposes (Customs report on responses to consultation, April 1996).

**21.9** Customs have power to make regulations to determine weight. They have done so by the *Landfill Tax Regulations 1996* (*SI 1996 No 1527*). The weight of material disposed of must normally be ascertained by weighing it at the time of disposal (unless that is a deemed time under *FA 1996, s 61*). If there is no weighbridge at the landfill site – or, although there is one, it would be costly to use it, e.g. because the waste does not normally pass near it or it is out of order – an alternative method of calculating the waste can be agreed with Customs. For example, the maximum permitted weight for the lorry could be used, or the volume of waste could be measured or otherwise ascertained and converted to weight. Customs Information Note, 4/96, 'Calculating the weight of waste' contains conversion factors for various categories of waste (Information Note 1/96, paras 7.1 and 7.2). The authority for this is *Reg 44* which allows the registrable person to agree a special method with Customs and *Reg 43* which provides that if they publish a notice specifying rules for determining weight it must be followed. Customs can withdraw from an agreement at any time. (*Reg 44(3)*).

**21.10** Customs can lay down rules to discount the weight of any water if water is present in waste only because either:

(i) it has been added to enable the material to be transported for disposal, e.g. moved by pipeline,

(ii) it has been used for the extraction of a mineral,

(iii) it has arisen or has been added in the course of an industrial process, or

(iv) the material is the residue from the treatment of effluent or sewage by a water treatment works.

The water cannot be discounted under (i) to (iii) unless it forms 25% or more of the weight of the material at the time of the disposal. In all cases the water cannot be discounted if the material is capable of escaping from the landfill site by leaching, unless either it is likely to do so in the form of water only or the leachate will be collected on the site and treated to eliminate any potential it has to cause harm (*Reg 44(6)(7)*).

Where the material falls within (iv) above, the water cannot be discounted unless it has been added prior to disposal. Naturally occurring water (such as rain or snow) cannot be discounted. It appears that if there is any such water in a load even the added water cannot be discounted although this is clearly not the intention.

**21.11** The person liable for the tax is the landfill site operator, i.e. the person who at the time of disposal holds the licence for the landfill site concerned (*FA 1996, s 41*). There is no obligation on the site owner to issue a landfill tax invoice but if he chooses to do so this must contain specific information, which is set out in *Reg 37* of the *Landfill Tax Regulations 1996* (*SI 1996 No 1527*). As bad debt relief is dependent on there being a landfill invoice it is likely that most site operators will choose to issue one. Landfill tax is not recoverable by the customer either by repayment or by offset against VAT. It is, however, an expense which is deductible in calculating taxable profits for income or corporation tax.

## Exemptions

**21.12** There are a number of exemptions.

(1) *Material removed from water (dredging, etc.).* The disposal of material removed from a river, a canal or watercourse (natural or artificial) or a dock or harbour (natural or artificial) and which before its removal formed part of or projected from the bed of the water concerned is exempt from the tax. This exemption extends to material removed from water within the approaches of a harbour and which was moved in the interests of navigation and to naturally occurring mineral material that has been removed from the sea in the course of commercial operations to obtain sand, gravel or other substances from the seabed (*FA 1996, s 43*).

(2) *Mining and quarrying.* There is an exemption for the disposal of naturally occurring material extracted from the earth in the course of either commercial mining operations (both deep and open-cast) or commercial quarrying operations. The material must not have been subjected to, or resulted from, any process separate from the mining or quarrying or any process which has permanently altered the material's chemical composition (*FA 1996, s 44*).

(3) *Pet Cemeteries.* A cemetery is not normally within the scope of the tax as the burial of human remains is not the disposal of waste. However a pet cemetery is licenced as a landfill site under the *Environmental Protection Act 1990*, so a specific exemption from the tax is needed for pet cemeteries. For the exemption to apply the only landfill disposals made at the site since 1 October 1996 must have been of the remains of dead domestic pets (*FA 1996, s 45*).

(4) *Material removed from contaminated land.* There is an exemption for the disposal of waste removed from contaminated land for which a certificate was issued by Customs. The certificate must be in force at the time the waste is removed and any conditions attached to the certificate must be met. The material must be removed before construction of any building or civil engineering work commences on the part of the land in question, or in the case of other qualifying land reclamation when the pollutants have been cleared from the relevant part of the site (*FA 1996, s 43A* inserted by the *Landfill Tax (Contaminated Land) Order 1996* (*SI 1996 No 1529*)). In other words, the exemption will not cover building waste or waste arising from landscaping, fencing or general site clearance. It is not clear when construction of a building commences for this purpose. It is probably not when a start is made on a foundation trench as logically the exemption needs to cover not merely contamination of the topsoil but the removal of deep contamination which is unearthed in the course of the construction of the foundations of a building.

The exemption does not apply if at the time the material is removed an enforcement notice has been served in relation to any part of the land in question requiring clearance of the pollution – unless the person carrying out the removal is a local authority, a development corporation under *s 135, Local Government, Planning and Land Act 1980* or its Scottish equivalent, the Environment Agency, the Scottish Environment Protection Agency, English Partnerships, Scottish Enterprise, Highland and Islands Enterprise or the Welsh Development Agency (*FA 1996, s 43A(4)(5)*). An enforcement notice for this purpose means a works notice under *s 46A, Control of Pollution Act 1974*, an enforcement, prohibition, order or remediation notice under the *Environmental Protection Act 1990* or a works notice under *s 161A, Water Resources Act 1991*. The purpose of this exclusion is to deny relief to the person who has himself created the contamination.

A certificate of contamination is issued by Customs on the application in writing by a person carrying out or intending to carry out a reclamation of the land in question once Customs are satisfied that the reclamation qualifies for exemption (*FA 1996, s 43B*, inserted by the *Landfill Tax (Contaminated Land) Order 1996* (*SI 1996 No 1529*)). A reclamation qualifies if:

(*a*) it is (or will be) carried out with the object of either facilitating development, conservation, the provision of a public park or other amenity, or the use of the land for agriculture or forestry, or of reducing or removing the potential of pollutants to cause harm;

(*b*) it constitutes (or includes) clearing the land of pollutants which are causing harm or have the potential for causing harm;

(*c*) unless removed the pollutants would prevent the development or other purpose being carried out; and

(*d*) all activities that have at any time resulted in the presence of pollutants on the land by the applicant or a connected person or by any other person on the land in question have either ceased or have ceased to create pollution (*FA 1996, s 43B(7)(8)*).

For the purpose of head (*d*) any activities carried out without the consent of the then occupier (or if the land is unoccupied, the person entitled to occupy it) can be ignored, as can the presence of pollutants which were borne onto the land by air or water. So can any activities not carried on by the applicant or a connected person of his (within *ICTA 1988, s 839* – see Appendix 1) or carried out by someone else but not on the land in question. The clearing of some pollutants can still be qualifying reclamation even though not all the pollutants on the land are removed (*FA 1996, s 43B (9)–(11)*). The application for a certificate has to be made at least 30 days before it is to take effect. By concession dated 27 May 1997 Customs agreed to remit tax paid before 30 June 1997 where the waste clearly qualified for exemption and at least some of the waste from the reclamation site had been certified. Customs refused to apply this concession to *Zenith Builders (L00001)* which appealed to the VAT and Duties Tribunal. The tribunal held that it had no jurisdiction and suggested the company should approach the Customs & Excise Adjudicator, although it expressed the view that the officer did not seem to have acted unreasonably. Customs appear to have refused the concession because there had been no previous certified waste from the site. They thought the company ought to have stockpiled it until Customs could inspect it. When Customs withdrew a contaminated land certificate because they formed the opinion that the soil was removed because of its engineering properties not because it was contaminated, the VAT and Duties Tribunal held that it was sufficient for one object of the removal to be because the land was contaminated, so the two motives were not mutually exclusive, and that the soil had been removed with the object of facilitating development with (*a*) above. It accordingly restored the certificate (*Taylor Woodrow Construction (Northern) Ltd – L00003*).

(5) *Temporary Disposals.* A landfill site operator can designate part of his site as set aside for temporary disposals pending the material being either:

(*a*) recycled or incinerated,

(*b*) used (other than being taken to another landfill site) either

(i) at a place other than a relevant site, or

(ii) for site restoration purposes at the landfill site itself, or

(*c*) sorted pending either

(i) its use for a purpose within (*a*) or (*b*) above, or

(ii) its disposal.

The definition of site restoration for the purpose of (*b*) and (*c*) above is the same as for *FA 1996, s 43C(1)* (see (6) below).

Landfill tax will not be payable on such materials provided that they are actually dealt with in one of these three ways within 12 months of being deposited (three years in the case of site restoration). The landfill site operator needs to maintain specified records in respect of materials deposited in a designated area. If the material is not used or removed in the 12-month (or three-year) period it is deemed to have been deposited for landfill at the end of that period so as to trigger liability for the tax. Customs can nullify the designation either by notice in writing, or if materials not intended to be dealt with as in (*a*) to (*c*) above are deposited in the designated area, or if material not dealt with in the 12-month or three-year period is not removed from the designated area within a further seven days. If they do so, all material in that designated area is deemed to have been landfilled at that time (*Regs 38–40, Landfill Tax Regulations 1996* (*SI 1996 No 1527*) as amended by the *Landfill Tax (Amendment) Regulations 2002* (*SI 2002 No 1*)). The power to designate part of a site to hold qualifying materials pending site restoration was introduced by *FA 2000, s 141* but the amending regulation did not come into effect until 1 February 2002. Customs allowed relief on an extra-statutory basis in the interim.

(6) *Site restoration*. For disposals after 30 September 1999, the disposal of qualifying material within *section 42* (see 21.8), i.e. inactive or inert waste, by depositing it on and using it in the restoration of the site or part thereof (*FA 1996, s 43C(1)* inserted by the *Landfill Tax (Site Restoration and Quarries) Order 1999* (*SI 1999 No 2075*)). The site operator must notify customs in writing prior to the disposal that he is commencing the restoration of all or a part of the site and must provide such other written information (again, it appears, before the disposal) as Customs may require either generally or in a particular case (*FA 1996, s 43C(1)(b)*). Restoration for this purpose means work which is required to be carried out to restore a landfill site to use on completion of waste disposal operations under either a planning consent, a waste management licence, or a resolution (presumably by a local authority) authorising the disposal of waste on or in land. It does not however include work to cap the landfill site (*FA 1996, s 43C(2)(3)*).

(7) *Quarries*. The disposal after 30 September 1999 of qualifying material within *section 42* (see 21.8), i.e. inactive or inert waste, at a qualifying landfill site (*FA 1996, s 44A* inserted by the *Landfill Tax (Site Restoration and Quarries) Order 1999* (*SI 1999 No 2075*)). A qualifying landfill site for this purpose is one which at the time of the disposal is (or was) a quarry for which it was a requirement of planning consent that it be wholly or partially refilled and the waste management licence (or resolution) authorising disposals on or in the land comprising the site permits only the disposal of qualifying materials (*FA 1996, s 44A(2)*). If the quarrying operations ceased before 1 October 1999 the planning requirement must have been imposed before 2 October 1999 (*FA 1996, s 44A(3)*). If a waste management licence did not permit only the disposal of qualifying material and an application is made to vary the licence so that it does so, the variation will be treated as effective from the making of the application provided it is finally resolved within two years. If it is not, the variation is deemed to have effect for the two years from the application, then to cease to have effect until the application is disposed of and then to have effect again (*FA 1996, s 44A(4)*). The logic of backdating the variation for two years from the application rather than for the two years preceding disposal of the application is not readily apparent. An application is disposed of for this purpose if it is granted, it is withdrawn, it is refused and there is no right of appeal against the refusal, it is refused and the time limit for appeal expires without an appeal being made, or an appeal against refusal is dismissed or withdrawn and there is no further right of appeal (*FA 1996, s 44A(5)*). Effectively this allows inactive or inert waste to be deposited on the site free of landfill tax for two years (or until rights of appeal are exhausted if earlier) even if at the end of the day the licence is not varied. If the application is not granted within two years there seems no

point from a landfill tax point of view of continuing to pursue it; the application or any pending appeal might as well be abandoned. Neither this exemption nor that for site restoration extends to site engineering activities such as the construction of cells, haul roads, daily cover, etc. (Business Brief 9/98), presumably as such operations do not amount to site restoration or the refilling of a quarry.

(8) *Power to vary.* The Treasury has power by statutory instruments both to grant new exemptions and to withdraw existing ones (*FA 1996, s 46*).

## Registration

**21.13** Anyone who carries out taxable activities has to register for landfill tax (*FA 1996, s 47(1)*). There is no *de minimis* exemption. A person carries out a taxable activity if either:

(*a*) he makes a taxable disposal in respect of which he is liable to pay tax, i.e. he is the holder of the site licence of a landfill site,

(*b*) he is liable to pay tax in respect of a taxable disposal made with his permission by another person, e.g. a lorry driver, or

(*c*) he is the person liable to pay tax (because he is the site operator) in relation to a taxable disposal made by some other person even though that disposal is made without his knowledge (*FA 1996, s 69*).

If at any time a person who is not registered forms the intention of carrying out taxable activities he must notify Customs of his intention (*FA 1996, s 47(3)*). A registrable person will be registered with effect from the time he begins to carry out taxable activities, irrespective of when he notifies Customs (*FA 1996, s 47(5)*).

**21.14** Application for registration needs to be made on a statutory form (LT1 plus LT2 if the applicant will operate more than one site and LT3 if it is a partnership). Application must be made within 30 days of the earliest date after 1 August 1996 on which the person has the intention to carry out taxable activities (*Reg 4, Landfill Tax Regulation 1996* (*SI 1996 No 1527*)). If a person discovers an inaccuracy in his application form or any of the information shown on the form changes he must notify Customs within 30 days. Such notification must not only reveal what was wrong and the date a change occurred, but why any information provided was inaccurate and the date on which the inaccuracy was discovered (*Reg 5*).

**21.15** A person who at any time ceases to have the intention of carrying out taxable activities must also notify Customs within 30 days of that change, giving the date on which he ceased to intend to carry out taxable activities and, if different, the date on which he in fact ceased to do so. Customs must then deregister him from the earliest practicable time after he ceases to carry out taxable activities – but only if they are satisfied that he will not carry out any further taxable activities, he has paid all the tax for which he is liable and there are no outstanding credits due to him. Customs can in any event at their discretion deregister a person who has ceased to carry out taxable activities and must deregister someone if they are satisfied that he never fulfilled his intention to carry out taxable activities and has decided not to do so (*FA 1996, s 47(4)(6)(7)(8)* and *Reg 6*).

**21.16** Where the right to carry on a taxable business is transferred, it is transferred as a going concern, and the registration of the transferor has not already been cancelled but as a result of the transfer it will fall to be cancelled, the transferor and transferee can jointly apply (on form LT4) for the registration of the transferor to be cancelled and for the transferee to be registered with the transferor's registration number. As with the transfer of a VAT registration number, the transferee takes over any outstanding liabilities of his predecessor to pay tax or to make a return, and all past actions of the predecessor are deemed to be the actions of the transferee (*Reg 7*).

**21.17** In the case of a partnership all the partners are jointly and severally liable for landfill tax responsibilities but once they have been complied with the obligation of the other partners is released (*Reg 8(3)*). There is similar joint and several liability for the responsibilities of other unincorporated bodies. The persons liable are the president, chairman, treasurer, secretary or any similar office holder. If there are no office holders it is the members of the management committee and if there is no such committee it is the members (*Reg 8(1)(2)*). If a registrable person becomes bankrupt or incapacitated (or in the case of a company goes into liquidation, receivership or administration) Customs can treat any person who carries on the business as if he were the registrable person. Such person must notify Customs of the bankruptcy or incapacity and the date on which it began, within 30 days of commencing to carry on the business (*Reg 9*).

**21.18** A body corporate that carries on business in divisions can apply to register the divisions separately (*FA 1996, s 58(3)*). A group of companies can opt for a single group registration. If they do so all the tax is due from the representative members but all other members of the group are jointly and severally liable. Companies can form a group if one controls the others or one person (or two or more individuals carrying on business in partnership) control them all. Customs can refuse a group registration if it appears to them necessary to do so for the protection of the Revenue (*FA 1996, s 59*).

## Accounting for the tax

**21.19** The landfill site operator must make a quarterly return, and pay the tax shown as due on it, by the end of the month following the period to which it relates. Customs will decide what accounting quarter a particular operator should use so as to spread their work load (*Regs 2, 11*). The return requires details both of tax payable and weight of materials deposited. If an operator does not submit his return Customs have power to assess him in estimated figures (*FA 1996, s 50*). There is an obligation to keep and preserve accounting records for six years (*Reg 16*).

**21.20** Interest is, of course, payable on tax paid late. This is at a penal rate – 10 percentage points above the normal Customs' rate for unpaid tax, i.e. if the Customs' rate is 7.5% the interest on overdue tax is 17.5% Furthermore it is compounded with monthly rests. Where an assessment is made by Customs in the absence of a return the penal rate again applies. Where a return is made but an assessment is raised to recover further tax, e.g. Customs believe there is an underdeclaration, interest is at the normal rate until the date the assessment is notified to the taxpayer and at the penal rate thereafter (*FA 1996, Sch 6 paras 26, 27*). Customs or the VAT and Duties Tribunal both have power to reduce or waive the interest (*Sch 5 para 28*). Interest on repayments is payable by Customs – at the normal rate only (*Sch 5 para 29*).

**21.21** Interest (and penalties) in respect of landfill tax are not deductible for income or corporation tax purposes (*ICTA 1988, s 827(1C)* inserted by *FA 1996, Sch 5 para 40*).

**21.22** Deductions can be claimed for various 'credits'. These fall into three categories: removals of material from the site, bad debts, and contributions to bodies concerned with the environment (Environmental Trusts and Companies) (see 21.35). A removals credit arises in two circumstances only. The first is where the site operator notifies Customs before the waste is landfilled that some or all of it will be recycled, incinerated or removed for use (not to another landfill site) and the removal of the material takes place within 12 months of its being landfilled (five years where water was added to facilitate disposal) (*Reg 21(2)*). The second is where the Environment Agency (or its Scottish or Northern Irish counterpart) order the material to be removed because the deposit was in breach of the site licence, the material has been landfilled elsewhere and the site operator has paid landfill tax in relation to the new deposit of the material (*Reg 21(4)*). In both cases the amount of the credit is the tax originally paid on the material actually removed (*Reg 21(6)*).

**21.23** In the case of a transfer of a going concern any credits that become payable will be given to the transferee, not the transferor, irrespective of whether or not he has opted to take over the transferor's registration number (*Reg 7(5)*).

**21.24** A credit for a bad debt can be claimed only if the person who deposited the material was not a connected person (within *ICTA 1988, s 839* – see Appendix 1) of the site operator, the operator has accounted for tax on the deposit, the debt is written off in his accounts as bad, he issued a landfill invoice in respect of the debt within 14 days of the material being deposited (or such other period agreed with Customs) and the invoice has remained unpaid for a period of at least 12 months. The regulations lay down detailed record-keeping requirements. Where there are several amounts owing by the same customer any receipts from him must be set against the earliest invoices first unless a payment was both allocated to a different invoice by the customer at the time of payment and that invoice was settled in full. Writing-off of the debt needs to have been done both in the operator's annual accounts and in a 'landfill tax bad debt account' which is required by the Regulations to be maintained (*Regs 22–29*).

**21.25** On disposals after 28 July 2000 the 'controller', i.e. the person in actual control of the landfill site, is liable for the tax if the holder of the waste management disposal licence, the 'operator', does not pay it. In some cases the operator is not involved in the day to day running of the site. For example, he may be a farmer who has leased out the site to the operator. A person is the controller of all or part of a site at a given time if he is entitled to determine what disposals of materials can be made at that site or that part of it (unless he does so only as an employee or agent) (*FA 1996, Sch 5 para 48* inserted by *FA 2000, Sch 37*). Where the controller controls part of the site he is of course only liable for the tax on disposals on that part. If the operator is entitled to offset credits (see 21.22) the controller can take the benefit of them in proportion to the amount of the operator's tax to which he is liable (*FA 1996, Sch 5 para 50*). Customs can collect tax from the controller only if they serve notice on him of the amount payable within two years of the end of the accounting period by reference to which the tax is due (*FA 1996, Sch 5 para 51*). Customs can similarly collect from the controller tax assessed under *FA 1996, s 50* (see 21.19). They must notify him that they intend to do so within two years of the issue of the assessment (*FA 1996, Sch 5 para 52*). Where Customs decide to assess the controller that does not relieve the operator of liability; both are jointly and severally liable but Customs cannot collect in total more than is due (*FA 1996, Sch 5 para 57*). The Controller is of course also liable for interest on the tax (*FA 1996, Sch 5 para 58*). He has a right of appeal to the VAT and Duties tribunal against a notice or against a decision that he is the controller (*FA 1996, Sch 5 para 59*). When a person ceased to be the controller he and the operator must together ensure that notice of that fact is given to Customs (*FA 1996, Sch 5 para 57*).

## Administration

**21.26** The administrative provisions are set out in *FA 1996, Sch 5*. They broadly follow the VAT rules. Customs have power to inspect documents (*para 3*); to enter and inspect business premises (*para 4*); to enter and search premises and remove anything thereon and to search any person on the premises who they reasonably believe to be in possession of any relevant documents or other things when they suspect a fraud offence of a serious nature and obtain a search warrant from a Justice of the Peace (*para 5*); to arrest anyone who they have reasonable grounds for suspecting has committed a fraud offence (*para* 6); to obtain access to records of third parties if a Justice of the Peace so orders because he believes that an offence (not necessarily a fraud offence) has been or is about to be committed (*para 7*); and to take samples from material that has been or is intended to be landfilled if they suspect either a mistake or fraud (*para 10*). A fraud offence is one for which criminal penalties can be imposed under *para 15(1)* to *(5)* – but not *para 15(6)* which makes it a criminal offence to enter into a landfill tax contract (or make arrangements for someone else to do so) with reason to believe that the tax in respect of the disposal will be evaded, or *para 15(7)* which makes it a criminal offence to operate a landfill site without giving any security for the tax that may have been required by Customs.

**21.27** Landfill tax is a preferential debt in an insolvency to the extent that it fell due in the six months prior to the insolvency (*para 12*). Customs have a right of set-off against any amount owed by them in respect of other taxes, but cannot set a debt arising before the commencement of insolvency procedures against one arising subsequent to that time (*Regs 45–47, Landfill Tax Regulations 1996* (*SI 1996 No 1527*)). They also have power to distrain on goods and chattels of the site operator (but in the case of assessed tax (other than an assessment made in the absence of a return) cannot distrain until the period for appeal against the assessment had ended) (*para 13* and *Regs 48* and *49* as amended by the *Landfill Tax (Amendment) Regulations 1996* (*SI 1996 No 2100*) and the *Distress for Customs and Excise Duties and Other Indirect Taxes Regulations 1997*). If tax is overpaid there is no obligation on Customs to repay it unless the operator makes a claim in such form and supported by such documentary evidence as they may specify – and even then need not repay it if to do so would unjustly enrich the site operator (*para 14*).

**21.28** There are both criminal and civil penalties for landfill tax evasion. The criminal penalty on summary conviction is up to six months' imprisonment, a fine of up to the statutory maximum (£5,000) or three times the tax if greater, or both. On indictment it is up to seven years' imprisonment, an unlimited fine, or both (*para 16*). Customs have power to mitigate these penalties (*para 17*). The civil penalty for evasion is an amount equal to the tax evaded or sought to be evaded (*para 18*). In the case of a body corporate, Customs can switch the penalty from the company to a director or manager whose conduct gave rise to the dishonesty (*para 19*). There is a 5% serious misdeclaration penalty which is not payable if the understatement of tax is disclosed before Customs begin enquiries (*para 20*). The penalty for late registration is the greater of 5% of the tax or £250 (*para 21*). For failure to furnish information required by Customs the penalty is £250 plus £20 a day after the imposition of the initial penalty (*para 22*). The penalty for a regulatory breach is £250 and that for breach of a walking possession agreement is 50% of the tax (*paras 23 and 24*). Customs have power to mitigate (or reduce to nil) all the civil penalties (*para 25*).

**21.29** Customs can require a taxable person to give security (or further security) for landfill tax as a condition of his running a landfill site (*para 31*). Customs have power to disclose information to the Environment Agency and similar regulatory bodies (*para 35*). They also have the right to publish the Landfill Tax register (*para 36*) and have done so. If a person issues a landfill tax invoice and no tax is in fact chargeable, the amount shown thereon is nevertheless recoverable as a debt due to the Crown (*para 44*). If a landfill invoice is issued within 14 days after material has been deposited the invoice date is treated as the date of the landfill unless the site operator notifies Customs in writing that he wants to adopt the actual landfill date. Customs have power to extend the 14-day period at the request of a site operator (*FA 1996, s 61*). Customs have power to direct that where material is disposed of it must be regarded as qualifying material if it would in fact be such material but for a small quantity of non-qualifying material. The direction may be made, either generally or at the request of a site operator in relation to a specific site (*FA 1996, s 63*).

**21.30** There is no general right of appeal against decisions of Customs. However, a right of appeal is specifically given in relation to most such decisions (*FA 1996, s 54(1)*). Experience with VAT suggests that the VAT and Duties Tribunal will lean over backwards to try to bring something within their jurisdiction if they can. An appeal cannot be brought unless the decision has first been reviewed within Customs. An application for a review must be made within 45 days of written notification of the original decision having been given and Customs have 45 days from the day on which the review was required to give a decision (if they do not respond within that time they are deemed to have confirmed the decision (*FA 1996, s 54(3)–(8)*). A person who is under a duty to make landfill tax returns cannot pursue an appeal (but can request a review) unless he has made all the returns due and paid all the tax shown as payable in those returns. Similarly an appeal as to whether tax is chargeable in respect of a disposal (or how much) or against a Customs' assessment cannot be entertained unless either the tax in dispute has been paid or Customs or the tribunal accepts that it would cause hardship to do so (*FA 1996, s 55*). It should be noted that the relief for hardship does not apply where a return has been made and the disputed tax is shown as payable on that return. The VAT rules for settling appeals by agreement and for the enforcement of tribunal decisions also apply to landfill tax (*FA 1996, s 56*). Curiously the VAT power to leap-frog an appeal from the tribunal direct to the Court of Appeal does not apply; a landfill tax appeal must proceed via the High Court.

**21.31** From 31 July 1998 the *Provisional Collection of Taxes Act 1968* has been extended to landfill tax. This will enable changes to rates to take effect provisionally from the time of the appropriate budget resolution (*FA 1998, s 148*).

## Adjustment of Contracts

**21.32** If work is carried out under a construction contract made before 30 November 1994 (when landfill tax was first announced), the work results in a need to landfill materials and the contract made no provision as to the disposal of such materials, the contract price is deemed to be increased 'so as to reflect' the tax chargeable on the disposal (*FA 1996, Sch 5 para 46*). It is not clear what this means. It does not necessarily mean that the contract price is to be increased by the amount of the tax; it appears to require one to ascertain what the contract price would have been likely to be had the existence of the tax been known. The provision will apply to a contract for site preparation or demolition as well as to a building or civil engineering contract (*FA 1996, Sch 5 para 46(3)*). *Paragraph 46* will not apply if there is some provision to the contrary in the contract. There could not have been a specific reference to landfill tax, but a provision that the price is inclusive of all taxes or something similar would probably stop it applying. There is no statutory provision to adjust a contract entered into after 29 November 1994 even though so little may have been known about the tax that it would have been impracticable to incorporate it in the contract. The then government considered that the parties could have included some sort of generalised provision had they wished.

**21.33** Similarly, where a lease or other agreement for the use of land entered into before 30 November 1994 provided for a rent or royalty or some other sum to be calculated by reference to the turnover of a business, landfill tax is to be ignored in calculating turnover if it can reasonably be expected that such a provision would have been included had the agreement been entered into after that date (*FA 1996, Sch 5 para 47*). This ensures that the landlord of a landfill site does not benefit from the introduction of the tax and his rent will be based on what it would have been had landfill tax not been introduced (ignoring, of course, the behavioural changes that the tax aims to bring about).

**21.34** If the rate of landfill tax changes (including a change from no tax to tax becoming chargeable) after the making of a contract under which materials are to be landfilled, the contract is to be adjusted to reflect the landfill tax that actually falls to be paid (unless the contract provides otherwise). It is immaterial when the contract was made or whether or not it relates solely to the landfill or covers other things also (*FA 1996, Sch 5 para 45*).

## Environmental Bodies

**21.35** To encourage the restoration of the environment a landfill site operator is allowed to deduct from his landfill tax liability 90% of a contribution that he makes to a qualifying environmental body (*Reg 31, Landfill Tax Regulations 1996* (*SI 1996 No 1527*)). Not only can he deduct contributions during the quarter to which the return relates but he can also deduct contributions made in the month following the end of the quarter (but before the return for that quarter has been submitted). Prior to 1 January 2000 he could only deduct contributions made in the month following the end of his landfill tax year from the tax due in the last quarter of that year. He could not carry back contributions during the year. The total deductions for contributions during any one landfill tax year is limited to 20% of the tax payable (less any amount repayable) for the operator's tax year (*Reg 31(3)(7)*). From 1 January 2000 an operator can vary his landfill tax year (which by default ends on the anniversary of his registration) to bring it into line with his accounting year but can only do so once in any 24-month period.

**21.36** A person can still deduct from his landfill tax liability a payment that he makes to a qualifying environmental body if he does not bear the cost because it has been reimbursed by a contributing third party, i.e. a person who has made or agreed to make a payment to him to induce him to make a qualifying contribution or to reimburse in whole or in part a contribution he has made. From 1 January 2000, he needs to maintain and pass on to both ENTRUST (see 21.40) and the qualifying body specified details of contributing third parties. The qualifying body is deemed to have received the funds from the third party not from the company that makes the payment, although the third party itself is not entitled to a deduction for its contribution (*Reg 32*).

**21.37** A qualifying environmental body is a company, trust partnership or other incorporated body that meets the following conditions.

1. Its objects are (or include):

   (*a*) Reclamation, remediation, restoration or any other operation intended to facilitate economic, social or environmental use of any land the use (for such a purpose) of which has been prevented or restricted because of the previous carrying on of an activity on the land which has ceased.

(*b*) Carrying out operations to prevent or reduce the potential for pollution, or to remedy or mitigate the effects of pollution in relation to land which is (or may have become) polluted as a result of some activity previously carried out on it which has ceased.

(*c*) Research and development, education or the collection and dissemination of information either about:

(i) waste management practices in order to encourage the use of more sustainable waste management practices (including waste minimisation, minimisation of pollution and harm from waste, reuse of waste, water recovery activities and the clearing of pollutants from contaminated land), or

(ii) the development of products from waste or the development of markets for recycled waste in order to encourage the development or use of such waste.

(*d*) The provision, maintenance or improvement of a public park or other public amenity in the vicinity of a landfill site (other than one that is to be run with a view to profit) where it is for the protection of the environment, and is not work required by a planning or other statutory consent or under a *s 106, Town and Country Planning Act 1990* agreement.

(*e*) The maintenance, repair or restoration of a building which is either a place of religious worship or of historic or architectural interest, is open to the public, is not operated with a view to profit and is in the vicinity of a landfill site, where such work is for the protection of the environment.

(*f*) The provision of financial administration and other similar services to other qualifying environmental bodies (but not to anyone else).

An object does not however fall within head (*a*) or (*b*) if the operation to be carried out by the environmental body either is such that any benefit from it will accrue to any person who carried out or knowingly permitted the pollution, etc., involves work that is required to be carried out by an order under the *Control of Pollution Act 1974*, the *Environmental Protection Act 1990* or the *Water Resources Act 1991*, or which is wholly or partly required to be carried out under the terms of a planning or other statutory consent or an agreement under *s 106, Town and Country Planning Act 1990*. In other words, work can qualify only if there is no one else that can be required to do it or that has a vested interest in doing it.

2. It is precluded from distributing and does not distribute any of its profits or other income.

3. It applies any profit or other income to the furtherance of its objects (whether or not falling within (1) above).

4. It is precluded from applying any of its funds for the benefit of any of the persons who make qualifying contributions (i.e. those attracting a landfill tax deduction) to it or where qualifying third parties make contributions to these parties in relation to such contributions (except where those persons may benefit because they belong to a class of persons that benefits generally).

5. It is not controlled by one or more local authorities (or companies under local authority control) or by landfill site operators who are registered for landfill tax

6. It is not controlled by either:

   (*a*) one or more of a local authority, a company controlled by a local authority or authorities, a registered person, or a person connected with one of the above,

   (*b*) a person who was concerned in the management of another approved body whose approval has been revoked, a person convicted of an indictable offence, a person who is disqualified from being a trustee for a charity, or a person connected with any of them, or

   (*c*) a person who is incapable by reason of any mental disorder.

7. No one within 6(b) above is concerned in its management.

*Reg 33* as amended by *Reg 6, Landfill Tax (Amendment) Regulations 1999* (*SI 1999 No 3270*).

8. It has been approved by the regulatory body (see 21.39 below) and pays its required fee (which must not exceed £100).

**21.38** An approved body must apply its contributions only to approved objects, must not benefit (except incidentally) persons who have made contributions to it, must keep specified records and notify the regulatory body within seven days of any transfer of contributions to another approved body, must pay a fee of 5 per cent of all qualifying contributions to the regulatory body and must comply with other specified conditions (*Reg 33A* inserted by *Reg 7, Landfill Tax (Amendment) Regulations 1999* (*SI 1999, No 3270*).

**21.39** The use of contributions to pay running costs of the body is treated as use for a qualifying purpose but only if these do not exceed the proportion of qualifying contributions from landfill site operators (plus the income produced from such contributions) that such contributions bear to the total funds at the body's disposal, e.g. if an environmental body derives £100,000 of income from qualifying contributions and £50,000 from elsewhere, not more than two-thirds of the £100,000 can be used to meet running costs. The use of contributions to contribute towards the running costs of the regulatory body (see below) is also treated as a qualifying purpose.

**21.40** To qualify for a deduction the environmental body has to have been approved by a regulatory body – which is in turn approved by Customs. The regulatory body can charge an application fee to environmental bodies that seek approval and can require them to make a contribution to its running costs. It can give approval subject to conditions, including as to records and accounts. It can revoke approval at its discretion. It must maintain a register of approved bodies and their registered numbers which it must publish and keep up to date. Its main function though is to satisfy itself that the qualifying contributions received by an environmental body have been used only in the furtherance of its objects falling within head (1) above (*Reg 34*). Customs can only approve one regulatory body at any time. They can revoke the approval and appoint a different body in its place. If Customs revoke approval and do not approve a replacement body they must notify all the approved environmental bodies in advance that when the revocation takes effect Customs itself will take over the functions of the regulator. If they do not do so the approval of all the environmental bodies lapses on the revocation (*Regs 34(2) and 35*). Customs have approved a non-profit company, The Environmental Trust Scheme Regulatory Body Ltd (ENTRUST), for this purpose. By December 1997 Entrust has enrolled over 750 environmental bodies.

**21.41** A contribution to an approved environmental body qualifies for a landfill tax deduction only if it is made subject to a condition that the body will spend the sum paid and any income derived from it in the course or furtherance of its approved objects (i.e. objects within (1) in para 21.37). A transfer to another approved body subject to a condition that it will only use it for its approved objects is also permissible.

**21.42** If Customs believe that an approved environmental body has not spent a contribution or the income therefrom on its approved objects they have power to require the landfill site operator who claimed the deduction to pay over the tax he saved (*Reg 36(1)*). If a contribution is repaid to the contributor by the environmental body or by the contributor to a contributing third party he must account to Customs for the tax saved, i.e. repay to them 90% of the amount refunded (*Reg 36(3)* as amended by *Reg 10* of *Landfill Tax (Amendment) Regulations 1999* (*SI 1999 No 3720*)).

# Miscellaneous

## Is a Company the Best Vehicle?

**22.1** Many people considering property transactions automatically adopt a corporate vehicle. This is frequently a mistake. As much consideration ought to be given to the structure of a property transaction as to the carrying out of the transaction itself. There are two basic considerations; the protection of limited liability may be vital, but a company is an inefficient way to hold appreciating assets from a capital gains tax point of view and in many cases also increases the effective long-term rate of tax on income.

**22.2** To what extent is limited liability needed in a property situation? Clearly if a taxpayer buys land with his own funds which he will resell later without having carried out significant improvements, limited liability is unlikely to be very important. It is difficult to envisage any likelihood of sizeable liabilities ever arising. If part of the funds is borrowed, limited liability becomes of greater importance, but except where the price includes a substantial element of hope value, there may still be little risk that the property cannot be resold at a price that will at least cover the borrowings. Where a property is being developed there is a far greater element of risk and the protection of limited liability in such circumstances may well outweigh the tax disadvantages of holding an investment property in a corporate form. Obviously one needs to consider how real the limited liability is before opting for a corporate structure for protection. If the development is being wholly financed by an 'institution' and the developer is required to give personal guarantees to the institution it will be wholly illusory. If the developer has to give a personal guarantee to the main contractor a company may not be worthwhile to provide protection from other creditors as the amounts involved may be comparatively small.

**22.3** The capital gains tax problem is that if an appreciating asset such as a property is held through a company there are two levels of capital gains tax; an increase in value of the property will bring about an increase in the value of the shares in the company as well. This effectively means that in order to pass the gain through to the shareholders a total tax charge of up to 58% will be borne – 30% in the company and 28% (40% of the 70% left in the company after payment of the tax) at shareholder level. Indexation relief is a help to alleviate this burden but property investments very rarely increase in value in line with the retail prices index. Taper relief will significantly alleviate this problem where the property is a business asset though. If there is a spread of shareholdings the £7,700 CGT annual exemption may also alleviate the problem but this is frequently not of great significance in the context of increases in property values. These figures are a little exaggerated as in most cases the gain could be extracted even more cheaply as dividend than by way of a liquidation. Nevertheless, unless corporation tax is payable only at the 20% small companies rate (when the effective rate is 40%), in most cases the effective tax rate for a 40% taxpayer will be in the region of 48%, a significant increase on the 40% payable on a gain made directly by an individual.

**22.4** Some other factors that can influence the decision whether or not to use a company are the following.

(*a*) The taxpayer's objective. If he is trying to build up a vehicle that he can sell or float, the limited company is often the only practical form to adopt. However, if a likely purchaser for the building is a pension fund, a corporate form is not necessarily attractive. If he is trying to build up a 'pension fund' for his old age, personal ownership is likely to be more sensible to avoid two levels of tax on the income – where possible, ownership by a self-administered pension fund may be even better. If he is trying to build up assets for his children, a family trust may be the preferred solution.

(*b*) If the property transaction being entered into is a dealing transaction a company will probably pay tax at 30%. If the small companies rate applies this is 20% on the first slice of profits (£300,000 if the company has no associated companies) and an effective 32.75% on the next slice (up to £1.5 million if the company has no associated companies). In practice most property companies tend not to pay the small companies rate of tax. On the other hand, 60% of the profit available in personal hands, where it can be spent or invested as the taxpayer wishes, can often be of far greater use than 70% of it locked inside a company. Once a profit is made in a company the total effective tax rate to get it into personal hands increases to around 46.33% if the profit is extracted as salary. If it is extracted as dividend the effective total tax becomes 47.5% (more on profits suffering 32.75% corporation tax) and 40% on profits taxed at only 20% – although that assumes a very low profit for a property transaction). In most cases this extra tax burden in the longer term is likely to outweigh the benefit of the seven percentage point saving in the short term. It also needs to be borne in mind that, depending on the choice of accounting date, an unincorporated business can pay one-half of its tax up to almost nine months after the year end and the other half up to 15 months after it. To the extent that profits exceed those of the previous year, tax on the excess is payable up to nearly 21 months after the year end. With a company, the tax on undistributed profits and profits distributed as dividends is payable nine months after the year end with that on profits distributed as salary payable within a maximum of six weeks of the distribution. A further point to bear in mind is that trading losses of an individual can be set against other income. Although this also applies in a company an individual is more likely to have other income than a company. However, the changes to business asset taper relief have tipped the balance the other way if the shareholders are prepared to wait for their money. Property dealing is a trade. Accordingly, the shares in a property dealing company are business assets for taper relief purposes. Curiously the exclusion for a property or share dealing company that is normally made when granting tax reliefs for trading companies does not apply to taper relief. This means that if a property dealing company is set up now and the shares retained for two years the effective capital gains rate on a liquidation (or on extracting the funds using Extra-Statutory Concession C16) will be only 10%, giving an overall tax burden of 37% (30% corporation tax and 10% of the 70% post-tax profit). Taper relief for shares acquired before 6 April 2000 is more complicated. Whether or not they qualified for business asset taper depended on the size of the shareholding. Most shareholdings of under 25% will not have qualified as business assets under the original rules but will do so now. The effective tax rate on a disposal of such shares does not drop to 10% until 2010/11.

(*c*) A direct investment in a property by an individual attracts capital gains tax taper relief from 1998/99. This can be very attractive if the property is a business asset. As explained above the effective capital gains tax rate is only 10% once the property has been held for two years (four years for disposals before 6 April 2002). If the property is an investment property, i.e. it was acquired to let out not for use in the owner's business, taper relief is far less generous. The effective rate reduces to 25% but the full reduction is given only where the property has been held for 10 years (nine years if it was held at 17 March 1998). If the property is held in a company, although the shares will attract taper relief the property itself will not do so; it will attract indexation. Depending on the rate of inflation (and thus the indexation relief), the gain within the company, the potential tax which the purchaser will normally want to reflect in the price, is likely to be significantly greater than the taxable gain on the shares after taper relief. The reduction in the purchase price will therefore eliminate much of the benefit of the taper relief. It also needs to be borne in mind that if the company owns several properties the option of selling the shares rather than the property is unlikely to be available.

(*d*) Once an individual has been labelled as a property dealer it may be difficult to convince the Revenue that all future property transactions are not also dealing. Accordingly a decision to carry out dealing transactions as an individual should not be taken too lightly. On the other hand now that the tax rates on income and capital gains for an individual are the same, the only benefit of establishing a transaction as a capital gain is taper relief. Accordingly it is not unduly disadvantageous to be a dealer unless the property will be held for a number of years when the taper relief becomes significant. Indeed, it could be positively beneficial, as it is often easier to shelter income than capital gains and the tax is in any event payable later by a dealer.

A discretionary trust pays income tax at a maximum rate of 34%. A trust may therefore be a good vehicle for property dealing activities. A possible problem is that as trustees are personally liable for debts of the trust it may be difficult to find trustees willing to enter into such transactions. A trust can also be a sensible vehicle in which to hold property investments. It avoids the inheritance tax problems of appreciating assets being held by individuals and also avoids the double capital gains tax problem of a company.

(*e*) It is easier to spread value around one's family if a company is used as shares can readily be gifted. On the other hand, a trust is equally a very effective inheritance tax planning tool. A limited partnership can in some circumstances also be an attractive tax planning vehicle, as this can give children or trustees most of the tax benefits of trading as an individual without taking on the risks of unlimited liability.

(*f*) It should be remembered that interest payable by an individual or a trust is not deductible for CGT purposes. On the other hand it will be deductible in computing rental income in many cases. A company can set interest payments against its capital gains as deficits on loan relationships.

(*g*) Because the limited company is the normal form of business organisation in this country many bankers are reluctant to lend substantial sums of money to other types of organisation, particularly where the money is needed for general purposes, not to buy a specific property on which it can be secured. It may therefore sometimes be necessary to use a company in order to be able to raise finance regardless of whether or not this is a sensible structure from a tax viewpoint. This problem can sometimes be solved by drawing up a *pro forma* consolidated balance sheet for the whole of a person's business interests so that his banker can appreciate what his business activities embrace in a form with which he is familiar.

## Group Structures

**22.5** If a corporate structure is to be used, a subsidiary question that arises is, 'How many companies are needed?' In some cases it may also be desirable to keep certain companies or individual properties outside any form of group structure which is used for the main part of a person's property interests.

**22.6** The decision is likely to be very much influenced by the owner's individual circumstances. There is no 'best' structure for a group of property companies. There are, however, a number of basic principles that should be borne in mind. Dealing and investment activities should normally be segregated into separate companies. Although in theory a company can carry out both dealing and investment activities, it is in practice far more difficult to establish that a property that is sold at a substantial profit was bought as an investment if the company carries out dealing transactions than if it has never done so. There is something to be said for initially putting each investment property into a separate company. If one is sold shortly after purchase and the Revenue dispute that it was acquired as an investment, a relabelling of that property as a dealing property is unlikely to affect other properties, whereas if the company owning it also owned other properties the reclassification of one is likely to cast doubt on the status of the others. If, at the time of acquisition of a property, it is uncertain whether it will be retained or sold, there may be merit in putting it into a new property investment company to preserve as much flexibility as possible. It can also be commercially attractive to put developments into separate companies to isolate the development risk from other investments, although a large number of separate investment companies is unlikely to be attractive in the long term.

**22.7** There is not normally any tax advantage to be obtained by putting dealing properties in separate companies. Indeed, as there are restrictions in setting losses in one company against profits of another, it is not normally desirable to have more than one dealing company in a group.

**22.8** Another question to be asked is whether the companies should be grouped or whether each should be held direct by the shareholders. Direct holdings have the merit that one company can be sold and the proceeds passed direct to the ultimate shareholders. The main benefit of grouping is that losses/deficits on loan relationships and excess management expenses in one company can be set against profits of another in the same year under the group relief provisions. There may also be legal problems in one associated company pledging its assets to support borrowings by another, whereas if they are both members of a group there is far more commercial logic for doing so. The structure to adopt is likely to depend on the facts of each individual case. If in doubt, it is worth remembering that if companies start life as parallel, it is relatively easy to form them into a group at a later date without adverse tax consequences; if they start as members of a group it may be difficult, if not impossible, to separate them at a later date without a heavy tax charge on an unrealised profit, which would need to be funded from somewhere. It should also be borne in mind that the definition of a group for VAT purposes is different to that for corporation tax. It is possible for associated companies to register as a VAT group while remaining parallel companies for income and corporation tax purposes.

## Farming and Agricultural Land

**22.9** All farming and market gardening in the UK is to be treated as the carrying on of a trade and is therefore taxable under Case I of Schedule D (*ICTA 1988, s 53(1)*). All the farming – but not, apparently, market gardening – carried on by a single taxpayer must be treated as one trade (*ICTA 1988, s 53(2)*). Accordingly, if a farmer in, say, Somerset sells his farm and acquires a new farm in, say, Northumbria he will not have a cessation of one trade and a commencement of another. It is not clear what happens if there is a gap of several years between the sale of the first farm and the purchase of another. It is possible that the farming activities could be regarded as one continuing trade that was in suspension during the intervening period. The problem does not appear to have come before the courts. The Revenue normally contend that there is a cessation of trade and the later start of a new farming trade if the gap exceeds twelve months. In *Bispham v Eardiston Farming Co (1919) Ltd (40 TC 322)*, where a company operating two farms sold one of them, it was held that the *subsection* allowed losses on the farm sold to be carried forward against future profits from the retained one. From 29 November 1994 short rotation coppicing (see 16.1) is treated as farming (*FA 1995, s 154*). The status of such activities before that date is unclear.

**22.10** 'Farm land' means land in the UK wholly or mainly occupied for the purposes of husbandry but excluding any dwelling or domestic offices and excluding market garden land, and 'farming' is to be construed accordingly (*ICTA 1988, s 832(1)*). The meaning of husbandry is considered in 10.146 above. 'Market garden land' means land in the UK occupied as a nursery or garden for the sale of the produce (other than land used for the growth of hops), and 'market gardening' is to be construed accordingly (*ICTA 1988, s 832(1)*). In the past the Revenue generally accepted that two-thirds of the running costs of a farmhouse relate to business use and the balance to personal use. They are no longer prepared to do so; the split will be based on the facts of the case for each year (Tax Bulletin, Issue 6).

**22.11** A sum payable to an individual by virtue of a scheme under *Agriculture Act 1967, s 27* (grants for relinquishing occupation of uncommercial agricultural units) is specifically excluded from capital gains tax (*TCGA 1992, s 249*). It has been held that compensation for disturbance under *Agricultural Holdings Act 1948, s 34* is also not liable to capital gains tax (*Davis v Powell (51 TC 492)*). The Revenue regard grants under the Arable Payments Scheme as income, whether or not there is a set-aside requirement and, if there is, whether or not the set aside land is left fallow or is used to grow eligible non-food crops (Tax Bulletin, Issue 10, February 1994, page 108). They similarly regard 'SLOM compensation', which is paid by the European Community to certain milk producers unfairly deprived of milk quota because they were participating in an EC non-production of milk scheme in 1984, as income (Tax Bulletin, Issue 11, May 1994, page 126). Compensation paid for the loss of milk quota in June 1991 following a re-vamping of the quota scheme is, however, accepted as capital (Tax Bulletin, Issue 11, May 1994, page 127).

**22.12** The Revenue have agreed that under a share farming agreement based on the Country Landowners Association model, both parties can be regarded as carrying on a farming trade provided that the landowner takes an 'active' part in the venture, at least to the extent of concerning himself with details of farming policy and exercising his right to enter onto his land for some material purpose even if only for the purpose of inspection and policy making (CLA Press Release 19.12.1991). This means not only that the landowner's income will be taxable under Schedule D, Case I not Schedule A, but also that the landowner will qualify for capital gains tax roll-over relief, retirement relief and business asset taper relief. In share farming a landowner enters into a joint venture with an operator under which the operator farms the land and the two share the profit generated. If the landowner does not take an active part in the venture his share of the profit will be a receipt taxable under Schedule A and the land will probably not qualify for business asset taper relief.

**22.13** As mentioned in 16.1 the cultivation of short rotation coppicing is farming not forestry. The Revenue regard the initial cultivation of the land including spraying, ploughing, fencing and planting of the cuttings as capital. Costs following planting are revenue but direct costs such as weeding, disease prevention, harvesting and the cost of the first cut should be reflected in the annual stock valuation. Further details of the Revenue's views can be found in Tax Bulletin, Issue 19, October 1995.

**22.14** The ECJ has held that compensation paid to a farmer in return for an undertaking not to harvest at least 20% of his potato crop is not a supply for VAT purposes (*Landbuden-Agrardienste v Finanzamt (Case C–384/95) (1998 STC 171)*). This is because there is no consumption (and VAT is a general tax on consumption). The farmer does not supply goods or services to an identifiable consumer. Nor does he provide any benefit capable of constituting a cost component of the activity of some other person in the commercial chain. A similar result was reached in *Mohr v Finanzamt Bad Segeberg (Case C–215/94) (1996 STC 328)* in relation to milk quotas. See also 17.289.

**22.15** Customs and Excise have agreed some guidelines with the National Farmers Union in relation to VAT input tax recovery on repairs, maintenance, renovation, etc. of a farmhouse.

(*a*) In the case of a normal working farm where the VAT registered person is actively engaged in running it, 70% of the input tax can normally be claimed.

(*b*) In the case of an alteration, such as building an extension, the recoverable amount will depend on the purpose of the work. If the dominant purpose is a business one 70% can be claimed; if it is a personal one Customs would expect the claim to be 40% or less – possible none, depending on the circumstances.

(*c*) Where farming is not a full-time business and occupation of the VAT registered person the amount claimable will be significantly less. VAT tribunals have tended to adopt a figure between 10% and 30%.

(*d*) If the farming trade is carried on by a company and the occupant of the farmhouse is a director (or a connected person) only tax on supplies used for other than domestic purpose is claimable (see 17.297). Where a room is used partly for business a proportion can be recovered but only if suitable records are kept to justify the business portion being claimed.

(Business Brief 18/96). These are guidelines only. They are not binding on the taxpayer and will not necessarily be applied by Customs if the facts suggest a lower business element. When, in reliance on (*b*) above, Mrs Walthall and Mrs Crisp (*15976*) who formed a partnership claimed 40% of the tax on the conversion of a building within the curtilage of the farmhouse to form a residence for Mrs Walthall (under a planning consent that permitted it to be used only in connection with the residential part of the farmhouse) Customs restricted the claim to 10%. The VAT tribunal upheld this, although mainly on the basis that the facts put before it were so sparse that it was not possible for it to say that Customs were wrong. Customs' 10% figure was based on the fact that there was already a farmhouse on the land and the dominant purpose of the conversion appeared to be to provide a second residence, although it was accepted that some business activity was carried on from it.

## Mines, Quarries, etc.

**22.16** Profits or gains arising out of land are taxed under Case I of Schedule D – although they are not specifically to be treated as the carrying on of a trade – if they derive from one of the following 'concerns':

(*a*) mines and quarries (including gravel pits, sand pits and brickfields);

(*b*) ironworks, gasworks, salt springs or works, alum mines and works, and water works and streams of water;

(*c*) canals, inland navigations, docks, and drains or levels;

(*d*) fishings;

(*e*) rights of markets and fairs, tolls, bridges and ferries;

(*f*) railways and other ways; and

(*g*) other concerns of a like nature to those in (*b*) to (*e*) above.

(*ICTA 1988, s 55*).

**22.17** It has been held that the receipt by the owner of a foreshore of payments by a contractor to remove shingle did not constitute the carrying on of a 'concern' (*Duke of Fife's Trustees v Geo Wimpey & Co Ltd (1943 SC 377)*). Similarly, payments by a quarry-master for taking stone from spoil banks adjoining the quarry were held to be rents not payments for trading stock (*Craigenlow Quarries Ltd v CIR (32 TC 326)*). A farmer was held not to be carrying on a mining concern within *section 55* when he received from a mineral merchant payments for material excavated from old lead mining dumps on the farm (*Rogers v Longsdon (43 TC 231)*). Receipts from such activities are accordingly taxable under Schedule A.

**22.18** Rent payable in respect of any land or easement which is used, occupied or enjoyed in connection with one of the above concerns, or where the lease (or other agreement under which the rent is payable) provides for the recoupment of the rent by way of reduction of royalties or similar payments in the event of the land or easement being so occupied, is taxed under Schedule D not Schedule A (*ICTA 1988, s 119(1)*). The *subsection* does not specify a particular Case of Schedule D.

**22.19** If the rent is paid not in cash but in produce of the concern, the above provisions do not apply. Instead the market value of the produce received is to be treated as a receipt taxable under Case III of Schedule D (*ICTA 1988, s 119(2)*).

**22.20** For the purpose of *section 119* 'rent' includes a rent service, rentcharge, fee farm rent, feu duty, or other rent, toll, duty, royalty, or annual or periodical payment in the nature of rent, whether payable in money or money's worth or otherwise; and 'easement' includes any right, privilege or benefit in, over, or derived from, land (*ICTA 1988, s 119(3)*).

**22.21** If rights to work minerals in the UK are let for a year of assessment the lessor is entitled to deduct in calculating his rental income sums wholly, exclusively and necessarily disbursed by him as expenses of management or supervision of those minerals in that year to the extent that such sums have not otherwise been allowed as a deduction for income tax purposes (*ICTA 1988, s 121(1)*). It should be noted that the expenditure must have been necessarily incurred – which is far tighter than the normal Schedule D Case I test for deductibility. Similarly, a company is entitled to deduct any sums disbursed by it wholly, exclusively and necessarily as expenses of management or supervision of the minerals in the accounting period in computing its taxable income from the letting of rights to work minerals in the UK (*ICTA 1988, s 121(3)*).

**22.22** Prior to 1 May 1995 tax at the basic rate had to be deducted from the rent. This could be retained by the tenant to the extent that it was paid wholly out of profits or gains brought into charge to income tax. To the extent that it was not paid out of such income the tax deducted had to be paid over to the Revenue (*ICTA 1988, s 119(1), 348, 349*). This requirement was repealed by *FA 1995, s 145(1)*. Where the mineral rights were let, the tax deducted could be reclaimed to the extent that money was wholly exclusively and necessarily disbursed as expenses of management or supervision.

## Taxation of Mineral Royalties

**22.23** Where a person who is resident or ordinarily resident in the UK is entitled to receive mineral royalties under a mineral lease or agreement:

(*a*) only 50% of the royalties are chargeable to income tax (or corporation tax on income) and only 50% of any management expenses available for offset against the royalties can be deducted; and

(*b*) the other 50% of the royalties receivable under the lease in the year of assessment or accounting period is chargeable to capital gains tax (or corporation tax on chargeable gains).

(*ICTA 1988, s 122(1)(8)*).

**22.24** This provision overrides *ICTA 1988, s 119(1)* (see 22.18 above) with the exception that the requirement under that *subsection* for the payer to deduct income tax at the basic rate when making a royalty payment prior to 1 May 1995 still applied (*ICTA 1988, s 122(1)*). If the deduction exceeded the income tax payable the excess was set against the CGT liability and any balance repaid (*ICTA 1988, s 122(4)*). This did not apply where the recipient was chargeable to corporation tax, but the normal corporation tax rules (*ICTA 1988, s 7(2)*) gave the same result. The requirement to deduct tax at source was abolished by *FA 1995, s 145* so this provision for repayment is no longer relevant.

**22.25** For the purpose of this provision 'minerals' means all minerals and substances in or under land which are ordinarily worked for removal by underground or surface working, other than water, peat, top-soil and vegetation. A mineral lease or agreement means:

(*a*) a lease, profit *à prendre*, licence or other agreement conferring a right to win and work minerals in the UK;

(*b*) a contract for the sale, or a conveyance, of minerals in or under land in the UK; or

(*c*) a grant of a right under *Mines (Working Facilities and Support) Act 1966, s 1* (other than an ancillary right).

(*ICTA 1988, s 122(6)*).

**22.26** For the purpose of (*a*) in 22.23 above management expenses available for set-off against royalties are the sums brought into account as expenses of management or supervision under *ICTA 1988, s 121(1)(2)* (see 22.21 above) or, if the royalties are taxable under Schedule A, any sums deductible under the Schedule A rules in respect of management of the property concerned (*ICTA 1988, s 122(2)*). 'Mineral royalties' means so much of any rents, tolls, royalties and other periodical payments in the nature of rent payable under a mineral lease or agreement as relates to the winning and working of minerals. The Revenue are empowered to make regulations to provide whether and to what extent payments made under a mineral lease or agreement that relate only partly to the winning and working of minerals are to be treated as mineral royalties (*ICTA 1988, s 122(5)*). These regulations, the *Mineral Royalties (Tax) Regulations 1971*, limit the mineral royalty element to the royalty value of the land (excluding any buildings, etc. on it) on the basis that it could only be used for the working of minerals. The entire royalty can, however, be treated as a mineral royalty if at least 90% of it qualifies under this test.

**22.27** The amount taxed as a capital gain under (*b*) in 22.23 above is 50% of the gross royalties. No deduction can be made in calculating the gain for expenditure incurred (*ICTA 1988, s 122(3)*). Where a capital loss accrues during the currency of a mineral lease or agreement, the following special rules apply (*TCGA 1992, ss 202, 203*). They operate only where, on the expiry or termination of a mineral lease or agreement or on the disposal (or a deemed disposal under any provision of *TCGA 1992*) of the 'relevant interest' the person who immediately before the occurrence of that event was entitled to receive mineral royalties under the lease or agreement had an interest in the land to which that lease or agreement related (i.e. the relevant interest) (*TCGA 1992, ss 202, 203*). If the relevant event is the expiry or termination of the mineral lease or agreement, the taxpayer can elect to be treated for CGT (or corporation tax on chargeable gains) purposes as if he had disposed of and re-acquired the relevant interest at its market value. The election (or one under *para* 6, see below) must be made within six years of the relevant event and can only be made if an allowable capital loss will accrue to the taxpayer on this deemed disposal (*TCGA 1992, ss 202, 203*). Such loss is called 'the terminal loss'. The election cannot be made if the expiry or termination of the lease already gives rise to a *TCGA 1992* disposal. The terminal loss can either be treated as an allowable capital loss for the year of assessment or accounting period in which the lease or agreement expires, or be carried back and set against the capital gains element of the royalties received under the lease in years of assessment or accounting periods falling wholly or partly within the preceding 15 years. The election must specify which of these options the taxpayer wishes to adopt. If the relevant event was a *TCGA 1992* disposal of the relevant interest the taxpayer can similarly elect to spread it back over the previous 15 years. He cannot elect to treat it in any other way as it is, of course, already a capital loss for the current year under the normal *TCGA 1992* rules. If the election to carry back the loss is made, the loss is set against the gains of the latest possible years. The loss can only be carried back against the capital gains element of mineral royalties under the mineral lease or agreement in question. This probably prevents it being set against gains arising from a prior lease of the same site even if it was to the same operator. If the carry-back does not exhaust the loss the balance is treated as an allowable loss arising in the year of assessment in which the relevant event occurs (*TCGA 1992, ss 202, 203*).

## Rent in Respect of Electric Line, etc. Wayleaves

**22.28** Rent payable in the UK in respect of an easement enjoyed in the UK in connection with any electric, telegraphic, or telephonic wire or cable is also taxed on the recipient under Schedule D unless the recipient has Schedule A income, in which case the wayleave rent is included as a receipt of his Schedule A business (*ICTA 1988, s 120(1)(1A)*). Prior to 1997/98 it was always taxable under Schedule D. In addition it was required to be paid under deduction of tax. The payer could elect to make the payments gross if the rent for the easement did not exceed £2.50 p.a. (this figure remained unchanged since the provision was first enacted in 1950).

**22.29** If a wire or cable was used by the payer of the rent in carrying on a trade which includes the provision of a radio relay service, the rent was deductible as a trading expense despite *ICTA 1988, s 74(q)* (which prohibits the deduction of rents, etc. payable under deduction of tax), but the tax deducted had to be paid over to the Revenue even if the payer had taxable income to cover it (*ICTA 1988, s 120*).

**22.30** For the purpose of *section 120* the definitions of rent and easements in 22.20 above again apply; the reference to easements enjoyed in connection with any electric, telegraphic, or telephonic wire or cable includes easements enjoyed in connection with any pole or pylon supporting the wire or cable or in connection with any apparatus – such as a transformer – used in connection with any such wire or cable. Up to 1996/97 'radio relay service' meant the transmission by wire to their customers of broadcast programmes (including television) which the operator receives by wire or wireless from the BBC or from the persons outside the UK who broadcast the programmes in question (*ICTA 1988, s 120(5)*). The tax legislation did not recognise the existence of independent television! This definition is no longer needed as *section 120*, where it is used, does not apply for 1997/98 onwards.

## Tied Premises

**22.31** Rent receivable from the lessee of tied premises is treated as part of the lessor's trading receipts, not taxed under Schedule A or, if the property is outside the UK, Case V of Schedule D (*ICTA 1988, s 98(1)(2)(4)*). He can deduct as a trading expense any rent that he pays for those premises but cannot claim a deduction for notional rent payable where he owns the premises. Premises are tied for this purpose only if in the course of his trade the lessor is concerned (either as principal or agent) in the supply of goods sold or used on those premises and he deals with his interest in those premises as property employed for the purposes of that trade (*ICTA 1988, s 98(1)*).

**22.32** Where part of a property is tied and part not the rent received must be apportioned on a fair and just basis, the non-tied portion being taxable under Schedule A (*ICTA 1988, s 98(3)*). Prior to 17 March 1998, where a lease comprised both tied premises and other premises the Schedule A charge was first computed ignoring *section 98*, and the Schedule A liability was then reduced to eliminate the part attributable to the tied premises (*ICTA 1988, s 98(5)*). The purpose behind this somewhat strange procedure is not readily apparent but it has now been repealed. Prior to 17 March 1998 a lease was expressed to include an agreement for a lease if the term to be covered by the lease had started. It also included any tenancy but did not include a mortgage

(*ICTA 1988, s 98(8)*). If the person carrying on a trade was entitled in equity to the interest of a lessor of the premises he is to be treated as if he were himself the lessor and as if the rent were receivable by him (*ICTA 1988, s 98(7)*). He was also to be treated as owning the non-tied land for the purpose of applying *subsections (4), (5)* and *(6)*. From 17 March 1998 the statutory reference to a lessor has been replaced by a person having an estate or interest in the premises, which is wide enough to embrace all such interests.

**22.33** The trader is also treated for capital gains tax roll-over relief purposes as occupying as well as using the premises for the purposes of his trade (*TCGA 1992, s 156(4)*).

## Other Occupation of Land

**22.34** The occupation of land in the UK (other than for farming or market gardening) is treated as the carrying on of a trade taxable under Case 1 of Schedule D if the land is managed on a commercial basis and with a view to the realisation of profits, unless the land comprises woodlands or is being prepared for use for forestry purposes (*ICTA 1988, s 53(3)(4)*).

## Housing Associations, etc

**22.35** Special rules apply to approved co-operative housing associations. The rent received from members is ignored and interest payable by the association is apportioned amongst the members who were tenants during the year and deemed to be payable by them personally – so that they can claim relief for such interest against their personal incomes. There is also an exemption from corporation tax on capital gains on the sale of a property which was occupied by a tenant of the association. The detailed rules and the conditions for approval are not considered here. They can be found in *ICTA 1988, s 488*.

**22.36** An approved self-build society is similarly exempted from tax on its rents and on chargeable gains accruing on the disposal of land to a member of the society. The conditions for approval and the detailed rules are contained in *ICTA 1988, s 489*.

**22.37** Special rules also apply to chargeable gains arising on a disposal of land between the Housing Corporation, Housing for Wales or Scottish Homes and a housing society. The sale is deemed to take place at such a price as would secure that neither a gain nor a loss accrues on the disposal (*TCGA 1992, s 218*). This also applies where the Housing Corporation, etc. disposes of land to a registered housing association, one registered housing association disposes of land to another, or a registered housing association or unregistered self-build society disposes of land to the Housing Corporation, etc. (*TCGA 1992, s 219*).

## Housing Grants

**22.38** A grant or other contribution to expenses made to any person under any enactment relating to the giving of financial assistance for the provision, maintenance, or improvement of housing accommodation or other residential accommodation is not to be treated as a receipt in computing income for any tax purpose (except to the extent that it is made in respect of expenditure which gives rise to a deduction) (*ICTA 1988, s 578*). Such a receipt may of course still be within the scope of capital gains tax.

## Annual Value of Land

**22.39** For income and corporation tax purposes the 'annual value' of land is the rent which might reasonably be expected to be obtained on a letting from year to year if the tenant undertook to pay all usual tenant's rates and taxes and if the landlord undertook to bear the cost of repairs and insurance and any other expenses necessary for maintaining the subject of the valuation in a state to command that rent (*ICTA 1988, s 837(1)*). *Section 23* of the *General Rate Act 1967* (adjustment of gross value by reference to provision of, or payment for, services, etc.) applies for this purpose as if it extended to the whole of the UK not merely England and Wales (*ICTA 1988, 837(2)*).

**22.40** As this definition is the same as that of gross value for rating purposes, the gross rateable value is normally adopted by the Revenue as the value under *section 837*. The last rating revaluation for non-domestic properties was based on rental values at 1 April 1998. Houses and other domestic properties have not been subject to rates since 1 April 1989. Where the property was in existence at that date the Revenue still seem content to use the old rateable value which is actually the value in 1973 terms (1985 in Scotland). Certain concessions were made in Scotland to limit the effect of the 1985 revaluation. (Inland Revenue Press Releases, 23 July 1985 and 22 November 1985). Where a residential property does not have a rateable value, they will estimate what that value would have been had rating continued (Inland Revenue Press Release, 19 April 1990).

## Meaning of United Kingdom

**22.41** The UK means Great Britain and Northern Ireland (*Interpretation Act 1978, Sch 1*). For all income tax, capital gains tax and corporation tax purposes the territorial sea of the UK is also deemed to be part of the UK (*TCGA 1992, s 276(1)*; *ICTA 1988, s 830(1)*). For certain purposes any 'designated area' under *Continental Shelf Act 1964, s 1(7)* is treated as UK property (*TCGA 1992, s 276(3)–(8)*; *ICTA 1988, s 830(2)–(5)*). This is intended to enable the UK to tax North Sea oil profits.

## Meaning of Land

**22.42** Land includes buildings and other structures, land covered with water, and any estate, interest, easement, servitude or right in or over land (*Interpretation Act 1978, Sch 1*). For CGT purposes 'land' includes messuages, tenements, and hereditaments, houses and buildings of any tenure (*TCGA 1992, s 288(1)*). This extends the above definition; it does not displace it. For inheritance tax, 'land' is expressed to exclude any estate, interest or right by way of mortgage or other security (*IHTA 1984, s 284*). Again this definition does not displace the *Interpretation Act* definition but supplements it.

## Special Provisions Affecting Property Dealers

**22.43** In computing the profits of a property dealer so much of the cost of woodland in the UK which are purchased in the course of his trade as is attributable to trees or saleable underwood growing on the land is to be disregarded. The part of the sale proceeds attributable to such trees is also disregarded if they have not been felled by the time the land is sold (*ICTA 1988, s 99(1)* – see 16.2 above).

**22.44** Where a property dealer is taxed under *ICTA 1988, s 34(1),(4)* or *(5)* (see 3.2–3.8 above) in respect of a premium received in relation to a lease of land which forms part of his trading stock the amount on which tax is so charged is excluded from his trading receipts (*ICTA 1988, s 99(2)*). Any amount taxed under *ICTA 1988, s 35* or *36* (see 3.13–3.22 above) is similarly excluded from trading receipts. If part of the tax assessed under *ICTA 1988, s 36* is repaid by virtue of a claim under *ICTA 1988, s 36(2)(b)* (see 3.20 above) the trading profits for the year in which the deemed premium was received – not that in which the claim is made – must be recomputed to exclude only the reduced figure (*ICTA 1988, s 99(3)*).

**22.45** Except where he has trading losses brought forward – which cannot be set against Schedule A income – it is accordingly generally of little concern to a trader to grant a lease within *sections 34–36* as the aggregate of the Schedule A and Case I assessments will equal the Case I assessment that would otherwise have arisen if no part of the premium had been taxable. As a lessee can obtain relief in certain circumstances where part of a premium is taxable on the landlord (see

12.45 above) a property dealer may well be able to obtain a better price for the sale of a short lease that he holds if he grants a sublease for the term less one day than if he assigns the lease itself.

## Sch E Charge on Occupation of Living Accommodation

**22.46** Where a person (or members of his family or household) is provided with living accommodation by reason of his employment he is treated as if he had received additional salary equal to the value to him of the accommodation for the period for which it is provided, less so much as is properly attributable to the accommodation of any sum made good by him to the person providing the accommodation (e.g. the rent, if any, that he pays) (*ICTA 1988, s 145*). The value of the accommodation is the greater of the annual value under *ICTA 1988, s 837* (see 22.39 above) or the rent payable for the accommodation by the person providing it (who will, of course, normally be the employer) (*ICTA 1988, s 145(2)*). In practice the charge under *section 145* is normally based on the gross rateable value of the property, which is far below the current rental value as it is the rental value in 1973. Special rules apply in Scotland where there was a rating revaluation in 1985. Where a property does not have a rateable value, e.g. because it was built or substantially altered after 1 April 1989, the employer is expected to provide an estimate of what that value would have been had rating continued. The annual value will then be agreed with the District Valuer on that basis (Inland Revenue Press Release, 19 April 1990). This probably means what the value would have been had the building existed in that state at 1 April 1973, although this is not clear from the Press Release.

**22.47** The charge is restricted to the extent that a claim could be made under *ICTA 1988, ss 198* or *332(3)* (allowable expenses of an employment) in respect of business use of the premises. No charge at all will arise if the employee is in 'representative occupation', i.e. where either:

(*a*) it is necessary for the proper performance of the employee's duties that he should reside in the accommodation;

(*b*) the accommodation is provided for the better performance of the duties of the employment, and it is employment of a kind in which it is customary for employers to provide accommodation for employees; or

(*c*) there is a special threat to the employee's security and he resides in the accommodation as part of special security arrangements.

(*ICTA 1988, s 145(4)*).

**22.48** A company director cannot come within (*a*) or (*b*) above if he owns a material interest in the company; or if his employment is not as a full-time working director (unless the company is non profit-making or is established for charitable purposes only) (*ICTA 1988, s 145(5)*).

**22.49** If the employee is a director or is in higher-paid employment he is also taxable as remuneration on the whole of any expenses in relation to the property borne by the employer or some other person, including rates, utilities, repairs and maintenance. Where, however, he is in representative occupation, no charge arises in respect of rates (*ICTA 1988, s 145(4)*) and the aggregate charge in respect of heating, lighting, cleaning, repairs, maintenance, decoration and the provision of furniture and other effects which are normal for domestic occupation is limited to 10% of the employee's salary less certain deductions (*ICTA 1988, s 163*). The Revenue have said that the exemption for rates also applies to council tax (IR Press Release, 16 March 1993). From 30 November 1993 this concession also applies for national insurance purposes (DSS Press Release, 9 November 1993). As stated at 15.4 above, the Inland Revenue consider that, in the majority of cases, where a UK house is owned by an overseas company but occupied by a UK resident the UK resident is likely to be a shadow director of the company (irrespective of whether or not the company is owned by trustees). Such a claim, if successful, will bring these provisions and, more importantly, *section 146* (see 22.51 below) into play. There may well be a similar risk where a UK property is occupied by a person who is non-UK resident – as the benefit could be taxable as UK source income.

**22.50** If the employer pays the employee's council tax the full amount is assessable as a benefit, and a payment in respect of council tax following a move to a more expensive housing area cannot attract relief under Inland Revenue Extra-Statutory Concession A67. Reimbursement of council tax on a second home where that is temporary accommodation while the employee is working away from home will not necessarily give rise to a benefit though. The same principle applied to the community charge (ICAEW Technical Release TR 795, 14 June 1990 and IR Press Release, 16 March 1993).

**22.51** Where a charge in relation to the use of accommodation arises under *section 145* (or would arise if the employee paid no rent for the use of the accommodation) and the cost of providing it exceeds £75,000, an additional Schedule E charge also arises. This is the rent which would have been payable for the period of occupation if the premises had been let to the employee at an annual rent equal to the appropriate percentage of the amount by which the cost of providing the accommodation exceeds £75,000 (*ICTA 1988, s 146(3)*). The appropriate percentage is the rate of interest prescribed for beneficial loans at the beginning of the year of assessment in question (*ICTA 1988, s 146(11)*). This is 5% for 2002/03. For earlier years it was 14.5% for 1989/90, 15.5% for 1990/91, 13.5% for 1991/92, 10.75% for 1992/93,

7.75% for 1993/94, 7.5% for 1994/95, 8% for 1995/96, 7.25% for 1996/97, 6.75% for 1997/98, 7.25% for 1998/99 and 6.25% for 1999/00 to 2001/02. The cost of providing the accommodation is the expenditure on acquiring the property (i.e. the estate or interest in the property held by the person providing the accommodation) plus any expenditure on improvements to it prior to the start of the year of assessment (*ICTA 1988, s 146(4)*). If the employee reimburses all or part of the cost of the property or of the improvements or pays a premium for a grant of a tenancy of the premises, the amount reimbursed or paid is deducted (*ICTA 1988, s 146(5)*). Where the employee pays rent that rent is deductible from the amount of the *section 146* charge to the extent that it exceeds that under *section 145 (ICTA 1988, s 146(2)*).

*Example 44*

Norman was provided throughout 2001/02 with the use of a London flat by his employer, Opeequeue Ltd at a rent of £2,000 p.a. The gross rateable value is £1,500. The flat cost £100,000. In 1991/92 Opeequeue carried out improvements at a cost of £24,000. As part of the work was done at Norman's insistence he agreed to reimburse one-third of the cost of such works.

Norman's assessable benefit in kind for 2001/02 is

| | £ | £ | £ |
|---|---|---|---|
| *Charge under ICTA 1988, s 145* | | | |
| annual value | 1,500 | | |
| less rent paid by Norman | 2,000 | Nil | |
| *Charge under ICTA 1988, s 146* | | | |
| Cost of flat | 100,000 | | |
| Cost of improvements | 24,000 | | |
| | 124,000 | | |
| *Less* reimbursement by Norman | 8,000 | | |
| | 116,000 | | |
| *Less* first £75,000 | 75,000 | | |
| | £41,000 | | |
| 6.25% thereof | | | 2,562 |
| *Less* rent paid by Norman | | 2,000 | |
| *Less* set against *section 145* charge | | 1,500 | 500 |
| Assessable benefit | | | £2,062 |

**22.52** If the property was held by either the person providing the accommodation, the employee's employer or any connected person (within *ICTA 1988, s 839* – see Appendix 1) of either, throughout the six years prior to the time that the employee first occupied the property (and this was after 30 March 1983), the value of the accommodation will be the market value of the property at the date of such first occupation plus expenditure on improvements since that date (*ICTA 1988, s 146(6)–(8)*). The market value for this purpose is the price which the property might reasonably be expected to fetch on a sale in the open market with vacant possession, no reduction being made in estimating the market value on account of any option in respect of the property held by the employee or a person connected with him or by the employer or a connected person (within *ICTA 1988, s 839*) of the employer or, if different, of the person providing the accommodation (*ICTA 1988, s 146(11)*).

**22.53** If the employer provides more than one property to the employee, the £75,000 threshold is applied separately to each property. Prior to 1988/89 the Revenue considered that the limit applied to the aggregate cost. Under *ICTA 1988, s 206* any assessment raised late for years prior to 1988/89 will be based on the Revenue's previous approach (Inland Revenue Press Release, 22 November 1990).

**22.54** The charge under *ICTA 1988, s 146* can be reduced by a claim for business use under *ICTA 1988, ss 198* or *332(3)* to the extent to which the relief exceeds the charge under *section 145* (*ICTA 1988, s 146(9)*).

**22.55** It is arguable that if a property is owned jointly by the company and the employee no charge can arise under *section 145* as living accommodation is not 'provided for' the employee – he is already entitled to occupy the property by virtue of his joint ownership. No charge will arise under *section 146* either as it is a precondition of that *section* that *section 145* already applies. For 1996/97 onwards *sections 145* and *146* apply even if the provision of accommodation is taxable under some other provision, but the tax charge under that other provision is then limited to any excess over the *section 145* and *146* charge (*ICTA 1988, s 146A* introduced by *FA 1996, s 106*). This prevents the application of the *Heaton v Bell (46 TC 211)* principle under which it might have been contended that no charge could arise under *section 145* if the employee takes a small salary reduction in return for the right to live in the house, with the ability to increase the salary by surrendering the right.

**22.56** Where an interest in premises belongs to a charity or an ecclesiastical corporation and in right of that interest a person (or persons) holding a full-time office as clergyman or minister of any religious denomination has a residence in those premises from which to perform the duties of the office, the following special rules apply to determine the amount of the emoluments assessable on the clergyman under Schedule E:

(*a*) the making good to him as holder of the office of statutory amounts payable in connection with the premises or statutory deductions falling to be made in connection with them are to be disregarded except to the extent, if any, to which they are attributable to a part of the premises in respect of which he receives rent;

(*b*) so is the payment on his behalf (except as in (*a*)) of any such statutory amounts;

(*c*) unless he is in director's or higher-paid employment, expenses incurred in connection with the provision in the premises of living accommodation for him are to be disregarded provided that they are incurred in consequence of his being the holder of the office;

(*d*) 25% of any expenses borne by him on maintenance, repairs, insurance or management of the premises can be deducted from his salary; and

(*e*) if he rents a dwelling-house any part of which is used mainly or substantially for the purposes of his duty as clergyman, up to 25% of the rent can be deducted from his salary.

(*ICTA 1988, s 332*).

**22.57** When considering the provision of living accommodation by a company for a major shareholder the capital gains tax position also needs to be borne in mind. The company is not entitled to the benefit of the private residence exemption and a company is in general an undesirable vehicle for holding investment property because of the double capital gains tax effect. The CGT indexation allowance is some help but house prices tend not to rise in line with inflation. Some people feel that the problem can be overcome by granting the employee an option to buy the house at a future date at its current value. They contend that such an option has no – or very little – value at the time it is granted and that when it *is* exercised the benefit is obtained *qua* option holder not *qua* employee. The author is sceptical as to both of these claims. Many property dealers would in all probability be prepared to pay a substantial sum in 2002 for an option to buy for £100,000 at any time prior to, say, the year 2012 a house which is worth £100,000 in 2002. If such an option is given to a director for no consideration the author considers that its value would be a perquisite of the employment taxable under *ICTA 1988, s 131*. It is also felt that the benefit obtained when the option is exercised is obtained by reason of the employment and is thus taxable under the benefit in kind provisions (see *Cheatle v CIR (56 TC 111)*).

## Valuation

**22.58** If the matter in dispute on an appeal in relation to capital gains tax or corporation tax on chargeable gains relates to or includes the question of the value of land or of a lease of land that question must be decided by the appropriate Lands Tribunal (not by the Special or General Commissioners) if the land is in the UK (*TMA 1970, s 47*). If the land is not in the UK jurisdiction apparently remains with the Commissioners. Curiously, it appears that where a question as to the value of land arises in an appeal in relation to income tax or corporation tax on income it must be decided by the Commissioners – who do not seem to have power even to refer it to the Lands Tribunal for assistance. Indeed it is specifically provided that any question as to the 'annual value' (see 22.39 above) of land is to be determined by the General Commissioners (*ICTA 1988, s 837(3)*). This appears to preclude this being considered by the Special Commissioners, which seems very strange. Where there is no right of appeal to the Lands Tribunal a reference by consent can be made under *section 1(5)* of the *Lands Tribunal Act 1949*. The Revenue have said that for stamp duty purposes they will normally consent but where questions of both law and valuation arise in relation to an appeal they would wish to resolve the legal issue prior to any determination of value by the Lands Tribunal (Tax Bulletin, Issue 18, August 1995). It seems likely that they would similarly normally agree to a reference in other valuation issues. Inheritance tax appeals on the question of the value of land are made to the Lands Tribunal. If the value of the land is relevant to the settlement of a dispute before the Special Commissioners or the High Court they must refer the valuation questions to the Lands Tribunal (*IHTA 1984, s 222* as amended by *FA 1993, s 200*). Before that date the taxpayer had to run two appeals, to the Commissioners and to the Lands Tribunal, with it being unclear how the two interacted. This problem was highlighted in *Alexander v CIR (1991 STC 112)* – see 22.61.

**22.59** For CGT purposes the 'market value' of an asset is the price that it might reasonably be expected to fetch on a sale in the open market. In estimating such value no reduction is to be made on account of the estimate being made on the assumption that the whole of the assets are to be placed on the market at one and the same time (*TCGA 1992, s 272(1)(2)*). However, if inheritance tax is chargeable on a person's death (on his personal estate) and the value of an asset forming part of his estate has been ascertained for inheritance tax purposes, the value so ascertained must be taken as the market value for capital gains tax purposes at the date of death (*TCGA 1992, s 274*). The Inland Revenue consider that a value has not been 'ascertained' where the 100% business property relief applies. It is arguable whether this is right as the relief takes the form of a deduction and it is questionable whether a deduction can be made from an unascertained amount. They have also expressed the view that if an asset is wholly exempt or relieved from IHT neither the deceased's personal representative nor the Revenue can require the value to be ascertained. Even where tax is payable they also see a distinction between their 'considering' the value and its being ascertained (Tax Bulletin, Issue 16, April 1995). It seems unreasonable that a person's CGT liability should vary dependent on whether the Revenue choose to ascertain a different person's liability, or to merely consider it, or to simply ignore it because it does not affect the amount of a tax liability. Nevertheless their view has found favour with the Special Commissioners in *Stonor v CIR (2001 STC (SCD) 199, SpC 288)*, where the view was expressed that, for a value to be ascertained there is an implication that some formality or agreement is required and also that if a transfer of value is exempt (in that case as a gift to charity), tax was not 'chargeable'. That case was concerned primarily with *s 191, IHTA 1984* (see 18.37), not *section 274* though. When considering a 5 April 1965 or 1 March 1982 valuation, the asset needs to be valued as it stood at the relevant date. This is not always easy to ascertain as is apparent from the case of *Henderson v Karmel's Exors (58 TC 201)* which is considered at 11.73.

**22.60** The Revenue take the view that the inheritance tax decision in *Lady Fox's Exors v CIR (1994 STC 360)* (see 22.64) applies equally for capital gains tax where the statutory hypothesis on which the valuation is based deems the assets to be disposed of together, e.g. an acquisition of assets by personal representatives under *TCGA 1992, s 62*, or a beneficiary of a trust becoming absolutely entitled to the settled property under *TCGA 1992, s 71(1)*. Where the statutory hypothesis requires the disposal of a number of single assets, e.g. rebasing to 6 April 1965 (see *Henderson v Karmel's Exors (58 TC 201)* at 11.72) or 31 March 1992, or a non-arm's-length disposal under *TCGA 1992, s 17*, each asset must be valued separately (Tax Bulletin 24, Aug 1996).

**22.61** Market value for inheritance tax is the price that the property might reasonably be expected to fetch if sold in the open market at the time it falls to be valued. That price must not be assumed to be reduced on the ground that the whole property is to be placed on the market at one and the same time (*IHTA 1984, s 160*). In an estate duty case (the forerunner of inheritance tax) it was held that knowledge of local conditions and requirements – including the existence of a 'special purchaser', i.e. someone who has a special reason for wanting the property and would be prepared to pay above market value to get it – are factors properly to be taken into account in determining the open market value of a house (*CIR v Clay (1914–15 All ER 882)*). In another estate duty case it was held that a large estate should be divided into its natural units for valuation purposes if such 'lotting' would produce a greater aggregate value than if the entire estate were placed on the market at the same time (*Duke of Buccleuch & Another v CIR (1967 All ER 129)*). If a property acquired under the 'right to buy' provisions of the *Housing Act 1980* falls to be valued for inheritance tax purposes during the period in which repayment of part of the discount would be triggered by a sale, it must be assumed that the hypothetical purchaser could acquire the property without triggering any repayment, but would acquire it subject to having to make the repayment if he were to resell it during the five-year period, i.e. he will stand in the shoes of the previous owner (*Alexander v CIR (1991 STC 112)*). As the open market would include potential occupiers as purchasers it seems unlikely that the value on that assumption would be much below the market value shorn of any obligation to repay. In *Alexander* the District Valuer was prepared to accept a discount of around 20% because he found that 75% of purchasers of flats in the block concerned resold within two to six years of purchase. The Lands Tribunal held in *Executors of G A Baird v CIR* (14 June 1990) that a non-assignable agricultural tenancy has a value. The District Valuer assessed this at 25% of vacant possession value. This was accepted by the tribunal as no alternative value (other than nil) had been put forward by the taxpayer. In the circumstances it should not necessarily be taken as indicative of the value of such a tenancy in other cases, particularly as it was effectively rejected by the Court of Appeal in the *Walton* case considered below.

**22.62** It is important to identify correctly what needs to be valued. In *Walton decd v CIR (1995 STC 68)* the deceased held a one-third interest in a farm which was let under an agricultural tenancy to a farming partnership of which the deceased and his son were the partners sharing equally. The vacant possession value of the farm was agreed at £400,000 and the value of the freehold subject to the tenancy at £150,000. In dispute was the value of the partnership's tenancy. The Revenue valued this at half the marriage value, namely £130,000. It was held to be the profit rent to the next rent review, a mere £12,645. This was because the value of a tenancy depends on the circumstances of the parties. The marriage value could be realised only if the landlord wished to obtain vacant possession at an early date and the tenant was prepared to stop farming the land. Although the buyer and seller are hypothetical it is not necessary for the operation of the statutory hypothesis of a sale in the open market of an interest in a tenancy that the landlord should be a hypothetical person, and similarly regard should be had to the actual intention of the actual surviving partner, not to a hypothetical partner. A purchaser of the deceased's interest in the partnership could not unlock the marriage value without the consent not only of the other partner but also of the freeholders.

**22.63** Normally what has to be ascertained for inheritance tax purposes is the fall in value of a person's estate. Where part only of an asset is disposed of this is effectively the difference between the value of the asset concerned prior to the disposal and its value after the disposal. For example, if the owner of a freehold property gifts a 20-year lease, what needs to be valued is not the 20-year lease but the freehold and the freehold reversion on the lease, the difference between the two being the reduction in the donor's estate. Where the value of any property comprised in a person's estate would be less than the appropriate portion of the value of it and any related property, its value must be taken to be the appropriate portion of that aggregate (*IHTA 1984, s 161(1)*). Property is related if it is owned by the transferor's spouse or if it has within the previous five years been owned by a charity or a National Heritage body and was gifted to it by the transferor (or spouse) by way of an exempt transfer (*IHTA 1984,* *s 161*). If other assets owned by the transferor himself affect the value of what is being transferred, they are not related property but are automatically taken into account as such in determining the value being transferred.

*Example 45*

Roger owns a freehold field worth £10,000 together with a lease worth £3,000 of an adjoining field. His wife, Rita, owns the freehold reversion on the second field valued at £5,000. The unencumbered freehold of the second is worth £10,000. Roger transfers his freehold field to a discretionary settlement. The value of the two fields together would be £25,000 if they had both been freehold.

| | £ | £ |
|---|---|---|
| The amount of the gift is | | |
| Value of 2 freehold fields | | 25,000 |
| Value of field settled | 10,000 | |
| Value of lease of other field owned by Roger | 3,000 | |
| Value of reversion owned by Rita | 5,000 | |
| | £18,000 | |
| Value of assets in Roger's estate prior to gift 13/18ths of £25,000 | 18,056 | |
| Value of assets in Roger's estate after gift 3/8ths of £10,000 (value of second field) | 3,750 | |
| | £14,306 | |

**22.64** In *Lady Fox's Exors v CIR (1994 STC 360)* the Court of Appeal held that the hypothetical sale must be supposed to take the course which would get the largest possible price provided that does not entail undue expenditure of time and effort. Lady Fox had a 92.5% interest in a farming partnership and also held the freehold reversion in the land that was subject to the partnership's agricultural tenancy. It was held that the two should be valued as a package.

**22.65** For inheritance tax purposes, where the right to dispose of any property has been excluded or restricted by a contract made at any time, that exclusion or restriction is to be ignored in valuing the property except to the extent that consideration in money or money's worth was given for the restriction. If the contract was itself a chargeable transfer an allowance will be given against the inheritance tax on the transfer of the property for the value transferred by the prior contract (*IHTA 1984, s 163*).

**22.66** In valuing for inheritance tax purposes agricultural property that includes cottages occupied by persons who are employed solely for agricultural purposes in connection with that property, any additional value attributable to the fact that they might also be suitable for residential occupation generally is to be ignored (*IHTA 1984, s 169*).

**22.67** The Law Society have discussed with the Revenue the valuation of agricultural tenancies. The Revenue's normal approach is to adopt a percentage of the vacant possession value. In arriving at the value, account needs to be taken of the benefits attaching to the tenancy, such as residential accommodation, compensation for disturbance, improvements, manurial rights, together with any favourable level of the rent, the consideration of who might be in the hypothetical market for the tenancy, and the principle that there should be no automatic presumption that the value of a tenancy could be arrived at by a method based on a standard percentage of the vacant possession premium or value. If the taxpayer believes that the likelihood or otherwise of a bid by the landlord is a factor to take into account, he should adduce evidence of this at an early stage (Law Society's Gazette 18.3.1992). The statement of course predates the *Walton* decision (see 22.62).

**22.68** The Revenue operate a sampling scheme, the Multiple Land Valuation scheme, where a taxpayer disposes of 30 or more interests in land in an accounting period or year of assessment. For this purpose a group of companies is regarded as a single taxpayer. The scheme is operated by a special unit, the Capital Gains Tax Sampling Unit (CGTSU). The CGTSU selects a sample – usually between 25% and 50% of the properties — and refers these to the local District Valuers. The CGTSU will then discuss the DVs' valuations with the taxpayer, and reach agreement on those valuations. Based on the changes, if any, to the taxpayer's figures in respect of those valuations the CGTSU may suggest changes to the valuations of non-sampled properties, if the sample produces a reliable pattern of differences. If it does not, the sample may be enlarged – up to 100% if all the valuations look suspect – and non-sampled properties that appear to give rise to particular difficulties may also be valued individually. If the valuations of the sampled properties support the taxpayer's valuations the remainder may of course be accepted unchallenged (Tax Bulletin, Issue 12, August 1994).

**22.69** Where property is held jointly the Revenue normally accept a discount of 10% in valuing one of two joint interests. This derives from the 1917 decision of *Cust v CIR (91 EG 11)*. In the 1982 decision in *Wight and Moss v CIR (264 EG 935)* a deduction of 15% was given. The Valuation Office Agency Manual indicates that the deduction should normally be 10% as it is highly likely that an order for sale would be granted but a 15% discount would be appropriate where an order is less likely such as:

(i) where it would involve displacing a co-owner entitled to possession, or

(ii) where the purpose of the trust for sale has not been fulfilled but is still capable of being fulfilled.

(Valuation Office IHT Manual, para 4.3)

## Interest on Compulsory Purchase

**22.70** Where property is compulsorily acquired it frequently takes months or even years to agree the compensation payable. Interest on the compensation is payable from the date the authority enters on to the land. Such interest is not income for income tax purposes until it is received. However, when it is received the whole amount is taxable as income of the year of receipt even though the figure may represent interest for several years. This can adversely affect the tax payable and needs to be watched. The Revenue adopt the view that the taxpayer can avoid the problem by asking for an interim payment on account of the compensation, and if he does not do so he must accept any resultant distortion of his tax position. For corporation tax interest is recognised on an accruals basis from 1 April 1996 so this is no longer a problem for companies.

## Transactions at Other than Market Value

**22.71** For capital gains tax purposes, transactions between connected persons (see *TCGA 1992, s 286*) are treated as made other than by way of bargains made at arm's length (*TCGA 1992, ss 17(1)(a), 18*) and therefore must be deemed to be at market value. The legislation clearly envisages a distinction between the two, so it is undoubtedly possible to have a transaction which is not between connected persons and is nevertheless not at arm's length. Indeed, the Revenue may well draw an inference that any transaction not at market value is not at arm's length. Having said that, the market price of a site is what an arm's-length purchaser will pay for it, and in the absence of any indication to the contrary the price paid by a non-connected purchaser could well be the market price of the site even though it may differ considerably from the value put on the land by a valuer. If an asset which is disposed of to a connected person is subject to any restriction or right enforceable by the disposer, or a connected person of his, the market value is the value ignoring that restriction, minus the market value of the restriction (or, if less, the amount by which its extinction would enhance the value of the asset). If the right is of such a nature that it would destroy or substantially impair the value of the asset without giving any corresponding benefit to the disposer or the connected person, or it is an option or other right to acquire the asset (or to extinguish it by forfeiture, merger, etc.) the value of the right is ignored completely, i.e. capital gains tax is payable by reference to the unencumbered value of the asset (*TCGA*

*1992, s 18(6)(7)*). A mortgage or other charge or a right to forfeit a lease excercisable on a breach of a covenant does not trigger this restriction (*TCGA 1992, s 18(8)*).

**22.72** Other points to bear in mind from a CGT point of view are that a loss on a disposal to a connected person can be used only against gains on disposals to that same connected person (*TCGA 1992, s 18(3)*); and that where a disposal at an undervalue is between individuals and/or trusts or is a disposal of assets by an individual an election can sometimes be made to roll over the gain to the purchaser (*TCGA 1992, ss 165, 260*). It is not always sensible to make such an election.

**22.73** If a transaction takes place at other than market value, *ICTA 1988, s 770A* and *Sch 28AA* need to be considered. These are aimed at transactions between associated companies, although the test of association is wider than normal. However there is normally an exemption where both companies are within the charge to UK income or corporation tax (*Sch 28AA para 5(2)*) so in practice the provision is limited to transactions with non-UK companies that artificially reduce UK taxable income.

**22.74** *Section 770A* replaced *section 770*, broadly in respect of transactions after 30 June 1999. *Section 770* could apply to a transaction between two UK companies under 'common control', where the vendor was a dealing company and the purchaser acquired the property other than as trading stock at an undervalue, or the vendor was a non-dealing company and sold the property to a dealing company at an overvalue. Common control existed if the vendor controlled the purchaser, or vice versa, or both were bodies of persons (which could include a partnership) and some other person controlled both of them.

**22.75** It was confirmed in *Ametalco UK v CIR (1996 STC (SCD) 399)(SpC 94)* that *section 770* could apply to impute interest on an interest free loan. This is because *ICTA 1988, s 773(4)* extended it, with the necessary adaptations, to lettings and hirings of property, grants and transfers of rights, interests and licences and the giving of business facilities of whatever kind. Many people doubted that an interest-free loan falls within any of these categories. In practice the Revenue rarely applied *section 770* where both parties to a transaction are UK resident. If they were to do so the imputed interest would be taxable or deductible on an accruals basis as interest under either a loan relationship (*FA 1996, Sch 9 para 16*) or a deemed loan relationship (*FA 1996, s 100(3)*). *Sch 28AA* is more widely drawn. It refers to transactions which differ from those which would have applied had the parties been at arm's length rather than to purchases and sales. This is clearly wide enough to tax imputed interest on an interest free loan.

**22.76** Where *Sch 28AA* does not apply this does not necessarily mean that no adjustment need be made. In *Petrotim Securities Ltd v*

*Ayres (41 TC 389)* the court held that a transaction had taken place at such a substantial undervalue that it was not in the course of the company's trade. The company had therefore appropriated the item of trading stock for a non-trading purpose and the item needed to be taken out of stock at market value under the principle in *Sharkey v Wernher (36 TC 275)*. A similar finding was made in *Coates v Arndale Properties Ltd (59 TC 516)*.

**22.77** The courts will not necessarily adopt such a view unless the transaction is clearly not at market value. In *Jacgilden (Weston Hall) Ltd v Castle (45 TC 685)* they declined to allow a company to substitute market value which it estimated at £150,000 for the price of £72,000 paid to buy property from its shareholders.

**22.78** If trading stock is sold at arm's length to another UK trader, at other than market value on the discontinuance of the vendor's trade, *ICTA 1988, s 100(1)(a), (1A)(a)* specifically provide that the consideration is the price actually paid. It has been held that no adjustment to market value was competent in such circumstances in *Moore v R J Mackenzie & Sons Ltd (48 TC 196)* and *Bradshaw v Blunden (No 2) (39 TC 73)*.

**22.79** However if the parties are connected with each other the arm's length price must normally be substituted. If the aggregate market value on the transfer exceeds both the vendor's acquisition value of the properties sold and the price actually obtained for them on the transfer, a joint election can be made (within two years after the end of the year of assessment or accounting period in which the trade is discontinued) to treat the transfer as taking place at the higher of the vendor's acquisition value of the stock or the price actually paid on the transfer (*ICTA 1988, s 100(1A)(b),(1C)*). The acquisition value is the amount that would have been deductible in calculating profits had the stock been sold (*ICTA 1988, s 100(1D)*). This is, of course, cost unless the value of the property has been written down in an earlier year. The purchaser must of course acquire the property as trading stock. If stock is sold on the discontinuance of a trade to someone who does not acquire it as trading stock, (whether or not it is a connected person) market value must be substituted in calculating the vendor's profits if it differs from the actual sale price (*ICTA 1988, s 100(1)(b)*).

A transaction at an undervalue will normally be an occasion of charge to inheritance tax as the undervalue will result in a reduction in the value of the transferor's estate. The main exception is if it can be shown both that the transaction was not intended to confer a gratuitous benefit on any person and that the transaction was either one made between unconnected persons or was 'such as might be expected to be made in a transaction at arm's length between persons not connected with each other' (*IHTA 1984 s 10(1)*). In *CIR v Spencer-Nairn (1991 STC 60)* a disposal was unwittingly made to a connected person, i.e. the vendor did not know the purchaser was a connected person. The vendor had taken advice on the value – albeit not from a valuer. The adviser, mistakenly as it turned out, had thought that a liability for improvements of £80,000 attached to the land and had advised a sale at around £100,000. It was held that in determining whether a transaction is such as might be expected to be paid in a transaction between unconnected persons the price was no more than a single factor to be taken into account. In all the circumstances, particularly the taxpayer's mistaken belief that he was dealing with an unconnected person, the Commissioners were entitled to find that the exemption conferred by *section 10(1)* applied.

## Special Returns

**22.80** The Revenue are empowered to require any lessee or occupier of land (or a former lessee or occupier) or anyone else having (or who had) use of the land to give them such information as they may require as to the terms of the lease, occupation or use of the land and the consideration given for the grant or assignment to him of the tenancy (*TMA 1970, s 19(1)(a)(b)*). They can similarly require any agent who manages the land or has receipt of rent or other payments arising from it to give such information (*TMA 1970, s 19(1)(c)*). They can require a tenant to provide them with the lease or any other written instrument establishing his terms of occupation (*TMA 1970, s 19(1)(a)*) but it is not clear whether an agent can be required to produce such a document. (*Section 19(1)(a)* refers to 'information' whereas *section 19(1)(c)* talks of 'particulars', which may be wide enough to cover documents.) The Revenue can use this power only for the purpose of obtaining particulars of amounts taxable under Schedule A or in respect of premiums, etc. taxable under Case VI of Schedule D by virtue of *ICTA 1988, ss 34–36* (see 3.2–3.22 above). The Revenue cannot require a mortgagee to provide such information (*TMA 1970, s 19(3)*).

**22.81** Where a householder takes in lodgers the Revenue can require from him a return containing 'to the best of his belief' the name of every lodger or inmate resident in his house, and if any of those people has another ordinary place of residence at which they wish to be assessed to tax the address of that residence (*TMA 1970, s 14*). The provision applies only to a property which is a dwelling-house.

## Power to Enter Premises

**22.82** The Inland Revenue can obtain a warrant to search, if necessary by force, any premises in which there is reasonable grounds for suspecting that there will be found evidence of an offence involving any form of tax fraud (*TMA 1970, s 20C*). The Board of Inland Revenue itself must approve the application for the search warrant and it must be granted by a Circuit judge (or a sheriff in Scotland or a County Court judge in Northern Ireland) (*TMA 1970, s 20D*). The officer authorised by the warrant to make the search can seize and remove anything found on the premises which he has reasonable cause to believe may be required in evidence (*TMA 1970, s 20C(3)*). If so requested he must, however, provide the occupier of the premises (or any person having custody of the items taken before their seizure) with a list of the items taken (*TMA 1970, s 20C(4)*). This list does not apparently have to be provided at the time of seizure nor apparently within any particular time after seizure. In *CIR & Another v Rossminster Ltd and Others (52 TC 106)* it appears clear that at the time of seizure under this provision the Revenue simply stuffed into sacks every piece of paper they could lay their hands on and did not themselves know exactly what they had taken until some days after the raid.

**22.83** It should particularly be noted that the power is to forcibly enter any premises in which it is thought evidence may be found. There is no need for the Revenue to show that the owner or occupier of the premises is involved in, or knows of, the suspected fraud. The only limitation is that if the Revenue raid a solicitor's office or barrister's chambers they cannot remove any document to which professional privilege attaches.

**22.84** Any person so authorised by the Board of Inland Revenue is also empowered to enter on, and inspect, any land with a view to establishing its annual value where that value falls to be determined for the purposes of income tax or corporation tax (*TMA 1970, s 110*). He can be required to produce evidence of his authorisation by the Board and can only call at a 'reasonable time'. An Inspector of Taxes or other officer of the Board (but not any other person such as an outside expert) can similarly be authorised to inspect any other property for the purpose of ascertaining its market value for the purposes of *TCGA 1992 (TMA 1970, s 111*). The person having custody of that property must permit such inspection at such reasonable times as the Board consider necessary, which obviously implies a right to the Revenue to enter the premises on which such property is to be found. A similar provision applies for inheritance tax purposes (*IHTA 1984, s 220*).

**22.85** Customs and Excise have somewhat wider powers in relation to VAT. A Customs official can at any reasonable time enter premises used in connection with the carrying on of a business and can enter any other premises if he has 'reasonable cause' to believe that such premises are used in connection with the supply of taxable goods and that such goods are on those premises. This only gives them power to come in and look around; they cannot open cupboards and drawers. To do that they need to obtain a search warrant (which also obviates the need to enter premises at a reasonable time) from a Justice of the Peace if there are reasonable grounds for suspecting that a fraud offence of a serious nature has been, or is about to be, committed on the premises or that evidence of such an offence is to be found there. Unlike the Revenue,

Customs can also search any person found on the premises in certain circumstances (*VATA 1994, Sch 11 para 10*). The powers of Customs in relation to entering private premises are broadly similar to those of the police.

## Property Investment Under the EIS Scheme

**22.86** The Enterprise Investment Scheme legislation is designed to encourage individuals to invest in risk ventures. It does so by granting income tax relief for half the amount invested – up to a maximum of £150,000 p.a. (£100,000 p.a. up to 1997/98 and £40,000 less any BES investment for 1993/94) – provided that certain conditions are met. The EIS scheme is not in general suitable for property investment. The company must be carrying on a trade and most trades with a substantial property element have been excluded from the scheme. Property dealing has always been excluded and since 17 March 1998, so have property development, farming, market gardening, holding, managing or occupying woodlands, any other forestry activities or timber production, operating or managing hotels or comparable establishments or managing property used as a hotel or comparable establishment, operating or managing nursing homes or residential care homes, and managing property used as a nursing home or residential care home. The operation of public houses is still acceptable, but if a pub incorporates residential accommodation it might be excluded as a comparable establishment to a hotel. It is not clear if property development includes housebuilding. The indications are that it does not, although most people would describe housebuilding as development.

**22.87** Receiving royalties and licence fees is also an excluded activity. The Revenue have pointed out that licences may be granted as a means of exploiting an interest in land. If the grant of the licence is merely incidental to an activity of supplying services (e.g. a cinema ticket confers a licence to occupy the seat but is primarily an opportunity to see the film) they accept that the exclusion does not apply. On the other hand making sports facilities available to the general public with no provision of services (a rare occurrence) would be an activity of receiving licence fees. Even if there is no provision of services, e.g. a fee to use a tennis court or a ticket to view an ancient monument, if continuous work is required to keep the property in a fit state for use by customers the fee may relate primarily to the cost of such work in which case it would not be regarded as a licence fee (Tax Bulletin 54, August 2001). The Revenue also consider that the provision of self-storage warehousing facilities is an excluded activity as constituting leasing. They consider that such exclusion applies in any case where, subject to reasonable conditions imposed by the trader, the customer is free to use the property for the purpose for which it is intended (Tax Bulletin 54, August 2001).

**22.88** EIS relief is withdrawn or reduced if the investor obtains a benefit from the company during the qualifying period. There are exceptions for business expenses for certain directors' fees, for dividends not exceeding a normal return on the capital invested, for rent for a property occupied by the company which does not exceed a reasonable and commercial return and for interest not exceeding a commercial rate (*ICTA 1988, ss 291(3)* and *291A*).

## Gifts of Real Property to Charity

**22.89** From 6 April 2002 (1 April 2002 in the case of a company), a gift of land to charity attracts a tax deduction against total income for the year of assessment in which the gift is made (*ICTA 1988, s 587B(1)(2)(i)* as amended by *FA 2002, s 97*). In the case of a company, it is treated as a charge on income, which appears to allow any unutilised amount to be carried forward against future income (*ICTA 1988, s 587B(1)(2)(ii)*). Where property is sold to a charity at an undervalue the amount of the undervalue is apparently a gift for this purpose. The charity is treated for capital gains tax purposes as acquiring the property at nil cost, or in the case of a gift at an undervalue at the price it actually paid (*ICTA 1988, s 587B(3)(4)*). This is not relevant in most cases as a charity is not liable to capital gains tax unless and until it ceases to be a charity. Accordingly the sub-sections claw back the relief if that eventually crystallises.

**22.90** The relief also extends to the incidental costs of making the disposal (as defined at 11.7) (*ICTA 1988, s 587B(6)*). In the case of a sale at an undervalue, incidental costs are relieved only to the extent that the sale proceeds is below the vendor's capital gains tax base cost (*ICTA 1988, s 587B(7)*). If the donor (or a connected person) receives any benefit in consequence of making the disposal, the amount eligible for relief is reduced by the value of that benefit (*ICTA 1988, s 587B(5)*). The legislation gives no guidance as to how the benefit is calculated.

**22.91** The relief applies only to a gift of UK land which is either a freehold or a lease for a term of years absolute (*ICTA 1988, s 587B(9A)* inserted by *FA 2002, s 97(2)*). The gift must be of the whole of the donor's beneficial interest in the land (*ICTA 1988, s 587B(1)*). If a person makes a qualifying gift of land and also gifts to the charity an easement, servitude right or privilege so far as benefiting that land, the gift of the easement, etc. also qualifies for relief (*ICTA 1988, s 587B(9B)*). The gift of a qualifying lease while retaining the freehold reversion or head lease qualifies as it is regarded as a gift of the whole of the beneficial interest in the lease (*ICTA 1988, s 587B(9C)*). An agreement to acquire a freehold interest and an agreement for lease are not qualifying interests in land (*ICTA 1988, s 587B(9D)*). Accordingly, if for example a person were to contract to buy land and passed the benefit of the contract to the charity when the land increased significantly in value between contract and completion, he could not obtain relief for the amount of the increase.

**22.92** If the qualifying interest in land is held jointly by two or more people either as joint tenants or tenants in common, no relief is due unless all of the joint owners gift their interest to the charity (it has to be to the same charity) (*ICTA 1988, s 587C(2)* inserted by *FA 2002, s 97(5)*). The reason for this restriction is not readily apparent. Curiously, if one of the joint owners is the charity itself it appears to prevent the relief applying completely. Where all of the joint owners do gift a property it appears that the relief does not need to be claimed in proportion to beneficial ownership but rather that the donors can – indeed, must, as it appears that no relief will be given if they do not – decide amongst themselves how the relief is to be split (*ICTA 1988, s 587C(3)*). The logic of this is also not readily apparent.

**22.93** The relief must be claimed (*ICTA 1988, s 587A(2)*). The normal six-year (five years and ten months for income tax) time limit applies. A claim cannot however be made unless the charity has given the donor a certificate specifying the land concerned and the date of the gift and containing a statement that the charity has acquired the land (*ICTA 1988, s 587C(4)(5)*).

**22.94** The relief is withdrawn if at any time within the six years following the disposal (five years and ten months for income tax – i.e. 31 January following the fifth anniversary of the end of the tax year in which the gift was made) the donor or a connected person either

(*a*) becomes entitled to any interest or right in relation to all or part of the land, or

(*b*) becomes party to an arrangement under which he enjoys some right in relation to all or part of the land

unless he pays full consideration in money or money's worth for such interest, right or enjoyment. In the case of a joint gift the relief is withdrawn from all the donors if one of them or a person connected with one of them receives the interest, right or enjoyment (*ICTA 1988, s 587C(6)–(10)*). There is no clawback of relief if the person inherits or becomes entitled to the interest or right (but not an arrangement under which he enjoys a right) on a death of someone else (*ICTA 1988, s 587C(9)*).

# Meaning of 'Connected Persons'

## ICTA 1988, s 839

(1) For the purposes of, and subject to, the provisions of the Tax Acts which apply this section, any question whether a person is connected with another shall be determined in accordance with the following provisions of this section (any provision that one person is connected with another being taken to mean that they are connected with one another).

(2) A person is connected with an individual if that person is the individual's husband or wife, or is a relative, or the husband or wife of a relative, of the individual or of the individual's husband or wife.

(3) A person in his capacity as trustee of a settlement is connected with

(*a*) any individual who in relation to the settlement is a settlor,

(*b*) any person who is connected with such an individual, and

(*c*) any body corporate which is connected with that settlement.

In this sub-section 'settlement' and 'settlor' have the same meaning as in Chapter 1A of Part XV (see *section 660G(1)* and *(2)*).

(3A) For the purpose of sub-section (3) above a body corporate is connected with a settlement if:

(*a*) it is a close company (or only not a close company because it is not resident in the United Kingdom) and the participators include the trustees of the settlement; or

(*b*) it is controlled (within the meaning of *section 840*) by a company falling within paragraph (*a*) above.

(4) Except in relation to acquisitions or disposals of partnership assets pursuant to bona fide commercial arrangements, a person is connected with any person with whom he is in partnership, and with the husband or wife or relative of any individual with whom he is in partnership.

(5) A company is connected with another company:

(*a*) if the same person has control of both, or a person has control of one and persons connected with him, or he and persons connected with him, have control of the other, or

(*b*) if a group of two or more persons has control of each company, and the groups either consist of the same persons or could be regarded as consisting of the same persons by treating (in one or more cases) a member of either group as replaced by a person with whom he is connected.

(6) A company is connected with another person, if that person has control of it or if that person and persons connected with him together have control of it.

(7) Any two or more persons acting together to secure or exercise control of a company shall be treated in relation to that company as connected with one another and with any person acting on the directions of any of them to secure or exercise control of the company.

(8) In this section:

'company' includes any body corporate or unincorporated association, but does not include a partnership, and this section shall apply in relation to any unit trust scheme (as defined in section 26(1) of the Prevention of Fraud (Investments) Act 1958 or section 22 of the Prevention of Fraud (Investments) Act (Northern Ireland) 1940) as if the scheme were a company and as if the rights of the unit holders were shares in the company,

'control' shall be construed in accordance with section 416 of this Act,

'relative' means brother, sister, ancestor or lineal descendant.

**N.B.** Subsections (3) and (3A) did not apply in relation to transactions prior to 1995/96. The previous wording was:

'(3) A person, in his capacity as trustee of a settlement, is connected with any individual who in relation to the settlement is a settlor, with any person who is connected with such an individual and with a body corporate which, under *section 681* of the *Act* is deemed to be connected with that settlement ("settlement" and "settlor" having for the purposes of this subsection the meanings given by subsection (4) of that section).'

*Appendix 2*

# Enterprise Zones

An 'enterprise zone' is an area designated as such by the Secretary of State (or Department of the Environment for Northern Ireland). Areas so far designated are as follows.

*Zones still in force at October 2002*

Dearne Valley (6 zones) (from 3 November 1995, *SI 1995 No 2624*)
East Midlands (North East Derbyshire) (3 zones) (from 3 November 1995, *SI 1995 No 2625*)
East Midlands (Bassetlaw) (from 16 November 1995, *SI 1995 No 2738*)
East Midlands (Ashfield) (from 21 November 1995, *SI 1995 No 2758*)
East Durham (6 zones) (from 29 November 1995, *SI 1995 No 2812*)
Inverclyde (from 1 March 1989, *SI 1989 No 145*)
Lanarkshire (Hamilton) (from 1 February 1993, *SI 1993 No 23*)
Lanarkshire (Monklands) (from 1 February 1993, *SI 1993 No 25*)
Lanarkshire (Motherwell) (from 1 February 1993, *SI 1993 No 24*)
Mansfield (announced May 1993 but not yet designated)
Tyne Riverside (North Tyneside) (6 zones) (from 26 August 1996, *SI 1996 No 1981*)
Tyne Riverside (North Tyneside and South Tyneside) (4 zones) (from 21 October 1996, *SI 1996 No 2435*)

*Zones where the ten-year period expired*

Arbroath, see Tayside (Arbroath)
Belfast (expired 20 October 1991, *SR 1981 No 309*)
Chatham, see North West Kent
Clydebank (expired 2 August 1991, *SI 1981 No 975*)
Corby (expired 21 June 1991, *SI 1981 No 764*)
Delyn (expired 20 July 1993, *SI 1983 No 896*)
Dudley (expired 9 July 1991, *SI 1981 No 852*)
Dudley (Round Oak) (expired 3 October 1994, *SI 1984 No 1403*)
Dundee, see Tayside (Dundee)
Flixborough, see Glanford (Flixborough)
Gateshead (expired 24 August 1991, *SI 1981 No 1070*)
Glanford (Flixborough) (expired 12 April 1994, *SI 1984 No 347*)

Glasgow (expired 17 August 1991, *SI 1981 No 1069*)
Hartlepool (expired 22 October 1991, *SI 1981 No 1378*)
Invergordon (expired 6 October 1993, *SI 1983 No 1359*)
Isle of Dogs (expired 25 April 1992, *SI 1982 No 462*)
Kent (NW) (expired 30 October 1993, *SI 1983 No 1452*)
Lancashire (NE) (expired 6 December 1993, *SI 1983 No 1639*)
Liverpool (Speke) (expired 24 August 1991, *SI 1981 No 1072*)
London, see Isle of Dogs
Londonderry (expired 12 September 1993, *SR 1983 No 226*)
Lower Swansea Valley (expired 10 June 1991, *SI 1981 No 757*)
Lower Swansea Valley (No 2) (expired 6 March 1995, *SI 1985 No 137*)
Middlesbrough (Britannia) (expired 7 November 1993, *SI 1983 No 1473*)
Milford Haven Waterway (North Shore) (expired 23 April 1994, *SI 1984 No 443*)
Milford Haven Waterway (South Shore) (expired 23 April 1994, *SI 1984 No 444*)
Newcastle (expired 24 August 1991, *SI 1981 No 1071*)
North West Kent (Chatham) (expired 9 October 1996, *SI 1986 No 1557*)
Rotherham (expired 15 August 1993, *SI 1983 No 1007*)
Salford Docks (expired 11 August 1991, *SI 1981 No 1024*)
Scunthorpe (Normanby Ridge and Queensway (expired 22 September 1993, *SI 1983 No 1304*)
Speke, see Liverpool (Speke)
Sunderland (Castletown and Doxford park) (expired 26 March 2000, *SI 1990 No 794*)
Sunderland (Hylton Riverside and Southwick) (expired 26 March 2000, *SI 1990 No 795*)
Tayside (Arbroath) (expired 8 January 1994, *SI 1983 No 1816*)
Tayside (Dundee) (expired 8 January 1994, *SI 1983 No 1817*)
Telford (expired 12 January 1994, *SI 1983 No 1852*)
Trafford Park (expired 11 August 1991, *SI 1981 No 1025*)
Wakefield (Dale Lane and Kinsley) (expired 22 September 1993, *SI 1983 No 1305*)
Wakefield (Langthwaite Grange) (expired 31 July 1991, *SI 1981 No 950*)
Wellingborough (expired 25 July 1993, *SI 1983 No 907*)
Workington (Allerdale) (expired 3 October 1993, *SI 1983 No 1331*)
See 10.158 above as regards capital allowances for commercial buildings in enterprise zones.
See 20.86 above as regards exemption from the uniform business rate for properties in enterprise zones.

# Index

*Paragraph* *Paragraph*

*Paragraph*



*Paragraph*

*Paragraph*

*Paragraph*

Paragraph

*Paragraph*